Tactics and Techniques of Community Practice
Second Edition

Tactics and Techniques
of
Community Practice

Second Edition

Fred M. Cox
University of Wisconsin, Milwaukee

John L. Erlich
California State University, Sacramento

Jack Rothman
John E. Tropman
University of Michigan

 F. E. Peacock Publishers, Inc.   Itasca, Il., 60143

PREFACE

One of the most original thinkers in American sociology, W.I. Thomas, suggested a theorum that remains basic to the social sciences: "If men define situations as real, then they are real in their consequences. Holding aside the typical sexism of his era, Thomas had a point that illuminates one major problem of assembling this second edition. The definitions of what is encompassed by community practice have expanded and been elaborated since the first edition was prepared. And, indeed, these developments impinge very directly on what students, practitioners, and teachers can do.

It is no longer possible to include all emerging perspectives in a volume of less than encyclopedic proportions. We have tried hard to pick and choose among those that we consider the most important and the most promising. But the often vast differences that must be taken into account caused by geography, community history, organizational auspices, political climate, community involvement and the like make this a hazardous task at best. At the same time, we have tried to retain the "how-to-do-it" approach of the book. But, as before, and for the reasons suggested above, it cannot be simply followed like a road map. Immediate situational contexts must be taken into account. One of these for the balance of the 1980's is that a major battleground for funding and change at the community level will be the political arena — national, regional, state and local.

For a practice-oriented book like this, there clearly is a question about what we mean by words like "tactics" and "techniques." How do we distinguish between "tactics" and "techniques" and "strategy"? Strategy we see as "an orchestrated attempt to influence a person or system in a relation to some specific goal which the actor desires."[1] Tactics and techniques may be viewed as specific interventive devices or means that contribute to the operationalization of a strategy. Thus the key differences between strategy and tactics and techniques involve scope and duration. Tactics generally are more modest in these respects. For example, a strategy to establish a single parent program may require coordinated approaches to funding sources, community leaders, single parents and the organizational network currently providing services to

---

[1]Fred M. Cox, John L. Erlich, Jack Rothman and John E. Tropman, Eds., *Strategies of Community Organization,* 3rd Ed. (Itasca, Ill., F.E. Peacock Publishers, 1979), p. 280. An elaboration of this definition follows in that source.

single parents. Tactics and techniques which contribute to carrying the strategy forward might include setting up a community advisory group, writing an application for funding from the source selected, recruiting a community-based board of directors, and working with an advisory group of single parents to announce the new program through the media and local organizations.

Since the appearance of the first edition, the editors — as practitioners, teachers and administrators — have not escaped the current period of cutback and change. We have continued to struggle with how to be more effective, more accountable and, if not more financially viable, at least solvent. At the same time, the movement away from grassroots activities toward planning, program development and policy-making under long-established organizational and political auspices has been notable. It has not been easy to continue to find the best ways of converting our commitments into meaningful programs, plans with some hope of success and better human service delivery systems. The articles which follow have helped us find our way through this difficult time. We hope that they will do the same for you.

Fred M. Cox, John L. Erlich,
Jack Rothman and John E. Tropman

Contents

INTRODUCTION

The last quarter of the twentieth century is surely a pivotal time for community organization. National trends that demand the skills of community organizers are outlined by John Naisbitt in his book, *Megatrends,*[1] involving a shift from an industrial society to an information society. Such a change will leave both displaced workers and displaced cities. Naisbitt also refers to the move from institutional help to self-help. The need to bring together and coordinate people interested in self-help activities will call upon community organization skills.

Jack Rothman[2] lays out some of the social implications of the "oil shock" and its aftermath. Basically he argues that the last quarter of this century will be a period of retrenchment and downsizing, that the age of abundance is over. We will have increased need for efficiency in the allocation of resources—for local initiative in their development and application, and for social advocacy when certain groups are left out. The skills of the community organization professional will be in great demand in accomplishing these social goals. That old definition of community organization in the Lane Report of 1939—organizing community resources to meet community needs—takes on new meaning in these difficult times.

Another condition that cries out for community organization effort is the decay of the nation's infrastructure. Roads, public buildings, dams, and bridges are in bad condition. This problem may seem strange for community organization. Organizers have almost always taken physical planning for granted and have argued that social planning should be included as a necessary part of community development. Now community organization skills are needed to bolster physical planning and maintenance. Part of our hesitancy to repair physical facilities comes from economic decline. We were used to the money being there, and are not quite sure what to do when it isn't. But that is not the whole picture. Americans are accustomed to throwing things away and getting new ones. In some sense, it could even be argued that the whole development of Long Island was simply a new "New York City," built when the old one began to deteriorate. Yet, we cannot discard an entire infrastructure, and therefore collective attention will have to be paid to keeping it in shape. It is also true that Americans (and Naisbitt makes this point as well) have not gone in for long-range planning. Here again the

1

methods of community organization will facilitate attention to these very pressing problems.

The difficulty is not limited to the physical structure, however. Our social institutions are also under fire. It is widely believed that most institutions are not working well. Schools, it is said, don't really teach people how to read and write. Mental hospitals don't cure people. Prisons don't deter crime or rehabilitate criminals. Newspapers distort the news. The list could go on. The feeling that things are not run as well as they should be is the central theme of Peters and Waterman's book, *In Search of Excellence,*[3] which develops lessons from commercial companies and suggests some applications. The public at large seems to have exhibited declining support for institutions, government, and business as well as labor as Lipset and Schneider point out in *The Confidence Gap.*[4] Public confidence in institutions seems to be declining. Rather than a sense of pride in the functioning of crucial elements in our society, there seems to be a sense of resignation at the cascade of bumbling ineptitudes which many of us now find to be the daily fare in encounters with these institutions. It is crucial, therefore, that the kinds of skills that community organizers possess be brought to bear for purposes of repair and refurbishment.

Finally, one should not ignore the problem of competition from abroad, particularly from the Japanese. The Japanese threat is particularly interesting, because to some extent its success and vigor have been based upon the application in business organizations of principles analogous to those of community organization practice.[5]

The overall impact of these trends suggests that the kind of cooperative efforts which have been the hallmark of community organization practice are needed now more than ever. They are needed not just to improve the lot of the disadvantaged, though social advocacy techniques stress that role in particular. They are needed to address large-scale national problems: declining income, productivity and efficiency, physical deterioration, lack of confidence in major institutions, the problematic functioning of those institutions, and vigorous competition from abroad. Community organization methods won't solve these problems, but they may help us cope with them more effectively.

Not only will there be a need for community organization skills, stimulated by these trends in the future, but there are many contemporary indications of demand for and use of them today. The anti-nuclear movement, focusing on local and state referenda calling for a simultaneous, verifiable freeze in the deployment of nuclear weapons, is a prominent contemporary example. Concern and action against the persistent and rising incidence of accidents and deaths on the roads, caused by drunken driving, is evident in the work of MADD (Mothers Against Drunk Driving) and other similar organizations. The "anti-abortion" and "pro-choice" movements continue to be active. A large number of groups concerned about the desecration of the environment and mobilized by the actions of the Environmental Protection Agency and the Department of the Interior provide still another example. At this writing, a substantial push appears imminent in registering minority, unemployed, and poor people to vote, stimulated by Richard Cloward and Frances Fox Piven, looking forward to the presidential and congressional elections of 1984.

Increasingly, these efforts are focused on the local and state levels, with reductions in federal programs and the emergence of block grants to states in President Reagan's New Federalism strategy. And fewer of these movements employ paid community organizers than was true in the heyday of the poverty and model cities programs. But these functions are still being performed, and we suspect many professionals in the fields of health, education, and social welfare are involved, in one way or another. Although the demand has diminished, there are a number of professionals engaged in social planning and administration. Inevitably, their work, as well as that of many direct practitioners in nursing, social work, education, and other human service professions, includes responsibilities for community practice.

Like the first edition, this book is organized roughly according to the stages of the community intervention process. It also incorporates a distinction between planning, organizing, and developing, roughly comparable to the types of community organization practice Jack Rothman developed in his seminal paper "Three Models of Community Organization Practice," which also forms the organizing scheme for the companion volume to this work, *Strategies of Community Organization.*

The book begins with a number of pieces on the assessment process, focused on various types of entities practitioners are required to size up from time to time—community agencies, neighborhoods, and social problems. The first part also includes a discussion of the various methods by which assessments may be carried out (Warheit, Bell, and Schwab) and decisions reached (Rycus), and the value dilemmas involved in the decision process (Tropman). This part ends with an assessment of emerging minority communities by Rivera and Erlich.

The second part turns to the major modalities of community practice— planning, organizing and developing.* In Part Two A, various processes that may be used for planning purposes are discussed, with detailed attention to how they may be carried out—community action planning, putting together a community coalition, working with boards of directors, running meetings both in their formal aspects (parliamentary procedures) and informal dynamics, and advocating for policy and programs in a legislative context. A variety of important contemporary problems and contexts are used to illustrate these planning processes, including the problems of alcohol and drug abuse and of older citizens and the rural context.

---

*It should be noted that the term "organizing" is sometimes used to refer to "social action" as it is used in Rothman's "Three Models . . . ," as in the title to Part Two, B. At other times, it is used rather loosely in the sense of "putting something together," as in "How to Organize a Community Action Plan," "Organizing a Community Coalition," and "Organizing Domestic Workers."

Part Two B deals with organizing and developing, "organizing" in this context meaning to deal with problems about which there is considerable dissensus and "developing" meaning to work with problems about which there is considerable value consensus in the society.

Sherry and Lipschultz discuss consumer education as a strategy for empowering oppressed minorities and the poor to gain influence in the organization and delivery of health services. Their paper describes a series of eleven techniques, referred to as actions, which help to assure the success of the consumer education strategy. Haggstrom presents a detailed rationale for a grass-roots, democratic approach to helping. The League of Women Voters describes techniques for building a coalition and developing a campaign in support of an issue in the legislative arena. Maguire deals with networking, including specific techniques for promoting it within the context of groups aimed at self-help.

Part Three deals with administration and management. We do not argue that they follow, in time sequence, planning, organizing, and developing. Neither are they at the center of community practice. However, they support those central functions and are often performed by community practitioners who "double in brass" as managers or have managerial functions delegated to them. Written especially for this book, the lead piece by Kruzich and Austin discusses supervision and management in the context of community organization practice. Cox provides guidelines for handling personnel matters, with an emphasis on preparing personnel policies. The League of Women Voters offers guidelines for public relations based on its extensive experience in this area. Geller, who has worked as a grant review officer in state government, offers us his suggestions for successful grant writing, and Flanagan tells us what she has learned about asking for money in support of nonprofit organizations. The United Way's guide to budgeting should be useful because so many agencies are supported by United Way and follow their suggested budgeting procedures.

The final stage in any practice endeavor is to evaluate the results obtained from one's efforts. Part Four addresses the problems of evaluation and ways of going about it. Weiss reviews the difficulties of evaluating programs in real-life settings, including the tendency of program administrators to make mid-course corrections in programs, strains that arise in relations between evaluators and program personnel, and problems that arise from the fact that programs are embedded in organizations that shape and sometimes distort those programs. Armed with knowledge of the difficulties of evaluation, the reader can explore the process. Solomon asks and answers these questions: why evaluate programs? What information is needed? Who should evaluate? What are the steps in evaluation? And what are the practical problems in conducting an evaluation? Washington, then, presents several frameworks for evaluation: the systems, goal attainment, and behavioral models. Douglass discusses the ways to use and present community data, which may be useful in both problems assessment (Part One) and evaluation. Finally

Gottman and Clasen offer a brief review of the various techniques available for evaluation, which should help those who need more details find them or help practitioners talk knowledgeably with evaluators about the evaluation process.

In Part Five, we depart from the basic scheme of the book. Instead of dealing with one of the stages in the process of community practice (or with various classes of practice activity such as planning, organizing, developing and managing) we turn to the dilemmas of practice, the cross pressures of competing goods which are difficult and often impossible to attain simultaneously in the same set of actions. The ethical dilemmas of practice are illustrated by the National Association of Social Workers Code of Ethics and the commentary by Cohen on its development. Role dilemmas are illustrated by Chernesky's piece on women in administration, and Morales' piece on working with Third-World people. Organizational dilemmas are discussed in Levine's piece on the management of organizational decline in resources and in Zietz and Erlich's piece on job satisfaction and burnout.

The discussion of dilemmas in practice should help us address contemporary issues in practice and reduce paralysis or excessive hesitation in reaching decisions and taking action as we understand their implications better. Most of us came into this field because of a concern about values in action, and as we resolve the inevitable dilemmas of practice, we are in a better position to use and apply effective techniques, which are the focus of this book.

Fred M. Cox

Notes

1. John Naisbitt, *Megatrends: Ten New Directions Transforming Our Lives* (New York: Warner Books, 1982).
2. Jack Rothman, "Macro Social Work in a Tightening Economy," *Social Work* July (1979): 24:4:274–282.
3. Thomas J. Peters and Robert H. Waterman, Jr., *In Search of Excellence: Lessons from America's Best Run Companies* (New York: Harper and Row, 1982).
4. Seymour Martin Lipset and William Schneider, *The Confidence Gap: Business, Labor, and Government in the Public Mind* (New York: Free Press, 1983).
5. William Ouchi, *Theory* (New York: Davon, 1981). See also Richard Tanner Pascal and Anthony G. Athos, *The Art of Japanese Management* (New York: Warner/Simon and Schuster, 1981).

PART One

Assessment and Option Selection

Introduction

Canadian humorist Stephen Leacock writes of the young man who woke up enthusiastically one morning, jumped on his horse, and immediately galloped off in all four directions at once. This singular behavior may be attributed in part to youthful exuberance. It can also be described as a failure of assessment. The chap hadn't decided what his needs and wants that day were, or at least had not put them in any order of priority. Assessment is a method for helping to decide in what direction to go.

Community practice can be described as a process of problem solving. It requires the design of strategies, or approaches or directions for resolving critical social problems. Community organization is often defined as a practice "method." In this sense it entails a series of logically interlinked steps, which produce an intended outcome or achieve a desired goal— namely the prevention or amelioration of community problems. Assessment, one of the earliest steps, will be the focus of our attention in Part One.

Assessment as a function has received heightened attention in recent years, partly in response to demands by both consumers of services and legislative officials for greater accountability in the provision of human services. Consumers have asked that delivery of services be relevant to real need. Legislative and governmental officials have spoken to fiscal responsibility and cost effectiveness. In either case, pressures have been placed on agencies and professionals to be clearer, more explicit, and more rigorous in justifying their service patterns.

Although "assessment" has a contemporary ring to it, it has occupied a prominent position historically in the field of community practice. The important Lane Report of 1939, which was the first recognized attempt to define community organization systematically, gave as the central function of community organization "the discovery and definition of needs" and the balancing of needs and resources "in order to better meet changing needs"

(Lane, 1959, p. 65). That significant document viewed assessing needs and taking appropriate action as the heart of community practice professionalism.

Precursor Activities

An early step in any problem-solving activity is the analysis or diagnosis of the problem that is being confronted. One is tempted to say that assessment is the "first" step in this process, but this is not necessarily so. There are ordinarily precursors to assessment, what Brager and Specht (1973) have referred to as "preorganizing" (p. 89).

There is, in the first place, the matter of identifying the problem to be worked on. A practitioner is typically situated in an agency, which serves as employer and job definer. A job description or assignment involving a focal problem to be dealt with is often a "given." Even when the assignment is rather open, it is important for the practitioner to analyze the employing agency critically because this organizational structure determines the policy context, the resources, the legitimacy, and the power base within which problems can be appropriately addressed. Article 1 by Hasenfeld presents a scheme for such an organizational analysis, which can also be used to analyze external organizations related to a focal problem, including a target agency in which the specific problem is located. In that case the outline becomes a more direct assessment vehicle.

A profile of one's community setting offers additional important information at this stage. Community and neighborhood surveys have long been a vital tool of community practice, providing both contextual and substantive data to be employed for diagnostic purposes. The selection by the Warrens contains a useful framework for such a study. Community surveys can also examine needs more directly, particularly in regard to a needs-resources analysis wherein needs are related to existing services and available resources.

This early stage may initially entail organizing a constituency with which to work. The constituency can then become the medium through which assessment takes place. Assessment can be a fairly technical and solitary professional activity carried out in an office surrounded by computer printouts and area maps. On the other hand, it can be conducted on a collaborative basis in neighborhood clubs and meeting halls, with the professional and the constituency taking joint responsibility as partners. Often "planning" models of community practice employ the former and "organizing" models the latter.

A number of other precursor aspects are spelled out in a problem-solving-schema employed by the editors in a previous book (Cox et al., 1979, pp. 175–191), including an appraisal of the practitioner's personal capabilities and role set. There are also activities which follow assessment in a problem-solving framework. Assessment flows into decision making, mobilization and implementation, and evaluation. This book will cover all of these phases in subsequent sections.

Essentials of Assessment

Assessment entails gathering pertinent evidence and drawing inferences from that evidence about the nature of a given problem and about optimal action initiatives to deal with it. This process can involve an analysis at two different levels: the core problem in substantive terms, and the task or solution environment surrounding the problem. Let us start with the problem.

Analyzing the Core Problem

Several different questions need to be asked about the core problem itself. According to the problem-solving schema referred to above, some of the following are salient:

The population

Who comprises the population of clients or constituencies requiring attention? Who are the primary beneficiaries of the change effort? What are their social, economic, political, and demographic characteristics?

The type of problem

What is the nature of the problem including type (economic, psychological, organizational), scope (numbers affected), and degree (severity of the difficulty)?

Origin of the problem

What is the origin of the problem, and how has it changed over time? This may entail a theory of the problem—does it arise from structural factors including racism (as in the case of chronic unemployment), or from inadequacies of individuals (child abusers), or from chance events in nature (maternal incapacity because of a stroke)?

Defining Need

Different theories of the problem may be advanced in the assessment. In the same way, different concepts of need may be applied. Bradshaw (1972) has suggested a number of alternative concepts of need as defined among planners and researchers. A *normative need* is said to exist when a standard of service or of living is established and certain groups or individuals are found to fall short of enjoying that desirable standard. This standard is most often set by experts, professional bodies, or government bureaus. *Comparative need* is not based on a set standard, but rather on the relative position or condition of a group when measured against some other group. The disparity between two groups is the criterion for determining the existence and extent of need. *Felt need,* perceived by individuals experiencing the problem, may be equated with want and is phenomenological in

character. A felt need that is articulated as a demand is an *expressed need.*
Expression can take the form of asking for service, protesting, signing a
petition, or other action.

Alternative Perceptions of the Problem

In any given problem situation, different perspectives can be brought to
bear in defining the problem. Need assessment methods, accordingly, have
embedded within them varying assumptions concerning need. Warheit and
his associates in Article 3 describe some of the more commonly used
approaches. The need is defined, in each approach, by particular categories
of people:

- the key informant approach—professionals and community leaders
- the community forum approach—professionals, community leaders,
  and community people
- the rates-under-treatment approach—clients expressing demand for
  service
- the social indicators approach—experts using empirical data

The authors indicate the advantages and disadvantages of each of these
approaches and specify some of the main activities required to implement
them.

A Multiplicity of Assessment Techniques

Lauffer adds to the array of assessment tools. As the public pressure for
better assessment was felt, assessment tools became more refined and
increased in number. Included in Lauffer's enumeration are Delphi, the
nominal group technique, task analysis, force field analysis, and simulation
games.

Biases of Assessment Techniques

It should be evident that although assessment attempts to gain objectivity
in analyzing and understanding a problem, total "truth" in this connection
is evasive. Surveying clients reveals how the problem "feels" to them.
Speaking to professionals offers expert insight and experience. Consulting
social indicators displays facts on the basis of available data. The community
practitioner must decide which of these approaches (or sources) is most
critical in a given intervention situation or what combination might best
illuminate the problem. Even with an aggregate approach there remains
the problem of interrelating and weighting the multiple streams of
information.

Analyzing the Solution Environment

We have suggested that assessment entails a study of the solution environment as well as of the problem per se. In this case the focus of interest is on those factors pertaining to the potential for action. This may include resources that can be mobilized, the array of forces and parties favorable to or opposing a given initiative, past history in dealing with the issue and its attitudinal and political aftermath, and others. While the problem assessment is greatly concerned with "analytical tasks" of a cognitive nature, the action environment assessment may include a high proportion of "interactional tasks" involving relationships with people (Perlman and Gurin, 1972).

Action Feasibility

Brager and Specht (1973) refer to this aspect of assessment as gauging action feasibility. In part it involves determining if one has a "good" problem in terms of building an organized attack on it. In their view it includes consideration of such factors as the concreteness or immediacy of the problem. The more immediate and concrete it is, the greater its potential for explaining it to people and mobilizing their participation. Another consideration is the potential reward or benefit to be derived from taking action. If the alleviation of a problem offers greater or more immediate benefit, it has more mobilizing leverage. The prospect for successful outcome is a closely related factor. Others include degree of accessibility to targets, the extent of public support, and the amenability of the problem to a collective solution. From an assessment point of view a "good" problem is one that reflects a real need in the community, as well as one that shows some potential of movement in light of the outlay of energy and resources that will be applied to it.

The article by Lauffer in this section provides an excellent review of considerations to take into account in assessing the task or solution environment. Force field analysis in particular can be used effectively for this purpose.

Assessment and the Decision-Making Process

The accumulation of assessment data is a necessary but insufficient basis for determining the direction of intervention. Data have to be reviewed and interpreted. Then decisions must be made concerning the most advantageous course of action suggested by the evidence and one's professional judgment.

Kahn (1969) has written extensively on this subject and has referred to "planning as choosing." He indicates that one aspect of decision making is highly analytical as well as complex. He lists the following elements in rational planning for services: (1) define the problem in detail; (2) diagnose the causes; (3) seek relevant theories; (4) get realistic estimates of scope and scale; (5) consider the interrelationships of component parts; (6) project relevant variables into the future; (7) inventory present resources and estimate future resources; (8) compute presently available and potentially available manpower; (9) examine relevant legal rights, sanctions, precedents; (10) translate all this as appropriate into geographic or time units, or subdivide it by other critical variables; (11) assemble interpretations by others on these facts and appraise such interpretations; and (12) estimate consequences of various possible interventions.

Once the facts have been assembled, there remains the task of organizing and weighting them in a way that leads to a specific decision on action. Some rather technical procedures have been developed; Article 5 by Rycus provides an overview of some of these. Rycus provides an introduction to such methods as forecasting, decision trees, and minimax analysis. Students should not expect to be able to apply these complex techniques after reading this article. The intent is to heighten awareness and point to content that may be worth further study.

More qualitatively, Rycus suggests some factors to consider in arriving at an intervention decision, including the risk involved in the initiative, turbulence that might be created by the change, the uncertainty of attaining the objective, and the specific nature of the change that will be brought about if the initiative is successful.

Value Dimensions

However, as Kahn (1969) rightly points out, intervention choices are heavily tinged with value considerations. Faced with data about rising crime rates, some individuals will condemn offenders and urge more prisons and longer sentences. Others will place part of the blame on society and advocate for prevention and rehabilitation. Kahn indicates that what is involved is an interplay between knowledge and preferences. Therefore, the process of making planning more rational should include making value preferences among the interested parties more explicit. One way to do this is to encourage the parties' participation in assessment and decision making. Morris and Binstock (1966) state that "mixtures of rationality and value are involved in the basic decision" and that these are based to some extent on "judgments as to merit" (p. 93). Stephen Leacock's young man needed not only facts about road conditions, but also some awareness of his philosophy of life, in order to decide on a direction to go.

The Tropman piece exemplifies the weighting and balancing of values in arriving at a planning decision. He introduces such concepts and techniques as averaging, sectoring, and adjudicating, among others, as means for dealing with value conflicts in making planning decisions. While the context is planning for the elderly, the interplay of value choices and the process followed is of a general nature.

Assessment in Context

Over time there are shifts in the political and economic climate surrounding community practice. Different approaches, target populations, and objectives rise and fall in salience and popularity. For social workers it is important that in the face of such fluctuations there needs to be a continuing commitment to meeting the needs of those who share least in the benefits of society—the poor and minorities. For this reason we have included in this section an appraisal of the circumstances of ethnic minority communities in the decade of the 1980s by Rivera and Erlich. Clearly we prefer to place assessment in the context of humanistic values, including social justice, that have traditionally characterized and guided the human service professions.

Jack Rothman

References

Bradshaw, Jonathan, "The Concept of Social Need," *New Society* 30 (March 1972): 610–643.

Brager, George, and Harry Specht, *Community Organizing* (New York: Columbia University Press, 1973).

Cox, Fred M., et al., eds., *Strategies of Community Organization: A Book of Readings,* 3d ed. (Itasca, Ill.: F. E. Peacock Publishers, 1979).

Kahn, Alfred J., *Theory and Practice of Social Planning* (New York: Russell Sage Foundation, 1969).

Lane, Robert P., "The Nature and Characteristics of Community Organization— A Preliminary Inquiry," in Ernest B. Harper and Arthur Dunham, eds., *Community Organization in Action: Basic Literature and Critical Comments* (New York: Association Press, 1959).

Morris, Robert, and Robert H. Binstock, *Feasible Planning for Social Change* (New York: Columbia University Press, 1966).

Perlman, Robert, and Arnold Gurin, *Community Organization and Social Planning* (New York: John Wiley, 1972).

1. ANALYZING THE HUMAN SERVICE AGENCY

Yeheskel Hasenfeld

Social work practice is embedded in an organizational context. The characteristics of the organization—mandate and domain, interorganizational relations, service technology, and structure of work—determine to a significant extent how social workers discharge their professional responsibilities, and particularly the structure and content of their relations and transactions with client systems. To wit: organizational mandate and domain define the type of clients the worker will encounter; interorganizational relations influence the resources the worker will have to respond to client needs; and the service technology will prescribe the range of service techniques and procedures the worker can use. Most importantly, the degree of professional discretion available to the worker is organizationally determined.

To enhance their effectiveness, social workers must understand the organizational parameters and dynamics which shape their role performance and responses to client systems. Too readily, workers tend to blame the client, themselves, or their immediate superiors for perceived failures and difficulties in responding to client needs. Less often do they realize and recognize that factors inherent in the political economy of the organization constrain their behavior and professional effectiveness (Hasenfeld, 1983). Such misplaced "diagnosis"

renders the workers impotent in attempting to change and improve their performance. It is, therefore, incumbent on the social workers to understand the political economy of their organization, namely the determinants and processes by which power and resources are mobilized from the environment and allocated internally (Wamsley and Zald, 1976). Only with such knowledge can the workers hope to undertake organizational change strategies to enhance the effectiveness of their service delivery system (Hasenfeld, 1980).

Community practitioners must understand not only the organizational context of their own practice, but also the organizations that directly affect the welfare of the client systems on whose behalf they advocate. Effective advocacy, brokerage, and mediation—key roles for community practitioners—require a thorough understanding of the political economy of the targeted organizations. Similarly, community planning, and specifically mobilization of resources on behalf of community groups, requires careful analysis of the interorganizational relations among the key human service organizations in the community. In both instances, the organizational analysis is a prerequisite for the selection of appropriate community intervention tactics.

The purpose of the following "organizational map" is to direct the worker in gathering systematic information about the organization. The aim is to give the worker a basic knowledge of the organ-

---

Reproduced by permission of the author.

ization and to identify those elements requiring further inquiry. The first part of the mapping process focuses on the agency's interorganizational relations and includes sections on the agency environment, market relations, and regulatory groups. The second part directs attention to the internal features of the organization: its structure, technology, domain and goals, clients, and resources. Technical terms are defined at the point in the text where they are introduced.

THE AGENCY AND INTERORGANIZATIONAL RELATIONSHIPS

1. Agency Environment

To understand the behavior of any agency, it is necessary to be knowledgeable about the community in which it functions. A wide array of factors may influence agency behavior, but it is expected that these will vary among agencies and communities.

A. Locate, study, and summarize demographic data relevant to understanding the environment in which this agency exists. Included would be data about population composition and mobility, economic base, tax policy and situation, governmental, welfare, business and industrial structures, housing, medical facilities, and so forth. (Sources for the above data include: U.S. Census and Department of Labor reports, courts, city planning commissions, school census and planning reports, Chamber of Commerce, university library, etc.)

B. As far as possible, map the "organization set" for the agency being studied. Indicate differential types of relationships such as formal authority, regulatory, complementary, informal, etc.
   1. Of these relationships, which ones are perceived by the agency as most important in the transactions? Why? Which ones the least? Why?
   2. With which additional groups, organizations, institutions, etc., would the agency like to develop relationships? Why?
   3. Identify any major problems the agency has encountered in developing linkages with other groups.

C. What is the nature of the communication system between the agency and its "organizational set"?
   1. What mechanisms has the agency used or developed to secure and process information from its organizational set and the general environment?
   2. Identify formal and informal channels of communication.
   3. What is the quality of the information exchanged?
   4. What barriers and gaps to communication can be identified?

D. What planning, coordinating, or governing bodies exist between the agency and its organizational set?
   1. Does the agency have delegated representatives to such bodies? If so, to which groups? How are representatives selected?
   2. Is content from these activities considered in agency meetings or is the representation only of a pro forma type?

E. Identify the principal sources of material resources for the agency (e.g., taxes, fees, contributions, endowments).
   1. What strategies has the agency developed to secure and maintain resources?
   2. What problems has the agency encountered in this area?
F. Identify any major areas of conflict between the agency and members of the "organizational set." How has the agency handled such conflict?
G. As far as possible assess the relative power position of the agency to other groups in the organizational set.
   1. How much influence does the agency seem to have?
   2. What coalitions, if any, has the agency joined? Why?
H. Identify the principal sources of legitimation for the agency (e.g., political groups, governmental units, public at large, professional organizations, special interest groups).

In all of the above, indicate the impact of the various environmental characteristics upon the activities of the agency. For example, do certain characteristics of the "organization set" facilitate or constrain agency decision making?

From the perspective of the organization, what type of external pressures and forces have interfered most in the organization accomplishing its goals? What modes of influence and adaptation has the organization used to minimize such pressures?

II. Market Relations

Market relations are: (1) the complex of arrangements, exchanges, and contingencies the target agency (i.e., the agency under study) encounters in disposing of its output. The units which receive the agency's outputs are "receiving units" (questions A-J). (2) Its relations with other agencies offering complementary and similar (competing) services (questions K-T). Complementary services are those services provided by external units which assist the target agency in achieving its tasks with the clients, services given to clients concomitantly with those of the target agency, and services given to clients upon referral by the target agency.

A. Identify the major external units (families, communities, agencies, etc.) which import, purchase, or use the agency's outputs; in so doing, indicate the nature and proportion of the agency's output marketed to each of these units.
B. How does the target agency identify external units as actual or potential "receiving units"?
   1. Is information about the receiving units (e.g., their address, contact personnel, input criteria) readily available in codified form for appropriate staff in the target agency?
      a. If "no," how do staff know about potential receiving units?
      b. If "yes," provide illustrative examples and indicate how such information is maintained "current."

C. Where possible, for each of the units receiving the outputs of the agency, identify:
1. The amount of freedom they have in accepting or rejecting the output.
2. The nature of the preconditions, if any, they set up for accepting certain outputs.

D. Can you discern how these preconditions were set up and by whom?

E. What type of information, if any, is requested by each of these units about the output and in what form is it furnished to them? (For example, what information is given to a halfway house that accepts a client from a state hospital?)

F. Who in the agency is in charge of marketing the agency's outputs to these units? What is their training and status in the agency?

G. From interviews with these staff and analyzing clients' characteristics upon exit from the agency, estimate the extent to which the agency takes into account the preconditions and specifications made by the units receiving the outputs.

H. Are there any indications of difficulties, strains, and problems on the part of the agency in meeting these preconditions? Describe them.

I. What are the possible and actual reactions of the receiving units if some preconditions are not met?

J. Summarize the patterns of the relations between the target agency and each of its receiving units.

K. Identify the units which provide *complementary* services to the target agency. In so doing, describe:
1. The nature of the service given.
2. The kinds of clients (or staff) receiving it.
3. The frequency with which these services are provided.

L. Identify the preconditions, if any, that the target agency must meet to secure these services.

M. How do staff evaluate the importance of securing each of these services in terms of accomplishing their tasks?

N. What services, payments, or other resources does the target agency provide, if any, to each of these units?

O. Identify those agencies in the community which provide services *similar* to the target agency. Indicate the extent of the similarity in terms of services given and clients served.

P. How does the executive core of the target agency compare the agency vis-à-vis these agencies in terms of:
1. Tasks performed by staff?
2. Desired goals to be achieved?
3. Characteristics of clients?
4. Staff-client relations?
Indicate in the comparison what is perceived to be unique to the target agency by the executive core.

Q. Rank these agencies and the target agency in terms of budget size, number of clients served per year, and number of line personnel. (In the case of multifunction agencies, compare the subunits engaged in the same kinds of services.)

R. Does the target agency have any form of contact, arrangement, etc., with these agencies? If so, describe their content.

S. Is there competition for clients among these agencies? If so, how is it manifested?

T. Are there efforts underway to move toward complementarity, combines, or other forms of organization where the target agency and one or more other agencies provide similar services for clients?

III. Regulatory Groups

Regulatory groups are all the major organizations, legislative or legal bodies, associations, boards, etc., toward which the target agency must be *accountable* and from which it must receive approval, formal and informal, for its domain and the legitimacy of its activities. Such units may certify the agency, review operations of the agency as a whole or subunits of it, enact rules the agency must adopt, etc.

A. Identify the major units and organizations that periodically inspect, review, and evaluate various aspects of the agency's activities. In so doing classify the various units according to:
1. The regulatory function that each unit performs (e.g., certifies, accredits, makes recommendations, legislative review, etc.)
2. The aspect of the agency's activities of concern to each of these units.
3. The kinds of mechanisms each unit uses to maintain relations with the agency and vice versa

(e.g., representative from an agency's board, periodic meetings, etc.).

B. What criteria, if any, are being used by each unit to evaluate the agency's activities?

C. Were these criteria agreed upon mutually by the agency and the unit, imposed on the agency, suggested by the agency, or established in other ways? What is the agency's view of the legitimacy and utility of the regulatory unit's regulatory efforts?

D. What specific kinds of information are requested by these units and in what form is information furnished to them? Analyze the nature of the information given in terms of:
1. Is it intrinsic to the nature of the activities reviewed; that is, does the information directly describe the nature of the activities reviewed, or provide some indirect assessment of them?
2. Does each unit requesting the information specify the kind of questions, data, and analysis it wants, or are these left to agency personnel to decide?
3. Is the information provided on a continuous or discontinuous basis?
4. Does the information provided lend itself to further analysis beyond that done by the agency? If so, does the agency receive any feedback from the regulatory units about comparative performance, etc., vis-à-vis other similar agencies?

E. Who in the agency is in charge of

maintaining relations and working with these units? In each of the regulatory units who is in charge of maintaining contact with the target agency, and how is it done?

F. What are the possible sanctions that each of these units can impose on the agency? Rank the units in terms of severity of sanctions each can potentially impose. Can the unit freely impose the sanctions?

G. By interviewing the agency's executive core, find out which of these units they consider the agency is most dependent upon in terms of continuation of services and what reasons they give for their assertions.

H. Based on your observations, review of reports, etc., estimate the amount of effort, resources, and personnel time spent by the agency to meet the requirements of each unit.

I. For each of these units, what do the agency's staff conceive to be the regulatory group's expectations re:
   1. The characteristics of the clients?
   2. The desired changes to be achieved?
   3. The appropriate intervention techniques that need to be utilized?

J. What is the nature of any discrepancies between each unit's expectations and those of other units or the staff's expectations?

K. Assess the impact of the regulatory functions of each of these units upon the effectiveness and efficiency of the provision of services to clients by the agency.

L. Identify any civic groups which, though they do not carry regulatory functions, have been involved in supporting, challenging, or expressing concern about the mandate of the agency.
   1. Estimate the resources (financial, personnel, prestige, connections with other organizations, etc.) that each of these groups has or can mobilize.
   2. What types of pressures or support have they brought on the agency?
   3. Identify any conflicting expectations these groups may have in relation to the agency's operations.
   4. How does the agency handle its relations with each of these groups?

ORGANIZATIONAL ANALYSIS

1. Organizational Structures, Technologies, and Processes

A. Structure
   1. Outline the organizational chart of the agency, identifying the major formal structural components which can be used to characterize the organization.
   2. What various informal structures can be identified in the organization, and what effects, if any, have these structures had on organizational technologies and processes?

B. Technology
   1. Describe the various types of technologies in the organization.
      a. The organization's standards governing the perfor-

mance, control, and specification of that technology.

b. The kind of feedback mechanisms that exist or have been established to assess the technology.

c. The manner in which that technology is linked with other components of the organization.

d. The method of evaluating the output.

C. Decision making. Identify issues that have significant consequences for the service delivery of the agency.

1. Describe the factors that have led to the emergence of each issue.

2. Identify the roles and positions of the key participants in the decision-making process.

3. Evaluate the relative influences or power of each participant.

4. What position toward the issue did each participant take? What assumptions and ideologies underlay them?

5. Identify the processes and procedures through which decisions were reached or attempted.

6. What relations (i.e., locations, bargaining, competition) were formed among the participants in arriving at each decision?

7. Assess the degree of participation in the decision process of various staff groups and clients.

8. What organizational constraints played a role in affecting the nature of the issue and the resulting decision?

9. What mechanisms were developed to implement the decisions?

10. How will the decisions affect services?

D. Control-coordinating. Describe the formal and informal process of socialization and control of individual staff members, divisions or departments, and clients in the organization.

E. Conflict-communication

1. Identify and describe major areas of internal and external conflict.

2. What strategies and tactics have been used by the organization to resolve these conflicts?

3. What type of conflict has been viewed by the organization as functional? Why? What type as dysfunctional? Why?

4. What systems have been developed for transmitting information within and outside of the organization?

5. How does the agency evaluate the effectiveness of the received and transmitted information, both within and outside of the organization?

II. Organizational Domain and Goals

A. Organizational domain means the claims which the organization stakes out for itself in terms of: (1) the range of human problems, issues, and concerns it purports to handle. (These may include concerns about problems of malfunctioning as well as concerns about enhancement and improvement of individual and social functioning); (2) the services offered; and (3) the population entitled to use the service.

1. Identify and list the specific human problems and concerns that this agency is set up to handle. In so doing, classify these by (a) the unit to which the problem or concern is related (e.g., individual, family, community, etc.), and (b) what in the unit is the target of concern (e.g., occupational role of the individual, parent-child relations, organization of community health services, etc).

2. Identify and list the services that the agency offers vis-à-vis the problems and issues it attempts to handle.

3. Identify those units which are eligible for the services offered by the agency. In so doing enumerate the conditions and qualifications they have to meet in order to be officially eligible for services.

B. Organizational goals. The concept of organizational goals generates different meanings and different guides for action in various parts of the organization, varying with the frames of reference and objectives of those who define or interpret organizational goals. Yet, they should be distinguished from organizational domain. The domain defines the areas in which the organization will function, but not the desired ends and outcomes its members aim at achieving in these areas and the corresponding services. Such definitions are the function of goals.

1. Cite the official statements, if any, which describe the mission and goals of the agency. Have there been major changes in the content of such statements in the agency's recent past?

2. As a result of interviewing the executive core of the agency, how would you describe their perspectives on the organization's goals?

   a. What do they see as the agency's objectives in relation to the clients? What priorities do they establish among the several goals?

   b. What perceptions do they have about the relevant characteristics of their clients as they define them?

   c. What roles do they see the agency playing in the larger community?

   d. What aspects of the agency's programs do they see as best reflecting their objectives?

   e. What do they identify as the major problems or tasks that require prompt solutions?

3. Summarize the ideological commitments of the executive core, that is, their belief systems about the characteristics of the clients; the nature and purpose of the intervention technologies; the desired changes to be achieved in the clients and the role of line personnel vis-à-vis clients.

4. From interviews with line personnel answer the following:

   a. What do they perceive as their major objectives in relation to clients?

   b. Can you discern a priority

ranking among the various objectives mentioned?

c. What perceptions do they hold about the relevant characteristics of their clients?

d. What perceptions do they hold about the proper staff-client relations?

e. What role do they see the agency playing in the larger community?

5. From interviews with clients, answer the following:

a. What do they see as the major objectives of the agency?

b. What expectations do they have of staff?

c. What would they like the agency to do which it does not do currently?

6. Summarize the similarities and discrepancies among the perspectives of the executive core, line staff, and clients about agency's goals.

7. From observations of staff-clients relations, what are your conclusions as to actual tasks that staff perform?

8. From reviewing the agency's allocation of personnel, budget, and other resources to various work units, which tasks and objectives receive more priority?

9. Compare the existing priority given to various tasks based on allocation of resources to that purported by the executive core and other staff.

III. Client Inputs

A. Present a profile of the clients served by this agency.

1. If the clients are individuals or families describe:
   a. Age, sex, and race
   b. Socioeconomic status
   c. Place of residence
   d. Most frequent presenting problems or concern

2. If the clients are other organizations or associations, describe:
   a. The stated goals and functions of these organizations
   b. The major services they provide to achieve their goals
   c. The characteristics of their constituent population (see 1)
   d. The amount of resources (financial, personnel) these organizations have

B. What is the rate or extent of the problem in the community which the agency is designed to serve? What proportion of this possible case load is served by the agency?

C. What admission criteria do clients have to meet in order to benefit from the services of the agency?

D. How were these criteria established (e.g., were they externally imposed, based on individual staff decision, etc.); and how much control did the agency's staff have in setting them?

E. Observing staff, analyzing data on the clients' characteristics, and comparing those accepted for services versus those rejected, identify the *actual* mechanisms staff use to select and screen clients.

F. How do these compare to the formally stated admission criteria?

G. Identify and chart the different routes that clients can take in the agency, and indicate some of the major criteria used to route clients at each juncture (e.g., initial routing to major divisions in the agency, further routing to specific services, movement from one work unit to another, etc.). Develop a flow chart of initial client case processing.

H. In assigning clients to services, can you differentiate subcohorts of clients, each of whom is characterized by a common client profile and a common service (e.g., all clients of a certain age, race, income, and problem receive a certain kind of service)?

I. By interviewing and observing staff and clients, analyze the extent to which clients can actively negotiate their admission for services and be actively involved in decisions about the kinds of services that will be provided for them.

J. Can you identify what types of clients have better chances of negotiating successfully with staff as compared to those who have little chances of doing so?

K. What alternatives do clients have in seeking the needed services?

L. To what extent is the agency dependent on clients for financial support?

M. To what extent is cooperation on the part of the client essential for staff to perform their tasks?

N. Are clients referred to the agency by other organizations (or individual professionals)? If so,
   1. Describe the organizations engaged in referral and the extent of their referral.

2. Analyze the extent to which the target agency is dependent upon each of these organizations for receiving clients, financial support, professional services (e.g., testing, diagnosis, supporting services, etc.) and personnel.
3. To what extent is the target agency free to accept or reject referrals?
4. What kinds of services, if any, does the target agency reciprocate for referrals?

O. Identify any pressures exerted on the agency to accept and reject certain client cohorts:
   1. What are the agency's responses to these demands?
   2. What do you consider to be the organizational reasons for such responses?

P. Identify the people in the agency in charge of client intake, their professional status, and their position in the agency.

Q. What is the ratio of clients per line staff (e.g., average case load)?

R. Can you infer from observations and other information what types of clients the agency seems to prefer?

S. In some agencies clients are given some form of representation (e.g., P.T.A. membership, advisory board, etc.). Do clients in the target agency have any form of representation? If so, describe:
   1. The criteria used and the ways clients are recruited to such roles
   2. The formal tasks assigned to such a body
   3. The nature of the decisions made by this body

4. The role of staff vis-à-vis this representation
5. The amount of influence such a body has on the agency's policies and the amount of control staff have on the decisional processes of this group

T. Are there any segments of the agency's clients who are organized in some formal pattern, yet not represented in the agency governance structure (e.g., welfare recipients' associations)? If so,
   1. Describe the characteristics of the clients belonging to that association
   2. How did it come into being?
   3. What are its major objectives?
   4. What strategies are being utilized to achieve these objectives?
   5. How does the executive core react and respond to this association?
   6. Can you discern any influence such association has over the agency's policies?

U. What are the various methods used by the agency to assess clients' needs?

V. From the perspectives of the executive, various other staff, client community residents, or others outside the organization, what are the areas of conflicts and gaps in client services and types of service delivery patterns in the organization? What steps have been taken to resolve conflicts and close such gaps?

IV. Resources Inputs

By resources inputs we refer mainly to those external units which provide the target agency with its financial basis and those units which provide its personnel. You should note that many units will assume a number of functions in relation to the target agency, such as combining regulatory and funding functions. Hence there may be considerable overlap in your analysis of these units.

A. Financial
   1. Identify the major units which provide the agency with its financial resources.
      a. What proportion of the total agency's budget is contributed by each of these units?
      b. To what extent does each supporting unit specify the activities for which the funds are to be allocated?
   2. What criteria are being used by each of these units in determining their allocation of resources to the agency?
   3. Can you discern whether these criteria have been determined by the unit exclusively, by negotiation with the target agency, or what?
   4. What types of information are requested by these units, and in what forms are they furnished to them? Provide examples.
   5. Who in the agency is in charge of maintaining relations and working with the target agency?
   6. In each of the funding units, who is in charge of maintaining contact with the target agency?
      a. What forms do such contacts take?
      b. Does such a person par-

ticipate in the policy decision-making processes in the agency?

7. Through interviewing agency's staff in charge of contact with each unit, what do they perceive to be the specific preconditions and requirements that the agency has to meet in order to secure funds from each unit?

8. Based on your observations, review of reports, etc., estimate the amount of efforts, resources, and personnel time spent by the agency to meet the requirements of each unit.

9. Are there any indications of difficulties or strains on the part of the agency to meet the preconditions set by the funding units?

10. How do these external units check whether their requirements have been met by the agency?

11. Can agency's staff identify any expectations or beliefs on the part of each funding unit regarding:
   a. The characteristics of the clients?
   b. The desired changes to be achieved?
   c. The appropriate intervention techniques?
   d. The role of staff vis-à-vis clients?

12. How do these beliefs compare with those of the agency's staff?

13. Assess the impact that each funding unit has on the ways in which the agency renders its services (e.g., type of service

given, nature of personnel agency can afford to hire, number of clients served, etc.), through the requirements each makes, the amount of resources given, restrictions on their use, and the like.

14. What external units are considered to be the agency's immediate competitors for resources vis-à-vis each of the fund providing units?

15. Does the target agency provide any services to each of the funding units? Are there other agencies which provide similar services to these units?

16. Describe the budgetary process in the agency in relation to such factors as planning programs, determining cost, securing funds, allocating funds, etc.

17. Describe the method(s) the agency has used in an attempt to measure benefits (outcome). To what extent is the planned program congruent with the organization's outputs? What problems have been encountered internally and externally in justifying its program and budget?

B. Personnel
   1. Identify the units from which the agency's personnel are recruited.
   2. What criteria are used by the agency for hiring personnel for each major work unit (excluding building maintenance staff)?
   3. Analyze staff characteristics in terms of their formal education, training for current task, and prior experience.

4. What methods are used by the agency to recruit its staff? What problems does the executive core encounter in recruitment efforts?

5. In the eyes of the executive core what kinds of demands, questions, and contingencies are expressed by potential staff as conditions for employment?

6. How are these met and handled by the agency?

7. Are there any direct relations between the agency and the units which provide staff?
   a. Describe the nature of these relations.
   b. Does the agency provide any services (e.g., training, research, etc.) to these units?

8. Identify the major professional and occupational associations with which staff affiliate. Does their affiliation serve a regulatory function? If so, how?

9. Are there conflicts among staff groups with different professional and organizational affiliations in relation to their beliefs? How are these expressed in the agency?

10. From the perspectives of the executive core, which of these associations has had the greatest influence on the agency's ideologies in working with clients?

11. What formal and informal criteria are used for evaluating the performance of staff?

12. What is the agency's orientation to the use of paraprofessionals?

13. If there are paraprofessionals in the agency, what mechanisms, if any, are or have been used to integrate professional and paraprofessional staff?

14. Has the agency experienced any particular positive and negative consequences as a result of employing paraprofessionals?

CONCLUSION

The mapping of the agency's critical elements should provide you with a beginning understanding of its structure and operations. Moreover, it should sensitize you to those aspects of the agency which are most relevant to the community organization issue you are addressing. For example, should your concern be the increased access to agency services by clients from oppressed social groups, the mapping may indicate the magnitude of the problem by studying the client input patterns and point to potential barriers that may exist because of personnel characteristics and training, interorganizational relations, or the operationalization of agency domain and goals. Hence, the mapping process serves as a diagnostic tool in identifying organizational factors affecting community practice.

REFERENCES

Hasenfeld,Y., "Implementation of Change in Human Service Organizations: A Political Economy Perspective," *Social Service Review* 54(1980): 508-520.

_____, *Human Service Organizations* (Englewood Cliffs, N.J.: Prentice-Hall, 1983).

Wamsley, G.L., and M. N. Zald, *The Political Economy of Public Organizations* (Bloomington, Ind.: Indiana University Press, 1976).

2. HOW TO DIAGNOSE A NEIGHBORHOOD

Rachelle B. Warren and Donald I. Warren

To all human service organizations, public and private (with or without outreach programs), to school systems and parent-school organizations, civic groups, volunteer agencies and associations, to labor unions and social action groups as well as others who by tradition have treated neighborhoods with a certain sameness, this chapter is for you. Neighborhoods are different. Effective action requires approaches based on subtle but important differences. This chapter describes, step by step, a method to capture the distinctive interwoven helping patterns—the networks crisscrossing the neighborhood fabric. Identifying the sources of this uniqueness is the first step in designing effective outreach programs and organizing for citizen action.

A. THE ETHOS OF NEIGHBORHOOD ETHNOGRAPHY: A PRACTICAL STEP-BY-STEP GUIDE

The methodology employed in this ethnographic work consists of a form of open-ended interview-and-observation effort using a set of guiding concepts and dimensions of local community and can function systematically to assess the neighborhood and community as a behavioral setting for help giving and getting.

The knowledge gained from this type of research has a variety of implications, one of which is for the way that social services should be organized. By investigating how different populations solve problems, we will be able to qualify what constitutes a resource for a given population and to describe the nature of the problem-coping processes surrounding those formal and informal resources. In this way, this kind of study can provide valuable insights that have direct implication for citizens and organizations to be better equipped to plan service interventions that are consistent with the unique coping styles, culture, and helping networks of a given population.

Gaining Entrée: City Hall Has Its Place

When you first arrive in a community, it's a good idea to spend a short time getting a feel for the city as a whole. Go to city hall and look around—note the location of the building. Is it near other community service centers such as the library, the courthouse, a general community center, the social service offices? Where is the central business district? What else is available within the immediate vicinity? What offices are housed in the building itself? Who are the city officers? What type of government does the city have—city council? mayoral? city manager? Usually the names of these persons are readily available—you won't have to make an appointment with any official to get this information. Use your eyes and your

head; there's got to be a building directory, and there are usually pamphlets
telling about the city and city services on
display. Pick them up and look them
over. This type of general background
information will give you a hint as to
what's available from the city and how
accessible these services are, background
that will help you in understanding what
the people in the neighborhoods might
be talking about or concerned with.

Maps. Maps are probably the most
important and useful items that you will
be able to garner from the city hall. They
are vital and usually are available at only
a minimal cost. Get two *street maps* of
the city: one for yourself to make notes
on, and one to use in interview situations.

Make sure you get street maps and not
precinct maps. The precinct maps have
dark lines outlining voting districts and
may be confusing in cases where voting
precincts do not correspond with elementary school districts or what people
in general think of as "their" neighborhood.

Find the sample neighborhoods on the
map. On "your" map only, outline the
neighborhoods. You can pinpoint services, business districts, etc. A good map
enables you quickly and clearly to see
"your" neighborhood in relation to other
neighborhoods and to the city in general;
it enables you to locate people all over
the community.

The Phone Book. The telephone book
for your area is usually available free
from the telephone company. All you
have to do is to request it and give a
phone number—either your own home
phone or where you work. The phone
book is a great time-saver. Carry it with
you for easy access to addresses and
numbers. Use it at home to set up

appointments, to contact referrals, and
to find churches and pastors. Or just
thumb through it to familiarize yourself
with the area.

The Library. It's a good idea to drop by
the library while you're on your initial
data-gathering mission. The usefulness
of the information available there, in
respect to the neighborhoods themselves, varies from city to city, but
usually available are listings on adult-
education offerings, city recreation programs, and senior-citizen's activities that
will help to build your background
regarding the community at large. Some
communities have neighborhood-fo-
cused programs stemming from the library such as bookmobiles or children's
films in neighborhood parks. It's good to
know about these in advance.

Newspapers. Pick up a copy of the local
newspaper. This will brief you on current
community issues and events. Be sure to
check the "Community Calendar" for
events that might be occurring in the
neighborhood—potluck suppers, block
parties, etc. A glance at the want ads can
tell you about garage or yard sales and
also can give you some idea about the
selling prices of homes in the various
areas of the city.

The Chamber of Commerce. The
chamber of commerce should have a list
of community organizations and contact
persons that is available at a small
cost—usually from $0.50-$2.50. This list
is an invaluable source of potential
neighborhood contacts. Go over the list
and locate the presidents of various
organizations on your map. Find out
where they live. If any of these people
live in "your" neighborhood, you're in
luck. Through their public listing, you
can feel free to call them and ask for an
appointment to talk with them about

their neighborhood. Usually the organizations represented on the Chamber of Commerce list run the gambit from the PTA to M.O.M.S. (Mothers of Men in Service), from the local bicycle club to the lapidary society.

It usually will not be necessary to explain yourself or your mission to any of the above institutions in order to get the information you seek. If you do happen across an inquisitive bureaucrat, tell the truth about why you are there. You do not have to adopt any role in order to legitimate or justify yourself. These are the places that people turn to for information, and your requests are in no way suspect or unusual.

Once you have received the basic information you need from these city-wide institutions, *STOP!!* If, in the course of your work in the neighborhoods, you are referred to certain city-wide agencies or officials, you can always go back to talk with them; but the focus of study is the neighborhood, and you should have enough background information by now to proceed.

B. TAPPING INTO THE NETWORKS

Familiarizing Yourself with the Area

Drive through the area. Map businesses, parks, schools, and any other important or interesting landmarks. Get a feel for housing type, activity level, and the geographical make-up of the neighborhood. Record your impressions, either in notes or on tape if a recorder is available. Then, park the car and survey on foot.

Even though you can cover more territory faster by driving, you are not making the most effective use of your survey time. It isn't necessary to map every house on every street; just get a feel for the area and the people. Maximize use of interaction—stop and chat with people who are out, and *keep your eyes open*. It isn't necessary to carry a pad and pencil or even a map if you've familiarized yourself with the streets. Just remember where you've been and make note of it later. Record your initial impressions as fully as possible—you can go back to them after working in the area for a while and check for clues to dimensions that might not have been brought out in your talks with informants. If your initial impressions and the information you've received don't jell, this can point out pathways that you should pursue. For instance: if you noted a poorer or sloppier area of the neighborhood, but no one you are referred to lives there, find out why. Or if you noticed some physical characteristic of the homes, such as porch chairs, but you've never seen anyone sitting in them, maybe you should try going into the neighborhood at a different time—in the evening or on the weekend—to see if the chairs really are indicative of interneighbor interaction.

Defining the Boundaries

A neighborhood can be many things to many people. Since elementary school districts represent jurisdictional definitions, and since the "real" neighborhood boundaries and school-district boundaries may not correspond, in the course of your field experience you may find it necessary to redefine the neighborhood. If so, proceed by lopping off sections of the area rather than by dividing the area into subneighborhoods and then rating them separately. Here are some conditions under which you might wish to eliminate a part of the area.

1. Major Physical Boundaries. Highways, rivers, major streets that cut through the area and isolate some section from the core of the neighborhood.
2. Historical Affiliation. If an area of the elementary school district has only recently been annexed, and there is evidence that this area is not really a part of the neighborhood, or if it maintains allegiance with its former area.
3. City Boundaries. Some school districts exceed the city borders and draw students from neighboring communities. Unless there is evidence for including the other community as a part of the neighborhood, stick to the community under study.

We recognize that many neighborhoods house two or more social classes or ethnic groups. This, of itself, is not enough evidence to divide the neighborhood into its subareas. We are interested in observing the interaction between the areas and in discovering the nature and intensity of social similarities and differences that may exist. Arguments for subdivision must be based on observed interaction, values, and norms—not on housing characteristics, social class, or ethnic affiliation alone.

Making Use of What's There

Here are some ideas of things to be on the lookout for while in the neighborhood.

1. Houses for Sale. Where are they? Are they clustered or dispersed throughout the area? Are any for sale by the owner? If so, go and look at it. What realtors are handling the sale of homes? Are these realtors locally based?
2. Construction and Home Repair. Note any homes being fixed up. Who's doing the work—neighbors or a construction company? What time of the day is the work being done?
3. Coffee Shops, Restaurants, and Bars. Are they locally oriented or franchise? Who frequents them?
4. Service Institutions. Are there any in the neighborhood? What type of services do they offer? Are they focused toward the neighborhood or the greater area?
5. Clubs and Organizations. Are there any clubhouses here? Or hints that local organizations exist, such as a street sign urging you to drive carefully installed by the Pleasant Pines Homeowners' Association?
6. Churches. What denominations are represented? Who is the pastor? Does he/she live in the area? (Check in your phone book.)
7. Stores. Do they service local customers, or are they areal in orientation? What type of merchandise is available in the area?
8. Parks. Are they well maintained? Who frequents the parks? What facilities are available? How many people are there?
9. Garage and Yard Sales. Stop in. Who's running the sale? Is one family selling goods on behalf of several neighbors? Are groups in the neighborhood participating? Notice what type of merchandise is on sale. Look at brand names, prices. Start up conversations if possible. It is not

necessary to push for information—take your cues from what is for sale.

10. Type and Make of Vehicles. Are they old or new, large or small? Is there on street parking? Are there recreational vehicles, foreign cars, station wagons, trucks?

11. Window Signs and Bumper Stickers. Are there any signs or stickers on display? What do they say? Is there a topical concentration, or are thematic signs fairly well dispersed?

12. General Appearance and Upkeep. Is it uniform throughout the area? Are there fences, pools, swing sets?

13. Activity Level. Take note of the time of day, the time of year, and (in more changeable climes) weather conditions. Look for evidence of activity if no one's about. You can check your impressions later by talking with people.

14. People's Reactions to You. Do they stare? Wave? Smile? Do they look out furtively from behind the blinds or offer "nice day" as they walk by?

15. Social Interaction. Is it hostile or friendly? Are people going from house to house, talking over fences, etc.?

You should not spend more than two or two-and-a-half hours on the initial survey. Observe and take note of what's available in the area. You will always have slack time when you're in the field for further investigation—and a better idea of how to spend your time after more contact with the area residents themselves.

If no one's out in the neighborhood, don't despair. You haven't wasted your time. You know the streets, the houses, the layout, and you should have some clues as to what the people do. Now is the time to go to your lists, to set up appointments, and to make contact with the people who live in the neighborhood.

Making Contact

In your initial survey you may have happened onto people—on the street, at garage sales, etc.—who have been willing to talk with you about their neighborhood. Most likely you didn't, or when you tried to press for the type of information needed, you were met with silence. Don't worry. It is not likely that most people will open up to strangers in a public setting. What you have learned from them is very valuable and a test against what people will tell you in a more formal situation.

Now, however, is the time to get into longer, deeper conversations with neighborhood residents. Whom do you go to? Hopefully, your list of organizational chairpersons from the chamber of commerce has someone from the neighborhood. If so, this is a good place to start. Especially if the person is not heavily tied in with the neighborhood institutions, i.e., PTA, church, school, etc. Call them and ask for an appointment. You must be ready to answer questions about your presence and purpose in the neighborhood. People on the list will probably be willing to talk to you and will supply you with valuable background information for approaching the more formal channels. Your contact probably will give you referrals to other of her/his friends and neighbors.

The Elementary-School Principal

Your best bet is to get to the elementary-school principal pretty soon.

Call and make an appointment; it might be necessary to get the approval of the school superintendent before the principal is allowed to talk with you. The principal has a wealth of information about the neighborhood and is especially informative in fields that you might have difficulty probing in home situations. He/she can give you a general overview of the neighborhood; home values, occupational makeup, percentage of single-parent families, demographic similarities or differences, estimated income levels, and leisure-time activities of the residents. The principal should be aware of any particular church influence, especially if a number of the children attending the school go to any one church. In addition, the principal is a valuable source regarding the incidence of A.D.C. and welfare support, and the frequency and type of child abuse in the neighborhood.

It is important to determine the nature and the depth of the principal's involvement in the neighborhood in order to do a comparative analysis of the effectiveness of principals in inducing or sustaining neighborhood cohesion.

Finally, the principal can give you easy referral access to some important people in the neighborhood. You should find out the names of neighborhood leaders and activists such as the PTA president or the head of the volunteer program (if the school has one). Ask the principal to identify the "chronic griper" and any persons who are active with groups like Boy Scouts, Little League, etc., that are important to the area. Give the principal the chance to initiate other references, and remember to let her/him talk—you can gain valuable information by letting the principal carry the conversational ball.

Don't Forget These Folks

Here is a list of people to be on the watch for in "your" neighborhood. All of these may not be represented in any one area. These are suggestions of the type of people you should ask about and possibilities for contacting if you feel you need further information or are not satisfied with the quality of the information you are receiving.

1. Elementary School Principal. This is a MUST.
2. Pastors. Talk to the pastor of any church located in the neighborhood if he/she is also a neighborhood resident. If you discover that a large segment of the neighborhood population attends a specific church, make an effort to see the clergyman regardless of where he lives. You may find that church affiliation is not a crucial factor in the neighborhood. In that case, don't spend too much time in church-affiliated channels.
3. PTA Presidents and School Volunteer Organizers. Another must. Try to assess the effectiveness and involvement of the PTA. If there is a volunteer organization, in what ways does it differ from the PTA? Do the memberships overlap? These contacts can be asked to set up group meetings or to invite their friends over to talk with you.
4. Chronic Griper. Ask people you meet with to identify the "chronic griper" of the neighborhood. If there is one, be sure to contact her/him. This person's information usually differs in telling ways from the overall picture presented by the more usual resident.
5. Presidents of Clubs and Social Organizations. If any of these people

live in your neighborhood, it's good to meet with them. Find out if the club is neighborhood based. Referrals gained from these contacts are good checks against the more formal referral networks. If the president of a city-wide organization, like the League of Women Voters, lives in the neighborhood, he/she is also a good source of information about other neighborhoods in the community.

6. Homeowners' Associations. If you discover a homeowners' association that is presently, or once has been, active in the area, make an effort to talk with someone involved with that association. Even if the association is now defunct, you want to know what it did do and why it has disbanded.

7. Boy Scouts, Girl Scouts, Little League. If organizations like these are active, talk with their leaders. This is one way of making contact with men in the neighborhood.

8. Neighborhood and Community Leaders. If anyone is identified as a leader, talk with her/him. Find out what leaders do and why certain people are considered to be leaders.

9. Realtors. Realtors can give you good demographic information about the city and the neighborhood—population groups, income brackets, etc.—and they can set this information in an historical perspective.

10. Local Business People. These people can be good contacts, especially if the business services the neighborhood primarily. Examples: "Ma & Pa store," a local bar, etc.

11. Service Agencies. If there are any service agencies in the neighborhood, drop in. Caution: most service agencies have a broad, area-wide clientele and may not be particularly useful in neighborhood studies.

12. The "Deviant." Try to isolate the types of "deviants" in the neighborhood: social, property, sexual. You may want to make an effort to talk with one, especially if you sense that your regular contacts are feeding you a line.

13. People with Special Economic Roles. If you find out about anyone in the neighborhood who has a special economic role—anything from babysitting in the home to a home-based construction company—contact that person. Policemen, firemen, and their ilk are especially good sources of this type of information.

14. Referrals. Be sure to follow along at least two separate referral pathways. It is important to see if the networks overlap or if they present different pictures of the neighborhood. Entrance to referral pathways should be generated from independent initial contacts, and these contacts should be as socially diverse as possible. E.g., the elementary school principal, and the president of the bowling league.

15. Age Groups. Try to meet with someone from different age groups. If there are a lot of senior citizens in "your" neighborhood, make an effort to contact them. If there are a lot of teenagers, go over to a group and start a conversation.

16. Ethnic Groups. Be sure to make contact with members of all relevant ethnic groups. This may be a significant source of helping/referral and may link this neighborhood to community-wide networks.

A Note on "The Key Informant"

It is advisable to set up interviews with certain "key informants"—persons who you believe will have a knowledge of the total community, a sense of history. Principals are an example of this type of individual. When you believe someone holds a potential wealth of general and important information, go in a twosome. One can write while one directs the discussion, and immediate debriefing to get down the many fine points will allow you both to profit from the neighborhood perspective.

Remember, it is not necessary for you to talk with someone on every block or at every other house. Your job is to identify networks, pursue them, and to discover how the neighborhood operates.

Chit-Chat

During the first few minutes of your visit, both you and your host are likely to feel strained and uncomfortable. Chit-chat helps to break down this tension and to set the tone for a free-flowing conversation. You can talk about anything—the weather, something in the house, the traffic—make small talk and establish trust.

Explain Your Presence

Give a quick run-down of your interest. Mention that you're trying to find out what holds a neighborhood together and how people help each other in this neighborhood. Ask for questions. Answer any questions truthfully. Some people will require a fuller knowledge of the scope of your presence than others. Be willing and able to satisfy them with all the information that they want. Use your discretion here—it isn't necessary to bore the host with a twenty-minute detailed description of your theoretical perspective, but it is necessary to eliminate any doubts that the neighborhood residents may have about you, your legitimacy, or your motives.

Neighborhood Definition

We have defined a neighborhood as an elementary-school district for several reasons, among which are that it is a compromise unit with an institutional focus, and that it provides a manageable area for observation within a limited time span. But it is important to find out how the residents define their neighborhood. Some people see their neighborhood as "just this block," others as the whole city. Bring out your unmarked map and ask the informant to tell you what he/she thinks of as his/her neighborhood. People will usually start talking about their immediate neighborhood and then their extended connections throughout the area. Listen, and encourage the informant to continue. Get information about churches, shopping areas, housing, gathering places—anything physical. Ask if the neighborhood has a name, and how the informant tells other people in the city where he/she lives. Find out about residential mobility, houses for sale. The resident of the neighborhood knows more about this than you do, and may well get carried away with his/her own expertise and give you information you wouldn't have been able to know about or to discover through directed questioning.

Follow Up Leads

During her/his description of the neighborhood, the informant has probably mentioned points or issues that pertain directly to your objectives. Follow up on these leads now. The informant may have mentioned areas where the residents hold block parties, streets where friends live, or homes that are sloppy. Find out more about the leads they have given you, and *do* direct the conversation toward helping networks or activities. But, base your questions on the foundations that the informant has already established.

Initiate New Subjects

By now you've probably established a basis of trust with the informant. He/she may have asked what else you want to know. Remember the objectives of your visit and hit upon points that have not been covered yet. Two methods of inquiry are useful when the informant does not really seem to understand what you want.

Draw upon your own experience. You've lived in at least one neighborhood in your life, and you've had contact with many, many people and situations in your work in other neighborhoods. Draw examples from your own experience to illustrate situations you are concerned with—what people do at the time of death; how men help each other with construction or home repair; the activities of volunteer groups at school or church. This type of exchange of information is important. You can't expect people to open up to you if you just sit there silently recording their every word. By opening up yourself, you reassure the informant, and make it easier for her/him to talk with you.

Propose a hypothetical situation. There are some topics that are taboo for certain people. Remember the gentlemanly edict

that politics and religion are not topics for polite discussion. When you feel you are treading near the boundaries of a forbidden or sensitive subject, or one that is threatening to the people you are talking with, don't push it through direct questioning. Proposing a hypothetical situation is a good way to get information regarding commitment to the neighborhood, child abuse, treatment of deviants, etc.

Hypothetical situations are "What if?" questions: What if you won the lottery? Would you move? What if someone moved into the neighborhood who abused her/his children? What if you needed your house rewired? What if someone is causing trouble? Frequently the informants will respond to your hypothetical formulation with concrete examples of what *does* happen in their neighborhood.

Get Referrals

Ask about leaders, friends—people you should talk with, or people whom the informant knows who he/she thinks would be willing to talk with you.

Let the Informant Close the Interview

When you feel that you have covered all the points you are concerned with, don't just pack up and go. Ask if there's anything more the informant thinks is important of interest about her/his neighborhood. You may have missed something very important and, at least, this gives the informant a time to express her/his own gripes or concerns.

C. THE MORE THE MERRIER: SOME HELPFUL FIELD IDEAS

There are certain situations when you

will want to have two ethnographers working together at one meeting with informants—in group discussions and key-informant interviews.

The Group Discussion

Group discussions are fantastic ways to cover a lot of territory quickly. If at all possible, you should try to set up at least one such situation in each neighborhood. You can ask neighborhood organizational people, e.g., PTA, to get some of their members together to talk with you; or you can suggest that a contact invite some friends and neighbors over for your visit. You've got a room full of people, all hooked into the same network—a ready-made lab situation for observing interaction. Note who's there and who isn't. Find out where the people live.

Group situations almost always flow more freely than the one-on-one interview. You need two ethnographers just to record the information. One person's tale elicits another's, and the situation may approach mayhem. In order to gain the most from the group discussion, the members of the ethnographic team must be attuned with one another. Their pacing is vital—one can write while the other talks, or, they may find themselves each involved in separate conversation groups.

The team should reconstruct the discussion *immediately* afterward in order not to lose the sense of what happened and in order to record anecdotes that the ethnographers were not able to take full notes on. An hour's debriefing is usually the minimum time allotted here to record all the many anecdotes as accurately as possible.

Slack Time: Time Well Spent

There's always going to be a lot of time between interviews, or at lunch and dinner time, when you won't be scheduled to meet with anyone. Spend as much of this time in the neighborhood as possible. If there are restaurants or bars in the area, eat there. Go to the stores, parks, or hangouts. Cover garage and yard sales. Look at homes for sale. These informal contacts are more meaningful once you have some concrete knowledge of the neighborhood. You can always work on your field notes in the local coffee shop—if someone asks you what you're doing, tell them. It's a good conversation opener.

Getting into the Home

You may be invited in by someone you meet on the street, but don't count on it. The best entrée is to get appointments—from lists, from previous contacts, or from general information about the neighborhood. Call beforehand and allow yourself enough time to let the conversation flow.

Take note of the physical properties of the home, exterior and interior. Any special aspects, such as a lovely garden, handmade objects, paintings, or construction work, are good conversation openers. You should pay attention to the furnishings, upkeep, and general style of the home.

The Sustained Ethnographic Interview

Remember—as an ethnographer, you are *not* a formal interviewer. There are certain items you do want to get at, but this information should evolve out of the informant's framework, not yours. Take your time and find things out indirectly. Follow their leads, don't cut them off,

LISTEN—the informant will undoubtedly mention topics that you're concerned with. Follow up on these points before delving into unintroduced areas.

Before you go out for an interview, familiarize yourself thoroughly with the organizer's exercises at the conclusion of this article.* Make notes of the information you want to get. One or two words should do. These notes are to remind you of points that you want to cover. They are *not* to be an interview format or a list of specific questions to ask. You can glance at this list during the course of your visit to see what further information you need to get. Go over these notes quickly if the phone rings or if your host is out of the room, then try to guide the conversation toward the uncovered areas.

As you gain experience, you will probably find some means of structuring the conversation that you feel comfortable with. This should grow from your experience in the field situation, not from intellectual theorizing as to the "proper" logical order of an interview.

Open Time—Contingency Plans

Leave time open after talking with persons who might be key informants, the elementary-school principal, etc. These people might call while you are present to set up meetings for you right away with neighbors—and you should be flexible. Have in mind a contingency plan in case this doesn't happen—you could go up to the messiest house in the neighborhood and ask the owners if they'd talk with you or interview the local shopkeepers.

*See Warren and Warren, *The Neighborhood Organizer's Handbook*, for exercises at the conclusion of each chapter.

Travel Time

The time you spend driving to and from the community can be some of your most productive hours. Rehash your day; talk it out. Fill in notes and embellish stories. A lot of the information you've received is intuitive. It is important to verbalize your impressions in order to crystallize what you *do* know. Work up hypotheses about neighborhood interaction and formalize plans for testing them. You can plan your future work in the neighborhood—whom you should see, what you need to look for, and how to go about it. Debrief and discuss.

Budgeting Time

It should not take more than four-and-a-half field hours to complete the initial community data gathering and the neighborhood survey. You may not feel that you have all the information you need, but there's sure to be slack time during the days you've scheduled interviews, and this can be most effectively used in walking about the neighborhood, shopping, or just hanging out.

Scheduling Interviews

After you have a bit of a feel for the area, it's time to schedule interviews. Set up interviews in advance. Allow a minimum of two to two and a half hours between the beginnings of interviews. You can spend the slack time in informal neighborhood interaction. Try to fill your field days as full as possible. You should be in the neighborhood during all times of day. Evenings are good for meeting the men or with women employed outside the home or for talking with families. A morning interview, two in the afternoon, and one in the evening is not unreasonable.

Monitoring Yourself

You should be aware of yourself and your effort on the residents in all field experiences. Dress appropriately for the neighborhood and the situation—don't alienate someone by your dress or demeanor before you get a chance to talk with her/him. Pay attention to what you do and to the type of responses your actions elicit. Make note of this. Watch for body cues—note seating arrangements and their effects on interviews. In your interactions with the neighborhood residents, you cannot be the isolated observer. The residents are making as many judgments about you as you are about them. Act accordingly.

Keeping a Record

It is necessary to record both your observations and your impressions daily. Anthropologists have a tradition of keeping a field journal on "empirical" observations and a field diary of their personal impressions and reactions. This is a good policy for neighborhood ethnographers to follow. As you gain knowledge of an area, you can go back and check your impressions, change your judgments if necessary, and uncover pathways of investigation that you should follow.

Take as complete a set of notes as possible. It will be easier to take notes in some interview situations than in others. Try to be complete, but remember that eye contact is important in maintaining conversation flow. Record as many direct quotes and stories as possible— these are invaluable. They hold a sense of

the people, of the neighborhood, that retelling cannot match.

Steering an Honest Course

In neighborhood ethnography, it is at times tempting to assume a role, to tell a story, in order to legitimize or justify yourself in the neighborhood. In all cases we must caution against such deception. Although you may gain immediate access, entrée, or information by disguising your real purpose in the neighborhood, role-playing can backfire, and whatever you may have gained in the short run can result in a long-term loss of legitimacy.

Neighborhoods are not very big, and news travels fast. When you don't know the networks that exist in the area, you risk losing all access by being caught in a pose. Don't back yourself into a corner.

The "Dynamic-duo" Approach to Neighborhood Ethnography

Experience suggests that the optimal ethnographic approach is to pair two people in one community. This is possible where randomization of elementary school districts has allowed for work in two neighborhoods within reasonably close proximity to each other.

While each person is responsible for the main organizing, interviewing, mapping, and analysis of her/his neighborhood, there are many advantages to using the "dynamic-duo" approach. First, going in as a team allows you to check out your impressions and to compare notes. This may be done while driving, over lunch at the local "Burger Queen" (or exotic little bistro), or at any other times when your paths might cross.

Second, your teammate may be drawn upon as a resource person. There are two basic plusses to this. For one thing, whenever you are facing a situation where you feel it is best to have two ethnographers in on the action, this is the person to whom you have immediate access. This is a matter of scheduling in advance so that both of you will be available to chat with groups, certain key informants, and school principals in *both* neighborhoods.

As an outgrowth of this team interview, you will have made certain observations that would have been denied you had you been confined to one neighborhood. For example, while driving to an interview in your teammate's neighborhood you will take note of the differences in housing characteristics, interaction patterns, status display, etc. You may note certain things that have not as yet been noted by your teammate. Such observations should be shared as they may encourage your teammate to explore different pathways. During the interview itself, you may hear issues raised that were not as yet mentioned by residents of "your" neighborhood. You may then want to bring these up as "having heard about some other issues when you were talking with residents

from another part of the city," when you are back in "your" neighborhood. The corollary to this is that you may (with your teammate's prior consent) bring up issues that are salient to "your" respondents but which, as yet, have been unexplored in your teammate's neighborhood.

When you are asked at some later point in time to compare your neighborhood with others in the community, you will then have a somewhat better perspective than that gleaned from your work in only one neighborhood.

A Final Word

Let the following advice serve as a postscript to what we have already indicated. By all means make note of the effect you think your presence might have on future neighborhood interactions. Remember, you are there to look at behaviors, examine values, and discover support networks in the neighborhood. But you should be aware that the presence of outsiders always represents a potential source of change, however minimal and however unintentional. Please note your impressions and put them in writing.

Organizer's Exercises

Physical Description of the Neighborhood

1. Includes a mapping of each block in terms of housing characteristics (single dwelling, age, size, and construction). Description should also note areas of commercial development, churches, meeting places, and important natural barriers suggesting internal differentiation of the total area.

2. Special physical attributes include evidence of political activity (signs, stickers, etc.)

3. Types of automobiles and special decorative features of homes (e.g., lampposts, grillwork, painting of homes).

Organizer's Exercises (continued)

4. Evidence of general upkeep and neighborhood improvements or lack of service:
   Neighborhood appearance and upkeep:

0	1	2	3	4	5	6	7	8	9
Poor									Excellent

5. What is the extent to which the neighborhood has a physically isolated boundary? (You should indicate on each boundary how many are marked by major subdivisions, by differences in housing, by physical barriers, or in contrast where there is little differentiation between the end of this neighborhood and the beginning of another. Therefore, the discussion should include each of the directions and what is true of them.)
   Physical isolation of area from the rest of city in terms of its boundaries:

0	1	2	3	4	5	6	7	8	9
Physically separated									Physically blends in

6. What are the number and variety of behavior settings that are found in the neighborhood? (Here we are speaking about parks and recreation areas, local stores or churches, street corners, back fences, any special settings that can bring people together.)

   a. Number of *potential* gathering places observed in the neighborhood:

0	1	2	3	4	5	6	7	8	9
None									Many

   b. Number of *observed* gathering places:

0	1	2	3	4	5	6	7	8	9
None									Many

   c. Diversity of potential gathering places:

0	1	2	3	4	5	6	7	8	9
None									Much

   d. Diversity of observed gathering places:

0	1	2	3	4	5	6	7	8	9
None									Much

   e. Competition over gathering places:

0	1	2	3	4	5	6	7	8	9
None									Much

7. What is the extent of demographic similarities, i.e., homogeneity versus heterogeneity of the neighborhood? (This includes how similar people are in regard to social characteristics such as age, family life cycle — preschool children versus teenage children — income, education, occupation, ethnic-group identification, etc. It may be possible to point out that a neighborhood has two different, evenly divided groups or several groups or a majority of one group and a minority of another or whatever helps spell out the diversity of the area.)

0	1	2	3	4	5	6	7	8	9
Homogeneous									Heterogeneous

3. SELECTING THE NEEDS ASSESSMENT APPROACH

George J. Warheit, Roger A. Bell,
and John J. Schwab

APPROACHES AVAILABLE

Needs assessment programs vary in comprehensiveness, complexity, cost, length of time to be conducted, information received, and relative effectiveness. This section outlines the various approaches and offers a review of their design, techniques, problems, costs, and advantages and disadvantages.

Siegel and his colleagues (1974) categorize the assessment approaches into three major areas: (1) community non-survey, (2) social and health indicators, and (3) community survey approaches. Our own research and experience suggest similar categories, expanded into five specific approaches:

1. Key informant
2. Community forum
3. Rates-under-treatment
4. Social indicators
5. Field survey*

These approaches can be used as parts of an integrated, sequential program, or they can be conducted independently.

Reproduced by permission of the authors. From *Needs Assessment Approaches: Concepts and Methods* by George J. Warheit, Roger A. Bell, and John J. Schwab, 1977, pp. 19-39, 136-142.

*Editors' note: The field survey approach is not included here, as it is covered by the Warrens in Article 2. For detailed procedures, work sheets, etc., see the original work from which this excerpt is drawn.

The relative effectiveness of any one of them is best measured by its success in securing the information necessary to implement the goals outlined in the description, conceptualization, and operationalization process. Each approach has merit and will be discussed in this section; however, the primary focus of this paper is on the *rates-under-treatment* and the *social indicators* approaches.

THE KEY INFORMANT APPROACH

Definition

The key informant approach is a research activity based on information secured from those in the area who are in a position to know the community's needs and utilization patterns. Therefore, the selection of a key informant is based on the individual's knowledge of the community, its people and their needs, and the patterns of services. The kinds of persons normally sought as key informants include: public officials; administrative and program personnel in the health and welfare organizations of the community, including clergymen; health purveyors from both the public and private sectors, including physicians and public health nurses; the program clinical staff of agencies such as community mental health centers, vocational rehabilitation organizations, guidance clinics, and others engaged in either the delivery of primary care or the administration of health programs.

To initiate a key informant approach, the steering committee needs to define the objectives of the study in order to identify those in the community who are most likely to assist in securing as much pertinent information as possible.

The next step is to construct a questionnaire or interview schedule which permits those conducting the research to obtain comparable information from each of the informants. The committee should choose one method of securing information from these key informants. The most frequently used technique is the personal interview since it permits face-to-face contact, a free exchange of ideas, and a high response rate. Mailed questionnaires are also used, but the response rate tends to be lower (cf. Weiss 1971; Schwartz 1973; Buhl, Warheit, and Bell 1977). In addition, the kinds and amount of data obtained are limited by the constraints imposed on the questionnaire in terms of the items which can be used and their format. Telephone interviews may be successful in surveys such as the key informant approach where the randomness and representativeness of those being interviewed are not an issue. The principal shortcoming of this technique is the restriction on the time allowed for the questioning process. However, if the interview schedule is brief and highly structured, and if there is reason to believe that those selected as key informants will cooperate, the telephone interview may prove to be adequate.

These techniques are not mutually exclusive; a combination of methods may be used effectively. For example, a brief telephone contact with the selected informants could be used to outline the purposes of the study and to solicit their assistance. This could be followed by a mailed questionnaire, a method with the advantages of personal contact (which generally increases the response rates) and minimal cost.

After the informants have been contacted and interviewed or have returned their questionnaires, the information may be summarized and put into tabular form for use. As an extension of this approach, all of the informants could be brought together in a meeting or series of meetings to discuss the findings of the study, thereby providing a dynamic setting within which the community's needs and services could be reviewed and discussed. Providing for mutual participation by the informants increases the likelihood of cooperative planning and joint service programming of the community's human service agencies.

Advantages

The key informant approach is relatively simple and inexpensive. It permits the input of many different individuals, each with his own perspectives, and the addition of meetings encourages a broad discussion of the needs and services of greatest importance to the community.

Through the processes of discussion and interaction, lines of communication among human service agencies in the community can be established or strengthened, and a more concerted community-based approach to the establishment of priorities and the allocation of resources may take place. Also, the enthusiasm such programs generate is helpful to the agencies involved.

Disadvantages

The disadvantage of the key informant approach is its built-in bias, since it is based on the views of those who would tend to see the community's needs from their own individual or organizational perspectives. These perspectives, even collectively, may not represent an accurate appraisal of the totality or types of needs which exist in the community. Because key informants are not representative of the community in a statistical probability sense, it is also possible that they may not be aware of those who are not visible to them, e.g., the very young, the very old, the socially or geographically isolated, and/or the powerless poor. Consequently, services to these groups may not be planned for and their needs remain unmet.

Activities Checklist

1. Describe the goals of the program, develop concepts, and operationalize these goals and concepts by preparing a design-methods outline.
2. Identify and contact key informants. These persons are chosen on the basis of their knowledge of the community's needs and care patterns. They include a cross section of the community's human service agencies: hospitals, clinics, churches, governmental bodies, and, where feasible, individuals not officially involved in the community's formal organizations.
3. Construct an interview schedule or questionnaire to be personally administered or mailed to the key informants. The items should reflect the goals of the study and be designed to gather the information required to answer those questions which relate specifically to the community's needs and services. A checklist of needs-services priorities is prepared by the committee for the interview schedule or questionnaire. The informants are then asked to rate the needs and services priorities from the listing.
4. Bring the key informants together in a group meeting after they have been interviewed and the data have been tabulated. Their findings can be discussed and consensus regarding community priorities determined, not only for the agency doing the needs assessment survey, but also for some of the other organizations represented.
5. Prepare a final report.

THE COMMUNITY FORUM APPROACH

Definition

The community forum approach relies on individuals who are asked to assess the needs and service patterns of those in the community. Although similar to the key informant approach in that it is based on the views of individuals, some of the disadvantages are reduced by widening the circle of respondents to include persons from within the general population. A forum study is designed around a series of public meetings to which all residents are invited and asked to express their beliefs about the needs and services of the community. The approach is a flexible one: It can elicit information from any member of the community willing to attend a public meeting; it can also include input from specific age, racial, ethnic, or other groups with special needs.

The process involved in a community forum is similar to that of the key informant approach. Prior to the meetings, a steering committee outlines the objectives of the research by preparing questions designed to structure the sessions around the issues, yet providing latitude for spontaneity and candor on the part of the participants.

There should be a concerted effort to publicize the meetings and to encourage attendance from all segments of the community's population. Letters urging attendance can be mailed to individuals, families, and selected organizations. The mass media—newspapers, radio, and television—are logical sources for advertising.

If feasible, strategically located meetings ought to be planned so small groups can be formed to encourage individual participation. Large assemblies held in school auditoriums, churches, and other public centers generally are not conducive to the open interchange that is desired. The forum can begin in a large meeting where the objectives of the program are outlined, ground rules established, room assignments made, and other logistical tasks completed, e.g., the selection of a secretary-recorder and the introduction of group leaders.

As the meetings progress, it is helpful to record the ideas, attitudes, and perceptions of those present. These notes should be as comprehensive as possible with special efforts being made to list all of the suggestions offered by those attending. As a final step, a summary of suggestions regarding needs and services should be prepared with special note of items accorded a high priority or sharing a strong consensus. A checklist of priorities provided to each person at the end of the session could be completed and returned to the sponsoring agency for consideration.

Advantages

Community forums are relatively easy to arrange and inexpensive to conduct. They provide input from many segments of the community, often identifying areas of previously undefined needs. The importance of increased citizen participation has been documented by recent research, and ways to increase and improve such participation have been suggested by Windle (1973), Bertelsen and Harris (1973), and Weiss (1973). The forum also identifies citizens who may be valuable resources for the later implementation of programs.

Disadvantages

In large communities the task of finding a sufficient number of strategically located meeting sites may pose problems. Even more difficult may be the obtaining of a representative attendance at the meetings. There will be only a partial view of the community's perceptions of needs and services unless the meetings are well attended by a cross section of knowledgeable citizens articulate in expressing their beliefs and in sharing their information.

At another level, those planning a forum must be aware of the potential for negative outcomes. The forum may be transformed from a positive seeking of information on the part of agency personnel to a generalized grievance session if some group in the community takes over the meetings in a physical or organizational sense and uses them to express disenchantment with real or perceived injustices beyond the scope or control of the local agency. While all persons in a community ought to have an opportunity to express their feelings regarding social, political, economic or other perceived injustices, or to freely voice their concerns about the inadequacy of the human services system, it must be recognized that individual local agencies are relatively powerless to alter the institutional arrangements of a community or society. It is important for those conducting the forum to know the program's purposes may be lost if the meetings become focused on problems for which the agency has no responsibility.

Another disadvantage of the forum lies in the possibility that the meeting may heighten the expectations of those in the community in ways that cannot be met. Again, many factors associated with health and welfare problems and delivery of care are beyond the control of individual local agencies. Accordingly, those in charge of the forum must make it clear, from the time of early publicity, that the sessions are designed to obtain information which can be used by the agency for assessment and planning. Those attending should be aware of what realistic outcomes may be expected.

A final and very significant disadvantage of the forum is related to the kind of data obtained. What is secured is largely impressionistic information about the community's health needs and services. And, while interesting, particularly for those agencies planning to do more comprehensive programs, the data are not amenable to systematic analysis; neither is there guarantee that input is accurate or representative of all groups in the community.

Activities Checklist

1. Describe the goals of the program, develop concepts, and operationalize these goals and concepts by preparing a design-methods outline for each stage of the process.
2. List key questions around which the meetings will be structured. Since not all questions are of equal importance, those planning the meetings may want to set a time schedule for the major items. A period of time for input from the participants also is included.
3. Set up meeting places which are geographically accessible to all segments of the community.
4. Undertake a comprehensive program of publicity through posters, letters, and announcements in the mass media, including a listing of the specific purposes of the meetings, who is sponsoring them, as well as the time, place, and date.
5. Designate members of the committee or other persons to record systematically the ideas, attitudes, and information presented by those attending the various sessions. A checklist of needs-services priorities may be presented to each person attending the meeting with a request that he/she identify the items in terms of their perceived priority. In addition to the list prepared in advance by the committee (or in place of it), those attending ought to be given an opportunity to express their own list of priorities.
6. Tabulate and summarize the information. Attention can be given to the expression of need from various groups within the community; these can be compared to one another and/or to the perception of needs outlined by the committee.
7. Prepare a final report.

THE RATES-UNDER-TREATMENT APPROACH

Definition

The rates-under-treatment (RUT) approach to needs assessment is based on a descriptive enumeration of persons who have utilized the services of the health and welfare agencies of a community. The underlying assumption is that the needs of the community (population) can be estimated from a sample of persons who have received care or treatment.

Historically, this approach has been used in research on the prevalence of mental disorders and treatment patterns in general populations. One of the pioneer studies of mental health problems in the United States was the 1933 Mental Hygiene Survey of the Eastern Health District of Baltimore, Maryland; it was conducted by Cohen and Fairbank (1938a, 1938b). They successfully isolated distinctive sociodemographic patterns relating to mental health problems and treatment. About the same time, Faris and Dunham (1939) used a RUT approach in making estimates of the prevalence of mental disorders in Chicago. They found that first admissions to mental hospitals were highest among persons from the center of the city and lowest among persons from areas on the periphery. Later, Hollingshead and Redlich (1958) noted that persons in differing social classes had differential treatment patterns. Those in the higher socioeconomic groups tended to receive psychotherapy; those in the lower social class groups were treated more often with various types of somatic therapy. They also noted that referral patterns were class related. Other studies

in the field of psychiatric epidemiology directly or indirectly utilized RUT data. The work of Malzberg (1944), Leighton et al. (1963), Srole et al. (1962), and Langner and Michael (1963) is well known. More recently, a RUT approach to needs assessment was proposed by Moore et al. (1967), who suggested that agencies can secure useful information for program purposes by analyzing such areas as referral sources, patient characteristics, waiting lists, and types of services being provided. For the purpose of this manual, it is essential only to note that RUT studies, or epidemiologic field surveys with RUT components in them, are being used to make estimates of the health needs and service patterns of populations.

Design

As with all needs assessment approaches, the first task is that of the definition, conceptualization, and operationalization of the objectives and methodology of the study. The basic questions during the initial stages are generic ones, and, although some have been outlined above, they are reviewed here:

1. What do we want to know?
2. What data do we need to gather?
3. Where can we find the data?
4. How can we obtain the data?
5. How can we analyze the data?
6. What are the best methods for presenting the findings?
7. How can we use the findings to make judgments and recommendations regarding our programs?

Data Sources

In RUT surveys, analysis of the clients of one's own agency provides data for the baseline study:

1. The sociodemographic characteristics of the clients, e.g., age, race, sex, ethnicity, education, place of residence
2. The presenting problem or problems
3. The characteristics of care services provided
4. The frequency and duration of the care treatment process
5. The sources of referral
6. Where possible, the outcomes of treatment or services provided

A work sheet can be developed to record the pertinent facts relating to these six items. It need not be lengthy, but should be designed so that the data can be easily transferred to tape or cards for analysis, especially when the number of cases is large. The procedure for constructing schedules, questionnaires, and recording sheets is outlined elsewhere.*

Once data on one's own agency are gathered, other agencies and persons in the community who provide human services should be identified. Many RUT data are in the public domain and can be obtained if those asked for information know in advance why it is needed and how it will be used. Such sources include public records of admissions to state hospitals, number of persons receiving public assistance, and the number and characteristics of persons being treated or receiving services from public agencies such as community mental health centers, drug and alcohol treatment facilities, hospitals, clinics, vocational rehabilitation agencies, etc. Information from private practitioners

such as physicians, psychiatrists, psychologists, marriage counselors, and clergymen is usually more difficult to obtain than records from public agencies. However, these persons may cooperate by providing general kinds of information on the number of persons being treated and their presenting complaints. One of the major obstacles to securing information from all of these sources, public and private alike, is that of guaranteeing the *absolute* and *total anonymity* and *confidentiality* of the record. Unless these can be guaranteed, agency directors and private caregivers often either refuse to cooperate or provide limited data of little use.

Techniques which increase the anonymity and confidentiality of the data ought to be used. For a RUT assessment study, names, social security numbers, or other information which identify individuals are not necessary. The focus of the RUT approach is on broad sociodemographic and geographic information and on the types and duration of services provided, not on individual persons. When this is made evident to those being asked for data, the likelihood of receiving cooperation is increased.

Once the data sources are identified and access granted, the necessary information can be obtained by a number of alternative methods which depend on: (1) the specific goals of the project, (2) the kind and amount of data to be gathered, and (3) the resources available. The most comprehensive method is to gain access to an agency's records and to retrieve from all, or from a sample of them, the information needed. If the analysis is designed to cover an extended period of time, or if the records are voluminous, a sample from each of the agencies is adequate.

---

*Editors' footnote: See Warheit, *et al., Needs Assessment Approaches: Concepts and Methods* (Bethesda, Md.: National Institute of Mental Health, 1979), pp. 63-73.

Data from records may be retrieved by personnel associated with the agency doing the survey or be provided by the organization whose files are being used. Establishing professional communications and cooperation with other organizations in the community prior to asking for their assistance is greatly facilitated by many activities directly related to the baseline study of the community and to the key informant and community forum approaches.

Analysis

Data can be summarized by use of a calculator or, when necessary and feasible, with the aid of automated equipment such as computers. The information can be put in simple summary tables and/or it can be tested for statistical associations and correlations by a variety of available formulae. The types of analysis selected depend largely on the kind of data secured and the uses for which they are intended.

Advantages

The advantages of the RUT approach to needs assessment accrue from the availability of the data and the relatively low cost of securing and analyzing them. A secondary benefit is increased communications between the human service agencies and providers in a community which often raise the general level of sensitivity to the needs of a community and, at the same time, make greater integration of services possible. As a whole, a RUT study provides an excellent overview of the services being provided those in a community.

Disadvantages

The problem associated with guaranteeing anonymity and confidentiality, especially in getting information from private practitioners/providers, is a significant disadvantage of the RUT approach. At a theoretical level, one must also be very cautious in estimating the needs of a community's *population* from a *sample* of persons seen by the community's public and private care providers. Research has shown there is a wide gulf between the mental health needs of a community as determined by field prevalence surveys and the number of persons receiving mental health care in the same community. Persons being seen simultaneously by a large number of both public and private providers may give a false picture of general community needs. Conversely, many residents of a community may seek services from agencies/persons outside the community, such as private psychiatric treatment. And there may be important differences between those who seek or receive care and those who do not. In short, it is a precarious procedure to extrapolate from populations receiving treatment/services to the population at large.

Activities Checklist

1. Describe, conceptualize, and operationalize the goals of the study and the methods to be used.
2. Identify data sources, contact responsible officials or providers, and solicit their cooperation.
3. Prepare a data worksheet which permits systematic retrieval of information for later analysis and summary.

4. Gather data, first in one's own agency (these may have been included as part of the baseline study of the agency) and then from other agencies/providers.
5. Prepare the data for analysis and summary.
6. On the basis of the analysis and summary, make a series of recommendations for action in terms of time-cost priorities.

THE SOCIAL INDICATORS APPROACH

Definition

The social indicators approach to needs assessment is based primarily on *inferences* of need drawn from descriptive statistics found in public records and reports. The underlying assumption of the approach is that it is possible to make useful estimates of the needs and social well-being of those in a community by analyzing statistics on factors found to be highly correlated with persons in need. These statistics are regarded as indicators of need. Some factors commonly used as indicators include the spatial arrangements of the community's people and institutions; the sociodemographic characteristics of the population such as age, race, sex, income; the social behavior and well-being of people, particularly as it relates to crime, substance abuse, family patterns, and morbidity and mortality rates; and the general social conditions within which people live, e.g., substandard housing, overcrowding, accessibility to services, and economic conditions. These and other social indicators can be analyzed as constellations, providing important information about a community and its needs.

Historical Perspective

The social indicator approach to needs assessment is flexible, ranging from simplistic designs using one or two indicators, such as census data on housing or the number of persons per dwelling unit, to complex designs consisting of 40 to 60 variables which require statistical procedures, i.e., standard scoring (Grey, Warheit, and Schwab 1973), multiple regression equations (Bixhorn 1973; Bell and Mellan, 1974), and canonical factor regression (Allen 1973; Holzer et al. 1975).

Regardless of the complexity of the design, there are basic assumptions for social indicators approaches. Social indicators analysis builds on the conceptual and methodological assumptions of early sociologists at the University of Chicago. The works of Park, Burgess, McKenzie, Zorbough, Faris, Reckless, Dunham, Anderson, and others are well known as reference material in the field. (A review and criticism of their assumptions may be found in Theodorson 1961.) Although many of their basic propositions and research findings have been modified over the years, the notion of the city as a constellation of "natural areas" has persisted and proven useful as a method of describing the social subdivisions within communities. A "natural area" is defined as a unit within a community, identifiable by the shared characteristics which set it apart from other units. The variables most commonly used to identify natural areas include: (1) topographical features—rivers and terrain and land use patterns; (2) sociodemographic attributes—age, race, sex, ethnicity, income, education, occupation, and family patterns; (3) population factors—distribution, density, mobility, and migration; (4) the spatial arrangements of institutions; and (5) health and social well-being characteristics—mortality and morbidity rates for a wide range of illnesses, crime and arrest records, suicides, and the prevalence of alcohol and drug abuse.

The first major effort in the United States to relate residence within natural areas to rates and types of mental disorder was conducted by Faris and Dunham (1939). They found that areas characterized by high rates of "social disorganization," defined in terms of poverty, homelessness, suicide, crime rates, transiency, and joblessness, were also areas with high rates of mental disorders. They also found that differing natural areas within the city of Chicago manifested dissimilar kinds of mental disorders. Since the publication of their provocative research findings and accompanying explanations, many empirical investigations have corroborated their results (cf. Kohn 1973; Attkisson 1970; Pearl, Buechley, and Lipscomb 1962; Bodian et al. 1965; and Keller and Effron 1956).

In the majority of our large cities there is a relationship between geographic proximity to the urban core and certain social and personal pathologies. The correlation between proximity to urban-core areas and epidemiologically derived rates of social dysfunction forms a basic conceptual link between place of residence and the needs and service patterns of those within a community (Siegel, Attkisson, and Cohn 1974). Research shows, however, that this conceptual link is not limited to proximity to the urban core; pathologies are prevalent in all areas of our society. For example, Faris and Dunham (1939) found in their early work that some disorders, most notably manic depressive psychoses, are randomly distributed within the city. Dohrenwend and Dohrenwend (1969) report that epidemiologic studies conducted within Europe and North America do not evidence consistently higher rates among urban populations than rural ones. And evidence from a major epidemiologic study in the Southeastern United States indicates that long-term residents of rural areas had higher rates of psychiatric symptomatology than those living in urban settings (Schwab, Warheit, and Holzer 1972; Warheit, Holzer, and Schwab 1973). It is clear that the social indicators approach is useful in any area for which spatial, sociodemographic, health, social welfare, and other relevant data can be gathered.

Design

Data Needed. The first and foremost task is an outline of the objectives of the study. The next step is to determine what types of data best serve as indicators of need. For example, typical data in past studies have focused upon:

1. Population characteristics—density, race, ethnicity, national origin, marital status, age, sex, and family status
2. Housing characteristics—type of structure, owner- or renter-occupied dwellings, persons per dwelling, and substandard indices
3. Mortality and morbidity rates—tuberculosis, infant mortality, venereal disease, or suicide

4. Crime patterns and arrest records—those dealing with substance or personal abuses (D.W.I. or assaults)
5. Education
6. Income
7. Fertility and fecundity rates

These data can be obtained from the U.S. Government Printing Office; the U.S. Department of Commerce, Bureau of Census; county health departments; community mental health centers; private medical practitioners; comprehensive health planning agencies, and local community colleges and universities.

The final determination of which data to gather should be decided by the use to which the findings will be put. For example, if one is interested in alcohol use and its consequences for social groups in the community, data should be obtained on such things as arrests for driving while intoxicated, assault, and other crimes where alcohol was a factor.

Units for Analysis. In the past, in identifying the unit for analysis, most studies have utilized existing area units such as *census tracts, enumeration districts (ED), block groupings,* or *minor civil divisions.* The choice has important consequences. For example, if census tracts are chosen, their size tends to obscure the relevance of some data, since the tracts may be large and heterogeneous. On the other hand, if planners choose a smaller unit for analysis, such as block groupings (BG), they may find the data thin and the number of BG's unwieldy unless the agency has computer capabilities.

For census subdivisions as the unit for analysis, it is better to gather data at the enumeration-district level than at the census-tract level because enumeration districts are subdivisions of census tracts and the characteristics of the tract can be obtained by aggregating the ED data. On the other hand, data obtained at the tract level cannot be reduced to the ED without considerable additional work. For example, Bell and Mellan (1974), utilizing a social indicators approach as an adjunct to a major epidemiologic study of mental health needs and services, found only part of the county had been tracted. Consequently, comparable census tract data for the entire county were not available, making comparisons at the census-tract level impossible. However, since ED's had been established for the entire county, they were selected as the unit for analysis. The analysis permitted comparisons of the community's sociodemographic characteristics, the social behavior of the population, and the general conditions within all of the county's ED's.

Although planners may choose any of a variety of units for analysis, the divisions developed by the Bureau of Census, i.e., census tracts and enumeration districts, have great utility because they are used extensively by public and private organizations. This permits easy comparison of data gathered by an agency with the research findings of other organizations. In addition, because these census subdivisions have a degree of permanence, their data provide an excellent basis for longitudinal studies. The utilization of census subdivisions as the units for analysis (and census data as social indicators) is enhanced for those in the mental health field by the work of a number of persons at the National Institute of Mental Health (NIMH).

The NIMH group has developed a program for the economical, efficient, and practical use of data available through the dicennial census. Referred to as the Mental Health Demographic Profile System (MHDPS), it provides computer tapes which present profiles on the standard catchment areas in the United States. These profiles contain data specific to individual catchment areas; they also present comparable data for the United States as a whole and for the county(s) in which the catchment area is located. In addition, the MHDPS provides an easily accessible data base for making comparisons with other data from the catchment area such as service utilization rates, public health, vital statistics, and crime reports. Of special value to researchers, the MHDPS is flexible in design—it can be expanded or reduced in keeping with the specific interests of individual agencies. If for no other reason than the availability of this extensive and useful profiling system, community mental health centers ought to give precedence to census subdivisions and census data when planning needs assessment programs based on social indicators. The MHDPS tapes are available from state departments or divisions of mental health. For a detailed reporting of the development and uses of the MHDPS see: Goldsmith and Unger 1970, 1972*a*, 1972*b*; Redick and Goldsmith 1971; Goldsmith et al. 1973, 1976; Rosen 1973, 1975. A description of the MHDPS as it relates to small-area demographic profile analysis is reprinted in Hargreaves et al. 1974.

Collecting the Data. Once the social indicators are identified and the unit for analysis chosen, the next step is to collect the data. As a part of the definition of the social indicators approach, four kinds of information were outlined on which such programs rely: spatial arrangements, sociodemographic characteristics, social behavior and well-being, and social conditions. The number of data sources is determined by the objectives of the study, the accessibility of data, and the amount of financial and personnel resources available. Social indicator data are obtained from public reports, such as those provided by the U.S. Bureau of Census; the reports of national, regional, state, and local health, education, and welfare bureaus and agencies; crime statistics; court records; bureaus of vital statistics, and health planning councils.

Not all of these records are equally accessible. For example, census reports can be secured easily, but police and court records and information from local health, education, and welfare agencies may be difficult to obtain. When the study requires data from local agencies, the project director or some other person with authority may have to contact these organizations, establish rapport, and legitimate the study.

Prior to a final commitment regarding which information is to be obtained, preliminary explorations of the various agencies are advisable to make certain that consistent and comparable data are available. For example, if driving while intoxicated (DWI) arrest records are to be used as a social indicator, it is advisable to examine the format of the records in the various law enforcement agencies in the community to make certain they yield consistent data. Or, if suicide rates are to be an indicator in a community comprising more than one political jurisdiction, it is advisable to make certain that all or nearly all deaths which occur outside hospitals are followed by an official autopsy. Unless autopsies have been performed consistently, suicide rates tend to be unreliable and conclusions based on them questionable. Failure to explore the data sources to be used may result in unproductive effort and expense.

The actual retrieval of data from various sources is best accomplished by work sheets designed for easy transfer of information from the reports or records. They should be constructed for easy coding and, where the use of the computer is contemplated, designed for key punching.

Analysis and Presentation of the Data

As noted above, the methods available for analyzing social indicators data vary from easily designed descriptive summaries to sophisticated, computer-based, statistical techniques. Blum (1974) provides a useful description of the theoretical and methodological issues associated with the analysis of social descriptors, summarized by Siegel, Attkisson, and Cohn (1974). Either the complete work or the summary is recommended reading before beginning an analysis of social indicators data. See also the books and articles listed in the References which deal with social indicators, their uses, and methods of analysis.

The methods chosen for analysis depend on the complexity of the data, the technical competence of the agency staff, and the availability of outside resources, e.g., consultants and computer facilities. Where the units for analysis are census tracts and the data limited, a relatively simple and inexpensive technique is a series of maps which show, tract by tract, the indicators being analyzed. Another common approach which has been used extensively (McHarg, 1969; Stewart, 1974) is a series of transparent overlays,

each constructed to visually represent the distribution of the various indicators. Such transparencies placed on top of one another offer a comprehensive picture of the indicators by census tracts. A similar method uses dots, shaded areas, or thatchings to represent the occurrences of a given phenomenon.

While the techniques are relatively easy and the maps inexpensive to prepare, they have serious shortcomings if the study includes a large number of indicators of analytic units. For example, the New Haven Study (1967) employed 113 block groupings. Grey, Warheit, and Schwab (1973) focused on only 22 census tracts, but employed 44 variables in each one, thereby prohibiting almost all analytic procedures except those depending on electronic data processing. The catchment area analyzed by Bell and Mellan had 253 enumeration districts in it and involved 65 indicators.

These examples forcefully point out that the methods of analysis to be used must be given careful consideration at the beginning of the study, as part of the description, conceptualization, and operationalization process. Unless attention to this aspect occurs at this early stage, either a great deal of data gathered cannot be used, given the analytic resources available to the agency, or the quality of data will be insufficient in light of objectives of the assessment program.

Advantages

Among the numerous advantages of using a social indicators approach is its development from vast data pools already existing in the public domain, e.g., census reports, governmental agency statistics, etc. In addition to ready access, most social indicators can be secured at relatively low cost by persons with a limited amount of research training or technical expertise. Another advantage is the design flexibility of social indicator approaches; for example, they can be used with limited amounts of information about the local community or they can include comparable data from other communities and the country at large. A further illustration of their flexibility is the possibility of simultaneously including data from several different sources in a single design, e.g., data on sociodemographic characteristics, social behavior and well-being and community conditions. These data can be derived not only from public sources such as the census but from community surveys which collect information from individuals relating to their needs and service utilization patterns. These multiple sources of data permit a wide range of analytic schemes which can be used by agencies with differing levels of resources. And, lastly, the development of a sound social indicators program can serve as a foundation on which other needs assessment programs can be built and updated on a continuing basis with a minimum of effort and cost.

Disadvantages

Most disadvantages of the use of social indicators as needs assessment programs are theoretical in nature, one being that data utilized as indicators are only indirect measures of the needs they are supposed to represent. Consequently, there is reason to question the validity of some social indicators. For example, divorce, separation, and illegitimacy rates may be a valid index of lack of family stability and security for many groups in our society, but for other groups they may be invalid. Such an index may really be measuring the incongruity between differing social class values rather than indicating the ability of a group of persons related to one another by law or blood to perform the necessary instrumental and affectual functions which make family life stable and secure. Similar criticisms can be made of many other social indicators. Therefore, if the measures constructed are to be valid, reliable, and useful, those constructing the list of items to be used as indicators must be sensitive to their own personal or class biases.

There is a second set of theoretical criticisms of social indicators approaches relying heavily on ecological data which are labeled *ecological determinism* and *ecological correlations*. Ecological determinism is a danger when those who interpret types of social indicators attribute to spatial units (such as census tracts and enumeration districts) the social forms which are found within them. While the spatial characteristics of an area influence and limit the social conditions and relationships, they do not *determine* what these *must* be.

Another danger when analyzing social indicators data as measures of need is the fallacy of ecological correlations. Work in the social indicators field has attempted to relate characteristics of individuals within those areas as measured by rates, averages, and the like, to the average characteristics in these areas. However, correlations between rates or averages for areas need not and often do not accurately reflect the characteristics of individuals within the areas (Robinson, 1950).

These theoretical issues which are disadvantageous should not dissuade those considering using social indicators as a technique for a needs assessment program; social indicators have far too many advantages. What is being suggested is that conclusions about need based on the spatial characteristics of areas, on statistical correlations, or on indicators which reflect social class values rather than genuine human conditions ought to be interpreted with caution. To be valid, reliable, and useful, social indicators approaches should contain data from a wide variety of sources. Ideally, the data for social indicators studies should permit an analysis of the spatial, sociodemographic, social behavior and well-being, and social conditions of the communities. Comprehensive studies incorporate components of agency and community baseline studies, rates-under-treatment studies, and community surveys. Although social indicator studies can be used effectively without integrating all of these components into their design, findings are enhanced by an extensive approach.

Activities Checklist

1. Define the goals of the study; develop, conceptualize, and operationalize these goals and concepts by preparing a design-methods outline for each stage of the process.
2. Make decisions regarding the data, their sources, methods of collection, and techniques of analysis and presentation. A crucial component is the selection of indicators of demonstrated validity. For example, a large number of studies have shown a consistent relationship between lower social class status and mental health problems (cf. Dohrenwend and Dohrenwend, 1969). There tends to be a

significant relationship between social pathologies and proximity to the urban core of large cities.
3. Contact and solicit the assistance of those in the community who have needed data.
4. Gather, code, and analyze the data.
5. Report the findings and recommendations for action to the administrative officers and governing board of the agency.

REFERENCES

Allen, M. Construction of optimally reliable and valid composite measures: Canonical factor regression method. Paper presented at the annual meeting of the American Sociological Association, New York, August 27-30, 1973.

American Psychiatric Association. *DSM-II: Diagnostic and Statistical Manual of Mental Disorders.* Washington, D.C.: American Psychiatric Association, 1968.

Attkisson, C.C. Suicide in San Francisco's skid row. *Archives of General Psychiatry,* 23:149-157, 1970.

Bell, R.A., and Mellan, W. Southern Health and Family Life Studies: Vol. I. *An Assessment of Needs: An Epidemiologic Survey.* Florida Mental Health Evaluation Consortium, 1974.

Bertelsen, K., and Harris, M. R. Citizen participation in the development of a community mental health center. *Hospital and Community Psychiatry,* 24:553-556, 1973.

Bixhorn, H. Descriptive methodology for composite social indicators and measures of change. Paper presented at the Conference of Urban and Regional Information Systems Association, Atlantic City, N.J., August 28-31, 1973.

Bloom, B.L. *Changing Patterns in Psychiatric Care.* New York: Human Sciences Press, 1975.

Blum, H.L. *Planning for Health: Development and Application of Social Change Theory.* New York: Behavioral Publications, 1974.

Blum, R.H. Case identification in psychiatric epidemiology: Methods and problems. *Milbank Memorial Fund Quarterly,* 40:253-258, 1962.

Bodian, C.; Gardner, E.; Willis, E.; and Bahn, A. Socioeconomic indicators from census tract data related to rates of mental illness. Washington, D.C.: U.S. Department of Commerce, Bureau of Census, Working Paper No. 17, September 5, 1965.

Bohrnstedt, G.W. Observations on the measurement of change. *Sociological Methodology,* edited by E.F. Borgatta and G.W. Bohrnstedt. San Francisco: Jossey-Bass, 1969.

Boulding, K. The concept of need for health services. *Milbank Memorial Fund Quarterly.* Milbank Memorial Fund, New York, 1967.

Buhl, J.M.; Warheit, G.J.; and Bell, R.A. The key informant approach to needs assessment: A case study. Unpublished manuscript, Department of Psychiatry, University of Florida, 1977.

Campbell, D.T., and Stanley, J.C. *Experimental and Quasi-Experimental Designs for Research.* Chicago: Rand McNally and Company, 1966.

Cantril, H. *The Pattern of Human Concerns.* New Brunswick, N.J.: Rutgers University Press, 1965.

Cattell, R.B. *Factor Analysis.* New York: Harper, 1952.

Cohen, B.M., and Fairbank, R.E. Statistical contributions from the mental hygiene study of the Eastern Health District of Baltimore. I. General account of the 1933 mental hygiene survey of the Eastern Health District. *American Journal of Psychiatry,* 94:1153-1161, March 1938*a*.

_____. Statistical contributions from the mental hygiene study of the Eastern Health District of Baltimore. II. Psycho-sis in the Eastern Health District. *American Journal of Psychiatry,* 94:1377-1395, May 1938*b*.

Cohen, B.M.; Fairbank, R.E.; and Greene, E. Statistical contributions from the mental hygiene study of the Eastern Health District of Baltimore. III. Personality disorder in the Eastern Health District in 1933. *Human Biology,* 11(1) :112-129, 1939.

Cohen, B.M.; Tietze, C.; and Greene, E. Statistical contributions from the mental hygiene study of the Eastern Health District of Baltimore. IV. Further studies on personality disorder in the Eastern Health District in 1933. *Human Biology,* 11(4) :485-512, 1939.

Cronbach, L.J. *Essentials of Psychological Testing.* New York: Harper, 1960.

Davis, H.R. Change and innovation. *Administration in Mental Health Services,* edited by S. Feldman. Springfield, ILL.:C. C Thomas, 1973.

Dohrenwend, B.P., and Dohrenwend, B.S. The problem of validity in field studies of psychological disorder. *Journal of Abnormal Psychology,* 70(1):52-68, 1965.

_____. *Social Status and Psychological Disorder: A Causal Inquiry.* New York: John Wiley, 1969.

Dunham, H.W. *Community and Schizophrenia.* Detroit: Wayne State University Press, 1965.

Edwards, A.L. *Techniques of Attitude Scale Construction.* New York: Appleton-Century-Crofts, 1957.

Faris, R.E.L., and Dunham, H.W. *Mental Disorders in Urban* Areas. Chicago: University of Chicago Press, 1939.

Froland, C. *The Meaning and Use of Social Indicators in Mental Health Planning and Administration.* Paper completed under contract with Region X, ADAMHA, #RX-833-75; August 14, 1975.

Goldsmith, H.F., and Unger, E.L. *Differentiation of Urban Subareas: A Re-examination of Social Area Dimen-*

sions. Adelphi, Maryland: National Institute of Mental Health. (Mental Health Study Center. Laboratory paper no. 35), 1970.

————. *Identification Procedures Using 1970 Census Data.* Adelphi, Maryland: National Institute of Mental Health. (Mental Health Study Center. Laboratory paper no. 37), 1972*a.*

————. *Social Rank and Family Life Cycle: An Ecological Analysis.* Adelphi, Maryland: National Institue of Mental Health. (Mental Health Study Center. Laboratory paper no. 43), 1972*b.*

Goldsmith, H.F.; Unger, E.L.; Rosen, B.M.; Windle, C.D.; and Shambaugh, J.P. *Mental Health Demographic Profile for Prince George's County.* Adelphi, Maryland: National Institute of Mental Health. (Demographic analysis: working paper no. 3, Population Research Programs, Mental Health Study Center), 1973.

Goldsmith, H.F.; Shambaugh, J.P.; Windle, C.D.; and Rosen, B.M. *Demographic Structure of Mental Health Catchment Areas: Principal Component Factor Analysis with Varimax Rotation of 18 Factors.* MHDPS Working Paper No. 35. Adelphi, Maryland: National Institute of Mental Health, September 1976.

Grey, R.J.; Warheit, G.J.; and Schwab, J.J. An index of sociomedical well-being: A case study in assessing community health needs and services. Unpublished manuscript, Department of Psychiatry, University of Florida, 1973.

Guttman, L. The basis for scalogram analysis. *Measurement and Prediction,* edited by S.A. Stouffer. Princeton, New Jersey: Princeton University Press, 1950.

Hargreaves, W.A.; Attkisson, C.C.; Siegel, L.M.; McIntyre, M.H.; and Sorensen, J.E. *Resource Materials for Community Mental Health Program Evaluation. Part II.* San Francisco: National Institute of Mental Health, 1974.

Hollingshead, A.B., and Redlich, F.C. *Social Class and Mental Illness: A Community Study.* New York: John Wiley, 1958.

Holzer, C.E.; Robbins, L.; and Warheit, G.J. A mythology of social indicators. Paper presented at the American Sociological Association Meetings, New York City, September 1976.

Holzer, C.E.; Robbins, L.; Warheit, G.J.; Bell, R.A.; and Schwab, J.J. *A Comparison of Ranking and Factor Analytic Approaches to Social Indicator Analysis.* Interim Report of Grant MH24740-01, Department of Psychiatry, University of Florida, December 1975.

Hughes, C.C.; Tremblay, M.; Rapoport, R.N.; and Leighton, A.H. *The People of Cove and Woodlot.* New York: Basic Books, 1960.

Hyman, H.H., and Cobb, W.J. *Interviewing in Social Research.* Chicago: University of Chicago Press, 1954.

Keller, M., and Effron, V. Alcoholism in the big cities of the United States. *Quarterly Journal for the Study of Alcohol,* 17:63-72, 1956.

Kish, L. A procedure for objective respondent selection within the household. *Journal of the American Statistical Association,* 44:380-387, 1949.

————. *Survey Sampling.* New York: John Wiley, 1965.

Kohn, M.L. Social class and schizophrenia: A critical review and a reformulation. *Schizophrenia Bulletin,* 7:60-79, 1973.

Langner, T.S., and Michael, S.T. *Life Stress and Mental Health; The Midtown Manhattan Study.* New York: The Free Press of Glencoe, 1963.

Leighton, A.H. *My Name Is Legion.* New York: Basic Books, 1959.

Leighton, D.C.; Harding, J.S.; Macklin, D.B.; Macmillan, A.; and Leighton, A.H. *The Character of Danger.* New York: Basic Books, 1963.

Likert, R. A technique for the measurement of attitudes. *Archives of Psychology,* No. 140, 1932.

Longest, J.W., and Konan, M. *State of the Art in Measuring the Need for Mental Health Services and the Availability and*

Adequacy of Mental Health Services. Prepared under contract with the National Institute of Mental Health, #75-0028, October 1975.

Malzberg, B. Mental disease among American Negroes: A statistical analysis. *Characteristics of the American Negro,* edited by O. Klineberg. New York: Harper, 1944.

McHarg, I.L. *Design with Nature.* New York: The Natural History Press, 1969.

Miller, D. *Handbook of Research Design and Social Measurement.* New York: David McKay, 1970.

Moore, D.N.; Bloom, B.L.; Gaylin, S.; Pepper, M.; Pettus, C.; Willis, E.M.; and Bahn, A.K. Data utilization for local community mental health program development. *Community Mental Health Journal,* 3:30-32, 1967.

Nie, N.H.; Hull, C.H.; Jenkins, J.G.; Steinbrenner, K.; and Bent, D.H. *Statistical Package for the Social Sciences.* New York: McGraw-Hill, 1975.

Oppenheim, A.N. *Questionnaire Design and Attitude Measurement.* New York: Basic Books, 1966.

Park, R. Human migration and the marginal man. *American Journal of Sociology,* 33, 1928.

Parsons, T. Suggestions for a sociological approach to the theory of organization. *Administrative Science Quarterly,* 1:63-85, 1956.

Pearl, A.; Buechley, R.; and Lipscomb, W.R. Cirrhosis mortality in three large cities: Implications for alcoholism and intercity comparisons. *Society, Culture and Drinking Patterns,* edited by D.J. Pittman and C.R. Snyder. New York: John Wiley, 1962.

Redick, R.W., and Goldsmith, H.F. *1970 Census Data Used to Indicate Areas with Different Potentials for Mental Health and Related Problems.* DHEW Publication No. (HSM) 72-9051. Washington, D.C.: U.S. Government Printing Office. 1971.

Riley, M.W.; Riley, Jr., J.W.; and Toby, J.

Sociological Studies in Scale Analysis. New Brunswick, New Jersey: Rutgers University Press, 1954.

Roberts, A.O.H., and Larsen, J.K. *Effective Use of Mental Health Research Information.* Palo Alto, California: American Institutes for Research, 1971.

Robinson, J. Life satisfaction and happiness. *Measures of Social Psychological Attitudes,* edited by J. Robinson and P. Shaver. Ann Arbor: Institute for Social Research, 1969.

Robinson, W.S. Ecological correlation and the behavior of individuals. *American Sociological Review,* 15:351-357, 1950.

Rosen, B.M. A model for estimating mental health needs using 1970 census socioeconomic data. Paper presented at the Southeastern Psychological Association meeting, New Orleans, 1973.

Rosen, B.M.; Lawrence, L.; Goldsmith, H.F.; Windle, C.D.; and Shambaugh, J.P. *Mental Health Demographic Profile System Description: Purpose, Contents and Sampler of Uses.* Series C, No. 11, DHEW Publication No. (ADM) 76-263. Washington, D.C.: Superintendent of Documents, U.S. Government Printing Office, 1975.

Schwab, J.J.; McGinnis, N.H.; and Warheit, G.J. Toward a social psychiatric definition of impairment. *British Journal of Social Psychiatry,* 4(1), 1970.

Schwab, J.J.; Warheit, G.J.; and Fennel, E. Community mental health evaluation: An assessment of needs and services. Unpublished manuscript, Department of Psychiatry, University of Florida, 1973.

Schwab, J.J.; Warheit, G.J.; and Holzer, C.E. Suicidal ideation and behavior in a general population. *Diseases of the Nervous System,* 33(11):745-748, 1972.

Schwartz, R. Follow-up by phone or by mail. *Evaluation: A Forum for Human Service Decision-Makers,* 1(2):25-26, 1973.

Sells, S.B., ed. *The Definition and Measurement of Mental Health: A Symposium.* Washington, D.C.: U.S. Government Printing Office, 1968.

Selltiz, C.; Jahoda, M.; Deutsch, M.; and Cook, S.W. *Research Methods in Social Relations.* New York: Holt, Rinehart and Winston, 1959.

Shaw, M.E., and Wright, J.M. *Scales for the Measurement of Attitudes.* New York: McGraw-Hill Book Company, 1967.

Siegel, L.M.; Attkisson, C.C.; and Cohn, A.H. *Mental Health Needs Assessment: Strategies and Techniques.* National Institute of Mental Health Report, 1974.

Srole, L.; Langner, T.S.; Michael, S.T.; Opler, M.K.; and Rennie, T.A.C. *Mental Health in the Metropolis: The Midtown Manhattan Study.* New York: McGraw-Hill Book Company, 1962.

Steel, R.G.D., and Torrie, J.H., *Principles and Procedures of Statistics, With Special Reference to the Biological Sciences.* New York: McGraw-Hill, 1960.

Stewart, R. Methods of assessing mental health needs from social statistics. Paper presented at the California State Psychological Association meeting, January 1974.

Theodorson, G.A., ed. *Studies in Human Ecology.* Evanston, Illinois: Row, Peterson and Company, 1961.

Torgerson, W. *Theory and Methods of Scaling.* New York: John Wiley, 1958.

Warheit, G.J.; Holzer, C.E.; and Schwab, J.J. An analysis of social class and racial differences in depressive symptomatology: A community study. *Journal of Health and Social Behavior,* 14:291-299, 1973.

Warren, R.L. *Studying Your Community.* New York: The Free Press, 1965.

Weiss, A.E. *Consumer Model of Assessing Community Mental Health Needs.* California Data: Methodology and Applications, No. 8. Sacramento: Bureau of Biostatistics, Department of Health, 1971.

Weiss, A.T. Consumer model of assessing community mental health needs. *Exchange,* 1, 1973.

Weiss, C.H. *Evaluation Research; Methods of Assessing Program Effectiveness.* Englewood Cliffs, New Jersey: Prentice-Hall, Inc., 1972*a*.

––––––. *Evaluating Action Programs: Readings in Social Action and Education.* Boston: Allyn and Bacon, 1972*b*.

Windle, C. An invitation to community participation. *Community Psychology Newsletter,* Division 27, American Psychological Association, 1973.

4. ASSESSMENT AND PROGRAM DEVELOPMENT*

Armand Lauffer

None of us would consider development of an action plan without careful assessment of the problem to be addressed, its potential for amelioration, or the aspirations of those affected and of the resources in the immediate environment that might be activated to deal with that problem. Yet we often engage in program design and development paying only cursory attention to the assessment process, relying all too heavily on our intuition, assuming the correctness of our decisions on the basis of personal and professional commitments.

Because the methods and technology used in an assessment are often the same as those of an evaluation and because both activities may take place concurrently, the two terms are sometimes used interchangeably. The two, however, are conceptually distinct. Assessment focuses on the examination of what is, on what is likely to be, or on what ought to be. Evaluation focuses on what happened, how it happened, and whether it should have happened. I will deal only with assessment, by examining three alternative approaches: here-and-now, anticipatory, and normative assessment. I will then examine the implications of

each of these approaches for assessing the environments within which agencies operate and programs are developed, and the ways in which those programs and organizations are themselves assessed. I will describe a variety of tools that I have found useful in my work. In general, these will be relatively nontechnical, requiring no research sophistication or expensive hardware. I will resist the temptation to be comprehensive in order to focus more directly on those tools that I think you also will find useful.

ASSESSING WHAT IS, WHAT MIGHT BE, AND WHAT OUGHT TO BE

When we assess what is, we are directing our attention to the here and now. We might choose to examine the services currently being provided, the populations being served, or the relationships between providers, and between providers and consumers. We might also be looking at the environment that surrounds the provision of services. Wherever one focuses, it is important to know what questions to ask. When the program planner focuses on an actual or potential consumer population, the following questions might be asked:

1. To what extent are services of various kinds *available* and to whom?
2. To what extent are available services *accessible* (by dint of location, hours

Reproduced by permission of the author. From a Summary of Remarks for the Center of Rehabilitation and Human Development at Haifa University, by Armand Lauffer, April 7, 1981.

*An expanded discussion of assessment accompanied by specific step-by-step instructions on how to use these and other assessment tools is found in Armand Lauffer, *Assessment Tools for Practitioners, Managers, and Trainers* (Beverly Hills, Calif.: Sage Publications, 1982).

offered, removal of architectural and psychological or social barriers)?

3. Even if available and accessible, are services *responsive* to actual and potential consumers, and what kinds of *accountability* mechanisms are built into those services?

4. How *effective* are the services (that is, do they make a difference and for whom)?

5. Are they efficient (could one serve larger numbers or provide more comprehensive services for the same amount of money, or would a change in the scope of the program result in considerable cost saving)?

When one examines the relationships between service providers or between providers and consumers, at least three sets of questions are raised:

1. To what extent are services provided *comprehensively,* in such a way that one service complements another instead of competing for the client's allegiance or leaving large service areas uncovered?

2. Are services provided *continuously,* so that when one agency completes its service (for example, job training in an institutional setting), other agencies are ready to provide subsequent service (reentry counseling for the disabled person's family, job placement in the local community, and other supports leading to independent living arrangements)?

3. What *relationships* exist *between the institutionalized* and bureaucratized forms of services offered under public and private auspices, and the more *informal services* provided by natural helpers (family, friends, neighbors, and members of self-help groups)?

These are "here-and-now" types of questions. They focus on *what is.* In anticipatory assessment one asks the same kinds of questions, but the focus is on the extent to which these problems are likely to be felt in the future. One might make projections on the basis of anticipated or unanticipated changes. What might be the likely drain on existing services should unemployment double or triple in the next five years? Would one then wish to focus on the debilitating attitudes or on lack of marketable skills? Anticipating the possible consequences of cataclysmic events such as war or economic depression, would rehabilitation services face major reductions in funding? Or assuming current trends and the completion of the legislative processes aimed at linking all rehabilitation services under a common service structure, to what extent might one anticipate continued problems of availability, accessibility, accountability, effectiveness, or efficiency?

The advantage of anticipatory assessment is that it permits program planners to think ahead rather than to catch up with problems after the fact. It may make it possible for us to make decisions now that are likely to head off problems and their consequences for the populations for which we are mandated to provide services.

There is yet a third approach. Normative assessment begins with an image of a desired state. We might ask ourselves what kind of services we would like to see in place four or five years from now, or what kinds of capacities we would like to build into the disabled population. We also might begin by deciding what a minimally acceptable rehabilitation service might look like (perhaps in terms of such issues as availability, accessibility, accountability, effectiveness, and efficiency). In effect, what we would be doing is developing a "competency" model that describes the desired state of affairs.

When the government establishes minimum standards for service agencies, for example, it establishes a competency model. For assessment purposes, designing the model is only the first step. We would then examine where the population, or the service system, is now in relation to the norms that we have specified. It is the gap between current reality and the desired state of affairs that would direct us in our program development efforts. Once we have uncovered present levels of competency and compared them to the norms we desire, we would then specify our objectives and set priorities on the basis of salience and feasibility.

I have often been asked which of the three approaches works best. Obviously, there is no single answer. We often do the here-and-now kinds of assessments because we are concerned with problems in the here and now. Such problems confront us in the present and demand our attention. Yet agencies involved in ongoing planning and program development activities would hardly do themselves or their consumers justice if they didn't engage in both normative and anticipatory assessment activities.

FOCUSING ON THE ENVIRONMENT

I have always found it useful to explore the environment around a service agency, a program, or an issue that I am concerned with. I would like to focus on two aspects of the environment: the aspect that might be termed the "acceptance" environment, and that which is called by sociologists the "task" environment. I will explain. Around any program, issue, or proposed solutions to the problems there will tend to be consensus, indifference, or disagreement. Research on community intervention programs suggests that it is quite appropriate to use a collaborative strategy when there is consensus about the existence of a problem or a proposed solution. The planner might play an enabling role, serving as a guide or catalyst, a convenor, a mediator and consultant, or even a coordinator. Those in accord would be brought together in some structural relationship (through committees or task forces) in order to arrive at a mutually desired outcome. The presumption would be one of goodwill, of complementarity of objectives. The program planner or developer would perform most effectively as an orchestrator of that consensus.

But a planner would be required to play a very different role in an environment characterized by indifference. One would hardly be able to convene the interested parties if everyone is uninterested. When no one seems to care, or at least care very much, the program planner must engage in a campaign strategy to heighten public sensitivity and awareness, animating those who are most directly affected by the problem (for example, the disabled and their families). The planner's aim would be to move toward a consensus environment in which newly interested parties could be activated to work in collaboration toward a given end or ends.

But what if the environment is one in which there are differences of opinion, conflicts of interest, and disagreements over problems, ends, and means? Under these circumstances campaign efforts aiming to "sell" or to persuade the other side, or to bring the competing sides together, are not likely to prove successful. On the contrary, attempting to mediate a conflict that represents real differences and in which none of the parties see any advantages to accommodations may prove counterproductive. It might be more appropriate to increase the coercive or reward power of those parties that the planner represents, or whose interest the program aims to serve. Consumer groups might themselves be empowered to take action on their own behalf. Initially, at least, those who oppose the program would not be viewed as potential collaborators. To the contrary, they would be viewed as the opposition—to be isolated or overcome.

How the program planner defines the "acceptance" environment, then, has serious implications for planning strategy. You may have noticed that until now I have been discussing this form of environmental assessment from a here-and-now perspective. But what if we were to take an anticipatory or a normative approach? In the former, we might ask ourselves to what extent there is likely to be consensus, indifference, or disagreement at some point in the future. We might decide, for example, that disagreement today is likely to be diffused if we do not attack it directly and that moving from a climate of confrontation to an environment of indifference might lead to a greater chance of success. This might suggest a temporary strategy of benign neglect. By diffusing a currently conflictful environment, we could move progressively toward one in which consensus might lead toward collaborative efforts.

Using the normative approach, one might begin with a model of a desired environment. Decisions about what to do today or tomorrow would then flow from an assessment of the implications of one or more of those actions for the environment.

Now let's examine the task environment. It is composed of all those organizations and institutions, groups and populations without which a service program could not exist and without which it would have no function to play. The task environment is composed of:

1. those organizations and institutions that provide auspice and legitimacy to the program or organization
2. providers of necessary resources
3. the consumers of service
4. the competitors for both resources and consumers
5. the various collaborators that enhance the availability, accessibility, accountability, effectiveness, efficiency of programs and services

A word about each.

The nature of the program or the service to be developed is very much a creature of the organization or the legislation which provides its auspice and which gives it its legitimacy. By *auspice* I mean the organizational and legislative configuration that mandates the program or service and is responsible for seeing that it is implemented. The auspice may be a governmental department, a local service agency, a self-help group, or a collection of organizations.

Most service programs use a wide variety of tangible *resources:* money, facilities, equipment, and supplies. They also use intangibles like expertise, organizational and personal energy, political influence, and prestige. Intangibles are no less important than tangible resources. The availability of money and facilities, for example, while important, might yield little without the energy and commitment required to activate them. We are all familiar with excellent service programs that were developed without any external sources of financial support.

The more dependent a service organization is on a single source of supply, the less likely will it be able to respond flexibly to new challenges and demands. The same is true if it becomes dependent on only one or two types of resources. An organization that can shift its programs to accommodate ups and downs in financial support by increasing or decreasing volunteer and consumer inputs, for example, is likely to accommodate a challenge and respond to new opportunities. The program developer must be able to assess actual and potential sources of supply as well as the actual resources being used and possible substitutes. He or she must also assess the organization's capacity to accommodate or to develop new sources of supply and to use alternative resources.

To a large extent, this capacity may correlate with the organization's perceptions of its consumers. *Consumers* may be perceived of as "output" constituencies—that is those who are the recipients of the services of the organization. Consumers can also be defined as "input" constituencies, without whose contributions the agency's services would not be possible. When an agency organizes its clients into self-help groups or uses them as volunteers and aides with other more dependent clients, it has redefined at least some of its consumers from output to input constituencies.

Competitors are those elements in the environment that compete for resources or for consumers. These may include alternative kinds of rehabilitation programs or other human services. Competitors also include other sectors of the social and economic environment: the military, industry, the agricultural sector, and so on. Effective program developers have often seen the potential of turning competitors into collaborators. Agencies that compete for scarce resources to hire staff might benefit from trying a number of alternative collaborative arrangements. For example, Agency A might "lend" a staff member expert in family diagnosis to Agency B, which has neither the financial resources nor the experience to perform that kind of diagnosis. The staff member on loan would then operate as a member of the second agency's staff for an agreed-upon time period. An alternative might to to "outstation" staff members on the premises of another organization.

ASSESSMENT TOOLS

Mapping Exercises

How does this discussion relate to the topic of assessment? We might begin by examining where an agency or program fits into its task environment and then identify the range of connections it has to elements in the environment. In effect, we would be using a *mapping technique.* Let's draw a map (Figure 4.1). Place the program or agency in the center of a piece of paper. Along the left side of the page list all the providers of auspices and put each in a box of its own. Across the top of the paper list all the providers of resources and include the kinds of resources that they are currently providing to your organization or program. Along the right hand edge of the paper list all the organization's consumers—those populations being served or other organizations that are the recipients of your

FIGURE 4.1
Map Outline of the Task Environment

SUPPLIERS OF RESOURCES

AUSPICE PROVIDERS

Your
Agency

CONSUMERS OF SERVICE

COLLABORATORS AND COMPETITORS

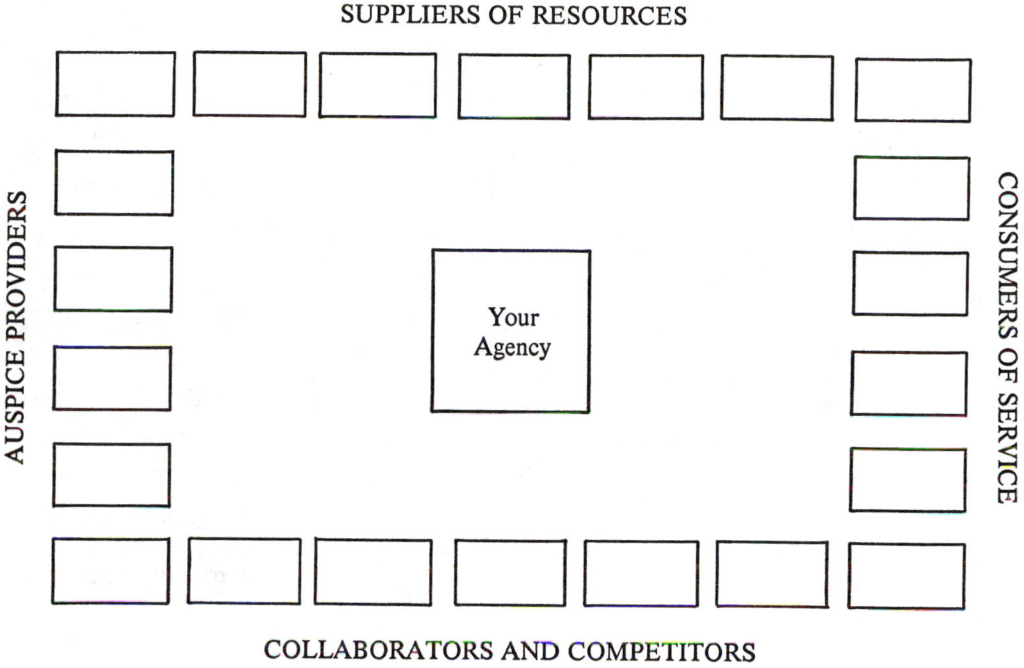

agency's services. And finally, along the bottom of the page list all those organizations that are potential competitors or collaborators.

In effect, what you now have is a map of the task environment in the here and now. You could also develop a map of what the environment might look like in the future, given what you know about changing resources or past trends. And there is no reason why you could not design the map the way you would like it to look; in other words, as a normative or competency model. If you have a large enough sheet of paper, or use overlays, you might show the here-and-now map in one color, the anticipated changes in a second color, and the desired state of affairs in a third. Together they should point you in the direction of an intervention or program development effort.

There are, of course, many aspects of the environment you might wish to map. Let's assume for the moment that you wanted to map current or desired linkages between your organization and potential collaborators in a service program. Start off with a blank sheet of paper and draw a large circle (Figure 4.2). Now draw a small circle in the center and a medium-size circle in between. Finally divide all three circles into pie slices. Let's say you divide it in half four times, making eight slices. Put your agency's or program's name in the central circle. In each of the segments of the outer circle write the name of an organization with which your agency or program actually does or might potentially collaborate. Use the blank segments between your

FIGURE 4.2
Linkage Map Outline

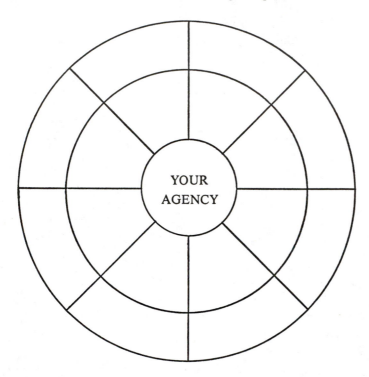

Names of other agencies go in outer ring segments

Types of linkages or exchanges go in middle ring segments

agency's circle and the collaborating agencies to identify all the actual or potential linkage mechanisms that might bring the organizations together.

We have already identified two linking mechanisms: loaner staff arrangements and out-stationing of staff. Consider also other linkages: case management, joint recruitment, collaboration on staff development activities, and so on. Consider exchanges of instructional material, the sharing of facilities, or client referrals. You might also engage in joint programs on a time-limited or permanent basis. For example, you might jointly develop volunteer programs or work in collaboration on the development of self-help and mutual aid groups, or share responsibility for a public awareness campaign. The current exchanges or activities might be listed on your map in one color and the potential or desired linkages in a second or third color. Again, you have used a mapping exercise to examine what is, what is likely to be, and what ought to be.

Mapping tools are rather easy to use. They are helpful exercises when you have a moment to sit down by yourself and think about your work. They are even more useful when done collaboratively with other members of your staff or with an interagency team. They help you systematize your thinking and structure the involvement of others in the assessment process. Like the other tools that I will describe next, they will help you retrieve information that may be locked into individual compartments of your memory or the collective memory of your organization. They will help point to elements in your environment that require systemic and systematic assessment.

I will now describe five other tools: (1) the nominal group technique, (2) the Delphi conference, (3) task analysis, (4) force field analysis, and (5) simulation games.

Nominal Group Technique

The nominal group technique was developed to involve people with diverse backgrounds and opinions in assessment and priority-setting activities. Unlike interactive groups, in which the dynamics of interpersonal exchanges are likely to influence each person's input, the nominal group technique guarantees each person's access to the process. There are many variations. Let's assume for the moment that the participants include faculty members at the university, representatives of various agencies at the community level, consumers of agency services, government officials, or a mixture of all of them. Participants at a meeting might be asked to list three to five needs to be addressed on small pieces of paper. You might wish to substitute for "needs" "problems to be addressed," "population groups to be served," "interorganizational linkages," "needed resources in the shortest supply," or something else. The group leader or facilitator then collects all the papers and groups them according to some logic inherent in the responses. For example, if the original inquiry focused on man-

agement problems within an agency, the responses might group themselves logically under such rubrics as "interorganizational exchanges," "intraorganizational communication," "staff morale," "appropriate allocation of work loads and responsibilities," and so on. Each of these headings might then be written on a chalkboard or at the top of a large sheet of paper. The problem descriptions written by the individual participants would be tacked or taped under each category and participants asked if some might be eliminated or integrated with others because of overlap and duplication. After this step, we might now find ourselves with seven or eight items under one category, three under the next, and so forth.

At this point the facilitator asks each person in order of the seating arrangement to argue forcefully why one or another of the items listed should be acted upon or should be ignored. There is at this point no group discussion. When the first person finishes the second person is given a chance, and so on until everyone has had an opportunity to speak. Each speaker might be limited to thirty or sixty seconds. It is now time for everyone to vote. If there are six or seven items under one category, participants might be asked to vote for the two that ought to be given priority. If there are only three or four items, perhaps they would only vote once. Once all the items have been voted on, the action priorities under each category are clear. It is now time to vote on whether to work on items under one category before another (say staff morale before interorganizational exchanges) or select the high-priority items under each category for action. In setting priorities, consider posing such questions as Which of these items should we work on first? Which problems are the most destructive to the organization? Which might be the easiest to deal with? and so on. In effect, what you would be doing is assessing the opinions of the key actors in a program development process and assessing their readiness to engage in change. The advantage of this technique over more interactive group processes is that it guarantees everyone's input. It reduces the likelihood of "group think" or of the excessive influence of one or two group members with a great deal of charisma, with clear personal priorities, or with higher social status. The Delphi conference provides similar advantages.

The Delphi Conference

Originally designed as a projective technique, using expert panelists to predict future events or trends, Delphi has increasingly been used for policy analysis and recommendation. Unlike the nominal group technique, the Delphi conference does not require face-to-face interaction or even the presence of the panelists in the same room or their participation at the same time. Delphi usually uses a structured questionnaire that goes through a number of repetitions. Respondents are called panelists and are selected in reference to their presumed expertise, perhaps because they represent particular points of view or specified populations. Effort is made to balance the panel with people who represent diverse positions. A "policy Delphi" is generally normative in its orientation. A number of future policies might be listed on a questionnaire, sometimes with pro and con arguments immediately following the policy statement.

An example of a policy statement might be "No one shall be released from the rehabilitation center until agencies from the client's local community have established a reentry plan and designated a responsible case manager." That statement might then be rated according to a number of different criteria such as feasibility, desirability, and cost. Respondents would be asked to rate each of the policy statements on a five-point scale according to the criteria selected.

Let's assume "desirability" and "feasibility" are the two criteria used. If the majority of respondents agree that a policy is both desirable and feasible, the policy decision is quite clear. But what if half of the respondents feel that the policy is desirable while the other half feel that it is not in any way desirable? Or what if the respondents agree as to a policy's desirability but conclude that it is not feasible? This is where the second repetition (second questionnaire) is required. The persons conducting the Delphi process would probe for the reasons why there may be differences between the respondents. A well-designed Delphi questionnaire often includes the opportunity for panelists to write in the reasons for their ratings. It also leaves space for them to add additional policy statements that they would like other respondents to react to. The Delphi process often goes through four, five, or six questionnaires. The process need not lead to consensus, but it does often lead to clarity.

Like the nominal group technique, the Delphi conference guarantees equal input by all parties. Unlike the nominal group, Delphi even protects the anonymity of the respondents whose identities need not be revealed on returned questionnaires. Studies of these processes reveal that participants generally feel that they lead to quicker and more effective decisions in which time is not lost in meaningless and often aimless discussions.

Future or projective Delphis, in contrast to policy Delphis, are designed to anticipate the likelihood of future events or conditions. The presumption behind them is that by selecting respondents for their individual or collective expertise, we are likely to make good predictions. Although the Delphi and nominal groups are likely to be used for similar purposes, they do not have common origins. Delphi emerged from the field of technological forecasting, while the nominal group technique is an outgrowth of the field of group dynamics.

Task Analysis

Task analysis has a somewhat different origin. It emerged from an effort during World War II to categorize all the tasks performed in the newly created United States Air Force. The intent was to group job descriptions and to articulate them functionally in order for the air force to perform its missions. Since then, task analysis has gone through a number of refinements. About ten years ago, for example, Sydney Fine, who had worked on the air force project, fashioned a national "task bank" in which 600 or more tasks performed by staff members in American public welfare agencies were categorized. Each task was defined in operational terms and typed on an individual McBee card similar to Figure 4.3. The performance standards for that task were also indicated either in qualitative or numerical terms, and the educational and experiential requirements for performing that task were identified.

A job, when properly designed, is composed of a number of tasks that are functionally interrelated. A work unit of several people in an organization would be considered functional if the tasks performed by group members are assigned so that they complement each other. By analogy, a work unit within an agency might perform its tasks best if it is functionally interrelated with other work units. And to take it a step further, service agencies or service programs would be functional if they perform their tasks appropriately in light of the tasks being performed by other programs and services in the community and the nation. Those familiar with systems theory and operational analysis will recognize the schema.

Let's take a step back and reexamine what we mean by *task*. Technically, a task is the smallest unit of work that can be described. The best way to identify a task is to think of the action verb that might be used to label it, for example, "writes," "organizes," "categorizes," "types," "counsels," "refers," and so on. The complete task statement requires more than an action verb, however. It specifies:

1. who
2. does what
3. to whom and to what
4. with what (tool, instrument, technique, or method)
5. for what purpose
6. under whose instructions or what directions

If you forget that sequence, try remembering this: (1) The butler (2) laces (3) Mrs. Scarlet's tea (4) with arsenic (5) in order to do her in (6) on behest of the upstairs maid. An example of a rehabilitation task might include the following: the (1) intake worker (2) refers (3) clients

FIGURE 4.3
Task Statement

Title of Task:	
Who	1
Performs What Action	2
To Whom or To What	3
Using What Tools or Methods	4
To What End or For What Purpose	5
Using What Direction or Under Whose Supervision	6

Entry Level Requirements:	Performance Criteria:
Rating:	
Importance Hi 5 4 3 2 1 Lo	Difficulty Hi 5 4 3 2 1 Lo
Frequency Hi 5 4 3 2 1 Lo	Hi 5 4 3 2 1 Lo

(4) to the appropriate service provider using standard agency procedures (5) in order to assure prompt and appropriate service (6) under the supervision of the rehabilitation coordinator at the branch office. We might label this task "referral" according to its action verb, "refer." If we were using a task statement of this sort to assess current agency practice, the here and now, we might then identify current levels of performance as well as entry requirements for persons performing referrals.

We might also use the task analysis technique for purposes of normative assessment. If we were to define a set of desired performance criteria and entry level requirements, we might then contrast what *is* with our perceptions of what *ought to be.* The same assessment tool can be applied to examining the functional relationships between departments within an organization, organization within a governmental department, or agencies, programs, and services at the community level.

Like the task analysis approach within an agency that involves all staff members in the assessment process, analysis within a larger arena is best when it includes representatives of those institutions and organizations that are likely to be affected by proposed changes. Remember, however, that this works best only when there is consensus around the issues to be addressed and/or approaches to be used to address those issues. When there is disagreement, it is often important to understand the forces that lead to conflicts of interest and how one might overcome those forces.

Force Field Analysis

Force field analysis is ideally suited for this form of assessment. Originating in Kurt Lewin's attempts to infuse the social sciences with the rigor of the physical sciences, force field analysis employs a more sophisticated mapping technique than described earlier (Figure 4.4). One might begin the process by defining a desired change or change goal. The next step would be to identify all driving and restraining forces. Driving forces are those that are currently or may potentially be activated in the direction of change. Here we might be talking about the weight of public opinion or the support of key individuals and organizations in the community, those we identify as elements of the consensus environment.

Restraining forces include all those against change (like inertia, poor experiences with similar efforts in the past, the state of the national economy, or resistance on the part of the client populations or others who might feel their vested interest to be threatened by the proposed change). In sketching a force field, you might wish to use different colors to record the actual and potential driving and restraining forces. The next step is to identify those forces over which we have control, over which someone else has control, and over which none of us have any control, such as the state of the economy or the potential catastrophes inherent in a major war.

There are, of course, many other ways to rate or rank each of these forces. Some planners talk about using "working," "framing," and "unpredictable" forces and ranking each according to how often one encounters them, their potency, and their amenability to change.

Simulation Games

As productive an assessment tool as force field analysis may be, the very fact that it leads us to examine dynamic

FIGURE 4.4
Force Field Balance Sheet

Change Goal

Antithesis of Change Goal

Amenability

Consistency

Potency

H/L/U

RESTRAINING FORCES (against change)

1.

2.

3.

4.

5.

DRIVING FORCES (for change)

1.

2.

3.

4.

5.

Who has control over these forces? CRITICAL ACTORS: A _____ B

No
One

US

C _____ D

Notes (scope of change, facilitating vs. critical actors, issue environment, prior experience, etc.

Potency

Consistency

Amenability

H/L/U/

relationships is also its limitation. It is difficult to display those dynamics adequately on a two-dimensional map. The forces we are concerned with, after all, can only be observed in the interplay of a social reality that exists in both time and space. For this reason some program planners gravitate toward the use of simulation games for assessment purposes. These can be played on computers much as a chess game is now played. Players might interact with the computer, or the computer program might include several simulated players. Alternatively, players might engage in a live situation in which people perform roles of bona fide players in interaction with each other.

About a decade ago I designed a game for the Rehabilitation Services Administration. It included roles for staff members of state and local rehabilitation agencies; the heads of other human service agencies (mental health, public welfare, job training, health, and so on); representatives of consumer groups; a variety of community influentials from universities, unions, and religious organizations; and funders or providers of other resources. You will recognize some of the elements of a task environment. In this game each of the players has access to different kinds of resources: personal and professional energy; manpower and professional expertise; charisma, esteem, and political influence; facilities; funds; and so on.

There are a number of issues that might potentially serve as a focus for interaction. These tend to be of greater or lesser concern to different players depending on their roles and what they perceive to be the interests of their constituents. In some cases, people at both local and state levels were clearly divided on whether or not to deal with an issue. The element of chance is simulated by using a deck of "chance cards" like those found in Monopoly that are likely to propel one or another issue to the fore. Any player, of course, can choose to work on any of the issues he or she is interested in, but in order to engage effectively in program development and design, resources must be properly orchestrated, support from others sought, and intelligence applied to the assessment of needs, feasibility, desirability, and so on.

A game's structure is particularly useful in simulating reality. Games are really nothing more than sets of rules. Think about football, or chess, or tennis and the rules that govern their outcomes. These are termination rules that tell you what the penalties are for various actions, who won and who lost, what the score is, or when the play of the game is over. Move rules are three kinds: those that govern personal choice (who does what, with whom, and when); those that reflect chance (like the flip of a coin or the roll of the dice); and those which are partially chance and partially choice. When the ball is tossed in the air at the beginning of a basketball game, for example, we observe a move that is partially chance and partially choice. The centers choose how they are going to hit the ball, but their choices are at least partially governed by chance. The taller the player (that is, the closer the access to the ball) or the more skilled, the more likely he or she is to optimize that choice. That is true, perhaps, with everything in life: the greater one's access or skill, the more likely one is going to optimize one's choices. Because moves quite clearly have an impact on ends, simulation games can be used to assess the impact of alternative strategies and to develop clarity regarding the implications of the various options before each of the players.

Note that players in a game, like the performers of any role, are likely to have their behaviors shaped by members of their role set. It is not possible, for example, to play a leadership role unless other players are interested in being led. If players perform their roles inappropriately, other participants are likely to let them know soon enough whether players perform their roles as individuals or as representatives of organizations in larger social structures. You will begin to see a parallel between role–role set behaviors, and those of organizations in their organizational sets or task environments.

The efforts by one actor to influence the behavior of others are in turn shaped by the efforts of others to shape the first actor's behavior. This is an important lesson for those who are concerned with the assessing of the feasibility or desirability of change. Change in a given direction doesn't occur just because one wills it. It requires a process of trade-offs and accommodations whether the acceptance environment is initially indifferent, in conflict, or in accord.

We seem to have come full circle. You will recognize the complementarity of many of these tools. The nominal group technique can become a component of a simulation game, or it might be used to identify the issues to be played out in that game. The Delphi process might lead to the identification of a number of policy objectives, which in turn are analyzed through force field analysis. Task analysis can help us understand the configuration of performers or players in functional terms. All six tools (mapping, nominal group technique, Delphi, force field analysis, task analysis, and gaming) can be used individually or with a large number of participants. Each can be used to focus on the here and now, on the likely future, or on a desired future state of affairs.

BIBLIOGRAPHY

General

Lauffer, Armand, *Assessment Tools for Practitioners, Managers and Trainers* (Beverly Hills, Calif.: Sage Publications, 1982).

Mapping Exercises

Lauffer, Armand, *Getting the Resources You Need* (Beverly Hills, Calif.: Sage Publications, 1982).

——, *Social Planning at the Community Level* (Englewood Cliffs, N.J.: Prentice-Hall, 1978), pp. 58–60.

Nominal Group Technique

Bales, Robert F., and Strodtbeck, Fred, "Phases and Group Problem Solving," in M. Alexis and C. Z. Wilson, eds., *Organizational Decision Making* (Englewood Cliffs, N.J.: Prentice-Hall, 1969), pp. 122–23.

Delbecq, Andre L., and Van de Ven, Andre H., "A Group Process Model for Problem Identification and Program Planning," in Neil Gilbert and Harry Speck, eds., *Planning for Social Welfare* (Englewood Cliffs, N.J.: Prentice-Hall, 1977), pp. 333–348.

——, and Gustoffsen, David H., *Group Techniques for Program Planning: A Guide to Nominal Groups and Delphi Processes* (Glenview, Ill.: Scott, Foresman and Co., 1976).

Schoenberger, Edward, and Williamson, John, "Deciding on Priorities and Specific Programs," in Wayne F. Anderson, Bernard J. Frieden, and Michael J. Murphy, eds., *Managing Human Services* (Washington, D.C.: The International City Management Association, 1977), pp. 162-63.

Van de Ven, Andre H., and Delbecq, Andre L., "Nominal Versus Interacting Group Processes for Committee Decision Making Effectiveness," *Academy of Management Journal* (June 1971): Vol. 14, No. 2, pp. 203-211.

Delphi

Dalkey, Norman, *The Delphi Method: An Experimental Study of Group Opinion* (Santa Monica, Calif.: Rand Corporation, 1969).

Dalkey, Norman C., Rourke, David L., Lewis, Roger, and Snyder, David, *Studies in the Quality of Life and Decision Making* (Lexington, Mass.: Lexington Books, 1972).

Delbecq, Andre L., Van de Ven, Andre H., and Gustoffsen, David, *Group Techniques for Program Planning: A Guide to Nominal Groups and Delphi Processes* (Glenview, Ill.: Scott, Foresman and Co., 1976).

Gustoffsen, David H., et al., "A Comparative Study of Differences and Subjective Likelihood Estimates Made by Individuals, Interacting Groups, Delphi Groups and Nominal Groups," in *Organizational Behavior and Human Performance* 9 (1973): 280–291.

Lauffer, Armand, "The Delphi Is No Oracle," in *Social Planning at the Community Level* (Englewood Cliffs, N.J.: Prentice-Hall, 1978), pp. 134–139.

Schoenberger, Edward, and Williamson, John, "Deciding on Priorities and Specific Programs," in Wayne F. Anderson, Bernard J. Frieden, and Michael J. Murphy, eds., *Managing Human Services* (Washington, D.C.: The International City Management Association, 1977), pp. 162–163.

Turoff, Murray, "The Design of a Policy Delphi," *The Journal of Technological Forecasting and Social Change,* 2 (1970): 149–171.

Task Analysis

Fine, Sydney, and Wiley, Reva W., *An Introduction to Functional Job Analysis.* (Kalamazoo, Mich.: The W. E. Upjohn Institute for Employment Research, 1971).

Lauffer, Armand, *A Manager's Guide to Task Analysis* (Ann Arbor, Mich.: The University of Michigan School of Social Work, 1980).

_____, "Working With Volunteers," in *Getting the Resources You Need* (Beverly Hills, Calif: Sage Publications, 1982), pp. 98-102.

The National Task Bank. U.S. Department of Health, Education and Welfare, Social and Rehabilitation Service, Office of Manpower Development and Training, Washington, D.C., 1972.

Force Field Analysis

Brager, George, and Holloway, Stephen, *Changing Human Service Organizations* (New York: Free Press, 1978), pp. 107–128.

Jung, Charles C., "Force Field Technique of Diagnosing a Problem," paper published by the Center for Research on Utilization of Scientific Knowledge, Institute for Social Research, University of Michigan, September 1966.

Kuriloff, Arthur H., *Organizational Development for Survival* (Washington, D.C.: American Management Association, 1972), pp. 132–136.

Lewin, Kurt, *Field Theory in Social Science* (New York: Harper & Row, 1951).

Gaming

Duke, Richard, *Gaming: The Futures Language* (Beverly Hills, Calif.: Sage Publications, 1975).

Horn, Robert E., and Cheaves, Anne (eds.), *The Guide to Simulation Games for Education and Training,* 4th ed. (Beverly Hills, Calif.: Sage Publications, 1980).

Lauffer, Armand, *The Aim of the Game* (New York: Gamed Simulations Incorporated, 1973).

Long, Norton, "The Local Community as an Ecology of Games," *American Journal of Sociology* 64 (1958): pp. 251-261.

5. DECISION ANALYSIS: SOME TECHNIQUES FOR CHOOSING AMONG ALTERNATIVE GOALS

Mitchell J. Rycus

FACTORS THAT AFFECT DECISION MAKING

Planners for the most part assist in decision making rather than make the actual decision. The mayor, council, city manager, and others who make decisions base them on a variety of sources, of which the planner can be one of the most important. One might expect that by the nature of decision making, some analytical methods exist that planners can use to make a case for either implementing or not implementing a certain decision. There is, in fact, a large body of literature on the nature of decision making* using some probabilistic techniques for selecting various choices. The techniques that use probabilistically determined outcomes are often called *stochastic models.* In stochastic models probabilities can be either assigned or determined without knowledge of any cause-effect relations. Techniques that depend upon the judgment of individuals, historical observations, or other nonrigorous procedures for assigning probabilities are called Bayesian analysis.

Two of these techniques stand out as the more common ones for planners: decision trees and minimax (or maximin) analyses. These techniques were developed under the relatively new engineering discipline of operations research to assist in making rational choices based upon probabilistic associations for multiple outcomes. Examples of these techniques can be found in the appendix at the end of this article.

Various methods for determining the probable outcome of a future event are available to those who assist in decision making for them to add credence to the acceptance or rejection of a decision. The inferential statistics discussed elsewhere in this book are available as valid methods to assist in making complex decisions; however, making decisions under uncertainty is probably the most common problem facing the decision maker concerned with the future. (See Lindblom, 1959, for a less rigorous account of decision analysis.) As a result, most of the mathematically rigorous methods are not as useful as one would hope. At least four nonmathematical factors act as the determinants of an outcome for any decision: risk, turbulence, uncertainty, and change.

RISK

Risk analysis has been developed in an analytical fashion, and some risk assess-

---

Reproduced by permission of the publisher and the author. This article has been modified from Chapter 4 of "The Planner's Use of Information" edited by Hemalata Dandekar, Hutchinson Ross Publishing Company, Stroudsburg, Pa., 1982. From *Decision Analysis: Some Techniques for Choosing Among Alternative Goals* by Mitchell Rycus.

*See the bibliography at end of this article.

ments can be performed on certain types of events. These types of assessments usually relate to technical events and involve the probabilistic assessment of a string of independent events. Analyses such as the risk of a meltdown at a nuclear power plant can be made in this fashion. The risk may change, however, as new factors are introduced or other analyses taking different factors into account are performed, so it is not always easy to come up with one probability associated with any single risky event. But more importantly, the decision maker must decide how much of a risk he or she is willing to take in making a decision. For example, if the probability of a serious nuclear accident at a power plant is 1 in 20,000 over a one-year operating period, then it may appear that it would be a safe decision to approve the construction of a nuclear power plant. However, if one further considers that there might be 200 nuclear power plants operating over a twenty-five-year period, then the probability of a serious accident is 1 in 4 in that period. But if a serious accident is defined like the accident that occurred at Three Mile Island in 1979, then the risk may be worthwhile if the benefits of the additional nuclear energy outweigh these risks. On the other hand, the United States currently has more electric generating capacity than it needs, so no new plants would be of benefit. But the majority of the operating plants burn coal, oil, or natural gas, fuels that either harm the environment when they are burned or are extracted, or are in dwindling supply.

This argument can go back and forth without the benefit of a rigorous numerical analysis even though quantifiable information exists. The risk that a decision-making body will ultimately take depends in large part on previously

taken risky decisions and the consequences of those decisions. Those assisting in decision making can present all the arguments and even numerically assess some of the risks associated with the decision, but the actual decision for the most part will be based on the decision makers' personal experiences.

The planner should learn the risks decision makers have taken in the past and either state them or be able to address them when presenting data. If the city of Middlesville's Environmental Engineering Department previously refused to pick up garbage downtown on weekends because of the fear of accidents during heavy weekend traffic, then Junior Planner should be prepared to address the issue when he makes his recommendation for a weekend pickup, no matter how rational his other reasons for making the recommendation may be.

TURBULENCE

A turbulent environment can be caused by a single event such as the evacuation of a community due to a natural or human-caused disaster or a combination of events—for instance, the transition of a community from one type of industrial base to another. A high level of turbulence is usually perceived as a negative factor, so decisions that can increase turbulence, no matter how short-lived that turbulence might be, will be avoided in general. Consider the clearing of an area having a particular land use such as residential to accommodate another land use, such as commercial or industrial. This type of decision will create turbulence for the residents and will also create resistance to making the final decision. Turbulence is not necessarily bad, but it can create problems if the decision in all other respects is an appropriate one for the entire community. Those who have avoided making decisions because they might create turbulence, no matter how short term, in all likelihood will continue to avoid such decisions.

Planners must be aware of turbulence-generating decisions and present their information by showing that short-term turbulence may be necessary for the overall benefit of the community, and a much more harmful, long-term turbulence may result from not making a decision. The decision to remove the residents from Love Canal in New York to avoid any further biological harm caused by exposure to toxic wastes created a turbulent situation, but the alternative of having the families stay in the area was potentially far more turbulent.

UNCERTAINTY

Even with good probabilistic analyses, a certain amount of uncertainty regarding any decision is always present. Each of us deals with uncertainty in our own way, and some of us are willing to accept far greater levels of uncertainty than others. Furthermore, the type of outcome associated with any decision will also determine how much uncertainty one might accept. If a particular outcome, such as a nuclear accident, no matter how small or localized, is totally unacceptable to a decision maker, then any amount of uncertainty associated with the possibility of a nuclear accident will not be accepted. On the other hand, if one is willing to accept a highly improbable, low-level nuclear accident (if there is such a thing), that person will also accept a certain level of uncertainty associated with a nuclear plant site.

Planners who are assisting decision makers will also have to understand their own personal level of acceptance of uncertainty, but more important, they must be fully aware that a decision maker or a decision-making body will have its own unique level of acceptance. As a result many planners are frequently frustrated by their inability to convince a decision making group to accept or reject decisions based on what the planner feels to be an acceptable level of uncertainty.

CHANGE

Almost all policy decisions lead to some change in either the behavior or appearance of the affected group and its environment. A fundamental premise of complex systems analysis is the system's ability to resist change no matter how valid or appropriate that change might be. Like uncertainty, the amount of change one is willing to accept varies from each individual and from each group. The difference is that change is more qualitative in nature, and the perceived change that may result from any particular decision is highly individualistic and frequently value laden. In many instances, prejudice and bigotry on the part of the decision maker will have a direct bearing on the type of change he or she perceives and is willing to accept. Zoning changes that appear to give some continuity to a community may be proposed to prevent perceived or real ethnic changes in a neighborhood. In fact, one of the first zoning ordinances passed by a city was to exclude laundries from San Francisco's Nob Hill area. The reason was not for environmental purposes, as some argued, but to prevent Chinese people from moving into the area.

Planners must be aware of the broad spectrum of changes, real and imaginary, that may result as the outcome of any decision and be prepared to address them. This may prove uncomfortable for and at times antagonistic to some decision makers, but unless the real and perceived changes are expressed, rational arguments may not lead to a desired decision.

MANAGEMENT TECHNIQUES USED IN DECISION MAKING

Planning analysis frequently requires synthesizing information solely on the basis of how the information is presented. Indeed the initial analyses of most problems are based on information presented in a format that best suits further analysis. Management problems involve complex interactions among people, tasks, and productivity, and usually they can be presented or arranged in such a way that a logical flow through can be analyzed.

Various planning management methods are described in this book; they include PERT (program evaluation and revision techniques) and CPM (critical path method). In these techniques, a collection of tasks is specified that, when complete, leads to a final outcome, which can be a program, a manufactured product, or a complex system. The project flows from task to task, with completion time estimated for each individual. Tasks are also represented leading to an overall assessment of how critical each task is and how each fits into the final outcome. These methods are extensively used in planning as are the techniques of planning, programming, and budgeting system (PPBS), matrix representations, and similar methods whereby information is synthesized into

a display useful for large program management. The bibliography at the end of this article covers these and other techniques in detail. Two examples of how such methods may be employed to communicate planning problems are presented here.

Most complex management plans require identification of non-quantitative processes, such as the various tasks to be accomplished, and who might do them, along with some fixed quantifiable variables, such as the time or money it takes to complete the tasks. Suppose that Junior Planner from Middlesville had to submit a program management plan to his planning director prior to initiating any other actions on the downtown trash problem. He might present the chart shown in Figure 5.1 indicating the time and effort expected to complete each task. Charts such as these, called *milestone charts,* are common management tools used to establish the overall cost and effort needed for completion of budgeted programs. They serve to check on the progress of the program and are useful in indicating potential cost and time overruns.

Another method for presenting information that guides managers in implementing an overall plan is in the use of a two-dimensional matrix presentation where some critical information about management needs and ways to meet them is given in each cell. We recently completed an energy planning and management program using this type of matrix for the U.S. Department of Interior, which will be used for parks and recreational areas. (See Figure 5.2.) The energy needs of various facilities, such as outdoor lighting, vehicle fleets, and swimming pools, are listed vertically on the matrix, and the fuels used to meet those needs are listed horizontally. The

FIGURE 5.1
Program Milestone Chart

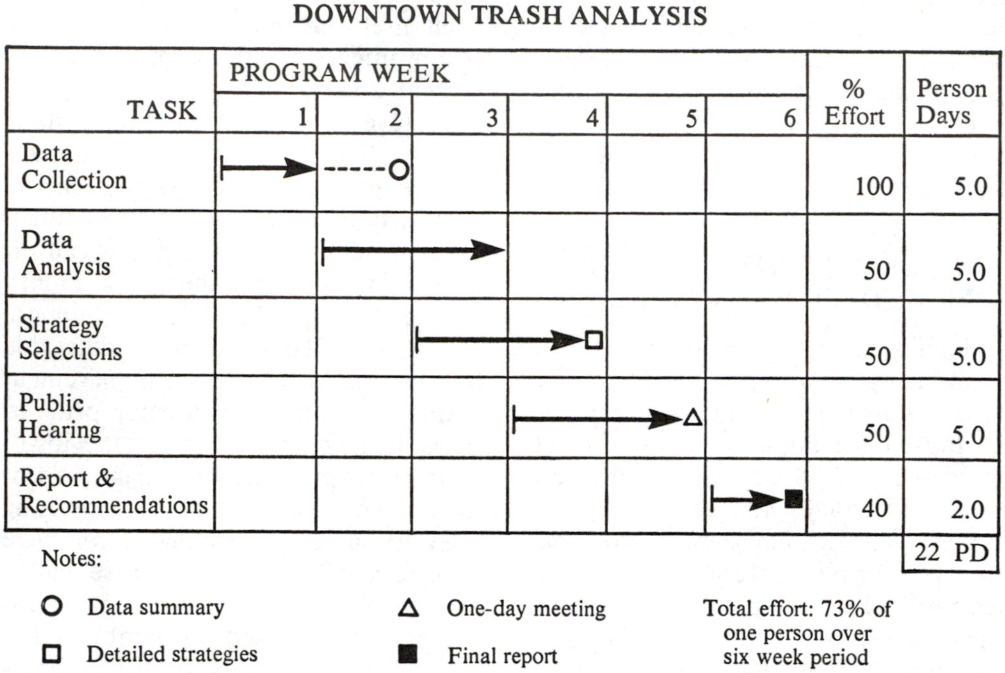

DOWNTOWN TRASH ANALYSIS

TASK	PROGRAM WEEK						% Effort	Person Days
	1	2	3	4	5	6		
Data Collection	├──►	----O					100	5.0
Data Analysis		├────	──►				50	5.0
Strategy Selections			├────	►□			50	5.0
Public Hearing				├────	►△		50	5.0
Report & Recommendations						├─►■	40	2.0
Notes:								22 PD

O   Data summary   △   One-day meeting   Total effort: 73% of
                                                    one person over
□   Detailed strategies ■   Final report   six week period

primary purpose of the program was to manage the park's energy budget so as to minimize the energy used while maintaining a high level of services. The information contained in each cell of the matrix summarized the cost and savings attributable to a particular conservation strategy applicable to the fuel used at the facility listed.

When completed, the matrix contained a large variety of strategies for use in developing an overall park energy management plan. The information for each facility was summarized at the end of each row, and the information for each fuel source considered was summarized at the bottom of each column. The summary information established an overall cost and the potential energy savings for the total implementation of all the strategies. The method is particularly valuable because it allows for the presentation of qualitative information, such as the political and institutional characteristics associated with implementing each strategy, by a color-coding process along with the detailed quantitative information. In this manner the park manager could select which strategy should be implemented and in which order implementation should occur. Since the costs and benefits of implementing strategies are cumulative, strategies having high costs and marginal

FIGURE 5.2
Energy Planning Matrix

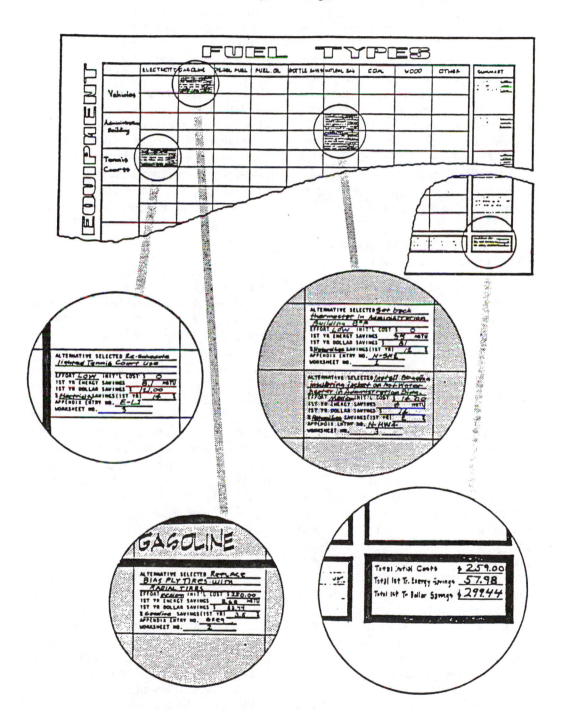

benefits could be implemented at a later stage of the program, or even not at all if the overall goals of the program are reached with the higher-priority strategies.

Planners who use such management tools for implementing programs should be aware that there is a lot of room for individual development of other methods. No one method is ideally suited for all management programs, and the creativity of the planner who is drawing upon methods developed by others is always challenged in developing new management programming tools.

FORECASTING TECHNIQUES USED IN DECISION MAKING

When planners discuss future events, they usually do this in terms of alternative futures. No unique future exists now, of course; rather a collection of probable futures exists, and by proper planning and appropriate decision making, a group can prepare for the futures with higher probability of occurrence.

The history of modern forecasting used by planners is relatively new, dating from around the end of World War II. Three primary reasons are usually stated as to why forecasting is used in planning: problem identification, consequence of actions, and normative judgment.

By observing trends and patterns over time, problems will surface that may not have been obvious without some type of forecasting process. By the same token, one can assess the consequences of one's actions not only by evaluating the primary effects but also by the secondary and higher-order effects of a particular action, which can be discerned over time. Various forecasting methods are quite responsive to these higher-order effects, and without them such effects would be almost impossible to predict. Finally, the outcome of decisions should lead to goals that are normative—in other words, within the accepted norms of the group affected by the decisions. Hence by appropriate forecasting, problems can be identified, the consequences of certain decisions surrounding those problems evaluated, and those decisions with the highest probability of leading to acceptable goals can be implemented.

Forecasting methods range from examining a single variable over time to complex multivariate interactions. The simplest types of forecasting usually involve only one variable, and based upon the patterns or trends observed, one can forecast the future behavior of that variable. More complex forecasting techniques generally include a number of variables, and either through some process or by using computer techniques designed to examine a large number of interactions, future events can be simulated and assessments made. These methods usually require quantifying the variables being examined—number of houses available in ten years, vehicle density in five years, number of different types of energy sources available in twenty years, amount of air and water pollution as a result of industrial growth in the next five, ten, and fifteen years, and so forth. But forecasting can be qualitative as well. Various methods are available that can offer some understanding of how the values of a group may alter future responses to various public and private acts. The current public awareness of environmental degradation caused by noncontrolled industrial processes is one example of how a change in societal values toward industrial growth can affect product cost and product availability of a region.

The *Handbook of Forecasting Tech-*

niques (Mitchell et al., 1977) details a large number of available forecasting techniques. An examination of a couple of the techniques will demonstrate how they might be used. Scenario generation is a common forecasting technique that is used to present different pictures of the future as a result of varying outcomes of major events. Scenarios can be both qualitative and quantitative. They can be generated from either the planner's knowledge of the problem or by random assignments to the descriptive information. An energy scenario for the year 2000 (Figure 5.3), along with a collection of other scenarios, each having different values assigned to the descriptive variables, can then be used in combination with other techniques to arrive at some U.S. energy forecast.

A method often employed with a collection of scenarios is the Delphi process. In this technique a panel of experts examines a range of scenarios similar to the one shown in Figure 5.3 and assigns some probability to the outcome of each scenario. The resultant probabilities are then shared by the panel who generally do not know which members assigned the probabilities to the various scenarios. After seeing all the probabilities for each scenario, the expert is asked to reexamine his or her original assignments and either to substantiate why they are different from those of the other experts or to change them, if he or

FIGURE 5.3
U.S. Energy Scenario, Year 2000

In the year 2000 the cost of gasoline has almost doubled over 1980 costs, and the availability of natural gas has decreased substantially. As a result the use of coal has dramatically increased without benefit of extensive pollution controls, leading to a considerable increase in environmental deterioration.

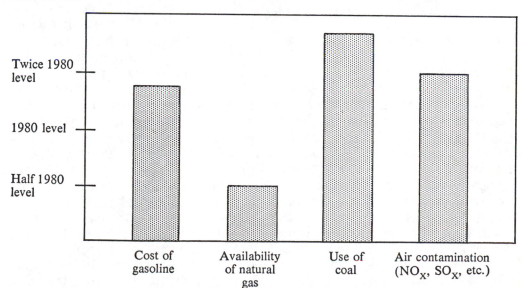

she so chooses. Finally, a consensus probability is calculated from all the experts' contributions for each scenario, resulting in a probabilistic forecast for the entire set of alternative futures.

Complex systems analysis using computers to handle vast amounts of data or calculations is also used to forecast future events. Forrester's *Urban Dynamics* (1969) is probably the most ambitious example of this technique. He took into account factors associated with housing, jobs, and industry to develop a complex model of urban interactions. By varying the rates of control variables, such as the rate of new job generation, changes in worker housing, and worker migration rates, forecasts for the future needs of cities in terms of new housing, new jobs, and industries could be generated.

Simulation/gaming also lends itself to forecasting. By having the players enact roles and make decisions in their roles, future events can be simulated. The knowledge of how decisions affect future outcomes in a game situation is easily extended to a forecast, if the underlying restrictions of the game model are kept in perspective.

Whichever forecasting technique the planner uses, a number of cautions must be observed. The most obvious is that the further into the future one forecasts, the more improbable the forecast. Long-range forecasting is not the most accurate tool for policy making, and planners should be aware of the accuracy of each technique. Another problem with certain types of forecasting is erroneously assuming causal relations between events simply because a correlation exists. Finally a forecast is only as good as the data used. Limited amounts of data, poorly measured data, and hastily reduced data will lead to inaccurate forecasts no matter how sophisticated the forecasting technique. Computer people refer to this as "GIGO" (garbage in; garbage out).

APPENDIX: BAYESIAN TECHNIQUES USED IN DECISION MAKING

Decision Trees

The decision tree is probably the most familiar technique. It uses the conditional probabilities associated with events that may be linked to a number of outcomes. The final probability of the linked outcomes can then be determined by multiplying the various outcomes along the branches to determine a final probability for a string of events. For example, suppose the mayor of Middlesville wants to know what effect ignoring the garden club's complaints will have on the upcoming city election. At this point, he knows that his opponent has as good a chance of winning as he does and that it is also a fifty-fifty possibility as to whether he will do anything about the downtown trash problem before the election because many problems need his staff's attention now. A quick analysis shows that if he does not do anything about the trash problem, 90 percent of the garden club will oppose his reelection, which can greatly affect his chances. In fact, if they resist his election, his odds of winning will drop from 50 to 40 percent. The question he needs to answer is whether to respond to the garden club now or wait until after the election.

A decision tree for this type of problem is illustrated in Figure 5.4. In this simple example, Figure 5.4 shows that the

FIGURE 5.4
Decision Tree of Mayor Lorch's Probability of Reelection

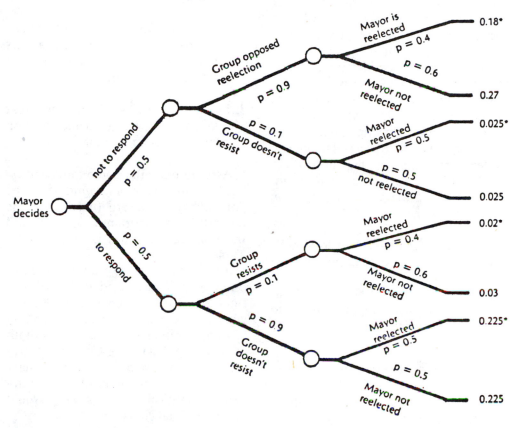

Reelection probability for Mayor Lorch will be the sum of reelection probabilities (*)
(.18 + .025 + .02 + .225 = .45)

mayor's chances for reelection are decreased if he does not respond to the group, and it resists his election. This results in a 0.27 probability of the mayor's not being elected and compares to a probability of 0.225 of being elected even if he does respond to their request. Indeed he has found that as a result of the garbage issue, his chances for reelection have changed from 50 percent to only 45 percent, which is calculated by totaling

the reelection probabilities on the decision tree. Therefore it is in the mayor's best interest to maximize his chances of winning by responding to their request immediately.

The example contains a number of statistical assumptions that must be validated before any action takes place; however, it demonstrates the use of probabilities in assisting decision makers.

Minimax Analysis

Other decision techniques, such as minimax and maximin strategies, are designed to allow the decision maker to select strategies that will, respectively, maximize the chance of getting at least the minimum benefit or minimize the chance of expending the maximum costs associated with program selection.

Consider the following simple example. A planning office is asked to prepare strategies for obtaining federal funds to develop a mass transportation program. After some deliberation two specific strategies emerge:

1. Political Pressure—Solicit local politicians to exert political influence on the federal agencies.
2. Business Pressure—Solicit local business and industry representatives to exert influence on the federal agencies.

Let us further suppose that there are three categories of federal funds available depending upon which program is solicited, namely:

1. Major Systems—Large-scale implementation of operational mass transit systems with funding reviewed annually.

2. Demonstration Programs—Small demonstration or pilot programs funded with possible major system development to follow.

3. Feasibility Studies—Small grants that establish the need for demonstration or major system funding.

Assume that after some initial investigation the planners found that the potential dollar award (payoff) for the three different programs associated with the selected strategies is as shown in Table 5.1.

From Table 5.1, we see that the minimum payoff associated with the political pressure strategy is $500,000, whereas the business pressure strategy has a minimum payoff of $100,000 (both of these payoffs are for feasibility studies). If one were interested in maximizing the minimum payoff (maximin), then the political pressure strategy would be the optimal course to follow.

Another way to present the information is to calculate the loss that might occur with the awarding of a program for

TABLE 5.1
Payoff in Millions of Dollars by Strategy and Program

If you apply this ↓ \ For this →	Major Systems	Demonstration	Feasibility	Minimum
Political Pressure	2.1	0.8	0.5	0.5
Business Pressure	3.6	0.5	0.1	0.1

a particular strategy. By subtracting the smaller amount associated with each strategy, we then have the potential loss (regret) realized by applying one strategy instead of the other.

Table 5.2 shows that if the political pressure strategy is employed, the city stands to lose $1,500,000 if a major system program is awarded. However, if the business pressure strategy is employed, then the city stands to lose only $400,000 if the feasibility study is awarded. If the planners want to minimize the maximum regret (minimax), then they should select the business pressure strategy.

Another way of evaluating the data is to try and maximize the maximum (maximax) possible payoff, which is $3,600,000, by employing the business pressure strategy. In fact the total dollar award possible for each strategy (assuming all programs can be awarded to the city) is $3,400,000 for the political pressure strategy and $4,200,000 for the business pressure strategy, making the business pressure strategy once again the strategy of choice. This assumes, of course, that there is an equal chance that each program will be funded regardless of which strategy the city chooses, but in

most cases that assumption would be very misleading. Obviously there are different probabilities associated with getting an award for each strategy. The methods for obtaining these probabilities are dependent upon some historical information or the judgment of individuals who have some knowledge about the award process, in other words, by Bayesian methods.

To carry the example a little further, assume these probabilities are obtained.

The "expected value," or average dollar amount obtainable for each strategy, is found by multiplying the probabilities from Table 5.3 by the amounts given in Table 5.1 for each program and then adding them all up. For the political pressure strategy this would be $970,000, and for the business pressure strategy it would amount to only $730,000, making the political pressure strategy optimal under this criterion. Given these probabilities, we should go back and reevaluate our minimax and maximin solutions using these probabilities in our analysis.

This little example demonstrates the type of reasoning that goes into maximin and minimax-related analyses. In many cases these analyses are very complex

TABLE 5.2
Loss in Millions of Dollars, by Strategy and Program

If this strategy applied / This program is awarded	Major Systems	Demonstration	Feasibility	Maximum
Political Pressure	1.5	0	0	1.5
Business Pressure	0	0.3	0.4	0.4

TABLE 5.3
Probabilities Associated with Awards

If this strategy applied ↓ \ For this program →	Major Systems	Demonstration	Feasibility
Political Pressure	0.2	0.5	0.3
Business Pressure	0.1	0.7	0.2

and require sophisticated linear programming techniques. However, in some cases an analysis as simple as this example can be done for some planning applications.

The methods detailed here are exemplary of the most commonly referenced Bayesian decision techniques. Such methods, where the probability of independent events is determined leading to the calculation of a probability of the outcome of a string of events, would be ideal if all events were indeed independent and the probability of occurrence for each event were well known. But this is not the case, and frequently probabilities have to be assigned based upon some heuristic method, such as the opinions of experts (called Delphi techniques) or upon best guesses by an experienced observer.

REFERENCES

Forrester, Jay W., 1969, *Urban Dynamics,* MIT Press, Cambridge, Mass.

Lindblom, Charles E., 1959, "The Science of Muddling Through," *Public Administration Review 19:* 79-88 (Spring).

Mitchell, Arnold, Burnaham H. Dodge, Pamela G. Kruzic, David C. Miller, Peter Schwartz, and Benjamin E. Suth, 1977, *Handbook of Forecasting Techniques,* 2 vols., INR Report 75-77, National Technical Information Service, Springfield, Va.

Rycus, Mitchell, Allan Feldt, Mark Hassett, Gregory Jones, and Matthew Rose, "Energy Planning and Management for Parks and Recreation," U.S. Department of the Interior, Government Printing Office, Washington, D.C., 1981.

BIBLIOGRAPHY

Dickey, John W., and Thomas M. Watts, *Analytic Techniques in Urban and Regional Planning,* McGraw-Hill, New York, 1978.

An excellent introduction and overview of the various analytic methods used by planners. Provides useful appendixes on basic mathematics and computer languages.

Forrester, Jay W., *Urban Dynamics,* MIT Press, Cambridge, Mass., 1969.

A detailed systems analysis of an urban area with projections of change in employment, housing, and industry based upon a complex but limited computer simulation model.

Krueckeberg, Donald A., and Arthur L. Silvers, *Urban Planning Analysis: Methods and Models,* John Wiley, New York, 1974.

A good, mathematically rigorous text

and reference work. Examples appropriate to planning are used throughout.

Lindblom, Charles E., "The Science of Muddling Through," *Public Administration Review 19:* 79-88 (Spring 1959).

The first statement of the now well-known and widely accepted critique of scientific decision making.

Mitchell, Arnold, Burnaham H. Dodge, Pamela E. Kruzic, David C. Miller, Peter Schwartz, and Benjamin E. Suth, *Handbook of Forecasting Techniques,* 2 vols., INR Report 75-77, National Technical Information Service, Springfield, Va., 1977.

A detailed description of thirty-one forecasting techniques. A practical and well-formulated handbook, with examples applicable to environmental, social, and economic forecasts.

Raiffa, Howard, *Decision Analysis: Introductory Lectures on Choices Under Uncertainty,* Addison-Wesley, Reading, Mass., 1968.

A sound mathematics text on decision theory. Readable for nonmathematicians with some statistics background and recommended for planners interested in decision-making analysis.

6. VALUE CONFLICTS AND DECISION MAKING: ANALYSIS AND RESOLUTION*

John E. Tropman

In complex urban society the community organizer and planner is required to make, or become involved with, complex decisions of great importance. Problems that were once considered the domain of the family—such as sex education—are more and more becoming elements of the public domain. Educational planning, health planning, social services planning, planning for children and the aged, for women going back to work and men leaving work—these and others are

Reproduced by permission of the author from *Community Development Journal,* October 1981, Vol. 16, No. 3.

*Portions of this article were supported by the American Values and the Elderly Project, sponsored by the Administration on Aging, Grant # 90-1-1325. Special thanks are given to Beverly LaLonde, Jane McClure, Sue Sweeny, and Terrence Tice for comments on an earlier draft.

becoming the subject of intensive social work activity.

Essential to these planning activities is the assessment process. Many kinds of assessments, and ones we talk about in other articles, involve demographic counts, community surveys, and even personalistic assessments of the worker's own orientations and involvements. One kind of assessment that is frequently left out, however, is what might be called a values assessment. Such an assessment differs from the process of "values clarification," which often involves a recognition of the individual worker's personalistic involvements in a situation. Rather, what is important is a sense of the structure of the values involved in the different groups. Planners often have no precedents to guide them. They frequently must rely on their subjective appraisal of the situation. Included in their appraisal are values of the community, values of the society, values of the client groups involved, and professional values, among others. This piece can provide a framework for making such an assessment, so that it is no longer necessary for the planner to "fly by the seat of her or his pants." While this piece provides no magic formula for making hard decisions, it does offer a new approach to analyzing the values involved in the planning process.

WHAT ARE VALUES?

Values are those gut-level feelings people have about fundamental aspects of life, which give it meaning and direction. Some of the more familiar values are family values, religious values, and work values. Values are ideas to which commitments are attached. There is no rule that they must be well-ordered, complete, consistent, or unambiguous. Indeed, as planners know, the reverse is the most likely situation.

Values have many complex, changing, and often conflicting meanings. People's values vary depending on their age, race, sex, income, education, and much more. To understand our own values, as well as those of others, we must realize that values intrude in subtle and unexpected ways. Values are so much a part of us that we are often not even aware of their influence. As a result, we often do not have the perspective we need to make appropriate decisions or to understand the actions of others.

Planners may be in the crucial position of making precedent-setting decisions involving fundamental values. It is therefore very important that they understand the complexities of values.

Values:

- vary among different people
- shift and change
- often go unrecognized
- often conflict with one another

The purpose of this paper is to aid practitioners in exploring their own and others' values and the ways they influence many different kinds of decisions affecting the planning process.

Value Conflicts

Our perspective on American values suggests that the values we hold often come in pairs, or sets of opposing beliefs. Part of the complex nature of values is our tendency to believe in values which compete with one another. For example, belief in family responsibility as well as individual fulfillment is one example. Americans tend to be committed to both parts of this pair of values: to the family as a central American institution, and to the importance of fulfilling our individual needs. When faced with a plan about responsibility to one's family or to one's goals, citizens are often placed in a value dilemma. Though both parts of the values pair may not carry equal weight, when we make a decision, we try to strike a balance between two desirable choices.

For example, more and more women are choosing to work while their families are growing. Though the public in general might be more accepting of this choice now than in the past, each woman still must find her own balance between independence, work, and responsibility to family. Social planners and community organizers need to be continually aware of the value tensions that are inherent in the system and make an assessment of these dilemmas and tensions a part of their ongoing "sensing" of the community or field of practice. Seven value dilemmas seem most critical.

individual ——— family

self-reliance ——— inter-dependency

secular ——— religious

equity ——— adequacy

struggle ——— entitlements

private ——— public

work ——— leisure

VALUES DILEMMAS IN COMMUNITY PRACTICE

Social planners and community organizers are continually involved in issues of assessment. These assessments involve, typically, money and personnel, issues and answers to the problems that beset the local community, the organization, or the subgroup. Planners and organizers continually struggle with finding solutions to community problems. What is often not so clear, however, is the fact that these problems involve value conflicts characterized by high ambivalence. As suggested, values upon which decisions are based are values which all of us hold. It is not "us" versus "them" but "us" versus "us" as well.

A second point involves us and our clients. The list of value conflicts suggests that the kinds of values our profession supports, on balance, tend to be on the righthand side of the list—family, interdependency, religious, adequacy, entitlements, public, leisure—tend to be subdominant ones, not, overall, as strongly held as those values on the left—individual, self-reliance, secular, equity, struggle, private, and work values. Thus our profession, our field, and to some extent, we ourselves, are in the position of advocating subdominant values. In fact, the very concept of "community" smacks of a subdominant value, linked more to interdependency than to self-reliance. Our client groups, too, often seem more linked to subdominant values than to dominant ones. Thus, to a certain extent, as we push the more subdominant values, we threaten the major value orientations in the society, in the community, and even within ourselves.

POLICY PLANNING AND PLANNERS

Under new guidelines, children of dependent elderly parents can be paid by the state for providing home care for their parents. Many people feel that children should do this as part of their family responsibilities without pay. Others feel that older people who need or want to work should be paid to provide home health care for other elderly people.

As a planner in the Department of Social Services, you have the option to propose payments to family members or to several elderly people who have been home care providers for many years. What do you recommend?

Planners as Policymakers

As a practitioner, you may not consider yourself a policy maker. But you are. Policy can be defined as a decision or series of decisions that apply to a group of people or to many situations. Policy that is made in legislatures is only one level of policy. It is then up to the practitioner to interpret the laws passed in legislative bodies.

Policy is a matter of making choices. Furthermore, the most difficult policy choices involve making a decision *not* between good and evil or right and wrong, but between two or more good choices or two or more unsatisfactory choices. Policy decisions often involve a serious conflict between two strongly held beliefs, so that it is very difficult for us to know which way to compromise.

The social planner is frequently involved in assessing situations where there is a turbulent environment, where feelings run high. Should a program be in a religious institution or a nonreligious one? Should a program be run under private auspices, or should public funds be found to support it? While the plan-

ners do not make policy, they are often involved in making the crucial recommendations that become policy.

Though these values may seem foreign and rather academic, some questions based on these values are familiar:

- How much should the government do for people?
- Does the government owe everyone an adequate income?
- Should people be allowed to work as long as they want?
- How much responsibility should the family take in caring for its older members?

These seven pairs are not the only values involved in decision making. Yet they seem to be involved again and again, whether in debate over the Social Security Act or in consulting with a client

TABLE 6.1
Value Dilemmas

1. individual/family	suggests the need to balance between our own needs and the needs of our family.
2. self-reliance/interdependency	emphasizes the strain between the desire to "go it alone" and the need to depend on others.
3. secular/religious	suggests the tension between looking for rational explanations for life's ups and downs and turning to religious sources for support.
4. equity/adequacy	refers to the conflict between fairness to all and the responsibility to help those most in need.
5. struggle/entitlement	suggests the tension between the importance of working for everything we get and being entitled to certain things just because we are human beings.
6. private/public	describes the conflict between use of personal or corporate means, and use of government to achieve desired social goals.
7. work/leisure	confronts the issue of work and its meanings. How much work should we do, and for how long? When should work stop and leisure begin?

about retirement. Everyone has value orientations which influence the style and approach they take with policy issues.

For each pair of values, Table 6.1 suggests a statement that a person holding that value might agree with. The values on the left—private, equity, work, and so on—tend to favor individual efforts and rewards. Over the years public opinion has tended to support the view that the welfare of each person is an individual or private concern. Values on the other side—public, family, adequacy, for example—tend to emphasize collective well-being. Government intervention, labor unions, and other community and social organizations are supported by these values. Only recently has public opinion tended to support these values in major policy issues.

Thus, certain values tend to be balanced by an opposite value. Yet, as our experience reflects, any value or set of values may conflict with any other. Depending on the issue, certain values

TABLE 6.2
Value Conflicts

"It is important that I consider my needs first."	
	"My family's needs are of first and foremost importance."
"I can get along best by myself."	
	"People need each other to do this."
"Problems can best be solved by thinking them through objectively and rationally."	
	"Problems become smaller if we have faith in a divine force."
"People should be treated the same, regardless of their needs."	
	"People most in need should get the most help."
"No one should have a good standard of living without earning it."	
	"Everyone deserves a decent standard of living whether he/she earns it or not."
"People should take care of themselves."	
	"The government should provide for people."
"Work is the most meaningful thing people do."	
	"Other activities are at least as important as work."

will be viewed as more important than others. In other cases, several values pairs may seem equally relevant. Value conflicts arise because selecting one value as the basis for action automatically raises an alternative view, whether we want it to or not.

Value conflict and compromise take place on many levels ranging from the national policy-making level to the agency-practitioner level.

PLANNER DECISIONS

You are a planner with an area agency on aging. There is a small, older area of town where a community of elderly people live, and have lived for years. The city wants the property for a new library and asks your help in developing a plan to move the people there out into institutional facilities, with their families, and so on. Two or three of the older residents come to the office and ask your help in developing a plan which will let them remain where they are.

What do you do?

Planning conflicts like this one are quite common. The issue is very complex because different legitimate views are represented. Many other examples of this kind of dilemma confront the planner, such as involvement in the merger of agencies, conflicts between city hall and other types of citizen groups, conflicts between "group home" advocates and those who oppose such homes—the list goes on and on.

As a planning and community organizing professional, you must carefully think through the issue, keeping in mind the values of all concerned. Five steps will usually be involved:

1. *Defining the problem*
   What are the basic issues?
   What information is needed, overall, about them?

2. *Developing alternative strategies for action*
   Consider the options and the consequences.
   Seek to balance values conflicts.

3. *Decision*
   This is the point at which those in authority make the decision. Additional balancing of conflicts goes on at this point.

4. *Operational planning*
   Working with those involved to develop an operational plan to carry out the decision.

5. *Implementation*
   Carrying out the decision and evaluating it.

Defining the Problem

Which is more important, the need of the city for the area, or the rights of the people in the area now? What alternatives are available for both groups? Is the group of older people a "community," in the sense that they share the concern of care for each other?

Developing Alternative Strategies

What is the range of alternatives here, including the takeover of the land and the possibility of the older people remaining in their own homes? Are there intermediate possibilities which need to be considered? What are the sets of values which need to be balanced? What may happen under these different possibilities? How can values of public and private, self-reliance and interdependence be blended?

Decision

Which authority, or combination of authorities, is going to make the decision? What are their values? What are the values to which they are likely to be sensitive? What kinds of compromises could be possible? Could the community be relocated elsewhere even if the buildings can not?

Operational Planning

Once the decision has been made, there is an operational planning process, which can itself involve a host of additional decisions. How can the decision be carried out in the best interests of everyone? What about individual and family interests here? Can these be accommodated?

Implementation

Putting the plan into effect requires an assessment of values, too. Equity and adequacy may be an issue in terms of what kinds of supports might be given to older people if they are forced to move. If the decision has gone the other way, then the city needs to find a new site that is adequate for its needs.

Values in Decision Making

While practitioners are often required to go through a formal evaluation process, they are not required to go through a formal decision-making process. Sometimes this is because the situation demands immediate attention. At other times, decisions are almost instinctual or "gut-level." At still other times, agency or client pressures prevail, and you make a decision against your better judgment. Recognizing the part that values play in all decisions can give you real insight into decisions. As a result you have more control over the decisions you make and participate in.

The worksheet in Figure 6.1 is a decision-making exercise that focuses on values. It will help you deliberately weigh the values, options, and consequences involved in a decision.

TACTICS FOR VALUES BALANCE

Given the fact that values come in opposing sets and we spend lots of our professional time trying to achieve a

FIGURE 6.1
Worksheet for Planning Decisions

Problem	Values Pairs	Decision Options	Compromises	Consequences
_____	_____	_____	_____	_____
_____	_____	_____	_____	_____
_____	_____	_____	_____	_____
_____	_____	_____	_____	_____
_____	_____	_____	_____	_____

values balance within a situation of potential or actual conflict, what are some tactics we might use, some ideas to list in the "options" column of the chart? Following are a few suggestions, by no means an exhaustive list, but one intended to provide a guide for the practitioner.

Averaging

Here the two value orientations are averaged. We have some public and some private, some secular and some religious, some individual and some family. This compromise idea is often useful, but it implies an equality of values, which is not always the case. Thus, there may need to be a *weighted average,* which takes account of the dominance/subdominance relationship.

Sectoring

In sectoring, the two values are used in different topics or in different places, or for different groups. Federalism is an example of values sectoring, in which topic and place vary. Some affirmative action programs are of this kind. Here the planner seeks to prevent value conflict through actualizing the values in different sectors. Ethnic service agencies, each emphasizing the values of the particular group in question, are an example.

Sequencing

In sequencing, the planner or organizer seeks to use time as the differentiating factor, rather than space, as in sectoring. One case might be a day program and a night program where different types of community needs are met at different times. Programs that are "improper" for schools in the day can be run at night, when the children are gone. Changing a program during the weekend because more men are likely to show up represents another approach to sequencing.

Adjudicating

Sometimes the planner or community organizer needs an authoritative interpretation; sometimes a choice must be made. Here an appeal to authority can be helpful. Sometimes such an appeal is through the courts, usually when other authority has failed to be convincing. Besides the courts, however, planners and community organizers can appeal to local authorities in the form of experts, political influentials, and so on.

Power

Sometimes the "merits" of a situation are not convincing, as in adjudicating, and community organizers seek to build coalitions of leaders and influentials to force their values (or the values for which they are advocating) to become dominant in the situation. "Political" associations are often of this type.

Decision Rule

Sometimes there are internal decision rules to which planners can appeal or organizers can use to solve a values dilemma. Sometimes these rules refer to *roles;* certain people do this, while others do that. Older and younger people may have such different roles, for example, as have men and women and parents and children. Sometimes a condition becomes the discriminating factor—in this situation, one type of behavior is all right; in that type of situation, some other type of behavior is all right.

Pragmatism

A popular solution is the pragmatic solution. Let's be "free" of values, it is argued, and do what seems natural and "works" in the situation. Pragmatism usually is not a rule in itself but relates to having a range of means for problem solution available—averaging, sequencing, sectoring, adjudicating, decision rule, and so on. At the means level the pragmatic person is one who has a range of ways to solve a particular values conflict and does not "value" any one over another one, in general.

CONCLUSION

Values always conflict, because there are many of them and because they tend to come in juxtaposed pairs. Much of the work a community practitioner has to do involves working through values dilemmas and providing solutions that permit the process of community development and improvement to go forward. Assessment is a key tool here. Solutions are not likely to be forthcoming if the multiple and dual aspect of the values system is not perceived by the practitioner.

A second problem of assessment lies in the different strengths of the paired values. It seems that one set of values in which we all believe is more dominant, the other more subdominant. For the values suggested here, those which fuel the social welfare enterprise in general, and community practice in particular, seem to be more on the subdominant side. If this is so, it means that progress toward achieving social work values is likely to threaten the society in general, the community in which the practitioner is working, and the practitioner. It is important to note that community practitioners, committed especially to the improvement of the condition of those who are less well represented in the system, such as minorities, the young, the old, women in broken families, are no less interested in the dominant values than others. Community practitioners must assess their own values, as well as those within the communities they serve.

If values are multiple, or in conflict, and if some values seem to be more dominant than others, how is the practitioner to resolve the inevitable differences of view within the community and within herself or himself? There are a number of techniques that can be used for this purpose, including averaging, sequencing, sectoring, and adjudicating. This suggested list mentions only some of the techniques—there are many variations that can prove very helpful, not only in assessment, but also in crafting a solution.

BIBLIOGRAPHY

Allison, David, *The R & D Game* (Cambridge, Mass.: MIT Press, 1969).

Baier, Kurt, and Nicholas Rescher, *Values and the Future* (New York: Praeger, 1982).

Banfield, E., and J. Q. Wilson, *City Politics* (Cambridge, Mass.: Harvard University Press, 1965).

Barbour, Ian et al., *Energy and American Values* (New York: Praeger, 1982).

Bell, Daniel, *The End of Ideology: On the Exhaustion of Political Ideas in the Fifties* (Glencoe, Ill.: Free Press, 1960).

Bengston, Vern L., and Mary C. Lovejoy, "Values, Personality and Social Structure: An Intergenerational Analysis," *American Behavioral Scientist* 16, no. 6 (1963): 893.

Braybrooke, David, and Charles E. Lind-blom, *A Strategy of Decision: Policy Evaluation as a Social Process* (New York: Free Press, 1963).

Degler, Carl N., *Affluence and Anxiety*, 2d ed. (Glenview, Ill.: Scott, Foresman, 1975).

Dunn, William, ed., *Values, Ethics and the Practice of Policy Analysis* (Lexington, Mass.: D. C. Heath, 1983).

Ekric, Arthur A., Jr., *Ideology and Utopias* (Chicago: Quadrangle Books, 1969).

Elder, Glenn, Jr., *Children of the Great Depression* (Chicago: University of Chicago Press, 1974).

March, James, "Theories of Choice and Making Decisions," *Transaction/Society,* Vol. 20 (November/December 1982): p. 29-39.

Marmor, Theodore, ed., *Poverty Policy* (Chicago: Aldine-Atherton, 1971).

Piven, Frances Fox, and Richard A. Cloward, *Regulating the Poor* (New York: Vintage Books, 1971).

Rokeach, Milton, ed., *Understanding Human Values: Individual and Societal* (New York: Free Press, 1979).

Tropman, John E., "The Constant Crisis: Social Welfare and the American Cultural Structure," *California Sociologist,* Vol. 1 (Winter 1978): pp. 61-87.

———, Milan Dluhy, and Roger Lind, eds., *New Strategic Perspectives on Social Policy* (Elmsford, N.Y.: Pergamon Press, 1981).

Tropman, John E., and Jane McClure, "Policy Analysis and Older People: A Conceptual Framework," *Journal of Sociology and Social Welfare,* Vol. 5 (November 1978): pp. 822-832.

Williams, Robin, *American Society,* rev. ed. (New York: Alfred Knopf, 1961).

7. AN ASSESSMENT FRAMEWORK FOR ORGANIZING IN EMERGING MINORITY COMMUNITIES

Felix G. Rivera and John L. Erlich

NEO-GEMEINSCHAFT MINORITY COMMUNITIES: IMPLICATIONS FOR COMMUNITY ORGANIZATION

Social work is running scared. As the era of "slash, cut and trim" descends

Reproduced by permission of the publisher and the authors. From "Neo-Gemeinschaft Minority Communities: Implications for Community Organization in the United States," in part, by Felix G. Rivera and John L. Erlich, *Community Development Journal,* Vol. 16, No. 3 (1981), pp. 189-200.

upon us, the fundamental weakness of the profession becomes painfully apparent. Of course, social work has been in retreat for some time. Since the early 1970s, programs directed to the needs of the minority oppressed poor have been phased out or diminished. Program controls have largely passed from the federal government and local communities to states and municipalities. From a political standpoint, it is understandable that confrontation-stimulating community organization efforts have given way faster than most other services.

However, given the demographic changes and inflation of the last decade, the profession is in the position of having to respond to rapidly expanding needs with ever-declining resources. It is not a comfortable position.

One of the most pressing issues of the decade of the 1980s will be the changing nature of ethnic minority communities as it affects community organizing. The changing and emerging communities are a result of the increase in the black, Latino and Chicano, Asian, Pacific Islander—especially the Indochinese refugee flow—and the Native American population, and the continued oppression of these communities. Many of the gains of the last twenty years have been eroded by a society that is threatened by education and job-related affirmative action, tired of refugee programs, and alarmed by the encroachment of minorities into previously all-white communities. The prognostications of the Reagan administration do not augur well for these efforts either. More backlash is just over the horizon.

The retreat from social justice has helped to set more rigid cultural, social and economic boundaries around many minority communities. Coupled with the resurgence of such racist organizations as the Ku Klux Klan and continuing racial oppressions suffered by all ethnic minorities, a unique revitalization of cultural, social and economic survival strategies has emerged. In part, this is a special response to the needs of new arrivals. The organization and complexity of these new communities presents a serious challenge to community organization. To meet the challenge, the profession must not only be able to support community empowerment but also join the struggle for group self-determination.

This paper addresses these issues within the context of community politics and structure. We will explore a model of the new communities that we hope will sharpen the analysis of questions about leadership, economics, power, culture, and social networks and how community organization may become an integral part of the helping process in working with them.

THE NEW EMERGING COMMUNITIES

Ethnic minority communities are growing dramatically, and with this growth come attendant problems that are further exacerbated by different languages, cultures, and traditions. A cursory look at demographic data only begins to touch on the multidimensional nature of this situation.

Between 1970 and 1980, the nation's white majority decreased from 87.5% to 83.2%, while the minority population grew from 12.5% to 16.8%, or 38.2 million. All major minority groups showed a steeper rate of growth than whites, whose number increased by 6 percent from 177.7 million to 188.3 million, while the total population grew from 203.2 million to 226.5 million.[1] The chief of the Census Bureau's ethnic and racial division noted; "It's one of the most significant changes in the racial composition of the U.S. population in any 10-year period."[2] Any significant undercount would, of course, tend to extend these figures further in the same direction.

Latinos and Chicanos

Among those listing themselves as "Spanish origin," there was a 61 percent increase from 1970 to 1980, from 9.1

million to 14.6 million.[3] A breakdown by subgroup was not available at the time this paper was prepared; however, there are such data for the 1978 population estimate of 12 million.[4] These figures break down into 7.2 million people of Mexican descent, 700,000 Cubans, 1.8 million Puerto Ricans, and approximately 2.4 million people from Central and South America. The Census Bureau estimates a growth rate of 14.4 percent from the 1970 census to 1978. Projections suggest that there will be close to 20 million Latinos and Chicanos by the year 2000 if undocumented aliens are taken into consideration.[5] With this increase in population has come a steady decline in Hispanics' relative economic position. Median income for Latino and Chicano families is $11,400 compared to $16,300 for the non-Latino. Puerto Ricans are the lowest on the ladder among their ethnic group with a median income of $8,000. Chicano and Latino unemployment rates hover at approximately 29 percent compared to the national average of 6 percent. Only 40 percent have completed high school compared to 46 percent for blacks and 67 percent for whites. High school dropout rates are estimated at about 85 percent for urban Latinos and Chicanos.[6] It must be pointed out that these statistics do not include the over 100,000 recently arrived refugees from Cuba nor those from El Salvador, Nicaragua, or Guatemala.

Blacks

Blacks represented 11.1 percent of the population in 1970 and 11.7 percent in 1980. Their numbers increased 17 percent from 22.6 million to 26.5 million.[7] The black community continues to be a horrendous showcase of racism. Unemployment rates hover at about 11 to 13 percent as a conservative estimate, while black youth unemployment rates stood at 40 percent as of 1977, compared to 16 percent for white youth.[8] Among blacks 46 percent, compared to 67 percent of whites, completed high school in urban areas. And 31 percent of blacks compared to 9 percent of whites were living in poverty.[9]

Higher socioeconomic status has not been of much help to the black community. Recent research continues to verify the trends of segregation. Blacks moving into white communities in any substantial numbers have precipitated the white withdrawal from that area with continued racial segregation being the result.[10] Furthermore, blacks living in suburbs continue to find themselves living in limited areas.[11]

Asians and Pacific Islanders

The largest proportional increase occurred among Asians and Pacific Islanders—from 1.5 million to 3.5 million, or 126 percent.[12] Until recently, this has been one of the most undercounted and ignored communities in the United States. The overly simplistic lumping of all Asians into one category in the census robs the community of its variety of languages, customs, and traditions that are as varied as a black Cuban's culture compared to a white Argentinian's. The community is composed of such diverse people as Pakistanis, Koreans, East Indians, Cambodians, Chinese, Filipinos, Guamanians, Japanese, Thais, Samoans, Yaps, Laotians, Vietnamese, and Hawaiians—and the list is far from complete.

The political and economic ramifications of the census miasma have been all too real for Asians and Pacific Islanders.[13] Some reasons given for a potentially serious undercount are language barriers, crowded housing conditions, fear of deportation, and non-Western cultural backgrounds of immigrants that worked to limit census takers' access to certain neighborhoods and discouraged community people from cooperating with the census takers.[14]

Native Americans

Those listing themselves as "American Indian, Eskimo, or Aleut" increased 71 percent from 800,000 to 1.4 million.[15] It marked the first time in census history that this group numbered over 1 million. A strong resurgence of involvement in tribal activities and family customs among younger Indians is partially responsible for increased numbers and visibility.

While these demographic changes have proved disruptive to many communities ill-prepared to welcome larger numbers of Third World people, they have also contributed to a very important strengthening of ethnic community ties. For example, Filipinos, Vietnamese, Cubans, and Haitians are bringing not only their racial characteristics to the emerging communities but a revitalization of their culture to the many little Manilas, Saigons, and Havanas. This cultural infusion is helping to make many of these cultural enclaves more self-conscious and active when compared to the assimilationist orientation of most earlier refugee groups. Both their cultural uniqueness and identity as victims of a majority society forces minorities to react in ways that are often similar as they cope and survive.

The political economy of minority communities is such that these communities continue to act as the mainstays of a dual labor market. And the difficulty these groups encounter in moving out of the peripheral or secondary sector makes for a continued (if forced) support of these communities that will not soon change.[16] Another shared experience has been the persistent theorizing about patterns of assimilation becoming almost an ideology of the more and sooner the better. Research has shown this to be a flawed perspective, thus further questioning the push toward white-determined integration of ethnic minorities into the dominant society. In fact, Cubans and Mexicans researched showed an increase in consciousness about their minority positions and the conflict associated with such roles.[17]

Another study has demonstrated that young, upwardly mobile blacks have not helped in closing the racial gap because of their consciousness and, "If anything, the progressive advance up the socioeconomic ladder by both races may result in greater disparities on certain participation-related attitudes."[18]

We need to define what we mean by an ethnic minority people within the context of the demographics presented and the new communities which we define next. The unique circumstances in which minority persons find themselves lead us to define them in several ways: (a) individuals of color different from the dominant society's, (b) individuals who belong to a community in crisis with inordinately high unmet service needs, (c) individuals who are monolingual in a language other than English, (d) individuals from Third World countries coming to the United States as refugees or emigrés, and (e) individuals who are poor.

By defining them in this way, we have set conditions that must be present for an individual or group to be so identified.

Thus Native Americans or blacks, even though they are citizens of the United States, are ethnic minorities because they may have high unmet human service needs and because they belong to different cultures, different races, and are poor. A black Cuban or Puerto Rican is also included in these categories because of the language barrier—if present—and because of race and unmet service needs. An elite colonel from Cambodia or Vietnam, even while politically distant from the poor people of his country, would still come within our definition because he too has unmet service needs, is monolingual, and is racially different. The colonel's problems may be exacerbated upon entering his own ethnic community, for he may be perceived as still being the enemy. The fact is that refugees and minority citizens of the United States continue to find themselves in hostile, poor environments and that their color and culture will be used as shibboleths of exclusion rather than inclusion in the mainstream of society.

ETHNIC MINORITY COMMUNITIES REDEFINED

In describing the current status of minority communities, the distinction made by Toennies between *gemeinschaft* and *gesellschaft* is useful. The gemeinschaft ("community") is a social system in which relationships are personal, informal, traditional, general, and sentiment-based. On the other hand, the gesellschaft ("society") is a system in which relationships are impersonal, contractual, utilitarian, specialized, and realistically based on market conditions. As Toennies noted, "In Gemeinschaft with one's family one lives from birth on, bound to it in a weal and woe.... There

exists a Gemeinschaft of language, of folkways, of mores, or of beliefs."[19]

The development of minority communities with their reinvigorated support systems strongly suggests that we define them as *neo-gemeinschaft*. Our model assumes that these communities' life experiences take place within a causal, deterministic reality, based on racism and economic exploitation. We are further postulating that these systems are essentially closed once individuals enter or leave them. By closed we mean that there are definite entry and exit points in the community with definite parameters based on the respective individual cultures, sociopolitical, and economic situations.

By identifying ethnic minority communities as being *neo-gemeinschaft,* we are arguing that the primary cultural, social, political, and economic interrelationships of such communities are of fundamental importance, because these qualities are seen as major determinants of daily life in them. We also conceive of them as "new" communities because we are identifying specific groups coming together in a new country or geographical area and attempting to salvage their traditions in the face of a largely hostile existing social order. The model is based not only on empirical evidence but also on conversations with members of the various groups as well as personal experiences of the authors. *Neo-gemeinschaft* communities are an excellent example of communities becoming and evolving within an antagonistic environment. The more survival skills that are mastered by these communities, the more unique they become, thereby requiring a new and enlarged definition for their experiences.

By redefining the ethnic minority

communities we get a better analytical tool for understanding how these communities are evolving. Traditional definitions of communities are like quicksilver. A summary of these definitions is presented by Effrat, who has condensed much of the literature and has arrived at three definitions: communities are categorized as institutionally distinct groups, as a solidarity of institutions, and as the arena for "primary" inter-action.[20]

Cox has described communities as context, demographic characteristics, shared institutions, social system, vehicle, problems, and power relationships.[21] While the above definitions have aspects of *neo-gemeinschaft* communities, they lack the variable of race and culture within a changing context as experienced by these communities with the constant influx of new arrivals, and our additional prerequisites for being defined as a minority person. Take, for example, the recent immigration of more than 100,000 Cubans into the Miami area (of whom perhaps 70,000 remain). These refugees bring with them a need for redefinition of the culture beyond the established Cuban culture. Rather than putting trust in a single individual, many of these refugee groups have organized along horizontal lines with no one individual recognized as the leader. Some of these communities have organized as economic collectives. Because they lack money, they employ bartering as the primary form of service sharing, putting into practice many of the craft skills learned in the home country. Indeed, many more economically secure Cubans who have been in Miami for years have partially altered their business practices to provide for barter as an alternative mode of exchange. This practice is prevalent in many minority communities.

The church has played a significant role in helping to bring groups and individuals within the community together. Churches have been required to adapt to the life-styles of newcomers. One day they may support a fund raiser, the next they will be baptizing an infant or getting involved in organizing a housing drive. English classes and basic survival techniques (sometimes billed as "community orientations") have been offered in many churches. More established residents have been mobilized to help provide emergency food and clothing. A more personalized church has thus been thrust upon the clergy and existing practitioners.

The physical appearance of the community is also shifting. It abounds with "mom and pop" stores, stores that often serve as centers for information exchange and informal discussions. The Latino *bodega* is one example. Billboard advertising, posters, newspapers, and magazines are in the community's native language. One telltale sign is that of cooking smells, an excellent barometer. This element of phenomenological assessment is often heralded as one of the most rewarding for obvious reasons. In coping with pressures of a dominant society, these communities are forced to turn inward for almost all needed support. One of these variables of mutual support is the social network. It is defined as:

a specific set of linkages among a defined set of persons [groups and institutions] with the ... property that the characteristics of these linkages as a whole may be used to interpret the social behavior of the persons involved.[22]

The main components of social networks with which we are concerned include support, access to new and diverse information and social contacts, communication of expectations, evaluation and a shared world view, and an orientation to getting things done to improve one's lot in this country.

As Stack describes the networking process:

The most typical way people involve each other in their daily domestic lives is by entering them into an exchange relationship. Through exchange transactions, an individual personally mobilizes others as participants in his social network.[23]

The reasons for the resurgent development of these social networks are varied. One is that the transition to new communities by ethnic minorities, some of whom may have been accustomed to leadership roles in the past, throws them into a state of powerlessness when they encounter racial and ethnic segregation. This lack of social integration and acculturation (not assimilation) into the dominant society often accounts for survival-threatening poverty, delinquency, and mental health problems.[24]

Social networks function as horizontally supportive webs throughout the community, for there are few governing elites among recently arrived individuals from the home countries or other areas. Because the communities either share the stigma of forced removal from their native countries or have left their homes because they had few options for improving their quality of life due to war, political, economic, and social turmoil, the people that arrive here may find themselves lost and anomic. And although they may be citizens, they are treated as second- or third-class citizens, still experiencing the racism and econ-

omic exploitation of their ancestors. This frustrating situation stimulates mutual support networks that have little respect for old-country leadership hierarchies. Table 7.1 illustrates some of the variables unique to *neo-gemeinschaft* communities and their implications for community organization practice when compared to gesellschaft communities. The Table is not meant to be exhaustive but illustrative, and serves to introduce students of community organization and community development to some of the more significant variables and their possible application to community organization strategies.

IMPLICATIONS FOR COMMUNITY ORGANIZATION PRACTICE

The phenomenon of new communities emerging from existing old ones is something community organizers have either not had to deal with or have little understood. One of the reasons is that organizers have assumed that the tenement buildings or housing projects or deteriorated neighborhoods have had some permanence, with the elements of community supports more or less in place. But this is not the case in the emerging communities, for although the buildings may be the same, the activities within present a unique challenge to organizers and other practitioners. For one thing, the literature has shown that evolving minority communities require intervention strategies that go beyond many of the traditional models of community organizing.[25] As Table 7.1 very clearly suggests, the kind of organizing we are talking about cannot be done by anyone simply with the "proper motivation." A deep and sensitive cultural awareness is required. Bilin-

TABLE 7.1
**Structural Variables in Gesellschaft and Neo-Gemeinschaft Communities
and their Implications for Community Organizing Strategies**

Variables	Gesellschaft Communities	Neo-Gemeinschaft Communities	Implications for Community Organizing Strategies
Culture (ethnicity)	The dominant society with culture and traditions not having a strong ethnic identification. English — main if only language spoken and no strong ties or identification with another country. Basically Anglo population.	Relatively homogeneous. English not spoken much, or a street variant of it. Strong traditions from the homeland making for isolated, autonomous pockets of Little Tokyos, Havanas, etc.	Knowledge of culture not enough, should be part of the culture and bilingual. Sensitive to cultural patterns and traditions. An appreciative posture a necessity.
Social Structure	Vertical. Limited extended family networks with no experience of oppression or racism.	Horizontal. Shared experience of racism and oppression. Many extended family networks.	Ethnic and cultural membership helps in understanding the complexities of the social structure, helps to provide access to family networks.
Power Structure	Mainly externally elite and vertical in nature. Community gives up its power in favor of "institutional trust."	Mainly internally pluralistic, decision making usually by consensus. No trust of outside power blocks and their institutions.	Knowledge of power analysis, the formation of coalitions, "winnable" issues and knowledge of power blocks inside and outside of the community.
Leadership Patterns	Leadership by political culture and party system. Extended influence and authority. Charisma and personalism less important.	Charismatic leaders, *personalismo*, strong feelings of alienation and anomie. Sphere of influence limited to that community.	Knowledge of and respect of the leadership patterns of the culture. An understanding of horizontal and consensual decision making, and leadership by age and wisdom.
Economics	All levels of economic ladder, but a strong middle class and much vertical mobility. Limited, if any, labor market segmentation.	Marginal to poor level of existence. Strong interdependence. Bartering for survival. Welfare a constant reality and reminder of their situation. Major contributors to labor market segmentation.	A thorough understanding of political economy and the need for a progressive analysis of same. The ability to identify short- and long-term issues to lessen failures. Knowledge of employment, housing, and community development strategies.
Physical Appearance	No unique "flavor" to the communities. A variety of housing patterns.	Strong ethnic flavor in signs, newspapers, magazines. Smells of different foods unique to the homeland. Rundown tenements and substandard housing.	Ability to understand the language and being part of the culture a necessity.
Social Networks	Less formal when present. Usually a "conscious" decision is made in developing them.	Strong and quite formal. Usually an integral part of the culture.	Ability to understand the language, relate to the culture, and respect network changes.

guality is clearly preferred, although supportive roles for English-speaking monolinguals may well emerge. For certain black and Native American communities bicultural experience and deep respect may take the place of specific linguistic skills. A full appreciation of a group's culture will most often require thorough knowledge of its historical experience—including traditions, political upheavals, and folkways.

The so-called mobilization style of organizing (set up shop in relation to a particular issue, mobilize around it, win what you can, and get out) will not work. Developing the trust necessary to understand, appreciate, and gain access to social networks is going to take a lot of time and patience, much of it beyond the normal workday. Some activities border on the quasi-legal and involve economic exchanges that keep money in the community rather than flowing to outsiders. One organizing key will be to figure out ways of building up existing social networks rather than generating new structures that will undermine these networks—as some of our community action agencies did during the War on Poverty. Rather than beginning with the problems, weaknesses, and inadequacies of these communities, our analysis suggests that strengths are to be noted first and foremost, and looked upon as the basis for organization building. What survival skills work best in that community? How is this shown? The thrust of organizing should be toward empowerment, which according to Solomon:

> ... enables the client to perceive his or her intrinsic and extrinsic worth. It motivates the client to use every personal resource and skill, as well as those of any other person that can be commanded, in the effort to achieve self-determined goals.[26]

The exercise of self-determination is central to the framework we have proposed. Furthermore, organizers should keep the concept of community sociotherapy in mind. Rein defines it as:

> ... the belief system which holds that such processes as organizing groups for self-help, protest, access to community facilities, or even revolution, can create a transformation of the individual personality. Participation in social action is viewed as a sociotherapeutic tool.[27]

This process of empowerment helps in not only giving people a sense of purpose, but a shared experience which will help in the development and nurturance of leadership, the identification of issues that are solvable and hopefully help to reduce the community's general feeling of malaise that may be hampering its development of self-determination and further animation.

CONCLUSION

In responding to the needs of new and emerging minority communities, we have a choice. We may offer what modest services we can to these communities while focusing primarily on the trendy, fundable programs as we have in the recent past. Or we can take hold and establish a real priority for developing extensive community organization programs in the new communities. This will not be either easy or simple. The environment of self-determining communities is hazardous at best. However, if we are to believe in our own rhetoric, do we have any choice but to find ways to support *neo-gemeinschaft* minority communities in defining themselves, their surroundings, and their futures?

NOTES AND REFERENCES

1. Bryce Nelson, "Percentage of Non-Whites in U.S. Rises Sharply," *Sacramento Bee,* February 24, 1981, p. A4.
2. Ibid.
3. Ibid.
4. *Current Population Reports: Population Characteristics, Persons of Spanish Origin in the United States: March, 1978.* (Washington, D.C.: U.S. Department of Commerce, Bureau of the Census, June 1979.)
5. Ibid.
6. Ibid.
7. Nelson, "Percentage of Non-Whites," p. A4.
8. *Task Panel Reports Submitted to the President's Commission on Mental Health, 1978, Volume III, Appendix,* (Washington, D.C.: U.S. Government Printing Office, 1978), pp. 824–825.
9. Ibid.
10. Arnold M. Denowitz, "Racial Succession in New York City, 1960–1970," *Social Forces* 59, no. 2 (December 1980): 453.
11. Wayne J. Villemez, "Race, Class and Neighborhood: Differences in the Residential Return on Individual Resources," *Social Forces* 59, no. 2 (December 1980): 428.
12. Nelson, "Percentage of Non-Whites."
13. For a detailed discussion on this issue see the papers in the "Census Issues" section of *Civil Rights Issues of Asian and Pacific Americans: Myths and Realities* (Washington, D.C.: U.S. Commission on Civil Rights, U.S. Government Printing Office, 1980), pp. 46–49.
14. Ibid., p. 82.
15. Nelson, "Percentage of Non-Whites."
16. See, for example, R. C. Edwards, "The Social Relations of Production in the Firm and Labor Market Structure," in R. C. Edwards, M. Reich, and D. M. Gordon, eds., *Labor Market Segmentation* (Lexington, Mass.: D. C. Heath, 1975); and R. L. Bach, "Mexican Immigrants and the American State," *International Migration Review* 12 (Winter 1978): 536–558.
17. Alejandro Portes, Robert Nash Parker, and José A. Cobas, "Assimilation or Consciousness: Perceptions of U.S. Society Among Recent Latin American Immigrants to the United States," *Social Forces* 59, no. 1 (September 1980): 220–224.
18. Bruce A. Campbell, "The Interaction of Race and Socioeconomic Status in the Development of Political Attitudes," *Social Science Quarterly* 60, no. 4 (March 1980): 657.
19. Ferdinand Toennies, "Gemeinschaft and Gesellschaft," in Talcott Parsons et al., eds., *Theories of Society* (New York: Free Press, 1961) 1:191.
20. Marcia Pelly Effrat, "Approaches to Community: Conflicts and Complementaries," *Sociological Inquiry* 43, no. 3–4 (1973): 1–28.
21. Fred M. Cox, "Alternative Conceptions of Community," in Fred M. Cox, John L. Erlich, Jack Rothman, and John E. Tropman, eds., *Strategies of Community Organization,* 3d ed. (Itasca, Illinois: F. E. Peacock, Publishers, Inc., 1979), pp. 224–234.
22. J. Clyde Mitchell, ed., *Social Networks in Urban Situations* (Manchester, England: University of Manchester Press, 1969), pp. 1–50; and Roger E. Mitchell and Edison K. Trickett, "Task Force Report: Social Networks as Mediators for Social Support: Analysis of the Effects and Determinants of Social Networks," *Community Mental Health Journal,* 16, no. 1 (Spring 1980), 27–44.
23. Carol Stack, *All Our Kin: Strategies for Survival in a Black Community* (New York: Harper Colophon, 1974), p. 43. Also see Bettylou Valentine, *Hustling and Other Hard Work: Life Styles in the Ghetto* (New York: Free Press, 1978).
24. For further elaboration of this issue see Robert E. Kopsis, "Powerlessness in Racially Changing Neighborhoods," *Urban Affairs Quarterly* 14, no. 4 (June 1979): 425–442; C. S. Fischer, "On Urban Alienations and Anomie: Powerlessness and Social Isolation," *American Sociological Review,* 38, no. 3 (June 1973): 311–326, and Lee Rainwater, *Behind Ghetto Walls: Black Families in a Federal Slum* (Chicago: Aldine, 1970); and Roger E. Mitchell and Edison J. Trickett, "Task Force Report."
25. For example, see Shirley Jenkins, "The

Ethnic Agency Defined," *Social Service Review,* 54 (June 1980): 250.

26. As cited in Armando Morales, "Social Work with Third World People," *Social Work* 26, 1 (January 1980): 49.

27. Martin Rein, *Social Policy: Issues of Choice and Change* (New York: Random House, 1970), p. 292.

PART TWO

Mobilization and Implementation: Planning, Organizing, and Developing

Introduction

In moving from assessment to mobilization and implementation, how goes it with community practice in the ninth decade of the twentieth century? The commonly held view in the field seems to be massive reduction—politically and economically—down to a shadow of its former robustness. But perhaps this view neglects the broad sweep of recent history. Certain goals that we have been advocating over the years are coming to be accepted by the society as a whole. For example, the Japanese method of management,[1] which at its core is involvement and participation, is a long-standing approach in community practice. It is "practicing community" within an organizational context. Or consider "community creation." Dahrendorf refers to this process in discussing life chances,[2] which are made of options on the one hand, and ligatures on the other. Ligatures especially concern us here. They are the connections between people. A society without ligatures is a society without community. The effort to create ligatures, or networks in our fragmented society, can be seen in everything from single parent groups to "self-actualization" weekend marathons and personal development institutes. Yankelovitch points out that nationally the "new rules" involve greater attention to family and others, reducing the concentrated focus on the self.[3,4]

Options concern us as well. The creation of options is the creation of opportunity. It has long been understood that much social action is required to develop and enhance opportunity, and vigorous effort is required to maintain it. While the development of ligatures refers to the "bonding" aspects of community practice, the pursuit of options refers to the "change" aspect. Development and social action require planning.

Wide Application

There are many kinds of planning, organizing, and developing. There are social planning, land use planning, hospital and health planning, and planning within large organizations, to name but a few. There are several kinds of organizing, such as block club organizing, union organizing, organizing a tenants' association, and the like. Activities as diverse as job interview workshops and intercultural festivals might qualify as development activities. Is there a common element? Indeed, and that something is a set of common techniques. Many of these apply to planning, organizing, and developing in a range of settings and serve a variety of ideological purposes.

Ideas and People

There is animated disagreement in community practice about the extent to which practitioners can do both organizing and planning. Some practitioners feel there are requisites of personality that make them "organizers" or "planners." Perhaps. What is certainly true is that some people find one or the other change mode more comfortable. But what is more important is that the mobilization of both ideas and people is typically required for the accomplishment of social tasks.

There are real differences between planning, organizing, and developing, however, which do require tactical variations. In one important respect, planning emphasizes the mobilization of ideas and information. Facts and figures are involved; making projections and analyzing trends through the use of numerical data are typical. The whole process of planning is driven, in great part, by information. Organizing and developing, on the other hand, involve the mobilization of people. The need for participation to influence the course of social and political life and to enhance the quality of social life requires the ability to bring people together in working groups of one kind or another. One might call planning "task"-oriented and organizing and development "process"-oriented.

The problem is that both are needed for the accomplishment of social purposes. Planners may be faulted for lack of attention to participation in the planning process. Dunbar and Morris point up the importance of citizen participation in rural social planning. Federal legislation frequently has required the involvement of citizens in advisory bodies. Yet all too often the professional planner has no training or experience in working with committees and boards.

The converse is also true. It is possible to place too much emphasis upon participation and not enough upon the factual basis and content of the decision. Involvement is characteristic of planning, organizing, and developing. It is required if plans are to have legitimacy. An overemphasis is partly a result of lack of attention to the need for balance in task and process elements in the accomplishment of social purpose.[5] Both are vital, and community practitioners who have skill in one area must master skills in the other.

Part of the problem in finding the right balance between task and process lies in the timing of interventions. One cannot do everything at the same time. For this reason, special attention must be paid to alternating emphasis on task achievements and process accomplishments. Problems of sequence and balance are likely to differ depending upon a careful reading of the larger "climate" in the community.

The Use of Committees

One place where the mobilization of ideas and people come together is a committee or board. Most planning, developing, and organizing efforts involve committee structures and meetings. The Rothman and Reed piece on organizing community action points to the committee structure required for such activities. Welsh's "Operation Independence" shows ways to pull together the network of agencies and services which can help older people in their own homes. An embryonic coordinating committee structure evolves, emerging within the interorganizational system.[6] "The Role of the Board in the Planning Process" by Tropman stresses the importance of a good board and provides some suggestions about how to compose one and what it should do. That thrust ties in nicely with the simplified parliamentary procedure provided by the League of Women Voters. All too often people in community practice have no knowledge of these basic rules of decision making. While these are appropriate at the board level, they may also be useful in grass-roots groups. In "For a Democratic Revolution," Haggstrom suggests a conceptual and practical base around which poor people may be organized against the forces which oppress them.

So much of the planning and organizing process is involved with meetings—meetings to develop ideas, meetings to develop support, meetings to bring ideas and people together—that the success of the meeting itself is often predictive of the success of the tactic. Jay's "How to Run a Meeting" stresses necessary skills and tactics.

The Politics of Approval

Committee activity is one essential. So often technical planning fails because legislative or other political approval is not secured. The piece by Dear and Patti is helpful here. Their purpose "is to suggest tactics that can readily be used by the part-time, single-issue advocates who make an occasional foray into the legislative arena to promote a bill of immediate interest to their agency or client constituency." City councils, hospital planning authorities, sewage districts, and regulatory bodies of all types are among those whose permission and authority are, at times, needed to accomplish community practice ends.

How do things get to the point of approval? That is one of the most important tasks of mobilization. One article speaks especially to the matter of issue generation and crystallization—the League of Women Voters' "Making an Issue of It." The League focuses upon lobbying and influencing the legislative process thereby. Sherry and Lipschultz provide a list of eleven specific techniques, such as focusing upon a specific event and stressing the commonality of concerns, which can serve to mobilize groups for action in a health context. But that in no way limits the general utility of these action tools.

Sometimes there exists a "latent" or "natural" structure in the community which can be activated by community practitioners and related to a more systematic vehicle. Maguire lays out some of the important details for community practitioners to consider, especially touching upon the sensitive nature of the practitioner-client relationship.

Mobilization involves generating appropriate resources for making decisions and carrying through with them within a community context. Mobilization may be necessary at many points in the planning process—assessment, goal selection, decisions on strategy and tactics, and so on. All too often the tactic of "calling out the troops" is limited to the meeting in which some decision will be made. While this is often necessary, it mistakenly locates the decision process at a single point rather than a series of points in an action process. The focus upon a single point in the decision process means that attention to the content of the decision is often ignored. Similarly, lack of attention to the later points in the process of decision means that the desired goal may not be achieved.

Implementation

"What happens after a bill becomes law?" Bardach asks.[7] Frequently, community practitioners fail to follow through on the details of funding, administrative revisions, and implementation. Good intentions alone may pave the way for programmatic failure.[8] The areas we discussed—committee process, planning, mobilization—become useful when practitioners realize that painstaking attention to detail finally makes a plan or program a success.[9]

The checklist developed by Gordon Chase covers a number of problems which can be anticipated and dealt with by community practitioners in a coherent manner.[10]

Conclusion

Despite broad acceptance of certain aspects of community practice, current practitioners are challenged to have a full repertoire of tactics and skills at their command. Funding declines have made this situation at once more immediate and more important. As we have suggested, most community practice is not limited to planning or organizing or developing. Rather there are key components common to all three, as well as those that

Implementation Assessment Outline

A. Difficulties Arising from Operational Demands
  1. People to be Served
     (a) Number of client transactions
     (b) Ease of reaching client
  2. Nature of Services
     (a) Number of discrete functions
     (b) Complexity of discrete functions
     (c) Coordination among functions
     (d) Replication
  3. Likelihood and Costliness of Distortions or Irregularities
     (a) Involving clients
     (b) Involving services
  4. Controllability of Program
     (a) Measurability
     (b) Uncontrollable critical elements

B. Difficulties Arising from Nature and Availability of Resources
  1. Money
     (a) Flexibility
     (b) Obtaining additional funding
  2. Personnel
     (a) Nature of personnel in place
     (b) Numbers, kinds, and quality needed
     (c) Availability of personnel in market
     (d) Attractiveness of program to personnel
  3. Space
     (a) Nature of the current facilities
     (b) Availability of facilities
     (c) Special problems in acquiring or using space
  4. Supplies and Technical Equipment
     (a) Availability and usability
     (b) Importance of technology

C. Difficulties Arising from Need to Share Authority
  1. Overhead Agencies
     (a) Number of transactions
     (b) Likelihood of favorable response
  2. Other Line Agencies
     (a) Extent of involvement
     (b) Critical nature of involvement
     (c) Likelihood of harmonious working conditions
     (d) Ability to pinpoint responsibility
  3. Elected politicians
     (a) Capacity to help or hurt
     (b) Inclination to help or hurt
  4. Higher Levels of Government
     (a) Extent of authority
     (b) Number of transactions
     (c) Nature of politics
     (d) Likelihood of favorable response
  5. Private Sector Providers
     (a) Need
     (b) Availability
     (c) Control
     (d) Political problems
  6. Special Interest Groups
     (a) Kinds and inclinations
     (b) Strength
     (c) Likelihood of helping or hurting
  7. The Press
     (a) Level of visibility
     (b) Power of the press
     (c) View of administration
     (d) Controversial dimensions

SOURCE: Reproduced by permission of the publisher John Wiley & Sons, Inc., New York, N.Y. From Gordon Chase, "Implementing A Human Services Program," *Public Policy* 27, 4(Fall, 1979), pp. 442-43.

are unique to each. Few practitioners have the luxury of confining themselves to a single practice modality. Keeping balance between the details of the practice process and demands of the more general political and social climate is required.

John E. Tropman

Notes

1. William Ouchi, *Theory Z* (New York: Avon, 1981) is but one example of the kinds of attention Japanese management has been getting. For a more critical

position, see Richard Pascale and Anthony Athos, *The Art of Japanese Management* (New York: Simon and Schuster, 1981).

2. Ralf Dahrendorf, *Life Chances* (Chicago: University of Chicago Press, 1979).

3. Daniel Yankelovitch, *New Rules* (New York: Random House, 1981).

4. In the introduction to the first edition of *Tactics and Techniques,* we pointed to some of the spheres where these developments were occurring.

5. For a general discussion of task and process functions, see Jack Rothman, "An Analysis of Goals and Roles in Community Organization Practice," *Social Work,* 9, no. 2 (1964): pp. 24-31.

6. For more information on committees and meetings see John E. Tropman, Elmer J. Tropman, and Harold R. Johnson, *The Essentials of Committee Management* (Chicago: Nelson-Hall, 1979), and John E. Tropman, *Effective Meetings* (Beverly Hills; Calif.: Sage Publications, 1980).

7. Eugene Bardach, *The Implementation Game* (Cambridge, Mass.: MIT Press, 1977).

8. See D. Bunker, "Policy Science Perspectives on Implementation Processes," in John E. Tropman et al., eds., *Strategic Perspectives on Social Policy* (Elmsford, N.Y.: Pergamon Press, 1976).

9. Ibid. Part II of this volume, called "Skill Phases in the Policy Process," deals with steps in the implementation process.

10. See also R. Elmore, "Organizational Models of Social Program Implementation," *Public Policy* 26, no. 2 (Spring 1978): pp. 185-228.

A. PLANNING

8. ORGANIZING COMMUNITY ACTION TO ADDRESS ALCOHOL AND DRUG PROBLEMS

Jack Rothman and Beth Glover Reed

Licit and illicit drug and alcohol use is a widespread phenomenon in most communities in this culture. Many people use chemicals moderately with few personal or social costs. Others become dependent on or compulsive users of particular drugs, or suffer negative consequences from their use (for example, alcohol-related driving offenses). Attitudes and values about different patterns and types of drug use vary widely as do opinions about what types of policies and programs are appropriate and effective. There is rarely much agreement about what chemicals should be of concern or what the community views as unacceptable drug-related behaviors.

Mobilizing a community to assess its needs and create an effective action plan to address its drug- and alcohol-related problems can be a challenging and rewarding task. It is also a complex and uncertain endeavor. Creation of a broad-based action council is one way of stimulating, organizing, and implementing such an action plan.

In this paper, we will describe some of the issues that must be considered in developing a community action plan. We will present varying directions that programs can take, and the stages involved in organizing for community action. Finally, we will make some recommendations about administrative and structural concerns.

IMPORTANT PRINCIPLES

Every Community Is Different

A community action plan must be based on a thorough understanding of the particular community for which it is designed, including a knowledge of the important characteristics of the community, the patterns and consequences of alcohol and drug use within it, the attitudes, knowledge, and values about the use of psychoactive chemicals, and the resources for prevention and treatment that already exist.

For example, communities differ in the types and sources of available drugs. In some communities, the availability of drugs other than alcohol is low; in others, a wide range of drugs, including heroin, is readily obtained. Various combinations of "street drugs" that may or may

Reproduced by permission of the authors. From an unpublished article.

not contain the drug they are purported to be can appear periodically. In still other communities, a few physicians may be freely prescribing large amounts of psychoactive drugs for weight control and minor anxieties. Each of these availability patterns would require different approaches in order to reduce problematic use since: (1) different types of people are likely to be regular users in each of these communities and for different reasons; (2) the different sources of drugs are likely to require quite different strategies to "contain"; and (3) the effects and consequences (for example, physical, legal) of use will also vary.

Thus, who is using what, how, and with whom, the reasons they are using, and where they obtain the chemicals all must be considered in developing a community action plan. Middle-class teenagers who use drugs to get high present very different issues for community organizers from adult heroin and polydrug users in the inner city, who use drugs to provide some excitement and meaning in their harsh and discouraging environment. Middle-aged drinkers who have gradually organized their lives around alcohol consumption and who are experiencing frequent blackouts represent a different set of concerns from thirteen- and fourteen-year-olds who drink on their way to school or a career woman who drinks to help her cope with conflicts among her multiple roles.

Communities also vary in the degree to which they regulate or support different types of drug use. The degree of involvement by organized crime and the presence of other types of distribution networks will vary from community to community. The presence and strength of drug subcultures and attitudes about

intoxication and drug dependence will also vary from neighborhood to neighborhood. These depend, at least partly, on the numbers and types of individuals involved, the length of time particular drugs have been present in the community, the functions drug use has served, not just for the individual but also for the community (for example, ceremonial), and other subcultural norms and values.

For all of these reasons, any guidelines to community action must not be perceived as a master plan to be adopted routinely. Rather, in each community, a group must be created that includes or can develop relevant expertise and that is representative of a cross section of key community components and viewpoints. The effectiveness and acceptance of any plans and programs developed will be largely a result of how well this group can educate itself and the community about the antecedents and consequences of alcohol and drug use, and can assess the community's attitudes, needs, and resources.

The Importance of an Open Mind

In developing a community action plan, members of the organizing group must recognize that they are entering a highly complex and uncertain area of endeavor. Even many well-informed experts disagree about the causes of problematic drug and alcohol use and what should be done to prevent, minimize, or treat these problems. They may even differ on what they define as a problem. Opinions in the general population are often strong and not well informed. Thus organizers must be prepared to study the problem objectively, to critique the available literature and range of existing options, and respond with frankness as new facts about chemical dependency and other drug and alcohol problems become available locally and nationally.

Even though it is difficult to suggest what a particular community action plan should incorporate, given the variations in communities described earlier, the uncertainty of our knowledge in many areas, and the diversity of opinion, much has been learned about what *not* to do. The following is adapted from a Kiwanis "Operation Drug Abuse" plan (early 1970s; see also Nowlis and Jackson, 1977, for a discussion of these issues).

Avoid specious reasoning, misinformation, and half truths. The whole field of drug education has been fraught with misinformation, superficial conclusions, emotionalism, and conjecture. A program cannot rest its case on obviously specious reasoning—for example, that marijuana must have chemical properties or produce pharmacological effects comparable to those of heroin, morphine, and opium because its use is regulated under the same state or federal statutes . . . or that if most heroin addicts admit to having used marijuana before they used heroin, it must follow from this reason alone that marijuana use leads to the use of heroin . . . or that if the percentage of drug addicts who have criminal records is higher than the percentage of nonaddicts with criminal records, this must be proof of a drug-crime relationship.

If a program is based on this level of reasoning, it will most certainly be recognized as superficial by even a young audience. Valid and factual information is increasingly abundant, and the well-informed participant will have no need to resort to the crutch of unsubstantiated dogmatism and authoritarianism. This is the reason for self-education.

Avoid "scare" tactics. If, from the information available, we select only the horrifying, the tragic, the bizarre examples of drug use and present these as the total and true picture of contact with the drugs of concern, we will lose the respect of those who know or will later find out that we have deliberately avoided the whole truth.

Don't focus only on drugs that "kids" use. It would further be dishonest to give the impression that today's drug problems are just another youth problem, symptomatic of a generation gap or youth rebellion. Our adult generation has produced an estimated 6.5 million alcoholics. The older generations have created a chemically oriented society in which United States physicians in 1968 alone issued 167 million prescriptions for amphetamines and barbiturates. Fortunately, these prescription rates have declined, but misuse of chemicals clearly cuts across age, ethnicity, and class differences. Even if a community action group wishes to target the youth of the community for special intervention efforts, the program developed must be clear that all age groups in society are involved.

VARYING PROGRAM DIRECTIONS

We have argued that because of community variability and scientific uncertainty that it would be presumptuous to prescribe a uniform solution for each community. Instead, we recommend that communities place their drug and alcohol problems on the community agenda and develop various mechanisms to allow citizens, representatives of relevant agencies, and professions to talk and work together to identify and address community priorities. The major steps that each community must take include:

1. Research and fact finding concerning cultural, social, and health dimensions of drug and alcohol use, both locally and in the nation.
2. Development of specific programs of intervention, early identification, and rehabilitation based on an assessment of local community needs and resources.

A range of program directions, emphases, and objectives should be considered in planning. In general, every community should eventually develop a multipronged approach, for a number of reasons:

1. *Problems with use or dependency on drugs and alcohol are usually multifaceted and multiply determined.* A recent National Institute on Drug Abuse (NIDA) publication (Lettieri et al., 1980) describes forty-three theories on causal factors for drug use and abuse (and several are not included in this compendium). It further separates them into how each addresses factors that influence movement through the progressive stages of drug use and dependency: initiation, continuation, transition, use to abuse, cessation, and relapse. A community action committee must become familiar with various theoretical perspectives and their relevance in their particular community. Careful and honest attention must be given to physiological, family, peer group, community, and societal forces that contribute, and usually interact, to create an individual who develops problems with use of chemicals. A single intervention strategy is not likely to address this complexity.

2. *Use of different chemicals by different types of people usually requires different intervention approaches.* As noted earlier, chemical dependency and other problems resulting from drug use crosses all age, gender, cultural, and class barriers. Prevention programs have usually tended to target youth, while treatment programs have largely been funded to combat drug-related social problems of concern to a community and the nation—most notably crime (resulting from the need to acquire money to buy illicit drugs) and highway safety problems (alcohol-related crashes). Many other social and health costs result from the use of chemicals, however. For instance, a large proportion of general hospital admissions are related to alcoholism or drug dependency; drug and alcohol use during pregnancy can affect the unborn; and family problems, work productivity, and accidents are often highly related to drug and alcohol consumption (National Institute on Alcohol Abuse and Alcoholism, 1982). A community action plan should consider the wide range of social costs incurred in many situations and groups, and identify their intervention targets accordingly.

In addition, various segments of a community will often require different approaches and services, not only because they use different chemicals for different reasons, but also because other aspects of their lives differ. For instance, adolescents must negotiate the difficult transitions into adult roles, separating from their families, adapting to rapidly changing bodies, emotions, peer groups, and societal expectations. The elderly face other transitions and may combine recreational use of chemicals with self-medication of emotional and health problems. They may also react to the complex interactions among various medications prescribed for particular physical conditions. Each of these groups encounters different societal caretakers and the form, location, and design of prevention and treatment programs for them would need to be quite different.

Men and women also differ from each other in their social roles, gender socialization, life circumstances, and coping styles, among other things. Intervention plans must take these differences into account or they will be primarily effective for only one gender or optimally effective for neither.

Different ethnic, racial, and socioeconomic groups are also likely to respond best to approaches that are sensitive to their cultural norms and nuances, located in accessible areas, and offering a comfortable atmosphere and compatible structure for that group. The materials that any planning group selects must be neither sexist nor racist, and should be multicultural and gender-sensitive, or they will perpetuate some of the problems they are trying to reduce.

3. *Planners should try to anticipate and reduce the system's inevitable resistance to change.* Every community is an ecological system with different interrelated components. Drug use is a complex behavior related to other behaviors and imbedded in a physiological organism living in a complex environment. Thus, interrelated factors to those being targeted must also change if the targeted changes are to occur and stabilize. One very simple drug-related example here is the interrelationship of supply and demand. Strategies that target the reduction of drug supplies without also trying to reduce the demand for them are much more likely to fail, and vice versa. At the individual level, educating about the risks of particular drug-related behaviors will not change these behaviors unless the individual can develop satisfying alternatives for those behaviors and reach a new physiological and behavioral homeostasis without the use of chemicals. Examination of the value system and social forces that support the drug use may also be necessary.

Similarly, at the community level, the current equilibrium in a neighborhood or community may resist needed changes. A planning committee should carefully analyze forces within the community likely to support the desired changes and those that may act as barriers to the changes. Increasing the forces for change may increase the resistance to change unless fears and reactions to proposed changes are anticipated and reduced. Many planning groups have been unpleasantly surprised to face intense neighborhood resistance that they did not anticipate after a successful campaign to create a new intervention program. Involvement of key people who will be affected by a change and who can influence others like themselves may take longer initially, but will be invaluable in later stages. In fact, a community may be able to move toward desired change most effectively simply by removing some of the barriers and resistances to the desired change.

4. *Every community also ought to have initiatives that address all stages and levels of use, if possible.* A community that worries only about those already dependent on chemicals will not be addressing the factors that promote drug dependency in the community. An overemphasis on prevention may not allocate the resources needed to help those already having difficulty with drugs.

5. *Similarly, every action plan should*

establish both short- and long-term priorities. Short-term goals can help maintain morale and build support, while long-term plans can serve as a framework for coordinated planning and more comprehensive objectives.

6. *A diverse, multifaceted plan allows many ways for people with different skills, orientations, and community connectedness to participate.*

As the reader can see, a balance and openness to experimentation will be necessary. Balance implies equilibrium — between preventive and rehabilitative approaches, between legalistic and educational ones, between short-range and long-range strategies. With all of this as context, we will now provide illustrations of a range of different types of initiatives and then discuss in more detail the stages and tasks a community action planning group can undertake.

Illustrative programs

1. A public discussion program to present some of the key issues in an objective way, in a calm atmosphere. One of the objectives could be to foster dialogues among groups with different points of view. In some communities, the emphasis might be on cross-generational dialogue; in others, dialogue may be more needed among different segments of the community, such as those emphasizing a law enforcement approach with those more educationally or human service oriented.

2. Alternatively, a public education campaign to convey to the populace the extent and types of problems related to use of drugs and alcohol along with what might be done about them.

3. Education and counseling programs with an emphasis on particular groups within the community, such as youth, or young mothers, or business people. These programs might combine information about the chemicals most used by that group, the risks associated with particular kinds of use, and the options available for changing problematic use patterns. Such a program also should address the factors most likely to support problematic use in the target groups.

4. Programs to make it more difficult to distribute and use drugs. These might encourage support for the police in surveillance and enforcement of existing laws, about selling and using illicit drugs, about public intoxication or selling liquor to minors. A group might decide to lobby for stiffer penalties for distributors or users, to try to revoke the license of a bar or liquor store that routinely sells to minors, or to work with the local medical association to take action about a physician prescribing numerous psychoactive medications that are inconsistent with recommended medical practice.

5. Alternatively, develop legal statutes that lessen severe penalties, so that the laws are consistent with medical and social evidence about the consequences of use of particular drugs. Work to move programs from the legal to the health and social arena.

6. Develop new treatment-rehabilitation services to address gaps identified in the service delivery network.

7. Create alternative activities within the community that are not linked to drug and alcohol consumption.

8. Help improve services that already exist through expansion, inclusion of

newer techniques, or better communication and cooperation among the agencies and their staff.

9. Create or strengthen local research programs investigating key aspects of drug and alcohol use and dependency.

As you can see, program alternatives are diverse and are not always compatible with one another. The mixture developed for any community should be based on the needs and resources in that community, and what the community will accept and can afford. A rational approach to planning requires an open mind, a willingness to study and incorporate new research evidence as it becomes available, involvement of a cross section of the community, and a balance and flexibility in program directions. This last is especially important if the planning group is to be able to adapt to new information and changing conditions and move in new directions if needed or useful.

STAGES IN ORGANIZING FOR COMMUNITY ACTION

Just as there are many approaches to drug and alcohol problems, there are various ways for communities to organize to do something about them. Following is an outline of an organizing format that has been successful in some communities and that presents a logical sequence of steps. It suggests the establishment of a community-wide broadly representative planning council. As before, we do not offer this as a blueprint. Communities should develop whatever variations best fit their local situations.

1. *A small informal initiation group.* Most community action programs start small and snowball, including more and more people and organizations as they develop. A useful first step is for a group of interested people (citizens, those recovering from chemical dependency, professionals, and others) to come together to test the extent of their own commitment and to ascertain generally whether a community program is needed. If there truly is a group that is willing to "start the ball rolling" and to provide work power and encouragement through the early organizing stages, then additional organizational effort is in order.

2. *Larger representative sponsoring group.* A larger planning group is necessary to survey the local scene and initiate the program formally. This group should represent wide community interests, including all who might be interested in addressing drug and alcohol problems within the community. Such a group can further test the feasibility of a unified community approach, share perspectives on the extent and nature of the problem in the community, and legitimate the whole venture.

In the earliest stage this group may want to engage in a period of self-education in order to be able to provide knowledgeable leadership (see Committee on Research and Evaluation under No. 4 for suggested activities).

Representatives from among the following kinds of groups might be invited to participate in this sponsoring group:

Parents

School representatives (elementary, junior high or middle, high)—administrators, faculty, students (Serious drug and alcohol use often begins by junior high, so it is important to have elementary representation.)

Courts (juvenile, family, traffic, felony)—judges, probation officers, other personnel

Rehabilitation agency staff—health care, social workers, psychologists, psychiatrists, counselors, administrators

Law enforcement representatives—sheriff, police (state and local)

Local drug or narcotics or alcohol control commission

Clergy (ministerial association) and church organizations

Kiwanis and other service clubs (Kiwanis has been active in drug problem prevention efforts.)

Youth organizations

Representatives of self-help groups (Alcoholics Anonymous, Narcotics Anonymous, Alanon, Alateen, Families Anonymous, Women for Sobriety, Parents Anonymous, Tough-Love, etc.)

Medical Association chapter

Professional association chapters (National Association of Social Workers, American Psychological Association, alcohol and drug counselors associations, etc.)

Pharmacists and pharmacologists

Mayor's office and city council members—local government representatives

Health Department

Civic groups such as League of Women Voters

Chamber of Commerce

Media representatives

United Community Services, United Way, and other such groups

Current and recovering chemically dependent persons

College students and professors

Early childhood education specialists

If other groups concerned about drug and alcohol problems exist within the community (this should be checked explicitly), contacts should be made in order to discuss mutual interests. Possibilities include a cooperative venture; the new group may choose to work through the structure of the existing organization to strengthen each other; the groups may divide tasks among them; or the older organizations may be replaced.

The planning group should also investigate how the state's drug and alcohol funding and licensing is coordinated. Most states have designated agencies to handle drug and alcohol policy development and coordination. Some states have one agency that handles both alcohol and other drugs, while other states still handle alcohol separately from other drugs. There are also likely to be regional or even county-level coordinating agencies in many states. These agencies can be important sources of information and support and at minimum should be informed of the group's plans as they evolve.

As a result of its deliberations, the initial sponsoring group should arrive at some *tentative* understanding of the nature of the problems locally and the programmatic measures likely to be useful. It should also be prepared to recommend a tentative organizational structure for proceeding with the work—that is, an executive or coordinating structure, necessary committees, means of funding the operation, and other matters.

An important part of this process would be to determine an appropriate name for the group. A group may or may not wish to include drugs, alcohol, substance abuse, chemical dependency, or other drug/alcohol-related terms in its title. Each of these labels will have different connotations, depending on the community. Including such words can make clear a group's purpose or stigmatize the group in some parts of the community. The group must weigh the pros and cons of different titles before assuming one.

After preliminary planning is completed, the group should prepare to present its tentative recommendations to an open community meeting. At this time the official action council would be established. It should select interim officers to preside at the meeting and prepare a list of possible committees (see listing later in this paper for examples). While preparing for the large public meeting, the sponsoring committee should work with news media in order to educate people locally about the issues and create interest for the open public meeting.

3. *Official launching at an open public meeting.** The opening public meeting or "community mobilization" signals the official launching of the local action council. Members of the community at large should be invited as well as the membership of all the organizations (plus any others relevant) listed in step 2.

The tentative recommendations about program and organizational arrangements should be presented for discussion and either approval or modification. Some open-ended time should be allowed for people to "sound off," discuss, or even debate the issues raised. A speaker or event of some educational, inspirational, or even entertainment

value might be included to enliven the program, although care must be exercised here not to sensationalize or polarize people about the issues. Tentative officers could be elected, and individuals should be asked to sign up for specific committees on which they would like to work. Dues or financial contributions could be solicited. Sign-up sheets should be passed around to obtain names of potential members and participants and to take an inventory of interest. Literature tables might be set up for purposes of community education. A wealth of materials is available from local, state, and federal sources (National Council on Alcoholism, National Institute on Drug Abuse, National Institute on Alcohol Abuse and Alcoholism, federal and state enforcement and coordinating agencies, and various private organizations— Hazelton Foundation, Kroc Foundation, Do-It-Now Foundation, and others).

4. *Program committee structure.* Form follows function, and committee structure should follow the specific goals and philosophy of a given organization. Again, there is no established committee organizational chart to suit all organizations and communities. They should be constructed to facilitate the purposes of the organization and the desired programs to meet these goals.

A listing of possible committees follows. These are presented suggestively, to be selected according to the action council's priorities and the requisites of the local situation. *Few communities will have the resources to undertake all these committee activities at once, especially in the early stages.* It would probably not be desirable to undertake all of them in any instance because the action council's efforts could become too diffuse. Most organizations tend to overstructure—to

---

*In some communities, it may be desirable to forego the large public meeting.

establish too elaborate and ambitious an organizational framework. *Modesty and simplicity would be the desirable orientation in the beginning.* Also, it is well for an organization to be somewhat fluid in its structure in the beginning, so that a natural pattern may emerge from the interests and personalities of the membership. Committees to consider include:

Committee on Community Information

Establish close working relationships with newspapers, radio stations, and television stations

Establish a speakers' bureau

Write and promote "spot announcements" for local radio and television stations to use for their public service requirement

Prepare news releases for the total program

Prepare a series of articles on chemical dependency for the local newspapers

Sponsor study sessions, seminars, and informational meetings for groups in the community

Prepare and disseminate "fact sheets" periodically

Establish a telephone "dial access" system on drug dependency

Serve in the role of disseminator for other committees

Form liaison with churches and synagogues

Form liaison with community organizations to (a) conduct their own drug-related programs, (b) contribute work power, funds and other resources to the community program

Literature distribution possibilities for this committee include:

1. Door-to-door to residences

2. Heavily visited offices and public places—doctors' and dentists' offices, public libraries, employment offices, supermarkets, and so on.

3. Business locations—drug stores, bank lobbies, barber shops, pharmacies, and so on. If there is a target group, places frequented by that group should be emphasized—for instance, for youth, video arcades, snack bars, and so forth.

4. Public reading racks in train stations, bus depots, churches.

5. At public functions such as forums, conferences, school assemblies.

6. To welfare and youth service agencies—recreation programs, child guidance agencies, vocational services.

7. To police departments, juvenile court judges, sheriffs' offices.

8. Through civic groups such as PTA's, Kiwanis, Chamber of Commerce, women's organizations, civic improvement associations.

9. To churches and other centers for family and personal activity.

Committee on Parent/Family Relationships

Conduct education programs on family dynamics and their relationship to chemical dependency—incidence, impact on the family, how to recognize it, what to do about it in the family.

Use a variety of means of presentations:

1. Authoritative presentation by a speaker

2. Panel discussion (health or mental health professional, members of chemically dependent families, domestic court representatives, others)

3. A film followed by discussion

4. Combined meetings of family members

5. A series of such meetings

Develop literature programs aimed at spouses (of both genders), at parents, at children and youth, for concerned relatives

Establish family counseling service for chemical dependency (by telephone or face-to-face)

Committee on Curriculum Development

Prepare a comprehensive status report on current instructional efforts

Determine whether or not current programs are appropriate and effective

Consider the desirability and feasibility of a formal, sequential instructional program in the local schools—kindergarten through twelfth grade

Prepare additional instruction units for new grade levels as deemed appropriate; determine the proper placement of instructional units in terms of subject-matter area

Determine the teacher qualifications necessary

Review drug and alcohol education material available

Plan for and implement workshop programs as a prerequisite to instituting new units of study

Create some adult education curriculum units

All phases of this program should be conducted with the cooperation of local school boards and principals. Many local and state boards of education and departments of education already have programs and may have tried several alternatives; care should be exercised to avoid duplicating efforts and repeating previous errors. Much is known about what to do and not to do in drug education efforts (for example, avoid scare tactics, don't emphasize charismatic recovering people, don't focus on information only; do base it in the area of health promotion, in the context of individual and community values about self-care and recreation, along with skill development in making personal choices, interpersonal communication, and so on. Contact NIDA, NIAAA, and the U.S. Office of Education for guidelines).

Committee on Multimedia Materials

Become familiar with the available guidelines on drug and alcohol-related media (contact Drug and Alcohol Clearinghouses, Rockville, Md.)

Preview and evaluate multimedia materials—for factual accuracy, avoidance of scare tactics, ethnic and gender sensitivity, age appropriateness, value orientations, goals

Prepare annotated bibliographies on materials with their recommended uses

Consider the feasibility of establishing a mobile and/or stationary drug and alcohol library

Set up and circulate displays in cooperation with other committees

Provide assistance in the selection and development of multimedia materials for use by other committees and in the schools

Develop appropriate discussion questions and critiques for each piece of media available (visual, audio, and printed)

Committee on Staff Development

Depending on the action committee's goals and objectives, identify key categories of persons in a position to provide education and referrals for the groups of concern in the community

Work with appropriate authorities to develop in-service and other types of training programs for these people, tailored to their roles and responsibilities

Secure and/or prepare materials, including training films, audio or video tapes

Prepare statements on practices and procedures for staff in various settings to use when an alcohol or drug user is identified or suspected (obviously these guidelines will be different for an employer than for a schoolteacher although there would also be some similarities)

Plan and implement workshops to train key staff members to serve in leadership roles within their setting in future in-service training

Again, to avoid duplication and promote acceptance of the program by appropriate authorities, close cooperation is important in the planning stages. This may be especially necessary within school systems where contact with PTA's, school boards, school administration and principals, and teachers' associations may all be necessary and useful.

Committee on Research and Evaluation*

Attempt to determine the extent and consequences of drug and alcohol use among all people in the community. Try to answer the questions: who is using what, with whom, for what reasons, in what circumstances and amounts, with what effects?

Identify the sources of drugs and alcohol in the community for particular groups of concern. Through what routes are they made available?

Review, digest, and disseminate research findings in the area

Design evaluation instruments to be used to determine impact of program activities for the total program

Work on identifying contributing factors to the development of chemical dependency and drug and alcohol-related problems—in particular, groups of individuals, and related to family, neighborhood, school, and even political considerations

Committee on Clinical Services

Assess the services currently available, the degree of coordination among these services, who is being served, gaps and duplication in services

Study the appropriate functions a drug or alcohol clinic should serve relative to prevention and/or rehabilitation services (and types of needed personnel related to objectives)

Determine the need, desirability, and feasibility of establishing new services. Prepare a cost analysis of these services in terms of location, space requirements, staffing, equipment, furniture, materials, and supplies

Study the funding options in light of community and state support

Committee on Police and Court Relationships

Form liaison with agencies of law enforcement and administration of justice

---

*In the earliest stages, the action council as a whole may wish to attend primarily to these tasks as a basis for all further activities. A committee would then supplement and continue these early research efforts.

Compile current information of incidence of investigations, arrests, and convictions in drug- and alcohol-related areas

Recruit police and court officials who can participate in community programs

Become and remain informed about drug- and alcohol-related statutes—be prepared to inform the organization and the community about them

Evaluate current legal and enforcement situations in terms of the action council's concerns and goals:

1. Are the laws adequate? How or why not?
2. If adequate, are they adequately and appropriately enforced?
3. Are the laws so severe that juries and courts are reluctant to convict violators?
4. Does enforcement focus on particular segments of the community?
5. Does it harass the small violator and ignore larger issues of organized crime, or violations by respected citizens?

The work of this committee overlaps to some degree the Committee on Legislation. The two could be combined, especially if resources are scarce or if coordination becomes difficult.

Committee on Legislation

Review, study, and evaluate current relevant legislation

Attempt to influence legislators to revise or change current legislation if appropriate

Identify limitations in current laws and attempt to initiate new legislation

Support legislation in process that would provide useful changes or resources for your community action plans

Work with other task force committees to gather supportive data and reactions to legislative proposals

Organize a political action plan to support and influence improved drug- and alcohol-related legislation

Committee on Programs and Resources in Other Communities

Establish liaison relationships with agencies, institutions, and programs in your state and the nation

Visit other cities for the purpose of gathering ideas and data to strengthen the local program

Share ideas, programs, and materials from the local program with others

Identify human resources in your state and elsewhere that might be used on a consultant basis to strengthen the local program

Share promising materials and practices with other appropriate committees

Prepare a compendium of promising programs based upon data gathered

ADMINISTRATIVE AND FINANCIAL COMMITTEE STRUCTURE

Program is the heart of any organization, but the organization must also set up an appropriate administrative structure to perform ongoing maintenance functions. A set of officers is ordinarily required, including the usual chair or co-chair, one or more vice-chairs, secretary, and treasurer. This group, together with all, or key, committee chairs, should sit as a steering committee to direct the overall policies and programs of the organization.

Besides the program committees described earlier, it might be useful to add a membership committee (to recruit new members as needed) and a finance committee (to raise funds). If the general program becomes moderately large, it would be useful or even necessary to add a paid clerical worker or to acquire professional staff assistance. A professional staff administrator may be hired directly by the organization (full or part time) or perhaps might be obtained on loan from a community agency with an ongoing strong interest in drug-problem prevention.

Most communities have a number of organizations and agencies with regular programs, personnel, and budgets whose functions include some attention to drug- and alcohol-related problems. These may include city officials' offices, the board of education, the police, alcoholism or drug clinics, United Community Services, the Chamber of Commerce, and others.

If the aid of one or more of such groups can be enlisted, they may offer funding as well as staff service to the action council. Such agencies might view a community approach as a beneficial extension or enrichment of their own program—in a sense, a way of fostering a broader implementation of their mandate.

One precaution is in order here. An agency providing such assistance might want to put its own personal stamp on the community program and thus make it parochial or one-sided. For example, board of education sponsorship might entail pressure to concentrate only on youth, police sponsorship to focus exclusively on stricter enforcement, and so on. If it's possible to obtain sponsorship from one of these agencies, the officers of the action council should explore thoroughly with the director of the agency whether it is willing to commit resources to a broad-based community structure and a multi-faceted community approach.

The action committee members also should investigate the philosophy and reputation of a potential sponsor. There is often competition among different types of agencies, and various components of the community perceive them as having different orientations. Some of these perceptions are likely to become associated with the action council's efforts as well.

If a potential sponsor is willing to support a broad-based community effort, the resources of the agency (money and/or staff assistance) can be powerful in getting the organization started and in sustaining it. If there is no such commitment, it would probably be better to seek other sources of funding. Agencies such as United Way or the Chamber of Commerce generally approach problems in broad community terms rather than from the standpoint of narrower program interests.

Other funding possibilities include:

Membership fees for participating in the organization (individual or organizational)

Voluntary contributions from individuals and organizations

Fees obtained from distribution of literature, films, speakers, and the like

Foundations

Grants from federal sources (although most of these require a research-evaluation component)

State funding (each state has an agency that allocates state and federal monies to alcohol and drug treatment and prevention activities)

CONCLUSION

We have attempted to lay out some guidelines for community action approaches to reducing problems with drugs and alcohol. Again, we would like to underline the fact that communities should view this text as a series of suggestions rather than a formula to be copied. Each community will need to assess its own values, needs, and resources and develop a program appropriate for, and acceptable to, that community.

In developing these activities, a group must recognize that widespread and problematic use of chemicals is always a multifaceted situation and usually indicative of broader problems and issues within the community and larger society. For instance, drug use in the inner city can be viewed as a reaction to the poverty and discrimination to which our racial minorities are subjected. Increases in drinking may be tied to increasing unemployment rates. Drug use by women may relate to a lack of meaningful roles and too much other-centeredness. Teenagers may be reacting to the materialism around them or to a sense of hopelessness about their future in a world threatened by atomic destruction and chemical waste contamination.

As communities address the manifestations of drug and alcohol consumption through programs similar to our suggestions, they should recognize that eliminating destructive use of chemicals depends also on solutions to these larger problems. Attention to these larger issues may be necessary if real and long-lasting progress is to be made.

REFERENCES

Lettieri, D. J., M. Sayers, and H. W. Pearson, *Theories on Drug Abuse: Selected Contemporary Perspectives,* DHHS Publication No. (ADM) 80-967 (Rockville, Md.: National Institute on Drug Abuse, 1980).

National Institute on Alcohol Abuse and Alcoholism, *Alcohol Consumption and Related Problems: Alcohol and Health Monographs No. 1,* DHHS Pub. No. (ADM) 82-1190 (Rockville, Md.: NIAAA, 1982).

Nowlis, H., and L. S. Jackson, "Role of education and prevention," in S. N. Pradhan and S. N. Dutta, eds., *Drug Abuse: Clinical and Basic Aspects* (St. Louis: The C. V. Mosby Co., 1977), pp. 535–543.

Selected Sources of Education and Materials in Chemical Dependency

Addiction Research Foundation
33 Russell Street
Toronto, Ontario M5S 2S1
Canada

Do-It-Now Foundation
P.O. Box 5115
Phoenix, AZ 85010

Hazelden Literature
Box 176
Center City, MN 55012

National Clearinghouse for Alcohol Information
P.O. Box 2345
Rockville, MD 20852

National Clearinghouse for Drug Abuse Information
P.O. Box 416
Kensington, MD 20795

All these organizations have catalogues, and the two government resources (last two) will send you one free copy of anything they still have in stock. Other government publications can be ordered through the Government Printing Office.

9. ORGANIZING A COMMUNITY COALITION: OPERATION INDEPENDENCE

Joyce C. Welsh

Operation Independence is a major effort within the voluntary sector to stimulate the development of services within the community for the most vulnerable older persons who need supportive services to live alone or to return to their homes after hospital or institutional care. Operation Independence places emphasis on a collaborative planning process and partnership between service providers from the public and voluntary sectors to meet this need in a community.

So that older persons may have the option of continuing to live in their own homes or other places of residence for as long as they wish, a variety of community-wide services are necessary to maintain social well-being, to enhance mental and physical health and to supplement self-care whenever necessary. Operation Independence is designed to encourage local communities and groups to develop and strengthen such services where needed.

Many older adults who are vulnerable due to factors of health, isolation, or frailties which sometimes accompany old age may be able to function adequately with the help of a single supportive service available to them either in their own homes or readily accessible in the community. However, for some

older adults living alone or as couples, the chances are that one or more additional services are required to keep open their option of continued independent living at home. Thus, it is essential that public and voluntary agencies committed to the goal of assisting older adults to remain in or return to their own homes work together so that the services of each, as well as those which can be provided through voluntary organizations, are appropriately related to one another. Many different clusters of services are possible, whether established under public, private nonprofit, or commercial auspices. The clusters will involve different combinations of professional, nonprofessional, and volunteer personnel in accordance with the types of services offered.

For example, a homemaker-home health aide program involves basically a combination of paraprofessional homemakers and professional supervisors. The team for a given case may include a homemaker, a social worker or a nurse, perhaps a physician, a nutritionist, a physical therapist, or others; or it may consist only of the homemaker and her supervisor. Usually the homemaker is on a part-time basis. Consequently, it is necessary in many situations for contacts on days when the homemaker does not visit, a need that can be met by an organized telephone program, staffed by volunteers. Often there is need for chore service, including minor household repairs, which can be supplied by

Reproduced by permission of the publisher and the author. From *A Guidebook for Local Communities Participating in Operation Independence* by Joyce C. Welsh, The National Council on the Aging, Inc., 1975.

either an employee of an agency providing chore service (frequently the local homemaker-home health aide agency) or by a volunteer from such an agency. Other supportive services may be added or substituted, which give the plus to the basic health and welfare service designated nationally as homemaker-home health aide services.

Another example of a widely needed service is a *friendly visitors program,* staffed by volunteers under professional supervision. The friendly visitors help to reduce isolation and stimulate continued social relations. Such visitors may observe the need for a variety of other services in the homes they serve. This may call for close ties with an information and referral service regarding public services or for development of a transportation service to take the older adults to health services, to the grocery store, etc.

The national nutrition program sponsored by the Administration on Aging under Title VII of the Older Americans Act uses the provision of meals as the core service. The congressional intent of Title VII envisions a wide-ranging cluster of related services to promote the health and welfare of individuals receiving the meals service.

Any group offering or planning to offer services to older adults in their own homes should evaluate the multiplied effect of a cluster of services on the well-being of those served and concomitantly the economies—in time, money, effort, staff—of multiservice programs as contrasted with single service operations. Inevitably one program will lead to others, so that the agency concerned with an initial service can hopefully provide a variety of protective and preventive services when and as needed in individual situations.

Services cannot "just grow" for persons in their seventies and eighties. They *must be carefully planned,* community by community, so they are readily available and accessible throughout a given geographic area—and, hopefully, throughout a state. They will not meet full need unless they serve all economic and social groups, whether on a free basis, a sliding scale of fees, or purchase at full cost. They must be adequate not only in quantity but also in quality.

It is important to note the complementary relationship between Operation Independence and national programs of the Administration on Aging of the U.S. Department of Health, Education and Welfare plus the regionalized planning and coordination efforts of state units on aging and area agencies on aging. The program objective of Title III of the 1973 Older Americans Act Comprehensive Service Amendments is to strengthen or develop at the state and area levels a system of coordinated and comprehensive services for older persons—services to enable older persons to live in their own homes or other places of residence as long as possible. Area agencies on aging are charged with:

1. Becoming focal points for aging.
2. Serving as advocates for older persons in connection with all issues confronting their lives.
3. Developing a cooperative network to serve older persons by providing comprehensive coordinated services to meet their needs.

Also, Title XX of the Social Security Act, effective October 1, 1975, and administered by state social services agencies, mandates three specific services for the aged. Operation Independence, with its mobilization of voluntary resources focused on the most vulnerable older people and the in-home, supportive services they need to maintain their independence, complements and cooperates with the broader focus of the area agencies on aging and of state agencies administering Title XX.

A local cooperative effort can result in the development of a service delivery system enabling older persons to live independently in their own homes by

1. Focusing or concentrating attention on that objective.
2. Planning more fully.
3. Eliminating unnecessary duplication of effort.
4. Filling unmet service needs.
5. Sharing responsibilities and resources.

There must be a specific focus on the vulnerable and handicapped older adults; those most in danger of unnecessary institutionalization. Priority in service delivery must be given to older persons with physical, mental or emotional conditions that may handicap their functioning capability or their ability to fully care for themselves. In addition to community services, these people also frequently need in-home services to maintain maximum functioning ability and to prevent further deterioration and loss of independence. They are:

• Homebound and isolated
• Neighborhood bound and lonely
• Visually handicapped or blind
• Physically, mentally or emotionally handicapped
• Deinstitutionalized and convalescing
• Subject to frailties

A community coalition promotes independent living for older adults through services that make it possible for the more vulnerable to continue to live in their own homes or other places of residence in the community as long as possible. The coalition is an advocacy group. While growing in its own awareness of the needs of this specific segment of the aging, the coalition in turn informs and educates the community at large.

COALITION DEVELOPMENT

Community coalitions that form around the objectives of Operation Independence will follow two patterns:

1. In communities where there is an organization(s) with well-developed planning responsibility and capability, this organization and/or its advisory council, board, or committee will logically assume the Operation Independence coalition role. Operation Independence does not aim to set up competing planning and service mechanisms in any community.

2. The establishment of a new Operation Independence coalition will occur in communities where there are high proportions of older persons and no well-developed planning instrumentalities. New coalitions will be formed more frequently in small towns and rural areas; here there tend to be few, if any, formal planning structures, and large percentages of older persons are struggling to remain in their own homes with few public or voluntary agency services readily available to help them.

Step I

It is important, then, to determine first who, if anyone, in the community is engaged in planning services for older persons. Typically, this function is carried out by specific types of organizations. The following observations should be made before attempting to form a new coalition:

1. Is there an area agency on aging serving the locality? (If you are uncertain, your county governmental structure or state commission on aging can provide this information.)
2. Is there a council on aging serving your community?
3. Does your Community Health and Welfare Council or local United Way (United Fund or Community Chest) have a committee with focus on aging?
4. Is your council of governments or local planning district involved in planning for the aging?
5. Are there any other organizations with planning capability now delivering services to older persons (county social services department, community action agencies, parks and recreation departments, voluntary action centers, private agencies such as senior centers, Senior Citizens' Services, Inc., etc.)?

Step II

If a planning mechanism for older persons does exist in your community, that organization and/or its advisory council, board, or committee may well assume the role of an Operation Independence coalition. If it is part of a planning and service area with a designated area agency on aging, the latter may wish to encourage formation of a local coalition in a rural county with many older persons but few services.

Operation Independence encourages such organizations to undertake this role, requiring that two criteria be met:

1. Adoption of specific focus on the more vulnerable older person and the in-home and supportive services they need to maintain their independence. This could be accomplished by expanding an existing community service to include a priority with respect to the more vulnerable older person or by initiating a new program either within one or more of the participating agencies or directly under auspices of the coalition.

2. Representation of public and voluntary groups. This could be accomplished by appointing a subcommittee or task force.

You or your organization can act as a catalyst and encourage organizations with existing planning structures to undertake leadership in the two action steps outlined above.

Step III

If there is no area agency on aging in your planning and service area—and no other planning structure exists in your community—the next step is to convene an initial meeting of representatives of public and voluntary agencies/organizations to accept a commitment to the goal of Operation Independence and to agree on a plan for action. To develop an effective membership, care should be taken to invite all public and voluntary agencies with a service which is, or might be, provided to older persons plus representatives of churches, service clubs, and fraternal organizations, etc., who have the authority to make group decisions.

Examples of agencies and organizations to be invited to the initial meeting are:

Community Health and Welfare Council
County/City Council on Aging
Area Agency on Aging
Council of Governments
County/City Health Department
County/City Department of Social Services
Social Security
Housing Authority
Parks and Recreation Department
Local affiliates of national voluntary organizations which are members of National Voluntary Organizations for Independent Living for the Aged (NVOILA), such as professional associations of doctors, home economists, librarians, etc.
Voluntary health and social welfare agencies, such as the American Red Cross, Visiting Nurses Association, Family Service Agency, Homemaker Service, etc.
Civic and fraternal organizations, such as Rotary, Lions, Kiwanis, Pilot, Altrusa, women's clubs
Religious organizations, such as ministerial alliances, churches, synagogues
Union organizations
Local institutions of higher education, community colleges
Senior citizen organizations and centers, including programs sponsored by civil rights and ethnic groups

Make certain that organizations serving the rural areas of your county or community have been approached:

Farm Bureau
County agents
Grange
Home demonstration agents
State Extension Service
Future Farmers of America
Future Homemakers of America
National Farmers Union
Green Thumb

EXAMPLE OF A COMMUNITY COALITION

Boulder (Colorado) County Steering Committee On Aging

Purpose:

1. To provide a representative group in Boulder County for research and development of the needs of the aging.
2. To act as an advocacy group which makes an effort to assure equitable distribution of Federal and state funds for aging.
3. To act as a coordinator of grant application for services for the aging.

Structure:

1. The membership is limited to a maximum of 25 persons.
2. The set meeting date is the second Wednesday of each month at 1:30 P.M. Special meetings may be held as needed.
3. Council membership is composed of department or agency heads or persons designated by such organizations to insure authority to make group decisions. An alternate is appointed by each member organization to insure continuity of action.

4. The chairperson is expected to request consumer representation when appropriate.
5. The chairperson and vice-chairperson are elected each January 1 on a rotating basis.
6. A secretary, recruited from outside the group, prepares a record of discussions and decisions (summary of actions taken).
7. Summaries of discussions and decisions made are communicated to three county commissioners, county representatives, state legislators and congressmen, as well as to mayors and/or city managers in Boulder County.

Composition (current membership):

Boulder Senior Citizen Center
Volunteer and Information Center— Information and Referral
Boulder County Health Department
Boulder County Department of Social Services
Nutrition programs
R.S.V.P.
City housing
County Commissioners
Church liaison representative
Senior Citizens Coordinating Committee
Nursing homes
Retirement housing
Senior Opportunities and Services section of Boulder
Economic Opportunity Council, Inc.
Mental health
Community Nurse Coordinator
Lafayette Parks and Recreation
American Red Cross

Broomfield Parks and Recreation
St. Vrain Council of Agencies, Senior Task Force
Residential Care Facility

Program accomplishments:

1. Development of the group from a steering committee to the Boulder County Council on Aging. Once it became clear that the area agency on aging expected to organize county councils in each county, the Boulder Steering Committee went to the county commissioners and asked that it be recognized officially as the County Council on Aging. This clear linkage with the area agency on aging has added a significant dimension to the council's effectiveness.
2. Development of a countywide coordinating and planning instrumentality that includes representatives of existing service providers. This group works cooperatively and jointly plans for future services.
3. Establishment of a directory of senior services for Boulder County.
4. Telephone reassurance program.
5. Adult health care conference (screening).
6. Development of the steering committee into a grant review committee for all funding proposals for senior programs in the county submitted by agencies within the coalition. The committee established and coordinated a comprehensive package of five service proposals for submission to the area agency on aging.

Formation process (1971):

1. The coordinator of the Volunteer and Information Center and the director

of the Boulder Senior Citizen Center were invited to be co-convenors of an initial meeting by the National Steering Committee. They sent out invitations to all agency people in the community that dealt with older persons. One hundred and thirty-eight national voluntary organizations elected to become part of an action program growing out of the 1971 White House Conference on Aging called the Steering Committee of National Voluntary Organizations for Services to Older Persons in Their Own Homes or Other Places of Residence. The Plan for Action of the Steering Committee called for designated individuals/organizations in over 400 communities to convene a meeting of representatives of private and public service deliverers and voluntary organizations. The meeting's purpose was to consider the possibility of working together for the planning, coordination, and provision of services to enable older persons to live independently in their own homes or other places of residence. Positive results were effected in more than half of the 400 communities, either in the encouragement of further efforts towards activities already under way or in the initiation of new coalitions for action.

2. Sixty persons responded and attended the first meeting, where the following actions took place:
   a. Identification of the needs of older persons at the local level.
   b. Identification of existing community services.
   c. Identification of gaps in services and unmet needs.
   d. Selection of an executive committee as a policy committee (directors of major agencies).

3. The Executive Committee met and determined 11 priority areas of need from the list identified at the initial general meeting (transportation, homemaker and home health care, adult health care, residential care, communication coordination and education regarding senior services, spiritual well-being, home renovation and repair, adult day care, housing, telephone reassurance, and nutrition).

4. A second general meeting was called, where the following actions took place:
   a. Division of the general group into subcommittees.
   b. Assignment of separate priorities to subcommittees.
   c. Initial work begun on coordinating existing programs and services/and developing new services to fill unmet needs.

Note: For the first two years there was no attempt to formally structure the group, which made the coalition less threatening, enabling it to remain operational through three stages: A city coalition to a countywide coalition to the County Council on Aging.

SELECTED PROGRAMS AND SERVICES HELP OLDER ADULTS REMAIN IN OR RETURN TO THEIR OWN HOMES

The goals of national, state, and local organizations, however varied, can include specific services to older Americans and, of course, they frequently do. Most organizations can provide a specific service directed toward helping older persons to remain in their own homes or other places of residence. In Operation Independence, public and private agencies serving the elderly join with affiliates of national organizations to promote and develop programs which enable older persons to live independently in their own homes.

The following is an attempt to list a number of action programs in which organizations can participate in some way. The participation may take place variously. The organizations may use their facilities for program headquarters, their publications to communicate program ideas; they may urge their membership to become involved on a paid or voluntary basis, use their funds to support such programs, or they may take the leadership role in organizing community action. Many of these programs offer an opportunity to enlist the skills and energies of older persons themselves, in itself a contribution to their continued health and well-being. Also, many programs can provide opportunities for older and younger persons to work together, bridging the generations.

A. Programs of Information and Referral

Through public media, newsletters, information centers, volunteer programs and other means, organizations can

TABLE 9.1
Clusters of Direct Service Programs for Older Persons

I. Consumer Issues
  Consumer education
  Cooperative buying

II. Creative/Leisure Activities
  Adult education
  Arts and crafts
  In-home library services
  Recreation activities
  Talking books, reading services for
    the blind

III. Health
  Health education/counseling
  Home health services
  In-home physical therapy
  Mail order drug services
  Multiphasic health screening

IV. Housing
  Home repair services
  Housing counseling

V. Legal Services
  Conservatorship/guardianship programs
  Financial counseling

  Legal aid
  Tax counseling

VI. Nutrition
  Congregate meals
  Food stamps
  Home-delivered meals
  Nutrition education

VII. Social Support Services
  Adult day-care centers
  Chore services
  Counseling services
  Equipment loan
  Escort services
  Foster home care
  Friendly visitors
  Homemaker – home health aide services
  Personal grooming
  Shopping services
  Telephone reassurance
  Transportation services – reduced bus
    fares
  Driver refresher courses

provide older persons with information to help them remain in their own homes, including:

1. Social Security
2. SSI (Supplemental Security Income)
3. Social service program
4. Protective services
5. Consumer services
6. Counseling services
7. Health programs
8. Food stamp eligibility
9. Housing relocation
10. Employment assistance
11. Volunteer programs

B. Programs of Direct Service

These programs can include service to older persons in their own homes or in group settings, as in a senior center. Bear in mind the multiplier effect of a cluster of services on the well-being of those served. (See Table 9.1.)

C. Programs of Advocacy

National organizations and their local affiliates, in conjunction with local public agencies, can help older persons remain in their homes by serving as their advocates. For instance, their members can work for the development of housing authorities. They can influence local school boards to provide facilities and vehicles for nutrition and transportation programs.

In many cases, this advocacy role can mesh with other special concerns of an organization. An organization concerned with the physically handicapped could work to influence rehabilitation agencies to focus on the elderly's rehabilitation needs. All organizations can underline and obtain support for the selection of the special issues that confront the elderly who are members of minority groups or who have special handicapping conditions.

10. THE ROLE OF THE BOARD IN THE PLANNING PROCESS

John E. Tropman

The planning process in community organization has historically involved citizens in decisions that affected them. Yet, we have not seriously attended to the problems of collective decision

Reproduced by permission of the author.

Special thanks to Kathryn Walter who materially assisted in the preparation of a longer version of this piece, and to Nancy Smith of Aurora Associates, Washington D.C., for her helpful comments.

making inherent in this involvement. Sometimes the problems resulting from this neglect catch up with us. Those instances in which human service organizations have been faulted for spending inordinate amounts of money on fund raising and fund procurement represent one example. Another is lack of proper and vigorous attention on the part of the organization's board of directors to take regular responsibility for policy decisions and direction. Alternatively, one is reminded—and injunctions for maximum feasible participation of the poor are one example—of the fact that board memberships have all too frequently tilted in the direction of the corporate benefactor rather than the beneficiaries. Such a tilt was inappropriate even in the days of charitable institutions, but now, since many clients (through insurance programs indirectly) are paying part of the freight for their own service, their representation on boards becomes even more imperative.

THREE ROLES FOR THE POLICY BOARD

Inherent in this planning process is decision making. And in human service organizations the boards represent the organization's policy center, or that place where decisions are made. A lot of organizational lore suggests that it is the executive and her or his cadre of associates who are really the "powers behind the throne" and the boards are "rubber stamps" bouncing, as it were, from issue to issue with no substantive input. Where this is the case, it represents a failure of both legal responsibility under most state charters, and of trusteeship responsibility in terms of the civic purpose that boards are charged to accomplish. Legally, for example, "directors of New York State not-for-profit corporations are required by statute to discharge their duties in good faith and with that degree of diligence, care and skill which ordinarily prudent men would exercise under similar circumstances in a like position" (Weber, 1975, p. 7). That standard of care which must be taken by the directors in the exercise of their duty means that many could be liable for various kinds of legal action if

it can be shown that they were too cavalier in their attitudes. The area of legal responsibilities is too complex to detail here, but all community organizers should familiarize themselves with the state codes governing not-for-profit corporations in their state and locality.

More complex is the board's responsibility in the planning process for civic purpose. Most boards get together because, ostensibly, they are interested in improving the civic climate in the area in which they live. The individual directors (board members) share in this wish. Yet, all too often, boards fail to accomplish the very civic purpose for which they are set up. Part of the reason lies in poor organization and poor decision-making styles. These difficulties are not unique to boards by any means, but relate to all kinds of decision-making groups. The piece by Antony Jay in this volume provides some suggestions for *meeting* structure that will be helpful in the board context as well as the planning committee context. However, there are a number of issues that deal with the board itself that need to be considered. The purpose of this paper is to suggest three of these issues in particular: the board as a decision maker and a decision overseer with some suggestions about ways in which the board can better handle those responsibilities; board responsibility for role appropriateness and internal and external functions, in particular; and the board as a trainer and developer of members and of the agency itself.

By way of introducing these topics, I suggest that the common term "board member" be changed to "director." In the corporate world people who serve on boards are called directors of the corporation. The word suggests greater power and vigor than does the more passive-sounding term "member." Under not-for-profit corporation laws, the term "directors" is used. They work jointly with the executive director to accomplish the organizational purpose from its definition to its implementation. Perhaps this change can move the perspective of many "members" from a more reactive posture to a proactive one.

The role of boards in the overall planning process is to make decisions and to see to it that those decisions are carried through. To do this, of course, boards work with the executive director and they share with the executive co-responsibility for the integrity of the organization's mission and role. The accomplishment of these purposes requires thought, organization, and structure. And to this end the remaining sections of this paper are devoted.

The target being addressed here is the formal board, one with bylaws, legal responsibilities, and a professional staff. The target is not the grass-roots association, or even some policy professional groups (local chapters of the National Association of Social Workers, for example). Those kinds of groups tend to be less formal and structured than the processes contemplated here. However, there are many times when less formal processes are appropriate and useful. Neighborhood groups may wish to use an approach that mixes task and process goals. One danger with using less formal approaches and procedures is the possible failure to accomplish the tasks through inadequate attention to the set of procedures and programs with which the group is charged. Overformalization is less likely to occur, but it also presents dangers. The key is balance.

All boards and directors groups *plan,* and to that extent they can use the suggestions outlined in this paper. They will need other procedures to meet other

goals and should be aware that multiple functions require multiple procedures, not the use of one set to the exclusion of others.

BOARDS AS DECISION MAKERS AND DECISION OVERSEERS

Policy and Administration

The role of the board extends beyond policy making to the overseeing of policy implementation as well. The line dividing "policy" functions from "administrative" functions is always unclear. I prefer the notion of intersecting sets as described in the Figure 10.1.

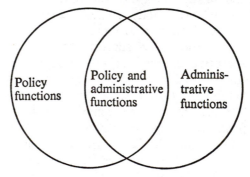

FIGURE 10.1
Functions of Boards of Directors

Industrial consultants suggest, and my own information confirms the idea, that approximately one-half of board time is wasted in unnecessary agenda items, items for which there is insufficient information and so on. Therefore, board organization represents one of the most important elements of decision quality. Referring to Figure 10.1, the entire board meets on policy matters. Subcommittees, the nature of which I will suggest in a moment, meet with the executive and staff in the policy-administration intersect area, and the executive handles the administrative matters. Obviously, there is no rule for neatly allocating one item or another into the various categories, but generally speaking, the broader the scope in terms of the organization, the larger the number of people a particular proposal affects, the more a particular proposal or organizational action will cost, or the more an organization is committed based on a particular action, the more such an action is likely to be policy and to require board approval. Thus, the board itself makes decisions. The subcommittee structure both oversees decisions and develops proposals for board action. Without an appropriate subcommittee structure it is very difficult to carry out the decision-making and oversight role. I have identified nine subcommittees that are important on an ongoing basis:

1. the executive committee
2. the budget and finance committee
3. the resource development committee
4. the personnel committee
5. the program committee
6. the public relations committee
7. the community relations committee
8. the nominating committee
9. the recruitment and training committee

The Executive Committee. The executive committee is composed of the president, officers, the executive director, and committee chairs from the board. It usually can take action in emergency situations when the board cannot meet, and it is often involved in sorting out those activities and proposals that need board approval. It coordinates the work of the other subcommittees and takes overall responsibility for the operation of the board itself.

The Budget and Finance Committee. The budget and finance committee deals with matters of budget generation and financial oversight, reviewing financial trajectories on a monthly basis at least and sometimes on a weekly basis. It is involved with the chief budget officer of the organization in preparing budgets and making proposals for new expenditures, handling emergencies, and so on. It is best to involve people from the financial community here so that access to banks and other kinds of financing can be facilitated when necessary. The budget and finance committee reports both overall budgetary strategy and specific budget proposals to the board.

The Resource Development Committee. This committee seeks to develop financial resources for the agency or organization. Its activity may involve seeking funds through public contributions, planning fund-raising events, securing grants, developing donations of property, and so on. It is important that all board members have an opportunity to serve on this committee, because raising resources is a difficult task and people "burn out." Also, the need to raise funds, as well as spend them, introduces a note of realism into the allocations process.

The Personnel Committee. The personnel committee develops the personnel practices guide for the organization, staying in touch with staff and their concerns, on the one hand, as well as the broader personnel community on the other. Issues involved can refer to compensation, burnout, holidays, and so on. It also typically handles grievances and selection of top agency staff.

The Program Committee. The program committee provides structure and purpose for the organized mission and role of the agency itself. Usually agencies have somewhat general missions and roles, which need to be given concrete programmatic manifestations. This or that activity needs to be undertaken while some other activity needs to be stopped; all activities need to be monitored and evaluated. The program committee, often composed of professionals in the area of concern, makes programmatic recommendations to the board. It generally works more closely with staff than other committees.

The Public Relations Committee. The public relations committee enhances and improves the agency's image with the general public. It prepares annual reports, news releases, and other pieces of public information. It seeks favorable publicity about the agency. Sometimes this committee is merged with the community relations committee, but its function tends to be focused more on media. Interviews with staff, preparing newsletters, and press releases are all tasks of the public relations committee.

The Community Relations Committee. The community relations committee focuses on the personal aspects of community involvement, for example, organizing tours of the agency, providing speakers for public functions, and interpreting the agency's mission and role to key people in the community. While the public relations committee tends to concentrate on involving the media, the community relations committee focuses on involving people. Often community relations links to political figures at local, state, and national levels.

The Nominations Committee. The nominations committee usually meets on a yearly basis, sometimes intensively for a period of time, to develop a slate of officers. At times it also reviews the appointments of top staff. It may also be

merged with the recruitment and training committee, although it is preferable to keep these functions separate. While the nominations committee moves people who have already participated in organizational life into officership, the recruitment and training committee works to secure people from the outside and to bring them into the organization.

The Recruitment and Training Committee. The recruitment and training committee seeks to interest previously uninvolved individuals in the organization and its mission and role. This committee may develop a list of potential members in advance of any specific vacancy. In the recruitment phase, its members meet with individuals, interpret the kind of job the agency is doing, and seek to promote involvement. Its training responsibilities include preparing the board members' manual, conducting annual training sessions for the entire board, and providing additional training for individual board members if they so desire. It is important that each board member of a human service organization have one personal improvement opportunity a year made available through board membership. The reimbursement policy for this effort should be part of the recruitment and training committee task.

How Big a Board

In general, the minimum number of members per subcommittee should be three. Thus, if three people were assigned to each of these committees, there would be a minimum board size of twenty-seven. There are usually at least three extra members for ad hoc assignments, resulting in a board of thirty. A rule of thumb for board size is the number of subcommittees plus one (for ad hoc assignments) times three.

Subcommittee Structure

The subcommittee structure just discussed may appear to some to violate the notions of openness, spontaneity, and freedom, which should characterize the human service board. I believe just the contrary. Most boards deal with technical legal issues of great importance involving quite a bit of money. These issues cannot be approached casually or in an offhand manner; rather, they must be given sustained thought. My view is that a board operates more effectively when working from a subcommittee's recommendation. Therefore, with rare exceptions, I recommend that boards assign upcoming tasks to subcommittees, requesting that the subcommittees study the matter with appropriate staff and other members of the organization and the community to develop a proposal for action with alternative considerations and present the proposal to the board. When this groundwork is laid, the board can deal with the matter much more effectively and efficiently than it can if it is trying both to make the decision and to acquire relevant information at the same time.

Subcommittee Functions

Basically, subcommittees have five major functions. The first is to generate decision options, the point I just made. Second, once a decision has been made in an area germane to the functioning of the subcommittee, it is the subcommittee's task to oversee the implementation of that decision. Oversight here does not mean scrutiny on a daily basis; rather it means that the subcommittee receives periodic reports on how things are going, raises questions, and gets to the executive, president, and full board if necessary. Third, subcommittees evaluate and pass recommendations to the board on activities in their area of concern and responsibility. Fourth, subcommittees become the center of the trusteeship-generating function because they seek to foresee problems. The finance committee that does not foresee difficulties is the finance committee that may find itself liable for civil action. The job and responsibility of subcommittees is to be proactive, to take leadership roles and to present suggestions based on these two orientations to the board itself. Fifth, through carrying out these four functions, the subcommittee educates the whole board and thus provides for board growth in its respective area of concern.

From Administrative Board to Policy Board—The Problem of Transition

One particular problem that boards in the human services field have is to accomplish the transition from "administrative board" to policy board. This transition occurs in the following way. Often a human service organization has been founded by a group of interested citizens who initially get together and *are* the agency. As time passes, federal or state monies may be acquired. As more stable funding becomes available, an executive director and perhaps a secretary are hired, and the organization is beginning to move from a very informal, nonbureaucratic, personal organization to one that is more formal and bureaucratic, and includes a board of directors legally chartered under the laws of the state. This transition often leaves the agency founders feeling left out, in second place, and needing to move on. And, indeed, some organizational analysts indicate that the kinds of people who are organizational founders are very different from those who are organizational maintainers. One cannot prescribe a solution to these problems any more than one can prescribe for a safe adolescence. One can only point out the kinds of problems and difficulties that are likely to occur, to alert people to expect them, and to be sensitive to them. One such problem stems from the need for founding directors to adjust their behavior to more of a policy role and to become less involved with the actual day-to-day operation of the agency. If the member desires such day-to-day interaction, it would be better to volunteer at another agency rather than to seek to maintain old relationships and patterns in the agency that member founded. A new member, brought in to join a board which was founded in this fashion, is likely to feel irritation and then resign. One has to understand the difference between involvement of founding members as opposed to maintaining members. While this does not mean that license should be given to founding members, an understanding of their perspective often helps to locate their interests and wishes more accurately.

Decision Accountability

One of the most important initial steps in evaluating decisions and being accountable for them is to make them in the first place. All too often when a problematic decision comes up, people ask, "When did we make that decision?" And, indeed, upon scrutiny of the records it becomes very unclear because the decision was not made at one point, but evolved at several points. The subcommittee system permits the specific identification of areas of responsibility and the development of decisional formats in those areas of responsibility. These decision proposals then go to the full board where they are acted upon and recorded in the minutes. At the end of the year or whatever time is appropriate, one can go back and ask the question, "What decisions did we make during the particular year?" and review the collective impact on the structure and quality of those decisions overall. Because it is often difficult to assess a decision's impact immediately after it has been made, such retrospective assessment is essential to accountability. Sometimes the wisdom or foolishness of a decision emerges only after time has passed. Such accountability review also takes into consideration the extent to which the information available at the time was sufficient and accurate. If an organization continually makes decisions that, as it later turns out, were ill informed, then the process of information generation needs to be studied.

The other aspect of accountability, of course, is implementation. Here the performance audit is useful. The performance audit means taking a specific look at some areas of organizational activity, assessing the speed, quality, integrity, and intelligence with which a decision was implemented. A board is not only responsible for making a decision; it is responsible for seeing to it that the decision is efficiently carried out. Generally, this responsibility falls to the executive director, and it is usually in concert with the executive that the board exercises implementive oversight and control.

BOARD'S RESPONSIBILITY FOR ROLE APPROPRIATENESS

Board members and the board itself are responsible for acting appropriately within the context of their role. We have discussed the individual requisites of that role, particularly as they regard legal responsibilities and the avoidance of acting in self-aggrandizing and self-profiting ways. More importantly, we have mentioned the positive aspects of one's personal role, that is, acting as a trustee of civic purpose and taking a proactive, accomplishment-oriented posture.

As a means to accomplishing these ends, there are particulars of role performance that are appropriate in carrying out one's organizational responsibilities. For example, there are appropriate ways for a chair to behave and there are appropriate things for a chair to do, which a chair *must* do if organizational purposes are to be achieved. Similarly, there are appropriate member, staff and executive roles. These will not be detailed here; they are discussed at length elsewhere (Tropman, 1980). Suffice to say that there *are* role requisites for chair, member, staffer, and executive. In addition, one can violate, through inappropriate personal behavior, these requisites. I use the phrase *appropriate* to indicate the convention as social rather than legal, but it has force nonetheless.

The Role of the Board: Internal Functions

In this section, I will discuss the role of the board itself, rather than the roles of the individual members. The board as an entity is responsible for acting appropriately. But what is "appropriate"? There appears to be a great deal of role confusion. I suggest seven functions that a board may perform and discuss them in terms of the different role behaviors that might be required when these different functions are being performed. Just as individuals may well be different at various points during the working day, depending upon the tasks they need to accomplish, so boards need to think about changing their own behavior as a group entity when tasks are different. The seven functions can be divided into two parts: internal functions and external functions. Internal functions relate to deciding policy, overseeing policy, and administering policy. External functions focus upon the interorganizational system.

Policy Decision Functions. These typically relate to the board as a whole and refer to those aspects of its role that involve formal legal authority as specified under articles of incorporation and under statutes of the state. Decisions made here are typically referred to as "policy decisions" although other types of decisions may have policy impact as well. Crucial to the policy-deciding function is adequate information, adequate time for review, adequate feedback from appropriate parties, and reasonably prompt action consistent with the available information. What needs to be avoided here is decisional pre- and postmaturity. Prematurity occurs when an item is brought to a policy-deciding meeting in advance of adequate available information. Typically, a great deal of time is spent on such an issue, and then it is postponed. Decisional prematurity is one of the most significant causes of decisional postmaturity. A decision delayed is, all too often, a decision denied. It is legitimate for a director to accuse a board of undue delay. The problem of what is "undue" is difficult. There is no issue on which more information cannot be garnered and on which additional perspectives would not be useful. However, there are often a series of external constraints such as grant deadlines, fiscal year deadlines, and so on, which make the very best informed decision useless if it comes too late. Therefore, within the policy-deciding function, boards need to achieve a balance between information on the one hand, and decisional needs and pressures on the other.

Policy-Overseeing Functions. Policy-overseeing functions—seeing that decisions are implemented—are typically accomplished through the subcommittee structure. They involve policy-generating and review components, as well as assessment and program audit elements. Policy oversight occurs once a formal decision is made by the board of directors, and not before. However, the concept of policy oversight involves a certain amount of policy proactivity—that is, the anticipation of upcoming events and the proposed adjustment of existent policies to take those new events into account. Members of policy-overseeing groups must be clear about the scope and extent of the particular policy that is being monitored and should neither overextend their role to encompass areas tangential to it nor ignore or minimize the responsibilities that they do have.

Policy-Administering Committee. During unique organizational situations, a policy-administering committee is set up by a board of directors. For example, in an agency crisis, power may be delegated to a small group along with appropriate financial resources, and secretarial and other logistical support to handle a particular situation. Most typically, fast-breaking type situations require the

development of such a task force; the task force dissolves when those situations have been resolved.

A second situation in which the administering committee appears is during the initiation stage of an organization. That is, a group of people get together to do a task, make the decisions as they go along, and get enjoyment and gratification from accomplishment of the task itself. Soon they "turn into" an "agency." They then must begin to play more of a "director's" role.

The Role of the Board: External Functions

Boards of directors of human service agencies play four external roles that are quite different in nature and quality from the internal roles. As agencies move into the interorganizational environment, they no longer have the imperative control given them by their charter and articles of incorporation. Rather, they move from a position based on authority to a stance based on cooperation. There are four external roles that boards may play (and sometimes they may create other community committees that play these roles, too): policy sharing, policy advisory, policy coordinating, and policy implementing.

Policy Sharing. Policy sharing is a role in which the board agrees to cooperate with other similar agencies, to acquaint them, and be acquainted with ongoing programs. It does not imply any adjustment in program, nor does it imply that any particular program is right, wrong, appropriate, or inappropriate. It simply reflects an agreement to get together and "show and tell" one's program. This reflects a cooperative posture only.

The Policy-Coordinating Functions. Sometimes policy sharing leads to a policy-coordinating function. For example, a board will be asked to perform roles with respect to other organizations in terms of program adjustment. "We'll handle young kids and you handle older kids," it might be suggested. Or "We'll handle boys and you handle girls." These types of adjustments require either prior agreement from the board or actual board agreement once the proposal is made. I suggest that policy coordination without board approval be permitted on a case basis only. Agency or organizational coordination requires conjoint planning and conjoint agreement.

Policy Implementing. Sometimes, within the interorganizational system, the board of directors becomes part of a team asked to implement a particular community-wide decision. Again, we are speaking of delegated functions and functions that require constant board oversight and approval. A board member joining a community-wide group for coordinating and implementing purposes does not mean that that individual carries any kind of board approval unless that approval has been specifically given. This is an important function for the board to play, and I strongly encourage boards to participate in policy-sharing, policy-coordinating, and policy-implementing activities at the community level. In such a situation, however, a special subcommittee might well be developed to handle the relationship of the particular organization to the constellation of organizations which are seeking to accomplish even larger social tasks.

Policy Advisory. Sometimes a board is asked for a collective opinion on a matter of community concern. The mayor, for example, may call and ask what your agency thinks about an issue. It is not sufficient to simply chew the matter around and then let the executive write up some kind of recommendation. Rather, the matter must be discussed and language must be prepared to reflect the board's perspective. It must be approved by the board and entered into the minutes. A "decision" is actually made during the policy advisory process, but the decision is a piece of advice!

There are certainly many other roles that boards as boards may play. However, these seven, divided between internal and external roles, represent the beginning of a perspective suggesting some of the differences that might be involved. I think that boards need to pay more attention to the external system than they have in the past—particularly in the human service community. Boards, as I have experienced them, tend to be more inwardly focused, playing roles as corporate citizens in the collective community less and less frequently. While it is appropriate that a balance be struck, the emphasis on the word *balance* suggests that some time, and I think more time, needs to be spent in collaborative, coordinating, implementive, and sharing types of roles. Decision-making boards often find it difficult to play these external roles because they relinquish the authority they are used to having when they deal with internal matters. This shift from authoritative posture to cooperative posture is difficult, but it must be carried out in any case.

THE BOARD AS A TRAINER AND DEVELOPER

Boards have a responsibility for training new members and for developing ongoing members. Nowhere has this need been more seriously recognized than during the efforts to provide "maximum feasible participation of the poor" during the 1960s in the United States. During that time many individuals lacking board experience were brought on to the governing body of nonprofit charitable organizations. Rarely were they provided with any kind of orientation. Joseph Weber and Nellie Hartogs (1974) found that executives rated orientation among the lowest of priorities, while finance and personnel were among the highest. Given the perspectives in this paper, orientation becomes an absolute necessity for new members, and ongoing training is even more a requisite for all directors because they are unlikely to know what to do. Beyond the members, there needs to be some assessment of the growth of the board itself. I will consider the last point first and then suggest ways in which members can improve themselves.

Board Growth and Development

How do we gauge whether the board is growing and moving in a more sophisticated direction and improving the quality of decisions? There is no one way, but many boards are moving to an annual program evaluation and assessment system. There are two categories of assessment generally used. One concerns itself with member meeting satisfaction, and the second is concerned with assessment of decision quality.

Meeting Satisfaction. To measure member meeting satisfaction, the board itself should develop an instrument to assess how well the members felt the meetings had gone during the year. There are a number of categories, such as length of time, pleasantness, adequacy of information, and so on. By developing its own instrument, the board has a greater investment and thus, it is much more likely to follow through on using it and

be identified with its results. The training and recruitment committee (one of the board's subcommittees) can be asked to take some responsibility here. It is important to keep in mind, however, that satisfaction with the meetings does not necessarily mean that good decisions were made, although dissatisfaction with the meetings is more likely an indicator that poor decisions were made.

Decision Quality. Implicit here, of course, and an assumption of any decision quality assessment, is that the minutes are so written and the board processes so structured, that it is possible to pull from the minutes a list of decisions made by the board. These must be listed in terms of their substantive content and orientation, not simply listed as "approval of the budget," but rather sentences and phrases which indicate the nature of and the direction of budgetary thrust for the year. These should be listed on a sheet and reviewed during an assessment session. People are now asked what they think of these decisions. Has any information come up that suggests that they were ill considered? The board rates its decisions on a scale of 1 to 10, A to Z, or any other appropriate scale. The very act of sitting down and reviewing decisions is, in itself, a positive process.

Review and Refurbishment. In addition to reviewing decisions, there is the policy review and refurbishment function. I feel that every seven years boards need to take an in-depth look at their mission, role, and articles of incorporation to ascertain whether any adjustments are necessary. During each year of the six intermediate years, one specific area of agency board relationships is selected for review and refurbished and improved, if needed. Personnel policy might be scrutinized one year, financial policies in another year, and so on. Thus, at the end of the seventh year, all of the subparts of the organization will have been reviewed. Meeting satisfaction and decision quality assessments, when combined with policy review and refurbishment and supplemented with information from the program audits, provide a useful overview of the organizational activity. These reviews could be accomplished during a yearly one to two-day retreat, or at a special meeting in which people can look at the organization, and in doing so, reconsider their own role in it.

Assessment of the Member. Assessment of the member is considerably more difficult because of its personal nature. It is best, therefore, to begin on a positive side. I think that each member should have the opportunity for at least one personal growth experience per year. Typically this means attendance at a professional meeting or workshop paid for by the organization. I feel very strongly that this type of compensation (if indeed it is compensation) should represent a priority activity for agencies. Many agencies are very scrupulous about seeking staff development but completely indifferent to board development. In any event, one should assess with members whether there has been the opportunity for personal growth experience and whether that has added to the overall functioning of the board.

In addition, development programs should be run by the organization for board members (and possibly staff) once or twice a year. There are numerous training films available for board members, an outside expert could be invited to speak on board problems and activities, or a relevant article could be distributed and a board discussion organized. It is important that individual members be given the opportunity, within the context of their board membership, to think about their role. That thinking and self-reflection will undoubtedly be positively applied to the specific board in question. There are a number of personal assessment instruments available (see Figure 10.2).

Using these assessments should permit individuals to think through their own roles in a challenging but nonthreatening situation.

Board Training

Every organized board should have a manual for directors. Again, I stress the use of the word "directors," not members, to emphasize the more vigorous and active director role.

The board manual should begin with a statement of mission, the purpose of the organization, and a brief history and "raison d'être" of the organization. The legal responsibilities of the organization should then be detailed and should refer the reader to the articles of incorporation listed in the appendix. Following this opening section, there should be a statement of the expected responsibilities of membership, which outlines the role of the director and details the subcommittees and their functions and purposes. A third section, which can be replaced regularly, should deal with the current operating structure of the organization: names, addresses, and telephone numbers of directors; past directors; advisory committees; training program plans; retreat dates; meeting schedules— all of the specific paraphernalia of directorship. It is useful to have the names and addresses of staff on a separate sheet, which can be updated as frequently as necessary. Another section should contain a compilation of annual reports.

FIGURE 10.2
Exercise: Am I a Good Board Member?

Is it possible to identify the attributes of the perfect volunteer board member? The question is academic because all human beings are a combination of strengths and of weaknesses. A good board, therefore, blends imperfect human beings into an effective working team.

There are certain attitudes which help to make good board members. Some of these are listed here.

0 = NO • • • • 10 = YES

Good Board Members:	I Am	Others Are
1. Are dedicated to helping others and modest in the light of their responsibilities as board members.		
2. Approach their responsibilities in the spirit of a trustee on behalf of contributors, their intended beneficiaries, and the public at large.		
3. Stand up for their convictions, even at the cost of misunderstanding or disapproval in business or social life.		
4. Back up other board members and staff, rising to their defense when they are unjustly criticized or attacked.		
5. Treat staff as a partner in a high calling, maintaining overall supervision and control, but not interfering with day-to-day administration.		
6. Avoid being overawed by others on the board, whether they be executive staff, tycoons of business, labor or society; professionals in social work, education, medicine, etc.		
7. Welcome information and the best available advice but reserve the right to arrive at decisions on the basis of their own judgment.		
8. Respect the right of other board members and of staff to disagree with them and to have a fair hearing of their points of view.		
9. Accept as routine that decisions must be made by majority vote and will at times go against one or more members.		
10. Criticize when necessary, in a constructive way, if possible suggesting an alternative course.		
11. Recognize that time and energy are limited and that overcommitment may prove self-defeating.		
12. Endeavor to keep disagreements and controversies impersonal, and to promote unity.		
13. Maintain loyalty to their agency, within a higher loyalty to the welfare of the community and humanity as a whole.		

SOURCE: "Volunteer Board Member in Philanthropy," National Information Bureau, 419 South Park Avenue, New York, New York 10016 (Reprinted with permission).

This gives each member an opportunity to see what the agency has done over time and consider what it is likely to do in the future. Future or projected plans can also be listed here. In addition, it is useful to have a single summary sheet giving historical demographic facts about the agency, such as its annual budget, per capita expenditure on children, and the like.

Finally, if the board feels that there is any pertinent reading material essential to the board member, it can be included as well. This is only a skeletal suggestion for a board manual. Some are more simple and direct; others are more complicated and intricate. What is important is that the board develops its own manual. Following well-accepted practices of community organization, the involvement of the board in developing its own guidelines should be an important guiding principle.

New Director Training Session

One of the most important types of board training activities is the new director training session. If the suggestion made earlier in this document is followed and the two-tier involvement process used, the new director will not begin from zero. This is too often the case, however, and it frequently takes six months to a year for the new director to become a useful participating member. In either case, whether the new director has participated in ancillary groups or is an inexperienced person in this area, there should be an orientation process. It need not be long, but it should include certain basic matters. First, the substantive thrust, purpose, mission, and commitments of the organization should be explained. While the new director may feel that his/her motives for membership are being changed or detracted by this kind of orientation, substantive contributions will come later; the board member needs to know what he or she is getting into first.

A second aspect of the training should deal with the principles of good group decision making. Often this section of the new-member training program can be linked to a training program offered to other individuals on the board. Mutual education involving discussion, participation, and the acquisition of new knowledge is one very good way to establish the new member-old member bonding required for effective and efficient decision making.

CONCLUSION

This paper has presented some systematic concerns and perspectives on the modern board. It is a much more complex, intricate, and involved process than anyone previously considered. The model board represents one of the essential vehicles through which the pluralism of American values is expressed and through which the historic striving for democratic involvement and participation for decisions which affect individual lives can be orchestrated. And yet, despite these important large-scale social functions, as well as the crucial day-to-day decision functions, board membership is casually, if not shabbily, treated. This casualness and shabbiness is a conspiracy of everyone—members who accept directorships without proper scrutiny and review, those of us who extend invitations to directorship in a thoughtless and offhand manner, executives who put board training at the bottom of the list of priority activities, and society itself, which tends to undervalue, if not devalue, group activities.

Human service organizations, whether they be philanthropic or nonprofit, must receive leadership, stewardship, and trusteeship from their boards of directors if they are to survive for the future. No area of the modernization process has been as ignored as the board of directors in terms of research, training, or suggestion. Those who are seeking to learn more about this area and improve it, hone it, and fine-tune it, are to be commended. It is not a job full of praise and thanks. Rather, one is likely to be greeted with some indifference, ambivalence, and lack of concern. It reminds one of the story of the board training session in which a man said ignorance and apathy are the two major enemies of board activities. A listening board member looked at another and said, "Do you think that is right?" The other board member replied, "I don't know and I don't care." That's the problem as it lies before us. This paper represents a small attempt to move things in the other direction, to reduce apathy and ignorance.

REFERENCES

Tropman, John E., *Effective Meetings* (Beverly Hills, Calif.: Sage, 1980).

Weber, Joseph, *Managing Boards of Directors* (New York: The Greater New York Fund, 1975).

———, and Nellie Hartogs, *Boards of Directors* (New York: Oceana Publications, 1974).

BIBLIOGRAPHY

Bennis, Warren G., "RX for Corporate Boards," *Technology Review* (December/January 1979).

Bennis, Warren G., "The Crisis of Corporate Boards," *Technology Review* (November 1978).

Bridges, Edwin M., Wayne J. Doyle, and David J. Mahand, "Effects of Hierarchical Differentiation on Group Productivity, Efficiency and Risk Taking," *Administrative Science Quarterly* 13 (1968).

Glover, E. Elizabeth, *Guide for Board Organization and Administrative Structure* (New York: Child Welfare League of America, 1972).

Greenleaf, Robert K., "1. The Servant as Leader," "2. Trustees as Servants," "3. The Institution as Servant," and "4. The Servant: Retrospect and Prospect," *The Servant Series* (Peterborough, N.H.: Windy Row Press, 43 Grove St., Peterborough, N.H. 03455, 1973).

Griggsby, C., "Separable Liabilities in Directory Trusts," *California Law Review* 60, no. 4 (1972).

Hawkins, A. J., "The Personal Liability of Charity Trustees," *The Law Quarterly Review* 95 (January 1979): 99-116.

Hone, Michael C., "Responsibilities of the Directors of Non-Profit Corporations Under the Proposed Revision of the Model Non-Profit Corporation Act." Paper presented at the American Bar Association Annual Meeting, August 1981 (unpublished paper, School of Law, University of San Francisco).

Levy, Leslie, "Reforming Board Reform," *Harvard Business Review* 59 (January/February 1981): 166-172.

National Information Bureau, "The Volunteer Board Member in Philanthropy," (New York: National Information Bureau, 1979).

Oleck, Howard L., *Non-Profit Corporations, Organizations and Associates* (Englewood Cliffs, N.J.: Prentice-Hall, 1980).

Palmerie, Victor H., "Corporate Responsibility and the Competent Board," *Harvard Business Review* 57 (May/June 1979): 46-48.

Pascarella, Perry, "The CEO of the 80's," *Industry Week* (January 7, 1980).

Perham, John C., "Non-Profit Boards Under Fire," *Dun's Review* 114, no. 4 (October 1979): 108-113.

Prospects, "How to Make Boards of Directors Effective in the Modern World," *Technology Review* (December/January 1979).

Prybil, Lawrence D., "Accountability Invested Trust," *Hospitals* 50 (April 1, 1976): 48-50.

Solomon, Louis D., "Restructuring the Corporate Board of Directors: Fond Hope—Faint Promise?" *Michigan Law Review* 76, no. 4 (March 1978).

Topinka, James E., Barbara H. Shilling, and Carolyn Mar, *A Guide to the California Non-Profit Public Benefit Corporation Law* (San Francisco: The Management Center, 150 Post St., Suite 640, San Francisco, CA 94108).

Trecker, Harley, "Boards Can Be Better: The Productive Board Meeting" (Hartford, Conn.: Community Council of Greater Hartford, April 1980).

———, "Boards Can Be Better: Board and Staff, The Leadership Team" (Hartford, Conn.: Community Council of Greater Hartford, May 1980).

———, "Boards Can Be Better: Overview" (Hartford, Conn.: Community Council of Greater Hartford, February 1980).

———, "Boards Can Be Better: An Annual Check-up for Boards" (Hartford, Conn.: Community Council of Greater Hartford, June 1980).

Tropman, John E., "A Comparative Analysis of Community Organization Agencies," in I. Speigal, ed. *Community Organization: Studies in Constraint* (Beverly Hills, Calif.: Sage, 1972).

———, *Effective Meetings* (Beverly Hills, Calif.: Sage, 1980).

———, Harold R. Johnson, and Elmer J. Tropman, *The Essentials of Committee Management* (Chicago: Nelson-Hall, 1979).

Weber, Joseph, *Managing Boards of Directors* (New York: The Greater New York Fund, 1975).

———, and Nellie Hartogs, *Boards of Directors* (New York: Oceana Publications, 1974).

Weihe, Vernon, "Are Your Board Members Dressed for Their Role?" *Canadian Welfare* 52 (1976).

———, "Keeping Board Members Informed," unpublished paper, School of Social Professions, University of Kentucky, 1979.

Williams, Harold M., "Corporate Accountability," *Vital Speeches* 44, no. 15 (May 15, 1978): 558-563.

Zelman, William, "Liability for Social Agency Boards," *Social Work* 22, 4 (July 1977): 270-274.

11. SIMPLIFIED PARLIAMENTARY PROCEDURE

League of Women Voters of the United States

MEETINGS

Minutes should reflect what was *done,* not what was *said,* at a meeting. The common tendency is to report in too much detail. Minutes should contain:

- the date, place, time and type of meeting (regular, special);
- the names of the presiding officer, the secretary and, in boards and committees, the names of those present;
- action taken on the minutes of the previous meeting and corrections, if any;
- exact wording of each motion, the name of the maker and the disposition;
- the name and topic of guest speakers (their speeches need not be summarized);
- time of adjournment.

At all meetings (referred to in *Robert's Rules* as "assemblies") it is up to the presiding officer to use the rules of parliamentary procedure appropriately so that good order and reasonable decorum are maintained and the business of the meeting goes forward. At times, the technical rules of parliamentary procedure may be relaxed as long as the meeting accomplishes its purpose and the rights of absentees and minorities are protected. Conventions and large meetings are conducted more formally than the meetings of small boards and committees.

The Role of the Presiding Officer

The presiding officer (chair) should:
- Be ready to call the meeting to order at the time set.
- Follow the agenda and clarify what is happening and what is being voted on at all times.
- Deal firmly with whispering, commotion and frivolous or delaying debate and motions.
- See that debate is confined to the merits of the question and that personal comments are avoided. No one should speak more than twice on a subject, and no one should speak a second time until all who wish to speak have had a chance to do so.
- Talk no more than necessary. Except in small boards and committees, the presiding officer should not enter the debate without giving up the chair to a substitute until the motion under debate has been voted on.
- Remain calm and deal fairly with all sides regardless of personal opinion. To preserve this impartiality, the presiding officer abstains from voting except by ballot or to cast the deciding vote on an issue.

Order of Business

A minimum number (*quorum*), as prescribed in the bylaws, must be present before business can be legally transacted.

Reproduced by permission of the publisher. From *Simplified Parliamentary Procedure,* Pub. #138, League of Women Voters of the United States, 1979, pp. 5-11.

The presiding officer should determine that there is a quorum before beginning the meeting. Every organization is free to decide the order in which its business will be conducted, but most agendas follow a standard pattern:

1. **Call to order.**
2. **Minutes** are read by the secretary and corrections requested. The presiding officer says: *If there are no corrections the minutes stand approved as read.*
3. **Treasurer's Report** is given and questions called for: *The Treasurer's Report will be filed.*
4. **Reports of officers, the board and standing committees.** Recommendations in reports should be dealt with as motions at this point.
5. **Reports of special committees.**
6. **Unfinished business.** Items left over from the previous meeting are brought up in turn by the presiding officer.
7. **New business:** *Is there any new business?*
8. **Program.** The program chairperson is called upon to introduce a speaker, film or other presentation.
9. **Announcements.**
10. **Adjournment:** *Is there any further business?* (Pause) *The meeting is adjourned.*

Motions

Business is conducted by acting on motions. A subject is introduced by a **main motion.** Once this has been seconded and stated by the presiding officer, nothing else should be taken up until it is disposed of. Long and involved motions should be submitted in writing. Once a motion has been stated, the mover may not withdraw it without the consent of the meeting. Most motions must be seconded.

While a main motion is being considered, other **parliamentary motions,** which affect either the main motion or the general conduct of the meeting, may be made. The ones most frequently used are described in general below, but it should be noted that there are exceptions and modifications that cannot be included in this brief text.

1. **Amend.**   **Debatable; majority vote**
   Used when the intention is to change, add or omit words in the main motion.
   Amend the amendment: Used to change, add or omit words in the first amendment. This motion *cannot* itself be amended.
   Method: The *first* vote is on the amendment to the amendment. The *second* vote is on the first amendment either as changed or as originally proposed, depending on the first vote. The *third* vote is on the main motion either as introduced or as amended.
2. **Refer.**   **Debatable; majority vote**
   If a motion becomes too complicated through amendments or if more information is needed, a motion may be made to refer it to a committee for study or redrafting. This committee must report back or act as instructed.
3. **Postpone.**   **Debatable; majority vote**
   Consideration of a motion can be delayed until a more suitable time, until other decisions have been made or until more information is available by a motion to postpone to a stated future time.
4. **Lay on the table.**   **Not debatable; majority vote**
   I move that we table this motion. This postpones consideration in such a way

that the motion can be taken up again in the near future if a majority decides to "take it from the table."

5. The previous question.   Not debatable; two-thirds vote

I move the previous question. This motion is used to end debate that has become lengthy or repetitious. When it is seconded, the presiding officer immediately puts the question on closing debate. If this receives a two-thirds vote, the pending motion is voted on at once without further discussion.

6. Reconsider.   Usually debatable; majority vote

A vote may be reconsidered through this motion, which must be made on the same day or the day following the vote by someone who voted on the prevailing side. A motion can be reconsidered only once. The *first* vote is on whether the motion shoud be reconsidered. If this passes, the *second* vote is on the motion itself.

7. Point of order and appeal.

A member who feels the rules are not being followed may call attention to the breach by rising and saying: *Point of order.* The chair says: *State your point of order.* Upon hearing it, the chair may say: *Your point is well taken,* or *Your point is not well taken.*

One dissatisfied with the ruling may appeal to the meeting for a final decision: *Shall the decision of the chair be sustained?* This appeal is debatable, and the presiding officer may enter the debate without giving up the chair. A majority of *no* votes is necessary to reverse the ruling; a tie sustains it.

8. Questions and inquiries.

Whenever necessary, advice may be asked as to correct procedures (**parliamentary inquiry**), facts may be requested (**point of information**), or a change may be sought for comfort or convenience (**question of privilege**). The presiding officer responds to the question or refers it to the proper person.

9. Adjourn.   Usually not debatable; majority vote

If the time set for adjournment has arrived or there is no further business, the presiding officer declares the meeting adjourned without waiting for a formal motion. A member may move to adjourn at any time except when a speaker has the floor or a vote is in process. If the motion carries, the meeting is immediately adjourned.

Voting

The vote needed to pass a motion or elect an official is based on the votes actually cast, unless the bylaws or rules provide otherwise. Thus, a majority is more than half of those voting; abstentions and blank ballots are disregarded

- By using **general consent,** a formal vote can be avoided on routine matters where there is no opposition. The presiding officer says: *If there is no objection* (pause) . . . and declares the decision made.
- A **voice vote** (aye and no) is common practice but should not be used where more than a majority is needed.
- A **show of hands** is a good alternative in small groups.
- If unsure of the result, the presiding officer should order a **rising vote** or an actual **count**. If this is not done, a member can insist upon a rising vote by calling out **"division"**; a count can

be forced only by a motion made, seconded and approved by a majority vote.

- A motion for a **ballot** (secret written vote) can be made if the bylaws do not already require one. This motion is not debatable and requires a majority vote.

NOMINATIONS AND ELECTIONS

Normally, a nominating process is used for elections, although any eligible member may be elected whether nominated or not. Most organizations use a **nominating committee** to prepare a slate of nominees for the offices to be filled. Service on a nominating committee does not prevent a member from becoming a nominee.

After presentation of the nominating committee's report to the assembly, the presiding officer calls for nominations from the floor. Many organizations require that the consent of the nominee be obtained in advance to avoid a futile election. Seconds are not necessary for either committee nominations or nominations from the floor.

When all nominations appear to have been made, the presiding officer declares that nominations are closed—or a motion to this effect may be made. It is not debatable and requires a two-thirds vote.

A motion to reopen nominations requires a majority vote.

The method of voting is usually fixed in the bylaws. A ballot is the normal procedure if there is more than one nominee for an office. If there are several nominees and the bylaws do not provide for election by a plurality vote (that is, the largest number, but not necessarily more than half of the votes cast), several ballots or votes may be needed before one candidate achieves a majority.

Where election is by ballot, the presiding officer appoints tellers (or an election committee) to collect and count the votes. The tellers' report, giving the number of votes cast for each nominee, is read aloud and handed to the presiding officer. The presiding officer rereads the report and declares the election of each official separately.

A Postscript to the Presiding Officer. The rules of parliamentary procedure are meant to help, not hinder. Applied with common sense, they should not frustrate the meeting or entangle it in red tape. Retain control at all times, give clear explanations, and keep things as simple as possible. Good advice from the chair as to the wording of motions and the best way to proceed will avoid needless complications. When in doubt, your rule should be: Respect the wishes of the majority, protect the minority and do what seems fair and equitable.

Order from League of Women Voters of the United States, 1730 M Street, NW, Washington, DC 20036. Pub. No. 138. Prices on request.

12. HOW TO RUN A MEETING

Antony Jay

Why have a meeting anyway? Why indeed? A great many important matters are quite satisfactorily conducted by a single individual who consults nobody. A great many more are resolved by a letter, a memo, a phone call, or a simple conversation between two people. Sometimes five minutes spent with six people separately is more effective and productive than a half-hour meeting with them all together.

Certainly a great many meetings waste a great deal of everyone's time and seem to be held for historical rather than practical reasons; many long-established committees are little more than memorials to dead problems. It would probably save no end of managerial time if every committee had to discuss its own dissolution once a year, and put up a case if it felt it should continue for another twelve months. If this requirement did nothing else, it would at least refocus the minds of the committee members on their purposes and objectives.

But having said that, and granting that "referring the matter to a committee" can be a device for diluting authority, diffusing responsibility, and delaying decisions, I cannot deny that meetings fulfill a deep human need. Man is a social species. In every organization and every human culture of which we have record, people come together in small groups at regular and frequent intervals, and in larger "tribal" gatherings from time to time. If there are no meetings in the places where they work, people's attachment to the organizations they work for will be small, and they will meet in regular formal or informal gatherings in associations, societies, teams, clubs, or pubs when work is over.

This need for meetings is clearly something more positive than just a legacy from our primitive hunting past. From time to time, some technomaniac or other comes up with a vision of the executive who never leaves his home, who controls his whole operation from an all-electronic, multichannel, microwave, fiber-optic video display dream console in his living room. But any manager who has ever had to make an organization work greets this vision with a smile that soon stretches into a yawn.

There is a world of science fiction, and a world of human reality; and those who live in the world of human reality know that it is held together by face-to-face meetings. A meeting still performs functions that will never be taken over by telephones, teleprinters, Xerox copiers, tape recorders, television monitors, or any other technological instruments of the information revolution.

FUNCTIONS OF A MEETING

At this point, it may help us understand the meaning of meetings if we look at the six main functions that meetings will always perform better than any of the more recent communication devices:

1. In the simplest and most basic way, a meeting defines the team, the group, or the unit. Those present belong to it; those absent do not. Everyone is able to look around and perceive the whole group and sense the collective identity of which he or she forms a part. We all know who we are—whether we are on the board of Universal International, in the overseas sales department of Flexitube, Inc., a member of the school management committee, on the East Hampton football team, or in Section No. 2 of Platoon 4, Company B.

2. A meeting is the place where the group revises, updates, and adds to what it knows *as a group.* Every group creates its own pool of shared knowledge, experience, judgment, and folklore. But the pool consists only of what the individuals have experienced or discussed as a group—i.e., those things which every individual knows that all the others know, too. This pool not only helps all members to do their jobs more intelligently, but it also greatly increases the speed and efficiency of all communications among them. The group knows that all special nuances and wider implications in a brief statement will be immediately clear to its members. An enormous amount of material can be left unsaid that would have to be made explicit to an outsider.

But this pool needs constant refreshing and replenishing, and occasionally the removal of impurities. So the simple business of exchanging information and ideas that members have acquired separately or in smaller groups since the last meeting is an important contribution to the strength of the group. By questioning and commenting on new contributions, the group performs an important "digestive" process that extracts what's valuable and discards the rest.

Some ethologists call this capacity to share knowledge and experience among a group "the social mind," conceiving it as a single mind dispersed among a number of skulls. They recognize that this "social mind" has a special creative power, too. A group of people meeting together can often produce better ideas, plans, and decisions than can a single individual, or a number of individuals, each working alone. The meeting can of course also produce worse outputs or none at all, if it is a bad meeting.

However, when the combined experience, knowledge, judgment, authority, and imagination of a half dozen people are brought to bear on issues, a great many plans and decisions are improved and sometimes transformed. The original idea that one person might have come up with singly is tested, amplified, refined, and shaped by argument and discussion (which often acts on people as some sort of chemical stimulant to better performance), until it satisfies far more requirements and overcomes many more objections than it could in its original form.

3. A meeting helps every individual understand both the collective aim of the group and the way in which his own and everyone else's work can contribute to the group's success.

4. A meeting creates in all present a commitment to the decisions it makes and the objectives it pursues. Once something had been decided, even if you originally argued against it, your membership in the group entails an obligation to accept the decision. The alternative is to leave the group, but in practice this is

very rarely a dilemma of significance. Real opposition to decisions within organizations usually consists of one part disagreement with the decision to nine parts resentment at not being consulted before the decision. For most people on most issues, it is enough to know that their views were heard and considered. They may regret that they were not followed, but they accept the outcome.

And just as the decision of any team is binding on all the members, so the decisions of a meeting of people higher up in an organization carry a greater authority than any decision by a single executive. It is much harder to challenge a decision of the board than the chief executive acting on his own. The decision-making authority of a meeting is of special importance for long-term policies and procedures.

5. In the world of management, a meeting is very often the only occasion where the team or group actually exists and works as a group, and the only time when the supervisor, manager, or executive is actually perceived as the leader of the team, rather than as the official to whom individuals report. In some jobs the leader does guide his team through his personal presence—not just the leader of a pit gang or construction team, but also the chef in the hotel kitchen and the maître d'hôtel in the restaurant, or the supervisor in a department store. But in large administrative headquarters, the daily or weekly meeting is often the only time when the leader is ever perceived to be guiding a team rather than doing a job.

6. A meeting is a status arena. It is no good to pretend that people are not or should not be concerned with their status relative to the other members in a group. It is just another part of human nature

that we have to live with. It is a not insignificant fact that the word *order* means (a) hierarchy or pecking order; (b) an instruction or command; and (c) stability and the way things ought to be, as in "put your affairs in order," or "law and order." All three definitions are aspects of the same idea, which is indivisible.

Since a meeting is so often the only time when members get the chance to find out their relative standing, the "arena" function is inevitable. When a group is new, has a new leader, or is composed of people like department heads who are in competition for promotion and who do not work in a single team outside the meeting, "arena behavior" is likely to figure more largely, even to the point of dominating the proceedings. However, it will hardly signify with a long-established group that meets regularly.

Despite the fact that a meeting can perform all of the foregoing main functions, there is no guarantee that it will do so in any given situation. It is all too possible that any single meeting may be a waste of time, an irritant, or a barrier to the achievement of the organization's objectives.

WHAT SORT OF MEETING?

While my purpose in this article is to show the critical points at which most meetings go wrong, and to indicate ways of putting them right, I must first draw some important distinctions in the size and type of meetings that we are dealing with.

Meetings can be graded by *size* into three broad categories: (1) the assembly—100 or more people who are expected to do little more than listen to the main speaker or speakers; (2) the council—40 or 50 people who are basically there to listen to the main speaker or speakers but who can come in with questions or comments and who may be asked to contribute something on their own account; and (3) the committee—up to 10 (or at the most 12) people, all of whom more or less speak on an equal footing under the guidance and control of a chairman.

We are concerned in this article only with the "committee" meeting, though it may be described as a committee, a subcommittee, a study group, a project team, a working party, a board, or by any of dozens of other titles. It is by far the most common meeting all over the world, and can perhaps be traced back to the primitive hunting band through which our species evolved. Beyond doubt it constitutes the bulk of the 11 million meetings that—so it has been calculated—take place every day in the United States.

Apart from the distinction of size, there are certain considerations regarding the *type* of meeting that profoundly affect its nature. For instance:

Frequency. A daily meeting is different from a weekly one, and a weekly meeting from a monthly one. Irregular, ad hoc, quarterly, and annual meetings are different again. On the whole, the frequency of meetings defines—or perhaps even determines—the degree of unity of the group.

Composition. Do the members work together on the same project, such as the nursing and ancillary staff on the same ward of a hospital? Do they work on different but parallel tasks, like a meeting of the company's plant managers or regional sales managers? Or are they a diverse group—strangers to each other,

perhaps—united only by the meeting itself and by a common interest in realizing its objectives?

Motivation. Do the members have a common objective in their work, like a football team? Or do they to some extent have a competitive working relationship, like managers of subsidiary companies at a meeting with the chief executive, or the heads of research, production, and marketing discussing finance allocation for the coming year? Or does the desire for success through the meeting itself unify them, like a neighborhood action group or a new product design committee?

Decision Process. How does the meeting group ultimately reach its decisions? By a general consensus, "the feeling of the meeting"? By a majority vote? Or are the decisions left entirely to the chairman himself, after he has listened to the facts, opinions, and discussions?

Kinds of Meetings

The experienced meeting-goer will recognize that, although there seem to be five quite different methods of analyzing a meeting, in practice there is a tendency for certain kinds of meetings to sort themselves out into one of three categories. Consider:

The *daily meeting,* where people work together on the same project with a common objective and reach decisions informally by general agreement.

The *weekly or monthly meeting,* where members work on different but parallel projects and where there is a certain competitive element and a greater likelihood that the chairman will make the final decision himself.

The *irregular, occasional, or "special project" meeting,* composed of people whose normal work does not bring them into contact and whose work has little or no relationship to the others'. They are united only by the project the meeting exists to promote and motivated by the desire that the project should succeed. Though actual voting is uncommon, every member effectively has a veto.

Of these three kinds of meeting, it is the first—the workface type—that is probably the most common. It is also, oddly enough, the one most likely to be successful. Operational imperatives usually ensure that it is brief, and the participants' experience of working side by side ensures that communication is good.

The other two types are a different matter. In these meetings all sorts of human crosscurrents can sweep the discussion off course, and errors of psychology and technique on the chairman's part can defeat its purposes. Moreover, these meetings are likely to bring together the more senior people and to produce decisions that profoundly affect the efficiency, prosperity, and even survival of the whole organization. It is, therefore, toward these higher-level meetings that the lessons of this article are primarily directed.

BEFORE THE MEETING

The most important question you should ask is: "What is this meeting intended to achieve?" You can ask it in different ways—"What would be the likely consequences of not holding it?" "When it is over, how shall I judge whether it was a success or a failure?"— but unless you have a very clear requirement from the meeting, there is a grave danger that it will be a waste of everyone's time.

Defining the Objective

You have already looked at the six main functions that all meetings perform, but if you are trying to use a meeting to achieve definite objectives, there are in practice only certain types of objectives it can really achieve. Every item on the agenda can be placed in one of the following four categories, or divided up into sections that fall into one or more of them:

1. *Informative-Digestive.* Obviously, it is a waste of time for the meeting to give out purely factual information that would be better circulated in a document. But if the information should be heard from a particular person, or if it needs some clarification and comment to make sense of it, or if it has deep implications for the members of the meeting, then it is perfectly proper to introduce an item onto the agenda that requires no conclusion, decision, or action from the meeting; it is enough, simply, that the meeting should receive and discuss a report.

The "informative-digestive" function includes progress reports—to keep the group up to date on the current status of projects it is responsible for or that affect its deliberations—and review of completed projects in order to come to a collective judgment and to see what can be learned from them for the next time.

2. *Constructive-Originative.* This "What shall we do?" function embraces all items that require something new to be devised, such as a new policy, a new strategy, a new sales target, a new product, a new marketing plan, a new procedure, and so forth. This sort of discussion asks people to contribute their

knowledge, experience, judgment, and ideas. Obviously, the plan will probably be inadequate unless all relevant parties are present and pitching in.

3. *Executive Responsibilities.* This is the "How shall we do it?" function, which comes after it has been decided what the members are going to do; at this point, executive responsibilities for the different components of the task have to be distributed around the table. Whereas in the second function the contributors' importance is their knowledge and ideas, here their contribution is the responsibility for implementing the plan. The fact that they and their subordinates are affected by it makes their contribution especially significant.

It is of course possible to allocate these executive responsibilities without a meeting, by separate individual briefings, but several considerations often make a meeting desirable:

First, it enables the members as a group to find the best way of achieving the objectives.

Second, it enables each member to understand and influence the way in which his own job fits in with the jobs of the others and with the collective task.

Third, if the meeting is discussing the implementation of a decision taken at a higher level, securing the group's consent may be of prime importance. If so, the fact that the group has the opportunity to formulate the detailed action plan itself may be the decisive factor in securing its agreement, because in that case the final decision belongs, as it were, to the group. Everyone is committed to what the group decides and is collectively responsible for the final shape of the project, as well as individually answerable for his own part in it. Ideally, this sort of agenda

item starts with a policy, and ends with an action plan.

4. *Legislative Framework.* Above and around all considerations of "What to do" and "How to do it," there is a framework—a departmental or divisional organization—and a system of rules, routines, and procedures within and through which all the activity takes place. Changing this framework and introducing a new organization or new procedures can be deeply disturbing to committee members and a threat to their status and long-term security. Yet leaving it unchanged can stop the organization from adapting to a changing world. At whatever level this change happens, it must have the support of all the perceived leaders whose groups are affected by it.

The key leaders for this legislative function must collectively make or confirm the decision; if there is any important dissent, it is very dangerous to close the discussion and make the decision by decree. The group leaders cannot expect quick decisions if they are seeking to change the organization framework and routines that people have grown up with. Thus they must be prepared to leave these items unresolved for further discussion and consultation. As Francis Bacon put it—and it has never been put better—"Counsels to which time hath not been called, time will not ratify."

Making Preparations

The four different functions just discussed may of course be performed by a single meeting, as the group proceeds through the agenda. Consequently, it may be a useful exercise for the chairman to go through the agenda, writing beside each item which function it is intended to fulfill. This exercise helps clarify what is expected from the discussion and helps focus on which people to bring in and what questions to ask them.

People. The value and success of a committee meeting are seriously threatened if too many people are present. Between 4 and 7 is generally ideal, 10 is tolerable, and 12 is the outside limit. So the chairman should do everything he can to keep numbers down, consistent with the need to invite everyone with an important contribution to make.

The leader may have to leave out people who expect to come or who have always come. For this job he may need tact; but since people generally preserve a fiction that they are overworked already and dislike serving on committees, it is not usually hard to secure their consent to stay away.

If the leader sees no way of getting the meeting down to a manageable size, he can try the following devices: (*a*) analyze the agenda to see whether everyone has to be present for every item (he may be able to structure the agenda so that some people can leave at half time and others can arrive); (*b*) ask himself whether he doesn't really need two separate, smaller meetings rather than one big one; and (*c*) determine whether one or two groups can be asked to thrash some of the topics out in advance so that only one of them needs to come in with its proposals.

Remember, too, that a few words with a member on the day before a meeting can increase the value of the meeting itself, either by ensuring that an important point is raised that comes better from the floor than from the chair or by preventing a time-wasting discussion of a subject that need not be touched on at all.

Papers. The agenda is by far the most important piece of paper. Properly drawn up, it has a power of speeding and clarifying a meeting that very few people understand or harness. The main fault is to make it unnecessarily brief and vague. For example, the phrase "development budget" tells nobody very much, whereas the longer explanation "To discuss the proposal for reduction of the 1976-1977 development budget now that the introduction of our new product has been postponed" helps all committee members to form some views or even just to look up facts and figures in advance.

Thus the leader should not be afraid of a long agenda, provided that the length is the result of his analyzing and defining each item more closely, rather than of his adding more items than the meeting can reasonably consider in the time allowed. He should try to include, very briefly, some indication of the reason for each topic to be discussed. If one item is of special interest to the group, it is often a good idea to single it out for special mention in a covering note.

The leader should also bear in mind the useful device of heading each item "For information," "For discussion," or "For decision" so that those at the meeting know where they are trying to get to.

And finally, the chairman should not circulate the agenda too far in advance, since the less organized members will forget it or lose it. Two or three days is about right—unless the supporting papers are voluminous.

The order of items on the agenda is important. Some aspects are obvious—the items that need urgent decision have to come before those that can wait till next time. Equally, the leader does not discuss the budget for the reequipment program before discussing whether to put the reequipment off until next year. But some aspects are not so obvious. Consider:

1. The early part of a meeting tends to be more lively and creative than the end of it, so if an item needs mental energy, bright ideas, and clear heads, it may be better to put it high up on the list. Equally, if there is one item of great interest and concern to everyone, it may be a good idea to hold it back for a while and get some other useful work done first. Then the star item can be introduced to carry the meeting over the attention lag that sets in after the first 15 to 20 minutes of the meeting.

2. Some items unite the meeting in a common front while others divide the members one from another. The leader may want to start with unity before entering into division, or he may prefer the other way around. The point is to be aware of the choice and to make it consciously, because it is apt to make a difference to the whole atmosphere of the meeting. It is almost always a good idea to find a unifying item with which to end the meeting.

3. A common fault is to dwell too long on trivial but urgent items, to the exclusion of subjects of fundamental importance whose significance is long-term rather than immediate. This can be remedied by putting on the agenda the time at which discussion of the important long-term issue will begin—and by sticking to it.

4. Very few business meetings achieve anything of value after two hours, and an hour and a half is enough time to allocate for most purposes.

5. It is often a good idea to put the finishing time of a meeting on the agenda as well as the starting time.

6. If meetings have a tendency to go on too long, the chairman should arrange to start them one hour before lunch or one hour before the end of work. Generally, items that ought to be kept brief can be introduced ten minutes from a fixed end point.

7. The practice of circulating background or proposal papers along with the minutes is, in principle, a good one. It not only saves time, but it also helps in formulating useful questions and considerations in advance. But the whole idea is sabotaged once the papers get too long; they should be brief or provide a short summary. If they are circulated, obviously the chairman has to read them, or at least must not be caught not having read them. (One chairman, more noted for his cunning than his conscientiousness, is said to have spent 30 seconds before each meeting going through all the papers he had not read with a thick red pen, marking lines and question marks in the margins at random, and making sure these were accidentally made visible to the meeting while the subject was being discussed.)

8. If papers are produced at the meeting for discussion, they should obviously be brief and simple, since everyone has to read them. It is a supreme folly to bring a group of people together to read six pages of closely printed sheets to themselves. The exception is certain kinds of financial and statistical papers whose function is to support and illustrate verbal points as reference documents rather than to be swallowed whole: these are often better tabled at the meeting.

9. All items should be thought of and thought about in advance if they are to be

usefully discussed. Listing "Any other business" on the agenda is an invitation to waste time. This does not absolutely preclude the chairman's announcing an extra agenda item at a meeting if something really urgent and unforeseen crops up or is suggested to him by a member, provided it is fairly simple and straightforward. Nor does it preclude his leaving time for general unstructured discussion after the close of the meeting.

10. The chairman, in going through the agenda items in advance, can usefully insert his own brief notes of points he wants to be sure are not omitted from the discussion. A brief marginal scribble of "How much notice?" or "Standby arrangements?" or whatever is all that is necessary.

THE CHAIRMAN'S JOB

Let's say that you have just been appointed chairman of the committee. You tell everyone that it is a bore or a chore. You also tell them that you have been appointed "for my sins." But the point is that you tell them. There is no getting away from it: some sort of honor or glory attaches to the chairman's role. Almost everyone is in some way pleased and proud to be made chairman of something. And that is three quarters of the trouble.

Master or Servant?

Their appointment as committee chairman takes people in different ways. Some seize the opportunity to impose their will on a group that they see themselves licensed to dominate. Their chairmanship is a harangue, interspersed with demands for group agreement.

Others are more like scoutmasters, for whom the collective activity of the group is satisfaction enough, with no need for achievement. Their chairmanship is more like the endless stoking and fueling of a campfire that is not cooking anything.

And there are the insecure or lazy chairmen who look to the meeting for reassurance and support in their ineffectiveness and inactivity, so that they can spread the responsibility for their indecisiveness among the whole group. They seize on every expression of disagreement or doubt as a justification for avoiding decision or action.

But even the large majority who do not go to those extremes still feel a certain pleasurable tumescence of the ego when they take their place at the head of the table for the first time. The feeling is no sin: the sin is to indulge it or to assume that the pleasure is shared by the other members of the meeting.

It is the chairman's self-indulgence that is the greatest single barrier to the success of a meeting. His first duty, then, is to be aware of the temptation and of the dangers of yielding to it. The clearest of the danger signals is hearing himself talking a lot during a discussion.

One of the best chairmen I have ever served under makes it a rule to restrict her interventions to a single sentence, or at most two. She forbids herself ever to contribute a paragraph to a meeting she is chairing. It is a harsh rule, but you would be hard put to find a regular attender of her meetings (or anyone else's) who thought it was a bad one.

There is, in fact, only one legitimate source of pleasure in chairmanship, and that is pleasure in the achievements of the meeting—and to be legitimate, it must be shared by those present. Meetings are *necessary* for all sorts of basic and primitive human reasons, but they are *useful* only if they are seen by all present to be getting somewhere—and somewhere they know they could not have gotten to individually.

If the chairman is to make sure that the meeting achieves valuable objectives, he will be more effective seeing himself as the servant of the group rather than as its master. His role then becomes that of assisting the group toward the best conclusion or decision in the most efficient manner possible: to interpret and clarify; to move the discussion forward; and to bring it to a resolution that everyone understands and accepts as being the will of the meeting, even if the individuals do not necessarily agree with it.

His true source of authority with the members is the strength of his perceived commitment to their combined objective and his skill and efficiency in helping and guiding them to its achievement. Control and discipline then become not the act of imposing his will on the group but of imposing the group's will on any individual who is in danger of diverting or delaying the progress of the discussion and so from realizing the objective.

Once the members realize that the leader is impelled by his commitment to their common objective, it does not take great force of personality for him to control the meeting. Indeed, a sense of urgency and a clear desire to reach the best conclusion as quickly as possible are a much more effective disciplinary instrument than a big gavel. The effective chairman can then hold the discussion to the point by indicating that there is no time to pursue a particular idea now, that there is no time for long speeches, that the group has to get through this item and on to the next one, rather than by resorting to pulling rank.

There are many polite ways the chairman can indicate a slight impatience even when someone else is speaking—by leaning forward, fixing his eyes on the speaker, tensing his muscles, raising his eyebrows, or nodding briefly to show the point is taken. And when replying or commenting, the chairman can indicate by the speed, brevity, and finality of his intonation that "we have to move on." Conversely, he can reward the sort of contribution he is seeking by the opposite expressions and intonations, showing that there is plenty of time for that sort of idea, and encouraging the speaker to develop the point.

After a few meetings, all present readily understand this nonverbal language of chairmanship. It is the chairman's chief instrument of educating the group into the general type of "meeting behavior" that he is looking for. He is still the servant of the group, but like a hired mountain guide, he is the one who knows the destination, the route, the weather signs, and the time the journey will take. So if he suggests that the members walk a bit faster, they take his advice.

This role of servant rather than master is often obscured in large organizations by the fact that the chairman is frequently the line manager of the members: this does not, however, change the reality of the role of chairman. The point is easier to see in, say, a neighborhood action group. The question in that case is, simply, "Through which person's chairmanship do we collectively have the best chance of getting the children's playground built?"

However, one special problem is posed by this definition of the chairman's role, and it has an extremely interesting answer. The question is: How can the chairman combine his role with the role of a member advocating one side of an argument?

The answer comes from some interesting studies by researchers who sat in on hundreds of meetings to find out how they work. Their consensus finding is that most of the effective discussions have, in fact, two leaders: one they call a "team," or "social," leader; the other a "task," or "project," leader.

Regardless of whether leadership is in fact a single or a dual function, for our purposes it is enough to say that the chairman's best role is that of social leader. If he wants a particular point to be strongly advocated, he ensures that it is someone else who leads off the task discussion, and he holds back until much later in the argument. He might indeed change or modify his view through hearing the discussion, but even if he does not it is much easier for him to show support for someone else's point later in the discussion, after listening to the arguments. Then, he can summarize in favor of the one he prefers.

The task advocate might regularly be the chairman's second-in-command, or a different person might advocate for different items on the agenda. On some subjects, the chairman might well be the task advocate himself, especially if they do not involve conflict within the group. The important point is that the chairman has to keep his "social leadership" even if it means sacrificing his "task leadership." However, if the designated task advocate persists in championing a cause through two or three meetings, he risks building up quite a head of antagonism to him among the other members. Even so, this antagonism harms the group less by being directed at the "task leader" than at the "social leader."

Structure of Discussion

It may seem that there is no right way or wrong way to structure a committee meeting discussion. A subject is raised, people say what they think, and finally a decision is reached, or the discussion is terminated. There is some truth in this. Moreover, it would be a mistake to try and tie every discussion of every item down to a single immutable format.

Nevertheless, there is a logical order to a group discussion, and while there can be reasons for not following it, there is no justification for not being aware of it. In practice, very few discussions are inhibited, and many are expedited, by a conscious adherence to the following stages, which follow exactly the same pattern as a visit to the doctor:

"What Seems To Be the Trouble?" The reason for an item being on a meeting agenda is usually like the symptom we go to the doctor with: "I keep getting this pain in my back" is analogous to "Sales have risen in Germany but fallen in France." In both cases it is clear that something is wrong and that something ought to be done to put it right. But until the visit to the doctor, or the meeting of the European marketing committee, that is about all we really know.

"How Long Has This Been Going On?" The doctor will start with a case history of all the relevant background facts, and so will the committee discussion. A solid basis of shared and agreed-on facts is the best foundation to build any decision on, and a set of pertinent questions will help establish it. For example, when did French sales start to fall off? Have German sales risen exceptionally? Has France had delivery problems, or less sales effort, or weaker

advertising? Have we lost market share, or are our competitors' sales falling too? If the answers to all these questions, and more, are not established at the start, a lot of discussion may be wasted later.

"Would You Just Lie Down on the Couch?" The doctor will then conduct a physical examination to find out how the patient is now. The committee, too, will want to know how things stand at this moment. Is action being taken? Do long-term orders show the same trend? What are the latest figures? What is the current stock position? How much money is left in the advertising budget?

"You Seem to Have Slipped a Disc." When the facts are established, you can move toward a diagnosis. A doctor may seem to do this quickly, but that is the result of experience and practice. He is, in fact, rapidly eliminating all the impossible or far-fetched explanations until he leaves himself with a short list. The committee, too, will hazard and eliminate a variety of diagnoses until it homes in on the most probable—for example, the company's recent energetic and highly successful advertising campaign in Germany plus new packaging by the market leader in France.

"Take This 'Round to the Druggist." Again, the doctor is likely to take a shortcut that a committee meeting may be wise to avoid. The doctor comes out with a single prescription, and the committee, too, may agree quickly on a single course of action.

But if the course is not so clear, it is better to take this step in two stages: (a) construct a series of options—do not, at first, reject any suggestions outright but try to select and combine the promising elements from all of them until a number of thought-out, coherent, and sensible suggestions are on the table; and (b) only when you have generated these options do you start to choose among them. Then you can discuss and decide whether to pick the course based on repackaging and point-of-sale promotion, or the one based on advertising and a price cut, or the one that bides its time and saves the money for heavier new-product promotion next year.

If the item is at all complex or especially significant, it is important for the chairman not only to have the proposed course of the discussion in his own head, but also to announce it so that everyone knows. A good idea is to write the headings on an easel pad with a felt pen. This saves much of the time wasting and confusion that result when people raise items in the wrong place because they were not privy to the chairman's secret that the right place was coming up later on in the discussion.

CONDUCTING THE MEETING

Just as the driver of a car has two tasks, to follow his route and to manage his vehicle, so the chairman's job can be divided into two corresponding tasks, dealing with the subject and dealing with the people.

Dealing with the Subject

The essence of this task is to follow the structure of discussion as just described in the previous section. This, in turn, entails listening carefully and keeping the meeting pointed toward the objective.

At the start of the discussion of any item, the chairman should make it clear where the meeting should try to get to by the end. Are the members hoping to make a clear decision or firm recommendation? Is it a preliminary deliberation to give the members something to go away with and think about? Are they looking for a variety of different lines to be pursued outside the meeting? Do they have to approve the proposal, or merely note it?

The chairman may give them a choice: "If we can agree on a course of action, that's fine. If not, we'll have to set up a working part to report and recommend before next month's meeting."

The chairman should make sure that all the members understand the issue and why they are discussing it. Often it will be obvious, or else they may have been through it before. If not, then he or someone he has briefed before the meeting should give a short introduction, with some indication of the reason the item is on the agenda; the story so far; the present position; what needs to be established, resolved, or proposed; and some indication of lines of inquiry or courses of action that have been suggested or explored, as well as arguments on both sides of the issue.

If the discussion is at all likely to be long or complex, the chairman should propose to the meeting a structure for it with headings (written up if necessary), as I stated at the end of the section on "Structure of discussion." He should listen carefully in case people jump too far ahead (e.g., start proposing a course of action before the meeting has agreed on the cause of the trouble), or go back over old ground, or start repeating points that have been made earlier. He has to head discussion off sterile or irrelevant areas very quickly (e.g., the rights and wrongs of past decisions that it is too late to change, or distant prospects that are too remote to affect present actions).

It is the chairman's responsibility to prevent misunderstanding and confusion. If he does not follow an argument or understand a reference, he should seek clarification from the speaker. If he thinks two people are using the same word with different meanings, he should intervene (e.g., one member using *promotion* to mean point-of-sale advertising only, and another also including media publicity).

He may also have to clarify by asking people for facts or experience that perhaps influence their view but are not known to others in the meeting. And he should be on the lookout for points where an interim summary would be helpful. This device frequently takes only a few seconds, and acts like a life belt to some of the members who are getting out of their depth.

Sometimes a meeting will have to discuss a draft document. If there are faults in it, the members should agree on what the faults are and the chairman should delegate someone to produce a new draft later. The group should never try to redraft around the table.

Perhaps one of the most common faults of chairmanship is the failure to terminate the discussion early enough. Sometimes chairmen do not realize that the meeting has effectively reached an agreement, and consequently they let the discussion go on for another few minutes, getting nowhere at all. Even more often, they are not quick enough to close a discussion *before* agreement has been reached.

A discussion should be closed once it has become clear that (a) more facts are required before further progress can be made, (b) discussion has revealed that the meeting needs the views of people not present, (c) members need more time to think about the subject and perhaps discuss it with colleagues, (d) events are changing and likely to alter or clarify the basis of the decision quite soon, (e) there is not going to be enough time at this meeting to go over the subject properly, or (f) it is becoming clear that two or three of the members can settle this outside the meeting without taking up the time of the rest. The fact that the decision is difficult, likely to be disputed, or going to be unwelcome to somebody, however, is not a reason for postponement.

At the end of the discussion of each agenda item, the chairman should give a brief and clear summary of what has been agreed on. This can act as the dictation of the actual minutes. It serves not merely to put the item on record, but also to help people realize that something worthwhile has been achieved. It also answers the question "Where did all that get us?" If the summary involves action by a member of the meeting, he should be asked to confirm his acceptance of the undertaking.

Dealing with the People

There is only one way to ensure that a meeting starts on time, and that is to start it on time. Latecomers who find that the meeting has begun without them soon learn the lesson. The alternative is that the prompt and punctual members will soon realize that a meeting never starts until ten minutes after the advertised time, and they will also learn the lesson.

Punctuality at future meetings can be wonderfully reinforced by the practice of listing late arrivals (and early departures) in the minutes. Its ostensible and perfectly proper purpose is to call the late-

comer's attention to the fact that he was absent when a decision was reached. Its side effect, however, is to tell everyone on the circulation list that he was late, and people do not want that sort of information about themselves published too frequently.

There is a growing volume of work on the significance of seating positions and their effect on group behavior and relationships. Not all the findings are generally agreed on. What does seem true is that:

1. Having members sit face to face across a table facilitates opposition, conflict, and disagreement, though of course it does not turn allies into enemies. But it does suggest that the chairman should think about whom he seats opposite himself.

2. Sitting side by side makes disagreements and confrontation harder. This in turn suggests that the chairman can exploit the friendship-value of the seats next to him.

3. There is a "dead man's corner" on the chairman's right, especially if a number of people are seated in line along from him (it does not apply if he is alone at the head of the table).

4. As a general rule, proximity to the chairman is a sign of honor and favor. This is most marked when he is at the head of a long, narrow table. The greater the distance, the lower the rank—just as the lower-status positions were "below the salt" at medieval refectories.

Control the Garrulous. In most meetings someone takes a long time to say very little. As chairman, your sense of urgency should help indicate to him the need for brevity. You can also suggest that if he is going to take a long time it might be better for him to write a paper. If it is urgent to stop him in full flight, there is a useful device of picking on a phrase (it really doesn't matter what phrase) as he utters it as an excuse for cutting in and offering it to someone else: "Inevitable decline—that's very interesting. George, do you agree that the decline is inevitable?"

Draw out the Silent. In any properly run meeting, as simple arithmetic will show, most of the people will be silent most of the time. Silence can indicate general agreement, or no important contribution to make, or the need to wait and hear more before saying anything, or too good a lunch, and none of these need worry you. But there are two kinds of silence you must break:

1. The silence of diffidence. Someone may have a valuable contribution to make but be sufficiently nervous about its possible reception to keep it to himself. It is important that when you draw out such a contribution, you should express interest and pleasure (though not necessarily agreement) to encourage further contributions of that sort.

2. The silence of hostility. This is not hostility to ideas, but to you as the chairman, to the meeting, and to the process by which decisions are being reached. This sort of total detachment from the whole proceedings is usually the symptom of some feeling of affront. If you probe it, you will usually find that there is something bursting to come out, and that it is better out than in.

Protect the Weak. Junior members of the meeting may provoke the disagreement of their seniors, which is perfectly reasonable. But if the disagreement escalates to the point of suggesting that they have no right to contribute, the meeting is weakened. So you may have to take pains to commend their contribution for its usefulness, as a

pre-emptive measure. You can reinforce this action by taking a written note of a point they make (always a plus for a member of a meeting) and by referring to it again later in the discussion (a double-plus).

Encourage the Clash of Ideas. But, at the same time, discourage the clash of personalities. A good meeting is not a series of dialogues between individual members and the chairman. Instead, it is a crossflow of discussion and debate, with the chairman occasionally guiding, mediating, probing, stimulating, and summarizing, but mostly letting the others thrash ideas out. However, the meeting must be a contention of *ideas,* not people.

If two people are starting to get heated, widen the discussion by asking a question of a neutral member of the meeting, preferably a question that requires a purely factual answer.

Watch Out for the Suggestion-Squashing Reflex. Students of meetings have reduced everything that can be said into questions, answers, positive reactions, and negative reactions. Questions can only seek, and answers only supply, three types of response: information, opinion, and suggestion.

In almost every modern organization, it is the suggestions that contain the seeds of future success. Although very few suggestions will ever lead to anything, almost all of them need to be given every chance. The trouble is that suggestions are much easier to ridicule than facts or opinions. If people feel that making a suggestion will provoke the negative reaction of being laughed at or squashed, they will soon stop. And if there is any status-jostling going on at the meeting, it is all too easy to use the occasion of someone's making a suggestion for the opportunity to take him down a peg. It is all too easy and a formula to ensure sterile meetings.

The answer is for you to take special notice and show special warmth when anyone makes a suggestion, and to discourage as sharply as you can the squashing reflex. This can often be achieved by requiring the squasher to produce a better suggestion on the spot. Few suggestions can stand up to squashing in their pristine state: your reflex must be to pick out the best part of one and get the other committee members to help build it into something that might work.

Come to the Most Senior People Last. Obviously, this cannot be a rule, but once someone of high authority has pronounced on a topic, the less senior members are likely to be inhibited. If you work up the pecking order instead of down it, you are apt to get a wider spread of views and ideas. But the juniors who start it off should only be asked for contributions within their personal experience and competence. ("Peter, you were at the Frankfurt Exhibition—what reactions did you pick up there?")

Close on a Note of Achievement. Even if the final item is left unresolved, you can refer to an earlier item that was well resolved as you close the meeting and thank the group.

If the meeting is not a regular one, fix the time and place of the next one before dispersing. A little time spent with appointment diaries at the end, especially if it is a gathering of five or more members, can save hours of secretarial telephoning later.

Following the Meeting

Your secretary may take the minutes (or better still, one of the members), but the minutes are your responsibility. They can be very brief, but they should include these facts:

1. The time and date of the meeting, where it was held, and who chaired it.
2. Names of all present and apologies for absence.
3. All agenda items (and other items) discussed and all decisions reached. If action was agreed on, record (and underline) the name of the person responsible for the assignment.
4. The time at which the meeting ended (important, because it may be significant later to know whether the discussion lasted 15 minutes or 6 hours).
5. The date, time, and place of the next committee meeting.

13. BUILDING RURAL COMMUNITY PARTICIPATION IN THE PLANNING PROCESS: IS IT POSSIBLE?

Ellen Russell Dunbar and Lynne Clemmons Morris

Planning and the planning structures of the 1970s were characterized by growth of increasingly powerful regional, national, and international organizations, which attempt to shape processes of economic and social development throughout the world. Contemporary planning models have been characterized as systems that promote the development of societies controlled by powerful technocratic elites. Many rural communities have undergone disruptive changes that were the result of decisions made by state or federal planners or corporate decision makers in distant metropolitan areas. Industrial firms make decisions to move a plant from one region to another, creating a major depression, taking away the principal source of livelihood in one town, and creating the chaos of "boom" in the other. Federal decision makers, for example, have decided to eliminate the Community Service Agency because it was small, powerless, and "ineffective" in the national scene. With that decision, the administrative, evaluative, and coordinating systems in thousands of counties and small towns across the nation were eliminated. Social planning can be criticized as an elitist model and as an urban model of practice. Additionally, planning systems have been rightly

described as the last bastions of male supremacy, resulting from an identification with the power structure.

Can anything be done to improve this situation? Is rural America eternally delegated to the periphery of the social systems? Can social planning exist in an environment other than that of the elite? Can social planning be a part of the solution to local problems of rural communities? Are women making any inroads into this male-dominated environment?

CRITIQUE OF TRADITIONAL FORMS OF SOCIAL PLANNING

Social planning is often regarded as an elitist process that dispenses goods and services in accordance with the wishes of the most powerful. It is an effort to control the course of future social events, the distribution of resources, and the delivery of human services. The elitist planning perspective identifies the source of influence and control over those events as being principally in the hands of people in positions of authority, power, and prestige in the society or community in question. A democratic approach to planning perceives the system in such a way as to place the ultimate power or control in the general population, in "the people." Elitist planning tends to emphasize technology and manipulation of larger systems and organizations. Even the Great Society programs of the 1960s that did so much to raise public consciousness about citizen participation were themselves essentially the product of a planning process that included only national leaders and intellectual elites who were insensitive to political and social relationships in local neighborhoods or rural counties.

Because of its reliance on technocratic skills and involvement of large, powerful formal organizations, social planning increasingly is being questioned as a model of community practice appropriate for work in rural areas. In their review of strategies for organizing in contemporary rural communities Woehle, Dwyer, and Askerooth conclude that "social planning is the least useful, and possibly the most damaging C.O. approach for rural America" (1981, p. 54). Proponents of colonialism theory as a framework for analyzing problems and developing strategies for change in rural areas have been particularly critical of social planning as an instrument for colonization of rural people (Lewis, Johnson, and Askins, 1978). This critique of traditional methods of social planning in rural areas can be summarized as follows:

1. Planning is a mechanism for imposing technocratic control on rural communities. We have previously defined planning as an attempt to control future social events, particularly the distribution of resources. As contemporary society confronts the condition of an increasingly limited environmental resource base for economic development, the term "rural" usually means land, water, timber, and energy resources which somebody else wants. Planning is the process used to establish outsiders' (usually multinational absentee corpora-

tions and metropolitan areas) control over rural resources, to direct those resources outside the community, and to minimize compensation to the communities from which these resources are taken.

2. Citizen participation in the planning process is the principal mechanism through which rural people are co-opted into the planning process, and through which their acquiescence to outsiders' takeover of community land and resources is secured. Often local citizens are not adequately informed or are deliberately misinformed by large, powerful organizations that control the planning process. As local communication networks become filled with inaccurate information, social ties based on trust and mutual respect may be severely eroded (Gold, 1979).

3. Social and health services planning assumes, in rural communities, a social control function similar to the functions of public assistance as described in Cloward and Piven's classic analysis, *Regulating the Poor* (1971). When rural communities protest the takeover of their land and resources, they are accommodated through the allocation of funds for the development of health and social services. In many rural communities, planning for social and health services begins with the assumption that outside takeover of local resources for purposes of development is inevitable and that the purpose of planning is to moderate its anticipated negative impacts on the local community.

ADAPTING TO A DEMOCRATIC CITIZEN PARTICIPATION MODEL

Citizen participation, that is representative citizen participation, requires some adaptation of a traditional social planning model. The significant adaptations relate to: (1) sequence of events, (2) selection of participants in the planning process, (3) communication style and networks, and (4) time orientation. As we will point out later, these are the areas that require different approaches in rural areas as well.

The sequencing of events in a planning process tends to be flexible. Kahn (1977), in his model, has emphasized flexibility by suggesting that planners may return at any time to an earlier stage of the planning process. A citizen participation process, however, needs to begin with the citizen participants. Regardless of what may be the ordered later events, the selection and involvement of citizens is the first step in the process. This was illustrated by Darlington (1976) in his descriptive study of neighborhood development projects in England. On their first attempt, they developed lovely plans and then put them on display in the community. They met with community people, solicited and accepted their recommendations, and incorporated many of the recommendations into their plans, but still were met with considerable opposition and criticism when the plans were operationalized. In the second neighborhood, they began with a representative group of citizens, who in turn decided what improvements they wanted. The latter approach was not only more accepted in the community, it was also more successful in accomplishing their principal goal, to stimulate owners to improve their properties.

The second consideration is who shall participate in the planning process? Traditional planners select community influentials and representatives of relevant political constituencies. Citizen participation implies broader represen-tation to include consumers. It does not mean token representation selected by the elite for a planning body that is controlled by the elite. To represent a constituent population, citizen participants need some attachment or identification with that population. That is best accomplished if a constituency selects the representatives or is the source used to identify potential participants.

Selecting participants begins with some analysis of the population affected by the planning process, be it a community or the elderly of the state. The analysis, including age, income, geographic location, and special interests, will be a guide for determining a numerical balance. A determination of whether the particular persons are in tune with their constituencies, and whether they could be identified by them as representatives, calls for careful exploration of community relationships and tapping into new social networks. Tapping social networks may require some communication adjustments—our third adaptation.

Communication styles and systems need adjustments to incorporate the citizens effectively. Most important may be the communication that occurs in the selection of participants. It is not sufficient to call existing board or committee members for recommendations. If there is a need for a person to represent a working-class community that is predominantly Hispanic, it will be necessary to contact their social networks. Planners tend to invite people who are like themselves or their elite board members to make recommendations and later are surprised when the community represented is not pleased. There is not space here to delineate the potential social networks in any community, but let us give a few examples from rural situations and women's networks. For representation from rural communities, we might tap Cooperative Extension, church conferences, the school personnel, booster clubs, or other local service clubs, health districts, local newspaper editors, or the Tribal Council. For women's networks, we might contact the National Organization of Women (NOW), homemakers' clubs, churches, local college women's centers, health districts, the League of Women Voters, Deltas, or Links. Representative participation requires communication with the social networks that are to be represented.

The communication style of meetings may also need adapting. The "Snap, Crackle, and Pop" of business style with a long, wordy, and complex written report will leave the person with less education and different life experience lost and frustrated. Written material needs to be brief and clear without professional jargon. If each participant can be contacted in advance of meetings to discuss the issues and the material and to see if there are questions or problems, communication problems can be avoided or corrected.

Rural people will tend to expect communication to be personal. All of life is more personalized in small towns. There is not anonymity, and therefore life is accommodated to that life-style. Formal memos are not compatible with the informality in communities where people know one another over a long period of time. These long-term relationships also mean that communication has to account for existing rivalries, antagonisms, and friendships.

Time orientation is a fourth adjustment for citizen participation. Professional planners tend to be ethnocentric in their orientation to time, assuming there is only one logical orientation. Some rural communities have as much time as it takes to reach consensus (Vidich and Bensman, 1968). Time rhythms go with seasons and/or harvests. Some people have to travel far using a lot of time to get to meetings.

Rural culture is more oriented to the present than to the future. Rural folks are more likely to view events as being the result of fate (U.S. Department of Health, Education and Welfare, 1979). Contrary to the basic premise of planning, the fatalist attitude with a present orientation would not see the possibilities for altering the future and may be more sensitive than the planner to systemic, "unanticipated" consequences that various change efforts might precipitate. That attitude allows events to take their "natural" course. This "here-and-now" orientation makes it difficult to conceptualize future events or to anticipate with some measure of realism that a particular change is about to occur. It is difficult to be motivated to plan for something that one cannot foresee. Because change is less likely to occur, rural persons often are not oriented to change and do not see the urgency often felt by urban planners. All activity and persons are highly visible in a small town and anyone out of pace, moving in a different time, is very noticeable. We know no formula for handling time orientation conflicts, but it is essential to shed the ethnocentrism and explore, with participants, what can be achieved, how long it will take, who will be present, and when to accomplish the goals.

CITIZEN PARTICIPATION STRATEGIES IN RURAL PLANNING

Given the important criticisms of traditional approaches to social planning in rural areas, there is a clear need either to (1) develop workable democratic approaches to rural planning, or (2) abandon planning as a useful method of community practice in rural areas. We have identified several approaches to citizen participation in rural planning which address problems of technocratic control linked with traditional social planning. These approaches suggest that social planning can be adapted to serve the interests of local communities and that rural citizens can play meaningful roles in the planning process. All of the following strategies expand the functions of citizen participation considerably beyond the traditional role of "giving input" or "voicing concerns."

1. Teach planning skills to local citizens. Train local residents so that they can carry out actual planning tasks. Residents' familiarity with community values, history, and physical environment are assets which can be incorporated into the planning process. Training can include both acquisition of technical skills (Dyballa, Raymond, and Hahn, 1981) and activities which help citizens to envision alternative futures and conceptualize planning possibilities (Morris and Morris, 1981).

2. Develop citizen participation roles that include the retrieval of community history as a key process in community revitalization. An important issue for planning in small communities is citizen articulation of not only "What do we want to change?" and "What do we need?" but also "What do we want to retain?" "From what patterns of social interaction (for example, festivals and mutual aid activities such as volunteer fire departments) do we derive a sense of community purpose and accomplishment?" "What features of our communi-

ty do we value and want to preserve?" Community history projects also provide key roles for elderly residents, an adaptation particularly important for planning in small communities with large numbers of older persons. Excellent descriptions of the uses of community history in rural planning are found in Poston (1950) and Robertson and Robertson (1978).

3. Combine planning and community development approaches in rural community organization practice. A critical planning task in small communities is to decide which problems lend themselves to solution through a local community development approach emphasizing self-help resources within the community and which problems require coordination with larger resource systems located outside the community, as emphasized in regional planning. Local citizens are the major source of knowledge of informal networks and self-help capabilities, and this knowledge must become part of the planning process. While residents' experience with sophisticated data-collection techniques may be limited, there is a greater general knowledge of the community because it is easier to see relationships in smaller systems and because there may have been considerable community stability over time. Planning in rural areas is characterized both by wide diversity among communities in terms of culture, ethnicity, income, types of employment, history, terrain, and climate, which require planning at the local level, and by problems that cut across communities and require planning at a regional level.

4. Emphasize citizen participation in both resource assessment and needs assessment. Many rural communities are characterized both by need for additional

employment opportunities and social services and by lack of control over the outflow of existing resources. Assessment processes that generate both types of information are critical in addressing the social services/social control dilemma previously mentioned. Resource assessments of control over land, employment, and mineral resources conducted by local citizens such as the recent Appalachian lands study (Appalachian Alliance Land Ownership Task Force, 1981) have encouraged reassessment of coal and timber lands, building a stronger and more equitable tax base in many rural communities. Through participation in planning, local citizens are gaining skills in obtaining and interpreting vital information that controls their futures. This is an illustration of the ways in which physical and social planning are critically interrelated in rural communities.

5. Develop a network for exchanging information among local communities. In many areas of the United States, rural communities are beginning to build a body of information about planning based on the experiences of others and are developing networks for exchanging this information. Sometimes this is done through leadership development institutes sponsored by regional colleges and universities or through national organizations such as Rural America and Rural American Women. Rather than cooptation of local communities into traditional planning structures, participation in planning may, in some areas, be building a network for future coordinated political action and policy initiatives supported by an organized rural constituency.

6. Include within the citizen participation process a community examination of the costs and benefits of different planning alternatives. Costs and benefits often are quite different for (1) the larger society, (2) the local community as a whole, and (3) various groups within the local community. Through the experiences and efforts of local communities, some changes have occurred in the ideological and legal bases of planning which, in the past, have justified the taking of societal and outsider control of local resources in the public interest. Concepts such as "eminent domain" and "appropriative water rights" are being challenged by local communities. For example, efforts directed at preservation of agricultural lands have encouraged replacing "production of maximum monetary profits" with "production of food" as the highest and best use definition of prime farmlands (Wolf, 1981).

"RURBANIZING" PLANNING: ADAPTATIONS IN THE RURAL ENVIRONMENT

Current planning systems are generally based in urban headquarters or state capitals. Rural areas are on the periphery of the planning process and generally are conceptualized as that space between urban areas. Yet strangely it is in these small towns and counties where the massive national plans are most likely to interface. It is here that plans for aging services, for the developmentally disabled, and the mentally ill are administered, supervised, or even carried out by the same person. It is here that economic development under the community action agency and economic development under the economic development agency are handled by the same committee. We might be able to separate mental health from social service in Washington, D.C., but not in Colville, Washington. In order to prevent being like a few chickens to whom twenty people are each throwing a few grains, the rural communities need some organizational framework from which to orchestrate and to participate in the powerful planning organizations. The Kellogg Foundation has funded some programs to attempt to develop such alternative structures. Other organizations that might assist but have been part of the rural structure for some time include Cooperative Extension, the Grange, Farm Bureau, and public welfare agencies. These latter have not expanded to incorporate the new service networks and programs.

Another alternative which has been suggested in Wisconsin is the Ruralplex.

The basic idea is for a group of small cities within close proximity to plan for and provide various public and private services for the total group of communities. One community might be the site of the junior college or trade/technical school, while another provides a regional hospital, and a third community acts as a major light industry or high technology center. (Blakely and Bradshaw, 1981, p. 17)

Smaller sizes make the issues more clear cut and often more easily resolved. Smallness also limits resources and means that no single organization could support the efforts of a planner. The planning model increasingly utilized in rural areas is that of the circuit rider planner who works with a number of small communities within a particular region (Watts, 1980). The circuit rider model is particularly adapted to the dual needs for both local and regional planning in rural areas.

RURAL CITIZEN PARTICIPATION

Rapid societal changes, including development of management informa-

tion systems, centralized budgets and budget controls, and rapid transportation and communications systems make it increasingly difficult for rural organizations to remain in isolation from the broader society. There are increasing demands to enter the larger systems but at the same time they see that they are easily swallowed up in bigness if they do not have alternative organizational structures. There is, in other words, increasing need for organization and planning.

The adaptations needed for citizen participation apply to rural as well as urban environments. In addition, there are other factors that need to be considered when planning is applied to the rural community. First, because planning has not been institutionalized or legitimized in most rural communities, that process has to occur. Planners should not expect the same level of status as they may receive in the urban area. The challenge is to earn that acceptance. Rural residents first will assess the ability and credibility of the individual planner and his/her efforts to resolve specific local problems. Rural planners should be prepared to sell themselves as competent persons and demonstrate that planning is useful in addressing a specific, concrete issue (Getzels and Thurow, 1979). Second, resources are different and often scarce in rural areas. This requires a creative use of what exists and an ability to recognize a resource in a different form than what is found in the more highly technical urban environment. Third, because timing is different in rural cultures (the hurried urbanite looks rather ridiculous when Moses Lake is waiting for the wheat to ripen), planners have to relate to the rhythm of the environment in which they are working and not vice versa. Where life has for generations related to forces of nature, not futuristic planning, there is a strong cultural barrier to overcome and this should be accepted as a part of the process. Fourth, to counteract the tendency for rural communities to be on the periphery, catching leftover crumbs, there is a need to organize rural-based systems crossing some geographic barriers to establish a rural power base. Fifth, communication style and networks are different in rural than in urban environments and planning has to adapt to that style whether it be talking more slowly or arranging meetings on different schedules. The existing service networks such as those of agriculture or education must be recognized and tapped.

EXAMPLE: PARTNERSHIP FOR RURAL IMPROVEMENT

The Partnership for Rural Improvement (PRI) was established in 1976 with a grant from the Kellogg Foundation. The original goals were to: (1) strengthen community problem-solving capacity, (2) increase the effectiveness of educational institutions and public service agencies in contributing to the solution of community problems, and (3) develop and evaluate communication and organizational linkages among educational institutions, public service agencies, and local communities (Schwalbe and Hagood, 1981).

The major thrust of the program is to use resources, including faculty, of the universities and colleges to help rural towns and counties develop their ability to solve problems and to facilitate planning. The development of local capacity is classical community development with a multiorganizational approach. The projects that have developed in the

six years of this program are varied. Two of them illustrate rural planning adaptations. The first example is the development of a domestic violence task force in the county seat of Ferry County, a sparsely populated lumbering and mining community. The population includes the descendants of early settlers, a few miners, workers of the lumber industry, "back to the landers," and some urban expatriates. A domestic violence program was needed, as a mental health professional explained, to "get out the word that spouse beating and child abuse is not acceptable."

PRI activity is initiated by a community consultant (planner/organizer) based at the community college. In this case the community consultant learned from the state office of domestic violence that they had designated some funds for the development of a rural domestic violence program. Not untypically, the staff of the domestic violence program had no conception of how to approach the eastern side of the mountains, the large rural area. Negotiations began for PRI staff to assist in their program development. Those negotiations were slow partly because there was considerable caution on the part of the women involved in domestic violence programs.

In the meantime, the community had solicited the participation of a social work faculty person to work with her to provide some board training and staff consultation at the Community Service Center, the agency that provides services for the county in the areas of mental health, aging, developmental disabilities, and alcohol and drug abuse. This was part of another project, but one of the mentioned needs during those sessions was domestic violence information, prevention, and treatment. A linkage was made, and PRI staff with staff from the state domestic violence program traveled to the north and met with the woman on the community service center staff who had shown interest in the development of a program. They decided to organize a local task force. Planning who might be included and how to get started all occurred at that meeting. The local mental health professional did the local organizing work but relied heavily on materials, information, and support that were offered her from PRI staff and from the state domestic violence and sexual assault programs. The task force, now in operation, includes police, the local judge, school personnel, social services, mental health, health department, and a chiropractor. Their major goal at this time is community education, but the effect has already been felt in the first year, particularly with the referrals from the judge. Another interesting factor is that in most cases, in contrast to urban programs, the treatment begins with the man, the batterer, rather than with the victim. This illustrates use of a rural-based system, PRI, to pull resources into several communities simultaneously, using a process sensitive to local communication networks and local timing.

The second example is in a somewhat desolate wheat-farming desert-like county near Spokane that has been selected by the giant Washington Water Power Company as the site for a future coal-fired electric plant. When the location was selected in the mid-1970s, the lure of progress was overwhelmingly more compelling than any concern for environmental pollution or loss of country life-style. There was strong local support for the project. They did not suffer for lack of help with planning. The Council of Governments for the two affected

counties received a grant from Farmers Home Administration to hire a circuit-rider planner. She worked with the local officials and Cooperative Extension. She also brought in the Eastern Washington University Planning Department and Partnership for Rural Improvement as resources. They organized educational meetings and workshops. Financial workshops for local government officials were well received. At those sessions they worked on projecting their own budgets into future conditions.

Meanwhile, without local input, President Carter designated this area as one of five demonstration areas, and the state of Washington received a planning grant and placed three planners (socioeconomic impact team) in Creston, a town with a population of 310. Washington Water Power also hired a consultant planner from a Texas-based firm. So we have one planner hired with funds requested by local people and four gifts from afar. The impact team organized citizen groups, wrote plans and impact statements, and left.

The federal-state "shot-gun" approach was to provide results in the form of impressive documents. This approach may get more grant money but does not change the status or structure of the community. The circuit-rider planner, using a citizen participation process, helped local officials produce some plans they could call their own and behind which they could stand firm when developers came with money for a trailer park where there were no planned sewers or transportation.

EXAMPLE: THE CITIZENS' GRASSROOTS COMMITTEES

Originally organized through the assistance of the South Carolina Division of

Rural Development and Special Economic Assistance, the Grassroots Committees or Councils exist in every county in the state. They are currently the major vehicle within the state for citizen participation in public and social services planning. The Grassroots Committees or Councils have identified in their purposes a range of community organization activities such as participation in planning, advocacy, and community development. They include:

a. citizen participation in public/government affairs.
b. self-help improvement.
c. community motivation and *unity*.
d. relaying needs of rural communities to appropriate agencies/officials/others.
e. monitoring the "powers that be" in communities, e.g., city, county council, school board; DSS [Department of Social Services].
f. providing information to grassroots citizens on public programs, services available and how to go about getting funds.
g. serve as a forum for the discussion of rural needs and concerns.
h. serve as an advocate of rural people (South Carolina Division of Rural Development and Special Economic Assistance, 1980).

In addition, the Grassroots Committees and Councils have provided important training opportunities for leadership development. Several council members have been elected to the state legislature. Current activities of the Grassroots Committees and Councils include:

1. Publicizing the needs of communities with high levels of rural poverty. These have been identified through research conducted by the Division of Rural Development. The governor and other public officials have been invited to make visits to these communities, with appropriate press coverage. Public agencies for providing community services also are identified and interviewed.

2. Serving as a network for reaching rural people to encourage public participation in social services planning. Currently, the state Department of Developmental Disabilities is conducting hearings in each county concerning needs of developmentally disabled persons in rural areas. The Grassroots Committees and Councils have been effective in generating a high level and diversity of citizen participation. They are less successful in monitoring the actual use of this information in state planning and policy making.

3. Holding annual statewide meetings to exchange information, conduct workshops for membership, and engage in meetings and discussions with state elected and administrative officials.

SUMMARY

Although traditional social planning often has been based on an elitist, technocratic model, our review of planning efforts in rural communities suggests that, yes, citizen participation in the planning process is still possible. Believing that social planning models can be adapted to the rural environment, we have analyzed several planning systems existing in rural environments, examining their applications of citizen participation approaches. These planning efforts identify ways in which "planning with people" can become a reality in rural communities and offer models of the diversity of creative approaches to citizen participation in planning which currently are being developed in, by, and with rural communities.

REFERENCES

Appalachian Alliance Land Ownership Task Force, *Land Ownership Patterns and Their Impacts on Appalachian Communities* (Boone, N. C.: Center for Appalachian Studies, 1981).

Blakely, Edward J., and Ted K. Bradshaw, "Implications of Social and Economic Changes on Rural Areas," *Human Services in the Rural Environment* 6, no. 2 (1981): 11–22.

Cloward, Richard A., and Frances Fox Piven, *Regulating the Poor: The Functions of Public Welfare* (New York: Random House, Inc., 1971).

Darlington, Richard, "Successful Public Participation Experiments," *Planning and Administration* 3, no. 2 (Autumn 1976): 35–44.

Dyballa, Cynthia D., Lyle S. Raymond, Jr., and Alan J. Hahn, *The Tug Hill Program: A Regional Planning Option for Rural Areas* (Syracuse, N.Y.: Syracuse University Press, 1981).

Getzels, Judith, and Charles Thurow, *Rural and Small Town Planning* (Chicago: Planners Press, 1979).

Gold, Raymond, "Industrial Trespass at Colstrip, Montana," in William Burch and Daniel R. Field, eds., *Land Use and Community: A Biosocial Approach to Environmental Assessment* (Ann Arbor, Mich.: Ann Arbor Science Publishers, 1979).

Kahn, Alfred J., "Definition of the Task: Facts, Projects, and Inventories," in Neil Gilbert and Harry Specht, eds., *Planning for Social Welfare: Issues, Models, and Tasks* (Englewood Cliffs, N.J.: Prentice-Hall, 1977), pp. 78–86.

Lewis, Helen Matthews, Linda Johnson, and Don Askins, *Colonialism in Modern America: The Appalachian Case* (Boone, N.C.: The Appalachian Consortium Press, 1978).

Morris, Lynne Clemmons, and Judson Henry Morris, Jr., "Preparing Human Service Workers for Practice in Boom Communities," *Human Services in the Rural Environment* 6, no. 1 (1981): 22–28.

Poston, Richard, *Small Town Renaissance* (New York: Harper and Row, 1950).

Robertson, James, and Carolyn Robertson, *The Small Towns Book: Show Me the Way to Go Home* (Garden City, N.Y.: Anchor Press, 1978).

Schwalbe, Michael L., and Richard A. Hagood, "Partnership for Rural Improvement: Washington State University, Pullman," in *Rural Development and Higher Education: The Linking of Community and Method* (Battle Creek, Mich.: W. K. Kellogg Foundation, 1981) pp. 151–165.

South Carolina Division of Rural Development and Special Economic Assistance, "Keeping Grassroots Groups Alive and Well," Columbia, S. C.: 1980).

U.S. Department of Health, Education and Welfare, *Mental Health and Rural America: An Overview and Annotated Bibliography,* DHEW Publication No. (ADM), 78-753 (Washington, D.C.: U.S. Government Printing Office, 1979).

Vidich, Arthur J., and Joseph Bensman, *Small Town in Mass Society* (Princeton, N.J.: Princeton University Press, 1968).

Watts, Ann, "Planners' Perceptions of Rural/Small Town Issues," *Human Services in the Rural Environment* 5, no. 5 (1980): 15–21.

Woehle, Ralph, Judy Dwyer, and Gary Askerooth, "Changing Rural Society and Its Implications for C.O.," *Social Development Issues* 5, nos. 2 and 3 (1981): 53–61.

Wolf, Peter, *Land in America: Its Value, Use and Control* (New York: Random House, 1981).

14. LEGISLATIVE ADVOCACY: SEVEN EFFECTIVE TACTICS

Ronald B. Dear and Rino J. Patti

It is often said that the legislative system is more effective in defeating bad bills than in enacting good ones. Indeed, the legislative process can be characterized as a series of obstacles that collectively constitute a formidable barrier to the passage of legislation, good or bad. The most telling evidence in this regard is that roughly one in five bills introduced in state and federal legislatures becomes public law.[1] For some this may be a source of comfort, but for the human services professional seeking enactment of a bill that will have a positive impact on the health and welfare of a population, these are poor odds.

The purpose of this article is to present tactics that will increase the advocate's chances of obtaining a favorable outcome on legislation as demonstrated by empirical evidence assembled by the authors and others. The tactics fall short of a complete model of legislative advocacy. Omitted from consideration are such efforts as involvement in political campaigns, the use of community pressure, coalition-building, and the wielding of interpersonal influence. Although these and other tactics are potentially important to a fully articulated model of advocacy and have received some attention in the literature, there is yet little empirical evidence that systematically links them with legislative outcomes.[2]

The primary concern in what follows is to suggest tactics that can readily be used by part-time, single-issue advocates who make an occasional foray into the legislative arena to promote a bill of immediate interest to their agency or a client constituency. Such people are generally not immersed in the legislative culture or aware of the nuances and subtleties of the legislative process. They seldom have the opportunity to develop the resources, skills, and credibility that are the stock-in-trade of the seasoned lobbyist. Notwithstanding these limitations, part-time advocates can play a crucial role in promoting constructive social legislation if they focus on using time and energy appropriately. The seven tactical guidelines presented in this article are reasonably concrete steps that increase the probability of obtaining favorable legislative outcomes. In general, the tactics suggested are those that may be implemented by advocates with limited power and resources.

BACKGROUND

The authors' research, which provides much of the basis for this discussion, involved an analysis of all 183 social and health services bills introduced in the forty-fourth session (1975-77) of the Washington State legislature and subsequently referred to the Social and Health Services Committees of the house and senate. The data collected on each bill included legislative outcome; process characteristics, such as source of request, date of introduction, number of sponsors, nature of sponsorship, committee deliberations, and number and magnitude of amendments; characteristics of sponsors, such as the prime sponsor's party, the number of terms served, committee membership, positions of leadership, occupation, age, and sex; and substantive characteristics, such as subject matter, magnitude of change proposed, nature of change proposed, and fiscal impact. The data were aggregated and analyzed to determine the relationships, if any, between the outcome of each bill and its process, sponsor, and substantive characteristics.

For purposes of this study, outcomes were defined in terms of whether a bill remained in, or was reported out of, the Social and Health Services Committee to which it was originally referred. It was necessary to resort to this restricted definition because the number of bills in the sample that ultimately became public law was so small as to preclude meaningful analysis. In addition, since a committee's decision in the house of origin is by far the most critical obstacle a bill must traverse, this criterion arose as the best surrogate measure of a bill's success or failure. The authors also conducted a pilot study on social and health services bills in the forty-third session (1973-75) of the Washington State legislature. This article also reports some findings from that study. When it was possible to equate the data obtained from the two studies, this was done. The seven suggested tactics follow and are accompanied by a discussion of the empirical findings on which they are based.

EMPIRICALLY BASED TACTICS

1. Introduce the bill early in the session or, ideally, before the session has begun.

Any politician, lobbyist, political scientist, or careful observer of government readily acknowledges that the legislative process—the trail from idea to enactment—is a tortuous one beset with an incredible number of stumbling blocks, hurdles, and pitfalls.[3] To make matters worse, the constitution in most states permits the legislature to be in session only sixty to ninety days, often in alternate years, and the bill cutoff date—the last day a regular bill may be introduced—is usually about halfway into the session. This is why some political scientists contend that "no single factor has a greater effect on the legislative environment than the constitutional restriction on the length of session."[4]

In spite of short sessions and early cutoff dates, in the 1975 and 1976 sessions approximately 200,000 bills were introduced into the fifty state legislatures in this country. For most states the number of new bills averaged between 2,500 and 4,000, although the number ranged from under 1,000 in several states to an astonishing 34,000 in New York.[5] Clearly, there is no way each piece of this bewildering volume of legislation can be considered with equal seriousness, especially by part-time citizen-legislators buffeted by constant and conflicting storms of special interests.

Given these constraints, it has been suggested that introducing a bill early in the session, or even before the session begins (prefiling the bill), increases the chances of favorable consideration. There are a number of reasons why this is considered a good tactic.

First, bills that are introduced early in the session frequently are better pieces of legislation because the sponsor or sponsoring group has had the time to do the necessary research and a greater opportunity to see that the measure is well drafted. A striking example of the value of careful drafting can be seen in the success rate of bills drafted by the Legislative Council, the former research office of the Washington State legislature. An astounding 93 percent of all measures drafted by the council were passed into law. All these bills were drafted prior to the beginning of the session.[6]

Second, the early introduction of bills allows the advocate more time to lobby legislators and committee staff about the positive features of the bill and to press for hearings, muster community support, counter potential opposition, and negotiate changes. Third, early bill introduction is one of the best ways to avoid the last-minute legislative logjam. In the frantic rush of the closing days of a session, many bills are voted down after being given scant consideration.

The authors' research clearly supports the desirability of early bill introduction. For example, of eighty-one bills introduced into the house and senate Social and Health Services Committees of the forty-fourth biennium of the Washington State legislature during the first four weeks, 61 percent were reported out of committee, whereas only 51 percent of the bills introduced thereafter were reported out of committee. Moreover, a bill's chance of becoming law deteriorated rather markedly as the session progressed. That is, the chances were better if the bill was introduced in the first ten days of the session, dwindled somewhat in the second ten days, and were worse yet after the legislature had been in session more than twenty days. The authors' pilot study of the forty-third session uncovered a similar pattern: bills introduced early in the regular session had a fifty-fifty chance of being reported out, whereas only one in three of the bills introduced later were reported out. At least one other study offers further empirical support for early bill introduction.[7] It should be noted that measures can be introduced late in the session and still move through all phases of the legislative process and pass into law. In such instances, though, there is usually a majority in support of the measure at the start or a powerful sponsor who sees that significant opposition is overcome.

2. It is advisable to have more than one legislator sponsor a bill. Bills with multiple sponsorship tend to have a better chance of making their way through the legislative obstacle course than those with a single sponsor. This is what one might expect. Additional sponsors increase the likelihood that a bill will be heard. Since the volume of legislation is so great, legislators can read only a small portion of the hundreds of bills introduced into each of their committees and are likely to be knowledgeable about only a tiny fraction of the thousands of bills active in the legislature in any one session. Naturally, they must rely on their colleagues to advise them on the great bulk of bills they have neither the time nor interest to read. In this context, multiple sponsors serve two important functions: they are likely to make the bill more visible, and they multiply the power that can be applied to push the bill past crucial legislative obstacles. In essence, then, multiple sponsors not only tend to give a stamp of credibility to a measure, they can also become all-important advocates who can be called on to muster collegial support within the legislature, press for hearings, make the necessary trades and compromises to move a bill out of committee, push to get it scheduled by the rules committee, and apply pressure to get it passed by both houses.

The value of multiple sponsors tends to be enhanced even further when at least one of the sponsors is a member or a chair of the substantive committee or the rules committee. Such legislators can be particularly effective, because one common practice used to determine which bill will be given a hearing is to allow each member of the committee (usually by rotation) to select the measure they want heard that day. Additional sponsors in the legislative chamber can thus use their individual and collective influence to have a bill reported out of the substantive committee and also out of the rules committee and onto the floor of the chamber for a vote. Finally, the more sponsors a bill has, the more legislators to whom the advocate will have access and the opportunity to influence.

Data obtained in the authors' study support the proposition that bills with more than two sponsors are more likely to be reported out of committee. In the forty-fourth biennium, there were 183 bills introduced into the Social and Health Services Committees. Seventy-three bills had two or fewer sponsors, and the remaining 110 bills had three or more sponsors. Less than one-half (48 percent) of the bills with one or two sponsors were reported out of committee, as opposed to 60 percent of the bills with three or more sponsors.

Analysis of all bills that successfully passed the Washington State legislature during one entire biennium (this includes all bills, not just those dealing with health and welfare matters) strikingly illustrates the efficacy of multiple sponsorship. There was a total of 465 successful bills; 225 were originally sponsored in the house, and the other 240 in the senate. Table 14.1 leaves little doubt that the more sponsors a bill has, the better its chance of passage.

This table warrants serious attention by advocates who may question whether it is really worth the effort to seek more than one sponsor on a pet measure. Of the 225 successful house bills, 200 originally had more than one sponsor. Thus, an astonishing 89 percent of all house bills that were initially reported out of committee (the authors' criterion of success in their analysis), passed both houses, and were signed into law had multiple sponsorship. Moreover, one-third of all successful bills had six or more sponsors. Conversely, only 25 of the 225 successful house bills—a mere 11 pecent—originally had a single sponsor, and of those 25 bills, 14 later gained additional sponsors. Thus, only 11 bills, or less than 5 percent of all the bills that passed the house, had a single sponsor. This means the chances a bill that retains a single sponsor has of becoming law is about one in twenty—even worse odds than one would expect from chance alone, which would be about one in five. Further analysis of the data in Table 14.1 indicates that the modal number of sponsors on successful bills was three, and the mean number of sponsors was between five and six.

A similar picture emerges from analysis of the 240 successful Washington State senate bills, although the data are less striking, possibly because the senate is a smaller body tending to consist of a higher proportion of senior legislators. Of the 240 bills signed into law, less than 10 percent had a single sponsor. Both the mean and modal number of sponsors on successful bills was three.

3. The advocate of social legislation should seek to obtain the sponsorship of the majority party, especially when the majority is Democratic. It is even more beneficial to obtain meaningful biparti-

san sponsorship with the primary sponsor a member of the Democratic majority. It is sometimes said that political parties are not as influential as they were at one time.[8] In spite of what may be a lessening of party influence and control, the fact remains that 96 out of 99 state legislative chambers in the United States are elected on a partisan ballot.[9] Wise advocates tailor their tactics to the reality of partisan politics.

TABLE 14.1
Number of Original Sponsors of 225 Successful House Bills in the Washington State Legislature, Forty-Fifth Biennial Session, 1977 – 1979

Number of Original Sponsors[a]	Bills[b]		Total Number of Sponsors
	Number	Percent	
1	25	11	25
2	27	12	54
3	47	21	141
4 – 5	55	24	238
6 or more	71	32	807
Total	225	100	1.265

[a]The table shows only the number of original sponsors. By definition, committee bills always have the sponsorship of the majority of the members of the committee. Such bills almost always gain more sponsors than they had when originally introduced.

[b]The total of 225 successful bills includes all committee legislation and special request legislation — legislation requested by governmental agencies or by the governor. Almost one-half (47.5 percent) of the 225 bills became committee bills, and over one-fifth (21 percent) were special request legislation.

SOURCE: Compiled from data in *Legislative Report, 1977: Final Edition, Forty-fifth Regular and Extraordinary Sessions* (Olympia. Washington: House and Senate Research Center. July 1977).

A study of Democratic and Republican votes in Washington State on selected key human service issues, such as social services and income maintenance, points to the partisan nature of voting on social legislation.[10] Only contested votes were chosen for this study because they were the ones that were thought to reflect genuine party differences most accurately. There were twenty-four contested votes in the house and eleven in the senate. Every legislator was given a score based on his or her voting record on these key human service measures. A "perfect" score would be 100 percent and would indicate that the legislator had voted in favor of all contested social legislation.

In the senate, the scores for Republicans ranged from a low of 11 percent (presumably the most conservative) to a high of 91 percent, with a mean score for all Republican senators of 65 percent. Senate Democrats ranged from a low of 64 percent (again, the most conservative or anti–human-service Democratic legislator) to a high of 100 percent, with a mean percentage of 89. Fifteen Democratic senators voted in favor of all contested social legislation and were given scores of 100 percent.

In the house, the voting records of its ninety-eight members were assessed in regard to twenty-four contested human service votes. The lower chamber was evenly divided with forty-nine Democrats and forty-nine Republicans, a most unusual and awkward political phenomenon. As might be anticipated under such circumstances, the partisan flavor of the legislature was even more striking, especially as it pertained to social legislation. The forty-nine Republican representatives had a mean percentage of forty-five, meaning that they voted against more than half of all key human service legislation. Scores ranged from a low of 9 percent to a high of 79 percent. Democrats had a mean percentage of 93, with a range from 71 to 100. Only one Republican scored higher than the lowest Democrat.

These findings are consistent with those of other research that links party affiliation with voting behavior. However, it is not clear whether the tendency of Democrats to support social welfare policy is attributable to these legislators' urban bases with low-income and minority constituencies or to their party affiliation. Regardless of the reason for Democratic support of welfare policies, it is enough of a reality for Rothman to advise,

In keeping with popular views on the subject, Democrats are natural allies for programs necessitating government intervention. . . . Working through Democratic legislators . . . would appear to be a useful strategy for furthering many human service objectives.[11]

Advocates would be well advised to adjust to and develop tactics that recognize the partisan characteristics of the legislature they wish to influence.

Although conventional wisdom buttressed by the empirical data recorded here might well lead the advocate to think that partisan support is sufficient, this is not the whole story. Additional evidence indicates that, in some instances, bipartisan sponsorship may improve the chances of passage. The study of the forty-fourth legislative session indicates that social and health legislation with bipartisan sponsorship does just as well, and at times much better, than measures with only partisan support. Data from this research show that equal percentages of partisan and bipartisan bills were reported out of committee. The pilot study of the forty-third session found that 40 percent of the bipartisan bills were reported out of committee, whereas only 20 percent of partisan bills left the committee of their origin. Neither study found that partisan sponsorship (even of the majority party) was an advantage over bipartisan sponsorship.

Successful legislation is based on compromise, forming coalitions, gaining support, and nullifying opposition. It is important to gain the support of those normally seen as allies as well as those with whom one may not be in ideological agreement. Too often, those advocating a measure, particularly in social legislation, tend to write off the other party (usually the Republican party) as too conservative. This could be a fatal error for the advocate. In short, bipartisan sponsorship is a way of extending the influence of the majority party by making the measure more acceptable to a broad range of legislators.

4. Whenever possible, the advocate should obtain the support of the governor and of relevant state agencies. No bill becomes law unless it is signed by the chief executive. During a recent biennium, the governor of Washington State vetoed or partially vetoed 6 percent of all legislation passed by both houses. If for no other reason than to avoid the possibility of a veto, it is wise to gain executive support.

Since state agencies also have a significant influence over the fate of legislation, it is a good idea not to have opposition from them, although at times it is not possible to avoid such conflict. This is especially true when agencies perceive the legislation as working against their interests, a not uncommon occurrence in social welfare. Moreover, the position taken by representatives of relevant state agencies is usually listened to most seriously by legislators. This is understandable when one considers that people in state agencies are usually viewed by legislators as the experts in the substantive area of legislation. They are the ones who must live with the law, translate it into administrative procedures, and see that the legal intent is carried out. As a consequence, opposition from the department of social services tends to decrease a bill's chances of passage. The opposite is also true. When a bill is supported by the relevant state agency or, better yet, requested by it, chances of passage are high.

How well does agency-sponsored legislation do? The findings in the Washington State studies indicate that such bills do well. In each study, agency-requested legislation had a significantly better chance of being reported out of committee than bills without such requests. In the forty-fourth session, for example, 75 percent of all agency-requested bills were passed out of committee, compared to 55 percent of all bills. In the pilot study, 39 percent of all 227 bills were reported out of Social and Health Services Committees, in contrast to 54 percent of all department-requested bills.

Other data lend strong support to the contention that agency-requested legislation has a high probability of success and an excellent chance of becoming law. In the analysis of 465 successful bills from the forty-fifth biennium, 115, or a full 25 percent, were agency-requested legislation.

5. The advocate should seek influential legislators as sponsors of proposed legislation, provided that they are willing to exercise their influence in promoting the bill. Given the obstacles to the passage of legislation in state legislatures, it seems logical to select as sponsors individuals who enjoy power and influence with their colleagues. Influence is at best an elusive phenomenon, easier to observe in concrete instances than to measure systematically in a global way. Since most advocates do not have the opportunity to become intimately familiar

with the distribution of influence in a legislative chamber, it often becomes necessary to use readily observed characteristics as a basis for inferences regarding the possession of influence. Three such characteristics are thought to be particularly important in this regard: party leadership, committee leadership, and committee membership.

The influence of party leaders, including the majority and minority leaders, whips, and caucus officers, derives in large part from their experience and skill in the legislative process and their central role in formulating policy strategy on critical issues and in seeing that this strategy is implemented on the floor. In addition, as Truman suggests, party leaders often exert influence on their colleagues by virtue of the credibility and trust that they have come to enjoy over years of service.

Legislative skill, usually acquired only after considerable experience in a law-making body, creates its own following; less experienced or overly busy members will often be guided by a skilled veteran when a vote is called for, and in a fashion that cannot be explained simply in terms of party loyalty or the trading of votes.[12]

Committee chairpersons tend to be particularly powerful in regard to the fate of bills that fall under their committee's jurisdiction. The following comment, although it may overstate the power of chairpersons, suggests something of the central position that such legislators occupy:

The chairman of a committee ... was in a particularly powerful position. He was responsible for scheduling committee meetings and had considerable leeway in determining the extent to which the committee met.... He had control over the agenda, and given a surplus of bills could easily exercise a strategy of delay. Majority party members were faced with many committee assignments ... sufficient to distract them from the procedural preferences of committee chairmen. ... The fate of much legislation could be determined by ... the chairmen.[13]

The power of chairpersons is not this unbridled in many states, but even when their discretion is circumscribed by rules, procedures, or party discipline, these individuals are influential in determining the outcome of bills that are within the purview of their committee.

Committee members are also likely to be influential with bills that come under the scrutiny of the committees on which they serve. Legislators, faced with an enormous range of issues in diverse fields, seek to handle this load by dividing the labor among committees. Members of these committees are expected to develop a special expertise in specific areas. Others, preoccupied with work in their own committees, come to rely on the judgment and advice of these specialist colleagues in a given area, although legislators known for hard work, loyalty, and playing by the rules also come to enjoy the respect and trust of colleagues.[14]

One study of influence patterns in Washington State tends to confirm these observations regarding the influence of certain legislators. When lawmakers were asked to indicate fellow legislators who were most influential in legislative matters, party leaders, committee chairpersons, and members of key committees were most often nominated. Party leaders were perceived as generally influential, and chairs and members of committees were thought to have a disproportionate influence in their areas of specialization.[15]

The data from the study of legislative outcomes in the forty-fourth session of the Washington State legislature again bear out these observations. Of the 183 bills referred to the senate and house Social and Health Services Committees, 101, or 55.2 percent, were reported out of committee. The rate of success experienced by the chairpersons and members of these two committees who were prime sponsors of bills was somewhat greater than that of nonmembers. Nonmembers succeeded in getting favorable committee action on slightly less than 45 percent of the bills for which they were prime sponsors. Chairpersons had 65 percent of their bills reported out, and members of the committees succeeded with 59 percent.

The authors' data do not support the contention that party leaders are particularly effective prime sponsors of social legislation. To begin with, such persons sponsored relatively few such bills in the forty-fourth session. Moreover, their success in achieving favorable committee action was about the same as that of other legislators and decidedly less than that of chairpersons and committee members. One possible explanation of this finding is that party leaders must attend to a wide array of issues, some of which, such as taxation and appropriations, are likely to have higher legislative priority than health and welfare measures. Lack of time and a disinclination to expend political capital on bills that touch the interests of a narrow constituency may have contributed to the relative ineffectiveness of party leaders as sponsors of social legislation.

Although the chairpersons and members of human services committees who sponsored legislation had better success in moving their bills out of committee than other legislators, the differences were not as great as some observers of the legislative process have contended. In part, this may be attributable to the fact that members of these committees, including the chairpersons, sponsored a disproportionate share of the bills that came to their committees—almost 74 percent of the total. Some of these bills were no doubt sponsored merely as a courtesy to constituents or out of a desire to be associated with a cause that had some popularity among voters but little chance of being enacted. In any case, this large workload may have forced them to focus energy, time, and influence on the bills that were considered most important or most likely to be acted on.

This suggests that although committee leadership or membership confers power on legislators, it remains only potential power until they exercise it with respect to a particular bill. Therefore, although it behooves the advocate to seek sponsors who have influence with their colleagues, it is equally important to determine, so far as possible, whether the lawmaker will exercise this influence in promoting the bill. This may be difficult to determine, but the policy priorities established by the legislators' party caucus and their voting records on related issues may provide some important clues. In addition, research suggests that on controversial issues, legislators with secure electoral margins are more likely to be responsive to proposals from interest groups and to work for unpopular causes; the evidence also suggests that when a bill touches on the vital interests of the legislator's constituency, active sponsorship is likely to follow.[16]

6. The advocate should press for open committee hearings on the bill and when such hearings are held, attempt to arrange for testimony in behalf of the bill by expert witnesses. It is generally recognized that open hearings are not the most effective forum in which to inform and persuade legislators. Milbrath, in his study of legislators and lobbyists, found, for example, that hearings had less impact on legislators than either personal contacts or presentations of research results. This is not to say that hearings lack any value as a means of persuasion. For legislators who are wavering on issues or who are looking for additional information to buttress a decision that has already been made, hearings can have an impact.[17]

Perhaps the major value of hearings for the advocate, however, is the opportunity they afford to draw public attention to a bill. Truman argued that a primary function of hearings is to create a channel for propaganda.[18] Especially if a hearing draws the attention of the media, the interested public can be sharply expanded and thus can indirectly influence legislative decision-making. Hearings often reveal sources of both support and opposition to a bill. Thus, although hearings may extend the constituency of a measure, they also involve the risk of providing a platform for legislators or groups opposed to a measure and giving them an opportunity to extend and consolidate their opposition.

Data from the authors' study suggest that hearings may facilitate the progress of social and health legislation. Of those bills heard in open meetings during the forty-fourth session of the Washington State legislature, 71 percent were reported favorably out of committees in the senate and house. Conversely, only 22 percent of the bills not heard in public hearings were reported out of committee. However, the data do not support a conclusion that hearings lead to favorable committee action. It is possible, indeed likely, that a decision to schedule a bill for hearing reflects a favorable disposition to the bill. Nevertheless, the strong association between positive committee action and hearings supports the notion that pressing for a hearing is, in general, a desirable tactic.

When such hearings are held, it is helpful to arrange for testimony by expert witnesses, especially staff members from relevant governmental agencies. There is some evidence that informed presentations based on systematic study or intimate familiarity with the subject can be persuasive to legislators. Rothman, for example, cites several studies that support the conclusion that advocates should seek the involvement of relevant governmental agencies in their lobbying efforts.[19] Smith's review of the literature on interest group influence suggests that legislators are receptive to groups that have factual knowledge about matters they are considering.[20] The authors' study supports this conclusion. When the Washington State Department of Social and Health Services testified in behalf of bills, over 81 percent of these measures were favorably reported out of committee. When personnel from that agency testified against a bill or adopted a neutral stance, only 50 percent of such bills received favorable committee action. Obviously, the fate of these bills was not influenced solely by the testimony of agency witnesses, but this does appear to have at least a marginal impact. This is not to suggest that only agency witnesses should be recruited to appear at hearings. Depending on the nature of the bill, other people, including former or potential clients, front-line workers, community leaders, representatives of special interest groups, and independent professionals, can also be effective witnesses.[21]

7. The advocate should use the amendatory process as a strategy for promoting a favorable outcome for a bill. The authors have observed elsewhere that advocates should expect to compromise on the substance of their proposals at every step in the legislative process.[22] Indeed, there is probably nothing more axiomatic in the legislative process than the notion that successful action requires an accommodation to diverse and sometimes conflicting interests.

The amendatory process in legislatures is one of the vehicles through which these accommodations are expressed. In standing committees, on the floor, in conference committees, and in negotiations with the governor, the language of the bill may be changed to neutralize opposition or gain support for the bill. To the extent that advocates are parties to these decisions, they have to decide whether the cumulative impact of the changes is a worthwhile price to pay for passage.

Data for the authors' study of social and health services bills in the forty-fourth session of the Washington State legislature strongly support the relationship between the amendatory process and favorable outcomes. Of the 183 bills under consideration in both houses during that session, 31 were amended and 152 were not. Nearly 97 percent of the amended bills were reported out of committee, and only 47 percent of those not amended were reported out. Even more significant was the finding that 64.5 percent of the amended bills were signed by the governor and became law; a mere 5 percent of the unamended bills achieved this status.(The authors' study of social and health services bills in the forty-third session yielded similar findings.) These figures must be interpreted with caution because the probability that a bill will be modified increases as it progresses through the legislative process. Thus, the extent to which amendments to a bill contribute to or result from the legislative process cannot be determined. In any case, the findings reported here, when joined with the widely recognized importance of compromise in the legislative process, argue for the tactical value of amendments as a means for promoting desired bills.

DILEMMAS TO BE FACED

Thus far this article has suggested tactics that appear to increase the probability of bill passage, all other factors being equal. Unfortunately, other things, most notably the substance of bills, are seldom equal. Bills vary considerably along a number of dimensions, including, for example, the extent of social change called for, the cost, and the target groups affected. Table 14.2 suggests the relationship between these substantive variables and legislative outcomes.

In a conservative political and economic climate, for example, proposals that seek to substantially extend benefits or services to some undervalued group, such as recipients of Aid to Families with Dependent Children, are unlikely to receive favorable legislative consideration, the tactical skill of the advocate notwithstanding. This poses a critical dilemma for professionals who are attempting to effect significant social change through the legislative process. In the face of anticipated resistance, the

advocate has two alternatives. The first, described by Howe in her recent analysis of the strategy employed by the New York City Human Resources Administration, is to reduce the scope and costs of proposals to avoid likely rejection by the state legislature.[23] A second alternative is to proceed with the measures, even though the prospects for enactment are slim, hoping that through compromise some incremental policy improvements can be achieved. There is no happy way to resolve this issue. The first strategy, based on considerations of feasibility, may increase the likelihood of success, but it often requires the advocate to defer proposals that deal with significant and pressing social problems. The second course may focus attention on the magnitude and urgency of a social problem and the real costs of adequately addressing it, but it is a course likely to result in failure. How is the advocate to decide? Several considerations seem important.

1. If the advocate has the skill and resources necessary to mobilize an active constituency around a measure, it may be feasible to pursue legislation that calls for far-reaching change at considerable cost.

2. In some cases the advocate may wish to proceed with a more ambitious proposal to dramatize an issue or to introduce a policy principle into legislative consideration. In this instance, the purpose is not to achieve immediate success, but to establish a basis for future advocacy.

3. When the advocate is pressing several proposals, it may be wise to defer introducing ambitious measures to conserve legislative cooperation and support for measures that stand some chance of passage.

TABLE 14.2
Relationship Between the Content of a Bill and Its Chance of Passage

Low Probability of Passage	High Probability of Passage
High fiscal impact: Implementation would require large appropriations of money.	*Low fiscal impact:* Implementation involves little or no cost.
Major social change: Implementation would affect many people, programs, and agencies.	*Minor or no social change:* Implementation may involve merely a regulatory or housekeeping matter.
Unpopular content: The bill deals with a subject or group unpopular with the public.	*Popular content:* The subject of the bill or the group it affects is well thought of by the public.

4. When the advocate is interested in building a reputation as a political realist, it may be necessary to focus on bills that have some prospect of succeeding. This can help establish the credibility that is often an important asset in advocating for major change.

Although these considerations provide little help in resolving the problems of a conservative political and economic climate, they may help the advocate assess the costs and benefits of alternative courses of action.

In summary, empirical research indicates seven tactics of legislative advocacy that are associated with favorable outcomes for human services legislation: (1) prefiling or introducing a bill early in the legislative session, (2) obtaining multiple sponsorship for the measure, (3) arranging for sponsors who are members of the majority party, preferably the Democratic party and, if possible, obtaining bipartisan sponsorship, (4) seeking the support of the state agencies that would administer the proposed legislation, (5) seeking sponsorship by influential legislators, such as committee chairpersons, provided they are willing to

exercise their power in promoting the bill, (6) pressing for open hearings on the bill, and (7) using the amendatory process to acquire support and neutralize opposition.

These tactics by no means account for all the variance in legislative outcomes. However, used singly or, preferably, in combination, these tactics appear to increase significantly the probability of favorable legislative action on social welfare legislation. Unfortunately, in a climate of political and fiscal conservatism, bills that propose extensive and costly social programs for disadvantaged and often undervalued groups are likely to be rejected by legislators regardless of the tactical skill of the advocate. This reality poses a critical dilemma for the professional seeking significant social change through the legislative process. Recognizing this dilemma and resolving it, however imperfect the solution, may be the advocate's most difficult challenge.

A number of tactics frequently proposed as a means of promoting desired legislation have not been considered in this article because there is insufficient research that links their use to legislative outcomes. The hope is that research can be extended to examine the effectiveness of other tactics, such as campaign support for legislators, the introduction of a bill in successive legislative sessions, the use of constituency pressure, and various forms of interpersonal influence. As research on tactics used in advocacy is extended, it will be important to know what combinations of tactics have the greatest impact. The investigation of these and related questions will help establish an empirically based model of legislative advocacy in social welfare.

NOTES

1. Of the nearly 200,000 bills introduced into the fifty state legislatures during the 1975 and 1976 legislative sessions, only 42,445 were passed into law, a scant 21.4 percent of all bills filed. See *The Book of the States, 1978-79,* Vol. 22 (Lexington, Ky.: Council on State Governments, 1978-79), pp. 36-38.
2. *See,* for example, Maryann Mahaffey, "Lobbying and Social Work," *Social Work,* 17 (January 1972), pp. 3-11; and Peter Rossi, "Power and Politics: A Road to Social Reform," *Social Service Review,* 25 (December 1961), pp. 359-369.
3. *See,* for example, Rino J. Patti and Ronald B. Dear, "Legislative Advocacy: One Path to Social Change," *Social Work,* 20 (March 1975), pp. 108-114.
4. Malcolm E. Jewel and Samuel C. Patterson, *The Legislative Process in the United States* (New York: Random House, 1966), p. 138.
5. *The Book of the States,* pp. 36-38,
6. Personal communication from James Gunther, past executive secretary of the Legislative Council of the Washington State legislature.

7. Wayne L. Francis, "Simulation of Committee Decision-Making in a State Legislative Body," *Simulation and Games,* 1 (September 1970), p. 257.
8. *See,* for example, Richard Reeves, "Why Congress Is Weak," *Seattle Times,* October 11, 1979.
9. Thomas R. Dye, "State Legislative Politics," in Herbert Jacob and Kenneth N. Vines, eds., *Politics in the American States: A Comparative Analysis* (Boston: Little, Brown & Co., 1971), p. 165.
10. Personal communication from Arthur Wang and Dick Van Wagenen, "Human Service Votes in the 1979 Legislature." Unpublished manuscript, Olympia, Washington, 1979. Mimeographed.
11. Jack Rothman, *Planning and Organizing for Social Change: Action Principles for Social Service Research* (New York: Columbia University Press, 1974), p. 232.
12. David B. Truman, *The Governmental Process* (2d ed.; New York: Alfred A. Knopf, 1971), p. 345.
13. Francis, op. cit., pp. 243-244.
14. *See* Truman, op. cit., p. 345.
15. James Best, "Influence in the Washington House of Representatives" (mimeographed, no date), p. 17.
16. Rothman, op. cit., pp. 233-240.
17. Lester Milbrath, *Washington Lobbyists* (Chicago: Rand McNally & Co., 1963), pp. 214 and 230-31. *See* also, Truman, op. cit., pp. 376-377.
18. Truman, op. cit., pp. 272-273.
19. Rothman, op. cit., pp. 244-245. *See also* the previous discussion on the importance of state agency support in pressing for legislation.
20. Virginia W. Smith, "How Interest Groups Influence Legislation," *Social Work,* 24 (May 1979), p. 235.
21. *See,* for example, Truman, op. cit., p. 374, for a discussion of the point that persons without technical knowledge are sometimes used to draw attention to the issue under consideration.
22. Patti and Dear, op. cit., p. 109.
23. Elizabeth Howe, "Legislative Outcomes in Human Services," *Social Service Review,* 54 (June 1978), pp. 173-188.

B. ORGANIZING AND DEVELOPING

15. NETWORKING FOR SELF-HELP: AN EMPIRICALLY BASED GUIDELINE

Lambert Maguire

The community-based practitioner cannot rely solely upon the resources of other formal organizations. He or she needs to link actively with and engage the support systems of individuals, groups, families, and communities, and help them to affect each other. In other words, the practitioner needs to *network*, which can be defined as the process of developing multiple interconnections and chain reactions among support systems (Barnes, 1972; Maguire, 1980).

When this process is established using individual-social networks or the natural networks of communities for the purpose of self-help, the practitioners can be more effective in their interventions by following certain specific techniques and models of intervention. This article examines several of those networking interventions and provides guidelines for using them in a manner that stimulates

the use of one's own network resources to effect change. It is networking for self-help.

I see six reasons for this rise in the use of networking. First is the political and economic necessity. Since the federal government has withdrawn from its traditional and historical commitment to help in the area of human services, a need has developed to coordinate limited resources more effectively and to find and utilize natural human resources wherever they exist, which is essentially what networking is all about. Second, there is a seeming disenchantment with professionals and experts, whether they are politicians, economists, child psychologists, or psychotherapists (Chu and Trotter, 1974; Gross, 1978). The public has come to realize that we don't have all of the answers.

Third, there has been the rise of the self-help movement in the areas of advocacy for causes or oppressed groups (Pollard, 1979) or in mutual help groups (Gartner and Riessman, 1980; Lieberman and Borman, 1979; Silverman, 1980). Another reason that networking has become more widely used lately has

Reproduced by permission of the author. This is an unpublished article. An in-depth description of each of the models described appears in the author's *Understanding Networks: Intervention Strategies with Individuals, Self Help Groups, Organizations and Communities,* Sage Publications, 1983.

been the perceived lack of more dramatic outcomes, particularly in mental health (Garfield and Bergin, 1978), where the longer-term, psychodynamically based approaches are still the mainstay, and in social services, where the vast health and welfare system is perceived as insensitive. So the alternative of using people's own social networks or the natural helping networks within communities becomes viable.

Next, recent advances in research methods, statistical procedures, and data analysis have all combined to give us a far greater capacity to examine not just simple quantitative measures dealing with human interaction, but also qualitative assessments of how and why people develop friendships (Fischer et al., 1977) or go to certain friends or relatives as opposed to others for favors, support, help, or whatever. This ability to analyze networks and their patterns of influence and communication can be statistically very complex (Barnes, 1972; Boissevain and Mitchell, 1973; Holland and Leinhardt, 1979; Wellman, 1981; Gottlieb, 1981). However, it can be used positively in clinical interventions by simply asking people some basic questions which I will discuss later.

The sixth reason is the fact that a tremendous amount of epidemiological and social survey research indicates that supportive networks do serve as a general buffer against stress (Antonovsky, 1979), or as a correlate with a wide variety of health and mental health problems (President's Commission on Mental Health, 1978, Vol. 1–4; Caplan and Killilea, 1976; Gottlieb, 1981; Nuckolls, Cassel, and Kaplan, 1972; Rabkin and Struening, 1976; Barrera, 1981; Dean and Lin, 1977). Obviously, we cannot say that the lack of a social network or close social support system would cause health or mental health problems, but there certainly is a diversified body of research that indicates that there is some consistent pattern of relationship between social networks, health, and mental health. In fact, some of this research indicates that the networks for "normal" people are both qualitatively and quantitatively very different from the networking of those with psychiatric problems (Tolsdorf, 1976; Pattison et al., 1975).

INTERVENTIONS

Because of those factors, there has been a proliferation of strategies developed in recent years, which might generally be considered as networking approaches. Four of these have application in practice. They are personal networking, networking for mutual aid and self-help, human service organization networking, and networking within communities for community empowerment.

Personal Networking

Most of the well-established casework approaches or models of treatment preferred in social work recognize that the worker needs to identify carefully and assess the client's strengths and resources as well as problems and difficulties before going on to help the client realistically examine what can be done interpersonally as well as intrapersonally to alleviate the problem, using all available resources (Roberts and Nee, 1970; Turner, 1979). Personal networking is no different except that its emphasis is on preventing problems before they require in-depth treatment, and it uses a network paradigm to develop a more precise analysis or a mapping of those resources before linking the resources together. Furthermore, the approach is based upon two bodies of research on personal networks. One is in the area of qualitative and quantitative differences in the personal networks of "normals," the neurotic, and psychotic individuals (Pattison et al., 1975; Tolsdorf, 1976). These studies indicated that the networks of psychotics tended to be very small (four to five people), composed primarily of family and unidirectional in their helping (that is, the network of family helped the ego or psychotic central figure, but the help was not reciprocal). "Normals" tended to have personal networks of twenty to thirty people composed of friends as well as family, and the helping process was reciprocal.

The other body of network research pertinent to personal networking is that which concerns differential types of helping for various problems. Some research does indicate that tightly knit small networks tend to help with emotional concerns, whereas larger networks with loose ties are often more helpful in situations which require specific types of help or information not usually available to close friends and relatives (Fischer et al., 1977; Craven and Wellman, 1973; Hirsch, 1981; Mitchell and Trickett, 1980).

Based in a strong tradition of social casework and diverse research on personal networks, the personal networking approach developed utilizes three stages of intervention. These stages are identification, mapping, and linking.

Identification involves a preliminary attempt to assess whether personal networking will be feasible or whether a more traditional approach would be best. It involves helping the client to define the problem in a clear way while weighing various options relevant to solving the problem. It also is the beginning of a process of developing a relationship with the client, which will serve to further any subsequent work. At this phase there is a focus upon the client's own existing resources in relation to his or her own personal strengths as well as resources from family, friends, neighbors, work colleagues, and others. There is an attempt at this phase to assess "networkability," or linking potential with others. This "networkability" is a function of the client's interpersonal abilities in relation to actual or potential network members. In other words, how willing and able is the client to define potential linkages and then to activate them? If there is potential, then mapping or a network analysis is developed.

Mapping is a form of social network analysis which has been described in various technical ways by social scientists (Barnes, 1972; Boissevain and Mitchell, 1973; Gottlieb, 1981; Holland and Leinhardt, 1979; Wellman, 1981). However, this author recommends either of two clinically oriented mapping approaches. One involves using a diagram consisting of four concentric circles like Figure 15.1. The circle is divided into six pie-shaped sections: Family, Friends, Neighbors, Work Associates, Professional Associates, and Other Significant Individuals. On the chart one places initials to depict each person's relative closeness to the client. When the individuals designated have been placed in the circles, lines are drawn connecting each person in the support system with others they know, representing their own networks.

FIGURE 15.1
Map of Personal Networks

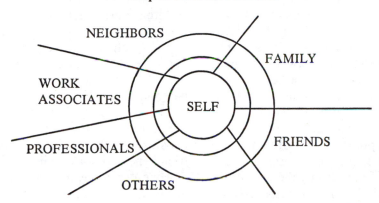

Another clinical mapping method involves an intake questionnaire that asks the client to answer, with the worker's help, the following questions:

1. Who are the people in your life who would be really helpful for the types of problems we have discussed? Please list them.
2. For each person, please define your relationship to them as either relative, friend, neighbor, work colleague, professional helper, or other (please define).
3. How often do you see or talk to this person (daily, weekly, twice monthly, monthly, yearly, less than yearly)?
4. Who usually initiates the contact?
5. How far does this person live from you in minutes, using your usual mode of transportation?
6. Do you feel you give more than you get, get more, or that the relationship is fairly even?
7. How long have you known this person?
8. Now, can you diagram for me which of these people know each other? (A rough sociogram or a variation of one of the social network analytic approaches described in the preceding references can be used, or the exercise described prior to this method might be attempted).
9. List the organizations with which you are currently or recently involved, including clubs, church groups, unions, ethnic organizations, or community activities.
10. List the professionals you have seen at any time in recent years who have helped with the problems we discussed or even any similar problems. Please include doctors, lawyers, ministers, police, pharmacists, social workers, counselors, etc. (This list of suggestions should be developed specifically as a cue for each client.)

The mapping stage involves extensive discussion afterward with the client about the real potential for using these network resources.

Linking, which is the third and final stage of personal networking, involves making the necessary connections with and for the client to alleviate the problem.

It involves the client, or the client and

the worker, meeting and calling first- and sometimes second-order network members, that is, individuals who are only indirectly linked to the client through an intermediary or another individual. First-order networks are used for more emotional or personal problems because the interconnectedness of paths or intimacy of relationships among members is close and multiple and provides support of a more intimate nature. The larger and looser network linkages are facilitated by the worker for concerns of a social or interpersonal nature, or where negative environmental forces, including health, work-related stress, and social welfare problems are apparent. Their resources are more diverse but less personally supportive. Workers are encouraged to use such group work factors as altruism, acceptance by peers, universality, and cognitive restructuring (Yalom, 1976). Furthermore, providing useful information and guidance by a concerned network of individuals having experience with the problem is no less helpful in networks than it is in formal groups. These group work skills allow the worker a greater capacity to establish and support the linkages among network members without feeling it necessary to control the linking process totally. Some of this linking can even be performed on the telephone between the worker and members, and between members themselves. The goal is simply to share ideas and resources and get network members to communicate with each other to solve the central figure's problems.

An example of this sort of personal networking is a case of a depressed, recently divorced male who was unemployed. He began drinking to excess, had considered suicide, and was angry enough at his ex-wife to consider physically hurting or even killing her, since she kept him from his three young children. Fortunately for him, he had a close, supportive extended family as well as many other relatives, old neighborhood friends, and associates from his old job. He had returned to live with his parents in the home in which he was raised, and his tightly knit ethnic neighborhood consisted of a great many cousins, aunts, and uncles as well as friends he had known since childhood.

After identifying tremendous potential in his personal network, and then mapping a total of twenty-two network members, it was clearly evident that networking with this potentially highly supportive system would yield far greater practical results than traditional treatment. The mapping stage itself was in fact rather therapeutic, although he protested that he would be reluctant to ask these relatives and friends for any form of help. Ultimately, he did not ask for help from any network member other than his immediate family. Most of the others were contacted but for informal purposes such as a family reunion and a series of dinners and nights out with his old friends and a few of his former work colleagues. This socializing not only ultimately gave him the social support he needed to break a cycle which was leading toward a serious reactive depression, but it also linked him up with friends who helped him find a new job and gradually reconcile with his wife. A full-scale depressive reaction was prevented by utilizing the personal network.

Mutual Aid/Self-Help

Mutual aid and self-help groups are excellent examples of networking in action. They usually begin with nonprofessionals who have a concern or problem and who link themselves up with others who share the same concern. It inevitably involves multiple linkages and chain reactions, or many people affecting each other to share their fears, their knowledge and their ways of coping. The mutual aid and self-help members are networking whether they are formal and have a name and meeting time and list of goals and objectives, or whether they are informal and remain as simply a group of friends who share a common problem. Networking for self-help and mutual aid can be used by professionals in two ways.

One is through serving as a *Clearinghouse Network* for mutual aid or self-help groups. For instance, I work with the Information and Volunteer Services and the Volunteer Action Center in Pittsburgh. These organizations have helped to locate mutual aid groups where they exist (which in itself is a difficult task), and serve as a clearinghouse for professionals in health and welfare who may want to know more about these groups or how to get clients linked up to them. As mentioned before, self-help and mutual aid groups are growing at a tremendous rate but exist almost as parallel systems to the professional system. At times there is a mutual distrust or disdain between the professional system, composed of social workers, psychologists, nurses, psychiatrists, and others, and the nonprofessional or informal system of mutual aid and self-help. This distance between the two systems has rapidly decreased in recent years and, in fact, it is misleading even to refer to the two as separate or parallel systems, since the overlap has become so great. But networking is needed in which the professional does several things. First, he or she has to locate the group

and get the name of its leaders. When dealing with one of the many anonymous groups, get at least a phone number or post office box. Next one needs a description of the group which includes:

1. The group's goals or objectives
2. Its membership criteria (that is, who gets in, in terms of the type of problem or concern, as well as whether there are any guidelines or restrictions based on age, race, sex, income, marital status, political or sexual orientation)
3. Its meeting times and places
4. Its format for meetings (for instance, AA and Recovery, Incorporated, have quite specific and rather rigid rules for how meetings are to be conducted whereas Theos, a self-help group for widows, describes its format as being totally flexible to the changing needs of its members)
5. Its dues or membership costs
6. Its sponsorship, if any (e.g., a church, social service agency, etc.)
7. Whether professionals are allowed or encouraged to be involved in any capacity (as active group members), which is rare, or as occasional speakers, board members, consultants, referral sources, and so on

Besides gathering and disseminating this information, networkers can sponsor self-help fairs. At these fairs, self-help groups in the area are invited to set up booths, make presentations about their group, serve as panelists around certain topics, pass out literature, or simply informally meet and get to know the professionals in the community. Typically, such a fair must include a weekday or two, plus a weekend day or two, with some daytime and evening times, so that everyone's schedule is accommodated. The purpose is to get the self-help group and the professionals to interact and get to know each other, so that they can develop their own networks of interactive systems.

Networking with Self-Help Groups: Developer/Facilitator

The other role of a networker for self-help/mutual aid is as a developer-facilitator. To further the goals of primary prevention, a social worker or other may take a more active role in helping to start a self-help group where one is needed in a community but does not currently exist. While some would encourage the professional to take an active role in running the first few sessions, then gradually withdrawing (Gartner and Riessman, 1980), I would advocate that the networker take more of a secondary role in the process of developing and facilitating a self-help group. Specifically, I suggest that the networker provide ten resources: (1) meeting place, (2) funds, (3) information, (4) training, (5) referrals to them, (6) referrals from them, (7) credibility in the community, (8) credibility in the professional community, (9) buffer, and (10) social and emotional support for leaders (Maguire, 1981).

Let's look at some concrete, clinical examples. Let's say you are working in a family service agency and the case load of the agency has a half dozen single mothers who are becoming depressed and overwhelmed by the demands on them. They may not necessarily need professional, one-to-one or group treatment. What they may need is a self-help group such as the single parent project sponsored by the Community Service Society in New York or a group called

Parent Care or they may choose to join a self-help consciousness-raising group such as those sponsored at many YM/YWCA s or through the National Organization of Women. If you have been networking in the clearinghouse capacity, you will have available a list of possible appropriate groups for them. If you do not have such a list, you can still find out about a self-help group for them by calling or writing any of the eight major national clearinghouses which will often provide you with a list of such organizations, by problem or by geographic location (Gartner and Riessman, 1980).

Otherwise, you can network by being the facilitator-developer, and either start the women's group going before gradually leaving them, or by linking them up with a national self-help group, which will provide them with some guidelines or frame of reference and then provide the resources mentioned before. So you may simply offer a conference room one night a week for them, bring some coffee to get the first few meetings begun, and then make a few phone calls to all single women with children who need support but not necessarily treatment. From there, you may need to make particular linkages with potential group leaders and suggest ways of getting started or formats which might be successful. Encourage their own leadership. If or when they want new members, suggest other names to them. Be available for advice, or just to listen to the group as a whole or for those who emerge as the leaders.

This type of networking with mutual aid and self-help groups can also be used preventively for alcohol and drug abusers who, as a target population, tend to respond rather poorly to traditional individual treatment as well as group treatment in diagnostically heterogeneous groups. Mutual aid is also a potent preventive force where a physical health problem can develop into a serious mental health problem. By getting potentially depressed, angry, or alienated people with arthritis, heart disease, cancer, paralysis, or almost any other serious health problem into a mutual aid group where he or she can share with others, the likelihood of more debilitating emotional problems will be greatly diminished.

Networking with Professionals and Organizations

There are two networking models with other professionals or organizations. One involves instances where a specific client presents himself or herself to an agency. The social worker at intake will recognize that the person may have a variety of social service, health, and mental health complaints. For instance, a forty-year-old single divorced woman who is on welfare may come in with complaints of sleeplessness, loss of weight, suicidal tendencies, sexual dysfunction, and lack of enough money to buy her family food or clothes. Networking or case management coordination is no doubt the best way to proceed. The networker will have to link this person up with an employment or vocational counselor, a therapist, a doctor for a physical exam and possible follow-up, and the welfare office. If done on a case-by-case basis, this is extremely time-consuming and inefficient.

Instead, a prevention-oriented, ongoing network of social service, health, and mental health professionals is recommended (Curtis, 1979; 1981; Project Share, 1981; Delahanty and Atkins, 1981). A human service network accomplishes two important things at the same time:

1. It allows agencies to maintain their separate identity while working closely together, and
2. It places a value or emphasis on cooperation rather than competition among agencies. In many ways, this is a complex process, but it can be developed by starting cooperatively on individual cases or projects, such as the case example already mentioned. It ultimately develops into an ongoing network, which can minimize the incidence of a wide variety of disorders by quickly and effectively channeling people at risk into the appropriate health care system or systems, and by maintaining communication and sharing resources and information among professionals and agencies.

This particular approach has tremendous potential as a preventive force in communities, but it is also a difficult task. A networker who wants to establish such a human service network which uses team management needs to recognize four essential facts. One is that agencies are territorial and do not want to share their professional roles or areas of reputed expertise with others. Thus the health professional involved will likely become angry or leave the network if a non-health-related professional speaks authoritatively about what should be done with a health problem. All network members need to be able to define their boundaries or areas and have those boundaries respected. For this reason, it would not be wise for the network to include two agencies that overlap excessively and that are already in competition for nearly the exact same funds or client populations. The competition would possibly lead to undermining each other rather than cooperating.

Second, professionals in different fields are status conscious. Social workers, nurses, and others become very angry at medical doctors or those with doctorates in psychology who presume leadership roles on the basis of their degrees. True leadership in these networks develops not on the basis of one's degree or professional affiliation. It develops when an individual merits it on the basis of the ability to inspire confidence, carry out tasks, delegate authority, and encourage useful dialogue. Structurally, it is best to maintain equality among all organizations or members and that equality must be recognized, developed, and maintained. However, as tasks begin to be pursued and assignments delegated, certain individuals will become the so-called first among equals.

Third, human service networks are only as powerful in the community as their members. In order to succeed, the network needs the agency directors, who can actually commit agency resources. The agency that refuses to send its director is implicitly saying that the network is too likely to infringe on his or her territory, and he does not want it to succeed.

Finally, human service network building is largely the function of the development of personal, trusting relationships. For this reason it is important for the atmosphere to be as open, supportive, and helpful as is realistically possible. The networker must serve as a model, therefore, in establishing the type of social environment.

Community Empowerment

One network model which has a clear concentration in linkages within the area of mental health involves the Neighborhood and Family Services Project (Biegel and Naparstek, 1982). This project, which was established in neighborhoods in Baltimore and Milwaukee, uses what is called a community empowerment model or process. The directors of the project had several goals. The first was to create community awareness of neighborhood strengths and needs. In this project, they were careful to build on the existing community organizations and leaders, not bring in or "parachute" in outside experts. Their orientation was more toward finding strengths as perceived by the neighborhood residents. Their second goal was to strengthen neighborhood helping networks. That part of the process was done by developing linkages among natural helpers in the community, among helpers and neighborhood leaders, and among neighborhood residents themselves. Third, they strengthened the professional helping networks by organizing a professional advisory committee in each city, which served to advise what was clearly a community-directed process. Fourth, they formed linkages between the lay and professional helping networks. In most instances, this involved the various community residents inviting the professionals to join their committees and to offer expertise. Their fifth goal was to form linkages between the lay and professional helping networks and the macro system. In other words they did such things as helping the local community residents to put together a data base of information regarding state and local mental health and human service plans,

United Way patterns, aging program plans, major federal legislation, and other topics. Sixth, they institutionalized the process, creating a mental health constituency, integrated but not assimilated or taken over by the human service system.

This process was long, because it involved not only getting community residents to know and trust the professionals, but it also required that the professionals both respect and turn power over to the people of the community. Prevention of mental health problems as well as improving the quality of life and social fabric of a community can be enhanced by using any of the various networking approaches that seem to appreciate the capabilities of the community leaders and natural helping networks that thrive all over the country.

SUMMARY

Whether we are talking about community networking approaches that involve community systems or any of the approaches that recognize natural helping networks around specific problems such as child or spouse abuse, practitioners in the communities need to recognize that their task is essentially a matter of networking people with others in their community who share the same concerns. People will help each other when asked, when given some support and encouragement, and when given some advice and suggestions. The professionals will have to continue to use and develop their treatment and rehabilitation strategies with individuals, but when it comes to prevention, they need community leaders, networks of people, and not only the

involvement but ultimately direction and leadership from the masses of people who could ultimately be affected. The lay helping network includes not only friends, neighbors, and family, but also within communities, the clergy, teachers, pharmacists, social clubs, self-help groups, union locals, neighborhood organizations, natural helpers, and ethnic organizations. By being linked together with each other and with the professional helping network to solve developing problems such as drug abuse, theft, teenage pregnancies, truancy, alienated or isolated elderly, child abuse, or virtually any other problem area which the professional system traditionally ends up treating rather than preventing, we are saving a great many people from a great deal of unnecessary pain and anguish. Professionals cannot do it alone, particularly given the very limited funds available.

Each of these approaches implicitly and explicitly recognizes the fact that the community-based practitioners can be most effective by working with the networks and support systems available to the client system or community, and helping them to achieve their greatest potential.

Whether working with personal networks, mutual aid and self-help groups, networks for coordinating human service organizations, or networks within communities for the purpose of community empowerment, all of these interventions involve coordinating and developing networks for self-help.

REFERENCES

Antonovsky, A., *Health, Stress and Coping* (San Francisco: Jossey-Bass Publishers, 1979).

Barnes, J. A., *Social Networks.* Addison-Wesley Modules in Anthropology no. 26 (Reading, Mass.: Addison-Wesley, 1972).

Barrera, M., "Social Support in the Adjustment of Pregnant Adolescents: Assessment Issues," in B. Gottlieb, ed., *Social Networks and Social Support* (Beverly Hills, Calif.: Sage Publications, 1981).

Biegel, D., and Naparstek, A., "The Neighborhood and Family Services Project: An Empowerment Model Linking Clergy and Agency Professionals," in A. Jeger and R. Slotnik, eds., *Community Mental Health: A Behavioral Ecological Perspective* (New York: Plenum Press, 1982).

_____eds., *Community Support Systems and Mental Health, Practice, Policy and Research* (New York: Springer, 1982).

Boissevain, J., and Mitchell, J. C., eds., *Network Analysis: Studies in Human Interaction* (The Hague: Mouton, 1973).

Caplan, G., and Killilea, M., eds., *Support Systems and Mutual Help* (New York: Grune and Stratton, 1976).

Chu, F. D., and Trotter, S., *The Madness Establishment: Ralph Nader's Study Group Report on the National Institute of Mental Health* (New York: Grossman Publishers, 1974).

Craven, P., and Wellman, B., "The Network City," *Social Inquiry 43* (1973): 57–88.

Curtis, W. R., *The Future Use of Social Networks in Mental Health* (Boston: Matrix Research, Inc., 1979).

_____, *Managing Human Services with Less: New Strategies for Local Leaders. Human Services Monograph Series,* No. 26 (Rockville, Md.: Project Share, September, 1981).

Dean, A., and Lin, N., "The Stress-Buffering Role of Social Support: Problems and Prospects for Systematic Investigation," *Journal of Nervous and Mental Disease,* 165, no. 6 (1977): 403–417.

Delahanty, D. S., and Atkins, G. L., *Strategic Local Planning: A Collaborative Model,* Project Share, *Human Services Monograph Series* no. 23 (Washington, D.C.: U.S. Department of Health and Human Services, 1981).

Fischer, C.; Jackson, R.; Stueve, C.; Gerson, K.; and Jones, L., *Networks and Places* (New York: Free Press, 1977).

Garfield, S., and Bergin, A., *Handbook of Psychotherapy and Behavior Change: An Empirical Analysis,* 2d ed. (New York: John Wiley and Sons, 1978).

Gartner, A., and Riessman, F., *Help: A Working Guide to Self Help Groups* (New York: New Viewpoint Books, 1980).

Gottlieb, B., "Social Networks and Social Support in Community Mental Health," in B. Gottlieb, ed., *Social Networks and Social Support* (Beverly Hills, Calif.: Sage Publications, 1981).

Gross, M., *The Psychological Society* (New York: Random House, 1978).

Hirsch, B. J., "Social Networks and the Coping Process: Creating Personal Communities," in B. H. Gottlieb, ed., *Social Networks and Social Support* (Beverly Hills, Calif.: Sage Publications, 1981).

Holland, P. W., and Leinhardt, S., eds., *Perspectives on Social Network Research* (New York: Academic Press, 1979).

Lieberman, M., and Borman, L., *Self Help Groups for Coping with Crisis* (San Francisco: Jossey-Bass Publishers, 1979).

Maguire, L., "Natural Helping Networks and Self Help Groups," in Milton Nobel, ed., *Primary Prevention in Mental Health and Social Work* (New York: Council on Social Work Education, 1981).

Mitchell, R., and Trickett, E. J., "Task Force Report: Social Networks As Mediators of Social Support (An Analysis of the Effects and Determinants of Social Networks)," *Community Mental Health Journal* 16, no. 1 (Spring 1980): 27–44.

Nuckolls, K. B.; Cassel, J.; and Kaplan, B. H., "Psychosocial Assets, Life Crisis and the Prognosis of Pregnancy," *American Journal of Epidemiology* 95 (1972): 431–441.

Pattison, E. M.; Francisco, D.; Wood, P.; Frazier, H.; and Crowder, J., "A Psychosocial Kinship Model for Family Therapy," *American Journal of Psychiatry* 132 (1975): 1246–1251.

Pollard, W., *A Study of Black Self Help* (San Francisco: R & E Research Associates, 1978).

President's Commission on Mental Health. *Task Panel Reports* submitted to the President's Commission on Mental Health, 2 (Washington, D.C.: U.S. Government Printing Office, 1978).

Project Share, *Networking Among Human Services Agencies, Human Services Bibliography Series* (Washington, D.C.: U.S. Department of Health and Human Services, 1981).

Rabkin, J., and Struening, E. L., "Life Events, Stress, and Illness," *Science* 194 (December 1976): 1013–1020.

Roberts, R. W., and Nee, R., *Theories of Social Casework* (Chicago: University of Chicago Press, 1970).

Silverman, P., *Mutual Help Groups: Organization and Development* (Beverly Hills, Calif.: Sage Publications, 1980).

Tolsdorf, C. C., "Social Networks, Support and Coping: An Exploratory Study," *Family Process* 15 (1976): 407–417.

Turner, F., *Social Work Treatment: Interlocking Approaches,* 2d ed. (New York: Free Press, 1979).

Wellman, B., "Applying Network Analysis to the Study of Support," in B. Gottlieb, ed., *Social Networks and Social Support* (Beverly Hills, Calif.: Sage Publications, 1981).

Yalom, I., *The Theory and Practice of Group Psychotherapy,* 2d ed. (New York: Basic Books, 1976).

16. CONSUMER EDUCATION AS A COMMUNITY ACTIVATOR

Susan Sherry and Clair Lipschultz

The realization of Health Systems Agency (HSA) goals is in large part dependent on the effectiveness of consumer participation in the health planning process. Yet obstacles to involvement by consumer-oriented volunteers and public have prevented meaningful representation of their constituencies' interests. A significant number of these barriers can be impacted by consumer-oriented education programs aimed at empowering those interests which have lacked a powerful voice in health planning. Specifically, those interests would include but not be limited to such constituencies as blacks, Chicanos, Asians, Native Americans, the disabled, allied and mental health workers, low-income groups, organizationally identified seniors and women, unions, and rural-oriented organizations. This program would provide a base of information from which consumers and

Reproduced by permission of the authors and the California Public Interest Research Group (CALPIRG).

community-based organizations can critically analyze the health and medical care system and develop health plans and strategies responsive to their groups' needs.

The education program must go beyond provision of substantive health planning information. It must be designed and implemented in a manner which (1) enhances the leadership and advocacy capabilities of the program participants, (2) develops their identification with and accountability to their constituency group, and (3) promotes a network among individuals within and outside the HSA who have common concerns and can develop cohesive positions and plans. Each aspect of the education program must reflect this goal of supporting the organization and efficacy of representative groups and individuals.

The program should be directed toward members of the target communities, both in and outside the agency. An educated and activated community outside the agency, in their capacity as interested public, can serve as a pool for future HSA volunteers; require accountability from representatives presently on HSA bodies; present their positions effectively, which is necessary for true community-based planning; and mold and support HSA implementation efforts.

Consumer-oriented education can and should be integrated throughout all aspects of HSA functions. The many actions and responsibilities of the volunteers and public lend themselves well to "on-the-job" training. The staff position of technical assistant to governing body volunteers, especially consumers, could result in important educational opportunities as the debate on issues is expanded by addressing the consumer perspective.

One important component of the integrated educational program is a series of training workshops with a set curriculum and timetable. The benefits from such a program are reflected in the successful outcomes of the Consumer Health Advocacy Training, which was conducted by the San Diego California Public Interest Research Group (Cal-PIRG) from November 1978 to February 1980. Community actions that resulted from the training include:

- Twenty-three participant appointments to HSA committees, subarea councils, and the governing body
- The creation of an active health advocacy organization, the San Diego Health Action Coalition
- The dissemination of health planning information to 4,500 persons through the outreach efforts of the trainees
- The delivery of twenty-five pieces of testimony before HSA public hearings by workshop participants

Educational programs similar to Cal-PIRG's can be conducted by HSA's to catalyze community participation. The following discussion outlines the key elements of a program which simultaneously educates and stimulates consumer-oriented involvement in health planning and health policy development. Although these steps are directed at a consumer health policy workshop effort, they highlight and summarize the essential activities for any organizing campaign geared toward mobilizing those groups who have traditionally had little access to policy decision making.

OUTLINE FOR COMMUNITY ACTION: CONSUMER EDUCATION AS ORGANIZING TOOL

Involving consumer constituencies in HSA activities, especially those constituencies that have not been forcefully represented in the past, is essential to fulfilling the spirit of P.L. 93-641 [the National Health Planning and Resources Development Act of 1974, authorizing a three year effort aimed at ensuring equal access to quality health care at a reasonable cost] as well as to developing a community support base for continued government resource allocations to health planning. Educational workshops are one of the most important mechanisms an HSA has at its disposal to foster ongoing community participation in its activities. As explained in more depth below, educational events provide a unique opportunity to invite participation from consumer groups not currently involved with the agency, as well as to extend the commitment of those groups who are peripherally active with the HSA.

Workshops will serve as a vehicle for increased consumer-oriented participation only if the definition of an educational event is expanded to include specific kinds of preparation, implementation, and follow-up efforts. Sponsoring workshops that focus on the actual educational delivery to the exclusion of important steps that must precede, accompany, and follow the event will merely bolster participation from those groups and individuals already adequately represented in HSA decision making.

The following discussion is based on the distillation of eleven strategies that were believed to account for the success of CalPIRG's Consumer Health Advocacy Training project. It is important to note that each of the following eleven guidelines were utilized in as many phases of the workshop design as possible:

- Recruitment
- Development of workshop materials
- The educational event itself
- Sustainment of participant involvement
- Advocacy activities generated beyond the training

Although each HSA will necessarily adapt the phases of the educational effort to meet its particular needs and constraints, attention needs to be paid to each phase to utilize the training as a community/consumer organizing tool.

ACTION #1: Focus on a *specific event* that will invite active and/or passive participation from the target community groups.

The concept of "workshop as event" is the key to generating community enthusiasm for participation in the training. For those groups who have been excluded from the health planning process, a workshop series designed with a community flare can provide participants with networking contacts, needed technical information, and an inspiration to engage in the policy-making process.

The "workshop as event" concept needs to be clearly communicated to the targeted constituencies in the recruitment efforts as well as in the actual educational sessions. For example, selected media coverage in the form of feature newspaper articles, television talk shows, public service announcements, radio interviews, community calendar entries, and live reporting at the training site can build a momentum for the workshops.

Besides media utilization, there are numerous ways to generate a community spirit around the training sessions. Establishing an application process for the workshop series which emphasizes the requirement of a time and advocacy commitment from the trainees can underscore the seriousness of the effort. Encouraging constituencies to send a "delegate" to the workshop(s) as part of their acknowledged organizational priorities also gives the event an increased stature. Inviting speakers who are outspoken and/or controversial, and who invite a lively dialogue with the audience continues the theme of "workshop as event." Developing a high profile for the training series is important because it directly influences the level of investment the trainees will make to the public policy decision-making process after the training has terminated.

If some agency resources can be devoted to sustaining participant involvements, a workshop series which extends over the course of three to nine weeks is preferable to one-time training. The series approach provides the time necessary for important organizational and interpersonal ties to develop among trainees, a critical factor in coalition and caucus building. Additionally, a sequential training program can explore and then replay the various issues relevant to health planning decisions. In this same vein, a two-day conference would be more useful than a one-day event, although some of the limitations of a one-time session can be countered with intensive preparation and follow-up work.

Training sessions that blend both active and passive participation from the trainees are best suited to community groups. Presentations followed by small group exercises work well. A lecture format, wherein pointed and sometimes confrontive questions are encouraged, is a particularly valuable way of communicating information and building the group's esprit de corps.

ACTION #2: Extend outreach efforts to the greatest number of individuals within the target group to increase the base of eventual activists.

The central idea behind this action guideline is that recruitment for the workshops is simultaneously extensive and selective. The first step in this type of outreach is to identify not only the specific constituencies that are targeted for participation, but those subgroups within constituencies that are more likely to support an advocacy model of public participation. Once the appropriate groupings are identified, it is important to devise outreach methods that will expose members of the targeted groupings to the short- and long-term goals of the training.

Developing a comprehensive mailing list, which reflects those organizations potentially inclined toward citizen activism, is essential. A mail-out piece that includes (1) an overview of the health care crisis from a consumer perspective; (2) a suggested article on the training for easy inclusion in the organization's newsletter, and (3) a visually attractive workshop flyer for posting is one way to begin the recruitment process. Additionally, it can be useful to publicize the workshops in the alternative and grass-roots newspapers of the areas.

Oral presentations delivered before the relevant groups are a particularly effective recruitment mechanism. A brief talk before a group already convened for its monthly meeting can elicit participation in a very time-effective way.

Ideally, outreach should continue on a limited basis throughout the workshop series. Each session topic has the potential of drawing out a number of people who for one reason or another would find it difficult to attend an entire series. For example, a "Barriers to Service" workshop might invite additional participation from the ethnic minority communities, as might a "Prevention" workshop from the holistic health or environmental health community. For this kind of one-time participation, constituency leaders should be encouraged to attend the workshop. In this way, trainees are exposed to various key actors in the community, and key leaders are exposed to the growing network of health advocates.

ACTION #3: Find *key leaders* (formal and informal) within each target group who will actively support the program and promote participation by their group.

Every constituency group has a network of influential personalities. One of the first tasks of successful community organizing is to identify these leaders and then to map out their policy interest areas and their general orientation toward advocacy and coalition building. Once identified, these leaders can be asked to lend their assistance to the training program in a number of ways: (1) suggest names of potential trainees and personally invite these individuals to attend the workshops; (2) encourage their group to designate an official representative to participate in the workshops; and (3) convey the names of other leaders who can provide additional entrée into the constituency.

Generally, the key leaders will not themselves participate in the training because of time constraints. Appealing specifically to those constituency members who are *not* already overburdened with community leadership responsibilities is generally a sound approach to organizing. Training sessions are an effective way of locating those individuals who are not yet pulled into volunteer activities. These are the types of individuals who generally have the extra time and energy to devote to consumer-oriented activities either as an HSA volunteer or as a coalition advocate.

ACTION #4: Activate involvement of different constituency groups by appealing to their particular vested interests.

To involve groups not only in a training series, but more importantly in resulting caucus, advocacy, or coalition efforts, it is vital to articulate clearly the limitations of the current health care system as it particularly affects that group. For example, in recruiting labor representation it should be pointed out that as health care costs rise astronomically, the increased costs of health care insurance benefits directly cut into wage increases. From that vantage point, the cost containment features of the Certificate-of-Need (CON) Review process can be explained, again continually integrating the various facets of the health planning process with the original concerns of the constituency group.

Once the self-interests of the group are addressed, the linkages to other critical issues can be developed. Continuing this example, after underscoring the connections between rising health care costs and wage constraints, one can then address the interplay between rising costs and the resulting barriers to service to low-income groups.

The training materials as well as the content of the sessions need to reecho the specific ways in which the present health care system works against a group's self-interest. More specifically, the speakers of the session should be prepared to address the specific, local concerns of several of the groups represented in the audience. Small group exercises, which place individuals from the same constituency group together to identify and solve problems around mutual concerns, also underscore a group's vested interests. The written materials need to highlight statistics, facts, and policy decisions that apply to specific constituency groups.

ACTION #5: Identify and relate to participants as representatives of their constituency rather than autonomous individuals. Instill a sense of accountability to their group.

As mentioned before, the bulk of the workshop trainees needs to be recruited from organized groups and should represent those groups at least informally. In recruiting, it is important not to overlook those organizations and agencies with paid staff who represent the targeted constituencies (such as social service agencies, legal services, and community clinics). These kinds of participants can be held directly accountable to their organizations, and often the sponsoring organizations will release the participants to do additional advocacy work on the agency's time.

If individuals without an organizational affiliation are interested in participating in the training, it is often possible to encourage those individuals to join an organization whose interests they may be able to represent. This provides an organizational context for their activities and also includes yet another group into the broader goals and efforts of the training.

Recruitment of organizationally identified participants is merely the first step in building a network of advocates who can relate to group concerns rather than individual ones. The workshop itself is the primary arena in which organizational accountability is stressed. In the CalPIRG series, every effort was made in introductions, announcements, and small group assignments to refer to a participant's organization rather than to a person's individual identity. For example, individuals were assigned to small group exercises not by name identification, but by group or organizational affiliation.

Additionally, the content of several small group exercises focused on coalition and constituency building. In one exercise, the participants were encouraged to work with their organizations to identify a health-related issue which had the potential for community action. This kind of "homework" exercise not only prompted the trainees to relate to their organization, but it also provided a mechanism for generating interest in advocacy beyond the training.

Those trainees who received active support for their participation in the training from their organizations were more accountable to their group and shared more policy and advocacy information acquired through the training with their group. The CalPIRG staff encouraged this informal and formal support by contacting organizational key leaders throughout the program to share information and offer technical assistance to their groups. On a number of occasions, key constituency leaders were invited either to attend workshops or to speak at workshops. Also, at the beginning of the project, a letter that explained the goals of the training was sent to the leadership of all the participating groups. The letter identified their representative at the training and also praised the group for identifying health policy as an organizational priority.

ACTION #6: Stress the commonality of concerns among diverse groups to build solidarity and emphasize the potential of collective action.

One of the uniting themes of the workshop series was that different groups, whether they be ethnic, disabled, women's, seniors', or labor groups, have basically the same health needs. Furthermore, a parallel theme was that there are specific, identifiable, and systemic forces that obstruct the provision of quality health care for the groups represented at the training. These themes were woven into the speakers' presentation, the training materials, the small group exercises, and in the advocacy activities which followed the series.

For example, the maldistribution of health care resources was discussed from a number of vantage points, with a particular emphasis on the relationship between the maldistribution of resources and the lack of primary health care services in the community. Each additional perspective served to extend the definition of the problem to include an expanding number of constituencies. In particular, the workshop facilitated a growing understanding among five constituencies who are concerned with the lack of appropriate primary care: ethnic minorities, women, labor, industry, and holistic health. The problem was initially defined by minority participants in terms of access and barriers to care, by women participants in terms of appropriate obstetrical and gynecological care, by labor and industry representatives in terms of cost containment and unnecessary hospital overutilization, and by holistic health representatives in terms of invasive medical procedures and excessive use of prescribed drugs. As the workshop series unfolded, these participants gradually enlarged their criticism of the current allocation of health resources to include the concerns of other groups, largely because they perceived the causes of the maldistribution to be essentially the same for each of the affected groups.

The potential for collective action was stressed in a number of ways. The written materials contained several case studies of coalition advocacy efforts throughout the nation around both health planning and policy issues. Several of the audiovisual documentaries also highlighted the force of group activity. The importance of united action was underscored both by CalPIRG staff and by workshop speakers. Workshop speakers, primed on local issues, often suggested issue areas or HSA activities that could serve as a focal point for coalition efforts.

ACTION #7: Underscore inequities in the system to impact participants on an emotional level. Concurrently, direct participants to immediate outlets for action.

Although it is important to cite health service injustices in recruiting efforts, action guideline number 7 is implemented primarily in the context of the workshop event itself. Much of the success of mobilizing a workshop group to action rests with the creation of a lively training environment, one which encourages participants to question traditional assumptions and one which uses enjoyable group learning techniques (such as role-playing, mock situations, and simulation games). The creation of an atmosphere that invites controversial and stimulating audience participation is the same atmosphere that fosters group activism beyond the workshop.

The person who convenes the workshop (in this case, the staff), not the speaker or the resource people, controls the emotional tone of the workshop. An informal atmosphere that encourages participants to share both their analytical and impassioned reactions to health policy issues brings culturally diverse participants together through a uniting common experience. Again, this facilitates coalition building and future collective action.

Choosing workshop speakers who can convey substantive information with local examples and a sense of community spirit can further the cohesiveness of the group. The selected speakers need to feel comfortable in articulating stands that the traditional health industry may not support, particularly in a panel discussion situation in which various interests that are not necessarily community-oriented may be represented.

To prepare a group to engage in community action, the content of the workshops must be technically sound and must emphasize the policy implications in human, day-to-day terms. For example, the CalPIRG workshop on excess hospital capacity was entitled "Hospitals: Is Bigger Really Better?" The workshop examined the historical and regulatory forces influencing excess capacity, but it also spoke to the more galvanizing issues of unnecessary surgery, lack of primary care in the inner city, and medical empire building.

The educational experience provided a catalyst for community action outside the workshop. The participants were regularly encouraged to attend meetings, hearings, and rallies on community health care issues. In particular, trainees were requested to fill out applications for the various HSA committees to exert a direct influence on the local HSA decision-making process.

Probably the most important mechanism in channeling the activism of the participants was the emergence of the Health Action Coalition (HAC). The San Diego Health Action Coalition formed during CalPIRG's first training series. It provided the participants with an ongoing structure—with regular meetings and specific issue campaigns—to join.

The Health Action Coalition used the network created by the training sessions as a base of mass support for its activities. Training participants were often invited by the coalition to testify before health policy boards and to provide audience support for coalition efforts. Since the workshop provided a common perception of the inadequacies and injustices of the health care system, the coalition was able to mobilize workshop trainees without significant value conflicts.

ACTION #8: Involve participants in events that will provide them with tangible rewards and outcomes that are likely to be successful.

The advocacy network (Health Action Coalition) that grew out of CalPIRG's first series provided participants with specific, local examples of victorious community action. These successes ranged from defeating a Certificate-of-Need application before the HSA to sponsoring a lively organizing session on hospitals' Hill Burton obligation.* Throughout the workshop series, staff and the speakers were able to refer to the successes of the coalition to illustrate the value of advocacy activities.

If the workshops are being sponsored in an area that does not already have the beginnings of a health advocacy group, they can be structured to nurture the spontaneous growth of such an organization. In the workshop context, HSA staff can support consumer coalition development by: (1) using written materials and speakers that cite case examples from other successful consumer/advocacy groups across the nation; (2) encouraging the participants as an informal group to attend hearings, ask questions, and deliver short pieces of testimony at these

meetings; and (3) explaining the ability of HSA staff to give substantial technical assistance to consumer or community groups if so requested. Once a small group has formed that is working on a community health issue, it is much easier to involve the participants in activities that are likely to meet with success.

Informing workshop trainees of the ongoing "steps" of a community action as it occurs through time is an effective way to involve participants in specific activities. This approach emotionally invests workshop participants in the outcome of an effort as it emerges. Once trainees have observed the workings of a successful campaign from a close distance, they will be more apt to participate actively in the next project.

In attempting to create rewarding situations, it is essential to recognize that the success of an organizing endeavor rests largely with goal definition. It is important to select short-range goals and to celebrate modest triumphs. For example, placing members of the workshop network on strategic HSA committees, organizing five speakers to testify at a hearing or having a participant quoted in the local newspaper should be seen as a victory. This type of an approach brings new members into the effort and sustains the involvement of the current activists. Each small success creates new resources upon which to base another, more extensive organizing effort.

There are several other immediate "rewards" that were integrated into the CalPIRG program. Small stipends were available for those participants who needed child care or mileage reimbursement. A certificate of completion was awarded to participants at the end of the training.

---

*Under the Hospital Survey and Construction Act of 1946—known as the Hill-Burton—joint federal and state funding was provided for construction of hospitals and neighborhood health centers. Modified in 1964, funding was provided for regional, or areawide, voluntary health facilities planning agencies.

ACTION #9: Implement the organizing efforts, considering a form and style with which the community can identify.

Community organizers have followed this age-old dictum for years. In the CalPIRG project, this lesson was best exemplified by the actual workshop event. Speakers were chosen who work extensively with their communities and identify with the perceptions of constituency advocates. The workshop site was selected for its central location, disabled access, and previous association with grass-roots groups.

The creation of an informal workshop atmosphere is also important to meeting this "form and style" criterion. An environment must be created wherein participants, both in small groups and in larger sessions, can challenge resource people, brainstorm about upcoming community activities, divide up the tasks of a successful coalition effort, and agree to support one another in controversial situations.

ACTION #10: Provide substantive information in a manner that is comprehensible, relevant, and usable by the community advocate.

Written, oral, and group exercise information needs to be communicated to workshop participants with three objectives in mind: (1) exposure to the extent of the problem and its causes, (2) identification of short- and long-term solutions to the problem, and (3) delineation of the here-and-now action steps which directly relate to the identified solution. For each workshop topic, staff and speakers constantly need to draw the connection between the theoretical overview of the problem, the local situation, and specific organizing strategies that the group could realistically pursue.

Although it is essential to include technical information in the workshop series, it is equally important to teach participants how to look beyond the technical to the social equity and political implications of a particular policy issue. By and large consumer and community-based trainees are concerned with the right to quality health care, the promotion of health maintenance, and the affordability of health care services. If a given planning/policy issue directly supports or attacks this value base, community groups will master the technical piece of the policy in an attempt to advocate for their constituency. It is, therefore, the responsibility of the staff and resource speakers to relate technical information in a way that can be used in public policy advocacy work.

Small group experiences provide an excellent opportunity for individuals to grapple with complex issues as well as to learn specific participation skills. Such exercises should encourage critical listening and analysis, assertive questioning, extemporaneous speaking, and the ability to defend one's opinion in a conflict situation. Other skills that should be reviewed for the trainees are lobbying, effective use of the media, and effective utilization of local and statewide consumer resource people.

On each topic, printed material including a fact sheet, several graphic representations, a brief background article, a bibliography, localized information, and a list of statewide and national resources should be distributed to the trainees. Optimally, a small group exercise and participant self-test would also be included in the packet.

In preparing the printed information

for the trainees, staff need to be aware of the various national publications that provide an in-depth consumer-oriented perspective. Some of these journals are *Consumer Health Perspective* (New York); *Health Law Project Library Bulletin*—soon to be out of print, but their back issues are worth your while (Philadelphia); *Health/PAC Bulletin* (New York); *Consumer Health Action Network: C.H.A.N.* (Washington, D.C.); and *Health Law Newsletter* (Santa Monica, California).

ACTION #11: Structure into each phase of the organizing effort activities that will meet the personal and social needs of those involved.

If a sustained community advocacy effort is to emerge from the workshop series, then meeting the personal and social needs of participants is an essential ingredient of the workshop design. Again, this guideline needs to be integrated into several of the workshop phases: recruitment, the educational event itself, and continued participant involvement in the workshop series.

In the recruitment and continued involvement phases, personal staff contact (in-person or phone) significantly increases participant investment in the process. Additionally, official recognition of trainees' participation by their constituency group also influences commitment to the workshop series.

The workshop event can promote the informal interactions that encourage local network and coalition building. Therefore, social hours, coffee breaks, wine and cheese receptions, and small group exercises are crucial to the workshop structure. The workshop speakers also have a definite role to play. Approachable resource people add another dimension to the workshops' informal interactions. If workshop speakers offer their technical assistance, phone numbers, advice, and so on to the participants' network, the statewide network is expanded by yet another local group of advocates, and the local advocates have experts to call upon to assist them in developing future policy positions.

Additionally, the direct contact that staff as "organizers" make with the participants cannot be underestimated. Staff can often provide an initial binding force which can be instrumental to the successful emergence of a caucus/coalition. For these reasons, staff should try to free themselves from logistical tasks during the workshop as much as possible.

The personal and social networks that were built over the course of the Cal-PIRG training were one of the most valuable features of the project. This could not have been accomplished had the project sponsored a number of "one-shot" workshops. HSA's need to consider seriously this dynamic in planning for the consumer education needs of their volunteers and the community.

BARRIERS AND SOLUTIONS TO IMPLEMENTATION

The foregoing discussion outlines the important elements of an HSA-sponsored consumer education program which can activate participation in health planning. But the potential successes and outcomes of such a program may generate resistance to its very implementation. Other obstacles may develop from real or perceived institutional limitations. Therefore, it is important to anticipate the barriers to implementation, which may be created by the internal workings of the agency, staff responsibilities, and volunteer/community responses, and consider the various solutions to these barriers.

Agency leadership—staff and volunteer—may feel threatened by the active participation of a community and volunteer force that has developed a sense of purpose, identity, and investment in effectively representing their constituency. Their assertions may require alteration of set work programs, timetables, staffing patterns, and agency resource allocation. They may challenge the processes and behavior of staff and volunteers that promote decision making by consensus approach and discourage the forceful representation of differing perspectives. In short, the status quo may be disturbed, and the agency may either have to shift resources to respond or deal with a disgruntled group. Traditionally, the inclination toward institutional stability makes an agency defensive about citizen participation that includes criticism.

The agency leadership may fear a provider backlash and resulting noncooperation if resources appear to be supporting the development of an effective consumer voice that generates "conflict" in the planning process. Agencies that do not acknowledge the existing differences between consumer and provider interests and the benefits that can be derived from active consumer input will find it difficult to respond to provider reactions to the debate and controversy that the agency has helped foster.

The lack of acknowledgment of differing perspectives will also challenge the very need for an educational program that primarily provides a consumer-oriented analysis of health/medical care issues. Further, the agency may question the need for selective outreach methods necessary to recruit participants who will represent consumer-oriented interests.

Finally, the agency may cite administrative limitations that create obstacles to implementation of the program. Staff may hesitate to assume additional responsibilities that the program might entail. There may not be staff expertise in developing and implementing a consumer-oriented educational program. Financial resources may not be available for such an effort. And the timetables set for plan development, CON reviews, and other processes may create problems for inclusion of another project into the agency's work plan.

Most HSA's can justifiably claim these barriers. However, unless the leadership of the agencies is convinced of the merits of a consumer-oriented educational program to promote participation, the obstacles will work to inhibit implementation of such a program. These barriers must therefore be acknowledged and overcome.

The basic approach to confronting obstacles to educating consumer-oriented volunteers and community is to promote the value of constructive conflict as a valid mode of decision making. The HSA leadership must view the informed articulation of conflicting points of view and the debate that ensues as a positive consequence of an active, pluralistic society and one that induces constituency investment in the health planning process. The agency must initially agree that there are some conflicts of interest among different segments of the community and that certain of these interests lack effective representation. Without programs aimed specifically at empowering these interests, passivity, frustration, and ultimate withdrawal from the process by critical constituencies will follow. Not only will the health plans for the area and implementation capabilities suffer from lack of input from these groups, but the agency will lose community credibility and support, which are crucial for its efficacy, if not its existence. Therefore agency leadership must come to appreciate and support an informed and activated consumer-oriented volunteer and public voice.

Development of training programs directed toward consumer oriented volunteers can be justified by requirements of P.L. 96-79 [Health Planning and Resources Development Amendments of 1979]. According to Sec. 112(c), staff responsibilities must be assigned to provide technical assistance to governing body members with an emphasis on consumer volunteers. The redefinition of staff roles, commitment of resources to educational activities, and restructuring of work programs must be undertaken to fulfill the law's mandate. Programs aimed at community and consumer-oriented issues are appropriate under this regulation.

The targeted recruitment of participants is a key ingredient of a successful program and can be cited as a necessary means to bring together people with shared concerns and goals. Another approach would be an educational program open to all but having, among others, specific workshops that provide a forum for constituencies who have had little influence in the health planning process. Yet another method would be to have separate workshops for consumers and providers, thus giving both interests the benefit of training.

To overcome the restraints that staff may feel in initiating aggressive consumer-oriented education, consumer volunteers and community groups could be the advocates for such an educational program and request it from the agency. Consumers may need to know that such an option exists, so they can act accordingly. If the request comes from the volunteers or community they will have a further investment in active formulation and participation in the program. Therefore, it would serve the HSA well to support the ongoing development of community health advocacy groups that can maintain active involvement in health planning.

The agency must be willing to commit resources to the program. It is possible to supplement existing financial resources with grants specifically for educational programs. For instance, the Department of Health, Education and Welfare, Office of Consumer Education, has set as its funding priority proposals that further consumer involvement in decision-making bodies. Many private local foundations have expressed interest in supporting projects which enhance the quality of life in terms of citizen participation. Even without supplements there are ways to minimize agency costs. Many consumer advocates are willing to plan, implement, and participate in programs with no or small honorariums. There are often valuable resource people in the community who can be called upon. Materials generated for consumer-oriented training by other organizations can be duplicated. Since the quality of the programs is far more important than quantity, limiting the number of programs but doing an outreach, content and format development, and follow-up that build constituency identification and activism may be one solution to the limited-resource problem. And, in the end, there may be a need to change the ordering of agency priorities so that sufficient monies are allocated to support an effective consumer education program.

OUTLINE FOR COMMUNITY ACTION

1. Focus on a *specific event* that will invite active and/or passive participation of the target community groups.
2. Extend outreach efforts to the greatest number of individuals within the target groups to increase the base of eventual activists.
3. Find *key leaders* (formal and informal) within each target group who will actively support the program and promote participation by their group.
4. Activate involvement of different constituency groups by appealing to their particular vested interests.
5. Identify and relate to participants as representatives of their constituency rather than as autonomous individuals. Instill a sense of accountability to their group.
6. Stress the commonality of concerns among diverse groups to build solidarity and emphasize the potential of collective action.
7. Underscore inequities in the system to impact participants on an emotional level. Concurrently direct participants to immediate outlets for action.
8. Involve participants in events that will provide them with tangible rewards and outcomes which are likely to be successful.
9. Implement the organizing efforts, considering a *form* and *style* with which the target community can identify.
10. Provide substantive information in a manner that is comprehensible, relevant, and usable by the community advocate.
11. Structure into each phase of the organizing effort activities that will meet the personal and social needs of those involved.

17. FOR A DEMOCRATIC REVOLUTION: THE GRASS-ROOTS PERSPECTIVE

Warren C. Haggstrom

There are two basic approaches to getting things done. The traditional way is the top-down approach: the formation of undemocratic work, military, and other organizations. In these organizations, most people who carry out the tasks of the organization don't have much say in deciding what is to be done.

Reproduced by permission of the author. This is an unpublished article.

The second basic approach, the grass-roots approach, is rapidly expanding, but does not yet usually involve most of the hours of the lives of those in it. When ordinary people join together on a basis of equality to accomplish something, they are taking the grass-roots approach. Currently, in the United States, the grass-roots approach includes self-help groups (about 14 million people), neighborhood organizations (about 20 million people), and the tens of millions of people involved in grass-roots co-ops, political groupings, labor unions, religious organizations, issue movements, and other voluntary organizations—a large and growing population of Americans. The grass-roots approach not only can be more efficient than is the usual way, but it can also be more beneficial educationally and psychologically for those affected.

I anticipate that the grass-roots approach, as it becomes perfected, will gradually replace the traditional, undemocratic top-down approach for getting things done. It is that replacement that I call a *democratic revolution*.

Will the democratic revolution be good or bad? The answer to that question depends on its outcomes, all things considered, for people. What is best for the people of the United States? Although the answer to this question involves economics, it also involves something broader: the entire human being.

We can begin by considering how to create social arrangements which will lead us to act in such a way that our actions have the best possible outcomes for people. That is a question of effective *helping* of people.

Grass-roots organizing can be understood as a way to *help* people in need in our society. Helping is a *core* activity, *not* peripheral, and not necessarily involving altruism, in any complex society such as the United States. To evaluate and develop modes of helping, therefore, is to get at the very foundations of all aspects of American life.

HELPING

Each person leads a unique life and more or less continues that life in such fashion as to realize best his or her potential for happiness or accomplishment. The extent to which a person realizes his or her positive potentialities is the extent to which she or he *flourishes*. To *help* a person is to enhance his or her level of flourishing or self-realization or to stave off threats to it.

Help may be

1. *unintended* (which would happen if, for example, the pursuit of economic self-interest within a capitalistic system were to enhance some aspects of self-realization throughout a society)
2. *intended* (which includes rushing to the aid of someone in distress)
3. *official* (that is, what is described as helping in an official report)

Official helping includes medicine, public health, social work, and so forth. The most important single characteristic of helping is the extent of *net effectiveness* of a helper.

Definition 1: Given all the positive, negative, and other consequences of the helping activity, the net effectiveness of a helper is how many people are helped how much by the helper after subtracting the harmful consequences of his or her or its helping activity.

Also, I propose the following

Postulate 1: The net effectiveness of helping is increased in direct relationship with the extent to which the helper is under the control of the person(s) helped.

There are two main classifications of helping activity in the United States in which the helper is under the control of the person(s) being helped.

First, employees in top-down organizations help (*a*) those in charge of the organizations (executives, administrators, some board members), and also, but not necessarily, (*b*) those outside the organizations who are affected by them. For example, a worker in an automobile assembly plant helps the bosses and *may* also help those who buy the automobiles assembled by the plant. We can say that the employee as helper is controlled directly by the bosses and indirectly, just possibly, by automobile sales.

Workers also help themselves to the extent to which they define and control the work or its related benefits. They have very little control of work on an assembly line, but wages and fringe benefits help the worker outside the job itself.

Second, some enterprises, such as co-ops, are officially self-help in nature, and in these the helpers are usually *ipso facto* more nearly under the control of those helped than is the case in top-down organizations.

A third category in which helpers might appear to be controlled by those being helped consists of official helpers in private practice, for example, some physicians, clinical psychologists, clinical social workers, and so forth. However, efforts by the professions to be

self-regulating and keep their practices autonomous through a variety of strategies usually has effectively removed much impact on this kind of helping by those ostensibly being helped. Actually, however, private practice in the helping professions can best be characterized as a kind of self-help activity.

In most official helping, there is not even the extremely limited impact on the helpers by those ostensibly being helped as patients and clients have on private practice. For example, social agencies are almost invulnerable to initiatives of their clients even though some of them have powerless "advisory" boards of clients whom they select. Institutions of formal education are similarly relatively invulnerable to initiatives of students except during rare times of crisis.

Postulate 1 thus applies to most official helping, making it possible for us to derive:

Theorem 1: The net effectiveness of most official helping is far less than is that of helping in the two other main categories.

Within the official helping process, it is crucial to consider the extent to which those officially helped actually are helped. Normally, these diverge widely.

For example, consider foreign aid by the United States to El Salvador. It may be publicized as help to the people of El Salvador by the generous people of the United States. But those actually helped may turn out to be almost entirely a tiny elite in El Salvador and a tiny elite in the United States.

It would be instructive to examine the efforts of the professional organizations of the helping professions. Do those organizations act effectively to reduce unmet need? Or do they act primarily on behalf of the self-interests of their members? Such an analysis may reveal that, contrary to their carefully cultivated public images, they are primarily self-help efforts by people not in need. In that case, we would propose:

Postulate 2: The net effectiveness of most official helping is primarily an outcome of their self-help characteristics and is not related to the need of those being helped, and

Postulate 3: The net effectiveness of official helping is not closely related to the altruism of officially designated helpers.

Let us next illustrate Theorem 1 and Postulates 2 and 3.

If you "think through" the following illustration, the reasons for supposing the validity of the three postulates and of Theorem 1 will become apparent.

Official Helping (Poverty): An Illustration

Official helpers include physicians, psychiatrists, clinical psychologists, social workers, and members of many other recognized "helping" professions. Social work help is extended mostly through social agencies, nonprofit bureaucratic organizations often staffed in part by professional social workers. A child guidance clinic, a family service agency, and public welfare agencies all are social agencies. But this official social work approach to helping poor people is not effective for many reasons. Poverty is both economic and psychological. The economy of poverty has not been much affected in the United States for a long

time. What help poor people have gotten by this means has come about through increases in general economic prosperity or through the allocation of public funds through the political process (like cash welfare payments, food stamps, rent supplements, medicare, public housing, and so forth). Neither prosperity nor legislation results from social work practice. The psychology of poverty has only worsened during recent decades—and social workers, in headlong retreat from their traditional preoccupation with poor people, have not even tried to affect it significantly.

The economy and the psychology of poverty can be positively altered only by some kind of social change. For example, so long as 6 to 8 percent unemployment is planned as normal, poverty on a large scale is also being planned as normal.

In American history, arguments about social policies designed to tackle social problems (poverty, crime, and so forth) have been based on the *stability assumption:* namely, that our society can remain pretty much the same as it mobilizes money and people (especially experts and professionals) to tackle such problems. The arguments have tended to be about money to be spent on dealing with the problem, and the nature and organization of the people to be mobilized. The grass roots perspective arises in relation to the state of affairs resulting from the long reign of the stability assumption, a reign which has maintained, not diminished, most such problems.

Further, the creation of social situations in which poor people will tend to flourish, which will also benefit them psychologically, also requires planned social change. Given the extent to which business and political elites affect the expenditure of funds for helping purposes, social agencies cannot even try to work on any extent of social change which will make much difference without their funds being jeopardized. Social changes, then, do not and cannot help poor people very much.

Bureaucratic agencies are so structured that a key element in helping poor people remains unknown to the helpers. That element is the meaning of being poor, the collective psychology and subjectivity of poverty, as it exists within the communities of poor people. Without such understanding, it is impossible to enhance predictably the level of flourishing of poor clients.

Furthermore, the policies of social agencies are set by boards and administrators. But they are structurally removed by their positions from any direct acquaintance with the clientele of the agencies, or more seriously, those in greatest need, who may not be clients. Thus, the people in charge are the least able to make certain that help extended is appropriate for those who most need help. But even if boards and administrators had more knowledge, they do not have the right to decide for those needing help.

By working in bureaucratic agencies, social workers are led by their work situations to identify first with the agency or profession and only secondly with those needing help. The structured incentive system of agencies support agency maintenance and expansion, and there is no external force that requires attention to carrying out its intended goals. The result is that social agencies become self-absorbed narcissistic collectivities rather than instrumental to the determined perception and reduction of unmet need.

Traditional helping approaches separate helpers from those toward whom help is directed. As a result, it is in the interest of professional social workers to help themselves first. It is in the interest of professional social workers to reduce attention to people in need to, at best, a second priority. Official helpers act largely on the basis of their perceived self-interest. Impulses toward professionalization play a similar role, with similar consequences.

Most social workers haven't been selected for their interest in, or knowledge of, poor people, especially the invisible characteristics of communities of poor people. Social workers come mostly from two groups. One group, the largest, consists of people from nonpoor backgrounds, most of whom will remain ignorant of the experience of poverty and its meanings for their entire lives. The other group is made up of people trying to escape from their poverty backgrounds and from most poor people— they are those from among the poor who do not identify with, and who will never be of help to, persons with long-term low incomes. Furthermore, neither social work students nor the faculties of schools of social work have often been selected as people interested in, or educated for, social change efforts, and therefore, cannot even conceptualize what is needed if poor people are to be helped.

Because a broad public mistakenly believes that social work is dealing with the problems of poor people, the very existence of social work saps motivation and support for the implementation of alternative ways to meet needs and thereby diminishes the possibility that really effective help will eventually be extended to people who are poor.

There is little evidence of the effectiveness of social work intervention at any level. The research on the effectiveness of casework has produced results which can only be described as "profoundly discouraging" to caseworkers and their supporters. If social workers were concerned with helping people, they would be heavily involved in effectiveness research. They are not.

The knowledge base of contemporary social work appears to be weak. Although there are recipes for professional action, those recipes are often only distantly related to reasons or evidence. For that reason, it can be argued that social work is mostly superstition: a semiprofession based on a semimythology. Social work graduate students pay in money and time to acquire this dubious lore, oblivious to the comment of Socrates that "There is far greater peril in buying knowledge than in buying meat and drink." (Plato, Protogoras)

There is not, within social work, a language that promotes thinking and critical discourse. Nor are there arenas within which critical discourse can well occur. For example, such words as "empowerment," "problem solving," "help," and many others are used within social work imprecisely and in ways that violate their literal meanings. In the social work profession, matters of fact are supposed to be taken on faith. Crucial issues are thereby removed from analytic and critical discussion. Professional values thus make it impossible for the profession to advance except through the perfecting of whatever now exists.

The bureaucratic way of organizing helping leads to rule orientations and away from consequence orientations on the part of helpers. This not only ends in collective narcissism, but also leads to a disinclination to pay attention to, and relate to, unmet need.

Since the decisions of social agencies and their personnel affect actual and potential clients far more than do actual and potential client decisions affect social agencies, the agency-client relationships directly increase the dependency of those seeking help. The meaning of these dependency relationships communicates the inferiority of those needing help and therefore further harms them.

The bureaucratic organization of helping tends, because of the related self-preoccupation, to maintain the status quo regardless of external social changes which always are taking place, and also regardless of the existence of unmet need.

Unintentionally, traditional social work focuses on the inadequacies and disabilities of poor people (deficiencies which need remedying) and not on their talents, capacities, intelligence, and other strengths. This focus defines poor people by their disabilities and thereby ignores other possible definitions, which would be more helpful.

The units defined by social workers have usually ignored extended families and thereby helped to undermine mutual aid resources which traditionally have been valuable supports for them. Social agencies are defining institutions.

Are most social workers or other traditional helpers to blame for this state of affairs? I think not. It is the assumptions on the basis of which traditional helping has occurred which are responsible for the deficiencies.

In February 1917 Antonio Gramsci commented with searing love and indignation: "I hate those who are indifferent." It is true that indifference is the greatest insult which can be rendered to people in need of help. But what has caused the mass indifference, even within the helping professions, to people in great need? The motives of most of them are positive (if somewhat weak). It is rather that most traditional helpers have become entangled in evil social arrangements designed to serve political, economic, military, intellectual, and social elites, and to perpetuate and expand bureaucracies, regardless of the consequences for people. As a result, the interests of most traditional helpers have worked against their extending effective help to people in great need.

The most urgent need for help in the United States is the need of the tens of millions of poor people who not only suffer greater hardships than do affluent people (there is evidence that poverty itself shortens life expectancy in a population, increases the rates of a wide variety of diseases, and assaults the personalities of those subject to it), but who also can't afford to hire helpers for themselves.

A second problem of very great consequence is nearly universal. It is the decline during past decades of the meaningfulness of life for most people, a likely outcome of the rise of bureaucracy and consumerism and a concomitant decline in the extent to which most people take charge of and define their own lives in ways that centrally matter to them, given their life histories.

Effective Helping

On the basis of the preceding remarks, it is clear that the net effectiveness of helping has little to do with the intentions of helpers. Further, helping is a central characteristic of any society, not something restricted to a residual category.

This discussion has stressed only the effect of placing helping in the hands of those helped. But, if one does not take a

second step, the effectiveness of helping remains far below what is otherwise possible. For example, if one does no more than to place helping under the control of those being helped, then helping may tend to concentrate its benefits on small elites, and the helping may deviate from the flourishing of those helped into a pandering to their tastes, wants, pleasures, satisfactions, and prejudices, or to a small sector of their lives (as with solely economic help). Thus the net effectiveness of helping will be improved by the expansion of democracy in all facets of our society and an expansion of *thinking*. Thus, we can formulate Postulate 4 considering helping as follows:

Other things remaining the same, the net effectiveness of helping in which the helper is under the control of the person(s) helped is increased in direct relationship with the extent to which the helping process is democratic and characterized by a thinking through of how best to proceed in helping.

It now becomes plausible to assume that an optimal institutionalization of helping can occur through the creation of an expanding, rational, self-educative, mass social movement with enough power to effectuate its major goals.

THE GRASS-ROOTS SOLUTION

Grass-roots organizing is a "bottom-up" process through which ordinary people join together to accomplish something. A grass-roots organizer is one who helps ordinary people to take charge of and improve their own lives through collective action directed toward accomplishing some social change. The grass-roots approach, therefore, is democratic (run by members) and is in stark contrast to the approach of accomplishing things through elites running authoritarian bureaucratic organizations (in factories, offices, social agencies, educational bureaucracies, the military, and so forth).

One basic question to ask concerning any organization called "grass roots" is "who is really in charge?" Although there are few perfect examples of a grass-roots approach, if a leader or a clique really runs things (as in political, labor union, community, or other organizations), then it is not grass roots even though it may be called "grass roots." Since words concerned with grass roots are often popular, they are frequently taken up to give a positive ring to one or another authoritarian enterprise (for example, an organization for "economic democracy," a "community development" county department). Sophisticated and authentic grass-roots organizations typically ensure that there is much honest and open critical discussion concerning what is to be done, with the right of any person vigorously protected who wants to dissent from the rest. Some co-ops, neighborhood organizations, block clubs, political organizations, labor unions, churches, towns, and so forth are grass-roots organizations.

When grass-roots organizations join together on a democratic basis, or expand greatly without losing their democratic characteristics, in order to struggle toward securing some social change, they are trying to form a *grass-roots movement*. If they are actually to become a grass-roots movement, they must make some progress toward the change they seek. As is true of grass-root organizations, a grass-roots movement may have

much or little formal structure (that is, explicit and legitimated rules to guide their internal processes).

For the first centuries of its existence, Christianity was a religious grass-roots movement. The spread of the town meetings in New England early in the history of the United States was a political grass-roots movement. The spread of co-ops in many rural localities in the midwestern and southwestern United States and in parts of Canada formed a single economic grass-roots movement, which was especially prominent in the late nineteenth and early twentieth centuries. The fast spreading ACORN (Association of Community Organizations for Reform Now), a national congery of neighborhood organizations, is a grass-roots neighborhood movement which has acquired about 34,000 dues-paying member households, mostly during the past five years.

A grass-roots movement becomes most relevant to social change by developing power. The power of such a movement usually depends upon the number of participants; the intensity of their involvement; their "staying ability"; the extent to which it is organized; the money, information, skills, and other resources available to it; its relationships to opponent vulnerabilities; and the "levels of consciousness" of its participants.

Historically, social movements have been among the most important factors in securing basic social changes. We are now seeking to combine technological innovation (another historically important source of social changes) with a scientific grass-roots movement approach with the aim of bringing about a powerful permanent process through which Americans will take charge of their society in such fashion as to flourish maximally and in so doing move toward the resolution or alleviation of all social problems, including the renewal of meaningful activity for most of the population. The progress of the grass-roots neighborhood movement during the last two decades, now involving tens of millions of people, has provided experience, sophistication, hope, and determination for the future of the grass-roots approach in our country.

THE GENERIC GRASS-ROOTS MOVEMENT

The word "generic" refers to all aspects of people's lives: psychological, moral, social, spiritual, educational, matters of pleasure and fun, work, and so forth. The idea of the generic grass-roots movement is to create a movement that will become an effective scientific, rational, and good force for social change in our society, a movement involving most Americans that will permanently endure. We do not now know whether such a generic grass-roots movement is possible or, if it turns out to be possible, whether it can result in a major transformation of our society.

At present in our society, people with lower incomes tend to be more involved in staving off threats to their self-realization (the threat of unemployment, of being controlled by others, of being dependent, of welfare, of having to accept even worse alternative jobs, and so on), than in positive flourishing. Positive incentives are more available to those with higher incomes. It is that available incentive difference and the meanings related to it that account for much of the social class differences in vitality and activity, including intellec-

tual activity. We may, therefore, now state:

Postulate 5: Other things remaining the same, the grass-roots generic movement will contribute far more to the general level of personal self-realization than does the present top-down structuring of most of our society.

A DEMOCRATIC REVOLUTION?

Persons associated with the grass-roots movement will come to understand democratic administration (as opposed to the authoritarian approach), social change, the nature and history of social movements, power, the positives and negatives of a long-time perspective, thinking, meaning, truth, morality, relevancy, solidarity, and other topics. But, most central of all will be reality changing. Let me here briefly illustrate this essential concept. Reality consists not only of physical objects. It also consists of meanings. One meaning of a neighborhood may be that the people in it are inferior. That societally held meaning may ensure that most of the people of the neighborhood lack confidence, energy, hope, determination, much skill, and many other characteristics. That meaning of the neighborhood may have been internalized by its residents, making it difficult for them to escape it even when they leave the neighborhood.

A grass-roots organizer working in that neighborhood may begin to focus existing discontents and interests of the residents into a change process. If that organizing effort is successful, some years later the meaning of the neighborhood may become one of the adequacy, or even superiority, of its members. This new meaning, carried partly by institutionalized internal groups, will support members into greater happiness, education, constructive activity, self-esteem, a kind of self-education, and a sturdy confidence and persistence in relating to the people and institutions in the vicinity of the neighborhood. Although the physical objects (houses, streets, human bodies) of the neighborhood may have changed very little, the reality of the neighborhood would have changed a great deal. Such a process would constitute reality changing on a local scale.

The proposed generic movement can be regarded as a social invention. Like other inventions, we may know early the main outlines of what will work but still need a long struggle to perfect it, to make it practical and beneficial.

To sum up, when it comes to helping people, "realism" and careerism, given present social arrangements, are impractical and destructive even to those who engage in them. Although there is no guarantee of what will work, it is an idealism rooted in history which relates to the future through imagination, thinking, reasons, evidence, and analyses by

people trying to tell the truth, which promises to work best, to be genuinely practical. But these are the qualities associated with the idealism inherent in the grass-roots perspective as it may come to be expressed in a generic grass-roots movement.

A revolution is a deliberate, basic, and sustained social transformation in a society resulting from changes in the relative power of groups within it. A revolution need not involve violence. By a "basic" transformation I mean one with substantial consequences for the general level of, and/or major varieties of, personal self-realization. We do not presuppose that a basic transformation primarily depends on something happening to the economy, the polity, the culture, technology, or any other sector or feature of society. A *democratic* revolution is one of, by, and for the people of a society. Perhaps one can now initiate in the United States a generic grass-roots movement that will eventually create an unusually desirable democratic revolution, one which will continue as a change process that will permanently work to enhance the lives of the American people.

18. MAKING AN ISSUE OF IT: THE CAMPAIGN HANDBOOK

League of Women Voters of the United States

Campaigning on an issue, like campaigning for public office, is a communication

Reproduced by permission of the publisher. From *Making an Issue of It: The Campaign Handbook,* League of Women Voters of the United States, 1976.

ications process with a political goal—winning votes. In a legislative campaign, however, the focus of your efforts is more on the legislators who must vote your legislation into law than on the voting public.

Like an election campaign, a legislative campaign is a group effort demanding good organization and a large and willing work force. There aren't many legislators who will propose or vote for a law that they believe will be bad for voters or that their constituents would not support. The job of a campaign, then, is to demonstrate that the legislation you back is good for citizens and that support from constituents exists.

Whatever your goal—cleaner air, an end to discrimination in employment, improved housing, school finance reform—the moment will come when you must decide whether a legislative campaign is the best way to reach that goal. Your organization needs to ask itself if it can marshal the commitment, the resources and the know-how to convince public officials that legislative action is necessary.

Since many good causes fail because their supporters are unable to deal with the machinery of state, local or federal government, this article is designed to help you organize your campaign so that you can deal effectively with potential snags, whether they are caused by the complexity of government or people's reluctance to get involved, and to help you win your fight. It has been written to address the complexities of a statewide legislative campaign, but is applicable in principle to a smaller target, such as a city council, as well. Regardless of where you intend to focus your efforts, the handbook can help you zero in on problems and resolve them before they get out of hand.

BUILDING A COALITION—WHY AND HOW

Political coalitions exist on the state and local level in virtually every state where legislative action is pending. The reason is simple—few laws get passed through the action of a single citizen group.

Necessary as a coalition may be, it's important to remember that a coalition is not a marriage for life. It is really an ad hoc, "sometime" thing. Its strength is the strength of the individuals and organizations that are affiliated; it does not, in reality, have an identity of its own. Its function is to serve as a focal point, a clearinghouse and a coordinator; to make sure that participating organizations and other groups are doing all they can and what they are best able to do, to achieve a desired result.

Although a coalition may carry out agreed-upon activities—e.g. fundraising, public relations, oversight on local organization and lobbying efforts—it is not a substitute for commitment and action from member groups. In short, being represented in a coalition does not mean that an organization has done its bit and can sit back and "let the coalition do it."

A coalition's first task is to define why its goal is important—why legislation is necessary. The reason behind the goal will be important not only to convince legislators and the public but in soliciting campaign funds and volunteer efforts as well. The *why* should become a theme that permeates all campaign activities.

There are, of course, varying degrees of coalition participation, a fact that is readily apparent as the number of organizations lined up behind the legislative goal expands. Some organizations, for example, may not have a grassroots constituency that can be mobilized for local legislative district letter-writing or public relations efforts. That same group may, however, have a crackerjack lobbyist at the state capitol who can put some time and effort into the campaign.

All participating groups should be

encouraged to speak out in their own names, as well as under the coalition umbrella, in support of the goal. Obviously, the president of a state or local League of Women Voters has a higher recognition factor and carries more clout than does the chairperson of a newly formed, amorphous body with a name unfamiliar to the public. The mushrooming of special "committees" or "coalitions" during any election or legislative campaign is, by now, a fairly familiar phenomenon to both citizens and legislators. Very rarely do they swing much weight or many votes on their own. What counts are the joint efforts of each of the parties that have lent their name and support to the common goal.

Following are some general guidelines for working within a coalition.

Who Should Belong?

Ask *organizations* and *opinion leaders* who have, or should have, an interest in the legislation to participate. Contact state and local counterparts of national endorsers, but don't ignore a local organization just because its national affiliate has not endorsed. Similarly, do not ignore organizations or individuals merely because you disagree on other issues: *a coalition is formed for one purpose—to secure legislation.* All other agreements or disagreements can and should take a back seat. Once the prime goal is achieved, the members of the coalition go their own ways (though you may have found interesting new allies on other fronts).

When the constituency of the state or district in which the legislation is pending is predominantly rural, seek membership among organizations and leaders whose constituency is rural; home economics associations, visiting nurse associations, farm groups, church leadership.

Go after the organizations that have the greatest influence on your state or city legislative body. If they won't join, seek individual endorsements or behind-the-scenes backing. Sometimes powerful people are willing to help but unwilling to have it known publicly that they are doing so.

Some Rules of the Game

Make sure that everyone who joins the coalition—group or individual—understands and agrees to the rules of the game:

- The legislative goal should be clearly defined and stated; no one is empowered to speak for the coalition on any other issue.
- Each organization is free to act for itself, outside the coalition, but not in the name of the coalition except with appropriate authorization from other members. What is required for authorization should be delineated.
- The coalition will work best if its tasks are clearly defined and assigned. Decisions will be made by those empowered by the coalition members to do so. Probably a coordinating committee will be set up to coordinate the work of other committees, which are in turn responsible for specific functions within the coalition.
- Agree on the necessary and appropriate elements of a campaign. Assign responsibilities. If everyone can agree from the beginning that success is more important than individual or organizational prestige, later conflicts will be minimized (though seldom eliminated). In this kind of positive climate, tasks can be assigned to the individuals and organizations best able to perform them.

FIGURE 18.1
One Way to Organize Your Coordinating Committee

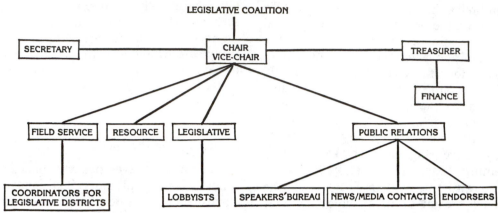

- Fund raising is necessary to both the largest and smallest campaigns. Who's paying for it—whether it is campaign literature, radio spots, or stamps and envelopes—is a question that even an all-volunteer campaign must face early in the campaign and be prepared to answer. Since money will be needed, determine a policy for fundraising and a tentative budget and try to stick to it. Money is the root of all evil only if you don't confront this issue right at the start.
- Decide how to maintain communication among member organizations—regular meetings? (schedule? place?) newsletters? telephone? etc.

It's one thing to list a number of parts that go into the makings of a successful coalition; it's quite another to achieve a well-coordinated, smooth-running coalition effort. Give-and-take is an integral part of coalition work. Every individual and every organization in a coalition has an identity (and probably an ego) of its own. It's important to keep in mind that organizations working in the coalition have different *raisons d'etre* and assign different values to the fight. Groups may differ on priorities, strategies, and/or tactics, and these differences can and do produce internal conflicts. Some groups are more successful in getting to the media. Is theirs the image that best serves the coalition's purpose? There can also be differences of opinion on when and how to lobby legislators—one group will want to push hard and early; another will favor a more passive, behind-the-scenes approach. "Activist" groups may devote more of their energies to the goal than do other coalition members and consequently to get a larger share of the spotlight. Reconciling these differences can get sticky. The task requires patience, tact, and the willingness to understand the reasons behind a group's advocacy of a particular approach.

There's no sure cure for settling internal organizational problems. However, solutions are more likely to be found if you have the pertinent facts at hand and are able to demonstrate conclusively the potential damage or advantage of a course of action. One of the main functions of a coalition is to gather and share intelligence and help all participants gain a clear understanding of political realities. The business of your coalition is the passage of particular legislation and, while it may not be the top priority for all member groups, coalition membership should be taken as a commitment to work for passage with maximum effort and efficiency.

If your coalition is effective, it should produce these results:

- Lobbyists know whom to talk to on what issues.
- Legislative attitudes are reported (particularly changes), and proper action results.
- Communications go to the right people in the right districts on the right issues at the right time.
- Visibility is promoted by a unified, cooperative campaign.
- Proponents *act* instead of reacting.
- The opposition is pinpointed and out-maneuvered.
- Everyone who wants to work has something useful to do.
- People and organizations with specific talents can use them most effectively.
- With constant interaction among committees (via task forces), no effort is wasted and action is directed effectively.

And "with a little bit of luck" it *should* also get that legislation passed.

Functions of a Coordinating Committee

To make daily decisions and determine common strategy and tactics, form a coordinating committee (by that or any other name). Occasionally, the coordinating committee (Figure 18.1) for a coalition's legislative action campaign has a *geographical* base: officers plus a coordinator for each legislative district. More often, it is *task-oriented:* officers plus a chairman for each major kind of responsibility. The second structure is represented in the sample table of organization below.

However you organize them, certain jobs have to get done, and a chairman must be assigned to carry out each major function. Where possible and appropriate, these functions, which are outlined below in terms of a state coalition, should be replicated at the local level.

Also, regular two-way communication must go on among the coordinating committee, district and local coordinators, and members of the coalition.

Five major committees (task forces) and their functions

1. Field Service (Operations)

Find coordinators in every legislative district.

Provide substantive information to district coordinators along with give-away material.

Provide "How-to" information (how to organize at the local level; how to get endorsers; how to set up speakers' bureaus; how to conduct a petition, letter-writing, or letters-to-editor campaign, etc.).

Keep district coordinators informed about political picture and strategy, scheduling, headcounts, where and what kind of pressure is needed.

Provide field visits and/or speakers from state coalition as needed.

2. Finance

Develop a budget.

Plan fund-raising activities: benefits (parties? speaking engagements?); direct mail, etc.

Plan personal solicitations of individuals and groups.

3. Resource or Research

Monitor opposition literature, speeches, etc.

Research answers to opposition *plus* positive arguments pertinent locally.

Research facts on the legislation and its impact. Provide fact sheets in simple, direct language to be used:

- by district workers;
- in news articles and releases, radio or TV programs;
- in flyers for public distribution;
- for briefing lobbyists and individuals who are answering or anticipating opposition publicly;
- in internal newsletters and bulletins for members of coalition organization;
- by legislators in committee or on the floor.

Know who supporters are.

Serve as clearinghouse for all information on the legislation.

4. Public Relations

Develop material (with Resource Committee) for public distribution (e.g. flyers, one-page fact sheets, logo, slogan).

Develop newsletter for workers to keep enthusiasm up, exchange good campaign ideas.

Set up clipping service, by district, to monitor press, pro and con.

Analyze positions of all relevant newspapers, TV and radio stations and get names of sympathetic reporters, publishers, producers; use them for advice and help in getting the proponents' story across.

Work on those elements of the media that are unsympathetic.

Analyze the power structure (ethnic, political, geographic, etc.); determine which segments of the population listen to whom.

Disseminate public information on substance, hearings and votes through news releases and stories; prepare sample news releases and stories for use by local organizations.

Set up TV and/or radio interviews or debates (in cooperation with Speakers Bureau).

As budget permits, develop radio and TV spots and newspaper ads.

Endorsers—subcommittee to PR Committee.

- Line up statewide endorsements for release at appropriate time, including prominent party leaders.
- Cooperate with district coordinators in lining up local endorsers, particularly in districts of crucial or swing votes.
- Keep building participating membership in coalition.
- Have someone specifically responsible for effort to recruit endorsements from a wide cross-section of key organizations and politically influential people.

Speakers' Bureau—subcommittee to PR Committee.
- Set up statewide bureau, get consent of all speakers, their availability schedules, how much reimbursement they'll need, etc.
- Train speakers as necessary. Provide sample speeches in simple, direct language (with help of Resource Committee). Include as part of training an interrogation session with the nasty questions raised by the opposition.
- Solicit speaking engagements at meetings, debates, radio, TV programs (with help of Public Relations Committee).
- Schedule speakers; coordinate with Field Service Committee for requests from local or district level.

5. Legislative

Set up and train a corps of lobbyists (easily accessible to the state capitol).

Maintain a regularly updated headcount (i.e., who is definitely for, who is opposed, who is uncommitted); double check the accuracy from as many sources as possible (without alienating your supporters).

Know who in the party *leadership* is with you; maintain regular contact so that you are fully informed and up to date about procedures, timing and the latest developments.

Coordinate who should call on which legislators for maximum impact and accurate assessment of position.

Determine the specific reservations or "anti" attitudes individual legislators are expressing. Inform Resource Committee, so they can come up with helpful answers.

Keep the Field Service Committee informed about what kind of grassroots activity is required (letterwriting blitz, contact by influential party member, attendance at hearing, etc.).

Anticipate hearings and votes so that Field Service and Public Relations Committees can generate public support and attendance.

Determine what organizations and individuals should testify at *hearings;* make sure all arguments will be presented without a lot of duplication.

Know your opposition: determine how best to neutralize it.

Work out strategy for *floor action;* line up influential legislators to carry the "pro" debate.

CAMPAIGN TECHNIQUES

Ready for Action

A legislative campaign has a goal with a deadline—the vote—just as a candidate's campaign ends on election day. Now that you know what your coalition committees must do, it's crucial to decide how and when they should go into action to meet the deadline. Three ingredients are essential to a successful campaign: good management, defined committee tasks, and a countdown calendar.

Campaign Management

The campaign must have a manager to make sure that the diverse elements in the campaign are functioning effectively and in unison. While it is possible to conduct a successful campaign without having a paid campaign manager (the

League of Women Voters has been doing it for years), it is impossible to meet campaign deadlines without good management.

Management must be appointed to set practical working goals for the campaign: how many volunteers, how many dollars, etc., are necessary (in January? in February?) to meet the schedule. And, as in a business where a regular profit and loss statement is an essential tool for analyzing whether goals are being reached, management must also plan periodic checks on how the campaign is going. Management must be willing to reconsider a particular strategy that proves not to be working, revise a schedule that has fallen behind, or decide if an interim goal is unrealistically ambitious and needs changing or is essential and requires redoubled effort.

Management also has the responsibility of coordinating all elements of the campaign in a way that makes sense. If there is no manager, however, this kind of thinking falls to the coordinating committee or task force chairman. For instance, it is important that the public relations chairman be aware of the positive impact that good PR will have on fundraising and on recruiting field workers.

Effective campaign management also includes good communications among all elements of the campaign. As the issue gets closer to a legislative vote, time pressures often preclude meetings. Good regular communications systems—newsletters, memos, etc.—are required to keep all elements of the campaign responding to each other as well as to the legislative goal.

A manager must also be responsible for anticipating the jobs to be done to reach the goal, assigning them in manageable amounts, and following up to make sure the work is being done. And because of the many diverse tasks in a campaign, authority must be delegated in turn to the people responsible for specific jobs in order for them to recruit workers, make work assignments, or purchase materials.

The oversight function of management is vital. Good management cannot try to do all the work, as well as direct it. Management must make sure responsibility is delegated well throughout the coalition. Otherwise members will have a tough time keeping a cool head as the campaign heats up.

Public Relations

Public relations, while not the focus of a legislative campaign as it is in a political candidate's campaign, nonetheless remains a crucial ingredient in achieving success.

A legislator will be reluctant to vote for legislation, if he thinks he will catch political flak from constituents for supporting it. Consequently, a vigorous public campaign on behalf of your legislative goal can be of invaluable assistance in gaining a legislator's vote.

Your first and most essential PR task is to identify the issue. It is not enough simply to state your goal. You must also tell the media and, through the media, the public *why* the goal is important.

The best indication that you know why the goal is important is that you can describe the goal briefly. When you can strip the issue down to bare facts, remove verbiage and confusing side issues, and succinctly explain why this legislation should be passed, you have added the ingredient basic to any successful campaign—the theme.

The theme is the tie that binds. It must be stated and restated throughout the campaign. It is your way of sticking to the issue and will help you avoid becoming sidetracked by issues raised by the opposition.

Having a working theme also enables controversy to work for you. Your comments on breaking news in a news release or a letter to the editor can effectively tie current issues to your legislative goal. Any hot issue that allows you once again to restate your theme can enhance your chances of success.

Tying your campaign in with other interests is also important, because different segments of the public will respond differently to your legislative goal. Parents of elementary school children may be for a school budget increase while senior citizens may oppose it. Commuting drivers may support a highway construction program that may be opposed by environmentalists. While opposition will exist on almost any piece of legislation, decreasing the opposition among the public is an essential function of PR.

As with the legislature, it is important that the resource or research committee identify opposing groups and that efforts to convince them be targeted at their particular interests. In this regard, it is not enough to tell the public why the legislation is important to you. It is also necessary to identify and communicate what's in it for them.

For practical information on how to reach the public through print and broadcast media, see *Getting Into Print*, LWVUS Pub. #484, and *Breaking Into Broadcasting*, LWVUS Pub. #586.

Headcounting and Legislative Coordination

The Legislative Committee keeps its finger on the political pulse at the state capitol. It carries out the direct lobbying with members of the legislature, anticipates the areas where concerted public relations, research, and field work must be carried out, and is aware of shifts in the political climate in time either to exploit them or turn them around. It's an all-encompassing and fascinating exercise in participatory democracy from which you will probably emerge exhausted but with an enormous amount of satisfaction. Lessons learned will be invaluable in other action campaigns.

Nothing is more important to a legislative campaign than an accurate headcount of legislators' attitudes. Without this headcount, your Coordinating Committee will have no idea where coalition efforts need to be focused in the field, nor can the lobbying be directed for maximum effect. The Legislative Committee should keep other committees constantly up to date on the status of the lobbying effort, the legislative schedule and the political picture, the districts where constituent pressure is essential (and what kinds of pressures will be most effective), and the kinds of substantive questions that must be researched. Information from the other committees must in turn be shared with the lobbyists and will enter into the Legislative Committee's determination of how to make lobbying assignments (see Lobbying).

Setting up and Using the Legislative Files

The Legislative Committee should maintain a central file somewhere in the capital city, preferably within walking distance of the state capitol, where it is easily accessible to the lobbyists. There are a number of ways to set up legislative files; the one suggested below can be adapted to your needs.

The Working Card File. The names of all legislators can be entered on 3×5 cards with minimal information including office address and phone, party, any past votes on similar or related legislation, sponsor of resolution, when and how often contacted in this session; comments. The cards can be color-coded: one color for supporters, one color for opponents and one color for uncommitted.

The cards can be handed out to lobbyists (keeping a central tabulation as to which lobbyist has which cards) to be used while they are lobbying **and returned to central headquarters with comments added or attached.**

The lobbying chairman (or an assistant good at detail, accuracy and interpretation), by keeping the color coding up to date in response to lobbyists' reports, will have a quick general view of how the campaign is going. When special effort is to be directed to holding on to proponents, for instance, all those cards can be easily pulled and assigned.

Worksheets. Worksheets listing all legislators either by district, by party or otherwise (depending on how lobbying assignments have been made) should be prepared. Opposite the names of each legislator, blank spaces can be ruled off to check his or her current attitude on a scale of 1 to 5: 1 = supports; 2 = leans favorable; 3 = neutral or uncommitted; 4 = leans negative; 5 = opposes.

At regular meetings with the lobbying corps, you can update attitudes from their own lobbying plus information

picked up elsewhere. Obviously, this system requires a new worksheet for each new "reading" after visiting a legislator. Regular meetings with the Coordinating Committee should note current legislative attitudes and get an overall *accurate* tally based on all possible contacts and analyses (e.g., a legislator might have told a League lobbyist he or she was uncommitted and told the secretary-treasurer of the local union that he/she would vote yes but couldn't say so publicly now). The current tally, in conjunction with information about opposition strength, analysis of questions that need to be answered for the public and for the legislature, and analysis of where and by whom pressure must be applied, form the basis for work by the Field Service, Public Relations and Resource Committees. These committees in turn relay information to the Legislative Committee for use in capitol lobbying.

Central Files. File folders should be maintained on every legislator. These files should *not* leave the office and should be accessible only to those authorized by the Coordinating Committee (e.g., off-the-cuff comments can be put in the central file for the information of lobbyists but should *not* be made public to the media or to unauthorized people who might exploit them).

The file folders should contain:

The legislator's name, district, party, home address and phone, professional address and phone, legislative address and phone.

A picture if available (If a lobbyist doesn't know a legislator, it's nice to get an idea of what he or she looks like.).

How long legislator has been in the legislative and committees he/she is on; special legislative interests.

Education and professional background; marital status (Does a legislator have an influential spouse who is a member of an organization sympathetic to your goal and who should be contacted?).

Prior recorded votes on similar or related legislation.

Major media in legislator's own district: *their* position on your goal; who reads or listens to them.

Outside interests: organizations of which legislator is a member; organizations and individuals who can influence him or her.

Position in legislative power structure. There are obvious signs, such as being a member of a major committee or the committee which holds hearings on the legislation; less obvious are such facts as that he/she went to school with the Speaker, or informally but not officially represents the governor's views, or was deposed from a chairmanship by the current Speaker, etc.

Report sheets on which a schedule of contacts made (by whom, when, where and how) can be entered, as well as comments on legislator's attitude, his/her analysis of the political scene and any hints he/she has dropped regarding colleagues (which would also go in *their* files).

Some of this information will be available right away and should help in briefing the lobbyists. Some of it will accrue as more and better contacts are made with the legislator and his/her colleagues. The more you can put together, the better off you'll be when the vote is approaching and special resources must be used to line up those last few votes.

Coordinating the lobbying

The first job, of course, is to pick your lobbyists, brief them on the substance and politics of the issue and train them in lobbying techniques (see *Lobbying*).

Make every effort to keep your issue away from partisan politics. Votes are needed from both sides of the aisle. Nevertheless, it makes common sense to assign lobbyists to legislators where as much potential as possible exists for agreement; Democrats should lobby Democrats and Republicans should lobby Republicans. It should also be self-evident that legislators who, for instance, are known to be opposed to labor should not be assigned to union lobbyists and so on. The lobbyists should be sensitive to the personalities and biases of the legislators, not forgetting that a nonthreatening, quiet approach (both in appearance and attitude) is generally the most effective.

Whether or not an exact and felicitous match can be worked out at the start, a lobbyist should in every case have been working with a legislator constructively enough and long enough in advance of any vote to establish credibility, so that the lobbyist can feel reasonably sure of an accurate headcount. If you discover on the day the floor vote is taken that you have lost by ten votes when your lobbyists' reports led you to think you were going to win by one, it's too late to recognize that the reports you were getting did not reflect the true picture.

The Legislative Committee is responsible for analyzing the lobbying reports, comparing them with reports received from the field and other sources, and determining how accurate the headcount is and how the political wind is blowing. The committee should know at all times who is seeing whom and should be prepared and *authorized* to make new lobbying assignments when any sign of inadequate or inaccurate reporting surfaces or when hostility has developed between a legislator and a lobbyist. If a vote took place in a prior session, the Legislative Committee should know how well the headcount agreed with the final vote. Any deficiencies in the headcount should be recognized and remedied early in the new session.

Lobbyists and others will be reporting on the individuals who should be enlisted to work on a particular legislator. They will also be reporting where constituent and/or organizational pressure should be applied. By keeping the Field Service and PR committees informed of these reports, committee resources can be used to reach the appropriate people. In addition, reports of which opposition arguments are penetrating the legislature should be referred to the Resource Committee and their answers made available to the lobbyists.

As a result of this constant oversight, reevaluation and communication, the Legislative Committee will be in a position to assure that **the right people are talking to the right legislators at the right time with the right facts.** These people will have established a relationship with the legislature so that an accurate headcount will be available before the vote. The committee should at the same time be able to anticipate political problems before they become potential disasters and rally all the coalition's resources into action.

Other Legislative Committee Responsibilities

Establish rapport and keep in touch with the majority leadership and the committee chairman in order to:

- get an early warning about the hearing date (arrange a mutually convenient date, time and place if possible);
- assure cooperation in the scheduling of proponents at the hearing;
- get early information about the reporting date and the schedule for floor action;
- get advice on effective use of legislative procedures;
- line up leadership support.

Coordinate hearing testimony of the proponents to achieve greatest impact (see *Testifying*).

Find out who key committee members are; work with them.

A strong minority report is essential, if lobbying reports indicate an unfavorable report is forthcoming. Check committee members favorable to your goal to see if they want help in writing the minority report or additional factual material; have Resource Committee prepare.

Line up influential legislators to floor manage and/or participate in floor debate in favor of the legislation; find out who would welcome prepared remarks or additional factual material; have Resource Committee prepare.

Lobbying

The Legislative Committee formulates the overall strategy and tactics and assigns lobbyists to specific legislators. In these assignments the committee *must* take into account the organizational and party affiliation of the lobbyist. Though an occasional mismatch is inevitable, a lobbyist who encounters real legislative hostility should not pursue the matter but should report back to headquarters with as much information as possible about the reasons for the hostility and who should make the follow-up contact.

Lobbyists can be especially important in assessing the strength of support or opposition of legislators representing districts with little or no constituency from the coalition's member organizations. Particularly when legislative opposition is anticipated (or when supporters need shoring up), the lobbyist can help determine which district forces will be influential in swinging the vote. Then the Public Relations and Field Service Committees can work to line up these forces in favor of the legislation.

There is nothing more satisfying, nothing more fun, than direct person-to-person lobbying for an issue you really believe in. The frustrations can be great, but the knowledge gained about both overt and covert political actions and reactions, the relationships established with major and minor political decision makers, and the gratification of having personally participated in the political process far outweigh the frustrations. Win or lose, a stint as lobbyist will leave you better equipped to move effectively in the political arena when the opportunity arises again.

Lobbying is not a dirty word. Lobbyists perform an essential function in our democratic process. Lobbying a public official is no more or less than using persuasion to convince a person to vote your way. The person has been elected to represent the views of his or her constituents and expects to hear from them. Human nature being what it is, the individual will respond more favorably to those he or she knows and respects. Therefore a *first rule of lobbying* is not to threaten or antagonize those whom you are trying to influence. You do your cause more harm than good, possibly slamming the door on further discussion

that might change the legislator's mind or even turning the person against you when he or she might have been favorably disposed to begin with. Furthermore, whatever the reasons for disagreement, threats or aggressively hostile behavior on your part can give political legitimacy to views that the legislator might not otherwise have seriously espoused.

The qualifications for a good lobbyist are:

- an intelligent command of the issue;
- a commitment to the cause, tempered by a tolerance for the human weaknesses of colleagues and elected public officials;
- enthusiasm and sincerity;
- a sense of humor, with a genuine liking of people and an ability to roll with the punches.

It is important to build rapport and understanding between the lobbyist and the legislator. Assuming a reasonably friendly relationship, legislators who are irrevocably committed either pro or con will usually tell you so quite candidly, *though you must listen carefully to what they say to be sure you're really hearing what they mean!* It is usually hardest to elicit an honest and accurate response from a legislator who claims to be neutral. Once mutual trust is established, however, the legislator will be more open in stating his position and the reasons for it, and the lobbyist will be able to make an accurate assessment of that position for headcount records.

Phone calls or organizational letters are less effective than personal visits, unless the legislator really knows who you are from prior contacts. The lobbyist who does not know the legislator should try to arrange to be introduced at the first visit by someone who does know him and has already established some credibility. After the first discussion, a lobbyist should make follow-up person-to-person visits periodically to present relevant factual material, discuss changes in the political picture or status of the legislation, or demonstrate support from influential endorsers (e.g., if the legislator usually votes with the Farm Bureau and its director has just come out in favor, the lobbyist should use this as a reason for a visit).

Some do's and don'ts for lobbyists

DO: recognize the legislator and the legislative staff as human beings; respect and *listen to* their views.

DO: get to know legislative staff and treat them courteously—their cooperation can make or break your chances to reach the legislators themselves.

DO: identify yourself immediately at each contact; public officials meet too many people to remember everyone.

DO: know the issue and the status of the legislation.

DO: know your legislator—past record on related legislation and/or votes; party and position in the legislative and political power structure; legislative and outside interests; how long he or she has been in the legislature; what kind of a personal interview will be most effective (sensitivity to legislative attitudes about appearance and approach is *essential*).

DO: be aware of any prior favorable commitment to your cause; enlist such a legislator to promote support among colleagues; ask his/her advice.

DO: commend legislators for actions you approve of, but don't feel as free to criticize.

DO: be brief with your appeal, then follow up periodically.

DO: give legislators succinct, easy-to-read literature with important facts and arguments highlighted.

DO: *keep off-the-record comments confidential.*

DO: keep the door open for further discussion even if legislator's attitude appears to be negative.

DO: report all contacts immediately to headcount headquarters so that appropriate district and capitol follow-up can be carried out.

DON'T: be arrogant, condescending or threatening.

DON'T: back recalcitrant legislators into a corner where they take a definite position against you.

DON'T: overwhelm legislators with too much written material, which they won't have time to read.

DON'T: make notes of a conversation while talking to a legislator.

DON'T: repeat off-the-record comments of one legislator to another.

DON'T: get into protracted arguments.

In addition to presenting arguments in favor of the legislation, the lobbyist is also on a fact-finding mission, intent on gleaning information for the central headcount files. Without asking direct questions, a good lobbyist can pick up clues on points like these:

- What questions has the legislator raised that must be answered?
- Which fellow legislators' opinions does he or she most respect?
- Does he/she respond to party pressure?
- Which coalition organizations are most respected by the individual?

Which ones generate the most hostility?

- What other organizations or individuals is the person likely to be responsive to? (e.g., church, service club, newspaper publisher, hometown mayor, etc.)
- What are his/her major legislative and nonlegislative interests? Are there individuals or organizations in these areas who might influence the person on the legislation in question?
- What does the legislator know about the political undercurrents affecting legislative positions of his/her constituents on your goal?
- If the person is friendly, does he/she have advice to offer? hints about how to work with other legislators?
- Is he or she influenced by rational arguments? by emotional appeals to human need and decency? by appeals from particular individuals or groups regardless of the emotional issues or facts?

Testifying

The major goal in testifying at a public hearing is to demonstrate to the committee, the media, and through the media to the public, that the proponents of the legislation know their facts, represent a broadbased constituency and can wield political clout. Good testimony and influential witnesses receiving good news coverage can serve to stimulate interest in the subject and overcome one of the weaknesses in many campaigns— namely, public apathy.

In many instances, the testimony presented at a legislative hearing has more effect on the people who read or hear about it than it does on the legisla-

tors themselves. To put it another way, as far as the legislative committee members are concerned, the lobbying you do with them before and after the hearing is more important than the hearing itself; nevertheless, it is essential that you present a case in the hearing that will give the public facts, attract public support and steer a course that takes account of political realities. Opponents must not be allowed by default to give the impression that support doesn't exist or to attract all the headlines.

A number of factors should be taken into account in determining who should testify:

- Will witnesses be more effective if they are from the districts of hearing committee members?
- Are there particular organizations and/or individuals who antagonize the legislators and thus should remain in the background?
- Which and how many witnesses will be needed to represent the largest cross section of the voting population?
- Which witnesses have the greatest publicity potential?
- Which witnesses can best overcome the arguments of the opposition and respond to committee questions?
- Which organizations and/or individuals *must* be included?
- Who should represent each party in order to demonstrate bipartisan support?
- What limitations on time has (or will) the committee set; how can the proponents' time be used best?

It is important that coalition members agree on who will testify. Give each witness a specific topic to cover according to his or her expertise, and make every effort to avoid repetition. Agree on the sequence in which witnesses should appear, in order to present the "pro" arguments most effectively. Where witnesses who are not members of the coalition are desirable, begin lining them up early, since refusals will necessitate further search for the kind of witnesses you want. Make every effort to find out which opponents are going to testify and to anticipate their arguments with refutations in the proponents' testimony.

In preparing testimony, legislative, public relations and resource or research people should all contribute their ideas: resource—facts to back the points to be covered; legislative—political knowledge of which approach will carry the most weight with the committee; public relations—the kind of language that has the greatest value in appealing to the media and persuading the public.

On the day of the hearing, report the arrival of witnesses to a coordinator to ensure that their presence is noted by the committee. Give the legislative committee chairman (whom you will already have convinced to cooperate on this matter) a list of witnesses in the order you want them to appear. Some member of the coalition should be responsible for collecting all statements of endorsement brought to the hearing and presenting them to the committee at an appropriate time.

The Public Relations Committee should prepare press kits, which might include: a factsheet on the legislation; status of similar legislation in other states; a flyer; copies of major testimony; the names of other prominent and influential endorsers; a press release summarizing the main points of the testimony.

Getting Endorsers

In addition to broadening the base of membership in a working coalition, the Coordinating Committee will want to enlist endorsements of the legislation from individuals and groups who may not be willing or able to join the coalition.

Endorsers are important because prominent names make news and because there are many segments of the general public and the legislature whose opinions and attitudes can be shaped and influenced by community and state leaders.

An early step in any major campaign should be a political analysis to decide how the voting population breaks down. Endorsers should be sought from all interests, but particular emphasis should be put on finding leaders whose opinions matter to those whom the coalition membership is least likely to influence.

Obviously, different kinds of endorsers appeal to different people. One person's views may carry great weight with influential legislators because the individual has control of a lot of political patronage; the general public may not even know who the person is. An outspoken clergyman may influence a large number of church members and yet extract little favorable response from the legislature. How you choose your endorsers and how you use their names and statements should thus be determined by the different groups you want to reach.

If labor is widely represented in the population, statements from prominent union leaders are needed; for a large rural population, farm and church endorsements. Leading sports figures, TV entertainers, radio talk-show MC's all have a following. Bipartisan political endorsements should be sought from influential politicians such as the governor, Democratic and Republican national committee members, state party chairmen, well-known and respected former legislators. At the district and community level, party chairmen and/or campaign managers, large contributors and local opinion leaders may be willing to make statements.

Few of these people will voluntarily and publicly endorse legislation unless they are asked to do so. Moreover, the more important the endorsement the more likely the man or woman is to be extremely busy and therefore somewhat inaccessible. A concerted long-range effort must be made to look for the leaders, to arrange for personal appointments in order to convince them, and to use the endorsements to the best political and public relations advantage.

Endorsements can be used in many different ways. A lobbyist could use the endorsement of a prominent farm leader when trying to convince a legislator from a rural district; endorsers' names and affiliations could be used on coalition stationery; a flyer could incorporate quotes of endorsement; endorsements can be the basis for news releases and articles; endorsements can be used on radio or TV debates or programs and in spot announcements or paid ads; and endorsements are always helpful when speeches are made.

The upshot is, lining up endorsers is a campaign in itself. Correspondingly, if you do a skillful job of it, you'll have moved further along the campaign trail.

Circulating Petitions

The coalition will have to determine early in the campaign whether or not a statewide petition drive is an effective use of organizational resources. As you consider a petition drive, take into account how the petitions will be used. Circulating petitions is a lot of work, so that a final special event should be planned to justify the effort and publicize the petition results.

There are two major reasons for using a petition drive: (1) it is a high-intensity, short-term activity that generates publicity about the issue; (2) it demonstrates to the state legislature that a large number of people support the desired legislation.

On the negative side, a successful petition campaign requires an enormous amount of preliminary organization and the enlisting of a large number of people to circulate the petitions. It is true that many people will take on a job of limited duration who might not do other things, so that a drive may be the answer to getting your co-members involved. Moreover, the names on the petitions are fertile ground for later contact when a home district letter-writing or telephone blitz is in order.

If you decide to go ahead:

Alert district coordinators early so that they can find local petition drive organizers, who in turn can start lining up workers. It is essential that no legislative district be left completely uncovered. If necessary, the state committee will have to collect signatures in those districts where no coalition members reside.

Appoint state petition drive head and committee.

Set schedule for collecting signatures and delivering them to the legislature.

Work out public relations strategy, including plans for the final event when the petitions are turned over to the legislators.

Prepare and disseminate careful instructions on timing, how to recruit and train workers, appropriate sites, how to organize during the actual drive, tips on local publicity and how, where and when to deliver the petitions to a central headquarters.

Prepare at least these materials:

- flyers for public distribution;
- Q & A's for workers;
- petition forms.

At the state level tabulate the signatures by district and work out appropriate ways of making delivery to the legislature, for maximum legislative and public relations impact.

Monitoring the Opposition—What to Expect

It is the nature of the legislative beast to be cautious: to maintain the status quo unless there is overwhelming reason to change. Because inertia favors the opposition, they need only to *raise questions that cast doubt* on the need for and the effect of the legislation. The opposition is seldom required to *prove* anything. The burden lies on the proponents of the legislation to provide the overwhelming reasons: the factual need, substantial constituent support, and the lack of a legitimate and sound basis for opposition. In short, it is the offensive, not defensive, campaign that wins.

It is always preferable to anticipate the opposition and answer their arguments positively before they surface publicly. One reason for a coordinated campaign countdown is to organize to get across your side of the issue in a believable fashion, so that opponents' last-minute scare tactics will receive no serious attention. One cannot, however, always know ahead of time exactly what new techniques and arguments the opposition will think of. It is therefore essential to work out a planned strategy for keeping track of opposition attacks and responding to them quickly and in kind.

The opposition's negative attacks are sometimes emotional ones, designed to appeal to the heart, not the head, and to exploit fear of the unknown. True, opponents often represent legitimate constituencies in your state and have reasons for opposition that are legitimate in their eyes. While their right to hold these views should certainly be respected, you should make every attempt to change their minds. Furthermore, whenever and wherever they speak out, rebut vigorously. Opposition leaders outside the legislature sometimes do *not* represent real constituencies. Just the same, they look for and get publicity that gives them an influence far beyond a natural power base. Proponents have to learn in a hurry to use techniques for exposing this kind of opposition and its motivation.

All sections of your Coordinating Committee play a part in monitoring and answering the opposition:

The Legislative Committee analyzes the lobbying reports for the kinds of negative arguments legislators are making and the sources from which these seem to be stemming (e.g., from the party ranks within the legislature? from rural residents? from outside the state?, etc.).

The Field Service Committee analyzes reports from the district coordinators: who the opposition is, what they are saying, where they're saying it and who's listening to them.

The Resource Committee does research and prepares the materials to counteract negative arguments and present positive favorable arguments. In order to present the positive, the committee must keep track of fast-breaking developments, such as recent court decisions which may be exploited by the opposition.

The Public Relations Committee monitors statewide media coverage of the opposition. District and local coalitions should have people monitoring district and local coverage. The Public Relations Committee should help the Resource Committee tailor promotional material to the interests of the people you're trying to reach (e.g., what convinces the rural housewife won't necessarily convince the city blue-collar worker).

Where the opposition is given coverage, the committee should be alert to demand equal time: with TV/radio and newspaper rebuttals; with proponent speakers where the opposition has appeared, etc. Plausible individuals must be chosen, persons who appeal to and influence the opinions of the people you are trying to reach (for instance, in promoting women's rights legislation, a militant female feminist, no matter how good her intentions, probably won't carry much weight at the state VFW convention; a nurse who's a veteran of the Second World War might).

Present the arguments for the desired legislation forcefully *over a sufficient length of time* so that the facts take hold in the minds of both the legislators and their constituents. The opposition's last-minute barrages of letters and descents on the state capitol in droves will then have minimal effect. Nevertheless, you should anticipate this final flurry of activity and be prepared to demonstrate constituent support with favorable letters and with the presence of a wide range of proponents at the statehouse. When gathering supporter constituents for this final push, be sure to remind them that, regardless of how much we may deplore the importance of appearance, it's a fact of life and must be taken into account when demonstrating in favor of legislation.

Suggested Calendar For Action

A gradual planned build-up through the various peaks ensures that you are organized ahead of time to anticipate crises and forestall the opposition; that publicity can be generated at the right times; that public interest can be stimulated; and that the enthusiasm and commitment of your workers can be sustained.

All this effort does not guarantee a favorable vote, but few legislators care to go against strong constituent pressure. You must generate that pressure from the constituency as a whole and from particularly influential segments of that constituency.

Following is an outline of the tasks required at various stages of the campaign and a calendar for planning their execution.

The start-up
Begin educational campaign, particularly with members.
Organize or join and strengthen a coalition; set up field organization.
Plan fund raising for campaign.

Determine your deadlines. It is often hard to determine exactly when peak points of a legislative campaign will occur, but certain deadlines are usually definite, and these dates should be known:

- When must the legislation be filed? Or is it an automatic carry-over from the prior session?
- What committee will it be assigned to? Must the committee hold public hearings? Is there a deadline for reporting the legislation to the floor?
- Does the legislature adjourn on a specific date?

The hearing

If the responsible committee in either house of the legislature is to hold a public hearing on the proposed legislation, the first peak of the campaign will occur then. If there is an *option* about holding a public hearing, proponents will want to consider whether or not the hearing would advance or retard their cause. If a hearing might be detrimental, consider asking the committee not to hold one. This is a strategy decision that must be made on the basis of the political realities in your own state.

Following are some tips on preparing for a public hearing (see *Anatomy of a Hearing,* LWVUS #108).

Consult with majority party and committee leadership to get a mutually advantageous hearing time and place.

Assign specific topics for testimony to members of coalition; seek additional testifiers with important constituencies and/or legislative influence.

Coordinate supporters' testimony and schedule witnesses to best advantage;

find out who is scheduled in opposition and refute their anticipated arguments in proponents' testimony.

Organize massive attendance at hearing; publicize date, time, place along with "pro" arguments.

Prepare press kits for distribution at hearing; make personal contacts with statehouse reporters and wire services to get good hearing coverage.

Assign responsibilities for the day of the hearing, such as coordinating scheduling of supporters' testimony; line up media interviews for supporters; monitor opposition arguments; etc.

The committee vote and report

The next peak would be the crucial committee vote. Unless a deadline exists, timing will be hard to determine, but certainly intensive lobbying should go on at the state capitol and in each district, with hearing committee members in particular, up until that vote is taken. Ask supporters on the committee whether or not they want coalition help in writing their report. If you expect an unfavorable majority, make certain that a very strong minority report is presented.

The week before the committee vote is expected, update the committee head-count daily and maintain daily contact with field organizations in committee members' districts for peak lobbying effort.

The floor vote(s)

The final peak(s) will be the debate and action on the floor. The three-month campaign countdown shown below works back from the projected date of a floor vote.

Three months before vote

(This is written to apply to the pre-floor-vote stage; but it applies equally to the pre-hearing phase, with appropriate modifications.)

A. Have general briefing session for members of the coalition's member organizations and/or begin series of bulletin articles (substance + techniques + stimulation to act) for coalition members.

B. Solicit an invitation for a proponent of your cause to address joint session of legislature

C. Anticipate sources and kinds of opposition. Prepare positive statements that answer typical "anti" arguments and publicize them before opposition surfaces publicly. Try to meet with potential opponents and move them into the neutral camp. The leaders of an *organized* opposition are not potential, they are real, but there are other influential citizens whose opposition can be reduced with a face-to-face discussion. The main objective is to identify them and convince them to *stay out* of the battle, even if they remain opposed.

With the help of your research committee, analyze your legislators and make a preliminary headcount; determine which techniques, organizations and individuals should be concentrated on whom; solicit help and advice of supporters on the legislative committee or committees responsible for writing the legislation and getting it to the floor for a vote.

D. Start lining up speaking engagements if you haven't done so earlier; organize and train speakers' bureau; prepare sample speeches.

E. Organize a plan for reaching each constituent in legislative districts. Decide which methods will be most effective, which ones you have the people power and/or finances to use.
—personal (house to house)
—postcard
—media
—distribution of material in public places
—petition drive (if you decide to hold one, workers must be found and trained well in advance of drive)

F. Organize for a letter-writing blitz from your coalition and other supporters.

G. Assign a coalition member or committee to establish media contacts; analyze their attitudes, and keep the media informed.

H. Start lining up endorsers from all concerned segments of the community (religious, business and labor, political, ethnic, rural, housewives, professional groups, etc.).

I. Make personal contact with individuals who influence legislators to solicit their active support (campaign workers and/or contributors; party leaders; labor, business officials; members' spouses, golf partners, college classmates, etc.).

J. Develop material for public distribution—flyers, news releases, posters.

K. Plan a big, publicity-getting event, such as a rally or banquet with a notable figure, to take place just before committee or floor vote. If it is a statewide effort, involving state or national figures who will speak out for your goal will produce better news coverage.

Two months before vote

A. Launch campaign publicly. Could

be by announcing a prominent figure as honorary chairman of coalition; launching petition drive; or having big kick-off rally for workers.

B. Use media contacts, radio spots, to intensify public education on the issue and to urge public support through writing legislators.

C. Conduct petition drive.

D. Set up speaking engagements, public meetings. A coalition member should be assigned to keep track of these and offer speaking services to groups you want to reach.

E. Maintain regular contact with legislative leadership.

F. Step up home district and state capitol lobbying. Now is the time to write and visit key legislators.

G. Solicit help of supporters in legislature (to testify, endorse publicly, work on colleagues, etc.).

One month before vote

A. Distribute promotional handouts in public places; door-to-door or postcard contact with voters.

B. Update pro/con headcount at least weekly for whole legislature.

C. Step up home district and state capitol lobbying.

D. Arrange to get supporters on interview programs; go after radio/TV news coverage.

E. Make regular announcements of prominent endorsers.

F. Stage one big event with a prominent name that can help the effort.

G. Present petitions to legislators with press release at press conference.

H. Set up letterwriting blitz to all legislators.

The week before floor vote

A. Make daily contact with field organization in districts for peak lobbying effort.

B. Organize a last letterwriting blitz.

C. Conduct persistent person-to-person lobbying with legislators at capitol—daily update of headcount.

D. Intensify public information efforts through media publicity and distribution of material.

E. Coordinate work with influential legislators who will carry "pro" debate on the floor (prepare speech material for them; work to ensure the attendance of proponents during the debate and vote).

Additional statewide efforts before the floor vote might include one-minute or 30-second radio spots. You might also consider rallies, torchlight parades, or sound trucks, when these measures are appropriate.

A good legislative campaign includes coordination, co-operation, and a well-focused approach. While the demands are many, they can spell the difference between failure and success. So it's really up to you to make sure that before you shout "full speed ahead" on an issue, you know where you want to head, and you've put in enough supplies and support to be sure you reach your destination.

PART Three

Administrative Leadership
and Management

Introduction

Because so many community practitioners must double in brass these days, taking responsibilities for agency leadership and management as well as their community work, and because so few have any special preparation for those important tasks, we decided to include articles on the subject of administration and management.

Administration may be distinguished from management because it involves basic decisions about the character and competence of organizations and pays attention to what is required to embody the special values and distinctive qualities for which an organization stands in the structure of the organization. Management is the art of control. How can the ends and related values served by the organization be achieved most effectively and efficiently with the available resources? Administration raises questions about the basic values of an organization while management is technical and takes those values as given. The articles in this section focus almost exclusively on problems of management. Therefore, it is useful to pause briefly to explore the meaning and significance of administration before examining problems of management.[1]

Consider those Planned Parenthood Associations which found themselves in the midst of great controversy in some communities two or three decades ago. Faced with implacable opposition to their goals, which include providing sexually active young people with the ability to prevent conception (and all the crushing responsibilities this usually entails for persons who have not completed their education and have few marketable employment skills), some of these organizations ventured into family counseling and downplayed their family planning objectives. Thereby, they

---

[1]This discussion is based on the seminal work of Philip Selznick, particularly his *Leadership in Administration* (Evanston, Ill.: Row, Peterson, 1957). It is highly recommended for those who wish to explore the subject further.

won broader community acceptance at the price of their major objectives. Other Planned Parenthood Associations accepted community opposition, recruited supporters who endorsed Planned Parenthood goals, did not try to win a place in local community welfare planning circles, sometimes raised more limited funds or raised their funds from a smaller group of supporters, and preserved their ability to pursue their special goals and values without compromise.[2]

These contrasting examples point to the role of leadership in administration. An institutional leader must identify the goals and values essential to the special character and competence of the organization she or he leads, and select the resources and structures that will further this pursuit. Who will be invited to sit on the board of directors? With what other groups will one form coalitions? From whom will one seek funding? What kind of personnel will be hired to carry out the work of the organization? These are among the character-forming decisions made by an institutional leader. If made without an awareness of the potential consequences for the organization's basic purposes and values, it may drift along and goals may be displaced or become diffuse.

Now consider another sort of organization, one that has had widespread application in recent years. These organizations, generally having a relatively brief existence, are designed to discover community problems and identify goals to be addressed by an entire community or metropolitan area over the next decade or two. Their general purpose is to develop a community consensus on a whole range of issues—economic development, crime and delinquency, health and welfare, cultural affairs, housing and community development, and so on. Imagine a leader faced with the enormous problem of finding a consensus in each of these sectors. One approach would be to gather together a small group of civic leaders, the local movers and shakers who normally get things done in the community. But such a step would violate the basic purpose of such organizations, the building of a general consensus on community goals that may serve to guide various community groups over an extended period.

Again, the significance of leadership in making the choices necessary to keep the organization true to its special values should be clear. The development of an agreement that the movers and shakers should not dominate the process, the consistent effort to involve widely divergent factions of the local community, the avoidance of premature agreement on issues, the involvement of the local press and other mass media in stimulating participation in the decision-making process all seem essential to the preservation of the special character of this type of organization.

Of course, the community practitioner, as institutional leader, seldom

---

[2]See Martin Rein, "An Analysis of a National Agency's Local Affiliations in Their Community Contexts: A Study of the Planned Parenthood Federation" (New York: Planned Parenthood Federation of America, Inc., 1961), mimeographed. See also: Martin Rein and Robert Morris, "Goals, Structures and Strategies for Community Change," *Social Work Practice 1962* (New York: Columbia University Press, 1962), pp. 127-145, which is more readily accessible.

enters the picture from the beginning, and is usually not able to make all such choices freely and unrestrained. But she or he can make an assessment to discover where choices exist or are foreclosed and come to a decision about what is possible in shaping organizational character. One may conclude that the disparity between aspirations for the organization and the conditions found when exploring a leadership position is too wide, and turn the position down. Or one may conclude that there is hope in building or training staff, recruiting board members and volunteers, forming new or reinforcing old coalitions or working relations with other organizations, and approaching new sources of funding. All such decisions are potentially character defining, and it is up to the community practitioner in a position of institutional leadership to choose carefully or risk the loss of values she or he wishes to infuse into the organization.

Not only does the institutional leader seldom enter the picture at the beginning before any character-defining decisions have been made. She or he is often not in a position to make them by virtue of the status and role occupied in the organization. Generally, the closer one is to the top, the greater one's discretion. But this perspective may be applied at lower levels in organizations. Community practitioners are seldom mere instruments carrying out technical functions serving values determined by others. One must probe the limits of one's assignment and search for ways to participate in the character-defining process at whatever level one finds oneself in the organization.

From this perspective, the skill of the administrator is in making choices that embody the special values of the organization. This discussion begs the question of where these values originate and who has the right to promulgate and shape them. The standard answer is that the policy-making body—the legislative arm of government or the board of a private organization—has the right and responsibility. But in employing a professional, a community practitioner or some other, the organization's policy makers are not hiring a cypher, a mere instrument of their bidding. Clearly professional perspectives and personal commitments, probed in every good personnel selection process of high-level employees, are part of what the policy makers are choosing when they hire. There must be some agreement on basic goals and values between administrator and policy makers, and to the extent this exists, there is a partnership in carrying out the organization's intentions. But often the policy makers are unclear in their mandate to an executive and expect the administrator to play an important part in shaping goals, objectives, and programs. Enabling legislation for many social problems is and has been less than precise on these matters, often containing conflicting elements. The administrator is expected to sort these out and shape them, not merely in the abstract but in basic decisions on staffing, funding sources, training, selecting outside organizations with which to collaborate, choosing clientele, and other basic, character-defining decisions.

Because the literature so frequently overlooks the value and character-defining consequences of such decisions, focusing instead on the technical problems that are also involved, the editor of this part of the book has digressed from what is otherwise the clear focus of the book on tactics and techniques, referred to here as management. The practitioner is asked to consider, in any decision, not only "Will it work?" and "How do I do it?" but also "What impact will it have on shaping the basic character and competence of the organization?" and "What commitments am I making that may be difficult to back away from later, and what are their value consequences?"

Turning now to management, one way to provide a framework for identifying its tasks is as follows: Some tasks are focused outside the organization, others within. Some have to do with building sentiments that support the organization or bind it together (or combating attacks upon or indecisiveness within the organization). Others are related to securing or organizing the means to accomplish the organization's task. This scheme is based on a modification of a typology originally put forward by Talcott Parsons.[3] When these two sets of attributes are organized into a fourfold table, they remind one of four very important classes of management tasks (see Figure).

Major Tasks Suggested by a Modification of Parsons' Scheme Vis-a-Vis the Organization

	External	Internal
Organization-Binding Sentiments	Building Legitimacy, Commitment, Support	Resolving Conflicts Among Organization Participants
Purpose-Achieving Tasks	Obtaining Resources for Organizational Use, e.g., Personnel, Funds	Organizing Resources to Achieve Organizational Purposes

DEVELOPING ORGANIZATION-BINDING SENTIMENTS EXTERNAL TO THE ORGANIZATION

Everyone who runs an organization knows how important it is to have a legitimate place in the community, to be acknowledged as having expertise in a particular kind of work, perhaps with a particular kind of clientele, or to be recognized as speaking for a particular constituency. This acknowledgment means people send you clients appropriate for your services or expect you to speak up authoritatively on issues in, say, the health or corrections field. Another kind of legitimacy has less to do with expertise than with legality. That is what is meant when it is said, for example, that the Intertribal Council has the right to speak for Native Americans in this community. Some of the tasks involved in managing this area of an

[3]Talcott Parsons, "General Theory in Sociology," in Robert K. Merton, Leonard Broom, and Leonard S. Cottrell, Jr., eds., *Sociology Today* (New York: Basic Books, Inc., 1959), pp. 4-7.

organization's work are:

1. Selecting board members and personnel with expert or legal authority to act in the area of the organization's work.
2. Engaging in public relations activities designed (*a*) to build community confidence and acknowledgment of expertise or the legal (or moral) right to act in a defined area, or (*b*) to counteract attacks on expertise, legality (or morality).
3. Obtaining appropriate licenses for the organization and employing personnel who hold appropriate licenses, credentials, or acknowledged ability.

This important group of tasks is exemplified here by the League of Women Voters' article on public relations, and by certain aspects of Cox's "Guidelines for Preparing Personnel Policies," particularly those dealing with recruitment and selection of personnel.

DEVELOPING ORGANIZATION-BINDING SENTIMENTS INTERNAL TO THE ORGANIZATION

In every organization there is a potential for divisiveness, based on background (for example, age, race, sex, religion, socioeconomic status, and the like); assigned responsibilities within the organization (such as employers and employees); organizing (which may include, for example, advocacy for the interests of some disfavored local constituency); or fund raising (which may be targeted to those at odds with such a disfavored constituency), and so on. Every manager must attend to such conflicts, minimizing them or resolving them in favor of one or the other party so that operations may continue more or less smoothly. Some of the tasks involved in managing this set of problems include:

1. Establishing clear expectations for employee performance.
2. Rewarding high-quality performance of expectations.
3. Resolving disputes that arise between individual employees or between departments.
4. Structuring communications within the organization.
5. Establishing clear lines of authority.

These tasks are addressed, in part, in Kruzich's and Austin's piece on supervision and in Cox's piece on personnel policies.

CARRYING OUT PURPOSE-ACHIEVING TASKS EXTERNAL TO THE ORGANIZATION

Every organization needs resources drawn from its environment: (1) clients, members, participants—the "raw material" of people-serving organizations; (2) personnel—employees of various kinds, board members and so on; (3) facilities—land, buildings, furnishings, equipment, supplies, and the like; (4) funds, the generalized resources which make it possible to obtain all the other necessary imputs. Someone or some group of persons must be assigned responsibilities for obtaining and maintaining the flow of these resources into the organization. The aspects of Cox's piece that deal with recruitment of personnel; the applications of the League of Women Voters' piece dealing with public relations which are applied to raising funds and recruiting personnel or members; the Geller piece on grant writing, and Flanagan's work on asking for money all bear on this set of essential functions.

CARRYING OUT PURPOSE-ACHIEVING TASKS INTERNAL TO THE ORGANIZATION

Every organization must organize its work, assign personnel to carry it out, communicate instructions on how the work is to be done, monitor the achievement of tasks, allocate resources to various tasks, account for the expenditure of funds and the use of other resources, and so on. This set of responsibilities is dealt with here, in part, by the Kruzich and Austin piece on supervision and the United Way piece on budgeting.

It has not, of course, been possible to be comprehensive in our coverage of management tasks. For example, we have not dealt separately with the techniques for establishing the legitimacy of an emerging organization (external tasks in developing organization-binding sentiments); for mediating labor-management disputes (internal tasks in developing organization-binding sentiments); recruiting members (external purpose-achieving tasks), or accounting for expenditures. Space does not permit comprehensive coverage, but we believe the pieces included here will assist the community practitioner who must double as a manager.

Fred M. Cox

19. SUPERVISION AND MANAGEMENT IN COMMUNITY ORGANIZATION AGENCIES

Jean Marie Kruzich and Michael J. Austin

There has been a significant increase in the literature on social service management and supervision over the last decade. Case materials, texts, and professional journals provide information on program evaluation, leadership styles, supervisory roles, and a host of other managerial topics. Yet, this literature tends to focus primarily on administration and supervision issues as they relate to direct-service agencies. While the administration of both direct-service and community-organizing agencies share some similarities, there are some important differences that relate to the unique characteristics of community-organizing agencies that impact supervisory and administrative practices.

Community organization approaches encompass (1) locality development with its focus on neighborhood or rural community involvement, (2) social planning with its focus on interagency problem solving and planning, and (3) social action, with its emphasis on social movements and political strategies seeking a redistribution of power, resources, and community decision making (Rothman, 1979). It is not unusual to find a community organization agency that incorporates one or more of these approaches. Thus, a neighborhood development association may be in-

Reproduced by permission of the authors. This article was written for this volume.

volved in the development of block clubs (locality development), in developing with the city a long-term plan for neighborhood improvement (social planning), and in organizing a chapter of the Gray Panthers in an effort to make the needs of senior citizens more apparent to city officials (social action). Just as an organization may incorporate more than one approach to community organizing, so too an agency may be involved in providing primarily direct services and secondarily seek to carry out specified community organizing activities. In fact, many community groups that began as activist social organizations have evolved into social agencies devoted to a wide variety of programs (Rosenbloom, 1981).

This article is designed to provide a general overview of the roles and functions of supervisors and executives of community organizing agencies. Such agencies include United Way Community Planning Councils, neighborhood associations, Tenants' Unions, Associations for Battered Women, and community action councils. Special attention will be paid to tasks and issues involved in supervising individuals carrying out organizing activities and some of the unique characteristics of citizen involvement with a focus on executive-board relationships. Our analysis begins with a discussion of the role of community organizing technology and its focus on community change, the organizer's work, and the ideology of the organizer. Community organizing technology clearly impacts the roles of agency supervisors and directors in a manner that is different from the performance of administrative roles in direct service agencies.

THE NATURE AND FOCUS OF THE SERVICE TECHNOLOGY

A major distinction between direct service to clients and community organizing is the technology used. Technology refers to techniques that are applied to some kind of raw material which the organization transforms into a product (Perrow, 1970). For the direct-service worker, techniques may include individual, family, or group counseling, case consultation, or skill training. Examples of such techniques include offering training in activities of daily living for a group of nursing home residents, offering group counseling for sexual abuse victims, workshops on parent effectiveness training, and offering case consultation to paraprofessionals in a residential treatment center. On the other hand, the technology of community organizing is likely to include writing proposals, organizing block clubs, developing a community needs survey, developing interagency coordination agreements, building coalitions to put pressure on a state legislature, or lobbying to get lower electricity rates for homeowners. While both caseworkers and community organizers work with individuals and groups (interactional tasks) and engage in problem solving (analytical tasks), these tasks are carried out through different methods.

One aspect of any technique is its visibility. Unlike the clinician where the bulk of the work is often carried out in an agency's office, the organizer's work is carried out in neighborhoods, other agencies, community centers, and residents' homes. Consequently, not only is the organizer's work more visible; it is also performed in a wider range of settings. In addition, the organizer often works in groups so that he/she is likely to be involved with larger numbers of clients than the direct service worker. In the same vein, the diversity of individuals that are part of the organizer's practice is likely to be greater.

The community organizer's relationship building often involves other professionals and politicians in addition to working with client groups. The skilled clinician and the skilled organizer both exercise considerable discretion, but most are limited in their autonomy by the sanctions and auspices of their employing agency. While the work of an organizer may be more visible than a clinician's, assessing job performance is no less complex. However, the ramifications of an organizer's work may be more immediate and sensitive when social change tactics aimed at social institutions are being used.

Besides using different technology, the community organizer's focus of change is also different from the direct-service worker's. While direct-service workers help clients to adjust to their environment by individual change, the organizer's focus involves changing environments in the community or in institutions such as prisons, schools, and welfare departments through the use of power, influence, and the reallocation of resources. This focus may often involve confrontation or conflict with political and bureaucratic officials. Requiring other groups or organizations to change may involve significant resistance and hostility, which is similar to that found in the counseling process.

In addition, the fact that community organizing as a method often attracts individuals who are strongly committed to client groups may well result in conflicts between the worker and executive, with the organizer's focus on maximizing client empowerment and the administrator's emphasis on agency survival.

The following three sections examine different aspects of managing community organizations: first, supervision of community organizers; second, the roles of the executive; and third, citizen involvement.

SUPERVISING COMMUNITY ORGANIZERS

In this section, supervision is discussed in the context of community organization agencies. The issues involved in the transition from organizer to supervisor are addressed. In addition, a framework is provided as an aid to the supervisor and worker engaged in articulating their understanding of community work. The importance of management by objectives and strategies as well as performance evaluation and staff development of organizers is discussed. The supervisory issues noted in this section are relevant for both the supervisor operating at the program level as well as the director of an agency devoted to community organizing activities.

Transition from Organizer to Supervisor

The transition from organizer to supervisor is rarely a smooth or easy process. Many issues emerge as one shifts from one role to another. The issues include the use of authority, decision-making style, orientation to relationships, orientation to effectiveness, and colleague orientation.

The changes in one's use of authority can be quite confusing. As an organizer, one's authority is derived primarily from the client group in relationship to one's expertise, experience, and relationship-building capacities. The organizer's reputation is built primarily in the community. In contrast, the supervisor's authority is derived from expertise in working with subordinates and from the supervisor's middle management position. In this position, the reputation is built primarily within the agency as supervisors exercise authority in seeking the cooperation of subordinates and compliance with organizational demands. The exercise of supervisory authority is also related to maintaining one's managerial credibility with supervisors. If you are unable to exercise authority in managing subordinates, your transition from organizer to supervisor may be incomplete.

The second transition issue involves decision-making styles. The primary decision-making style of the organizer is to be responsive to the client population and to optimize the group's capacity to act in pursuit of its own interests. In essence, organizers move with the flow of decision making which emerges out of citizen involvement. In contrast, the supervisor seeks to guide organizational decision making, which emerges out of staff involvement, in order to identify compromises. Such compromising results when subordinates compete for the supervisor's time and attention, which must be rationed across a group of subordinates in a manner by which subordinate capacity building must be shared equally and thereby not necessarily meeting all of the unique needs of each organizer. This can be most unsettling to the new supervisor seeking to continue the optimizing approach to decision making acquired as an organizer.

The third issue includes relationship building. One of the critical skills of an organizer is the capacity to build effective relationships with a client population whether it is the process of developing neighborhood cohesiveness, the goal orientation of strategies designed to change public policies, or the task orientation of an interagency planning group seeking to develop new services. In contrast, the supervisor-subordinate relationship reflects a different orientation, a concern for the productivity of staff members as well as a concern for the welfare of staff. The managerial relationship requires a special conserving of energy in order to maintain a balance of time and commitment in relationships with subordinates.

The fourth issue in making the transition from organizer to supervisor involves one's orientation to effectiveness. The organizer usually defines his or her effectiveness in terms of the results gained and capacity built by the client population. For example, if the organizer helped to get streetlights installed in the neighborhood, such an outcome could reflect on the organizer's effectiveness. In contrast, the supervisor tends to assess effectiveness in terms of a range of projects or programs which contribute to the goals of the agency. Effectiveness is more than the successes of one organizer. The viability and survival of the agency is frequently built upon the capacity of supervisors to document fully, assess, and interpret the combined effectiveness of staff across several projects or activi-

ties. One's orientation to effectiveness clearly differs in relation to one's position as an organizer or as a supervisor of organizers.

The last issue relates to one's colleague orientation. In most cases, organizers provide peer support to one another as they engage in the difficult processes of mobilizing people and resources. The collegiality among organizers, similar to that experienced by caseworkers, usually involves the sharing of successes and failures, the seeking of advice, and the sharing of personal life experiences. This orientation to colleagues clearly shifts into a new arena when assuming the somewhat lonely position of supervisor. This middle management loneliness is based, in part, on the perception that it is difficult to share supervisory worries with subordinates, and it requires special effort to build a peer support group of supervisors inside and/or outside the agency. Frequently, peer support inside the agency is difficult to achieve when competing with other supervisors for office space, additional staff, additional financial resources, or the director's attention. In the case of the executive assuming supervision of workers, no peer support in the agency may be available. The changes in one's orientation to collegial relations can be one of the most personally distressing aspects of the transition from organizer to supervisor.

The five transition issues have been identified primarily to alert all supervisors of the need to recognize and work on the dilemmas inherent in making a shift from one role to another. Ignoring these issues or denying their importance simply means that they will need to be addressed in the future (that is, pay now or pay later).

Understanding the Nature of Community Organizing Work

One's definition of community organizing will obviously vary according to the setting and the goals to be achieved. However, the major issue in this section is the recognition that supervisors must develop and articulate their own understanding of the nature of community organizing. This capacity is essential for assisting staff to understand their work, for advocating with staff the special needs of your unit, and for communicating with significant others in the community.

In an effort to demonstrate one approach to conceptualizing community organizing work and to stimulate discussion and debate, a framework was developed and is highlighted in Figure 19.1. The framework is built on three assumptions: (1) that community organ-

izing practice can be meaningfully divided into the three domains or methods: social action, locality development, and social planning; (2) that there are work functions common to all three methods involving outreach, resource mobilization, advocacy, and administration; and (3) within each work function there are essential tasks that are the major ingredients of a community organizer's job description.

Job functions or duties in Figure 19.1 refer to a constellation of essential activities carried out by an organizer. For example, outreach is defined in terms of case-finding and constituency-building tasks; resource mobilizing is defined in terms of mobilizing people and political influence as well as money and materials; advocacy is defined in terms of advocating for systems change related to either administrative or social policies; and the administrative role is defined in terms of

FIGURE 19.1
Framework for Conceptualizing Community Organizing Work

	Methods of Practice		
Major Job Functions	Social Action	Locality Development	Social Planning
1. *Outreach*			
Case Finding/Problem Finding	Tasks	Tasks	Tasks
Constituency Building	Tasks	Tasks	Tasks
2. *Resource Mobilizing*			
People and Influence	Tasks	Tasks	Tasks
Money and Materials	Tasks	Tasks	Tasks
3. *Advocacy*			
Client and Group	Tasks	Tasks	Tasks
Systems and Legislature	Tasks	Tasks	Tasks
4. *Administration*			
Intra-Agency/Organization	Tasks	Tasks	Tasks
Interagency/Organization	Tasks	Tasks	Tasks

FIGURE 19.2
Selected Tasks Relevant to the Job of a Community Organizer

(L.D. = Locality Development; S.P. = Social Planning; S.A. = Social Action)

I. OUTREACH

1. Develops information network with neighborhood residents in order to monitor unmet community needs. (L.D.)
2. Conducts community needs assessment surveys in order to develop interagency planning proposals. (S.P.)
3. Participates actively in local coalition of organizations in order to monitor violations of client rights. (S.A.)

II. RESOURCE MOBILIZING

1. Organizes campaign to recruit volunteers for developing a block watch anti-crime program. (L.D.)
2. Develops grant proposal to submit to a local foundation in order to meet an emerging community need. (S.P.)
3. Meets with union representatives in order to secure political support and financial resources for a consumer boycott. (S.A.)

III. ADVOCACY

1. Confers with city hall representatives about neighborhood public housing resident in order to influence a favorable decision for resident. (L.D.)
2. Testifies before state legislature in order to influence legislation affecting community agencies. (S.P.)
3. Organizes picket of local companies in order to change policies unfair to disadvantaged consumers. (S.A.)

IV. ADMINISTRATION

1. Prepares report on neighborhood conditions in order to develop new agency program to address those conditions. (L.D.)
2. Organizes campaign to approach several local foundations in order to seek financing for new service program. (S.P.)
3. Develops a telephone tree or network in order to alert consumers quickly about the need to write to their legislative representatives. (S.A.)

intra-agency tasks (such as record keeping, performance evaluation, maintaining tax exempt status) and interagency tasks (like coalition maintenance, newsletters, planning and implementing conferences or rallies).

The tasks within each cell can be defined as action or action sequences grouped through time with specified outcomes. Task statements include specific action verbs and outcome statements, which define worker behavior in terms of the work to be done in relationship to the worker and the work organization (Austin, 1981). Such specificity is useful for clarifying the nature of the job for both the supervisor and the organizer and can be used in job descriptions, performance evaluations, and career development activities related to up grading the knowledge and skills of the organizer. A list of selected community organizer tasks is noted in Figure 19.2.

Managing by Objectives and Strategies

Supervisors of community organizing staff need to expand the traditional administrative approaches of managing by objectives to include managing by strategy. Since supervisors actively model behaviors for their subordinates, they need to help organizers specify their objectives in relationship to a client population or a set of organizations. These objectives usually relate to the mission of the agency or organization that employs the organizer. Organizational auspice is a critical component of everyday practice about which organizers need regular reminding and reinforcement of the agency's mission.

Managing by strategy represents a more future orientation to organizing practice, whereas managing by objectives tends to reflect the past and present. Managing by strategy seeks to focus on specifying future goals and mechanisms which the client population needs to consider. Managing by objectives tends to emerge from extrapolational planning, which uses past and present information to guide practice. Managing by strategy utilizes transformational planning by which the future is defined in terms of the ideal and current practice is oriented toward reaching the ideal. Both perspectives are important components of the modeling done by supervisors for their subordinates. For example, a supervisor using management by objectives seeks to help the organizer carry out the agency's program goals and objectives as set out for the year and developed out of prior agency expertise. Still, the supervisor

also needs to include managing by strategy by involving the organizer in thinking strategically about the future in such a way as to develop emerging goals and objectives related to client needs but not yet formalized through agency planning and decision making. Management by strategy involves considerable creativity, risk taking, competence, and worker autonomy.

The day-to-day practice of organizers parallels the work of direct-service personnel. For example, case management processes are critical attributes of clinical personnel (Austin, 1981). Similarly, project or task group development and implementation are essential features of organizing work. The supervisor of organizers can relate to activities in terms of project consultation, process consultation, and program consultation. Project consultation, like case consultation, involves providing organizers with specific advice and assistance for conducting their day-to-day work. Process consultation can address the methods by which the organizer intervenes or works with a target population. Program consultation relates to the involvement of organizers in formulating programs relevant to the employing agency or organization which are then communicated across and up the organization. Program consultation relates back to managing by strategy in which the supervisor and his or her unit of organizers can influence the future direction of the employing agency by spelling out new directions and programs for community organizing.

Evaluation and Upgrading Staff

The final dimension of supervision addressed in this section includes performance evaluation and staff development. The mechanisms of good personnel management are available for both supervisors and community organizers, and they require an understanding of the difference between a periodic career development conference and the annual performance review. The career development conference is usually an annual or semiannual supervisor-subordinate meeting designed as a supportive and educational event devoted to the future learning needs and experiences of the organizer. It is built upon the premises of increasing professionalization and lifelong learning.

In contrast, the annual performance review is usually an agency requirement reflected in agency personnel policies. Performance review tools include the graphic rating form, the management by objective (MBO) approach, and the essay or the combined essay/graphic approach (Austin, 1981). The graphic rating form includes specific criteria relevant to the community organizer's job with rating categories ranging from excellent to poor. The criteria might include use of judgment, resourcefulness, self-control, planning capacities, and cost consciousness. The MBO approach is an outcome-oriented approach in which objectives are set at the beginning of the year and are assessed at the end of the year. The essay approach is simply a narrative report, which includes a description of the work performed, the strengths of the workers' performance and the areas of work performance requiring continuing attention or improvement. The essay/graphic approach combines these two methods by encouraging both narrative comments and ratings ranging from excellent to poor in such areas as accomplishment of job requirements, knowledge of job, reliability, communication capacities, and personal relationship

capacities.

Central to both periodic career development conferences and annual performance reviews are the supervisor's capabilities for giving and receiving feedback. These communication skills are essential in conducting such conferences and reviews. If supervisors are only critical or only laudatory of staff performance, they are depriving staff of relevant information necessary for career planning and effective job performance.

Staff development is obviously related to performance evaluation. The data generated from career conferences and performance reviews need to be jointly converted, by the supervisor and organizer, into plans for updating and upgrading staff. Poorly performed tasks can be translated into learning objectives to be met on the job, through in-service training, or through continuing education programs. Acquiring the capacity to perform new tasks as a result of job enlargement or job enrichment can also be addressed through staff development planning. At times, the supervisor acts as a trainer by tutoring staff, formulating growth-enhancing questions, sharing power by exploring new areas of knowledge and skill together, and assessing community educational resources for the purpose of guiding the education of subordinates.

It is particularly important for supervisors to conceptualize the range of knowledge and skill relevant for the effective job performance of organizers. The knowledge and skills should be related to the functions and tasks noted in Figures 19.1 and 19.3. Since all staff are by definition different, each organizer probably has different educational needs. Some of the knowledge and skill areas relevant to community organizing practice might include: (1) written and oral communication, (2) community and leadership analysis, (3) program development, (4) citizen participation, (5) community and organizational change strategies, (6) community needs assessment skills, (7) grant writing and fund raising, (8) political and legislative lobbying, (9) community impact analysis, (10) interorganizational relations, (11) community development techniques, (12) problem-solving and decision-making skills, (13) planning skills, and (14) task group management. Most organizers probably reflect different capacities to demonstrate excellence in these areas. There are obviously many other areas depending upon the domain of community organizing practice.

In the next section, we shall move from the perspective of the supervisor to the managerial roles of the agency or organization executive who is ultimately responsible for the job performance of all staff.

MANAGING COMMUNITY ORGANIZATIONS

Managerial Roles

The administrator or chief executive of a community agency is expected to wear many hats. Since some community organizations have only two or three permanent staff persons in addition to volunteers, student interns, or VISTA workers, the agency director may also have direct supervisory authority over workers—a task usually performed by middle managers and first-line supervisors in larger social service agencies. One useful way of looking at the executive's

FIGURE 19.3
Mintzberg's Ten Managerial Roles

Interpersonal Roles

Figurehead:	Performs duties of a ceremonial nature.
Leader:	Carries out staffing duties including hiring, training, motivating, promoting, dismissing.
Liaison:	Develops and maintains relationships with individuals outside the agency.

Informational Roles

Monitor:	Seeks information on internal operations and external events.
Disseminator:	Sends factual and value information to staff.
Spokesperson:	Transmits information to organization's environment.

Decisional Roles

Entrepreneur (Innovator):	Initiates and designs controlled change in organization.
Disturbance Handler:	Responds to involuntary situations and change beyond his/her control.
Resource Allocator:	Oversees system by which organizational resources are allocated.
Negotiator:	Negotiates with other organizations or individuals.

position is by examining the ten different roles that represent organized sets of administrative behaviors. Mintzberg (1973) identified three role clusters and ten roles that are defined in Figure 19.3. These role clusters group activities into three broad groups: interpersonal, informational, and decisional. Together, these role clusters comprise the major dimensions of the executive's job.

These roles provide a framework for the executive to organize tasks and clarify the amount of time spent in carrying out each role. An executive's analysis of *current* activities, which delineates the amount of time currently spent in the different roles, together with *future* projections, offers useful information to the board members in developing performance evaluation criteria for the executive. In a similar vein, an executive's analysis of his or her performance on either a role cluster or an individual role can provide valuable information on potential areas of improvement. By using roles to conceptualize the position, executives can move toward a clearer specification of the activities that comprise their job descriptions, offer clear criteria to board members for performance evaluation purposes, and identify areas of need for an executive development plan.

As *figurehead,* an agency executive of a local organization may attend the opening of a neighborhood bank cooperative or an honors dinner for high school youth in the neighborhood. A community development agency executive might be called upon to perform the figurehead role more often than, for example, the director of a planning organization where the agency is not part of a particular neighborhood or serving a specific target population. Though the amount of time spent in the role will vary with different types of agencies, it is part of any executive position.

The *leader* role involves virtually all interpersonal relationships between the leader and the led where the administrator seeks to integrate the workers' and organization's goals by involving staff in decisions regarding goals and objectives. Two different ways to achieve this integration are the democratic and bureaucratic leadership styles. In the former, workers are involved in decisions regarding goals and objectives, and cooperation among staff, board, and executive is cultivated with a view toward the personal development of each of the workers. A bureaucratic approach follows a hierarchical chain of command with staff having limited input into decisions. Rules and guidelines are used to control behavior with attempts to minimize the discretion of the staff person.

In general, a number of factors support community organizations operating at the democratic participatory end of this continuum rather than the bureaucratic end. Their size, which is generally smaller than other types of community organizations, together with the focus on empowering individuals, provides support for a more collaborative approach. In addition, boards of community organizations are likely to be composed of neighborhood residents or clients, whose position as consumer and regulator represents a major force in shaping agency policy and guidelines.

The administrator's *liaison* role includes interaction with other executive directors, membership on other community organizations' boards, and attendance at conferences and professional meetings. This role focuses attention on the agency's consumers, competitors, suppliers of resources, and regulators (Lauffer, 1978). By performing the liaison function, the manager can strengthen relationships with funders and find out how competitors and/or directors of similar agencies are responding to problems.

While these first three roles are primarily interpersonal in nature, the next three require skills in information processing. As *monitor,* the executive seeks information that helps detect changes in the environment, identifies problems, and builds up knowledge. The executive obtains information from four areas: (1) internal operations (for example, hearing that an employee is unhappy and planning to quit), (2) external events (for example, contacts with the city's Office of Community Development result in finding out that there is some money left over from their allocations that the agency might be eligible for), (3) analyses/reports (such as demographic data on the changing composition of the agency's neighborhood), and (4) pressures (like individuals and groups that make demands on the executive for different organizational priorities, support for another organization's involvement with the agency's clientele, and the like).

Just as the agency head needs to gather information, he or she also plays the central role in the way information is disseminated in the organization, thus the role of *disseminator.* The amount and kind of information shared with staff will depend upon the administrative style of the executive, the staff's understanding of the agency's mission and goals, and the director's capacity to articulate the mission and goals. In addition to articulating the agency's philosophy, the administrator must provide factual information that he or she alone is able to gather as a result of the status and connections that come with the position.

As *spokesperson,* the executive is involved in educating relevant publics about the agency activities and programs by speaking at community forums, using a newsletter, appearing on television or radio, attracting coverage in local newspapers, or through other forms of communication. This role is particularly important because of the visibility of the organizer's work and agency involvement with many different elements in the environment. While all employees have a part in communicating the agency's purpose, the executive has primary responsibility for representing the organization. Only if the executive has been able to provide leadership that successfully combines worker and organizational interests is the agency able to present a coherent picture to the public. The messages the executive or staff communicate to the task environment may range from annual financial reports to funding agencies to newsletters that give special recognition to agency volunteers.

The last role cluster is decisional, and it includes roles that use strategy development—a planning process whereby a series of decisions are made in order to deal with a problem or issue.

The manager as entrepreneur or *innovator* is involved in activities such as seeking funds to serve a population currently not included in the agency's target population or assisting in developing a new board training program. While the administrator may initiate and design a plan to bring about the change, there are at least three ways the change process may be handled (Mintzberg, 1973): (1) delegate all responsibility for the different phases of the change effort, based on the size of the change or expertise; (2) authorize staff responsibility for working out the details of the plan; but control signoff or approval before the plan is operationalized; and (3) maintain control and responsibility for the planning and implementation phases.

In the role of innovator the manager initiates change voluntarily, whereas in the role of *disturbance handler* he or she deals with involuntary situations and changes that are partially beyond the manager's control. A rent strike by members of a cooperative housing association or growing factionalism in a coalition of organizations addressing racism in the police department might require the director to take action. Losing a major funding source or the lease on the agency's building are also events that require decisive action on the part of the executive. These disturbances can be grouped into three types: (1) conflicts between staff, (2) resource losses or threats thereof, and (3) conflicts with other agencies regarding territory, responsibilities, or authority.

Organizational resources are money, time, material, equipment, man power, and agency reputation, and the executive as *resource allocator* plays a key part in this ongoing process—one usually characterized by conflict and bargaining. Everything from how the executive spends time to setting priorities for the use of staff time and travel monies is included. Once again, the degree of staff involvement in these decisions will depend on the executive leadership style.

The manager also plays a central role as *negotiator* because of his or her authority to commit resources. Negotiating a major contract with the Department of Housing and Urban Development (HUD) or participating in a collective bargaining session with an em-

ployees' union regarding staff compensation and benefits are both negotiating activities. In both instances it is the manager's ability to commit organizational resources that legitimizes this involvement.

A review of these ten roles describes the sets of behavior the executive needs to engage in if the organization is to succeed with its mission. By distinguishing between roles where the focus is the external environment (figurehead, liaison, spokesperson, negotiator) and roles primarily aimed at internal affairs (leader, monitor, disseminator, innovator, and resource allocator) the overview points up the major task of the executive, that is, constantly to operate on the boundaries, balancing the external demands of the environment with the internal needs of the agency and its staff.

CITIZEN INVOLVEMENT

An agency's board of directors is usually responsible for establishing policy guidelines, reviewing and adopting budgets, evaluating major programs, establishing job classifications, and selecting and evaluating the agency's chief executive (Lauffer, 1978). These responsibilities are impacted by the directors' perception of the usefulness of citizen involvement and by board activities. If the board is seen as a time-consuming burden or as a rubber stamp for executive decisions, the executive will have little reason to ensure that information is fully shared, particularly when the data might raise questions. If, however, the board is seen as an asset, as a group of individuals who act as advocates for clients and agency as well as liaisons between the community, other agencies, community groups, and elected officials, the executive will promote board involvement.

A strong board is usually capable of recognizing and dealing with ideological differences that may lead to such potential conflicts as disagreements over the respective functions of the board and the executive or different views about the future direction of the agency. While policy determination is a board responsibility and policy execution is the responsibility of the executive and staff, these responsibilities are frequently shared despite their different sources of authority and power. The board is the executive's employer, and yet the executive is generally held responsible for the results of the agency programs. Because of a sense of responsibility, the executive may see it in his or her best interest to not share information on agency problems that may reflect unfavorably on his or her abilities. This response limits how well the board can carry out its tasks. However, there are numerous mechanisms to help manage conflict and develop trust through cooperation. The following section on board development and training will highlight some methods of reducing conflicts that result from a lack of clearly defined roles and expectations.

A second area of potential ideological differences may be reflected in the composition of the board. While the boards of most direct-service agencies include community members, the majority are professionals and community leaders who share similar educational and work experiences as well as a socioeconomic status which frequently matches the attributes of the agency's executive. In contrast, the boards of community organization agencies are usually dominated by consumers and activists keenly invested in the specific programs of the agency. Examples of such organizations might be neighborhood development agencies, housing cooperatives, tenants' unions and citizens' action councils. The executive may well be faced with two unique issues when consumers of the service dominate the board. First, the board's concern for clients may be such an overriding factor that members fail to consider staff expertise, funding sources, and program strategies that will not alienate the larger community. A board with such a perspective may view the executive as conservative and unwilling to serve the real needs of people. From the executive's perspective, the board members lack the experience and expertise necessary to work with city officials and foundations; such a perspective may lead the executive to see the board as unrealistic and naive.

Board compositions that are primarily or totally consumers do not help create the same web of relationships. Thus, one would expect that the executive of a consumer-controlled board would need to spend more time performing the liaison role to ensure obtaining necessary information. In contrast, a board made up of professionals and other agencies' staff people plays a liaison role that is helpful in alerting the executive to changing political and economic realities. This kind of board also acts as a bridge to other agencies and their successes and failures with different strategies.

Just as a consumer-controlled board creates special challenges for the executive, different conflicts are likely to develop with a board composed primarily of professionals. While these individuals may help give the agency status and prestige, they could also be a conservative force that impedes the agency's choosing the most effective strategy or focus. Since most human service professionals operate on a collaborative or consensus approach, there may be little support for more activist strategies involving conflict. An executive who has had work experience as an organizer would recognize the importance of pressuring organizations to change at the risk of alienating some community institutions such as the police or schools. Board members unfamiliar with advocacy and social action strategies may be unwilling to support activist strategies.

Regardless of board composition, clarity about both the structure of the board/executive working relationship and the ideological focus of agency efforts is needed. Differences of perspective that are acknowledged, addressed, and worked through can result in a clear view and shared commitment to agency tasks and mission. In order to play a strong role in the agency, the board needs training. The next section discusses what is needed to help a board be effective and suggests ways in which staff and executives can assist in developing an effective board of directors.

Board Training Issues

In order to be effective, a board must include an adequate and qualified membership, a firm philosophical and rational basis for existence, an organizational framework from which to work, an understanding of the functions they are expected to perform, and the knowledge, skills, and assistance to accomplish these functions (Peterfreund, 1980).

The most important element of an effective board is active, committed, and informed members. The best way to ensure the selection of such board members is strategic recruiting after

locating individuals who meet the board's needs. Steps in the recruitment process include:

1. Assessing board membership needs, which includes:
   a. examining the composition of the current board in terms of age, sex, income level, and racial-ethnic backgrounds. Also, examining occupations, knowledge, skills, experience, and educational background to determine gaps in expertise. In addition note future projects and directions and assess gaps in skills needed to deal with issues effectively.
   b. recognize any requirements concerning board composition in by-laws or federal regulations. Examine any problems regarding turnover or excess absenteeism in an attempt to understand them.
2. Advertising for prospective board members: consider newspapers, especially local ones, flyers, posters, contacting community groups and individuals.
3. Screening, interviewing, and orienting prospective board members.

Once individuals are chosen, specially designed orientation programs can provide information vital to board member function by specifying roles and responsibilities. The following types of information are helpful (Peterfreund, 1980):

- History, purpose, philosophy of the agency
- An organizational chart, description of programs, client characteristics, agency finances
- Role and organization of the board, articles of incorporation, and major board and agency policies

While the board, the executive, and the staff should be involved in developing orientation materials, new board members should have the opportunity to meet with agency staff and the director, participate in workshops or training sessions focusing on the role of the board, ask questions after reading the orientation material, and engage in a "buddy system" where each member is assigned to an experienced member for the first six months (Peterfreund, 1980).

In addition to recruitment and orientation activities, there needs to be a recognition of the value of ongoing board development as reflected by the commitment of the executive director. In organizing the planning group, board members, executive, and staff need to be involved in designing a board development program which includes:

1. Assessing board needs—(compare actual performance with ideal performance)
2. Prioritizing areas identified by needs assessment (include consideration of time necessary from board and staff and other resources required)
3. Setting goals for accomplishment (need to be clear, measurable, and acceptable to all involved)
4. Developing a plan of action for board development (includes content areas and educational methods)

The content of development activities will vary according to type of agency and board composition. For a social planning organization composed primarily of professionals and lay leaders, board training may be aimed at increasing knowledge of advocacy and lobbying. If the board is composed primarily of low-income consumers with little exper-ience in working on committees, the board development program might stress the knowledge and skills of working in groups.

SUMMARY

The purpose of this article was to provide an overview of supervisory and management functions in a community organization. We began by describing some characteristics of community organizations that seem to set them apart from direct-service organizations. The technology of the community organizer is usually more visible, is performed in a wide range of settings, includes a larger number of individuals, and is aimed at changes in institutions or social arrangements. The community organizing technology attracts persons with ideological perspectives that are often divergent from those of the supervisor. All of these factors seem to influence supervisory and administrative responsibilities.

The supervisor must clearly understand the organization's functions and the tasks that flow from them. Clearly defined tasks inform and facilitate cooperative planning strategies; they also provide a base for performance evaluation and staff development. Just as the supervisor needs to conceptualize the organizer's work, the executive needs to examine his or her job. Managerial roles for describing executive functions provide a framework for assessing the executive's current and future job activities. These roles also act as a classification scheme that executives and boards can use to evaluate and assess performance.

The last section focused on citizen involvement particularly in relation to executive-board relations. The success of the administrator in implementing policy is in part dependent on the degree of support and involvement of a committed board. That section also identified potential sources of conflict in executive-board relations as well as possible methods to help develop and maintain an effective board.

REFERENCES

Austin, Michael J., *Supervisory Management for the Human Services* (Englewood Cliffs, N.J.: Prentice-Hall 1981).

Lauffer, Armand, *Social Planning at the Community Level* (Englewood Cliffs, N.J.: Prentice-Hall, 1978).

Mintzberg, Henry, *The Nature of Managerial Work* (New York: Harper & Row, 1973).

Peterfreund, Nancy, *Community Mental Health Center Board Development* (Washington, D.C.: U.S. Government Printing Office, 1980).

Perrow, Charles, *Organizational Analysis: A Sociological View* (Monterey, Calif.: Brooks/Cole Publishing Company, 1970).

Rosenbloom, Robert A., "The Neighborhood Movement: Where Has It Come From? Where Is It Going?" *Journal of Voluntary Action Research* 10, 2 (April-June 1981): 4-26.

Rothman, Jack, "Three Models of Community Organization Practice, Their Mixing and Phasing," in Fred M. Cox et al., eds., *Strategies of Community Organization*, 3rd ed. (Itasca, Ill.: F. E. Peacock Publishers, Inc., 1979).

20. GUIDELINES FOR PREPARING PERSONNEL POLICIES*

Fred M. Cox

Perhaps no other single area that seems as if it ought to be handled easily causes as much grief for organizers and planners (as well as administrators) as personnel policies. Indeed, poor, or nonexistent policies can make problems involving race, sex, or age almost insurmountable. Many organizers and planners carry administrative responsibility, often including personnel matters. Virtually all administrators in agencies doing organizing or planning must concern themselves with questions of personnel policy. For those practitioners in agencies which have no policies or policies needing improvement, this article offers some guidance in the policies building—or revising—process.

For those interested in a particular aspect of personnel policies, these guidelines are organized according to the following outline:

Why Have Personnel Policies?
How to Begin

Reproduced by permission of the author. This article was written for this volume.

*The author is grateful to John L. Erlich for a number of helpful suggestions in preparing this paper. However, the author must bear full responsibility for its content.

Who Should Participate in the Preparation?

What Should Be Included?

1. Variations in Employee Status
2. Hiring Policies:
   a. Authority to hire
   b. Source of employees
   c. Nondiscrimination and affirmative action policies
   d. Employment procedures
3. Compensation and Working Conditions:
   a. Methods of compensation
   b. Work schedule
   c. Methods of establishing compensation schemes
   d. Wage and salary structure
   e. Rationale for wages and salaries
   f. Rationale for adjustments in wages and salaries
   g. Should compensation be generally known or kept private?
   h. Compensation for work-related expenses
   i. Facilities
4. Benefits:
   a. Holidays
   b. Vacations
   c. Leaves of absence
   d. Employee security programs
5. Employee Rights and Responsibilities:
   a. Employee responsibilities
   b. Employee rights
   c. Grievance procedures
6. Employee Development:
   a. Orientation of new employees
   b. Probationary period
   c. Supervision and performance evaluation
   d. Staff development
7. Termination of Employment:
   a. Resignation
   b. Dismissal
   c. Reductions in force
   d. Retirement

WHY HAVE PERSONNEL POLICIES?

Personnel policies serve a number of purposes, including the following:

1. They provide a framework for consistent treatment of employees, reducing opportunities for feeling unfairly or arbitrarily treated. Thus, they help maintain morale.

2. They point out contingencies that require foresight, encouraging the formulation of plans for dealing with unexpected, and often unpleasant, developments such as the illness of an employee or unsatisfactory performance of duties.

3. They may help avoid painful and expensive legal troubles, such as may arise from failure to comply with the Fair Labor Standards Act or equal employment opportunity legislation.

4. They assist in the orientation of new board members and employees.

5. They help employees understand their responsibilities.

HOW TO BEGIN

For those employed by federal, state, or city agencies, it is mostly a matter of becoming familiar with existing policies, obtaining copies, and reading them carefully. Those who work for private, not-for-profit organizations, governed by a board of directors and an executive director, will be able to act much more directly.

1. If your agency has personnel policies, study them carefully.

2. If not, get copies of the personnel policies of comparable agencies in your locality or elsewhere. If your agency is part of a state or national organization, get copies of policies from that organization. The sample set of personnel policies that follows this article may be of some help.

3. Consider employing a consultant in personnel administration who can help you formulate policies or critique the ones you have.

4. Consult your agency's attorney to make sure your policies are consistent with the law.

5. Remember that personnel policies should serve as a general guideline. There is no need to try to cover every possible contingency or spell out every procedure in detail. Policies can always be amended, and procedures, if needed, can be developed in separate documents.

WHO SHOULD PARTICIPATE IN THEIR PREPARATION?

1. Clearly, the responsibility lies with the people who make the rules for the organization—for example, the board of directors in a voluntary agency. However, the responsibility may be delegated to a civil service commission, a personnel committee of the board, an executive, or a joint board-staff committee.

2. Those who must abide by the policies should have an opportunity to advise those in authority, reviewing and commenting on drafts. Most professional, supervisory, and administrative personnel, and in many agencies, especially the smaller ones, clerical and technical employees as well, identify strongly with the agency and may be expected to consider its interest along with their own self-interest.

WHAT SHOULD BE INCLUDED?

Not all of what follows should be included in a document entitled "Personnel Policies and Practices." However, these guidelines should inform the development of personnel policies and practices. They are intended to suggest what is common practice at this time in the United States, particularly in organizations engaged in community work. They are also intended to provide some basis for working out the "pros" and "cons" of various options.

1. Variations in employee status. Differences in status have an important bearing on differences in the treatment of employees under personnel policies. Variations commonly recognized in personnel policies include:

a. Full- and part-time employees

b. Persons employed for specified periods or indefinitely

c. Probationary or post-probationary employees

d. Administrative, supervisory, professional, clerical, technical, and so on.

Wages, working conditions, benefits, and conditions of termination typically vary with the status of employees. For example, part-time employees may be denied some benefits that are given to full-time employees, or given benefits proportional to the fraction of their employment. Employees working on time-limited contracts may be treated as performing services for a fee rather than for wages, and be offered no benefits. Probationary employees may have benefits withheld until they have successfully passed the probationary period, and may be dismissed without the procedural safeguards normally extended to post-probationary employees. Administrative and professional employees may be expected to work flexible hours; clerical and technical employees usually work fixed hours.

2. Hiring Policies

a. Authority to hire. The formal authority rests at the top of the organization, with the board of directors in a voluntary organization or the civil service commission or elected executive in a public agency. The board of a voluntary organization will normally not only retain the authority but also engage directly in the employment of the executive director, while delegating the hiring of other employees to the executive. In large organizations, appropriate supervisors are often delegated this authority. The extent of delegation of authority to hire depends upon:

(1) Size of the agency—the larger the agency, the more likely it is that hiring decisions will be delegated.

(2) Level of job—the more subordinate the position, the more likely the selection of employees will be delegated to an intermediate supervisor.

(3) The level of experience and trust the hiring authority has in those to whom the authority to hire may be delegated. An executive of a middle-size or large agency would soon be overwhelmed with details if he or she tried to make all hiring decisions personally, though it is appropriate for the executive to review such decisions.

b. Source of employees. There are at least three policy questions regarding the source of employees.

(1) Employing friends and relatives. There is a potential for favoritism in employment, promotion, termination, wages and salaries, and working conditions if relatives or close friends of top or middle management are employed. Administrators open themselves to criticism, warranted or not, when they employ relatives or close friends. If such persons are employed, administrators should go out of their way to demonstrate that such employees are not given special treatment. An employee should not supervise or have influence over salary increases or promotions of relatives or close personal friends.

(2) Internal versus external recruitment. "Promotion from within" is a policy followed by many businesses, and is considered a key to employee loyalty and morale. However, such a policy is limited by the size of the organization and the size of the pool of qualified persons for a particular position. Large organizations with a high percentage of well-prepared staff members from a wide variety of disciplines lend themselves to promotion from within, but most organizations doing organizing and planning are small. Perhaps the best policy for most organizations is to notify all employees of all job openings, and to encourage applications from and perhaps give preference to current employees who are qualified.

(3) Local versus broader recruitment. Some city and county governments limit their recruitment to local residents. When the necessary skills and abilities for particular jobs are readily available, this may work relatively well. But when the talents required are scarce in the community, then a broader search is in order.

(4) Methods of searching for employees. There are a number of ways to get the word out.

(a) Local newspapers take classified advertising. Large metropolitan papers, such as the *New York Times*, are often distributed outside their local areas and have special sections on jobs in the health and human services.

(b) Professional associations often publish newsletters that include job advertisements.

(c) Trade associations and national agencies often have newsletters or job services.

(d) National conferences in various fields typically offer opportunities for employers and job seekers to meet.

(e) Job lists are often maintained for graduating students by schools of social work.

c. Nondiscrimination and affirmative action policies.

Nondiscrimination implies a willingness to hire based solely on ability to perform. Affirmative action implies a good deal more: the willingness to search vigorously for qualified employees in categories underrepresented in particular types of employment.

d. Employment procedures.

(1) As a result of a search, job inquiries will be received. In response, the organization should be prepared to forward a detailed job description, giving information about the duties and responsibilities of the position, the education and experience requirements, the materials to be included in the application, to whom the application should be directed, and the closing date for its receipt. Some indication of wages and working conditions should be given, including employee status.

(2) Materials to be included with the application typically include the following:

(a) Resume of education and employment experience

(b) Names, addresses, and telephone numbers of three persons who may be asked for references.

(3) The employing authority, that is, the board of directors or its personnel committee or the administrator or person delegated employment responsibility for a particular position should review all applications and select a reasonable number that seem most promising for personal interviews. Three to five candidates is usually sufficient.

(4) It is wise to seek the advice of supervisors and fellow workers in the selection of personnel. They can provide insights that may have been missed by the employing authority and thereby improve the quality of the selection process. In addition, candidates should have an opportunity to talk with those with whom they will be working before accepting a position in order to assess whether the job, working conditions, morale, and so on, are satisfactory.

(5) If possible, arrange to pay the travel expenses of candidates selected for personal interviews. This signals the importance attached to the position, and the high regard for the candidates selected for interview.

(6) If possible, pay part or all of the moving expenses of professional, supervisory, or managerial employees recruited from outside the immediate area.

(7) Provide the candidate selected with a letter of offer, stating the terms and conditions of employment, a copy of the job description, and the organization's personnel policies. Require a letter of acceptance from the candidate before announcing that the position has

been filled.

3. Compensation and Working Conditions

  a. Methods of compensation

    (1) Hourly. Wages are paid for each hour of employment, requiring careful records of hours worked. Normally, this method is limited to clerical and technical employees.

    (2) Biweekly, monthly (or yearly) salary. This method is used, ordinarily, in compensating administrative, supervisory, or professional employees.

  b. Work schedule. Particularly with respect to hourly workers but also as a guide to salaried employees, it is important to establish a work schedule that will accommodate the organization's office hours and rhythm of work. For example, some community work requires evening and weekend hours.

    (1) The working week. Normally forty hours, the full-time work week may vary in length depending on local practices. A thirty-five-week is increasingly common.

    (2) The working day. Normally eight hours; seven is not uncommon. If a particular work schedule is important for a given job, that should be noted in the position description and letter of offer. A flexible working schedule, for example ten hours a day, four days a week, is increasingly used to meet the special needs of employees, such as working women. Job splitting, where two persons divide a full-time job to suit their individual needs, is increasingly coming into use. If these or other options are offered, they should be stated in personnel policies.

    (3) The organization's opening and closing hours. It is usually important that at least some employees arrive at work at the beginning of the working day, and that some remain until the end. These hours should be stated in personnel policies.

    (4) Overtime work. Administrative or supervisory permission to engage in paid overtime work should be required. The Fair Labor Standards Act requires pay at one and one-half times the normal hourly rate for over-time work beyond forty hours per week for eligible employees. For other hourly employees, compensatory time off is used to repay workers for overtime services. It is vital to keep accurate records of overtime hours worked for such employees.

    (5) Work records. It is essential that accurate records of hours worked be kept for hourly employees and of weeks (or months) worked for salaried employees. Such records are essential in preparing the payroll and in calculating such benefits as vacation time, severance pay, and other benefits that are related to length of time worked.

  c. Methods of establishing compensation schemes. They may be set by the board of directors or administration, worked out through negotiations between individual employees and the administration or board (very common with top management employees), or established through collective bargaining between unions of employees and the employer. Professional organizations, such as the National Association of Social Workers, may establish standards for salaries and personnel practices.

  d. Wage and salary structure. There are two basic ways in which compensation is structured.

(1) Pay ranges for each classification of employees are established, with or without intermediate steps. A common structure is a five-step scheme. The principal advantage of this approach is its openness to review and criticism by all concerned, and its contribution to equity of treatment. However, it creates certain rigidities which make it difficult to attract some desirable candidates and retain superior employees who reach the top of the range.

(2) Pay is established on an ad hoc basis, in order to take account of the special circumstances and conditions surrounding the employment of a particular individual, such as market conditions, reputation, length or quality of prior experience, quality of job performance, and others. However, it has the disadvantages of allowing inequities between employees of equal merit and breeding suspicions of favoritism, which can be harmful to morale.

e. Rationale for wages and salaries

(1) They may be determined on more or less rational grounds, through comparisons with compensation offered for similar work performed under similar conditions, that is, job security, fringe benefits, auspices, and so on. Check with professional associations, or associations of organizations working in the same field (often referred to as trade associations) such as United Neighborhood Centers of America.

(2) They may be determined by the limits of the organization's resources. It may not be possible for a developing organization engaged in community work to pay the going rate for the people it needs. Such organizations must depend on ideology, special commitment to the purposes of the organization, or various forms of unpaid compensation—opportunities for the inexperienced practitioners to gain valuable work experience, contributing to desirable social changes, and so on. Where these limits exist, such unpaid forms of compensation or other attractions need to be highlighted in recruitment efforts. Examples of such organizations include some churches and religious organizations, grass-roots citizens' groups, so-called "alternative" service programs, VISTA, and the Peace Corps.

(3) They may be determined by ideological considerations, such as egalitarian social objectives. On principle, equal or nearly equal pay may be offered for all jobs, and job assignment determined by individual abilities and training.

f. Rationale for adjustments in wages and salaries. The basis on which pay is adjusted needs to be stated in personnel policies. Some of the alternatives include:

(1) Passage of time, that is, seniority. Raises take place automatically at predetermined intervals if performance is satisfactory.

(2) Merit review. Increases are based on judgments of the quantity and quality of work performance.

(3) Cost of living. Particularly in times of rapid inflation in the cost of living, increases related to the rate of inflation are important to prevent pay from declining in real terms.

(4) Market conditions. When a valued employee is offered another

position at a salary increase, the organization may wish to offer an increase in pay (or in responsibilities and pay) in order to retain the employee.

(5) Inequities. For various reasons, inequalities in pay that are not based on rational grounds such as the above may arise. Thus, women and certain ethnic minorities such as blacks, Hispanics, and Native Americans earn less than others. When they are performing similar work of equal quality and quantity over comparable periods of time, the inequity should be rectified.

(6) Promotions. When similar work is organized in various ranks, whatever increases are provided for within a rank should be less than the increase offered when moving from one rank to another. A similar principle applies when one moves from one type of work to another, such as from technical to professional to supervisory. However, some overlap often exists in salary ranges of various types of work.

g. Should compensation be generally known or kept private?

Traditionally, one's wages or salary were considered a private matter, between one and one's employer. The trend, particularly in public employment, is to make wages and salaries public. Public disclosure reduces rumor and suspicion, which can erode morale. However, if there are obvious inequities in salaries, public disclosure can harm morale. On the other hand, employees generally compare and discuss salaries, so it is difficult to maintain secrecy.

h. Compensation for work-related expenses.

(1) Travel to and from work is generally regarded as a personal expense, both by employers and the Internal Revenue Service.

(2) Other job-related travel is typically reimbursed, either by providing the employee with an agency-owned vehicle to drive, paying so much for each mile of travel, or compensating the employee for actual expenses of using public transportation. Studies are available of the cost per mile of travel by automobile.

i. Facilities. In addition to adequate compensation, a number of supporting conditions are necessary for adequate performance of responsibilities. These include supervision, evaluation, and opportunities for vocational or professional development. Physical facilities appropriate to assigned responsibilities also need to be provided.

4. Benefits. Often referred to as "fringe" benefits, these are unpaid forms of compensation which are very commonly provided.

a. Holidays. Certain holidays are almost universal. Whatever paid holidays are given should be listed in personnel policies.

b. Vacations. Some period during the year, set aside for refreshment and recreation, is normally provided. The period may vary from a week to a month or more and typically varies with the length and status of employment. The paid vacation policy of the organization should be included in the personnel policies, including the basis for determining its length and timing. Vacation schedules should be organized so that their disruptive effect on the work of the organization is minimal.

c. Leaves of absence. Leaves may be granted with and without pay for a variety of reasons including (1) illness or disability, personal or of a close family member, (2) death of a close relative, (3) military duty, (4) jury duty, (5) maternity and, increasingly, paternity, (6) study. It is wise to check with your attorney to learn what leaves are mandatory in your state.

(1) and (2) Sick leave. Normally, sick leave accumulates at the rate of one or one and one-half days per month of employment, up to some limit, such as thirty or ninety days, and applies to personal illness or disability or the illness or disability of a close family member. In order to supplement sick leave with pay, some organizations offer disability insurance, paid by the organization or purchased by the employee, which provides some portion of one's salary for extended periods.

(3) Military leave. Federal law provides for job protection for those called to serve in the armed forces. Leave of absence to perform National Guard duty is required by law. The organization should pay the difference between military pay and the employee's normal pay for a period of up to two weeks.

(4) Jury duty leave. Normally, employees are paid the difference between their usual salary and payment received for jury duty, with no limit placed on the length of such leave. Employees subpoenaed as witnesses are treated similarly.

(5) Maternity and paternity leave. The usual pattern is to grant a leave without pay, although in other Western industrialized nations, leave with pay is common. Paternity leave is much less common, but is more frequently granted than in the past.

(6) Study leave. Organizations should consider granting leave for study for short periods, particularly when that study will contribute directly to the employee's effectiveness on the job or to promotion within the organization. Some large organizations provide not only for paid leave but also for payment of educational expenses, but most organizations are unable to afford such a policy. Paid leave, including payment of expenses to attend professional meetings, usually no more often than once a year, is quite common.

As indicated, personnel policies should state whether leaves are paid or unpaid. Personnel policies should also indicate whether the employee is eligible for other benefits during a leave. For example, does paid vacation time accrue during a sick leave? Does sick leave build up during a maternity leave? Does an employee continue to be covered by the organization's health insurance plan during an unpaid leave?

d. Employee security programs. Certain public programs are virtually required for all employees. If you think your organization may be an exception, check with your attorney. These include:

(1) Workman's compensation, required by state law, protects employees against the cost of injury and illness arising from job-related causes. Protection includes payment of compensation in lieu of wages, and medical, hospital, and related expenses.

(2) Unemployment insurance, also required by state law for most organizations, protects employees against involuntary loss of employment. Protection is provided by the

state, in the form of cash benefits for a limited number of weeks. The cost to the organization is based on the unemployment experience of its employees.

(3) Social Security, the federal government program which provides old age and survivors insurance, disability benefits, and payments toward the costs of health care for the aged and disabled who qualify. Benefits are paid for by a payroll tax on nearly all employees and employers.

Another group of employee security programs may be provided by employers on a voluntary basis or in response to a collective bargaining agreement. These include the following:

(1) Retirement benefits to supplement old age benefits under the Social Security program. Such benefits may take several forms:

(a) Fixed dollar payments related to salary, usually the highest salary paid during a given number of years, and the length of employment. This is a common pattern of state retirement systems.

(b) Fixed dollar payments related to the amount of contributions which are invested in bonds, mortgages, or other interest-bearing investments, and life expectancy. This is also known as an annuity and may be purchased from any private life insurance company.

(c) Variable dollar payments related to the value of the equities (stocks) in which one's contributions are invested together with life expectancy. Mutual funds and stock brokers sell such plans.

Such retirement benefits may be paid for by the employer, the employee, or both. Another feature of great importance to employees is the length of time that must elapse before benefits are fully vested in the employee, so that if an employee changes jobs, the benefits are fully retained or the employee receives a cash refund of all premiums paid on his or her behalf.

(2) Health benefits. Such benefits may take several forms:

(a) Ordinary health insurance pays all or some stated portion of the cost of specified services.

(b) Catastrophic health insurance pays virtually all costs of care for an illness or injury up to some very high limit such as $250,000 or $1 million.

(c) Health service plans, including health maintenance organizations (HMO's), undertake to provide a comprehensive set of health services for a fixed monthly fee, generally with few exceptions and very high, if any, limits. You are paying directly for the services of a hospital and a group of physicians and related health service workers rather than buying insurance which, in turn, pays for those services.

(d) Accidental death and dismemberment insurance provides a death benefit to survivors and so much for the loss of a limb or an eye due to an accident.

(e) Health indemnity insurance pays a fixed dollar amount for each day in the hospital or each day one is unable to work due to illness or disability to help defray the expenses of health care.

Most employers pay the full cost

of care for their employees of ordinary and catastrophic or health service plans, and many also pay part or all of the costs of covering other members of the immediate family.

(3) Disability benefits. To supplement disability benefits under the Social Security program, many employers provide paid sick leave, as noted earlier, and in some cases provide insurance which pays benefits designed to replace a portion of earnings, often two-thirds or three-quarters, for extended periods up to the time one becomes eligible for Social Security retirement benefits in cases of permanent disability that prevents reemployment.

(4) Life insurance benefits. To protect survivors against the loss of wages of an employee and supplement survivors' benefits under Social Security, some employers provide life insurance, usually term insurance which has no cash value, in some multiple of the employee's yearly earnings.

(5) Liability insurance. If you accidentally cause injury to someone in the course of your employment, you and the organization may be sued. Organizations normally carry insurance to protect themselves against liability arising from successful legal action. Employees are often asked to obtain liability protection for themselves and their employers if they use their personal automobiles in the course of their employment. Professional employees should consider obtaining malpractice insurance to protect themselves. Employers may or may not share in the cost of insurance protecting employees against general

and professional liability.

5. Employee Rights and Responsibilities

a. Employee responsibilities

(1) To fulfill the specific responsibilities of the *job* for which the employee is hired. This should be described in some detail in a separate job description, and a copy provided to the employee at the time the candidate is being considered for the job.

(2) To serve the *clientele* to the best of one's ability. This is a commitment to professional norms, putting work above personal interests while on the job, exercising judgment on what is in the best interests of the client, maintaining and developing professional skills, treating all clients fairly regardless of personal enthusiasms or antagonisms, establishing and maintaining good working relationships, and so on.

(3) To serve the *agency* to the best of one's ability. This is a commitment to the organization and its purposes and, generally, to bureaucratic norms. It includes doing what is necessary to advance the organization's programs; being flexible in varying one's work schedule and taking on extra responsibilities when necessary, such as during illness or crisis; exercising judgment that is broadly supportive of the organization in the formulation of policy; abiding by agency policy once it has been adopted; and working through the agency framework to change policy.

b. Employee rights

(1) To join with other employees and bargain collectively with the employer for wages, working conditions, and so on. In some places, this

right is guaranteed by law.

(2) To work through professional organizations to resolve disputes about personnel standards and practices and agency policies. While the employee has a responsibility to try to resolve differences through agency channels (supervisor, executive, board of directors), employees have a right to appeal to their professional organizations where differences cannot otherwise be resolved.

(3) To exercise the full rights of a citizen as guaranteed by the Constitution and statutes of federal, state, and local governments. However, the employee has the responsibility to make clear that such action is taken as a private citizen and not as an agency representative.

(4) To receive a copy of personnel policies and practices and a job description at the time of employment.

(5) To be treated by fellow employees, supervisors, executive, and members of the board of directors in a nondiscriminatory fashion.

c. Grievance Procedures. Grievances are inevitable, and plans should be made to handle them in an orderly way. Grievances that are ignored or not handled effectively can cause serious morale problems, unpleasant terminations, or even costly legal action. One basic principle is that grievances should be handled at the lowest level possible, that is, between the employee and his or her supervisor before appealing to higher levels. A second is that procedures for resolving disputes should be regarded as fair by all parties. Documentation should be required, but never in a way that inhibits resolution through discussion.

The outline for a relatively simple grievance policy follows:

(1) Any grievance or dispute between a staff member and the employing organization should be discussed between the employee and (a) his or her supervisor, (b) the organization's executive, and (c) the personnel committee of the organization, generally a committee of the board of directors (or the functional equivalent such as the civil service commission or its representative in a public agency) in that order in an effort to resolve the matter.

(2) If the matter cannot be resolved in this way, the matter should be referred to an advisory committee consisting of three members, one chosen by the grievant, one chosen by the executive director, and one chosen by the two advisory committee members representing the grievant and the executive director, who chairs the committee. Allowing for due process (but not necessarily all procedures followed in a court of law), the matter is considered by the advisory committee, and its chairperson prepares a written report and recommendations for the board of directors.

(3) The board of directors typically has the final authority to take action, except that the employee is always free to appeal to a court of law.

6. Employee Development

a. Orientation of new employees. New employees need to know something of the mission and goals of the organization that employs them. In large organizations, this may be done through in-service training programs provided for the newly employed.

b. Probationary period. The idea behind the probationary period of employment is that there is a relatively short time at the beginning of one's employment during which it is clearly understood by both employer and employee that the employer may terminate the employment contract with a minimum of formalities. During the probationary period the employee is generally not entitled to elaborate procedural safeguards, nor must the employer demonstrate gross unfitness, dereliction of duties, or other serious misbehavior as grounds for dismissal.

(1) The length of the probationary period should vary with the time required for the employer to assess the employee's performance thoroughly. Generally, this will be a shorter period for those engaged in clerical and some technical duties, and somewhat longer for those assigned to professional, managerial, or administrative responsibilities. Probationary periods of three, six, or twelve months are not uncommon.

(2) During the probationary period there should be periodic assessment of performance by the supervisor with regular communication to the employee, both written and oral. If the probationary period ends in termination, this should not come as a surprise to the employee.

(3) Personnel policies should specify which employee benefits apply during the probationary period.

(4) At the end of the probationary period, the new employee should receive a letter indicating that he or she has successfully completed the trial period or that he or she is dismissed.

c. Supervision and performance evaluation. Employees are entitled to know what is expected of them, to know whether the supervisor thinks they measure up, and to receive guidance in performing up to expectations if they fall below acceptable standards, and more generally, help in improving their performance even if their work is quite acceptable. For a number of reasons, evaluation is a difficult process.

(1) It is difficult to tell whether a community organizer or a planner is doing a good job because the indicators of successful performance are difficult to define and measure.

(2) Another difficulty is the visibility of job performance to the supervisor. Much of community organization and planning is done out of the view of a supervisor.

(3) Finally, the interpersonal ties of affection, admiration, and reciprocity (as well as disaffection and hostility) make it more difficult to give honest appraisals of performance.

Other considerations include:

(1) Demonstrated support for evaluation from the top of the organization. Because of the difficulties in performance appraisal, formal systems of appraisal are often ignored or performed in a perfunctory way. If personnel policies are to include performance appraisal, they should include appraisal of the executive director by the board and by the executive of those reporting directly to the executive, as well as the appraisal of subordinate employees. The way in which the appraisal process is carried out at the top levels of the organization will affect the way subordinates handle these responsibilities.

(2) Uses of evaluation. If merit is a consideration in salary and promotion policy, performance appraisal has obvious utility. Some form of performance appraisal is also important in improving organizational effectiveness, decisions on promotion, and in establishing the basis for disciplinary action or dismissal. Particularly in the latter case, careful documentation of instances of non- or mal-performance are essential

(3) Policy and procedural issues. In developing a system of performance appraisal, policies should include a statement of what purposes are to be served, who should do it, at what intervals, what is to be covered in the appraisal, what form documentation should take, and what steps the employee may take if he or she disagrees with the employer's evaluation.

(4) Employee participation in performance evaluation. One of the more effective approaches to performance appraisal places the emphasis on employee participation in the process and his or her contribution to organizational development and effectiveness. Employees are involved in defining the goals they are expected to achieve within a given period of time. Periodic reviews with each employee assess the extent of success and emphasize problem solving to improve performance. Only when these efforts fail, and the failure is well documented through this process, is disciplinary action considered. When disciplinary action is required, it is easier to take because the basis for it is well understood by both parties.

d. Staff development. Organizations engage in staff development activities because they are expected to improve organizational effectiveness and efficiency, and generate new ideas and better ways to solve problems. It is also clear that staff development may have considerable payoff for the individual employee.

(1) Types of staff development activity:

(a) Orientation for new employees, discussed previously.

(b) Group supervision and problem solving conducted by supervisors.

(c) In-service training related to specific tasks and operations, which may be conducted by:

(i) Specialists within the organization

(ii) External consultants from universities or professional consulting organizations

(d) Seminars and workshops offered by university extension, professional consulting organizations, and professional associations.

(e) Study for advanced degrees, sometimes related to improved performance in one's current employment but more often to career advancement and promotion.

(2) Policy issues

(a) In what ways and to what extent will staff development be encouraged? Will the organization offer paid or unpaid time off from work, or must the employee engage in some types of staff development activities after hours? Will the employer pay tuition and related expenses, or must the employee meet the expenses for some types of staff development?

(b) Must the staff development

activity supported by the organization be directly related to present duties, in preparation for other positions within the organization, or may they be for the professional development of the employee without these restrictions?

(c) What limits are placed by the organization on participation? Does the employer place a dollar limit on costs to be reimbursed within a specified period of time or a limit on the amount of time off?

(d) Policy should state whether the employee has an obligation to share what was learned. This is especially pertinent when a workshop, seminar, or independent study is directly related to agency problems or programs.

7. Termination of Employment. This is usually a sensitive matter, both because of the potential effects on interpersonal relations within the organization and employee morale and because of the moral, financial, and legal implication of termination. For example, the way in which an employee is terminated, voluntarily or involuntarily, will affect eligibility of unemployment insurance benefits. Organizational rules on severance pay and laws governing unemployment insurance may place an economic burden on the organization. Laws on nondiscrimination in employment and ethical obligations affect layoffs arising from program changes or funding constraints.

a. Resignation. Policy should provide for as much notice as possible to the employer. A minimum of one month's notice from professional and administrative employees and two weeks' notice from support staff is fairly standard. Personnel policies should include penalties for failure to provide minimum notice, such as loss of accrued vacation time.

b. Dismissal. The executive director should have the right to suspend the employee for misconduct or gross incompetence, pending application of established grievance procedures. The executive should consult with the personnel committee of the board of directors (or the functional equivalent in a public agency) prior to or shortly after suspending an employee. Normally, the grievance procedure is allowed to run its course before salary, benefits, and employment are terminated.

(1) The importance of an established process of staff evaluation occurring at prescribed intervals is especially important in this connection. (See supervision and performance evaluation, above.)

(2) It is essential that incompetence be documented carefully, pointing to specific behaviors and times that demonstrate the finding of incompetence. A pattern of incompetence, rather than isolated incidents, is normally required.

(3) A written evaluation of employee performance at established intervals should be routinely completed. When this is not a part of agency policy, it is nonetheless required to establish a pattern of incompetence. The employee should have an opportunity to discuss his or her performance with the supervisor as well as receiving a written evaluation, and should receive guidance on improving performance, followed by a reasonable period of time to demonstrate improvement.

c. Reductions in force. These result either because the organization's financial resources are insufficient to maintain all of its activities or because the organization has decided to change its programs. In either case, some employees must be terminated through no fault of their own, which raises the issue of severance benefits.

(1) Severance pay is a common benefit for employees who are laid off. Normally, such benefits are related to the length of employment, with some minimum and maximum. The benefit is normally measured in terms of the employee's rate of pay. The underlying theory behind this form of severance pay is that it is compensation for length of service and for the loss of seniority and accrued benefits.

(2) Another theory of severance pay is that it is compensation for loss of future wages. According to this theory, severance pay is redundant with unemployment compensation. Both theories are supported by legal precedent. Because unemployment compensation tax rates are related to an employer's experience with layoffs, one or more layoffs may result in increased taxes for the employer. Also, the receipt of severance pay may affect the employee's ability to collect unemployment insurance. The employer should check state law with the organization's legal counsel before establishing a policy on severance pay.

(3) Accrued vacation time is often added to severance pay at the time of layoff.

(4) Group insurance plans are often convertible to individual insurance policies at the employee's expense when employment is terminated.

d. Retirement.

(1) Organizations should consider providing one or more options for employees to provide retirement benefits to supplement Social Security. Particularly important are plans to supplement Social Security income and health insurance.

(2) Many organizations are recognizing the difficulty their employees experience when they retire. Increasingly, preretirement orientation programs are available to assist those nearing retirement to plan for the inevitable changes in their lives.

FINAL NOTE

Perhaps more than anything else, personnel policies need to be seen as facilitating, rather than impeding, the work of the organization and its employees. As part of this positive posture, the process for changing policies should be clear and readily accessible to all employees.

21. PUBLIC RELATIONS

League of Women Voters of the United States

INTRODUCTION

There are many definitions of public relations. Some call it the art of attracting attention. Others say it's the art of using radio, television, newspapers and magazines to inform and influence people. Still others say it is the means of communicating to the public what you or your group is all about. Public relations may be hard to define, yet you know it when you see it.

One thing is certain, the words "public relations" bring to mind a host of words—some positive and some negative. Words like plastic, phoney, slick, deceptive, come to mind along with words like influential, persuasive, constructive or beneficial. Public relations has been all of these things for better and for worse. But for your needs there's no doubt that public relations should be geared to all of the positive things that PR can be.

A good way to begin developing a long-range plan is to try to determine what image your organization already has and to think about the kind of image you want to project. What image do members have? Is it the same as that of leaders? What is your image in the community, especially among those you most need to reach? What does the "man in the street" or the "average woman" think of you? What do you wish they thought? What is your image among

Reproduced by permission of the publisher. From *Reaching the Public,* League of Women Voters of the United States, 1976.

those groups you most want to influence—be they legislators ... news media staff ... minority groups ... school personnel ... local "money bags"? What do you think it ought to be? How far can you move toward those goals in one year? in five years?

You may need to do a mini-survey to get some reliable feedback about your present image. Try a simple survey plus some interviews. Again, check out your members. If most of them think you exist almost entirely to give out neutral information and most of your leaders think you should be bringing about community change—or vice versa—well, you can see the problems that split can lead to. Now, take stock:

- What do you have going for you? What are your strengths? High degree of member activity? Sound finances? Some recent "big wins" in the legislature? The trust of other civic groups?
- What are your weak points? Poor media contacts? Too little financial support from the community? A "chicken" image when the going gets tough?
- Is your membership drawn from only one segment of the community? (You have to decide whether this is a weakness or a strength.)

What should your dominant, overall

image be? Getting agreement on this point may take a lot of consultation with leaders, members and friends of the organization. It's easier for a single-issue group. At least the subject is clear, and you can focus on style and stance. For a multi-issue organization, it takes more time and effort to develop a simple, inclusive, overarching statement, but it's time well spent. Once you get that established, all future PR on specific projects and campaigns can be kept compatible with that goal, that image.

Compatible with one another, too—because everything you do has ripple effects. Your PR efforts on behalf of, say, a fund-raising campaign will reverberate, affecting a later membership drive, a future lobbying effort, a current community service project.

Once you've squared away what kind of image you want to project (or think you already project), you may want to undertake some generalized PR efforts to reinforce that image. Perhaps a round of calls on media people with some brief background sheets on recent accomplishments or new emphases (accent on *recent* and *new*—a distant illustrious past doesn't turn on media types). Perhaps a discussion with the board about a facelift in content, looks and emphasis for all your publications, or at least for the basic leaflet that describes your organization. Perhaps some attention to who gets into the photos, who represents you at news conferences, as these affect your total image. Whatever you work out, be sure you don't work it out alone. First of all, that's bad internal public relations. Second, you need all the help you can get, and you need to involve as much of the leadership and the general membership as you can in this kind of thinking.

Lead time for this kind of groundwork may be nonexistent. You may find yourself plunged into a heavy PR effort for a specific organization activity. Don't despair. With everyone's head on straight about the general thrust for PR, you can undertake your short-term projects within reliable outside margins that have broad-based acceptance within the organization. Your tour of news media contacts can be tied to the job of the moment. That facelift on publications may start with the factsheet you need *right now*.

All this is not to say that every PR activity will have a cookie-cutter sameness, just because you have a broad-gauge definition of the image you want to project. Each organization activity has its own primary target audiences. And different projects have different priorities, different resources—budget, member interest—and different timetables.

Many Publics

Choose those audiences with discrimination. Be sure that you are directing your efforts where they will count. And it's not just numbers that count. It's also a question of getting the message to those people who can make a difference. If you need the help of a conservation group, for instance, to spike passage of some changes in regulations governing access to a rare bird sanctuary, you'd better not patronize them by explaining the term "endangered species." But if you want your whole community to back the preservation of that sanctuary, you'd better not put average citizens to sleep with more than they want to know. Worse still, don't confuse them with bill numbers, effective dates and multiple criteria. Keep it simple. Accent the broad benefits. Ask for one-shot citizen action.

Usually, you need to reach several kinds of groups. For example, your campaign to clean up a polluted waterway by dredging is not just news for other environmental groups. What about businessmen who ship goods? What about pleasure boat owners? What about residents who were concerned about the health hazards of the polluted area? By tailoring your message to fit the needs of particular groups, you are more likely to be able to broaden public support for your cause. If you turn over in your mind all facets of the issue you are pursuing, you can generally work up a far more varied list of target groups than first thought would indicate.

Setting Objectives

Good public relations doesn't just happen. It takes the same type of dedication you are used to in any other organizational commitments. A successful PR campaign not only requires study and analysis, it also demands a knowledge of how the media functions; know-how about the sources of support from which you can draw; a general knowledge of the forces for and against your agenda in the community; and a sense of the public's opinion of your group.

You've already determined what public image you want your organization to have. As part of the leadership team, you know what the goal for a specific project is. But that isn't enough, especially for a campaign on an issue. You need to take a closer look at the issue itself. The issue you want to bring to the media's attention must be well prepared before it makes its debut. Not only should you fully understand it; you must be sure others will be able to understand it just as clearly and as quickly as possible. That's why you will have to strip the issue down

to the bare facts, remove verbiage and confusing language and be sure the side issues have been separated from the principal point you wish to make. This preparation will go a long way toward assuring that in your effort to get the message across neither the audience nor the media will be sidetracked by other issues or get lost in confusion.

Having prepared the issue, choose the theme. A theme is the tie that binds. It's your way of succinctly letting the media know *why* you're doing *what* you're doing. In effect, your theme is determined when you're able to briefly state what you intend to say to the public.

Once you've chosen the theme, it's important that you stick to it and not get thrown off the track. This requires effort and planning. It demands that you carefully think through press releases, speeches and even what you plan to say when being interviewed so that you drive your points home time and again. Your impact on an audience depends on your determination to stick to the issue and to keep it in front of the media and the public as much as possible.

Getting the Message Across

Now that you've made that decision, you're on to the next plateau—how do you get your message across? The methods used in reaching the public run the gamut from the usual newspaper, radio and TV approaches to sometimes simpler and other times more far-out methods such as buttons and signs, telegrams and telephone calls, posters and flyers, parades or just buttonholing people.

To help reach the decision as to the best media or media mix for your purposes, try taking a hard look at the methods others have used to get their message across. What *may* have appeared to be a successful campaign in reality may be little more than fluff. So review carefully what others have done.

If the objective was to get people to think over a new idea, find out if thoughts *were* stimulated. If the goal was to get people to do something, *did* the audience respond and take action? If it's been a fund raiser, how much money was raised from the effort? Try to find out what costs were involved in their efforts and how much time was needed for the project. You can profit from the successes and failures of other groups, so time spent in checking out what's already been done in your area is time well spent.

But don't stop there. The information you've absorbed from other projects shouldn't be the only guidelines you use in making your decision on what media to use. Creativity also pays off. So turn loose your imagination. One word of warning: whatever method you intend to use, your plan should assure that your message will be direct and easily understood. It's important that you don't get so clever that you confuse the public about what you're trying to accomplish.

It's also important never to promise more than you can deliver. If your public relations campaign urges citizens to write in for free information or to call for additional material, be sure you'll be able to handle the responses. Your public relations will move into the minus column if you can't deliver on what you promised. Make sure, moreover, that you've squared away details on this before the campaign gets underway. If your effort proves to be successful, you won't have any time in the middle of the campaign to start deciding on how you will respond to requests.

When you're thinking about what media to use, do some hard thinking about how you may link your issue with breaking news. If a story in the paper dovetails with ongoing efforts in which you're involved, you may, for example, want to write a succinct and straightforward letter to the editor on the subject. While there is no guarantee that your letter will pop up in the paper the next day, often such letters are chosen. Remember, however, that this is just one PR technique, so don't overuse it.

If you're doing a press release for distribution regarding the latest developments in an issue, think about doing a windup paragraph at the end of the release recapping what your organization's role has been in the past on this issue. It's a good way of helping reporters to zero in on what you've been up to (For hints on press releases, see *Getting Into Print*.)

Whatever the issue, run with it and don't be afraid of controversy. A hot issue is likely to bring you more media attention. If you're willing to deal with controversy, to stand up and be counted on what you're backing and accept the criticism that always comes with controversy, then you stand a good chance of getting not only good media coverage but more respect from the community at large.

Time

A good PR campaign not only takes time to plan, it also demands that you meet time schedules as well. Be sure that you are well organized enough to meet newspaper, radio and television deadlines. The best PR material will only find its way to the wastepaper basket if an editor or program director finds that the material is old news.

If you find that you're in a time crunch but you need to comment on breaking news, think about calling the wire services with a succinct statement. (For details on the wire services, see *Breaking Into Broadcasting.*) In some instances, that quick but thoughtful comment hits the mark and is picked up by papers.

If you have plenty of time, you may think of developing a position paper spelling out the problem you are dealing with and giving information about your involvement in the matter. While this type of material will not be front-page news, it often helps a reporter or commentator get a better idea of where you are and why you are working on a particular issue. Backgrounders should not be long, however. In most cases you should be able to boil down the facts on the matter to a page or even less. A two-page maximum should be your guideline. Media people won't bother with lengthy tomes on a subject.

Your Committee

There's strength in numbers and that certainly holds true when undertaking a public relations campaign. So the PR chairman must also set to the task of creating a committee that is well organized, cohesive and knowledgeable.

Every member of the PR committee should have some specific responsibilities and at this point you would also do well to determine who will be the media contact throughout a PR campaign. Reporters and others need to have one person who has the facts that they can rely on. No media person trying to meet a deadline is willing to spend valuable time tracking down a spokesperson. In relegating duties, you have to get at least four of the following kinds of work done (none of which will divide up as neatly as in the list!):

- *Research*—finding the available media, the key media people, various audiences you want to reach, best ways to reach specific audiences, best PR opportunities and new PR techniques. Check out what other groups have done to get their PR message across.
- *Planning*—thinking about and deciding on the purpose of particular projects, brainstorming approaches and selecting media, budgeting PR efforts and assigning tasks.
- *Operations*—drafting releases, calling press, coordinating efforts, making arrangements, maintaining files with clips and other information.
- *Feedback*—finding out what you're doing both right and wrong, sending thank-you notes to those who made a special effort on your behalf.

If you are asking yourself whether one person should be in charge of operations and another in charge of research, the answer is: it depends. The size of your PR committee, your budget, special knowledge or experience of your committee members, and your committee's ability to work together will all enter into the decision. Try various forms of organization. Adjust membership and assignments on the committee as the short-term objectives and tasks shift.

Take the time not only to determine who your audiences will be, but to be sure you know who to contact with your material when you take on the PR campaign. The best PR material given to the wrong person will wind up in a wastepaper basket. That means know who to contact at your radio, TV stations and at your papers in order to get the best results. Put that information in a card file. It also means knowing the right contact person in each civic group, each neighborhood association, each business and labor organization. The accurate and up-to-date card file you've started for press contacts can also include other information on civic group contacts: names, emphases, agenda, biases, who influences who. This kind of card file is one important step in institutionalizing PR—making sure that the concepts, the contacts, the systematic pursuit of goals will survive a change of personnel. Drawing others into PR work, introducing them to news people and other contacts, sharing writing and other PR responsibilities are other forms of survival insurance.

Resources

As you proceed with your PR campaign, don't burn your bridges behind you. Hold onto that research you've done—not scraps on the back of envelopes, but the hard facts you dug up for this particular effort. It may come in handy next time around—or when a reporter decides to do a follow-up story at a later date.

You'll also want to hold onto those clips that you'll accumulate from a successful campaign. Other people in your organization may find them helpful to refer back to or to be used as evidence of a job well done.

Naturally, the more persons, dollars, time and talent your group can muster, the more your group can do. But whether you know it or not, you've got considerable assets at your command already since "one person can make the difference." So don't forget how each individual can help your effort. For example, in about an hour and for less than one dollar, it's possible for an individual to:

- call a congressman or state representative's nearby district office,
- call local papers and find out who's covering the issue you'll be working on,
- list contacts you and others already have that will come in handy,
- make a list for press releases, etc,
- research (from material in your daily newspaper) and write a letter to the editor or draft a possible press release,
- draft a public service message that your local radio station may run for free.

Your Members

Reaching the public and reaching your members go hand in hand. Your members are one of the best sources for getting your message to the community, so make sure they know what is going on and are aware of what points to emphasize when they come in contact with the public.

Good internal PR is part of any successful PR campaign. One way of assuring good internal PR is procedural fairness. That is, at least 95 percent of your members should feel that decision-making procedures are fair whether they agree on the outcome or not. Be sure that your organization's procedures assure every member a hearing and that they provide alternatives for those who are reluctant to speak up in groups.

If you really want to spread the word about something your organization is undertaking, the more help you have the better. But extra help is only a gain for your project if you've taken the time and effort to keep members up on what the project consists of and you've let them know how they can help. In other words, the art of communicating begins within your organization, not outside of it. Keep members apprised of developments in a PR effort. Remember that your members are likely to know a lot of the community, and they may be the way to help get to some community movers and shakers who are difficult to reach. Urge members to let you know who their contacts are and to *keep up their contacts* even after a PR campaign has ended.

Good internal communications require across-the-board sensitivity and problem-solving leaders. A good newsletter, sitter services, car pools for meetings—they're all ways of communicating that members matter.

Working with Your Community

One PR pro has defined public relations as giving credit where credit is due. So when your group learns of something worthwhile an individual or group is doing—sing out its praises. It's one thing to hear "our work is terrific," a self-serving statement even when true, and quite another to hear "*their* work is terrific" from somebody who isn't a member of the group. But be sure you give praise only when it's justified, or the value of it will go down.

And while we're on the subject of dealing with other groups, it's also wise to remember not to spread yourself too thin. Focus only on community projects within your group's expertise and program interest and learn to say "no" politely to community efforts that are extraneous to your purpose and programs. Remember, it's far better to do a few things well than a dozen things so-so.

Coalitions

Much work within the community will involve working in formal or informal coalitions. This type of work has its own special PR problems arising from individual egos, organizational pride, and a desire to get a fair—or perhaps more than fair—share of credit for the joint effort. So when you take on work in a coalition, guide your activities by the reputation your group wants six months after the coalition is gone and focus on the long-term interest of your group.

Before you begin work in a coalition, moreover, be sure to agree to a method by which you will be able to approve media material. If it is a small coalition, one spokesperson from each organization should be delegated to review the material that will be disseminated. If it is a host of organizations, you and other organizations may want to have a small group designated to review the material for the coalition. Regardless of the approach, material should not go out under coalition heading unless each group has been notified. This rule of thumb will save a lot of arguments and help you avoid misunderstanding. (For additional information on working with a coalition, see *Making An Issue of It: The Campaign Handbook,* Article #18 in this book.)

If you want to leave a lasting impression on the public, then your effort must be well timed, well planned, and well organized. While this may be a tall order to fill, particularly since you're bound to have other responsibilities and distractions during any PR campaign, careful planning often brings very satisfying results. If you undertake a well-planned media campaign to reach the public, you're likely to find that not only have you made an impact on the public but you've enlisted the support needed to solve the problem. Moreover, you've also gained more friends for your organization. And just as importantly, you've demonstrated that public relations can be a very positive tool for action!

22. SUCCESSFUL GRANT WRITING

Robert E. Geller

Do you have expectations for what you hope to get from this paper? If you don't, you should. My expectations for you are that when you finish reviewing it you will be able to: (1) write a clearer, more concise proposal, (2) implement a grant search, that is, look up in the source materials funding prospects, based on your subject, and (3) critique your own work, or someone's else.

BASICS

Grants are generally "seed" money. That is, no foundation, corporation, or federal agency is interested in "adopting" your agency. The most popular type of funding given is for new or innovative projects, and ones for which you have a plan for permanent funding once the grant has ended, generally one to three years.

Rumors to the contrary notwithstanding, money is still available, but the lines are longer and there are fewer lines. So you must be more selective and better informed in order to maximize results and minimize frustration.

Money is not given based on need! Sound strange? Do you know of anyone asking for money who will say that they don't need it? The key is what the grantor wants. It's the one giving the money away who decides what to spend it on.

The formula is simple. Us + them = $. To put it another way, be clear about what you want, find out what the grantor wants, and decide if you have a match worth pursuing. If you are after money for children's programs, and you haven't checked a foundation's priorities, what they give money for, and that foundation gives money only for senior citizens' programs, you blew it! Not only won't you get funded, but when foundation people get together, you may lose your credibility for future grant awards.

If you are selective, you enhance your chances for success by tailoring your proposal to meet the grantor's priorities. In other words, if the grantor wants to give money to projects serving children, and your proposal emphasizes such service, you are "in the ballpark." That will get you "up to bat." "Hitting a home run" will depend on how clear and well written your proposal is, establishing a personal relationship with the grantor, and timing. If you haven't missed the

Reproduced by permission of the author. This is revised from an unpublished article "Plain Talk About Grants: A Basic Handbook," 1982.

deadline, if there is currently money available, and if you can demonstrate your capability to follow through with what you are promising, you're on your way to home plate!

There are three ways to approach the grants business. You can be "reactive," wait for announcements to come across your desk, and decide which you want to pursue; you can be "proactive," develop an idea and go searching for potential funding sources; or you can do both. To be effective reactively, you have to subscribe to newsletters and get on mailing lists that fit your kind of program. To be effective proactively, you have to find out what granting agencies want to spend their money on, be clear about what you want to do and how much it will cost you to do it.

The "Idea Statement"

The first step is to have an "idea statement" in hand, a two-to five-page description of what it is you want to do and for how much.

I called on a federal agency in response to a request from someone in my agency to explore potential resources for a concept they had. When the contact person asked me questions like "How much?" "What's the staff composition?" "Is this a research or a demonstration project?" the best response I could muster was "I don't know." I was not ready to ask for anything because I couldn't articulate what it was I wanted.

Whether you are responding to an announcement or exploring a potential resource for your idea, you will need a clear, concise description of it. Then you can answer questions and determine if the resource is real. If not, you can save time by not applying to an agency that

would not have funding for you anyway. If it is a real prospect, you have begun to establish a relationship and can follow up with a visit by sending your idea statement, a fuller draft, or a formal application.

A word of advice: Take notes on any questions or suggestions by the grantor's representative and put the answers in your proposal. You will have the best consultation you can get, and it is free! If the funding agency will allow you to submit a draft for comments, you can get help from the funding source. You can use your modified idea statement as a draft. It is hard for a grantor's representative to critize your proposal in the review process if you've taken the advice given to you. If the grantor won't comment on a draft, submit your application early to allow the funding agency time to negotiate, ask for clarification, or explain what is missing or ask for a rewrite.

Whether or not a grantor will review and comment on a draft or your idea, you can ask for written guidance, forms, instructions, and other help. Be sure to get the review criteria, the scoring system that reviewers will use to rank your proposal. If you have a grant announcement from a federal agency, the review criteria are usually included with the instructions.

Nongrant Funding Sources

As I am sure you are aware, grants are only one source of funding. If your organization is a community nonprofit agency, then you may want to consider a variety of funding activities.

First, let's look at some statistics to illustrate a key point. In round numbers, statistics for 1981, 45 or 50 billion dollars were given in contributions. Of this total 84 percent came from individuals; 6

percent from trusts, bequests, and wills; 5 percent from foundations; and 5 percent from corporations. While our focus is on grants, there is a need for the perspective provided by these figures.

Tapping individuals requires a very well-organized plan, complete with giver-solicitors who will tap their peers. This requires knowing whom to tap, how much to request, and how many people and how much time to allow for the campaign. One source book you may find useful is *Successful Fund Raising Techniques* by David Lynn Conrad and the research and development staff of the Public Management Institute, 333 Hayes Street, San Francisco, California 94102. Of particular interest is the section on major gifts and the sample schedule from the section on capital campaigns which you may wish to adapt to your major gifts campaign.

Since more money was available from trusts, bequests, and wills than from either corporations or foundations, you may be missing a bet if you are not actively involved with trust officers at banks, attorneys, and accountants who do estate planning.

If you are not familiar with "testimonials," "parlor meetings," "opening nights," "card calling/open pledges," "memorial honor gifts," and "gifts in kind," you may be missing some fundraising options open to you. For a beginning orientation to fund-raising, you will want to read *The Art of Fundraising* by Irving R. Warner (Harper and Row, 1975).

Other Tips

Most granting agencies want some demonstration of local support, that is, evidence that the community is aware and supportive of your project. Such demonstrations may take many forms: Letters of support, matching funds, cooperation in referrals, volunteers and paid staff services, and board approval. Enclosing resumes of competent staff from other organizations who will work on the project is a good way to demonstrate support.

Try to persuade the prospective funding agency to visit your facility to build relationships and demonstrate your credibility. But make sure there are activities in progress. Have a knowledgeable and committed board member present. This demonstrates that you attach special importance to the grantor's visit.

Be aware of hidden costs in preparing grants. A major cost is staff time in gathering information and writing. Others may include the cost of long-distance telephone calls, duplication, and data gathering. With rare exceptions, you may not charge any of the preparatory costs to the grant.

When you are submitting a proposal, make certain what the deadline date means. If the deadline says May 15, it may mean postmarked May 15 or received by that day. If you aren't sure, ask.

FOUNDATIONS AND CORPORATIONS

The average grant is $5,000. Big grants are rare, usually given by large foundations which look for projects with national significance. Averages are deceptive, because that means many are larger and many smaller. The most meaningful numbers are the "average range." For example, the full range of grants given may be $200 to $100,000, which would not be helpful. But if the average range was $5,000 to $15,000, your grant application should fit within those numbers. If it does, you increase your chances of success.

Next, let's look at the different types of foundations:

Operating Foundation. As a general rule, an operating foundation solicits funds, but only gives them to a pet project, organization or to a program it sponsors. Don't apply to an organization that is exclusively focused on a single program or activity.

Community Foundation. A community foundation serves a specific geographic area, usually a city or one or more adjacent counties. The name usually indicates this. In some instances, an individual or family may not wish to set up a foundation so the will or gift may stipulate special restrictions on the use of funds received by a community foundation. One question you will want to ask is whether there are any restrictions or conditions you should be aware of.

General Purpose Foundation. These foundations tend to be large, they usually have staff, and generally carry the name of the original founders. As a rule, the board establishes the policy, and the staff make grant decisions. There is usually heavy competition, nationwide, and generally grants must have national significance.

Family Foundations. These vary greatly in size and areas of interest. Some have staff. The preferences and decisions of family members usually prevail, so it is essential that you know or have a contact who knows a family member.

Corporate Foundations. As a rule, corporations give where they have plants or where their employees live. Generally corporations prefer noncontroversial programs. It is advantageous if you offer services their employees can use, for example, day-care centers or alcoholic treatment programs. One resource you may wish to use as a means of identifying a corporate contact person is the *Taft Corporate Foundation Directory.*

Corporate giving differs from giving by a corporate foundation. Foundations are required to complete tax forms (990-A) that are open and available to the public. Corporate giving requires no such forms. If you are seeking corporate funds, it is best to know or have contacts who know upper management or corporate officers.

Although corporations may give up to 10 percent of their pretax income, overall they have given less than 1 percent. Some are making an effort to invest in their communities and to plan for increasing the size of their gifts. In some cities there are "Two Per Cent Clubs."

As a general rule, foundations will not have application forms, but ask when you make contact. Generally, you will submit a two-to five page proposal, and the foundation will write to you for any additional information or questions regarding what you have submitted.

The contact may be by phone, letter, or visit. A phone contact plus visit is recommended. The key in either case is to be prepared. Be brief. Take notes on questions and comments. Use your contacts to build confidence in your ability to carry out what you propose.

Who should go if there is an interview at the foundation office? The executive director or person who has written the proposal, if that person is substantially more knowledgeable about the project, a fiscal person such as the agency accountant, and a knowledgeable board member.

A mock interview or two before actually facing the foundation is part of solid preparation. The Foundation Center has identified a list of matters that are significant for foundations: (1) What is it that you wish to accomplish? (2) Why is the project needed and why are you not funding it yourself? (3) What are the qualifications of the staff involved? (4) Is the budget realistic? (5) Is your organization fiscally capable of handling the project? (6) Is the proposal realistic? (7) What is its importance to the community or society? (8) Is the project original and creative? (9) Is the project tied to the foundation's priorities? (10) Will the project be sustained when the grant ends? (11) What will the applicant contribute? (12) How do you plan to evaluate it?

You will want to know when the funding cycle begins and ends; to whom you address the application; if there are any instructions, forms, or restrictions; and when a final decision is likely.

Always write a thank you letter following such a visit. If you don't know the answer to a question, say so. And follow up with an answer in writing.

When you submit your application, prepare a one-to two-page cover letter to establish your credibility. It should include a reference to the phone contact, interview, or visit. What is the name of the agency making the application? How long has it been in operation? What are its basic purposes? What does it do? What has it accomplished? (Be selective, for example, naming some grants the agency has successfully managed.) In brief, what is the project you propose? What precipitated the project? How much money is needed? Tell the foundation you will call in seven to ten days to make sure they got the materials and to answer any questions.

It is harder to condense and be brief and clear than to write volumes. It can be done, however, and this exercise will help you in the future.

If you are turned down, write a letter thanking the foundation for considering your project. Ask for the reasons for not approving it, so that you may learn from the experience. Say you want to improve your application skills. Ask if you may apply again in the future, and if they can refer you to others who might be interested in this type of project. You may have just missed their grant cycle, or they may have liked your proposal but have limited funds.

Resources

The Foundation Center is a national organization located at 888 Seventh Avenue, New York, New York 10019, that is devoted to collecting and distributing information about foundations. It maintains two national libraries, one in New York and another in Washington, D. C. A cooperating collection is maintained by the Donors Forum of Chicago. There are regional collections in nearly every state. Your local public library should be able to direct you to the nearest regional collection, or call the Foundation Center's toll-free number: (800) 424-9836.

In most states, the attorney general's office will make available copies of the annual reports of foundations required by the U. S. Internal Revenue Service. The so-called 990 AR's contain the names of trustees, a list of grant recipients, amounts of assets, and grants. In some states, state-mandated annual reports augment this information. These reports are also to be found in the national and regional libraries of the Foundation Center.

In about two-thirds of the states, someone—often a nonprofit organization, a commercial enterprise, or the state's attorney general—publishes a directory of foundations located in that state. The regional libraries of the Foundation Center should prove helpful in locating these directories.

The *Foundation Directory*, published by the Foundation Center and distributed by Columbia University Press, contains information about roughly 3,000 of the largest foundations. It is revised every odd-numbered year.

The *Foundation Grants Index*, published yearly by the Foundation Center, indexes the grants of about 350 of the largest foundations. Published every two months in the *Foundation News*, it is compiled yearly. The index enables the user to identify foundations serving a particular state or region, giving grants to particular types of organizations, for particular purposes, or for particular segments of the population, and can be very useful in narrowing your choice of foundations to which you should direct inquiries.

Judith B. Margolin's *About Foundations: How to Find the Facts You Need To Get a Grant*, published by the Foundation Center, is a guide to using Foundation Center materials, state foundation directories, and 990 Annual Reports.

The Grantsmanship Center, a nonprofit tax-exempt educational organization at 1031 South Grant Avenue, Los Angeles, California 90015, publishes many useful reprints from its *Grantsmanship Center News*, which it publishes six times each year. It also runs workshops in various parts of the country for those interested in raising funds from a variety of public and private sources. For further information, its toll-free number is (800) 421-9512.

Finally, you may find a book by Craig W. Smith and Eric W. Skjei entitled *Getting Grants*, published in New York by Harper and Row in 1980, of some use in obtaining grants from both private and public sources.

FEDERAL FUNDING

There are literally hundreds of federal agencies, subagencies, or units within the federal government, any one of which might be a potential grant source. As is true for other types of grants, you can get newsletters or other types of announcements and see what might fit your organization's needs, or you can do a search.

Either way, develop an idea statement so you are clear on what you want to do and for how much. Whether you are responding to an announcement or searching for a grant source, you need to be able to answer questions and discuss your project, and verify that you have located a realistic prospect. You can't do that unless you have a very well-articulated idea.

There are several printed sources of information that you may wish to use in your search for federal funds. The *Catalog of Federal Domestic Assistance*, published by the federal government, sells for $20 but can be found in many libraries. It provides basic information on federal resources, including a profile of each program, eligibility, deadlines, funding levels, and places to contact with telephone numbers. It is updated annually. "How to Use the Revised Catalog of Federal Domestic Assistance" is a reprint made available by the Grantsmanship Center for $1.35 (Order No. 506). The *Federal Register* is a daily announcement, published by the federal government, which includes pending regulations and guidelines for new and revised grant programs established through federal legislation. It may be subscribed to for $300 per year, but it is available in many libraries. The *Commerce Business Daily* is also a federal publication, a daily announcement of government contracts awarded and available for bid. Its subscription price is $100 per year, but it is also available in many libraries.

Generally, the minimum processing time for federal grants is nine months. Deadlines for submitting proposals vary. Some of the things you'll want to check include: Is your idea among the priorities of a particular agency? Is your anticipated budget within the "average range" of grants to be awarded? Are there uncommitted funds? That is, is there money for new projects or just enough for continuations of previously approved projects? When will the next funding cycle begin? When is the final application due? May you submit a draft for review and comment? How can you get an application, guidelines, and review criteria? Will the agency make a site visit? A request for proposal (RFP), an announcement inviting applications, will often contain due dates, amount of funding available, and review criteria.

If you have obtained consultation through a telephone call, visit, or review of a draft, use whatever information you have received. If additional information is requested, make certain it has been included. Have a third party read the proposal for clarity and readability. Write in short sentences, break up the text with paragraphs, use italics, underline, check for typographical errors, use good English, and leave out or explain jargon. For reviewers, prepare the text with wide margins to allow space for comments.

If you are offered less money than you requested, hesitate before you accept it. Take less, but cut back your proposal proportionately. You can't promise to do $100,000 worth of services for $80,000.

It will look as though you padded your proposal. Consider what could be cut totaling $20,000 without destroying the major elements of the proposal.

If you are not funded, write a thank you letter expressing your appreciation for consideration of your application, and requesting politely the reasons for the rejections so that you may learn and improve your future applications.

COMPONENTS OF A PROPOSAL

The goals of this section are that after you have thoroughly reviewed it and have practiced writing a proposal, you will be (a) better organized, (b) a clearer writer, and (c) able to critize your own work or the work of others.

Length and approach depend on who the audience is. Your primary audience is the granting agency. As a general rule, foundations expect application narratives to be two to five pages. State agencies expect application narratives to be five to twenty-five pages, and federal agencies expect them to be twenty-five to seventy-five pages. If you have instructions, follow them!

Whether you have instructions or not, you should be able to use most of these ideas. The heading titles may be slightly different in the instructions, but you can use the approach to maximize clarity and ensure that you cover the kind of information a reviewer will be looking for. Experience has shown that these ideas work. Agencies receive grants when they use them.

An idea statement is essential whether you are searching for a grant, answering basic questions from a funding agency, tailoring a project to a funding source, or submitting a draft to the funding source for input before preparing the final application.

The components of a complete idea statement or narrative are: (1) Summary, (2) Introduction, (3) Need or Problem Statement, (4) Goals, (5) Objectives, (6) Method, (7) Evaluation, and (8) Cost.

Summary

Whether or not it is required, it is advisable to have a summary. In a federal application you will be required to squeeze a summary into a tight box on the face sheet of the application. It is very easy to underestimate the importance of the summary. Agencies receive dozens, sometimes hundreds of applications for a single grant program. A good summary will help a reviewer know whether your application should be given a careful reading. The first stage of a review is to read the summary to see if it matches the funding agency's priorities. The match should be clear from your summary or your application will be rejected without further review.

Write the summary last. In order to include key elements, words, and phrases that are in the narrative, you need to write it last. Take the time and do it well. Otherwise, it may be all the reviewer sees.

Introduction

The introduction tells who you are, any related experience you have that makes you qualified to conduct this project, and why your organization is better than another agency offering to do a similar project. This is your first shot at demonstrating your credibility as an organization the funding agency can feel comfortable entrusting with their money. You must convince them that you are capable and qualified and can be trusted to deliver what you are proposing. If there is a place for an introduction in the instructions, great! If not, find a place, even if you have to add a cover letter to the application.

Even if you know the funding agency liaison or contact person, and even if you have had phone conversations and visits, assume the review committee knows absolutely nothing about your organization.

Need or Problem Statement

The Need or Problem Statement consists of information that substantiates a need for this particular project. It is essentially the reason you should get the money. As noted earlier, grants are not given on the basis of your need, but on the basis of needs perceived by the funding source, usually identifiable in the form of priorities. The statement justifies the basis on which the project request is made. It must match the funding agency's priorities.

There are a number of approaches you can use in developing a need or problem statement. The following are separated for clarity, but can be used in a number of combinations:

A *key informant* is an expert or knowledgeable person who substantiates the need for the project. An example would be to quote someone expressing the need for the type of project you are proposing. This might be the executive director of the local United Way agency, the governor, a prominent person in your field, or an agency executive.

For each of these approaches there are good reasons why the technique may be useful, and also certain drawbacks. A key informant is generally easy to find, available at little or no cost. The only drawback which might diminish its impact is that the funding agency knows you would only quote someone in complete agreement with you.

A *community forum* consists of a meeting of community people. If you want to know what people need, you may call them together and ask them. The major benefits of a community forum are that (1) it is generally not expensive to arrange, (2) it can be set up in a reasonably short time, and (3) generally people welcome the opportunity to express their views.

There are some problems with this approach that you need to be aware of. Some people may say they represent a constituency when, in fact, they are only expressing a personal opinion and have not been authorized to represent any group. Several hundred people are in one room and may be hard to control. A few may use this opportunity to discuss their pet peeve which may, or may not, be relevant to your project. Finally, it is often difficult to bring people with varied backgrounds and experience to a consensus.

To avoid these pitfalls, have a moderator who sets out the ground rules at the start of the meeting. For example, if each person is given two minutes to make a statement and the moderator sticks to the rules, no one will be able to monopolize the time available. If it is agreed that the majority rules and straw votes are taken, then the problem of reaching a consensus is avoided.

Rates under treatment is projecting need based on others' utilization of services. You look at the rate of service utilization experienced by other organizations and project the level of need based on your findings. For example, if there are several programs that serve families, and there have been a number of requests for day-care services by their clients, then it is possible to verify the need for day care and to project the extent of need. Or if a city is attempting to determine the number of police officers it may need to maintain an acceptable arrest rate, it may study cities of similar characteristics and arrest rates to determine the number of officers it needs.

Such information may be readily obtainable at little or no cost. However, if the need you are trying to establish cannot be linked to utilization of programs or resources, then this technique may not be appropriate. Also, there is a logical fallacy in equating provision or utilization of services with needs. Severe needs may be present where no services are available, and people may demand help they do not need. However, if you are clear that need means demand for specific services, you may be able to estimate such need by examining rates of utilization found elsewhere under conditions similar to your own.

Social indicators are those figures available from reports done by others such as the census. These are community descriptors which may be of help to you in reinforcing your needs statement. The census is done once every ten years, and the information, while specific, may not directly relate to your project. However, other sources, such as public health statistics, may be quite useful.

The *survey method* is the most sophisticated tool available. Sampling the community through mailed questionnaires, telephone surveys, or in-person interviews is the most direct way to measure need. However, if you are doing a formal survey, be certain you have someone who is thoroughly familiar with methods of sampling and data analysis. Also, make sure you have a design that can give you the information you want. The survey method is the most costly and time-consuming of the approaches.

Third party referrals are clients sent to you for services. The third party that sends them, usually a state agency, pays a fee for the services, or has a contract with you to provide the service. Let's say the Department of Rehabilitation proposes to refer ten clients per month, if the service you are planning were to be developed. If you can get a third party to say it has clients waiting for service whom they will refer to you, you have established a need and you are assured of payment for services. The contract is a form of permanent funding you may use to assure the granting agency you can stand on your own when the grant ends.

Cost comparisons demonstrate that your project is a more cost-effective method of delivering services than one or more others currently used. If it costs $2,000 to care for an individual in a psychiatric hospital for a month, and $500 to provide a residential treatment program through your project, there is a strong fiscal incentive to test out your project.

Goals and Objectives

A goal is a broad statement of overall purpose. It identifies the general direction you are heading. Objectives have three characteristics. They are specific, time-oriented, and measurable. There are three types of objectives: (1) *Process objectives* indicate the process or method to be used rather than the end result. An example is counseling sessions. As it might appear in a proposal, "We will provide counseling sessions, twenty per month, during the project year." There is no reference to what the outcome of the sessions will be. (2) *Product objectives* are the development of something tangible,

a product. For example, "We will develop an independent living skills curriculum by the end of the project year." (3) *Outcome objectives* reflect the results, impact, or change arising from the service you plan to provide. For example, "We will reduce the rate of reported alcoholism by 25 percent in our clientele in the first year." You must have the baseline information from which to calculate the percentage of change. That is, you must know that there were some number, say one hundred, cases of reported alcoholism in your case load. To meet your objective, the next year your target is seventy-five or fewer cases of reported alcoholism. The base is one hundred, from which you make your comparison in the stated time.

Method

The method is the blueprint for how and when things are to be accomplished, the action plan for the objectives you have chosen. In a project intended to deliver services, you describe the services and identify the time table indicating each service or activity to be implemented. You include the data you will collect to report your results. If you say you will serve twenty clients per quarter, you describe how you will keep track of new clients entering the program under the project.

You must show how the project fits, administratively. Often, you must submit an organizational chart with existing positions identified by title and surrounded by solid lines and project positions identified by title and surrounded by dotted lines. This gives a picture of what you have and what you want in staffing. When reviewers look at the organizational chart, they are interested in seeing whether the positions and structure outlined are likely to be effective in achieving project objectives. For example, how many layers are there between the proposed positions and the executive? If there are more than one or two, it suggests that decisions related to the project must go through many levels and that the sponsor may not place a high priority on the grant-supported project. Or if the number of positions is inadequate to the quantitative objectives (the number to be served) or if the grant-supported project is not appropriately related to other programs of the sponsoring agency, questions will be raised about the wisdom of supporting the project.

Other information you will want to include in your methods section are (1) advisory groups, including their composition, the groups represented, how members are to be recruited and used; (2) matching funds or in-kind contributions, how they will be obtained and their sources, and particularly what your agency will contribute, and your permanent funding plan.

One other important factor: If the grant pays you after you have incurred expenses, that is, is in the form of a reimbursement, be aware! Reimbursement means you pay the bills, submit a bill with receipts, and wait for your money. It is not unusual for ninety days to go by from the time you make your payments for salaries and supplies until you get your money. You may have to work out a line of credit from a bank and raise the money to pay the interest on the loan.

It is not unusual to want the money now—whatever you can get—and put off thinking about what you'll do when the grant runs out. And it may even be necessary to do some "creative writing"

in order to sell the grantor on your permanent funding plan, even if it is more fiction than fact. Most granting organizations rate your permanent funding plan. To rank high enough to get a grant, you must convince the grantor that you will not be dependent upon them forever.

You'll want to change the fiction to fact as soon as possible if you get the grant. Nothing is worse than being funded for one year, hiring staff, demonstrating the value of a given program or service, and then having to fire everyone at the end of the year because you had no workable plan for permanent funding.

A grantor may insist that you contribute some of your own resources, called matching funds, to the grant project. A match is not required in some cases, but even so you must demonstrate that your agency is committed to this project. One of the best ways to do so is to point out what you are contributing. Be sure to include office space, clerical help, supplies, phone, and staff time. These are things which have value and will support the project, but will not be charged to it. In your budget section you should have two columns: requested and donated.

Evaluation

Evaluation should flow from the previous sections. If your objectives are clear and measurable, and you have said how you will carry out your objectives, then developing a plan for evaluation should not be difficult.

The plan for evaluation addresses two questions: How will you assess your progress? and Who will analyze the information? With clear objectives, you merely need to monitor your objectives and indicate how often you will prepare reports, what their content will be, and who will prepare them. For example, you said you would serve twenty clients per quarter, and you are the coordinator of the project and have agreed to do a quarterly report based on those figures. If you have an intake worker keeping track of the number served each month, you have your evaluation system and report format. Just follow that same reasoning with each objective.

If you are given instructions on the frequency and format for reporting, you must follow them. There is no prohibition against exceeding the minimum requirements. I recommend you do a quarterly report, if not for the funding agency, then as a management tool for your own program. If you said you would serve twenty clients per quarter, and you come to the end of the first quarter, and have only served five clients, you want to know that so you may take measures to solve the problem. If you determine your project numbers were too high, you can make a request to the granting agency to reduce the target number. Or you can develop a plan to increase referrals.

If you offer a service project and have clear objectives, you should not need a paid evaluator. You should be able to use existing clerical and service staff to keep track of referrals and client progress. If your project has a complex research design, you may need to hire an evaluator to plan the evaluation, collect data, and report findings.

Dissemination

Dissemination of information obtained through the project will depend on your audience. If you have a federal grant, and the only requirement is an annual report, then you must decide if that is as far as you want the information

to go, or if you would like to take the initiative in sharing your findings with others.

Usually federal agencies are looking for projects that can be replicated in other parts of the country and want information that can be used by others to get similar results. If so, you may be required to develop plans for disseminating information as a condition for receiving the grant.

There are many ways to share information, any or all of which could be in your plan. Some examples are: Regular reporting to the granting agency; reporting through your newsletter; presenting a paper at a conference; and setting up training seminars in various locations. If you were to do the latter, you would need funds, and those funds should be requested as a part of your grant.

Costs and Budget

Proposals are usually written by program people, people with primary experience in direct service who have limited knowledge of fiscal matters. There is nothing wrong with that, and it is nothing to be ashamed of. What is essential is that you recognize your limitations and get appropriate consultation on costs and budget preparation which may be available from another member of the agency's staff or a board member. No one person is an expert in everything.

It is easy to overlook expenses that should be charged to the grant. You may have checked on the monthly charge for a phone, but you may have not thought about the costs for installation. Or you may overlook fringe benefits, not know how to calculate indirect cost (overhead), forget to include cost-of-living and merit increases in multiyear proposals, forget about supplies, maintenance, or insurance.

Keep your worksheets, that is, details of your thinking and calculations in preparing the budget. Your worksheets may help you avoid paying back all or part of a grant if there is an unfavorable audit!

Two key ingredients in a sound budget are consistency and realistic figures. A grant reviewer often takes a brief look at the concept in the proposal, and then examines the budget to see if the concept is consistent with the budget, and the budget is realistic. A few quick examples of inconsistencies: An organization asks for a typewriter and has no clerical positions on the grant; or says it will serve 1,000 people but plans for one half-time counselor. The budget is the barometer for determining if an agency knows what it is talking about.

Some Final Thoughts

Write clearly and forcefully. Avoid such terms as, "We *feel* that. . . ." Say, instead, "We know that . . ." or "Our experience has shown that. . . ." Avoid jargon. Even if the funding agency uses jargon words in the grant announcement, either leave them out or explain what you mean by them. You may want to have someone who is not in your field

read your proposal to ensure that it is easily understood and clear to any reader.

In reading your proposal, do not force the reviewer to look for essential content. Sometimes in federal reviews each reviewer takes a different section of the application. If you have something in the appendix, explain in one or two sentences what point you are making, and add: "For additional information, see Appendix D." That way the reviewer knows the point and has the option of looking for more or taking your word for it.

A common mistake that applicants make is to build themselves up by knocking others, feeling it will enhance their position. Nine times out of ten, you look bad. Don't knock others! Just point to gaps that your project proposes to fill.

If you are dealing with a federal agency and your project is unique, stress that others around the country may also be able to use your approach.

Some common reasons for turning down projects include: (1) the identified problem or need is not met by the method, (2) the problem is not addressed by the project objectives, (3) the objectives are not measurable, and (4) the budget is too big or too small to accomplish the stated objectives.

23. HOW TO ASK FOR MONEY

Joan Flanagan

GRASS ROOTS FUND RAISING

I learned to do fund raising—as everybody learns—by doing it. You can't go to Harvard and get a Ph.D. in benefits, but you can learn how to raise money by doing it.

The good news is that you can learn to do it and you can become very successful at it. The bad news is that it is never easy. Fund raising is really hard work but also worthwhile because you are doing work for a cause you believe in.

When I compiled *The Grass Roots Fundraising Book,* I traveled around the country and interviewed about 650 people, asking what advice they would give people who wanted to raise money. "What do you wish you had known then that you know now?" "How did you get to be successful?" "What mistakes did you make?" The book incorporated their answers.

Then I did a series of workshops in 59 cities and talked to another 1,500 people. Again, I learned that people can learn to raise money by doing it; they don't need any particular educational background, economic status, or writing skills. The only thing necessary to be a good fund raiser is the desire or will to raise money.

Reproduced by permission of the publisher and the author. From *How to Sell and How to Ask for Money,* Joan Flanagan, copyright 1980, National Committee for the Prevention of Child Abuse, Chicago, Illinois.

If you believe in the organization and in the goals of the group, if you believe in what you are doing and have the courage of your convictions, you can raise money. The methods you use are actually relatively inconsequential; all you do is go out and ask for money.

Obviously there are a great many ways you can ask. Most people don't like to do this or don't begin by liking it, and if they end up on a fund-raising committee, they will probably have cold feet when they start. Your job is to make them do it and motivate them to like it; then they will want to come back for the next meeting and bring a friend. The committee will grow and grow, and you will get more and more askers.

The sources of funds include wealthy individuals, corporations, foundations, dues, and benefits. There are advantages and disadvantages of each.

Individuals

What is the advantage of going to individuals? The answer is simple: it's quick. If they like your program and you sell them on it, you have their check when you walk out the door. This immediate giving contrasts with foundation and government grants, which are often delayed while officials make up their minds.

Another advantage is contacts. This is a fraternity in which they all know each other; and there are more individuals than there are corporations. In addition to money, individuals can also give you services and advice.

Another advantage is personal involvement, but remember, you are never the only one asking; you are always in competition with everybody else. Wealthy individuals are not going to come to you and say, "Please take my money." You have to go to them and convince them that your cause is worthy.

As you establish a personal relationship with these people, you hope they get involved, even if they do nothing more than read your newsletter. Then you will have added one more important person in the community with affluence and influence who understands what you are doing and why you are doing it. The advantage of educating others is that they, in turn, will educate people they know. One of the biggest hurdles at the beginning is convincing people that the problem exists.

Are there any negative factors in taking money or going to somebody for money? We have all been in organizations in which some people give disproportionate amounts of money. They may have a lot of influence on the policy of the group or may be perceived as having more influence. This can make others think their vote doesn't matter, and you have to be very careful about this attitude. If it exists, do you want that cost of taking money? Some people will say, "I'll give you $100,000 if you put my name on the building." That might be fine; but if someone says, "I'll give you $100,000 if I can dictate the policies," that is not fine. Policy decisions have to be made democratically, and you have to

be sure that by taking one person's money, you are not in any way dampening the enthusiasm of everyone else.

Corporations

What is the advantage of asking a corporation for money? First of all, the contributions are usually ongoing. Secondly, it's in their self-interest to give to your organization. Corporations have a stake in the community. Their employees work in this community; the better the quality of life is in the community, the better it will be both for employees and for corporate customers. Giving is clearly a good investment that will pay off for corporations.

In addition to money, corporations can also give services and advice, as well as in-kind contributions—anything from buses and trucks to paper, envelopes, and desks. Corporations also have national networks.

What are the negatives in seeking corporate money? Almost invariably, the request has to go through a committee. Also, if you are seeking support for a national organization, corporations usually give only in their own communities. Every community has corporations, however, and they don't have to be big to support you.

Raising funds is frightening and can be difficult, especially if you are working with volunteers unfamiliar with corporate rules. In my experience in community organizing, you never ask your volunteers to go somewhere outside of their experience. If you are dealing with housewives, educators, and social service workers, they find it intimidating to walk into a bank, office, penthouse, or big boardroom. One solution is to have a housewife and an educator, for example, team up and make calls together. They will provide each other with moral support and will quickly build on each other's strengths. When you receive a contribution from a corporation, it's a real victory because you feel as if you've received some income that represents new money for your cause. Once you do it a couple of times, it gets easier.

Foundations

What is the advantage of going to foundations? The best foundations have good staffs. If you get to know them, they can give you much advice and service. More and more foundations are giving money along with what they call "technical assistance," which is simply advice. All of this is very helpful.

You can also get matching money from foundations—the best kind of money to get because it is a shot in the arm to fund raising. A foundation may say, "We will give you a dollar for every dollar you get." To encourage initial efforts, they might give you four dollars for every one dollar you raise. Knowing contributions will be matched is an incentive to your own members in their funding requests.

What else can foundations give you? They appreciate new ideas. Foundations can also introduce you to other foundations. If you get to know a few people in one foundation and they learn that you are a serious group whose members get results, they can introduce you to others.

The problem with foundations is that they are usually one-time or short-term sources. Foundations tell you this; it has absolutely nothing to do with the merit of your group. They fund new projects. You may think you are going to be bigger and better in two or three years, with more skilled leaders, a larger membership, and a list of accomplishments; thus, you will be so irresistible to the foundation that it will want to fund you again. But the foundation won't fund you again, although you may be referred to another agency that gives grants.

Since foundation support is short-term and will not be renewed, you have to plan how to replace that money. Otherwise your leaders may perceive the loss of funding as a reflection on the work they are doing, which it is not.

Obtaining a foundation grant can take a long time and demand much staff time. Fortunately, in the process, you learn how foundations work.

Foundations are very trendy and very clubby. For example, they tend to support civil rights programs, then mental health projects, followed by programs for the handicapped. If you happen to be doing something before or after the fad, you won't get the money. Even worse is requesting funds at the same time as the fad occurs and then receiving too much money, only to have it run out two or three years later.

Membership Dues

What is the advantage of dues? They alone build your organization. Dues are a built-in incentive for growth and the only method with any incentive for you to get more people to join. They also require a commitment. Dues work; they absolutely work. Members literally own a piece of the organization.

Dues also give you some solid money. You can do absolutely anything you want to with dues because they have no strings attached; it is your money.

Dues allow you to count your own membership and measure where you are being successful. You know if senior citizens are becoming members and teen-agers are not; if blacks are and whites are not; if suburban people are and city people are not; and if women are and men are not. You can measure exactly where you are succeeding in your outreach, and you can also measure exactly where you need to employ more effort. You can count where your supporters are and go to foundations, corporations, individuals, or the government and say, "We have recruited 500 members and are growing all the time." If you are growing and getting more members, you know you will succeed and have an impact. Knowing this can be heartening.

What is the problem with soliciting membership dues? Some people fear that dues exclude some people. I disagree. I think dues only exclude the people who do not want to belong to your group. The people who want your group will pay for it. Large community organizations have shown that people will pay for membership in a group because they feel it's important.

The biggest problem with dues is that most people don't want to go get them because that demands much time and hard work. You can go to a wealthy donor, get $10,000, and you are done. If you need $15,000 from dues, you have to do a thousand transactions.

The payoff comes in the long run. Even though recruiting members is hard work in the beginning, it will pay off in 5, 10, 20, or 30 years. Dues are the most dependable and most democratic way to make money and will continue to be year after year.

The best example of this is churches. As a general rule, churches raise all of their money from their own membership. They receive no government money other than a break on their taxes and seldom get any foundation money; yet they do not go out of business in a depression.

You can sell your organization as one that is as vital to people's lives as their churches. If you can make that sale, people will give to you year after year. Memberships are recession-proof and the best way to raise money.

Benefits

Many types of benefits are possible. You can provide entertainment by having a popular performer, sports figure, fashion show, or theater group. Many families will want to bring their children to make the occasion a family affair. Then there are bake sales, garage sales, walkathons. What are the advantages of benefits? Profits are high, and through repetition they can go higher. If you do a benefit every year, each time you will make more money by expending less time. A benefit is also great for public relations and for getting people involved. Planning a benefit offers a good opportunity to use the talents of everybody in your group, and people always excel at something they like doing. Best of all, a benefit is fun. Talking to patrons isn't, but people have a good time at a benefit. They know they are working hard, but the advantages of doing benefits are that the same people who work hard together and suffer and fight together in meetings can go to the benefit, enjoy themselves, and meet families, boyfriends, girlfriends, parents, and children. This is the glue that holds an organization together—people really get to know one another. The next time they go to a meeting, things will go more smoothly, and everyone will have a better time.

There are other advantages to doing

benefits. You can get corporate support and involve a whole range of new people who would not otherwise be involved. People are extremely busy with many demands on their time, but because a benefit is a short-term project, people can work on it and succeed easily. They love it.

People who hate meetings and will never come to one, although they might be perfectly sympathetic with the goals of the organization, will come to a benefit. Through the benefit they will get to know you, who you are, what you do, and how you do it. In the future, they may support the organization by coming to a meeting or to a hearing and giving testimony to the cause.

What are the problems with benefits? They are a lot of work, and you need the right organizational talent for them. Any group can do some things like a dance or dinner. Planning other types of benefits demands special talent in the organization. If you don't have it, you can't do that type of benefit. Benefits are also a costly way to raise money compared to getting funds from individuals or depending on dues, which net almost 100 per cent profit. Benefits do have advantages other than raising funds, however, as I've pointed out.

HOW TO ASK FOR MONEY

All you do when you raise money is want it and ask for it. The difference between the winners and the losers is that the winners want it and will work until they get it. The more you do fund raising, the easier it gets and the more successes you experience.

People have two reasons why they prefer not asking the public for money. The first is fear. This is a normal reaction. With the exception of a few very rare people, everybody is afraid to ask for money. Second, people have been taught not to talk about money, and you have to unteach them.

You can ask for money in two ways. The most common and one of the easiest ways is to begin by selling a product. Instead of saying, "Give us money because we think this is the most critical problem in society," you say, "Buy our tee shirts, bumper stickers, balloons, cookies, candy, fruitcakes, or cookbooks."

Remember, you are dealing with people who already are experienced consumers. Everybody buys things. People understand how this works. When you get more sophisticated, you can sell your program; your program itself—all of the things you are going to do for society—becomes your product. What you have to do first is educate your members on why your cause is worthy, why it is the best investment other people can make, why you get results, how you get results, and why people ought to pay for it. This is competitive. You need to persuade others that it is better to give you money than to buy some thing.

You make more money more quickly by selling your program through memberships than through products. Suppose an organization sells tee shirts for $5. Each shirt may cost the organization $4; so the net profit is only $1. If the goal is $100, the organization has to sell 100 tee shirts in about 100 transactions. In the process, probably no new members are signed up. On the other hand, if dues are $5, their costs to the organization may be minimal because membership paraphernalia is often underwritten by a corporation. Net profit is then $5 per person. If the goal is $100, the organization only has to do 20 transactions to get $100; and those 20 new members can go out and recruit new members. Every person has networks; every member you sign up gives you access to that many more people.

Therefore, if your goal is to make the most money in the least amount of time, the best thing you can do is sell your program to potential members.

Motivation

What will motivate people to become involved? For one thing, collect on a favor and make it very personal: "I want you to do this for me." People may return a personal favor the first time it's requested because they want to work with you and get to know you better. You hope that through their experience in working on a committee they will learn why you are working in this area and will want to do it again. You can only collect so many times on a favor, however.

What else motivates people? The good of the cause, and this is the best motivation. People basically have good motivations, and if you show them a good cause, they will give to it.

In the variety of incentives you can offer as motivation—prizes or cash incentives among them—usually it's recognition people really prefer. Put the names of the board committee people in your publicity and recognize them at your benefit. Bring your top ticket sellers and money raisers to the podium and introduce them. These people make it all possible and keep the organization alive. They are the blood and the oxygen of the organization.

The people who raise money ought to get the most recognition because fund raising is hard work. It's a real victory to go out and ask for money, and people who do so ought to receive recognition. Some groups have award dinners every year, at which they hand out plaques and other awards. The way you do it doesn't make any difference as long as you are absolutely sure everybody is lavished with recognition. The president should personally call people and say, "I'm really proud of you, and I appreciate your work." Whatever can be done to make these people feel good about their accomplishments is extremely important.

You personally need to believe your organization is worth the price of the membership fee. Currently you are giving your time, which is even more important than money. If your organization is so important to you that you will give your time, and if other people in your group are giving their time, sit down with them and talk about what the organization means to each personally, how it has changed each life, improved the immediate community, and improved the country.

Your group should also reflect on what you have done in the previous year and what victories you have won. Every newsletter should have a list of what you accomplished that month. If the accomplishment is getting the newsletter out, include that. You should accomplish something every single month and keep a record every year. A list of accomplishments is something tangible and positive to offer people, thus encouraging their support. More important, your list proves that your organization is a good investment because you are finding solutions to a particular problem. If you believe in the work enough to give your time, others ought to believe in it enough to give their money.

You can probably think of other ways to help people think positively about asking for money so that they will feel comfortable doing so. As committee members do it more and more, they will feel better about doing it. But when you start, it's hard.

One of the exercises fund-raising groups use is this: have people make up a list of the times they have given anybody money and why they gave it. Was it because of who asked you? Or did you want what was being sold? Or did you like the cause? Or what? Then make a second list of every time you almost gave money but did not. Add what the askers could have done differently to get the money. Finally, make a third list of people you would never give a nickel to under any circumstances. Analyze what they do wrong and why they will not get money from you.

You will discover that others ask for money, and you give it much more frequently than you yourself ask for it. You will also discover that when you give you feel good about it. It makes you feel good to give to an organization that is successful or to a candidate who wins. You want to do it and will do it year after year. If you feel good about it when you give to a worthwhile organization, you should assume that the people who give to you will feel good about it. You are not imposing on them when you ask for money. You are giving them an opportunity to support something that really matters in the community. If you analyze it in that way, it's easier for you and your committee to ask.

Remember why you are raising money, why you personally are doing it, and what your organization is all about. The danger when you do a lot of fund raising is that sometimes it seems as if the fund raising is an end in itself. You may think, "Oh, if I could only sell the dance tickets or if I could only get my five new members." The logistics seem to be an end in themselves. You have to remember that the reason you are raising money is to build the kind of committee and the kind of organization you envision. Raising money is simply a means to an end.

In the process both laziness and fear are normal. They should be expected, but nobody, virtually nobody, will talk about them. If you say to someone, "I want you to be on the committee and get 20 new members in the next month," you will get a million excuses. What people are saying is that they don't feel good about doing it, are afraid to do it, and don't know how. There are many ways you can give them support. If you teach them what it's all about, this can make it easier for them. Sit down, listen to them, and give them materials. Then watch while they ask for money, or have them watch while you ask for contributions. It's like selling anything—there are ways to train others, making it both easy and rewarding for them. The payoff is more money and a stronger organization.

Where to Go for Advice

You can find places in your own community that offer courses on fund raising. Very often one of the positive things the United Way does is to offer extremely inexpensive courses on how to raise money. They are primarily tailored to their own agencies, but other groups can sometimes get in. The Donors Forum of Chicago offers an excellent program called "Dialogue with Donors." Check with the librarian at your nearest Cooperating Collection of the Foundation Center for current course information. (See the list of organizations at the end of this article.)

Some city colleges and junior colleges offer fund-raising courses. Very often public relations courses teach virtually the same skills. Sometimes other community organizations offer courses specifically on how to raise funds. Find out what you want to do, who else in the community has done the kinds of things you want to do, and where you can go for help.

One resource I have used frequently is the person formerly called the society editor of the newspaper, now often called the life-style editor. This is the person at the newspaper who goes to benefits. Very often it's somebody who has been going to benefits for 20 years and who knows all of the successful fund raisers in the community. This person can give you good leads on where to go for help and advice.

SUMMARY

Everyone finds it hard to ask for money, but it's possible for people to learn how to do it and enjoy it. In successful fund raising, an agency will solicit funds from a variety of sources—individual contributions, corporation gifts, grants, dues, benefits, and product sales. If you're new to fund raising, a variety of community resources can help you get started.

RESOURCES

Readings

The Bread Game, Glide Publications, 330 Ellis St., San Francisco, CA 94102.

A how-to manual on securing grants to work for social change.

Can Do, The Donors Forum of Chicago, 208 S. LaSalle St., Room 840, Chicago, IL 60604.

A guide listing more than 60 technical assistance organizations in the Chicago area that provide workshops, individual consultation, seminars, and other assistance to not-for-profit organizations.

Foundation Annual Reports: What They Are and How to Use Them, The Foundation Center, 888 Seventh Ave., New York, NY 10019.

A cumulative listing of all U.S. foundations' annual reports on microfilm. Includes those reports published from 1970 to April 1974.

The Foundation Directory, Columbia University Press, 136 S. Broadway, Irvington, NY 10533.

A compilation of lists of grants published in *The Foundation News,* reviews of state foundation directories, and changes in foundations' activities.

The Foundation News, 888 Seventh Ave., New York, NY 10019.

Published bimonthly. Concentrates on nonprofit foundations.

Foundation Researching—Buy a Service or Do It Yourself? The Foundation Center, 888 Seventh Ave., New York, NY 10019.

A reprint from the March/April 1973 issue of *The Foundation News,* with information on research systems for foundation funds, independent nonprofit agencies, and resource libraries.

The Grantsmanship Center News, 1031 S. Grand Ave., Los Angeles, CA 90015.

A magazine about funding, planning, proposal writing, and resource development.

The Grass Roots Fundraising Book, by Joan Flanagan, The Youth Project, 1555 Connecticut Ave., NW, Washington, DC 20036.

A compilation of valuable how-to information on the techniques that can be used in community-based fund raising.

How to Write Successful Foundation Presentations, Public Service Materials Center, 104 E. 40th St., New York, NY 10016.

Uses sample letters and presentations to illustrate proven methods in preparing appointment letters and other material needed for applications.

Organizations

The Donors Forum of Chicago, 208 S. LaSalle St., Room 840, Chicago, IL 60604.

Includes a library of resources providing information on foundations around 'the country. Focuses particularly on foundations and corporations that fund programs in the Chicago area.

The Foundation Center, whose central office is in New York City, operates four national Reference Collections. Each collection offers a free library of foundations' materials, including all of the center's publications; books, services, and periodicals on foundations and philanthropy; foundation annual reports; newsletters; and press clippings. The Reference Collections operated by The Foundation Center are:

The Foundation Center
888 Seventh Ave.
New York, NY 10019

The Foundation Center
1001 Connecticut Ave., NW
Washington, DC 20036

The Foundation Center
Kent H. Smith Library
739 National City Bank Bldg.
Cleveland, OH 44114

The Foundation Center
312 Sutter St.
San Francisco, CA 94108

In addition, there are Cooperating Collections in free libraries in every state, Puerto Rico, and Mexico. These collections provide local information. For the Cooperating Collection closest to you, call the New York center's toll-free number, (800) 424-9836. Many of the Cooperating Collections also offer workshops and other services.

The National Self-Help Resource Center, Inc., 1800 Wisconsin Ave., NW, Washington, DC 20007.

Includes a resource library. Coordinates workshops on such topics as fund raising, public relations, use of volunteers, planning, management, and evaluation.

W. Clement & Jessie V. Stone Foundation, 111 E. Wacker Dr., Suite 510, Chicago, IL 60601.

Provides a variety of consulting services and will forward information and an application form upon request.

The Support Center, 1424 16th St., NW, Washington, DC 20036.

Provides public interest organizations with support in management, personnel, communications, and financial development. Fees are based on the client organization's ability to pay.

Federal Publications

The following books and publications are available from the Superintendent of Documents, U.S. Government Printing Office, Washington, DC 20402, unless otherwise noted.

Catalog of Federal Domestic Assistance

A major federal publication that lists almost all federal domestic assistance programs, who's eligible, how to apply, and deadlines. Loose-leaf manual with semiannual changes.

Commerce Business Daily

Daily publication of all federal government contracts over $25,000 let out for bidding, plus contracts awarded. Chief public distribution for Requests for Proposals (RFP's).

Congressional Directory

Official organization and membership manual of the U.S. Congress. Contains office numbers, committee membership assignments, and federal agency listings.

Federal Management Circular 74-7, Office of Management and Budget, Executive Office Building, 17th St. and Pennsylvania Ave., NW, Washington, DC 20006.

The "bible" of grants administration. Uniform administrative standards noted for assistance to state and local governments.

The Federal Register
Contains all proposed and final funding rules and regulations, as well as deadline dates.

Washington Information Directory, Congressional Quarterly, 141 22nd St., NW, Washington, DC 20037.

A directory of resource individuals and organizations. Includes congressional committees, federal agency bureaus, lobbies, and professional organizations.

24. BUDGETING: INTRODUCTION TO BUDGETING

United Way

The term "budget" may be defined as:

A statement of the financial position of an independent entity for a specified future period of time based on *planned* expenditures during that period and proposals for funding them.

The term "budgeting" may be defined as a systematic, calculative process through which budgets—as defined above—are created. The process of "budget-making" is essentially a *political* process. Conversely, "[i]n the most integral sense the budget lies at the heart of the political process."[1]

BUDGETING DISTINGUISHED FROM ACCOUNTING AND ALLOCATING

Experience indicates considerable

Portions of this publication are based upon "Budgeting—A Guide for United Ways and Not-for-Profit Human Service Organizations," copyright 1975 by United Way of America, the publisher; and some passages follow the publication verbatim. Such passages have been reprinted by F. E. Peacock Publishers, Inc., with the permission of United Way of America.

confusion among volunteers as well as professionals with regard to the three interrelated processes: accounting, budgeting, and allocating. Often the terms are used interchangeably as though they meant the same thing—particularly, budgeting and allocating. The brief discussion below is intended to clarify the distinctions.

Budgeting and Accounting

Budgeting and accounting are two closely related but distinguishable concepts. Both relate to finances and use of resources. However, while accounting is concerned primarily with the past and current fiscal events, budgeting is concerned mainly with the future use of resources. To put it differently, accounting tells the story of the entity's finances in terms of where the money came from and how it was used to accomplish which purposes in a given time frame; budgeting tells the story of the entity's finances in terms of predictions as to how the money will be spent to accomplish specified purposes and where the funding is expected to come from. A good accounting system is invaluable to budgeting, especially in the case of an ongoing organization.

Budgeting and Allocating

The distinction between budgeting and allocating is more problematic because the two terms have been used interchangeably to mean the same thing. However, a distinction must be made between the two concepts, since it is fundamental to this article.

It would be useful to distinguish the two concepts in terms of two distinct *functions* of different types of organizations. First, budgeting, as a functional activity, is common to every organization. Every formal organization must engage in some form of budgeting as discussed and defined earlier. The confusion stems from the fact that one often uses the term "allocation" as an *element of the budgeting function.* For example, in the process of budgeting, a budgeteer is said to allocate 50 percent for salaries, 20 percent for occupancy, 10 percent for supplies, etc. Here, "to allocate" is used in its literal meaning which is: to apportion, to distribute, to assign, or to designate. Thus, in that sense, the concept of allocation is subsumed under the concept of budgeting.

Allocating as a distinct function of an organization is another matter. As mentioned earlier, all formal organizations have budgeting as one of their functions, but *not* all organizations have an allocating function. Allocating, as a function, means distribution of funds and other resources to *other independent organizations.* In effect, the function of allocating establishes a certain type of relationship between two or more independent entities. The best examples of organizations having a major allocating function are federated fund-raising organizations, such as local United Way organizations and foundations. In effect, these organizations do both budgeting and allocating, but budgeting is limited to their own internal matters.

FUNCTIONS OF BUDGETING

In a broad sense, budgeting serves three masters: planning, management or execution, and control. But the three functions are hardly ever served with equal zeal. Usually, the orientation of the executive and/or the governing body determines which function gets emphasized in the operation of a budget system.

... In the context of budgeting, *planning* involves the determination of objectives, the evaluation of alternative courses of action, and the authorization of select programs. ... Management involves the programming of approved goals into specific projects and activities, the design of organizational units to carry out approved programs, and the staffing of these units and the procurement of necessary resources. ... *Control* refers to the process of binding operating officials to the policies and plans set by their superiors. Control is predominant during the execution and audit stages, although the form of budget estimates and appropriations often is determined by control considerations.[2]

In this instance budgeting is almost synonymous with managing or at least a prime tool for achieving the organization's purposes.

Further discussion and application of these concepts to human service organizations follow.

TYPES OF BUDGETING

The theory and practice of budgeting show various types of budgeting. Sometimes the same type of budgeting has been called by different names, adding to the existing confusion. It would be useful to identify the most common or talked-about types of budgeting and to note the distinctions among them. For the purposes of this article, the following types of budgeting are described and discussed briefly: (1) Line-Item or Object Budgeting; (2) Functional Budgeting; (3) PPBS or Planning-Programming-Budgeting Systems; and (4) for lack of better terminology, what may be simply called *Planned Budgeting, i.e.,* budgeting based on planned programs.

Line-Item Budgeting

Line-item budgeting is based entirely on *line-item accounting*. For many years, the method of accounting most common among voluntary human service organizations was "line-item" or *object accounting*. Thus, agencies recorded expenditures for the "things" bought, such as equipment, rental, salaries, travel, printing. This, in turn, became the financial information reported to the public. Budgeting followed the same "line-item" approach. In preparing their budget requests, agencies reviewed how much was spent for each line item in prior years, projected the amounts to be spent for each line in the current year, and then used those figures, plus a factor for inflation and other cost increases, as the basis for their budget for the ensuing year. This type of budgeting is usually tied to another type of budgeting known as *incremental budgeting*. Under this system, whatever is already in the budget is more or less frozen, and the focus is on current increments to that budget. The phenomenon of line-item budgeting can be explained in the context of the predominance of the "control orienta-

tion" of budgeting authorities. In discussing the "stages of budget reform," Allen Schick explains this control orientation as follows (in part):

In varying degrees of itemization, the expenditure classifications established during the first wave of reform were based on objects-of-expenditure, with detailed tabulations of the myriad items required to operate an administrative unit—personnel, fuel, rent, office supplies, and other inputs. On these "line-itemizations" were built technical routines for the compilation and review of estimates and the disbursement of funds.[3]

At the other end of the spectrum is what is known as *base-zero* or *zero-base* budgeting. Under this system no historical base is recognized. How much was spent on each item last year or the year before has no bearing whatsoever on how much will be spent on those items next year. Every item in the budget is considered to be on trial and must fight for its life each year and must compete for funds against all other items. Thus, one starts, so to say, with a "clean slate" each year.

While many small agencies—especially single-program agencies—continue to use the line-item method of budgeting, it is not recommended here. Relying exclusively on line-item budgeting tends to perpetuate obsolete programs. Zero-base budgeting, while seemingly rational and attractive, has proved to be impractical in a few places where it has been seriously tried, and thus not recommended for human service organizations.

Functional Budgeting

Functional budgeting is based on functional accounting. The concept was first introduced to the field of voluntary human service organizations on a nationwide basis in 1964, with the publication of *Standards of Accounting and Financial Reporting for Voluntary Health and Welfare Organizations.*[4]

Functional accounting requires that agencies report their financial activities in terms of the "programs" (or "services") they provide, as contrasted with the practice of line-item accounting referred to above. *Functional budgeting* is the distribution of all revenue and expenditures to: (1) the management and general function; (2) the fund raising function (if any); and (3) the separately identifiable programs operated by an agency. Within each of the functional categories, income and expenditures are reported by object or line item, as in the conventional system. However, the ultimate report distributes overhead costs (management and general, and fund raising) among program costs in order to arrive at an accurate accounting of the total costs of all the agencies' programs.

Functional budgeting is also known as *performance budgeting* or *program budgeting.* Purely functional budgeting does not incorporate the important element of planning. In most instances, it is merely a distribution of the object categories by various functional categories. This is the key distinction between functional budgeting and PPBS.

To conclude the discussion on functional budgeting, it can be said that this method of budgeting has been steadily gaining ground among voluntary human service organizations. It should be noted further that functional accounting is now required for year-end public financial reporting under *generally accepted accounting principles for voluntary health and welfare organizations.*

Planning-Programming-Budgeting Systems (PPBS)[5]

PPBS is a budgeting innovation of the sixties. The seeds were sown during the early reform movement to bring about greater efficiency and effectiveness in government and greater rationality in the allocation of resources. PPBS may be called the culmination of this twentieth-century reform movement to make government more responsive and rational via the vehicle of a sophisticated budgeting system. As one of the most significant innovations in public administration in recent times, PPBS has had volumes written about it during the past ten years. It is not intended to provide here an in-depth analysis of PPBS. The purpose here is to make some summary observations on PPBS as a discrete category of the budgeting method and to distinguish it from the other types of budgeting discussed earlier.

There are almost as many definitions of PPBS as there are advocates and critics. There is no consensus even among its advocates as to what PPBS is exactly. With that in mind, an attempt is made here to describe this new budgeting system rather than concisely to define it.

PPBS is a centrally coordinated mechanism for managing resources, particularly in the governmental sector. It unites the three fundamental functions of management—planning, programming and budgeting—into an integrated system. In PPBS we see the following things happening:

• Goals and missions of the entity are identified, developed and explicitly stated. This may be called the policy-planning stage.

- Specific, time-limited objectives are identified, developed and explicitly stated. These objectives are designed to show progress in the direction of achievement of the entity's goals. An attempt is made to specify objectives in a quantitative, or some other measurable, manner.
- All available facts are gathered as to "who needs what, how badly." New information is created through analysis.
- Some form of priorities is established.
- Existing programs are analyzed in terms of their effectiveness. Modifications are made where appropriate. Obsolete programs are abolished. New programs are created.
- Both in program modification and program development (new programs), alternatives are vigorously analyzed, and the best alternatives are chosen. Analysis includes cost-benefit or cost-effectiveness studies and comparisons.
- Programs are put in place and the machinery is made to function.
- Periodic analysis is conducted to ensure that programs are running on the right tracks, as planned.
- Systematic evaluation is conducted to ascertain whether the program achieved its stated objectives.
- Based on the last activity and new information on the changes in the environment, a new PPBS cycle is started.

The above outline description of a PPBS process is stated admittedly in ideal terms. When it comes to practical application of the theory, many compromises are made. However, a review of the literature on experiences with PPBS—primarily in the public sector—raises some questions as to its practical benefits when measured against the cost and effort demanded in its implementation. In places where it has been tried, little significant difference was discerned in the results.

Current literature on PPBS indicates three fundamental reasons for the failure of PPBS in the public sector.[6] First, PPBS concentrates too much on *ends* without adequate regard to the *means*. Second, its orientation to, and overdependence on, *economic rationality* underestimates the fact that decision making on goals and objectives with regard to what should be funded is essentially a *political process* and is rooted in consensus politics and not in scientific methods. Third, PPBS relies heavily on its requirements of centralization, coordination and comprehensiveness in the decision-making process of resource allocation—which is antithetical to our democratic traditions and the polyarchical nature of our society.

Is PPBS feasible or recommended for human service organizations? No, not at least in the terms described above and in the manner in which it was attempted in the public sector. This is because, under PPBS, the distinctions between budgeting and allocating do not exist. It is fundamentally unworkable because, in the non-for-profit arena, those who distribute funds—the allocating organizations—and those who provide services—the service delivery organizations—are sovereign entities. Does this mean one should discard PPBS altogether? No. The basic concepts and individual components of the PPBS process are sound. The trick is to sort out what is usable from PPBS and blend it in a customized process in the case of a given agency. The kind of *internal agency budgeting* suggested below and in the next section provides a basic framework of a program planning and budget process that uses some of the PPBS concepts and at the same time provides enough freedom for users to customize and experiment.

Planned Budgeting

Since *planned budgeting* is the central thesis of this article, detailed discussion of the concept is reserved for later. However, some summary observations are in order here.

Planned budgeting, as will be explained, represents a modest approach to budgeting based on *planned programs*. It accepts agency autonomy as a given. It is designed to operate in the environment of every type of known constraint and thus designed to function in the real world. It combines selected elements from line-item and incremental budgeting, functional budgeting and even PPBS. It may even be regarded as a miniaturized PPBS. In essence, it is a budgeting system grounded in the philosophy of *doing the doable*.

PROGRAM PLANNING

Agencies exist to provide programs. Programs are delivered on the basis of some form of planning. It is hard to conceive of a self-respecting, established agency that does not engage in some prior planning of its programs for the coming program-fiscal period. The question, then, is not "planning vs. no planning," but "how much" planning, and on "what" basis, and whether "systematic" planning or "opportunistic" planning.

This section is about *systematic* program planning. The discussion covers two general topics: (1) the nature of planning as a human endeavor; and (2) the program-planning process, that is, the process agencies must undertake to plan their programs.

As mentioned in the earlier discussion, the agency is seen here as the sole arbiter of its programs. Thus, it is up to the agency to decide whether to attempt systematic planning or not and if "yes," how much planning it should get into, i.e., how much of its resources it should invest in planning. The reason for reiterating this point is that the key to successful planning is self-motivation and a conviction of its intrinsic value. If planning is undertaken half-heartedly, merely as a gesture or ritual, it is not worth undertaking. The ensuing discussion in itself should help agencies decide whether they should attempt it or not, and to what extent they should get involved in a systematic program-planning process.

PLANNING AS A HUMAN ENDEAVOR

Formal definitions of *planning* are probably as many as there are planning theorists.[7] Definitions examined were found unsatisfactory or unsuitable for the purposes of this article. Thus, a new working definition of planning is proposed here. The dynamic concept of planning may be defined as:

a systematic, deliberative process of, first, determining specific objectives to be attained and, second, determining and laying out a course (or courses), of action to attain those objectives based on analysis of available relevant data, for implementation within some specified future time period.

Thus, the planning process defined above can be broken down into its five major components:

1. Consensus on broad goals or missions. This is implied in the specification of objectives.
2. Determination of specific objectives—implying consideration of alternatives among possible objectives.
3. Data gathering and analysis. One cannot decide which objectives to choose and what course of action to take in the absence of information.
4. Selection of the most feasible and effective course of action.
5. Laying out in detail the selected course of action, i.e., programming.

In simple language, planning can be called a process whereby one decides *what* it is that one wants to achieve and then *figures out* the most effective and efficient way of achieving it (the *"how"*).

THE PROGRAM-PLANNING PROCESS

The program-planning process described here is not intended to be an exhaustive treatment of the subject; nor is it a set prescription for mechanical application in every instance. The process is described in terms of identification of main segments, in rough sequence. Each segment in the process identified here may be broken down into tasks, sub-tasks and sub-sub-tasks, but that is not attempted here. Agency size,

programs and resources vary so much that it is impractical to provide here a detailed "work-book" type approach to program-planning suitable for every type of voluntary agency. Also, the process outlined below is presented as one possible approach for those who wish to try it. In sum, it is not intended to imply that what is proposed below is the only way to plan programs; many variations are possible using the basic concepts.

Gearing Up—The Preplanning Stage

This phase of the program-planning process can be called the preplanning stage. These are the initial activities or preliminaries to get organized, "gear up," for the formal program-planning process. This preplanning phase covers, in the main, two basic types of tasks: (1) organization of the program-planning structure; and (2) organization of some preliminary data. Brief descriptions of these two tasks follow.

Program-Planning Structure. A joint volunteer-staff committee should be created, with the agency's volunteer president as chairman. Included on the committee from the volunteer board members should be the agency's treasurer. On the other side, the committee should include, in addition to the agency's executive, its chief financial officer, its budget officer (if a separate staff member carries that responsibility) and key program staff, preferably at the supervisory level. The committee should not be too large. The desirable range suggested is between nine and fifteen members. The agency executive acts as the committee's secretariat. He or she is responsible for all logistics, scheduling and arrangement of meetings, preparation of material, etc.

Preliminary Data Collection. The

purpose here is to provide some basic material to get the group process started. The nature and format of data at this stage are very important. Essentially the data cover basic information on *the agency itself and its current programs.* The data answer the following broad question: "What do we have and what have we been doing?" This gets into some statement on the agency's total resources: staff, plant, equipment, supplies. It also gets into some preliminary data on the agency's beneficiaries (clients, patients, recipients, etc.). The responsibility to put together the preliminary data described above rests with the executive and staff.

The Program-Planning and Budgeting Process

With the structure in place and the preliminary data ready, the stage is now set to: (1) define (and, if already defined, clarify) the agency's broad goal and mission; and (2) state *tentatively* specific objectives to be attained during the period for which planning is undertaken.

Goals and Mission. Goals and mission statements should have some philosophical frame of reference, should be expressed in close to ideal terms, and should relate to the type of service the agency is providing and/or planning to provide. Usually the goals and mission statements define the *purpose* for which the agency came into being in the first place, and generally these statements are also found in the agency's articles of incorporation. The statement should provide a frame of reference to all future activities of the agency.

Tentative Objectives. The word tentative is emphasized here. The idea at this stage of the process is to expand the

minds of the committee members, not to make them feel too constrained. The committee here looks at the preliminary data as described above, and determines what the agency should be doing over the period under consideration, under reasonably favorable conditions. The purpose here is to provide a reasonable range or field of objectives for further study and analysis as to the feasibility of their being accomplished. Thus, at the end of this phase of the process, the committee says, "We would like to do thus and so. Now let us go out and find out if we are on the right track."

Data Gathering and Analysis

This is fundamentally a staff responsibility, but volunteer help may be requested depending upon the agency situation and availability of technical help. It should be noted immediately that the suggestion here is to collect only those data which directly relate to the agency's programs and other needs. There are three basic types of data and data analyses that are needed for *decision making* in the next phase of the process: (1) needs and problems data; (2) resource availability data; and (3) assumptions and constraints data. Each of these items is discussed below briefly.

Needs and Problems Data. The agency explores various available and existing avenues of information (see discussion below on sources of information) and comes to some judgment as to the nature and extent of need. The important point to keep in mind here is that the agency is not looking at *all* the needs of *all* the people in the community, because it is simply not practical for every agency to do so. The objective is clearly a *limited* one, as will be evident throughout the planning process. The agency (i.e., the committee) is simply trying to figure out the extent of need for the services it provides or plans to provide.

When the needs information is gathered, it should be analyzed and presented in an easily readable and understandable format for the use of the committee.

Resource Availability Data. This relates to sources of funding the agency's program. It is well established that voluntary agencies are perpetually in search of money to finance their programs. Thus, there would be no point in dwelling long on the importance of what is called here "resource availability data." What is visualized here is some systematic data gathering and analysis as to "who" has the funds to give to the agency, "where" the agency should look or inquire, and, in instances where funds are available, some summary analysis as to the consequences of acceptance of those funds (because there might be some strings attached or because it may compromise agency autonomy or it may have an adverse impact on the agency's other programs or its image).

This is certainly not a book about fund-raising and what is suggested here is *not* the actual fund-raising per se but some research into the availability of funds tied to the tentative objectives which have already been established and service needs which have been estimated. The point here is to build this important task into the systematic planning process.

Assumptions and Constraints Data. *Assumptions* are beliefs about the existing state of affairs or anticipation of events which are certain to take place and over which the agency has absolutely no direct control or influence. These refer primarily to social, economic or political conditions external to the agency but which may have some direct

impact on the agency's operation.

Assumptions can be beneficial or damaging. It is a neutral term and could predict propitious circumstances as well as foreshadow unfavorable events to occur. Examples of negative assumptions might be: a major increase in utility (oil, gas, electricity) cost; imminent election to office of individuals ill-disposed to the agency's programs; probable shut down of a major industry; a major strike, etc.

Constraints are *always* negative. Again, since the agency has no control over these external conditions, it had best take them into account systematically in the program-planning process. In this instance, constraints are seen primarily as they relate to program planning based on tentative objectives. Put simply, constraints analysis tells what is "safe" and what is unwise to attempt. What is suggested here is that the program-planning process should have built into it a systematic analysis of *risks* involved in undertaking certain programs which might be characterized as unpopular, unorthodox or "far-out." This is not to say that agencies should not consider controversial programs. The point to be emphasized here is that the decision to go ahead with a program that might be considered "far-out" by the community should be taken, not on an emotional basis, but on the basis of a conviction of the *value* of such a program and with full knowledge of the unfavorable consequences that might ensue.

Sources of Data. It is important to note that data gathering and analysis are very costly processes. Some judgment should be exercised during the pre-planning stage as to how much resources can be invested. No general guideline is feasible here because agency capacity and sophistication vary so greatly.

The three types of data-gathering and analysis suggested here are usually available somewhere in the community to some extent. [For example, the local United Way may have recently completed a communitywide needs assessment and/or priorities planning study.] In other words, no original research is suggested here. The following are sources of information for voluntary agencies:

- Formal and regularized or informal consultation with other agencies providing like services.
- National affiliate of the agency.
- Brother/sister agencies in other communities.
- Public and private libraries.
- Newspapers, periodicals, and other public media.
- Census Bureau.
- Academic and research institutions.
- Municipal and state planning departments.
- Information and referral agencies.
- The local United Way.
- Independent planning council (usually United Way–funded).
- Sample client survey or informal client interviews.
- Market survey.

Objectives Setting

Armed with the clarified statements of the agency's goals and mission, listing of tentative objectives and a systematic analysis of needs, resources, assumptions and constraints, the committee is now ready to sharpen its focus and determine the future course of action for the agency.

Objectives should be designed as highly specific statements about what is to be achieved in a given program area. Key elements of a well-designed objective are its specificity in terms of measurability and time frame. W. J. Reddin provides many good examples of objective-setting in industry. Some of these may be applied with discretion to voluntary agency services with appropriate modifications.[8] Reddin provides the following tests of sound objectives.[9]

Sound objectives can be easily distinguished from unsound ones by being tested against this list.

TESTS OF OBJECTIVES

SOUND	PROBABLY UNSOUND
Measurable (quantitative)	Nonmeasureable (qualitative)
Specific	General
Results-(output-) centered	Activity-(input-) centered
Realistic and attainable	Minimum or unattainable
Time-bounded	Time-extended

A word of caution is in order with regard to quantification of objectives. Quantification can be misleading if used improperly and artificially. In those instances where quantification is feasible and *meaningful,* it should be attempted. In those "soft areas" of human service endeavors, where quantification of results is not feasible, the statement of objectives should be so designed that the agency is able to look back and *assess* to some degree whether what had been planned was indeed attained or that some progress toward the objective was made.

Thus, going back to the objectives-setting session, the following takes place. Tentative objectives are considered in the context of the existing reality described in the material provided to the participants. There is discussion, debate, challenge and response. Through this process of group dynamics, participants are "educated" about unattainable or infeasible objectives which are systematically eliminated one by one. Feasible objectives keep floating. These are further thrashed out and sharpened to a high level of specificity and quantification where feasible and meaningful. Once consensus is reached on the selection and language of objectives, an attempt is made to establish some form of priority among them, where several desirable objectives are established and there is some question about funding all of them adequately.

Once objectives have been selected and prioritized, criteria should be established as to how the agency will ascertain whether progress was made toward attainment of each one of the objectives or whether the objectives were, in fact, attained as planned. The concept here is to provide a framework for a system of self-evaluation and self-policing.

Finally, objectives are placed in specific timeframes. Where feasible, objectives should be set over a three-year period in three to six months segments. The three-year period is suggested here as an ideal "long-range" planning timeframe. This is because a two-year period can hardly be called "long-range" and four or more years would be impractical for most human service organizations.

Programming the Objectives

This is the next step in the process and is essentially a staff responsibility.

Programming involves effective use of resources available to the manager in accomplishing the individual objectives which have been established in the preceding phase. Programming must be undertaken for the attainment of each one of the objectives established. It gets

into the assignment of individual tasks and responsibilities of each one of the staff members. It also gets into the effective use of plant, building, office space and various equipment. A good manager looks at the real alternatives available in programming an objective.

The programming process should include an evaluation system for staff performance assessment. This is a second level of assessment as compared with the evaluation system referred to in the objectives-setting phase. The first attempts to assess whether the agency succeeded in attaining its objectives. The second attempts to assess whether individual staff members successfully performed their tasks as assigned. Here again, some criteria should be established in advance as to how staff performance will be measured.

Preparing and Testing the Budget

This is the phase of the process where the manager gets down to "budgeting" in a literal sense, referred to earlier in this book. This is the "nitty-gritty" of budgeting—putting figures to words, filling out the innumerable forms, schedules and worksheets. Once the budget is completed, the manager tests it out, that is, processes it with the various sources of funding.

Since the next section is devoted to this subject, no more will be said about it here—except to indicate the sequence in which it fits into the program-planning and budgeting process.

Program/Budget Modification

The extent of work involved in this phase depends largely on the outcome of the prior phase of the budget testing. If the budget is "successful," i.e., it is accepted by the funding sources, this phase is eliminated from the program-planning and budgeting process. However, if there is a substantial difference between what is in the budget and what the agency finds out it can get, it takes the agency back into the program-planning process. In the event that substantially less funding is available than anticipated, the agency is faced with the following types of alternatives:

- Eliminate all or part of a program.
- Reduce the level of services planned under one or more programs.
- Attempt to operate the planned program more efficiently by making certain shifts and adjustments in the use of its resources.
- Attempt to make up the difference in budget by exploring new sources.

In some instances it is conceivable that substantially more funds are available than anticipated because of a sudden increase in need for a service or for some other reason. This, too, would necessitate a shifting of gears back into the program-planning and budgeting process. Thus, it is important to structure this phase in the program-planning and budgeting process. If budget modification necessitates a substantial impact on objectives already established, it goes without saying that the entire Program-Planning and Budget Committee should be extensively consulted, and the decisions should be made on that basis.

This leads to the final phase of the program-planning and budgeting process.

The Adoption of a Balanced Budget

This is the culmination of the program-planning and budgeting

process. After all the necessary modifications are made, the budget is revised so that anticipated expenses and outlays match anticipated public support and revenue.

The revised budget should be first approved by the Program-Planning and Budget Committee and then presented to the agency's board of directors for formal adoption.

CONCLUSION

The process outlined in this section is designed as a serious and intensive undertaking. Because of the intensiveness and extensiveness of the process it is suggested that it be undertaken not on an annual basis, but only every three years. If properly orchestrated, the process will take a good part of a year. Thus, a process conducted in 1982 will cover program years 1983, 1984 and 1985. If found productive and successful, the process will be undertaken again in 1985 with necessary adjustments based on experience. At the end of program years 1983 and 1984, some form of self-evaluation is conducted to check whether the agency is "on the right track," as planned. Adjustments should be made as necessary and appropriate. However, in the event of major unexpected changes in the economic, social, or political conditions, a fresh look at the entire program plan and the budget will be undertaken.

Before embarking upon a program-planning and budgeting process as recommended in this section, one basic point needs to be stressed: the agency board should carefully consider and understand what it is getting into. In particular, the board should consider the cost of such a process and whether it would be worth the anticipated result. However, once a decision is made to proceed, there should be full and whole-hearted commitment to the process.

BUDGETING

In the previous section it was shown that the program-planning process precedes the actual budget-making activity. Since, under this process, specific objectives have already been established and programming has been completed, the time has now come to put a price tag on human and material resources programmed to achieve the agency's objectives. While this is budgeting understood in a very narrow or literal sense of the term, it is all the same a very important and essential undertaking. The purpose of this section is to present a brief summary of the actual budget preparation and adoption. The purpose here is to provide some general guidelines with regard to some of the more important aspects of budget preparation.

Estimating Budget Needs

There are a number of general approaches to the process of any agency's preparation of budget estimates or requests. Moak and Killian[10] have suggested several different types of approaches to needs estimating which are in general practice among budgeteers; of these the following may be noted:

1. Open End Budgeting—Line officals are permitted to submit unlimited budgets according to their best judgment as to optimum program for agency.
2. Fixed Ceiling Budgeting—A dollar ceiling is established for each department or agency before the preparation of the budget.
3. Work Measurement and Unit Costing—Estimates based on units of program product or service desired based on per unit cost.
4. Increase versus Decrease Analysis—Items requiring increases and decreases in comparison with prior year's budget are sorted out and analyzed.
5. Priority Listings—Requests are submitted in order of priority.
6. Item-by-Item Control—Each item is questioned and justified in terms of its essentiality and desirability.
7. Alternative Proposals—Basic budget plus skeleton plans for alternative amounts and analysis of consequences for each alternative.
8. Historical Analysis—Requests for nonpersonal services items are based on past experience and current trends.

The approach—or a combination of approaches—to budget estimating selected usually depends upon the subject matter under consideration. For example, in determining personnel needs, work measurement is the primary factor to be considered, and the method used is usually a combination of *work measurement, unit cost,* and *historical analysis.* On the other hand, when the budgeteer is estimating the cost of materials and supplies, a combination of historical analysis and work measurement is the key. In instances of determining equipment needs, agencies tend to use the *fixed ceiling* approach under which a dollar ceiling is established either for the agency as a whole or each department within the agency, prior to the preparation of the budget.

Personal Services. In most agencies and organizations this is probably the largest item in the budget and thus requires much analysis and study. In general, the estimates in this regard are based on any one or more of the following: (1) prior years' experience; (2) work-load trends; (3) staffing patterns indicated on existing organizational charts; and (4) guesstimates.

Depending upon the size of the agency and the multiplicity of its programs, Moak and Killian suggest the following additional factors to take into consideration in estimating the cost of personal services:[11] (1) department manning tables; (2) work-load trends; (3) the classification plan; (4) estimates of salary savings; (5) the use of overtime and premium time; (6) management studies; (7) sick and annual leave; (8) quality of the working force; and (9) impact of new capital facilities.

With the sole exception of extremely large organizations, the concept of manning tables is not too relevant to the typical voluntary agency. Workload trends, on the other hand, can be an important factor in the estimating process because there is a direct relationship between the trend in work load and the number of people needed to do the job. The following factors usually affect workload trends and therefore should be kept in mind: (1) new agency policies or changes in existing policy; (2) planned program changes as a result of the program-planning process described earlier; (3) workload consolidations resulting from changes in programming; and (4) changes in systems and/or procedures.

Salary Savings. Experience tells us that, as a rule, the full amount put in the budget for personal services will not be used during the budgeted period for a variety of reasons. Therefore, it is common practice to have an item called "Salary Savings" [or "Personnel Turnover Factor"] to be deducted from the total estimate for personal services. The standard method used in computing this figure is past years' experience—the percentage of gross personal services budgeted which was unused during the current period adjusted by any known factors of change.

Overtime and Premium Time. Good management entails optimal use of human resources available to agencies:[12]

Few operations move in such measured cadence that management can avoid some "non-productive" time or can avoid the necessity for "overtime" to help meet peaks in work load.

Many persons view overtime as an evil in itself and a thing to be avoided. However, overtime has long been associated with well-managed operations. The problem is to keep it in proper relationship and control.

Contractual Services. Many voluntary agencies increasingly purchase services on a contractual basis. Usually contractual services are bought because of either cost considerations, degree of specialization of the task to be performed or because of board decisions to keep the number of permanent staff as low as possible. Also, depending upon the agency, seasonal or intermittent workload factors play an important role in opting for contractual services as opposed to permanent employees.

The types of contractual services budgeted are usually of a professional or technical nature.

Materials, Supplies and Equipment. The purpose here is to determine the agency's needs for the type, quality and quantity of materials, supplies and equipment required to carry out the purposes of the organization.

In determining the agency's needs for materials and supplies, the following key factors should be taken into account: (1)

review of current inventory and agency policies governing inventory in light of current conditions; (2) price levels; (3) changing patterns in the use of materials; and (4) changing rules in relation to methods of producing results.

Budgeting for equipment from operating funds is concerned primarily with equipment replacement; however, some portion of the annual equipment budget ... represents a net increase in the inventory of equipment. These two aspects of equipment requirements should be considered separately at all stages of the budget process. Of course, the line of demarcation becomes obscure when the replacement item is a substantial improvement over the replaced item.[13]

The purpose here is to determine the type, the quality and the quantity of equipment required by the agency to achieve its objectives. The basic tools in this regard are: (1) the maintenance of an inventory system, and (2) equipment replacement schedules. The standard inventory system includes the following types of information: (1) date of purchase; (2) purchase price; (3) location; (4) description; (5) condition [in terms of maintenance cost and volume of hours of usage]; (6) quantity on hand; (7) life expectancy; and (8) classification code number of equipment, if any.

Equipment replacement policies involve consideration of: (1) definition of the work to be done, measured in terms of the number and type of equipment required and their planned maintenance; (2) permanent inventory and maintenance records; and (3) procedures for inspection to insure that the item is truly in need of replacement.

Estimating Public Support and Revenue

Writers in the field of revenue estimating (primarily for municipal government

purposes) have identified six different methods for the preparation of revenue estimates:[14]

1. Automatic Method—Projected revenues equal revenues for the most recent completed fiscal year; also known as the "rule of the penultimate year."
2. Method of Averages—Estimates based on a three to five year average of increases and decreases.
3. Empirical Judgment Method—Estimates based exclusively on personal judgment and relies entirely on the competence of the estimator.
4. Method of Direct Valuation—Revenue forecast is made a few days after the beginning of the fiscal year.
5. Conditioned Judgment Method—Judgment based on analysis.
6. Systematic Methods:
   a. Correlation Analysis—Estimates based on an equation reflecting the past relationship between the tax and economic series.
   b. Questionnaire Sampling—Taxpayers are asked to compare anticipated tax liabilities with taxes paid in the current year.

Of the methods listed above, the one most applicable to the voluntary agency field is the "conditioned judgment method." This method combines the use of personal judgment with a methodical analysis of data on general economic trends and trends in allocations policies of funding bodies such as local United Ways and foundations.

The classification scheme for public support and revenue provided in the chart of accounts in the United Way of America's Accounting Guide can serve as a useful tool for estimating agency "income" on an item-by-item basis. The major public support and revenue captions are classified as follows:

Public Support and Revenue

DIRECT PUBLIC SUPPORT
  Contributions
  Contributions to Building Fund
  Special Events
  Legacies and Bequests
INDIRECT PUBLIC SUPPORT
  Collected through Local Member
    Units
  Contributed by Associated
    Organizations
  Allocated by Federated
    Fund-Raising Organizations
  Allocated by Unassociated &
    Non-Federated Fund-Raising
    Organizations
FEES FROM GOVERNMENTAL
  AGENCIES
GRANTS FROM GOVERN-
  MENTAL AGENCIES
OTHER REVENUE SOURCES
  Membership Dues—Individuals
  Assessment & Dues—Local
    Member Units
  Program Service Fees
  Sales of Supplies & Services to
    Local Member Units
  Sales to Public
  Investment Income
  Gain on Investment Transactions

For those voluntary agencies that receive financial support from local United Way organizations—or those expecting to receive support for the first time—there is an annual report compiled by United Way of America on local United Way allocations, which may be of some use to these agencies in looking at trends in funding similar programs in comparable communities. Similarly, major foundations publish annual reports and studies which may provide some guidelines of the types of programs funded. As for fees and grants from governmental agencies, various sources of funding are available at different governmental levels. Voluntary agencies should carefully analyze their prospects of funding from these sources and the consequences attendant on such funding.

Balancing the Budget

The concept of balancing the budget is a logical outcome of matching resources to proposed expenditures and reserves. There is general agreement among budgeteers on the desirability of balancing a proposed budget by either bringing revenues up to expenditures or bringing expenditures down to revenues.

The question arises whether, in the balancing act, provisions should be made for contingencies and whether appropriations should be made for reserves. On this issue, Moak and Killian suggest:[15]

> ... in line with current thinking and practice, a "balanced" budget in all probability will not be one in which the amount of projected expenditures is exactly equal to the amount of anticipated revenues. Budget projections are at best estimates. Some provision for flexibility should be built into the proposed budget when local conditions permit. This flexibility is provided by an amount set aside as a reserve for contingencies.

However, in the case of agencies funded by central funding bodies, it would be prudent to ascertain whether such reserves for contingencies are permissible under the "allocating policy" of the funding source in question.

Surpluses and Deficits

The use of actual or estimated surpluses and the provision of funds in the budget to cover any deficit spending in the current year are two problems encountered by almost every budgeteer.

Surpluses. The term "surplus" has been defined by the National Committee on Governmental Accounting as the excess of resources over the obligations of a fund.[16] In many municipalities and other not-for-profit organizations, surplus is an important factor in balancing the budget. In some instances, amounts accrued from unexpended appropriations and unanticipated revenues are transferred at year-end to a reserve fund, rather than treated as surpluses.

Deficits. The term "deficit" is defined as the excess of obligations over resources in a fund.[17] Theoretically, voluntary agencies funded by central funding bodies such as local United Ways should not have any deficits to speak of if they are funded on the principle of "deficit-financing." As a rule, these funding bodies do not assume responsibility for unauthorized deficits. Potential deficits should normally be anticipated and discussed with funding bodies. If reasons for modifying original estimates seem justified, an additional appropriation may be made to meet the revised estimates.

To conclude this brief discussion on surpluses and deficits, the following recommendations of Moak and Killian are worth noting despite the fact that they are made for government budgeteers:[18]

... it is desirable for a municipality to have some flexibility in the management of surpluses and deficits.

To be specific, it is recommended that each municipality make two determinations:

1. The amount of cash that may be necessary to carry forward as surplus in order to avoid frequent recourse to short-term bank loans because the cash needed in the early months of the year is greater than is likely to be collected from revenues.

2. The amount of a reasonable reserve which will enable the municipality to do a good job of fiscal management especially in order that temporary losses in income or occasional genuine expenditure emergencies may be met and still avoid a cumulative deficit position.

Once these two items have been determined, the finance officer should be in a position to develop a desirable policy for his city concerning the amounts of surplus which should *ordinarily* be carried over from year to year. He can conclude that no surplus is needed or he may conclude that surplus should be provided for (2) and not for (1). But the determination should be deliberately made.

The principles outlined above for municipalities may provide at least some insight or guideline for voluntary agency budgeting. However, these guidelines should be read in conjunction with specific agreed upon policies established by funding bodies where they exist.

NOTES

1. Aaron Wildavsky, *The Politics of the Budgetary Process,* 2nd ed. (Boston: Little, 1974), p. 5.
2. Allen Schick, "The Road to PPB: The Stages of Budget Reform," XXVI *Public Administration Review* (December 1966), p. 244.
3. Ibid., p. 246.
4. *Standards of Accounting and Financial Reporting for Voluntary Health and Welfare Organizations,* National Health Council and National Social Welfare Assembly (New York, 1964).
5. See generally *A PPBS Approach to Budgeting Human Service Programs for United Ways,* United Way of America (Alexandria, Va., December 1972).
6. For a provocative analysis of the failure of PPBS, see Aaron Wildavsky, *op. cit,;* see also the following publications by the same author: "The Political Economy of Efficiency: Cost-Benefit Analysis,

Systems Analysis, and Program Budgeting," XXVI *Public Administration Review* (Autumn, 1961), pp. 183-190; "Rescuing Policy Analysis from PPBS," XXIX *Public Administration Review* (March/April 1969), pp. 189-202; and *Budgeting* (Boston, 1975).

7. For various definitions of planning and the problems connected with them, see Michael P. Brooks, "Social Policy in Cities: Toward a Theory of Urban Social Planning" (unpublished Ph.D dissertation, Department of City and Regional Planning, University of North Carolina), pp. 4-24; Lyle C. Fitch, "Social Planning in the Urban Cosmos," in Leo F. Schnore and Fagin (eds.), *Urban Research and Policy Planning* (Beverly Hills, Calif.: Sage, 1967), p. 329; and Robert Norris and Robert H. Binstock, *Feasible Planning for Social Change* (New York, 1966), pp. 14-15.

8. W. J. Reddin, *Effective Management by Objectives, The 3-D Method of MBO* (New York: McGraw, 1971), pp. 81-89.

9. *Ibid.*, p. 88. Copyrighted material reproduced with the permission of McGraw-Hill Book Co., the publisher.

10. Lennox L. Moak and Kathryn W. Killian, *A Manual of Techniques for the Preparation, Consideration, Adoption, and Administration of Operating Budgets* (Chicago, 1963), p. 128.

11. *Ibid.*, p. 134.

12. *Ibid.*, p. 135.

13. *Ibid.*, p. 142.

14. *Ibid.*, p. 205.

15. *Ibid.*, p. 213.

16. National Committee on Governmental Accounting, quoted in Moak and Killian, *op. cit.*, p. 213.

17. *Ibid.*, p. 214.

18. *Ibid.*

PART Four

Evaluation

Introduction

Evaluating Programs

Evaluation research has a curious history. Indeed, the development of evaluation research reflects much the same forces, imperatives, and influences as make the area such a challenge for current community practitioners.

At the turn of the century some of the earliest efforts to evaluate public education and health programs can be traced to the sincere interest (and political necessity) to improve literacy rates, help provide people with basic skills necessary for employment, and reduce the rate of death and disability caused by infectious disease. In the period prior to World War II perhaps the single best known set of studies was that undertaken from 1927 to 1932 in Chicago at Western Electric's Hawthorne Works. Jointly sponsored by Harvard University and the American Telephone and Telegraph Company, these studies sought to guide management in improving worker productivity by identifying sources of employee satisfaction and dissatisfaction.

New Deal social planning programs generated many evaluation efforts. Stephan, for example, suggested one possibility in relation to public housing.

> Do slums make slum people or do slum people make the slums? Will changing the living conditions significantly change the social behavior of the people affected? The public housing projects may furnish the made-to-order test tubes to help in answering these fascinating and bewildering questions.[1]

The political response to the rise of fascism included support for the seminal leadership studies undertaken by Lewin, and later by Lippitt and White, that explored the efficacy of democratic and authoritarian

---

[1] A. S. Stephan, "Prospects and Possibilities: The New Deal and the New Social Research," *Social Forces* 13 (May, 1935), p. 515.

approaches. World War II served as the impetus for a number of evaluation studies, especially the work done by Stauffer and his associates on American soldiers.[2] Morale, personnel policies, and propaganda were evaluated. Comprehensive, publicly well-financed evaluation studies emerged through the late 1940s and 1950s. Typical research focused on delinquency prevention, slum "clearance," prison reform, mental health treatment modalities, and group work and community organization. Largely under the auspices of the United Nations, evaluations of community development efforts in emerging and developing countries were undertaken.

Burgeoning federal funds for evaluation enabled it to become—along with poverty—one of the growth industries of the 1960s. The retreat from social programs in the 1970s also brought with it a new emphasis on evaluation for accountability: Are we getting what we paid for? The political struggles intensified for control of what was evaluated, who did the evaluating, with how much money, and with what proposed consequences. In the most recent period, evaluation research has become a widely accepted part of social policy making and public administration. Since federal expenditures for evaluation research are currently estimated at almost the $1 billion level annually,[3] to say nothing of privately and organizationally internally supported evaluation, it would seem wise to regard the political and economic aspects of evaluation as no less significant than the programmatic ones.

Reviewing the historical development of evaluation sensitizes us both to the field's major directions and some of the constraints which shape them, and thus serves as a framework in which to consider how we might best go about appraising community programs.

At best the impact and effectiveness of community practice programs are hard to demonstrate. Probably no other area of social work presents as many difficulties for evaluators, administration, staff, and client populations. But the need for more precise measurement is clear and growing. Today practitioners must be prepared to be accountable for their work. At the same time, most programs can benefit greatly by better specification of the relationship between our efforts and goals to which they are directed. To try to remain aloof from more rigorous scrutiny of our work will increasingly deny important resources to community programs and eventually jeopardize their existence. If practitioners do not soon become more amenable to joining in the process of evaluation, they are likely to find influence over its terms and conditions beyond their grasp. The potential for improving social programs is enormous. However, the state of evaluation (science and art) suggests that skepticism as well as support is healthy.

How should evaluation be defined? One definition which we like because it is broad and emphasizes the relationship between aspects of decision making and evaluation is:

---

[2]S. A. Stauffer et al., *The American Soldier: Combat and Its Aftermath* (Manhattan, Kans.: Military Affairs/Aerospace Historian, 1949).

[3]For example, see P. H. Rossi and H. E. Freeman, *Evaluation: A Systematic Approach,* 2d ed. (Beverly Hills, Calif.: Sage, 1982), p. 19.

The process of determining the significance or amount of success a particular intervention has had in terms of costs and benefits and goal attainment. It is also concerned with assessing adequacy of performance, appropriateness of the stated goal, the feasibility of attaining it, as well as the value or impact of unintended outcomes.[4]

This perspective on evaluation seems particularly useful for those who must decide whether programs are to be continued, modified, drastically altered, or ended. Seeing evaluation as a process rather than a product also leads in the direction of policy maker, administrator, staff, and client involvement.

What basic criteria might be used to judge the success or failure of a given program? Suchman provides us with the following:[5]

1. *Effort*—What goes into the program (without regard to what comes out).
2. *Performance*—What comes out of the program (without regard to effort).
3. *Adequacy of Performance*—The relationship of the performance to total need (among the population addressed by the program).
4. *Efficiency*—The relationship of effort to outcome or impact in terms of costs, as compared with alternative approaches.
5. *Process*—How did the program get where it went (including unintended consequences, desirable and undesirable).

The commonsense quality of these criteria lends credence to the possibility that they be used to differentiate stronger and weaker program aspects and thus contribute to the improvement of social programs.

Another key perspective on the process of evaluation, suggested by Tripodi, Fellin, and Epstein,[6] involves looking carefully at the stages through which all social programs must go (at least those that manage to get underway). The first is program initiation, the stage at which ideas are translated into a basic strategy or plan of action and the necessary resources secured. The second stage is program contact, in which the program staff attempt to become actively involved with the target client group (and address both limiting and facilitating conditions in the physical and psychological environments). Finally, there is the program implementation stage, during which the intervention modes of the program are applied and services are delivered. These stages are important because often they must be considered separately, and judged on their individual merits. Thus, for example, the services provided during implementation may be hampered by an inadequacy in the mobilization of needed resources during program initiation rather than because of any deficiency in the service delivery system

---

[4]Robert Washington, draft manuscript on Program Evaluation, 1975, p. 4.

[5]Edward Suchman, *Evaluative Research* (New York: Russell Sage Foundation, 1967).

[6]Tony Tripodi, Phillip Fellin, Irwin Epstein, *Social Program Evaluation* (Itasca, Ill.: F. E. Peacock, 1971).

established. Each stage may be appraised in terms of specific subgoals or incremental goals instead of overarching program objectives. In general, the viewpoint of "differential evaluation"—assessment in terms of different program aspects—seems a modest but sound stance for the practitioner involved in program evaluation.

The authors selected for this section do not represent a single theory of, or orientation toward, evaluation. Rather they offer perspectives on the strategy, tactics, and techniques of evaluation that can be helpful to the practitioner whose program is being evaluated and to the practitioner-evaluator.

Carol Weiss's article is particularly appropriate because it addresses the tensions, controversies, confusions, and "politics" of the evaluation process. Clear and specific suggestions are made for how these may be lessened, including an appraisal of how practitioners can be contributing partners in the evaluation process.

While the context of Darwin Solomon's article is the small communities of Saskatchewan, the suggestions he develops seem applicable to program evaluation in large cities, even in the largest metropolitan areas. The reasons for evaluation, who should do the evaluation, steps in evaluation, and practical problems in evaluation are explored in turn. Taking a step backward for a broader perspective, Robert Washington's article presents four basic frameworks in which program evaluation can take place—the systems model, the goal attainment model, the impact model, and the behavioral model. The strengths and limitations of each approach are explored and assessed.

The article on utilization of data by Richard Douglass is an original attempt to lay out some basic ways of quantifying and depicting data. It is addressed to practitioners and the kind of community information with which they are very often confronted. Finally, John Gottman and Robert Clasen's "Troubleshooting Guide" is a handy index of basic evaluation concepts and offers illustrations of the ways in which they may be applied in action situations.

What is to be made of these articles in light of the special constraints and pressures of the 1980s? The increased scrutiny of human service programs, the drastic cuts in social services, and the sharply declining job market for community practitioners all need to be taken into account. The rapid changes in computer technology have led to a speed and efficiency of information flow for which community practitioners and program managers are ill-prepared. The tendency toward cost accounting and "sunset" perspectives has jeopardized many community-based efforts with hard-to-count objectives. It will be hard but necessary to balance the demand for accountability with desire for knowledge building and useful feedback.

At most, program evaluation is a difficult, complex task. At the least, it is so co-mingled with the survival needs of organizations and political pressures brought by interest groups that a clear focus on assessing and improving programs is well nigh impossible.

In the current era of budgetary restrictions and conservative ideology, evaluation will not often be separated from the political process. However, it must remain as a vital part of the assessment of social change efforts at the community level.

John L. Erlich

25. THE TURBULENT SETTING OF THE ACTION PROGRAM

Carol H. Weiss

A characteristic of evaluation research that differentiates it from most other kinds of research is that it takes place in an action setting. Something else besides research is going on; there is a program serving people. In fact, the service program is the more important element on the scene. The research is an appendage, an also-present, a matter of secondary priority. Researchers frequently propose changing the order of priority, and with some justification. If we do not find out whether the program is really doing what it is supposed to be doing, how do we know whether it is worth having at all? But whatever the cogency of the argument in any particular circumstance, the program almost universally remains the first order of business. The evaluation has to adapt itself to the program environment and disrupt operations as little as possible.

Obviously, some interference will take

Reproduced by permission of the author. Carol H. Weiss, *Evaluation Research: Methods for Assessing Program Effectiveness*, 1972, pp. 92–109. Reprinted by permission of Prentice-Hall, Inc., Englewood Cliffs, New Jersey.

place. For one thing, data have to be collected. Staff members and program participants will be asked questions, observed, asked to fill out forms. Certain research requirements are uncompromisable. But all too often, evaluators ask for more information than they need or will ever use. With a clear focus for the study and some self-restraint, they can lower their demands and lessen their intrusion. But however cooperative and congenial the evaluator may be, there are some features of an action setting that can create serious research problems. We will discuss three in this article: (1) the tendency of the program to change while it is being evaluated, (2) the relationships between evaluators and program personnel, and (3) the fact that the program is embedded in an organizational system and that the nature of the system will have consequences for outcomes.

THE SHIFTING PROGRAM

In an earlier chapter [not reproduced here] we anguished over the complexity of social programs and recommended serious attention to monitoring, describing, and classifying program characteristics. The conscientious evaluator, heeding this advice, completes his specification of the program and files it away. Then in midstream, while the evaluation is still going on, the program slithers out of his carefully constructed categories. Conditions change and the program changes.

It may change little by little, as practitioners see that present methods are not working and conscientiously innovate until they find satisfactory arrangements. Perhaps changes in clientele or in community conditions lead to subtle changes in activities and principles. Or the program may change quite suddenly. More money becomes available—or less. Staff members resign, and staff with different viewpoints or qualifications are hired. The political winds shift, and old relationships are shut off. A decision is made in Washington or the state capitol to discontinue certain styles of operation and adopt others. Such factors affect even programs set up as "demonstrations," "models," or "social experiments." The longer and more complex the program, the more likely it is to experience change. For the evaluator even to know that the program is changing requires periodic stock-taking. He has to be in close enough touch to talk to directors and staff, examine records, perhaps attend meetings or observe the program in session. One signal that should alert him to turn up on the scene is a change in top program management.

If the program has altered course, what does the evaluator do? If he goes ahead as if he were studying the same program, he will never know what it was that led to observed effects or the lack of them—the old program, the new one, the transition, or some combination of everything going on. If he drops the original evaluation and tries to start over again under the changed circumstances, he may lack appropriate baseline data. He may not have measures relevant to the new goals and program procedures.[1] Further, he has no guarantee that the same kind of shift will not occur again.

One thing he can do is update his original specification of the program through continuing observation and definition. He can develop a dynamic rather than a static model of the program to categorize it in terms of its movement as well as its conceptual location. This makes for a more complex description of what the program is, but one more in touch with reality.[2] That, you may think, is all very nice; we are certainly for program descriptions that are dynamic and accurate over those that are static and wrong. But in evaluation, we usually want to learn which component, which strategy, of the program is associated with success. How does even an accurate dynamic description help us here?

The Issue for the Evaluator

The way that the issue is frequently posed: How can we hold the program steady? The assumption is that when things are changing, there is no way of separating out the useful components from those that are neutral or counterproductive. Continuity of input seems essential for any fair test of what the effects of that input are likely to be. Observers have proposed a variety of solutions. Some authors, and Fairweather is a good example,[3] recommend that when innovative programs are being tested, the researcher should be in control of the entire operation. Then the program will be conducted with evaluation requirements in the forefront and random changes will be fended off. Even when the researcher is not in control, he can still play the role of advocate for program maintenance. Freeman and Sherwood suggest that the evaluator has the responsibility to hold the program to its original concepts and principles. He should stand over it "like a snarling watchdog" to prevent program practitioners from altering its operations.[4]

Mann, after reviewing several hundred evaluations, found that programs are too complex and variable in operation to provide fair tests of program principles. For drawing conclusions about the relative merits of different approaches, he gives up on action settings and recommends taking programs back to the laboratory. There small segments of program can be studied rigorously, and successful practices can be identified for given conditions. Once this type of basic knowledge is obtained, the individual components can be built back up into operable programs.[5] Weiss and Rein have looked at large-scale programs that are exploratory and unclear in orientation, that inevitably cast about for new directions and methods. In cases such as community-action or model-cities programs, they believe that it is better to discard the investigation of goal achievement altogether. The researcher will learn more from careful analysis of what is actually going on. He can investigate such pressing issues as why and how programs change, how agencies absorb new inputs of money and direction and emerge relatively unscathed, how adaptations are worked out between innovative programs and resistant systems.[6]

Perhaps it is possible to redefine the controversy. Holding the program

steady, let alone controlling it, is beyond the authority of most evaluators in most settings I have seen. There *are* programs that remain clear, coherent, and intact by themselves without the evaluator's cajolery or imprecations. But if they are under strong pressures to change, there is a limit to what he can do to hold back the tide. On the other hand, surrender to complexity and retreat to the laboratory look like a cop-out. It is true that many programs are rushed into the field prematurely without the painstaking developmental work required for effective service. We are in a hurry for solutions; we want to serve thousands of people right away. Although the program may be inadequately conceptualized, we hope that the whole thing will somehow work and that at our leisure, we can sort out the features responsible for the success. It is worth heeding Mann's advice that more research should be directed toward the careful development and testing of program components. Furthermore, for the accumulation of a body of tested knowledge about the relative effectiveness of strategies, a grab-bag collection of disparate evaluations is hardly the ideal basis.

But the laboratory is not the real world. In the artificiality of the laboratory, all manner of things seem to work that do not survive their brush with operating conditions. Even optimum program components will get contaminated when they emerge, and further research will have to be done under an almost limitless set of circumstances to define the "best" components for each contaminated condition.

Some Practical Approaches

To cope with such problems, Suchman has proposed a four-stage developmental process.[7] He differentiates a pilot phase, when program development proceeds on a trial-and-error basis; a model phase, when a defined program strategy is run under controlled conditions; a prototype phase, when the model program is subjected to realistic operating conditions; and an institutionalized phase, when the program is an ongoing part of the organization. It is only in the model phase that the program must be held stable for experimental evaluation. At other stages, less rigorous study suffices, and variation in input is not only tolerated but expected. If an agency were committed to such a rational course of development (and maintained it!), it would effectively resolve the issue of program shifts. The evaluator may find it rewarding to encourage the agency to move toward such clear demarcation of program phases, with appropriate evaluation at each step.

The approach that Weiss and Rein propose is, I think, refreshingly relevant for programs of the scale and ambiguity that they discuss, although they give only fragmentary clues to the methods by which such complex processes can be analyzed. What they recommend is basically a study of the implementation process, rather than evaluation. We know that implementation is a critical juncture between the best-laid plans of program developers and the "gang aft agley" of operation.[8] The differences in perspective between planners and operators, the pressures that beset the local program, the responses necessary for survival and support all alter and reshape the original concept. Understanding what happens in the political and social complexities of broad-aim intervention programs may well be a priority order of business if we are to learn how to develop programs more realistically, to reduce the slippage between intent and action, and to address social problems with greater effect. Present inattention to this facet of program life is difficult to understand or condone.

Nevertheless, study of implementation does not supplant evaluation of outcomes. Critical as it is to learn more about the dynamics of operation, it remains important to find out the effects of the resulting programs on people and institutions. The two research efforts should be complementary. As we learn more about implementation, we can begin to identify vital elements in the operating systems and move toward description and measurement of them. In time, we can combine the study of program process with the study of outcomes. In the interim, it is not unimportant to know how the intended beneficiaries of the program are faring.

Evaluators used to yell and pound on the table that program staff should not wait to call them in until the program was in operation. They wanted not only to be in on the ground floor when the program was being planned; they wanted to "help dig the foundation."[9] Many program people have learned the lesson; evaluators are often in from the start. Now, however, it becomes clear that there is such a thing as premature evaluation.[10] Evaluations begin before the program has found its goals, its functions, or generally accepted ways of work. An analysis of the system can help program developers as they seek direction. It is a rewarding research activity, but it is not evaluation. Evaluation comes later, when there is an entity, however complex and interrelated, that can be defined, tested, and replicated. In the interests of social policy, we cannot postpone this part of the study too long.

If there is some recognizable set of principles and procedures that can be called a program, I am not sure that it is necessary to hold it steady in the arbitrary and argumentative way in which most raisers-of-the-issue propose. Programs almost inevitably drift. If the program and the drift are classified and analyzed, it seems possible to attribute the ensuing effects to the program in terms of how it worked and will often work in this disorderly world. Here are some suggestions that may be workable:

1. Take frequent periodic measures of program effect (for example, monthly assessments in programs of education, training, therapy), rather than limiting collection of outcome data to one point in time.[11]
2. Encourage a clear transition from one program approach to another. If changes are going to be made, try to see that A is done for a set period, then B, and C.
3. Clarify the assumptions and procedures of each phase and classify them systematically.
4. Keep careful records of the persons who participated in each phase. Rather than lumping all participants together, analyze outcomes in terms of the phase(s) of program in which each person participated.
5. Press for a recycling of earlier program phases. Sometimes this happens naturally; on occasion, it can be engineered. If it is possible, it provides a way to check on earlier conclusions.
6. Seek to set aside funds and get approval for smaller-scale evaluation of (at least) one program phase or component that will remain stable for a given period.[12] For this venture,

experimental procedures can be applied, even though less rigorous and more flexible methods may be sufficient in other program areas.
7. If nothing works and the program continues to meander (chaos would be the proper word in some contexts), consider jettisoning the evaluation framework in favor of meticulous analysis of the what, how, and why of events.

RELATIONSHIPS WITH PROGRAM PERSONNEL

The evaluator works on the turf of another profession. His relationships with the program professionals (teachers, recreation workers, trainers, correction officers) can range from friendly and cooperative to extremes of hostility. Occasionally, an evaluation closes down before completion because of the effective resistance of operating program personnel. The more usual situation, however, is wary coexistence.

Sources of Friction

What causes friction? There are many contributing factors.

Personality Differences. Some observers cite the personality differences between people who go into program practice and those who go into research. The researcher is likely to be a detached individual, interested in ideas and abstractions. He thinks in terms of generalizations and analytical categories. His interest is in the long-term acquisition of knowledge, rather than the day-to-day issues of program operation. He seems cool, uncommitted to any program philosophy or position, without personal loyalties to the program or the organization. As Leonard Duhl has said, the researcher is a "marginal man."

The practitioner, on the other hand, is likely to be a warm, outgoing personality. (This at least is the common expectation in such service professions as teaching, therapy, health care, social work, and occupational counseling, although it is clearly not true of everyone and may not even be the norm in some occupations.) The practitioner generally is intensely concerned about people, specifics, the here and now. He is committed to action. He finds the researcher's skepticism uncongenial, and he finds it difficult to warm up to him as a human being.

Differences in Role. Other observers believe that differences in role are more significant than any underlying personality variables. Basically, a practitioner has to believe in what he is doing; a researcher has to question it. This difference in perspective creates inevitable tensions.[13] Whatever their initial personal or value characteristics, once they go about their divergent tasks, they are almost bound to see things differently. Paula Kleinman tells a story about her experience as a graduate student working on a "training-and-evaluation" project. The project had a staff of four. At first they were assigned interchangeably to training and to evaluation tasks. Everyone got along very well, but there was concern that their commitment to the training program might "contaminate" the evaluation data. In the interest of objectivity, the group was divided in half, two people assuming training roles and the other two assigned to evaluation. Almost immediately, the comradely relationships deteriorated and dissension developed. The main issue was that the training group wanted to use the data from the preprogram questionnaires in later training sessions in order to enrich the training; the evaluators opposed the release of the data on grounds that trainees' knowledge of Time 1 answers might artificially alter Time 2 responses. Differences in role and responsibility had introduced frictions.

Lack of Clear Role Definition. Evaluation often requires practitioners to take on new roles, such as referring people to the "experimental" program, adhering to the specific program approaches (curriculums, treatment modalities), being tested, collecting data, collaborating with the evaluator. The new roles may not be clearly defined in advance and become apparent only after a series of disputes with the evaluators. Even when roles are not new, the division of roles between practitioner and evaluator may be murky. Tensions can arise over differences in interpretation about who has responsibility for which functions. Particularly frustrating are uncertainties about the authority structure; it is often unclear who has authority to resolve the differences that arise.[14]

Conflicting Goals, Values, Interests, Frames of Reference. The practitioner is concerned with service. He sees evaluation as a diversion and possibly even a threat. It seems to take things away from the program—money, time, administrators' attention—and promises the dubious return of a "report card." The evaluator, after all, is judging the value of his work, and by extension, his professional competence and *him*. The ultimate result of the evaluation, if it is used in decision making, will affect the future of his particular project and perhaps his own job. It may be perfectly true that the purpose of the evaluation is to add to knowledge and to rationalize social policy making, but it is he and his project who will bear the consequences if the results show project failure.

Sometimes practitioners see the

evaluation as part and parcel of an innovation in programming that violates cherished concepts of service and tradition. They visit their dislike on both the program and its evaluation component. If the program runs counter to traditional agency values (for example, if it stresses social factors in the rehabilitation of mental patients when the accepted emphasis has been on psychological factors), they may actively or passively undermine the program and—as a consequence—the evaluation.

The practitioner sometimes questions the worth of the evaluator's research tools. He sees the measuring instruments as crude, good enough only to pick up gross changes. He doubts their ability to detect the subtle effects—such as growth in a person's self-confidence—that are vital effects of the program. The program practitioner on the spot sees growth and achievement that the evaluator, with his "insensitive measuring devices," misses.

On the other hand, of course, the practitioner is an interested party, and he may be seeing changes that are not actually there. While the practitioner levels charges of "insensitive indicators," the evaluator counter-charges with "self-serving observation." There may be some element of truth on both sides, but the implications for the evaluator are clear. First, if he is to win the support of practitioners, he has to develop instruments that measure the factors that practitioners believe are the key effects of the program. They may believe that they deal in attitudes and values, perceptions and beliefs; if these are important program effects, he should find effective ways to measure them. Second, he may seek to convince practitioners that programs are almost always behavioral in intent. They aim to change what people *do*. His measuring tools will be designed to detect the vital effect—the change in behavior.

There is another aspect to this general resistance. In human service professions, practitioners deal with individuals. They are very much aware of individual differences, and they gain esteem and professional recognition from their sensitivity to the facets that differentiate one human being from another and their ability to tailor service to individual needs. The evaluator, on the other hand, deals in statistics—means, percentages, correlation coefficients—gross measures that lump people together. (He may, of course, break out the data by sex, age, race, length of program experience, and other factors, but that does not vitiate the practitioners' pervasive sense of mass data.) In confronting the evaluation data, the practitioner seldom sees that the conclusions are relevant to the specific people with whom he is working. It may be true, for example, that long periods of incarceration are associated with poor postprison adjustment, but the correctional officer cannot really believe that this datum deserves much weight when he has all his knowledge and experience and Johnny Jones standing in front of him.[15]

Institutional Characteristics. When an agency has a history of internal conflict, evaluation may be viewed with particular suspicion. Staff are apt to see the evaluators as management hatchet men— or as the agents of one faction out to do in another. Evaluators' secrecy—their refusal to share data prematurely, their insistence on the confidentiality of individual records—may look threatening in a troubled organization. In fact, the staff of any agency where grievances are strong and satisfaction low may resent the evaluation as another cross to bear.

Other aspects of the institutional

setting have consequences as well. Evaluator-practitioner relationships are affected by such aspects of the agency as the administrative structure, the fiscal and bookkeeping arrangements for the evaluation, supervisory practices, openness of communication channels, and the state of relationships with cooperating agencies who refer participants, receive referrals, or offer complementary services.[16] Where ambiguity and fragmented authority flourish, the evaluation is apt to suffer the strains of misperception, conflicting goals, and inadequate support.

Issues That Lead to Friction

What are the issues that provoke conflict?

Data Collection. The request that practitioners administer questionnaires, interviews, and tests to clients is a frequent source of trouble. Often, the evaluator wants the practitioner too to fill out forms or submit to interviews and observation. The practitioner is trying to get a job done. He finds the intrusion time-consuming and disruptive.[17] Since he sees no obvious payoff to the program from the information collected (much of it looks like pretty abstruse and irrelevant stuff), he boggles at the amount of time away from the task at hand. Even when the evaluator has his own staff to collect the information, there are occasional conflicts over access to people, annoyance, and scheduling.

Changes in Record-Keeping Procedures. If the evaluator seeks to collect information from the agency records, another set of squabbles may arise. The records are almost never complete enough and well enough kept for his purposes. (This appears to be a good generalization no matter what the type of

agency.) Once he starts asking that practitioners get the records up to date and fill in the missing information, he encounters resistance. If in addition, he has the temerity to ask that the records be kept in a different form, with information items coded to suit the purposes of the evaluation, the disruption of established ways of work can create further friction.

Selection of Program Participants. The evaluator usually wants a say in how participants are selected for the program. He is likely to opt for some kind of random procedure. Practitioners, on the other hand, usually want to choose participants on the basis of their amenability to help, the seriousness of their need, or other obvious or subtle characteristics. Random procedures negate their professional skills of diagnosis and service planning. But what the practitioner sees as responsible individual selection makes the participant group "special" in unspecified ways, and thus makes comparison between participants and controls useless as an indication of program effect. Further, the evaluator does not know to what other populations the results are generalizable. Selection, then, is a common bone of contention.

Control Groups. Another problem is control groups. Evaluators want them for the obvious purpose of ruling out rival explanations for the effects observed. Practitioners frequently regard them as a denial of service to needy people that violates all the ethical imperatives of service professions. Only when there are more applicants than available program slots are they likely to accept the researcher's requirements for controls. And when participants drop out of the program, it is not unknown for practitioners to raid the control group for new clients. Or they can upgrade services to controls who are supposedly receiving routine treatment in a competitive effort to "look good." It is difficult enough for evaluators to maintain contact and cooperation with controls who are not receiving the new showcase program, but when practitioners regard this as a "silly frill," they can further sabotage the effort.

Feedback of Information into the Program. Feedback—the communication of early evaluation information to affect later stages of the program—is another issue. Practitioners want to see the program improved by whatever means. If evaluation data can show them ways to increase effectiveness, they do not see why evaluators should object. (Isn't the purpose of evaluation to improve the program?) Of course, that may or may not be the purpose of a particular evaluation. When the purpose is longer range—for example; to decide on the worth of a particular program theory and approach—the evaluator wants the basic program model to remain stable for a long enough time to study its effects. He doesn't want his data to be used to shake things up drastically. But refusal to help is viewed as lack of commitment to the organization. The evaluator is refusing to come to grips with practical problems; he is not accepting any share of the responsibility for the program. (In the longer run, of course, when he has findings to report, he may play an active role. But in the interim, staff members see him as aloof and uncommitted.)

Status Rivalry. Practitioners on occasion resent what they see as the higher status accorded researchers. They slave away and do the day-to-day drudgery, while the evaluator observes, measures, writes a report, and collects all the kudos—programmatic, academic, and sometimes financial as well.[18] As they see it, the evaluator asks them to make all the sacrifices while he collects all the rewards, through publication and professional recognition. They are likely to be particularly resentful when the evaluator produces the report, turns it in, and goes away without acknowledging any further obligation to the program. He appears to be milking the program of opportunities to further his own career without giving much in return.

Of course, should the evaluator try to get a hearing for his report in decision-making councils, some practitioners will not be happy, either. For them, the report usually means some kind of impending change. No evaluation report finds *everything* in perfect shape.[19] They may or may not agree with the cogency of the findings, but the almost inevitable implication is that they should change their ideas and procedures and perhaps learn new skills as well. Change is hard, and the evaluator who suggests it wins no popularity contest. If the evaluation is less than convincing, then they see little reason to depart from ways of work that have long stood them well.

Lessening the Friction

This is an imposing catalog of sources of conflict, and it may seem that evaluators and practitioners are inevitably at odds. This is not necessarily so. With good communication and careful planning, most evaluations can proceed in a calm and cooperative atmosphere. If practitioners and evaluators rarely become close chums, they can usually settle their disputes in amicable fashion under appropriate conditions. When it comes time to put the results of evaluation into practice, differences may crop up again. . . . Here we will talk about ways of assuaging potential frictions.

Very little empirical research has been done on arrangements and methods that lessen tension in applied research projects. We therefore have to depend for guidance on the "received wisdom," the generally accepted lessons of experience. Six main conditions appear to be most successful in enabling people to function together comfortably.

Support from Administrators. As previously mentioned, it is essential to involve project administrators and managers in planning an evaluation. Through dialog with them, the evaluator develops insight and focus, and the administrators gain commitment to the study and to its eventual use in decision making. The support of top administrators is also crucial to getting and maintaining the cooperation of the program staff. They provide incentive, recognition, and reward for staff members who help, rather than hinder, the evaluation enterprise.

Involvement of Practitioners in the Evaluation. Involving the practitioners in planning the evaluation has further payoffs. A first benefit of bringing them in is that they gain understanding of what evaluation is all about. They learn what it is for and how it proceeds. This knowledge dispels some of the sense of threat (Why are they investigating what I'm doing?) and some of the suspicion generated by the presence of alien characters asking questions. Second, they have information and ideas to contribute. They can teach the norms of the project, the realities of its operation, and its jargon. Their contributions often enrich the evaluator's understanding and the sophistication of his study and make the evaluation more relevant to the needs of the agency. They can also keep him from making *faux pas* or unacceptable requests. Early consultation often forestalls later explosions. Further, they are more likely to be cooperative about new procedures and extra work when they see the sense of the requests. They are particularly likely to cooperate if they have had a chance to *contribute* to the development of the new procedures. When group meetings have been held and each member has seen group consensus develop on acceptance of the evaluator's requests, support for the study solidifies.

Although involvement in the early phases of the evaluation is important, it is equally necessary to continue communication through the life of the project. Each person whose work is affected by the evaluation should be kept informed and be given a chance to express his ideas and concerns. Whatever part the program staff plays during the course of the evaluation, the end of the study signals another opportunity for involvement. The evaluator has a responsibility to present his findings to the staff. He may find it stimulating, too, to ask for their help in interpreting the results and drawing conclusions for future action. He is not bound to accept their interpretations, but more than one investigator has found that they have interesting insights. Once they overcome their defensiveness, they can be useful colleagues in understanding the causes of past successes and failures, the process by which the program got where it is, what should be done in the future, and how to make future directions palatable to interested parties.[20]

Minimizing Disruptions. Another tension reliever is adherence to the rules of the road. If evaluators have the good manners to recognize program priorities and limit their demands to indispensable issues, practitioners are likely to follow suit. The trick is to know which issues cannot be compromised and which are susceptible to negotiation. Far too often, evaluators impose heavier demands than their needs warrant. They ask eighty questions instead of twenty; they administer twelve batteries of tests when four would suffice. The reason is usually that they are not clear about what they are looking for, and they take all possible precautions not to miss anything that may turn out to be important. Better focus of the study at the outset—including clearer definition of the theory and expected process of the program—would lessen the zeal to cast a wide and undiscriminating net. Evaluators can become less of a nuisance as they become better informed.

Hiring research assistants to collect evaluation data, rather than asking already-burdened program staff to take on extra duties, is a good investment. Not only do they have more time and knowledge of research requirements, but their allegiance is not divided. Their commitment is to the quality of the data, not to the client or the program. When there is a separate research staff, however, the demarcation of duties should be clear to everyone. The researchers should not be suspected of invading the practitioners' domain or duplicating their work.

Emphasis on theory. Almost every evaluation is out to discover more than whether this particular program works in this particular time and place with this staff and these participants. Even the most practical manager wants to know whether it will work next year with different participants and some changes in staff and emphasis. It is important to be able to generalize about the basic approach that underlies the program. Is an educational film *as a technique* useful in changing people's use of medical services? Are small-group discussions more effective in changing attitudes on discrimination than lectures?

There is some kind of theory implicit in almost every program. If the evaluator can draw it to the surface and make it the central focus of the evaluation effort, he is on the way to alleviating the very real uneasiness that practitioners feel about being judged and having their performances critically rated. It is nice to think that if it is the *theory* of the program that is being judged, the practitioners can become eager partners in the investigation. This strikes me as overoptimistic. Practitioners realize that the evaluation, however theoretical in concept, is concerned with real events and can have real (and possibly baleful) consequences for the future of the program.[21] But an emphasis on theory can widen the perspective.

The Feedback of Useful Information. If the evaluator can provide information that managers and practitioners need, he gains their support, even for some of his more bothersome and esoteric enterprises. Sometimes he can happily provide the information with no unpleasant side effects. But sometimes feedback, by changing subsequent program inputs or by contaminating later responses, would jeopardize his study. In that event, the best solution may be a separate data collection effort, apart from the evaluation, to satisfy program needs. In-house evaluation departments can do this more easily, both psychologically and financially, than outside research organizations, and they are more amenable to churning out the required data (and maybe even a speech or two for program people to give). This kind of practical side benefit can serve as an illustration of the utility of research data and increase practitioners' regard for the usefulness of the evaluator and his skills.

Clear Role Definitions and Authority Structure. People should know what is expected of them and of others. There should be clear understanding of the scope and limits of their roles. If practitioners perceive some of their obligations to be incompatible (for example, teaching to the best of their ability *and* using only the one instructional method being evaluated), ways should be found to communicate, interpret, and—if necessary—change role prescriptions in *advance* of the onset of the program.

When differences arise between program and evaluation personnel that cannot be reconciled by negotiation, the lines of authority should be clear.[22] Everyone should understand the channels of appeal and the person or groups of persons who will make decisions. If interagency relations are involved, the situation may be complex but it is even more vital to establish clear lines of jurisdictional authority.[23]

THE SOCIAL CONTEXT OF THE PROGRAM

Every program takes place in a setting that has consequences for its effectiveness. The primary context is the organization that sponsors and conducts the program. Even if the programs themselves are highly similar, one would expect differences between the outcomes of a community organization program run by the Chamber of Commerce and one run by a radical student group, or between a foreign technical assistance program supported by the U.S. Department of Defense and one supported by UNESCO. Programs in turn have effects on the organizations that run them. The effects may be favorable (raising the prestige of the agency), competitive and draining (drawing the most competent and committed staff from the regular run of programs into the "special" program), destructive (diverting the organization from the mission at which it is skilled and enmeshing it in programs and conflicts it is poorly equipped to handle).

The larger social frameworks of neighborhood and community also affect programs and their consequences. So, too, do national systems of values, laws, and sensitivities. Family planning programs will be welcomed in one country and boycotted in another.['] Local mores even determine what can be studied and what cannot. Thus, new nations or those engaged in modernization may be extremely sensitive to studies revealing the extent of poverty or maldistribution of wealth.[24] In the United States, drug use is defined as a criminal activity. Programs for addicts have therefore been under pressure to regard abstinence from drug use as the only possible goal. Meyer and Bigman report that until recently, it was almost impossible for a program to aim for anything less than abstinence, or for evaluators to study program results in terms of improved social functioning without regard to whether the patient was on or off drugs.[25] Hardy souls have now raised questions about alternative goals and criteria of program success.

Just as the program is embedded in a social context, so too is the person who participates. He does not come to the program empty, unattached, or unanchored. He has beliefs and values, he has friends and relatives, habits, patterns of behavior, and ideas. Often the pull of his existing social arrangements works against the efforts of the program to bring about change. This may mean that program efforts are inundated by the flood of other influences which are part of his everyday routine. One implication for evaluation may be the value of exploring the supportive and inhibiting features of the interpersonal context. It might investigate the attitudes and behaviors of key people in the participant's environment (family, co-workers, teachers) during the time the program is trying to instill new patterns of behavior. For example, for in-service training programs that teach new styles of work, the responses of supervisors back on the job may be crucial for the retention or fade-out of the lessons taught. Brim found that among mothers urged to adopt new feeding practices, husbands' reactions—although they did not influence the probability of trying the advised procedures—were influential in continuation of the trials and eventual adoption of the new practices.[26] Unless participants receive support from their social environment, or are at least freed from some of its binds, program efforts may founder. The evaluator who locates the operative sources of support or obstruction can help program planners direct the attention to reaching and affecting these groups and thereby strengthen program impact.

Agencies are similarly affected by the pull of existing arrangements. Their efforts to run novel programs may run afoul of obligations to established constituencies, public reactions, or countervailing pressures. On the other hand, their most potent effects may be the rearrangement of traditional patterns of thought and behavior in other agencies. Legal service programs for the poor, for example, may have greater impact on the practices of public agencies that deal with poor people than their direct benefits to the clients themselves. Evaluation can find this out.

Evaluation need not be limited to local

effects or low horizons. Sometimes the most important influences on a program's success lie outside the program's immediate purview. Sometimes the most important consequences of a program are not the effects on participants directly but on other people, agencies, or community institutions. The lesson for the evaluator is: Be alert. The studies that are ultimately most practical and useful are often those that open our eyes to new elements on the scene.

NOTES

1. Sidney H. Aronson and Clarence C. Sherwood, "Researcher Versus Practitioner: Problems in Social Action Research," *Social Work*, Vol. XII, No. 4 (1967), pp. 89-96.
2. See Alfred P. Parsell, "Dynamic Evaluation: The Systems Approach to Action Research," SP-2423 (Santa Monica, Calif.: Systems Development Corporation, 1966).
3. George W. Fairweather, *Methods for Experimental Social Innovation* (New York: John Wiley, 1967), pp. 24-36.
4. Howard E. Freeman and Clarence C. Sherwood, "Research in Large-scale Intervention Programs," *Journal of Social Issues*, Vol. XXI, No. 1 (1965), pp. 11-28.
5. John Mann, "The Outcome of Evaluative Research," in *Changing Human Behavior* (New York: Charles Scribner's Sons, 1965), pp. 191-214.
6. Robert S. Weiss and Martin Rein, "The Evaluation of Broad-Aim Programs: A Cautionary Case and a Moral," *Annals of the American Academy of Political and Social Science*, Vol. 385 (September 1969), pp. 118-32.
7. Edward A. Suchman, "Action for What? A Critique of Evaluative Research," in *The Organization, Management, and Tactics of Social Research*, ed. Richard O'Toole (Cambridge, Mass.: Schenkman Publishing Co., 1970).
8. In defining the career of social problems, Herbert Blumer lists five stages, the fifth of which is "the transformation of the

official plan in its empirical implementation." He goes on to say, "Invariably to some degree, the plan as put into practice is modified, twisted and reshaped, and takes on unforeseen accretions." "Social Problems as Collective Behavior," *Social Problems*, Vol. XVII, No. 3 (1971), pp. 301, 304-5. For a description of federal planners' "naiveté" about the complexity of translating official plans into operating programs, see Walter Williams, "Developing an Evaluation Strategy for a Social Action Agency," *Journal of Human Resources*, Vol. IV, No. 4 (1969), pp. 451-65. He notes three aspects that impinge on implementation: How well articulated the plan is, how administratively capable the local staff is, how much authority the federal agency has to force compliance (or obversely, how much political insulation the local agency has to resist change).

9. Elizabeth Herzog, *Some Guide Lines for Evaluative Research* (Washington, D.C.: U.S. Department of Health, Education and Welfare, 1959), p. 84.

10. Nelson Aldrich, ed., "The Controversy over the More Effective Schools: A Special Supplement," *Urban Review*, Vol. II, No. 6 (1968), pp. 15-34. The evaluator himself believed that the study was premature.

11. For example, Nathan Caplan, "Treatment Intervention and Reciprocal Interaction Effects," *Journal of Social Issues*, Vol. XXIV, No. 1 (1968), pp. 63-88.

12. For further discussion see Edward L. McDill, Mary S. McDill, and J. Timothy Sprehe, *Strategies for Success in Compensatory Education: An Appraisal of Evaluation Research* (Baltimore, Md.: The Johns Hopkins Press, 1969), pp. 66-71.

13. See Hyman Rodman and Ralph L. Kolodny, "Organizational Strains in the Researcher-Practitioner Relationship," in *Applied Sociology: Opportunities and Problems*, ed. Alvin Gouldner and S. M. Miller (New York: The Free Press, 1965), pp. 93-113. For further discussion, see W. L. Slocum, "Sociological Research for Action Agencies: Some Guides and Hazards," *Rural Sociology*, Vol. XXI, No. 2 (1956), pp. 196-99; Joel Smith, Francis M. Sim, and Robert C. Bealer, "Client Structure and the Research Process," in *Human Organization Research*, ed. R. N. Adams and J. J. Preiss (Homewood, Ill.: Dorsey Press, 1960), Chap. 4; William F. Whyte and Edith Hamilton, *Action Research for Management* (Homewood, Ill.: Dorsey Press, 1964), pp. 209-21.

14. Carol H. Weiss, *Organizational Constraints on Evaluation Research* (New York: Bureau of Applied Social Research, 1971).

15. See Francis G. Caro, "Approaches to Evaluative Research: A Review," *Human Organization*, Vol. XXVIII, No. 2 (1969), pp. 87-99.

16. Conflicts over these issues and others are discussed in Gwen Andrew, "Some Observations on Management Problems in Applied Social Research," *The American Sociologist*, Vol. II, No. 2 (1967), pp. 84-89, 92.

17. A frustrating attempt to add the job of research interviewer to that of social caseworker is discussed in Michael A. LaSorte, "The Caseworker as Research Interviewer," *The American Sociologist*, Vol. III, No. 3 (1968), pp. 222-25.

18. For further discussion, see Rodman and Kolodny, *op. cit.*

19. In fact, the tendency to negative findings is a common feature of evaluations to which we will return in the next chapter. [Not printed here.]

20. See M. A. Steward, "The Role and Function of Educational Research—I," *Educational Research*, IX, No. I (1966), 3-6.

21. Aronson and Sherwood, op. cit.

22. For a case where the structure was unclear, see Hans Nagpaul, "The Development of Social Research in an Ad Hoc Community Welfare Organization," *Journal of Human Relations*, Vol. XIV, No. 4 (1966), pp. 620-33.

23. A first-rate analysis of this and related issues is given in D. B. Kandel and R. H. Williams, *Psychiatric Rehabilitation: Some Problems of Research* (New York: Atherton Press, 1964).

24. Ralph L. Beals, *Politics of Social Research* (Chicago: Aldine-Atherton, 1969), p. 27.

25. Alan S. Meyer and Stanley K. Bigman, "Contextual Considerations in Evaluating Narcotic Addiction Control Programs," *Proceedings of the Social Statistics Section* (Washington, D.C.: American Statistical Association, 1968), pp. 175-80.

26. Orville G. Brim, Jr., "The Acceptance of New Behavior in Child Rearing," *Human Relations,* Vol. VII (1954), pp. 473-91.

26. EVALUATING COMMUNITY PROGRAMS

Darwin D. Solomon

WHY EVALUATE PROGRAMS?

The question—*Why evaluate programs*—may seem unnecessary. Do we not constantly ask ourselves whether a program was worth the effort? Did we like it? Were our clients satisfied? Was it what we (or they) expected?—Less frequently, we may ask what was learned from it.

We Evaluate to Economize on Effort

In one typical Saskatchewan community, it was found that eighteen individuals were devoting an average of forty-four hours per week to meetings and community activities of various kinds. Often only a few citizens are deeply involved in programs designed to meet individual and group needs. Most leaders are constantly looking for ways to improve these efforts: They would like to see their investment of time and energy pay better dividends. Accurate evaluations of past efforts, applied to the planning of future programs, can help them achieve this.

Reprinted by permission of the author.

We Evaluate to Improve Programs

In one community the recreation board had been sponsoring a number of recreation projects for two years. There were a Little League Ball Club, hockey and baseball programs for older boys, a swimming pool; a start had been made on beautifying the park. Then, as a basis for further planning, the board, with the help of the community council, decided to make a study of the utilization of recreational facilities. A sample of citizens was asked how they spent their spare time, whether they participated in available activities, what they liked and disliked about them, and what changes and additions they would suggest.

As a result of the survey, a number of important changes were made. Special committees were set up to develop recreational opportunities for girls, young adults, and the elderly. A half-day workshop on leisure-time use in the community was to be held every other year in connection with the annual sports field-day, in order to enable leaders to review recreational programs and make needed adjustments. In working out these plans, the board and its committees used the resources and advice of the Fitness and Recreation Office of the Department of Education, Arts Board, Adult Education Division, and social scientists from the Center for Community Studies.

In this instance, the focus of the survey was on program improvement. Evaluation led to the realization that flexibility was required to meet the varying needs of the community. Opportunity was provided for citizen participation in future evaluation and planning. The community was learning to improve, rather than trying to prove what a good job it had done.

We Evaluate to Get Support for Programs

Citizens need to know what the effects of a program are if they are to give it their continued support.

The Loamville community council kept the public informed about its activities through news media and annual community meetings. Every year the council held an evaluation meeting to review accomplishments and weaknesses. This was followed by a session to plan the next year's program. Both events were well publicized. At the end of the second year, a public meeting had been held so as to involve a wider segment of the community in evaluation and planning and in setting priorities. By the third year, the council was well-known and widely supported. This was largely due to the following factors:

1. The council was able to prove that it had assisted in important projects and contributed to the progress of the community. Each member organiza-

tion was given credit for the part it had played.

2. A degree of objectivity was ensured by wide participation in the evaluation process. Distortions of fact, often due to a desire to prove success, cannot remain hidden for long and, if allowed to persist, are self-defeating in the long run.

3. Thanks to periodic evaluation, the council was able to work on weak points and present a stronger program every year. Thus its public image became associated with worthwhile improvements.

4. The people saw the council as *their* organization: They felt responsible for it.

We Evaluate to Determine Change in Conditions or Behaviour

Community progress is usually measured in terms of physical things produced, such as the number of street lights installed, city blocks paved, or buildings erected. Sometimes the activities resulting from programs are listed; but rarely are changes in people or the quality of the relationship among citizens seen as measures of progress.

To build its community hall, Westend had to co-ordinate the efforts of a large number of organizations and resource agencies. To maintain the hall and regulate its use by various groups, a continuation of these co-ordinative relationships was necessary. Leaders and citizens could not go back to their old ways of thinking and acting.

In another Saskatchewan community, the council's stated objectives were:

1. To co-ordinate suggestions presented by various community groups;

2. To create leadership;
3. To encourage citizens to examine their community.

But when they took stock of accomplishments, did they mention these purposes? No, they reported:

1. A recreation program and a recreation board set up;
2. Water and sewage-disposal systems installed;
3. A community hall built and operated by one organization.

They did not talk about the increased effectiveness of their leadership, better communications among groups, greater awareness of community problems and world affairs, and improvements in organizational participation by citizens.

A complete evaluation requires that:

1. Before the program is started, a decision be reached on the evidence of change to be used, and on the ways and means of obtaining it;
2. The evidence be gathered systematically and submitted to those who are to evaluate the program;
3. Sufficient time be allowed for hoped-for changes to take place before an attempt is made to evaluate them.

We Evaluate to Provide Personal Satisfaction and Security

Where the object of evaluation is personal satisfaction and assurance that one's efforts have been worthwhile, the following conditions must be met:

1. Tangible signs of progress are needed, especially in the early stages of a new program or organization. Goals should be stated and programs planned in such a way that solid accomplishment can be shown. Short-term goals should be seen as steps toward long-range ones.
2. Unflinching commitment and support by key persons and decision makers is needed for effective evaluation. Uncertainty or doubt expressed by leaders may hinder community participation and prevent utilization of the findings in subsequent program planning.
3. Evaluation should be seen, and provided for, as an ongoing function of program planning. Trouble spots pointed out can lead to ultimate satisfaction only if ways are found to overcome them; otherwise, frequent evaluations may cause unhappiness and anxiety and destroy confidence.
4. If necessary, the planner must be willing to revise goals and set more realistic standards of accomplishment. The more certain citizens are of progress toward their objectives, the more satisfaction they feel and the harder they will work.

INFORMATION NEEDED FOR EVALUATION

Programs of development start with two important points of reference: (a) the present situation or condition, and (b) the situation or condition (goal) to be reached. The program or project is the means used to get from one to the other.

To find out how we are doing, either at some mid-point or at the end of a project or program, a number of key questions must be answered: How far are we from where we started? How close are we to our goal? Did anything unforeseen happen? What methods did we use, and how effective were they? What, besides the things we did, influenced the results? What difficulties did we have?—In short, we ask ourselves whether the program has helped us to reach our objectives and if so, in what way.

When the goals are physical facilities, such as new sidewalks or a community hall, the answer will be easy. But we may also want to know whether, as a result of our program, the community has become a better place to live; whether the people, and in particular, the leaders, have come to know more about themselves, their community, the world; whether they have learned to work together more effectively. Just what information is needed to answer questions like these?

What Difference Did the Program Make?

There are many aspects of a program that can be evaluated. However, the crucial question is whether it has brought about any changes. To answer this question, we must know the point from which we started and the situation that resulted. We need evidence that can be seen, understood, and accepted by all.

The Benchmark. Our starting point is indicated by a *benchmark.* This is not a complete description of the situation. For the sake of economy, only certain key aspects or *indicators* are selected. For example, if the object of a program is to combat delinquency, we may use police and court records as indicators. Similarly, numbers and values of businesses are indicators of the economic level of a community; years of schooling received indicate levels of education; member participation in programs provides a measure of the effectiveness of an organization; and so forth.

Without a careful record of such benchmarks, we would have to rely on subjective judgments and memory; evaluation would be affected by the hazards of forgetting and of changing opinions. It would, at best, be like navigating by floating icebergs. Only if we have objective indicators can we stop and "take a fix" on the permanent landmark, i.e., our starting point.

The Changes. After the program has been in operation for some time, we take another look at the indicators. For example, if a survey was used to establish our benchmark, we return to the same kinds of persons or records with the same questions as those used in the original survey. Differences in the findings obtained by the two surveys indicate the changes brought about by the program. If the indicators have not changed, it is reasonable to assume that we are not moving towards our goals—or that we have used the wrong indicators.

In the course of its development, a community will change in the following five areas:

1. Citizens' Knowledge and Skills. What experience have citizens gained in relation to community problems? How competent are they in organizing and planning? Do they know where to look for help? What things, besides their regular occupations, are they able to do and like to do?

Economic and physical assets are important, but the most valuable resources are skills and knowledge that are shared with others and used for the benefit of the community.

2. Community Organization. What groups are there in the community? What do they do, as individual organizations and in collaboration with other groups? What informal cliques are there? What kinds of businesses and services

does the community have? Who are the leaders, and how is leadership distributed or concentrated? Who is expected to do what? Where is there co-operation? conflict? compromise?

Understanding the nature of the relationships in a community—i.e., between organization leaders and members, businessmen and customers, officials and citizens—is as important as knowing that such relationships exist.

3. Community Feelings and Attitudes. How does the community feel about the sponsors of a program? About resource agencies and advisors from the outside? Has the program brought about changes in the way citizens look upon their community?

People's feelings about an activity and its sponsors will determine whether they are going to participate, how much they are likely to learn, and what resources they will use.

4. Outside Agencies. What do outside agencies and their workers know about the community? How effective are they in working with and serving the needs of the citizens? What have they learned as a result of programs in which they had a part? How influential are they?

An awareness of these aspects of the community-agency relationship is of value to both the community leader and the agency representative as they plan and work together.

5. Physical Aspects. How is the community laid out? How do its surroundings affect its shape, size, and other characteristics? How many homes and other buildings and facilities are there, and what is their condition? What physical resources does the community possess?

Physical factors may, on the one hand, aid or limit a community's development in specific ways; on the other, they are often indicators of past accomplishments.

Who Was Affected by the Change?

Community and agency leaders need to know who is being affected by a program and who is not. For instance, how many and what types of farmers have adopted a new variety of wheat? What kinds of leaders and organizations are using planning and meeting methods that were recommended in a leadership training program? Projects benefiting businessmen may actually bring hardship to persons dependent on fixed incomes or to the unemployed. A different approach may be needed for, say, low-income groups than for skilled workers.

Why Did It Happen This Way?

In one town, the community council gave high priority to rebuilding the hospital. Some funds were made available through a government agency. Then it was discovered that the town's resources were inadequate and its population too small to maintain the projected hospital. In order to qualify for provincial assistance, the community would have to co-operate with neighbouring municipalities. At this point the project died. Full information on why this happened is not available.

Frequently, when a project is in trouble, valuable energy is spent in complaining or blaming others. Knowledge of the causes underlying the problem might guide action into more constructive effort. It may be a matter of poor timing, or miscalculation of resources needed. Often, the difficulty arises from ignorance and lack of appropriate involvement on part of the public: For example, in one town, a check on negative votes on fluoridation of water supplies revealed that the citizens did not know much about the issue. An information campaign was launched by the community council. This resulted in a positive vote by a wide margin and a better understanding by all of the purposes and problems of the whole community.

We are often members of several groups at once, each with its own standards and goals. We are influenced by these groups in different ways at different times. We may be torn by conflicting pressures. Knowledge of these ties and influences is crucial in understanding why things happen as they do.

How Consistent and Widespread Is the Change?

In order to judge the effectiveness of a program, it is not enough to ask who or what has changed. We also need to know how permanent and how widespread the change is. Some physical improvements—e.g., sewer and water installations—are once-in-a-lifetime propositions. However, others, such as a clean-up campaign, are relatively impermanent unless they are accompanied by changes in the citizens' thinking and habits.

This is a particularly important consideration in the case of leadership training projects. Questionnaires filled out at the end of a leadership institute may show that a certain number of people have "learned" (in words) what the instructors were talking about. Yet a survey made six months or a year later to find out whether, and how consistently, leaders are applying their new knowledge may reveal that the learning was merely transitory and produced no observable lasting effects.

Were There Any Unforeseen Side-Effects?

Some Community Members May Suffer. Programs often produce *side effects* that were neither planned nor anticipated. For instance, one seldom thinks of a sewer and water system as a hardship for anyone in the community. However, the increase in property taxes may further impoverish pensioners and others on low incomes. Obviously such an effect would not have been deliberately planned.

Conflicts and Divisions May Develop. Riverton had been trying for years to get a community skating rink. A local service club had started raising funds. The club's representative welcomed help from the community council, which sponsored two community meetings. At the first meeting, a fund-raising committee was set up. At the second meeting, this committee submitted a progress report. It was decided that the funds it had collected should be turned over to the service club, and that the latter should build the rink.

One unexpected result of the community council's involvement was the withdrawal of the service club from the council. Although the club's representative had invited help, and although the club was, in the end, entrusted with the construction of the rink, some members resented the "interference" of the council and the fund-raising committee: they wanted the rink to be seen as *their* project. The fact that the leadership of the council and that of the club held opposing political views may have contributed to the split. Moreover, the club's and council's respective roles were never clarified. It is possible that the success of the fund-raising committee was seen as a threat to the club's prestige in the community.

Leadership May Shift. Effective programs are likely to bring forth new leadership, especially if they are concerned with the development of the human as well as the physical aspects of the community.

When a large industry moved to Parkville, the town's new needs and interests led to a change of mayors. The program initiated by the community council gave several hitherto inactive citizens a chance to demonstrate their leadership abilities. Thus, community progress may be expected to result in the advancement of some leaders and in the replacement of others. Such shifts can easily create conflict and friction.

Precedents Are Set. Any organization creates expectations through its programs. In one community, the council sponsored a fund-raising drive for an outside agency. Soon it began to receive requests to sponsor similar drives for other groups.

In another community, the council had no function other than channelling requests for action to its constituent organizations. Before long, the council's importance had declined to a point where it no longer rated the support of the citizens.

The expectations and precedents an organization sets early in its life can be decisive in determining its influence and effectiveness in the community.

New Obstacles May Defeat Long-Range Goals. The leaders of one community wanted to join a larger school unit. However, they were fearful that the high school might be located in another town. To improve their bargaining position, they decided to develop their school and expand the attendance area as much as possible. They increased taxes, issued bonds, constructed new buildings. These moves produced some unforeseen and unwanted results: (a) Local ratepayers in effect were subsidizing students from surrounding low-tax areas who had moved to the town for the duration of their high school attendance. (b) It became difficult to negotiate consolidation with surrounding low-tax areas unwilling to raise their taxes to assist with the retirement of the school bond debt. (c) Any increase in tuition rates for those commuting or residing in town only during the winter would have resulted in a loss of students and support to neighbouring units. The town kept its school, but at the cost of high rates and new obstacles to consolidation.

In evaluating programs, we should be alert to side-effects which might jeopardize our ultimate objectives.

WHO SHOULD EVALUATE?

Facts do not speak for themselves. Someone has to interpret them, to decide what they mean. Who, then, should help the facts to speak?

The town of Lost Lake, concerned about juvenile delinquency, had for a number of years employed a recreation specialist to keep young people occupied during the summer months. Although most citizens agreed that the program had produced some benefit, many were questioning the continued value of the expenditure involved. The recreation board therefore decided to have the program assessed. They asked the community consultants at a nearby university for help. A staff member was assigned to the task.

A brief survey of existing recreation facilities and needs had been made at the beginning of the program. This, together with police, welfare, and school records, provided the benchmark—i.e., a measure of where the community had stood before the program started.

At a community-wide meeting called by the recreation board, the consultant proposed the appointment of a steering committee, representing interested agencies, to direct the evaluation study. This suggestion was readily accepted. The committee's job, as defined at the meeting, was to determine *(a)* what the original objectives of the program had been; *(b)* to what an extent the program had succeeded in meeting these objectives; and *(c)* whether the public considered such objectives adequate for a community recreation program.

Through informal talks with the recreation board and other community leaders, the steering committee established that the program's major purpose had been to keep young people out of trouble by providing constructive leisure-time activities for them. To assess its effectiveness in accomplishing this purpose, a subcommittee was set up to check agency and community records for any changes that might be due to the program. Another subcommittee was to plan and conduct an opinion poll to find out *(a)* what citizens had originally expected of the program, and what they thought of it now; *(b)* how they were using their leisure time; *(c)* what new or expanded facilities and opportunities they would like to have; and *(d)* whether they would be willing to pay for such facilities and opportunities.

In planning and carrying out its assignment, the poll subcommittee secured the help and advice of both the provincial recreation specialist and the community consultant. Volunteers, recruited through personal contacts and appeals to community organizations, conducted the interviews, tabulated the results, and, with the help of the two specialists,

interpreted the responses. The steering committee and recreation board, meeting in small groups for several evenings, prepared a report on the findings of the study and made recommendations for further programming. An editing committee was put in charge of the final drafting and reproduction of the report which was issued jointly by the steering committee and the recreation board. Every household in the community received a copy.

A week later, a second public meeting was called to discuss the report, question the findings, revise recommendations, and approve proposals for continuing and new programs.

To sum up: The recreation program was evaluated by the *whole community.* Citizens not only had a chance to express and compare opinions; they also took responsibility for collecting and interpreting new facts and for deciding on future action. They used *specialists'* broader experience to (a) help check the accuracy and completeness of their information, (b) locate resources they might not have thought of themselves, (c) select suitable yardsticks for evaluation, and (d) provide guidance for effective procedure.

Frequently specialists are hired, not as consultants (as in the Lost Lake case), but to assume responsibility for the entire evaluation process and its product. However, unless such assessments are fully understood and accepted by the community as their own, the motivation to further action may be lacking. The subjective judgments of citizens, in the final analysis, provide the motive power for community action. More objective viewpoints, introduced from outside, may be more accurate but cannot replace citizen evaluations in the planning of community-based programs.[1]

STEPS IN EVALUATION

We can look at evaluation as a series of steps whereby groups reach some common judgment of what they have accomplished. Whatever the procedure, certain principles should be observed. The case of one community may serve to illustrate those principles.

Arden Evaluates Its Recreation Project

In Arden (pop. 3000), the building of a community recreation center had been proposed. The town was located about sixty miles from the nearest city. The arguments for and against the center were many and varied.

Some were concerned over an increase in juvenile delinquency. Others thought that a home-grown program and good facilities would slow down the trend for youth and whole families to seek recreation in, and hence take business to, the city. Better recreational opportunities for all age groups might increase loyalty to and pride in the community and strengthen family life.

On the other hand, many felt that too much emphasis on recreation might lead to distraction from school and home life. Then there was the question of costs. Was there a real need for a new building? Taxes were already high: Who would pay for the proposed structure? If outdoor sports facilities were to be added, the cost would be even higher. Moreover, a number of other community projects were competing for funds and leadership.

The citizens finally agreed to set up a two-year experimental recreation project making use of existing facilities. At the end of this period, the question of new buildings would again be approached.

A temporary recreation board was set up to co-ordinate the various parts of the project and the survey that was to accompany it. Areas that might be affected by a recreation program included school, home life, business, attitudes toward the community, and trends in responsibility and delinquency among youth and adults. The indicators that were to measure changes in these areas were decided upon. The Home and School Association, in co-operation with the school administration, agreed to sponsor a study of student grades, study habits, and classroom problems. The Board of Trade was to collect facts about business volume and trading patterns during the same one-month period in two consecutive years. A survey of a 50 percent sample of all local households was made to determine how family members spent their free time, what shopping and service centers they used, what their recreational preferences were, and how they felt about the community.

Facts were to be collected before the program started and again two years later. The results of the study would determine whether the proposed recreation center should be built. Thus from the beginning evaluation was seen as one of the objectives of the program.

What were the most important steps in evaluation in this case?

Build Evaluation into Planning

Program evaluation cannot be considered apart from program planning.[2] In Arden, arrangements had been made for the gathering of information before, during, and after the project; results would be weighed in relation to the community's goals and expectations. In Lost Lake, evaluation was related to past objectives so as to provide a basis for future plans. In both cases, it became a part of programming and action. Both communities utilized an assessment of the success of one phase in their planning for the next phase.

Set Clear Program Objectives

General purposes of agency programs are often statements of lofty social values, irreproachable, all-inclusive umbrellas like the following: "To create a healthy society"; "to meet people's needs"; or "to provide a medium through which desirable ... environments are brought into existence whereby rural people may help themselves or obtain help in meeting their needs ... solving problems, and accomplishing their desires and goals."[3] Similarly, the purposes of community programs are often stated in very general terms. Where objectives are as vague as these, it becomes impossible to measure progress.

In Arden, one early short-term objective was to get complete and reliable information on the effects of a recreation program on various areas of community life. In their long-term goals, the townspeople went beyond the mere provision of facilities in seeking to improve their community generally by stimulating local business, reducing delinquency, encouraging positive attitudes and community responsibility among citizens, etc. Their procedure allowed them to become increasingly specific in their objectives as their planning progressed.

Decide on Indicators of Progress

Indicators are the means by which we gauge, estimate, or measure progress toward goals. For example, if we are building a recreation center, evidence of completed or partially completed facilities will be an important indicator of progress. If, however, the goal is to strengthen community and family life or to reduce delinquency, recreation being seen merely as a means to that end, then the choice of indicators becomes more difficult.

The following indicators were used in the Arden study: *(a)* The Board of Trade's figures on *volume of trade* during the same month in two consecutive years were compared to assess the effect of the program on business activity. *(b)* A comparison of *students' scholastic records* for the year immediately preceding the experiment and the first year of the study showed whether the program had affected scholarship. *(c)* Each year, students in the junior class were asked to keep a record of their *leisure-time activities* during three designated one-week periods. *(d)* To measure the effect of the program on home life, *records of activities of the members of a sample of households* for the same ten-day period in each of the two years were compared. *(e) Opinions* of heads of families about the program were obtained through interviews.

Select, and Plan for Appropriate Use of, Procedures and Tools

To ensure valid evaluations, we need a reasonably complete and accurate picture of how things have gone.

Two types of information may be sought: One reflects people's feelings about the program—whether they think it was good, useful, effective, etc. The other deals with the specific ways in which the program has been good, useful, effective; whether, for example, it has increased business activity, reduced delinquency, strengthened family or community ties, and so forth. Arden tried systematically to obtain both kinds of information.

Facts can be secured in several ways: *(a)* by asking others; *(b)* by observing for ourselves; and *(c)* by studying records and documents. Procedures range from informal talks with neighbours to surveys conducted by means of questionnaires; from simple interviews to formal tests and scales; from consultations with groups of officers and leaders of organizations to the study of agency records or newspaper files; from the efforts of community volunteers to the employment of specially trained observers. Different methods usually produce different kinds of information.[4]

In selecting procedures and tools for assessing the effects of a program, the following pointers may be helpful:

1. If possible, get some experienced help and advice. Such advice might come from social science departments of universities, social science research workers in government departments, commercial polling agencies, organizations like the Center for Community Studies, and extension and social agency field workers with some previous experience.
2. Plan for collection of the information needed for evaluation during every phase of the program.
3. Keep records of important aspects of the program as it develops.
4. Use procedures that are "reliable," i.e., that produce the same results regardless of who uses them (provided the information-gatherer has received a minimum of instruction).
5. Procedures should fit the type of information sought as well as the conditions under which the facts will have to be collected.
6. Procedures should come within the limits of available resources. Thus it is important to know what a given procedure requires in terms of skills, money, equipment, and time.

Decide What It All Means

Findings need interpretation. This should be done by those most directly

concerned, i.e., the leaders of groups affected by the program. Too frequently, citizens are unwilling to spend the time necessary to discover the meaning of the information they have gathered. Or, they may feel that the expert should do this for them.

Expert opinions are most useful for *added* insights and more general testing of local judgments. When the findings of the Lost Lake survey had been summarized, the consultant was asked to explain their meaning. He, however, insisted that the citizens put forward their own interpretations; he challenged their thinking by raising more questions than he answered in the discussions that followed. The resulting conclusions and recommendations were validated by the whole community at a public meeting.

The following guides will help groups to make the most of their data:

1. Add up all the facts and arrange them in logical order. It is easy to jump to unwarranted conclusions on the basis of incomplete information.
2. Raise as many questions as possible about relationships among the various findings and between these findings and other known facts. For example, let us suppose that in community X, (i) many of the elderly say they are lonely or do not know what to do with themselves; (ii) little organized activity exists for such persons. We might then ask ourselves whether it is hobbies they want, or opportunities to get together and talk, or a chance to do something useful for others, etc.
3. List interpretations and try to reach agreement on them. Test them against known facts and past experience.
4. In attempting to make recommendations, list as many courses of action as possible. Examine each for strengths

and weaknesses. Let each member of the group have his say. Probe for the causes underlying disagreements.

5. Involve those responsible for action in the drawing up of recommendations. As suggested earlier, the facts have meaning not only for what has already happened but, more significantly, for what is to be done in the future. If groups and individuals responsible for next steps are a party to the recommendations, the likelihood of action is greater.

PRACTICAL PROBLEMS

For most of us, evaluation is an automatic part of our thinking. To improve it, we must become aware of the blocks that often hinder effective evaluation.

Failure to Build Evaluation into Program Planning

As indicated above, it is difficult to do a good job of evaluation if it is not built into the original program plan. Evaluation takes the fuzziness out of planning; good plans take the fuzziness out of evaluation.

Adequate Procedures Cost Time and Resources

Most people are far more interested in getting things done than in *post-mortems*. If each project is seen as an end in itself, unrelated to the next step, there seems to be no point in reviewing methods and results: Once the job is finished, we lose interest.

However, where, as in the case of Arden, a project is perceived as merely one phase in a program leading to increasingly effective leadership and

action in succeeding stages, citizens are willing to invest time and resources in evaluating their efforts.

Changes in Adults Come Slowly

It may take years before changes become measurable. Persons who change quickly are usually not highly regarded by their fellows: they are considered "undependable." Studies show that ten or more years are required before a majority of farmers will adopt even simple new farm practices.

The individual who has learned how to do things better may have to wait for the group to catch up. Nowhere is this more evident than in leadership methods. Organizations and communities, accustomed to operating in a particular manner, cling to the ways that are familiar to them. They will not accept and effectively use a new method, no matter how good, until they have practised it for some time and become comfortable with it. The group puts pressure on its leaders not to change too rapidly if they value their position.

Some Changes Do Not Last

In the leadership clinics held in several communities, participants' knowledge and attitudes toward leadership and methods of problem solving had changed measurably. However, a subsequent survey showed that, a year later, these leaders had reverted to the attitudes and views held before the clinics. Perhaps they had been retaught by their communities; or they may not have been confident enough in their new learning to apply it, so that they lost it through disuse.

It Is Often Difficult to Distinguish Between Cause and Effect

Even if we can show that changes have occurred, it is not always easy to prove that they were the result of our program. They might have happened anyway. Simple cause-and-effect relationships are rare; and there are always unexpected side effects. In evaluating programs, it is useful to look for explanations of change other than the apparent ones.

Conflict Between Professional Standards and "Do-It-Yourself" Attitudes

There is a tendency to separate the things people can do for themselves from those that should be done by experts. Anything requiring special skill or knowledge usually is in the latter category.

The professional working with a community should learn to bridge this gap; he should meet leaders where they are and offer them his help. One agency representative failed to do this. He spent an evening telling local leaders what he thought they ought to do. As a result, they became angry and did nothing. Similarly, a research technician may be too much of a perfectionist to help a community improve its fact-finding procedures. On the other hand, citizens often do not know how to use the expert. They seldom ask for assistance in improving on the methods they have been using. Rather than seeing him as a resource, they ask for a judgment which they can either wholly accept or reject.

Some of Our Motives Get in the Way

Often unconscious wishes and attitudes distort our perception. Wishful thinking may get in the way of objective evaluation. An awareness of motives such as the following can help us to deal with them:

1. Fear of evaluation may be due to uncertainty about our objectives.
2. Positions of leadership are sometimes used for personal ends rather than for the benefit of the group or community being served. Although this is always the case to some extent, we find it difficult to admit publicly.
3. We tend to place all responsibility for the actions of our organizations on the elected officers, and to criticize or desert them if they have failed. A more democratic philosophy, and one leading to stronger organizations in the long run, sees two centers of authority—namely, the membership *and* the officers. The latter are elected for specific functions, but not for *all* functions. Final responsibility should rest with the membership.
4. Where evaluation is seen as personal criticism, it is often considered a sign of distrust of leaders and hence, reprehensible. If programs are a group responsibility, evaluation is less likely to carry such implications.
5. Judgments of goodness, rightness, and even effectiveness are often based on feelings or habit; we may resist having such judgments challenged by provable and demonstrable facts. The opposition to water fluoridation is a case in point.
6. Some things are honoured by tradition and custom. They were, it seems, evaluated long ago and once and for all; they are above questioning. This is true of many religious and patriotic matters, education and school routines, and, to some extent, of the recognized rights and privileges of various groups.
7. An all-or-none attitude sometimes

prevents us from taking small steps to refine our present procedures and habits. If we cannot run, we are not going to walk. Because our present approaches to evaluation are so far from the ideal, we may hesitate to attempt improvements of the planning procedures and the collection and use of information that make measurement of progress easier.

SUMMARY OF PRINCIPLES OF PROGRAM EVALUATION

From the foregoing discussion, some general principles can be drawn which may be helpful in other community situations.

1. All program planning and action should include some systematic evaluation. This will enable us to understand why we have reached, or failed to reach, our objectives. In community programs, we want to know whether, and in what ways, the community has changed, and what procedures were most effective.
2. Start in simple ways, by using easily available and observable indicators at first, but seek increasingly accurate and dependable means of measuring progress toward planned changes.
3. Plan to evaluate the effectiveness of your program in relation to short-term, tangible goals as well as to learning and human-relations objectives. The former include such things as physical facilities, community calendars, or numbers of meetings held. The latter have to do with ways of working together, with relationships among organizations, with techniques and procedures. Both kinds of objectives are essential to

community change: While one gives citizens a feeling of accomplishment, the other is important to human development.

4. Provide enough resources to carry out the evaluation you have planned. The minimum required is the time of volunteer workers and some knowledge of procedures. As more accurate data are desired, specialists, trained interviewers, and facilities for tabulating and analyzing findings will be needed.
5. Involve as many people as possible and appropriate—resource persons, officials, leaders, and all those who play a part in the program. When analyzing information about planned changes and unplanned side-effects it is particularly helpful to have a wide variety of views; this will ensure interest in and support for the next steps.
6. Do not attempt an evaluation unless you are prepared to face some hard facts. The sweepings under the rug may be found. New and unexpected problems may appear.
7. Divide the program into manageable units for evaluation. Rather than attempting to assess the whole program at once, select one project at a time, or focus on changes in key aspects of the community, such as organization, distribution of leadership, levels of income and standards of living, or morale. Then study the relationship of these changes to the various parts of the program. By adding up such partial assessments you will obtain your total evaluation.

By making it possible to analyze the weak points of a generally successful program, or the bright spots in an unsuccessful one, this bit-by-bit approach will yield information more useful for further planning than overall judgments of accomplishment.

8. Evaluate the psychological conditions, or climate, of change. Citizens' attitudes towards leaders, resources, or agencies are important in determining the success or failure of a program. In a favourable climate of feeling, a relatively ineffective program, especially if traditional in character, may continue almost indefinitely. On the other hand, little will be accomplished if attitudes toward a program or its sponsors are negative. Without participation and support, the best-laid plans will lack the motive power necessary to translate them into action.

9. Do not be afraid to try different procedures for gathering or evaluating information. This will encourage an experimental and enterprising attitude among leaders and members of a community.

10. Before launching a program, consult social scientists and others experienced in planning and collecting social information. Consultation does not commit you to any particular line of action, but it may provide valuable ideas and help to prevent unnecessary mistakes.

11. Begin where people are, and do not expect too much too soon. We are all in the habit of judging actions, people, and things—usually on the basis of very limited impressions or chance observations. Similarly, communities have their own built-in evaluation processes: Some rely heavily on the judgment of one or two persons; others depend on informal exchange of opinions, on the chance encounter, back-fence conferences, barbershop discussions, or after-church comments. Most communities use methods developed in an age of simple face-to-face interaction. We now need more reliable procedures for gathering information from and about events and persons we seldom see. As changes in individuals and groups take time, patience, and planning, so does the development of effective evaluation skills and habits and, above all, of the ability to suspend judgment until all relevant facts have been collected and analyzed.

Community programs are becoming big business; mistakes and poorly laid plans may be costly in terms of money, effort, and time. To an increasing degree, community decision-making must be based on facts evaluated in an objective and reliable fashion.

NOTES

1. This does not deny the value of more systematic program evaluation by outside experts in determining government policies. It is especially important when deciding whether to continue or discontinue a policy or a program.

2. For further discussion of this point, see also Key to Community No. 2, "Community Program Planning," by H. R. Baker.

3. Quoted from objectives of field service divisions of departments of Saskatchewan Provincial Government as reported in *A Self-Survey of Agency Resources,* coordinated by the Center for Community Studies, 1961.

4. For further discussion of community fact-finding procedures see Key to Community No. 3, "The Self-Survey in Saskatchewan Communities," by V. W. Larson.

27. ALTERNATIVE FRAMEWORKS FOR PROGRAM EVALUATION

Robert Washington

There are at least four conceptual models which are generally accepted as analytical frameworks within which to conduct evaluative research.

The term "conceptual model" is used here to refer to an explanatory frame of reference within which certain social and behavioral science concepts are used as tools for circumscribing evaluative behavior. This explanatory system offers the evaluator a way of thinking which defines the means to be employed as well as the ends to be served in evaluative research. The term also suggests that there are precisely formulated concepts drawn from business and public administration which provide us with clues as to what it is about human service delivery systems that should be studied and evaluated. In other words, a conceptual model provides us with a "change" or "intervention" theory which forms the analytical framework within which the evaluation will be conducted.

Since outcomes from most services imply directed social change, it is useful to have a "change" or "intervention" theory. Such a theory tends to identify what constitutes the desired change to be measured as well as to provide clues as to how the change should be measured. Usually, the change or intervention theory developed by the evaluator will be couched in a particular discipline. For example, some evaluators use organizational theory as their analytical framework. Organizational theory uses

Reproduced by permission of the author.

the rigorous methods of economic analysis, but also incorporates findings of behavioral science research. Using organizational theory then, the evaluator is likely to conceive of a human services program as a complex social system. This framework, for example, provides the foundation for the *systems* model of evaluation.

THE SYSTEMS MODEL

The systems model of evaluation is based upon efficiency and relates to questions of resource allocations to produce certain outputs.

The systems model assumes that certain resources must be devoted to essential non-goal activities such as maintenance and preservation of the system. From this viewpoint, the central question in an evaluation of the effectiveness of an intervention should be: How close does the organization's allocation of resources approach an optimum distribution? Etzioni (1969), a central proponent of this model, suggests that what really is important is whether there exists a balanced distribution of resources among all organizational needs rather than the maximal satisfaction of any single organizational requirement.

The systems model of evaluation assumes that the evaluator must answer at least four questions: (1) how effective is the coordination of organizational subunits? (2) how adequate are the resources? (3) how adaptive is the organization to environmental and internal demands? and (4) were the goals and subgoals met?

While the measurement of general organizational goals is central to the systems model, proponents of the systems model tend to minimize the need to measure how well a *specific* organizational goal is achieved. They contend that such a strategy is unproductive and often misleading since an organization constantly functions at a variety of levels with a variety of goals which are sometimes conflicting. Moreover, they contend, overattention to a specific goal will lead to underconcern for other programmatic functions. The fact that an organization can become less effective by allocating excessive means to achieve a particular goal is viewed by systems protagonists as just as detrimental as withholding such resources.

The systems model of evaluation tends to be more productive in decision making among organizations which employ program budgeting. The general idea of program budgeting is that budgetary decisions should be made by focusing upon overall goals. In other words, program budgeting is a goal-oriented program structure which presents data on all of the operations and activities of the program in categories which reflect the program's goals. Inputs, such as personnel, equipment, and maintenance, are considered only in relationship to program outcomes. Program budgeting, then, lays heavy emphasis upon relating costs to accomplishing the overall goal.

Program budgeting has two essential characteristics: (1) the budget is organized by programs rather than by objects of expenditures, and (2) the program shows not only current needs but also future needs for resources, as well as the financial implications of the programmed outputs.

From the perspective of the evaluator, program budgeting contains two important pieces of information. First is the organizational goals and objectives. The second piece of information needed is a statement of the financial resources required to achieve the goals and objectives.

Drawing from program budgeting procedures, the two most frequently used evaluation strategies employed in the systems model are cost-effectiveness and cost-benefit analysis.

Cost-Effectiveness Analysis

There are many and varied reasons why it may be of limited value to apply cost-benefit techniques to a particular human services program. However, such a program may be effectively evaluated with a slightly modified version of cost-benefit analysis known as cost-effectiveness analysis. Unlike cost-benefit analysis, which attempts to quantify benefits of a program in money terms, cost-effectiveness analysis utilizes output variables in nonmonetary forms to serve as indices for benefits of specific programs. The output variables are specified by various goals of a specific program, such as number of persons trained in a given skill, employment, or level of proficiency on a standardized test.

Cost-Benefit Analysis

Cost-benefit analysis involves the use of economic theories and concepts. It is designed to tell us why a program or one of its components works in addition to how well it works. The concept of "cost-benefit" defines the relationship between the resources required (the cost) to attain certain goals and the benefits derived. One of its basic premises is that many decisions involving the allocation of limited resources are often made on the basis of how those resources can be most optimally used, avoiding waste, duplication, and inefficiency. Cost-benefit analysis is a tool for decision makers who need to make choices among viable competing programs designed to achieve certain goals. It is not designed to favor the "cheapest" nor the "costliest" program, but rather the optimal program in terms of the available resources and the explicit goals.

Usually cost as well as benefits are given a dollar value over time, and benefit over cost ratios are computed. A ratio in excess of one indicates worthwhileness from an investment point of view. The higher the ratio, the greater the value and worth.

The cost-benefit calculus is not a wholly satisfactory tool for evaluating human services programs, because of its incapability to measure "psychic" or "social" benefits. Psychic and social benefits are defined here to refer to the state, or well-being of the recipient or the changes that take place in attitude and behavior as outcomes. Weisbrod (1969) argues that an evaluation design built around cost-benefit analysis is likely to reach negative conclusions about the effectiveness of any human services program, since only "economic" benefits and costs are taken into account. (Remember, an evaluation design built upon the systems model is concerned primarily with "allocative efficiency.")

One of the precautions in interpreting cost-benefit data relates to the fact that, while a particular human services program may be judged inefficient, it may not necessarily be considered undesirable. It may, for example, have certain favorable income redistributional consequences that are socially preferable to other benefits.

In applying cost-benefit analysis to evaluation of compensatory educational programs, Thomas Ribich (1968) in his study argued that the kinds of educational changes put into effect through the use of Title 1 ESEA funds, is not the kind of impact or change measured by the "payoff-rate" concept. He concluded: "New measurements are needed that have a more direct bearing upon current policy." Thomas (1967), supporting this point of view, noted:

... the social benefits of education, whose value is almost impossible to express in quantitative terms, are a major portion of education's output. Examples of these non-quantifiable benefits are reduction of civil strife, greater social harmony between persons of diverse ethnic and social backgrounds, less capacity for the political process to be seriously influenced by extremist groups, etc. The problem for the evaluator is that such benefits, while impossible to quantify, are nonetheless of crucial importance relative to the basic justification of a particular program.

There is general agreement that the utility of a cost-benefit model as an evaluative tool lies in its emphasis on a systematic examination of alternative courses of action and their implications. But it is important to note that data from such a model should be only one piece of evidence in the appraisal process; and, from the vantage point of the evaluator who is concerned more with "social" than economic benefits, such data may not be the most significant piece of evidence. When programs have goals that go beyond simply maximizing the return on public investments irrespective of who receives the benefits, a simple cost-benefit ratio is an insufficient indicator of program effectiveness.

THE GOAL-ATTAINMENT MODEL

Of the models to be presented, the goal-attainment model of evaluation is the most commonly used. This model, given prominence by Sherwood (1964) and expanded upon by Levinson (1966) stems from a conception of evaluation as the measurement of the degree of success or failure encountered by a program in reaching predetermined goals.

The goal-attainment model of evaluation relies heavily upon strategies which measure the degree of success in achieving specified goals. It assumes that specific goals can be assessed in isolation from other goals being sought by the program. The goal-attainment model is derived from theories of motivation (forces which energize and direct behavior) and Lewinian field theory. This model is very useful in measuring abstract goals and functions "to define the indefinable and to tangibilitate the intangible" (Mager, 1972, p. 10). A basic premise of the goal-attainment model of evaluation is that if the ultimate goal is met, then a series of prior accomplishments were fulfilled. This model emphasizes the measurement of outcomes rather than inputs, assuming that if the goal is met, then the appropriate combination of inputs was made.

The evaluator does not measure the phenomena he is studying directly. Rather, he observes and measures empirical manifestations or indices of these phenomena. It is not criteria themselves which are measured, but their equivalents—indicators. For all practical purposes, the goal-attainment model employs the ex post facto research design. Since the fundamental question asked by the model is *was the goal met?* empirical inquiry can take place only after manifestations of the independent variables have already occurred. Therefore, the focus of the model is upon the clarification of goals and program objectives, and the evaluation of their accomplishment. The evaluation of accomplishment is intended to test the hypothesis that a certain form of intervention has a beneficial outcome.

Goal-Attainment Analysis

Analytically, measuring goal-attainment involves five steps. They are as follows:

1. *Specification of the goal to be measured.*

In using the goal-attainment model, the evaluator must make clear distinctions between goals and objectives. A goal for our purpose is a statement which represents in general terms an end to which a planned course of action is directed. A goal statement should also state, explicitly or otherwise, the outcome behavior of the consumer and/or a desired state or condition once the planned course of action is completed.

2. *Specification of the sequential set of performances that, if observed, would indicate that the goal has been achieved.*

A level of performance achieved within some temporal context which represents an approximation toward the goal is defined as an objective. An objective is operationally defined in terms of a beginning and an end point, so that either the existence or nonexistence of a desired state or the degree of achievement of that state can be established. It may be *qualitatively* or *quantitatively* defined. A qualitatively

defined objective is one that is either obtained or not in terms of empirical observation. A quantitatively defined objective is one that is obtained and can be measured in terms of degrees.

For purposes of evaluation, then, goals should as far as possible be defined operationally. That is, they should be expressed as discrete objectives. In this way, the degree of achievement of the various objectives or level of performance of the target for change can be a direct measure of goal attainment. Conceived in this way, goal attainment can be measured in terms of achieving certain objectives. Therefore, the achievement of all of the objectives should represent 100 percent goal attainment.

3. *Identify which performances are critical to the achievement of the goal.*

An evaluation process must identify proper criteria to be used in measuring program success. In the goal-attainment model, success criteria are stated in terms of benchmarks. The use of benchmarks presumes that certain levels of performances are more critical to goal attainment than others. These are treated as criterion tasks in that they constitute specific necessary conditions of goal attainment. Precise measures of achievement are set up, and data on them are collected systematically. Since achievement of performance is expected to occur in a time sequence, achievement of data should be expressed in terms of changes.

One of the major characteristics of the goal attainment model of evaluation is that it does not require that input factors be individually defined. For example, if one were evaluating a counseling program, one need not be concerned about the number of counseling sessions; the amount of money spent for counseling;

the amount of effort the counseling staff exerts toward the achievement of counseling goals; the nature and demands of the counseling component in relationship to other program components; the characteristics inherent in staff members which affect their ability to carry out the goals or the debilitating and facilitating features of the counseling environment. As already pointed out, the basic question is: was the goal met? Consequently, the evaluator can identify what goals were achieved, but he may or may not be able to explain why they were achieved or why others were not.

4. *Describe what is the "indicator behavior" of each performance episode.*

For the most part, indications of goal attainment will be observed as measures of changes in performance, using some normative criteria. Moreover, since achievement of objectives is defined in terms of beginning and end points, the achievement of an objective may represent the conclusion of a "performance episode." Therefore, the "indicator behavior" of a performance episode is some measurable behavior which can be observed in kind or amount within some time frame. For example, let's say that the goal is to improve morale among workers. The "indicator behavior" may be characterized as absenteeism. Measures of absenteeism are selected as *frequency* and *length*. In this case, the objective may be to reduce absenteeism each month more than it was the previous month over a six-month period. Benchmarks for measurement may be established as a reduction of at least one absence per month over the previous one.

5. *Test collectively whether each "indicator behavior" is associated with each other.*

In most cases, the indicator behavior should be the same for each performance episode. This facilitates standardization of measurement and makes it easier for outcomes to be compared from one episode to the other. Different evaluators studying the same phenomena may report different outcomes. Without standardization, there is a problem of determining whether the differences are in fact actual differences or differences in measures. When measures are standardized, one source of the differences—the measures used—is controlled and the likelihood is then increased that the differences observed reflect differences in the phenomena.

In some situations, the nature of the change being measured will dictate different indicator behaviors from one performance episode to the other. The evaluator, therefore, must be sure that he adheres to proper research methodology to ensure this; multiple measures are preferred because they yield higher validity than single measures.

Measurements of goal-attainment yield, principally, information about outcomes. For program planning, the human services worker may also need a more detailed description of the social environment that produced outcomes. More often than not, program administrators need information on what were the specific levels of input, what resources they require and how these levels of input relate to outcomes. In other words, did a particular level of input make a difference?

Strengths and Limitations of the Goal-Attainment Model

One of the major limitations of the goal-attainment model is that as an ex post facto study, the evaluator cannot always attribute goal attainment to a specific set of input variables. Also, goal attainment may be the result of environment factors over which the human services worker has no control, or there may be factors which neither the worker nor the evaluator can account for.

A third limitation of the goal-attainment model centers around the fact that evaluators often ignore the distinction between ends and means, or output and input. As Terleckyj (1970) suggests, the mere expenditure of funds for a certain goal is often equated with the intended achievement.

A fourth limitation of this model is that it may be too narrow in its evaluation methodology and too formal in its consideration of goals. Also, it may not take into account sufficiently the informal goals that emerge or the unanticipated events that produce new goals and activity.

A strength of the model is that it assumes that individual goals in a program can be evaluated in isolation from other program goals. Another strength is that the model is considered an objective and reliable analytical tool because it omits the values of the evaluator in that he is not required to make any judgments about the appropriateness of the program goals.

A third and important use of the model is its capacity to measure abstract goals by operationalizing the goal into discrete measurable objectives. Finally, perhaps, one of the major strengths of the model is that the measurement of goal attainment need not be rigidly quantitative. For example, the achievement of an objective signifies that the goal has been met to some degree in terms of some defined event. When all the objectives have been achieved, the goal is said to have been met. This argument is based upon the assumption that the goal is met if a series of prior accomplishments are fulfilled.

When to Use Goal-Attainment Model

Evaluations may be classified in a number of ways. They may be classified by *what* is being evaluated, by *who* conducts the evaluation, by the *decision* that is to be affected by the evaluation, and by the *method* used. The appropriate classification used depends upon the purpose of the evaluation.

Evaluations may also be classified in terms of their purpose. They may be conducted in order to make decisions about resources allocation, program changes, capacity building and for measuring accountability.

The goal-attainment model of evaluation seems to be best suited for capacity building. In other words, it serves the purpose of developing a data base, improving in-house capacity to collect and assemble relevant outcome data and measures, and provides rapid feedback on problems requiring technical assistance.

The goal-attainment model of evaluation is relatively easy to carry out but the conclusions that may be drawn are necessarily limited. Therefore, this evaluation strategy can be justified only when the relationship between inputs (as independent variables) and goals (as dependent variables) has already been demonstrated or will be tested in subsequent studies.

THE IMPACT MODEL

The next model of evaluation to be discussed is the *impact* model, which involves the formulation of hypotheses that are to be tested. It employs experimental designs in which hypotheses are stated in terms of the comparative effectiveness of certain program inputs. It begins with the premise that since human services programs are designed to improve the social position of recipients, the experimental hypotheses should be stated in a manner which predicts that the intervention will be more beneficial to the recipient than the usual social practice (control condition). As implied from the foregoing, an essential difference in the application of the impact model and the goal-attainment models is in the assumptions made in the use of the impact model. One assumption is that in order for the evaluator to estimate the effects of a particular human services program, it is necessary to compare the experiences of the recipients of services with those of some reference group. Comparisons of the outcomes of the reference group represent what would have happened to the consumers in the absence of the program or intervention.

A second assumption is that the impact model is predicted upon the notion of cause and effect. It consists of (1) a set of theoretical concepts or ideas which trace the dynamics of how it is expected that the program will have the desired effects, and (2) a theory which logically interrelates a set of principles and procedures, which imply that certain decisions rather than others be made with respect to day-to-day program situations.

Since most program outcomes are influenced by multiple causal factors, a search for cause-effect relationships becomes largely one of testing for associations between some arbitrarily selected causes and the hypothesized effect. The question raised by the impact model is: *"What difference does the intervention make?"* In this sense, the impact model is more rigorous than the goal-attainment model. It assumes that in order to determine what differences the intervention makes, it is necessary to measure the relationships between the program goals (the dependent variables) and a variety of independent variables, including the personal characteristics of participants, the program components, and the conditions under which the program operates. The notion that most of the dependent variables with which the evaluator deals are functions of more than one independent variable is essential to the model. Therefore, the analysis should treat simultaneously all of the independent variables which are believed to be relevant. To omit some variables in the analysis may lead to distorted conclusions due to correlation or interaction among these variables and those independent variables which are included in the analysis.

This line of reasoning calls for the use of multivariate techniques. Proponents of the impact model often complain that the weakness in the goal-attainment model is that few investigators use regression analysis, for example, as a means of controlling for the effects of population in determining differences between programs.

To maximize the use of experimental techniques, Freeman and Sherwood (1970) suggest that the impact model should incorporate three kinds of hypotheses: (1) *Causal hypothesis*—A statement concerning relationship between the input and the outcome. "A statement about the influence of one or more characteristics or processes on the condition which is the object of the program. The hypothesis assumes a causal relationship between a phenomenon and the condition or behavior in which change is sought." (2) *Intervention*

hypothesis—A statement about what changes the input will produce. "A statement which specifies the relationship between the program (what is going to be done) and the phenomenon regarded, in the causal hypothesis, as associated with the behavior or condition to be ameliorated or changed." (3) *Action hypothesis*—A statement about how that change will affect the behavior or condition the worker is seeking to modify. The action hypothesis is necessary in order to assess whether the intervention, even if it results in a desired change in the causal variable, is necessarily linked to the outcome variable, that is the behavioral condition that one is actually seeking to modify. This hypothesis is also necessary because although the chain of events may be true in a real life situation, it may not necessarily hold true when it is brought about by intervention.

Impact evaluations should provide five essential sets of information. They should provide all of the data necessary: (1) to determine if a particular program should be continued; (2) to determine which of alternative programs achieve the greatest gains for a given cost; (3) to present information on the components of each program and the mixes of components which are most effective for a given expenditure so that maximum operating efficiency can be achieved; (4) to provide relevant information for determining which programs best serve individuals with particular demographic characteristics; and (5) to suggest new program thrusts.

The impact model is essentially an experimental design. Therefore, it insists upon random assignment of subjects to the experimental and comparison groups. Herein lies the limitation of the model. Developing designs based upon controlled experimentation in evaluative research has always been troublesome. While it is always desirable, it is not always essential nor possible.

One of the basic principles of controlled experimentation in evaluating human services programs is that treatment and control conditions must be held constant throughout the period of intervention. Under these circumstances, experimental designs prevent rather than promote changes in the intervention, because interventions cannot be altered once the program is in process if the data about differences engendered by intervention are to be unequivocal. In this sense, the application of experimental designs to evaluation conflicts with the concept that evaluation should facilitate the continual improvement of the program. Dyer (1966) makes the following observation:

> We evaluate, as best we can, each step of the program as we go along so that we can make needed changes if things are not turning out well. This view of evaluation may make some of the experimental design people uneasy because it seems to interfere with the textbook rules for running a controlled experiment. . . . There is one kind of evaluation to be used when you are developing an educational procedure. . . . I would call *concurrent* evaluation. And there is a second kind of evaluation ... I would call *ex-post facto* evaluation; it is what the experimental design people are usually talking about when they use the word evaluation. (p. 18)

The objective of the impact evaluations is to be able to say definitively that a particular intervention has led to a particular outcome that would not have occurred otherwise. In the absence of experimentation, this is not wholly possible. But the larger problem in conducting an experimental evaluation in the human services field is related to the ethical problem of denying services

in order to have a truly experimental model.

In a true experimental study, random assignment of subjects is based upon the probability theory that each subject has an equal chance of being assigned either to the control or treatment group. In the regular course of service, consumers are almost never assigned to programs on this basis.

THE BEHAVIORAL MODEL

The newest model is derived from behavioral constructs. It places a heavy emphasis upon measuring goal-attainment, but regards goal statements as statements which define the dependent variable only in terms of behavior(s) the consumer should be able to demonstrate at the end of the service intervention. It differs from the impact model in that it places little importance upon controlled experimentation on the ground that the selection of comparison groups which match up in all respects except for the intervention is rarely if ever possible.[1] The basic strategy of the behavioral model of evaluation (BME) is to use the "treatment" group as its own control by employing pre- and posttreatment measurement. In using this procedure, the assumption is that each subject is his own control and that the behavior of the group before the program intervention is a measure of performance that would have occurred if there had been no program service.

The BME places far less importance upon allocative efficiency than the systems model; however, one may apply cost-benefit analysis to program outcomes not defined as "psychic" benefits. The BME also uses process data for identifying independent and intervening variables.

The BME begins from the premise that the effectiveness of human services should be measured in terms of the extent to which desired changes in the behavior of consumers take place. This model is grounded in three important behavioral science concepts which argue that: (1) the phenomenon with which the evaluator deals is behavior (dependent variable) and the independent variables which control behavior are elements of the environment; (2) since behavior is a function of an environmental stimulus, then, the most effective way to change behavior is to change the environmental circumstances which influence it; and (3) since behavior is a function of the environment, the social function of human services programs is to provide the individual with the skills to cope with the environment.

The primary question raised by the behavioral model of evaluation (BME) is: *To what extent has the program intervention improved the consumer's ability to gain mastery over his environment?*

The BME appears to conform to a formative evaluation design, in which program administrators are looking for information on a feedback basis for strengthening program administrative patterns and service delivery. Therefore, the initial concern of the evaluator should be goal clarification.

SPECIFICATION OF GOALS

Goal clarification is an essential feature of the BME because the evaluator is concerned not only with goal attainment, but also with the appropriateness of the goal and the feasibility of attaining it, both in terms of costs of resources and effort and in aiding the consumer to gain mastery over his environment.

For purpose of analysis, a program is regarded as consisting of three subsystems: (1) *donor,* the group that allocates the funds and develops the policy, guidelines and mandate by which the program operates; (2) *the service delivery,* the program staff who are responsible for service delivery; and (3) *the consumers,* the persons who receive the services.

Program goals, then, should reflect the value orientations of all three subsystems. Very often, if evaluation takes place during early program development, the most significant contribution the evaluator makes to the program may be the clarification and reconciliation of the perceived goals of members of the three subsystems.

It becomes clear then that there is a distinct advantage, when using the BME, to have the evaluator on board at the time of goal setting. One of the initial ways in which the evaluator provides valuable technical assistance to the program administrator is by helping him to: (1) Clearly define goals in terms of behavioral outcomes; (2) specify quantitative measures and criterion conditions accepted as standards of program success; and (3) set up a data collection system for collecting the kinds of evidence needed to measure program success.

Since the BME calls for the evaluator to be an integral part of the organization from the outset, he can provide ongoing feedback about whether program development is consistent with the predetermined goals.

Specification of Indicators of Goal Attainment

Specifying goals as discussed in the

preceding section is as much a planning and program development process as it is an evaluation task. On the other hand, formulating indicators of goal attainment is regarded solely as a part of the evaluation strategy. This is so principally because such indicators must be both observable and measurable.

Indicators of goal attainment infer a state-change relationship. That is, the evaluator collects as evidence of goal attainment, data which illustrate a change in the state of the consumer on some baseline measurement. The context within which change (dependent variable) is defined is couched in the behavioral construct (man vis-à-vis his environment) and should represent mastery over the environment. Indices of mastery over the environment are measures of changes from one level of dependency to a higher level of independence or evidence of improved life chances.

Gil (1970) defined these as " ... changes in the quality of life or the level of well-being of society's members, as observed on demographic, biological, psychological, social, economic, political, cultural and ecological indicators." He categorized indices of mastery over the environment as:

1. Changes in the development of life-sustaining and life-enhancing resources, goods and services.
2. Changes in the allocation of individuals and social units of specific statuses.
3. Changes in the distribution to individuals and social units of rights and rights equivalents.
4. Changes in rewards, entitlements, and constraints, and in the proportion of rights distributed as rewards and entitlements.

5. Changes in the quality and quantity of real and symbolic resources, goods and services distributed.
6. Changes in the proportion of rights throughout society and in the degree of structural inequality of rights among individual members and social units.
7. Changes in the extent of coverage of a defined level of minimum rights for all members of society.
8. Changes in the extent to which the distribution of rights is linked to allocation of statuses.

Data Collection

Once the evaluator has specified the dependent variables against which to measure program effectiveness and goal attainment, he can begin to collect evidence. The behaviorally oriented evaluator relies heavily upon the use of questionnaires, observation, attitude scales, idiographic data and interviews as the primary bases of data collection.

Data Analysis

The basic design used by the evaluator is the pretest-posttest design; then applying an appropriate statistical test to determine whether the difference is significant.

As pointed out earlier, the analytical framework of the BME is the measurement of program effectiveness in terms of the extent to which the intervention helps consumers to gain mastery over their respective environment. However, the evaluator is also concerned with accountability of service delivery which is measured in terms of responsiveness to consumer needs.

Feedback

As already described, the BME emphasizes a formative strategy. That is, it is designed to provide feedback information to the program administrator and the staff at any time during program implementation. Feedback data are used to modify program operations and to make any changes which seem to foster the achievement of program outcomes.

Since the evaluator is an integral member of the project staff, he can provide client satisfaction information to members of the staff shortly after the completion of each episode of service. Inasmuch as client satisfaction is measured in terms of satisfaction with the process as well as with outcomes, the evaluator can also provide information to members of the entire delivery system about assessibility and continuity. Furthermore, since the evaluator usually has the responsibility for providing needs assessment data and determining whether goals and priorities conform to needs data, he can also provide authoritative data for program modification.

One advantage of the BME is that certain program inputs can be modified after each episode of service. In this way, the outcome data from one set of service delivery activities become the baseline data for the set of modified activities. This cybernetic approach in which outcome data are treated as input within some temporal dimension is a key element of the feedback process. In this way, the feedback process serves as the nexus between service delivery and accountability.

Another feature of the BME is that it consciously treats values, attitudes, program priorities, environmental and managerial constraints as input variables. The BME probably falls into

Kogan and Shyne's (1965) category of a tender-minded approach to evaluative research. However, Weiss and Rein remind us that the "tough-minded" approach often results in technical and administrative problems which minimize the utility of the evaluation data.

Perhaps, the feature that distinguishes most the BME from other models of evaluation is its theoretical base, the independent variables it espouses and its definition of dependent variables. For example, the BME begins from the premise that behavior is a function of the environment and the individual's perception of the environment. Therefore, one of the ways to change the behavior of the consumer is to change the environmental circumstances that impinge upon his behavior. Relating this to human services programs, the BME presumes that program effectiveness is measured in terms of the extent to which these programs aid in the reduction and elimination of social and economic inequalities through the redistribution of resources and social and economic opportunities. In this context, the dependent variable is always couched in terms of gaining mastery over the environment and the independent variable in terms of facilitating mastery over the environment.

The major limitation of the BME is that it is most effective only when the evaluator is on board at the outset of program planning. Since most evaluations are conducted in retrospect, essential features of the model are lost.

The absence of a control or comparison group often creates problems of internal validity. This is another limitation of the model.

CONCLUSION

This article set out to present four

conceptual models of human service program evaluation. An underlying premise is certain human services programs lend themselves to particular research designs and, in turn, particular statistical and analytical procedures. Another point presented in this paper is that each conceptual model represents a particular way of thinking which defines what evaluation questions should be asked. Each model also provides the evaluator with clues about what to measure and why.

The goal attainment model asks the question: *Was the goal met?* It usually employs the ex post facto research design, relying principally upon descriptive-inductive analysis. The impact model employs the experimental design. However, such a "tough-minded" approach to human services program evaluation often results in both technical difficulties and intraorganizational friction. It responds to the question: *What difference does the intervention make?* Since most program outcomes are influenced by multiple causal factors, such a design also calls for the use of multivariate techniques.

The systems model asks the question: *How close does the organization's allocation of resources approach an optimum distribution?* It presumes that certain organizational goals are nonconsumer related; and that certain resources must be devoted to system maintenance. The most popular analytical tool used by systems evaluators is the cost-benefit calculus. The lesson to be learned is that while cost-benefit analysis represents a major step toward rigor, program evaluation should not rest solely on cost-benefit analysis.

The behavioral model of evaluation (BME) is the newest model. It defines goals in terms of service intervention.

The BME asks: *To what extent has the program intervention improved the consumer's ability to have mastery over his environment?* It employs the pretest-posttest design on the assumption that each subject is his own control and that the behavior of the group before the program intervention is a measure of performance that would have happened if there had been no program service.

A major strength of the BME is that it requires the evaluator to consider the value orientations of the consumer as important as those of the service provider and the donor. Another strength of the model is its assumption that the reduction and eventual elimination of social and economic inequalities through redistribution of resources and economic and social opportunities is a core function of human services program.

The limitation of the model is that it is only effective when the evaluator is on board at the outset of program planning.

The very nature and variety of human service programs require different evaluation strategies. No single model accommodates the evaluation requirements of most programs. In most situations, the evaluator will need to select elements of several models in order to achieve a comprehensive evaluation strategy.

NOTE

1. More often than not, evaluations are conducted as ex post facto research. Therefore, the investigator cannot achieve random assignment of subjects to groups or experimental manipulation of independent variables. On the other hand, if subjects are randomly preassigned to groups or treatment for the sake of evaluation, program administrators are confronted with a moral dilemma.

REFERENCES

Dyer, Henry S., "Overview of the Evaluation Process," *On Evaluating Title I Programs* (Princeton, N.J.: Educational Testing Service, 1966).

Etzioni, Amitai, "Two Approaches to Organizational Analysis: A Critique and a Suggestion," in Schulberg, Herbert C., Alan Sheldon, and Frank Baker (eds.), *Program Evaluation in the Health Fields* (Port Washington, N.Y.: Human Sciences Press, 1970).

Freeman, Howard E., and Clarence C. Sherwood, *Social Research and Social Policy* (Englewood Cliffs, N.J.: Prentice-Hall, 1970).

Gil, David G., "A Systematic Approach to Social Policy Analysis," *The Social Service Review* 44, no. 4 (December 1970).

Kogan, Leonard S., and Ann W. Shyne, "Tender-Minded and Tough-Minded Approaches in Evaluative Research." Paper presented at the National Conference on Social Welfare, 1965.

Levinson, Perry, "Evaluation of Social Welfare Program," *Welfare Review* 4 (December 1966), pp. 5-12.

Mager, Robert F., *Goal Analysis* (Belmont, Calif.: Fearon Publishers, 1972).

Ribich, Thomas I., *Education and Poverty* (Washington, D.C.: The Brookings Institution, 1968).

Sherwood, Clarence C., "Methodological Measurement and Social Action Considerations Related to the Assessment of Large-Scale Demonstration Programs." Paper presented at the 12th Annual Meeting of the American Statistical Association. (Chicago: the Association, 1964).

Terleckyj, Nestor E., "Measuring Possibilities of Social Change," *Looking Ahead* 18, no. 6 (August 1970).

Thomas, Alan J., "Efficiency Criteria in the Urban School System." Paper presented to the AERA, New York City, February 18, 1967. Mimeographed.

Weisbrod, Burton A., "Benefits of Manpower Programs: Theoretical and Methodological Issues," in Somers and Wood, *Cost Benefit Analysis of Manpower Programs* (Kingston, Ontario: Queen's University, 1969).

28. HOW TO USE AND PRESENT COMMUNITY DATA

Richard L. Douglass

The demand for quantitative demonstrations of service needs, program effectiveness, and other aspects of accountability being made on community service providers increases each year. Federal, state, and local governments, private foundations, and other sources of philanthrophic support are demanding that service providers give an accounting, in quantitative terms, of their activities. A long-felt trend toward increasingly quantitative planning and decision making in other sectors of society including industry, business, medicine, and public health now has reached the service community. It is timely for human service professionals to accept the probability that the future of human services will be characterized by more, rather than less, emphasis on measurement of activities, services, and outcomes and the quantitative analysis of such measurements.

REASONS FOR INCREASING EMPHASIS ON QUANTIFICATION

The reasons for the trend toward more emphasis on measurement in the planning, managing, and evaluation of service programs are numerous. During the last several years the resources available for human service provision have been alternately abundant and scarce. Today, however, and in the foreseeable future, scarcity of fiscal and human resources appears to be an enduring problem. During the same period the number of units competing for those scarce resources has greatly enlarged, often including organizations with considerable sophistication in quantitative methods. The net effect has been an upgrading of quantitative sophistication among competing units bidding for resources and, more important, a greater expectation of quantitative information among governmental departments responsible for the distribution of resources. Thus, at the same time that the market for resources has become more crowded, demands for sophistication in measurement and analysis have increased. Success in this environment will depend increasingly upon the ability of the competitors to generate and use quantitative information.

Another social force that has increased the emphasis on quantification is the apparent failure of the many new programs aimed at solving social problems. The alarming expenditure of resources for poorly documented problems, the inadequate assessment of need, evalua-

tion of outcome, and determination of the efficiency of procedure has triggered a cry for accountability, especially from the governmental units responsible for distributing resources.

An immediate by-product of the interest in quantification of service needs and program activities and outcomes is that successful human service administrators discovered that improved information helps them plan and provide better services. Thus, the external demand for increased quantification generated a demand within the service delivery system itself for more precise and adequate measurement.

Underlying all of these trends has been a virtual explosion of new technologies to perform inexpensive measurement. Time-efficient systems, generally computerized, are prevalent and may soon be universal among the major service delivery organizations. Community data sources and local, state, and national statistical information are more accurate, current, and available for use at the local level. Professional boundaries are becoming less rigid, and a broader range of disciplines is providing man power for the human services. Frequently these new sources of manpower have introduced new quantitative skills to service systems with little quantitative tradition.

To summarize, the competition among human services for scarce resources, the demand for accountability, professional recognition of the value of accurate measurement for planning and administering services, and an influx of quantitatively skilled personnel and technologies have interacted to produce an emphasis on quantification in the human services. This trend has been long in coming. Most other fields have developed quantitative methods earlier.

However, many human service professionals have misgivings about translating the human condition into numerical abstractions and often are quite threatened by the trend toward quantification. Hopefully the information presented here will serve to reduce the anxiety.

WHAT ARE COMMUNITY DATA?

Practitioners frequently are unaware of many useful data sources bearing on community dynamics, population movements and changes, economic conditions, housing characteristics, etc. It is perhaps true that such collections of community data are not recognized because of a hesitation to use them. Community data are compilations of periodic measures of the status of the community, activities of specific organizations and services, and other descriptive information including health, vital statistics, housing, and economic conditions. Community data consist of records, often collected routinely for purposes of documentation. Any specific analysis of such information with the intent of identifying changes or trends, or of making inferences about social conditions is secondary to the purposes for which the data are collected. Thus, they are called "secondary data." In contrast, measurements specifically intended to be used for a particular analysis are referred to as "primary data." The utility of primary and secondary data for the community practitioner is largely determined by their characteristics. These will be discussed below.

PRIMARY AND SECONDARY DATA

Primary data are those sets of measurements collected by investigators for a specific purpose. Primary data include specially designed surveys of community residents, organization representatives, or service recipients. Primary data can take the form of special data collected during intake, termination, or follow-up interviews with the clients of social services. However, the overriding distinction between primary and secondary data is that primary data are defined and collected only for the specific analytic purpose at hand, while secondary data are routinely collected for various purposes including documentation and subsequent use by others.[1]

Primary data, unlike case records, are not prepared routinely by community service organizations. Special-purpose measurements, however, frequently are routinized. The difference between routine and routinized is subtle, but significant. Routinely collected data, such as client records, often are characterized by considerable missing information, less than optimum quality controls, and little or no understanding on the part of the personnel recording the measurements of why the data are being collected. Frequently, there is no perceived need for the data and the recording process is a burden to staff members.

Routinized data collection procedures are most common to primary data. The value and immediate utility of the measurements are usually well understood by the personnel involved in data collection. For these reasons, primary data tend to be specific and precise. Secondary data collection can be well supervised and the recording process routinized with adequate quality control. However, with the exception of secondary data collected by the Bureau of the Census and other highly skilled organizations, it would be folly to assume that secondary data generally approach the level of standardization and accuracy achieved in primary data collection.

Operational consistency of the data is the primary issue raised in routinizing or changing data collection methods. Operational consistency is defined as the comparability of measurements of a variable between groups or jurisdictions, or for single groups or jurisdictions over a period of time. Data collection is often poorly controlled. Routine data frequently have errors of recording, missing measurements, inconsistently defined meanings, and other shortcomings. Such negative characteristics reduce their utility for human service professionals. With the exceptions noted, primary data are more likely to be operationally consistent than are secondary data.

However, primary data are expensive to gather. Because the measurements are uniquely defined, designed, and collected, primary data collection requires the allocation of resources far beyond the requirements of acquiring secondary data.

In addition to being expensive, primary data cannot be collected to measure factors in the past. Furthermore, the collection of primary data may present problems of confidentiality and practicality. Thus, secondary data are often the only realistic source of community information. The likelihood of errors and operational inconsistencies in secondary data must be identified and understood before a reasoned analysis can be made.

Secondary data are available to community services from a variety of sources, discussed below. These and other sources of secondary data contain a wealth of information that is potentially useful for those who plan, manage, and offer services and evaluate community programs.

Major uses of secondary data in human service programs are: (1) to describe a community statistically, (2) to identify human service needs in the community, and (3) to test hypotheses of change in a social condition after a change in services or the introduction of a new program.

Accurate and useful description of change depends upon the operational consistency (or reliability) and the correspondence of the measurement used to the concept or idea being measured (or validity). While primary data often are more valid and reliable, secondary data may well be the only practical source of data because of constraints on staff, time, and budget. Fortunately, a careful search for secondary data often results in data adequate for the needs of the investigator at a minimal cost.

SOURCES OF COMMUNITY DATA

A practitioner should undertake a thorough search to identify sources of information available locally and their usefulness before considering the collection of primary data. Because special-purpose investigations are often costly, there is a considerable payoff if existing data are uncovered.

Possible sources of information include:

1. Federal and state government agencies, e.g., the Departments of Labor, Commerce and its Bureau of the Census, Housing and Urban Development, Health and Human Services, Education, comparable state agencies.

2. City and county planning departments and regional councils of governments.

3. State and local health departments

and specialized units such as the Public Health Service Center for Disease Control and the National Center for Health Statistics.

4. Federations of social, health, and recreation agencies such as community welfare councils and united community services.
5. Comprehensive regional health planning councils.
6. Mental health associations and community mental health agencies.
7. Funding agencies, both public (see 1 and 3 above) and private such as the United Way, united funds, and community chests.
8. Clearinghouses in many problem areas; e.g., the National Institute of Mental Health maintains clearinghouses which administer data banks and publish summary data on drug abuse, alcohol abuse, and mental health; its Biometry Branch publishes a useful "Statistical Note" series.
9. Universities, including departments, schools, libraries, research institutes, and individual faculty members with relevant research interests.
10. Libraries and local newspaper archives.

PRESENTATION OF COMMUNITY DATA

The statistical analysis of community data is beyond the scope of this article. However, the utilization of data eventually depends upon the clarity and accuracy of printed presentation. By this I mean the tables, charts, graphs, and other displays of numerical information that any data analysis ultimately requires. This section will describe the construction and variety of ways that numerical information can be presented.

Tables: Numbers, Titles, Rows, Columns, and Cells

A table is an orderly arrangement of numerical information in columns and rows. There are few hard and fast rules for table construction. Perhaps the wisest are those given by a former director of the Bureau of the Census who wrote in the foreword of a manual on tabular presentation,

In the final analysis, there are only two rules in tabular presentation that should be applied rigidly: first, the use of common sense when planning a table, and second, the viewing of the proposed table from the standpoint of the user. The details of mechanical arrangement must be governed by a single objective; that is, to make the statistical table as easy to read and to understand as the nature of the material will permit.[2]

Numbers. If more than one table is used in a report, each table should be numbered to indicate its place in the series. It is also easier to refer in the text to a specific table by use of its number.

Titles. Each table should have a title to indicate the what, where, and when of the contents of the table. Table 28.1 is used to illustrate these points. *What* the table contains indicates whether absolute numbers, computed numbers or both are used; the title indicates how the contents of the table have been defined. For example, the title for Table 28.1 states that both the number of deaths and death rates are classified by age and sex. The *where* indicates the geographic area to which the information applies, as the "United States" in Table 28.1. The *when* is the time for which the data apply; in Table 28.1 this is 1963.

The title should be as brief as possible; however, the content of the table should be absolutely clear from reading the title. Titles of more than two lines are usually avoided. Further information needed for the understanding of the contents of the table can be placed in a *headnote*. The headnote follows the title and may be printed in smaller type and enclosed in brackets or parentheses. The information in the headnote should apply to many if not all items in the table. Such information may also be given in a note to the table, as in Table 28.2.

In Table 28.1 the headnote indicates that the deaths included in that table are those occurring within the country, and deaths of U.S. citizens taking place outside the boundaries of the nation are not included. It also indicates that no fetal deaths are included in the numbers.

Columns. Each column has a caption to state what is referred to in that column. Sometimes several columns will be bracketed together and the *spanner*

head, the caption for this bracket, will apply to all columns under the bracket. In Table 28.1 two spanner heads are used, one with the caption "Number," indicating that the contents of all three columns under the bracket will be numbers of deaths for both sexes, for males, and for females in the separate columns. The second spanner head, "Rate per 1,000 Population," indicates that the numbers in the three columns under that bracket are rates.

In column captions and spanner headings, only the initial word and proper nouns may be capitalized. (In published tables, this depends on the style of the publisher.) In order to save space, there is a temptation to use abbreviations. These should be avoided unless the abbreviations will be readily understood, as those for the names of states, or days of the week. (In published tables, vertical

TABLE 28.1
Number of Deaths and Death Rates by Age and Sex, United States, 1963
(only deaths occurring within the United States; exclusive of fetal deaths)

Age	Number			Rate per 1,000 population		
---	Total	Male	Female	Total	Male	Female
Total	1,813,549	1,027,686	785,863	9.6	11.1	8.2
– 1	103,390	59,734	43,656	25.4	28.7	21.9
1 – 4	16,571	9,140	7.431	1.0	1.1	0.9
5 – 14	16,524	9,955	6,569	0.4	0.5	0.4
15 – 24	29,321	20,680	8,641	1.1	1.5	0.6
25 – 34	32,879	20,841	12,038	1.5	1.9	1.1
35 – 44	74,277	45,053	29,224	3.0	3.8	2.3
45 – 54	160,429	102,905	57,524	7.5	9.8	5.2
55 – 64	282,960	183,050	99,910	17.3	23.2	11.8
65 – 74	440,362	263,231	177,131	38.9	51.1	28.6
75 – 84	445,667	226,255	219,412	85.2	100.9	73.4
85+	210,541	86,472	124,069	210.1	224.6	201.1
Not Stated	628	370	258	—	—	—

SOURCE: Public Health Service, National Center for Health Statistics, *Vital Statistics of the United States, 1963,* Volume II, Part A. Government Printing Office, Washington D.C., 1965.

rules dividing columns are usually omitted in the interests of economy. In this case, period leaders go from the stub to the first column.)

Rows. The first column of the table is called the *stub column;* it contains *row headings,* which serve the same purpose as column captions, indicating what is contained in a particular row. The caption of the stub column indicates the variable that is classified in the row headings.

If data are stratified by more than one variable, for example, by age and sex, ethnicity, or cause of death, the variable which is stratified, or classified, in the stub column is mentioned first in the title of the table. In Table 28.1 the stub column contains the various strata of age, so age is mentioned before sex in the table title. Like column captions, only the initial words and proper nouns are capitalized in the row headings, and abbreviations are used only when they are readily understood.

If stratification of items in a table is by two variables, common sense suggests that the one which will have the greater number of categories will appear in the stub column. If classification is by age and sex or age and ethnicity, there will be more age groups than categories for sex and ethnicity, so that the age groups will appear as row headings in the stub column. If deaths are stratified by age and by all causes of death (as in a table appearing in an annual report of a health department), there would be many more causes of death than age groups, so that the causes of death would appear as row headings in the stub column while the age groups would be used for column captions.

The order in which row headings or column captions are arranged depends largely on whether or not there is progression. In a table presenting an age distribution, the youngest age group would appear as the first row heading followed by the other age groups in ascending order of magnitude. If the information in the table represents a time series, that is, information for different years, months, or days, the proper chronological order would be followed in the stub column or in the column captions.

If there is no progression from one group or another, as is usually the case with qualitative information, the order in presentation of row headings (or column captions) is determined by the size of the frequencies to which they apply. The category with the largest numbers should appear first, followed by other categories in descending order of magnitude of their frequencies. In Table 28.2, showing orphans of three types, it is shown that most orphans have lost only the father, which is the first type-specific column. Maternal orphans, in which only the mother died, follows the paternal column, and full orphans, with both parents deceased, is the third column under each spanner head.

Cells. Below the column captions, to the right of the row headings in the stub column, is the so-called *"field"* of the table, made up of *cells.* A cell is a space representing an interaction of a column and a row and containing a number or a symbol. The number may be an absolute number (as the number of paternal orphans) or it may be a relative number (a percentage of the child population in Table 28.2).

If the table contains computed values, such as percentages or rates, they should

TABLE 28.2
Orphans, by Type: 1940 to 1972

	Number (1,000)				Percent of Child Population			
	Total	Paternal	Maternal	Full	Total	Paternal	Maternal	Full
1940, October	2,930	1,890	960	80	6.1	3.9	2.0	0.2
1955, July	2,710	1,830	820	60	4.8	3.2	1.5	0.1
1960, January	2,955	2,055	840	60	4.5	3.1	1.3	0.1
1965, January	3,290	2,330	890	70	4.7	3.3	1.3	0.1
1970, July	3,260	2,300	890	70	4.6	3.2	1.3	0.1
1972, July........	3,074	2,166	838	70	4.4	3.1	1.2	0.1

NOTE: Beginning 1960, data include Puerto Rico and Virgin Islands. Covers children under age 18 who have been orphaned at any time. Paternal orphan refers to loss of father, maternal orphan to loss of mother, full orphan to loss of both parents. Percentage of child population based on Bureau of the Census estimated population of children under 18, as of July 1. Data not exactly comparable for all years because of changes in methodology.

SOURCE: U.S. Social Security Administration. Data appear regularly in *Social Security Bulletin, Statistical Abstract of the United States, 1973,* p. 313.

all be expressed with the same number of decimal places. One would not record such value as:

25.485	but as	25.5
12		12.0
3.61		3.6
.7149		0.7
11.6		11.6

Percentages and rates are usually expressed with one decimal place to show that they are computed values, not absolute numbers. If rounding to the nearest tenth gives a whole number, this is written with a 0 in the tenths position, as the 12.0 above. If the value is less than 1, this is written with a 0 in the units position, as 0.7.

If computed values are included in the table, the reader should be informed as to what they represent. If they are rates, are they rates per 100, per 1,000, or per 100,000? If the computed values are rates per 1,000 this information may sometimes be included in the title, in a headnote, in a column caption, or in a spanner caption. Occasionally, the information may be given in a footnote.

In some tables both column and row totals will be given (Table 28.1). In others only one set of totals will be given, as Table 28.2 which includes only row totals. Occasionally, no totals will be given in a table, as one which might give the number of births and deaths in Michigan for each year from 1900 to 1976. In such a table, neither row nor column totals would have any meaning.

If the totals are considered to be important, of more importance than individual items in the table, column totals will appear at the top of the columns and row totals will appear on the left, in the first column following the stub column. If the totals are of less importance than other items in the table, however, the column totals will appear at the bottom of the columns and the row totals in the column on the extreme right.

Graphs: Bar Chart, Histogram, Polygon, Time Series

A graph presents numerical information in pictorial visual form. The graph does not present the information more accurately than does a table, but presents it in such a form so that contrasts and comparisons are more readily seen than in a table. Graphs are most meaningfully used in combination with tabular presentations of the same information.

Bar Chart. Such a chart or graph consists of a series of rectangles, equal in width, equally spaced, but varying in length, the length of each rectangle or bar being dependent upon the amount that it represents.

Bar charts are usually used with qualitative variables (such as type of housing, type of treatment) with quantitative variables when measurements have been grouped into categories (such as age groups divided into under 15 years, 15-64, and 65 years and over), for comparison of geographic areas, or for chronological data when there is a wide gap between years, such as 1920, 1960, and 1970.

The bars may be horizontal or they may be vertical. While it is by no means a rule, there is a tendency to use vertical rather than horizontal bars when the information is for time periods.

To construct a bar chart, a scale is first drawn. If bars are to be horizontal, the scale appears at the top of the graph; if vertical bars are to be used, the scale will appear at the left. The scale must start at 0 and extend to some value beyond the

highest amount represented by any of the bars. The scale is divided into equal intervals, with the intervals usually being 2, 5, 10, 25, 100, etc., depending upon the quantities represented by the bars. If the scale is to be a part of the completed graph, the scale should have a caption indicating what the numbers represent — population in thousands, rate per 100,000 population, etc. If the scale is eliminated in the final graph, this information must be conveyed to the reader in the title or in a footnote.

All bars are equal in width and equally spaced, the space between bars usually being approximately one-half the width of the bars and the first bar being placed this same distance from the scales. The length of each bar is determined by the scale, although it is often necessary to approximate its length.

If there is progression, bars would be arranged in order of that progression. In Figure 28.1 each age group, 18, 19, 20, 21, 22, and 23 years of age, appears in order, regardless of the bar lengths. With most qualitative variables there is no such progression, and bars are arranged in order of length, with the longest horizontal bar appearing at the top or, if vertical bars are used, at the left.

Each bar should be labeled to indicate *what* and *how much* it represents. If all bars are quite long and if the labels are short the information may appear on the bar itself. It is also possible to label the bars on the right, but a better practice is to put the part of the label indicating *what* the bar represents on the left, the amount on the bar itself.

In order to show more contrast the bars should be colored or crosshatched. Generally the same color or the same crosshatching pattern will be used rather than using a different color or a different pattern for each bar.

FIGURE 28.1
Vermont Late Night,
Single-Vehicle Accidents with Male Drivers,
by Age of Driver, 1971

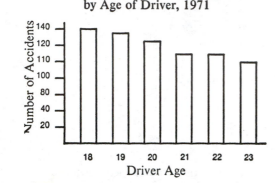

FIGURE 28.1
Vermont Late Night,
Single-Vehicle Accidents with Male Drivers,
by Age of Driver, 1971

SOURCE: Highway Safety Research Institute, University of Michigan.

The scale on the vertical axis should always start at 0, as the picture will be distorted if the scale starts at some value other than 0. The scale on the vertical axis would be divided into equal intervals, the intervals being 2, 5, 10, 25, 100, or even higher values, depending upon the highest frequency in the distribution. If the highest frequency were 79 the scale would be set up in intervals of 10, going up to 80; if the highest frequency were 790 the scale would be set up in intervals of 100, going up to 800.

Like a table, a graph should have a title telling the what, where, and when of the information portrayed. If the graph is for display purposes only, the title may appear at either the top of the graph or below it. For graphs included in reports or publications, it is common to find the title below the graph. If more than one graph appears in the series, they are numbered and are referred to as Figure 1, Figure 2, and so on. (In publications, double numbers such as 29.1 indicate the chapter or reading number, plus the table number.)

Histogram. This form of graph is used to show a frequency distribution, preferably a distribution with groups of equal intervals. A histogram has two scales, one on the vertical axis, and one on the horizontal axis. The vertical scale usually presents the frequency (size) of the concept or variable. The horizontal scale is used for some set of characteristics of the population or subject of the graph. These conventions are clearly shown in Figure 28.2.

FIGURE 28.2
Washtenaw County, Michigan, Late-Night, Single-Vehicle Accidents with Male Drivers 18-to 20 Years Old, 1968 – 1973, in Six-Month Intervals

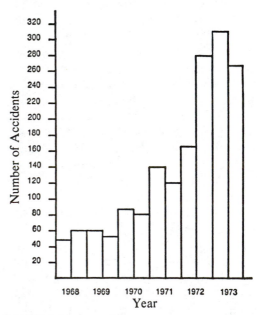

SOURCE: Highway Safety Research Institute, The University of Michigan.

The horizontal scale starts at the lower boundary of the lowest measurement group. For example, if the ages of all persons in the United States were of interest, the scale would start at zero. However, if only those who were eligible for Medicare were of interest the scale would start at 65.

Each scale should have a caption, indicating what the measurement is (on the horizontal scale) and what the frequency represents (on the vertical scale). When very large frequencies are involved, the scale on the vertical axis might have a caption "Number in thousands" or "Number in millions," thus reducing the number of figures used on the scale itself.

In Figure 28.2 for the first measurement group, the first half of 1968, a line is drawn parallel to the horizontal axis from the lower boundary (the first part of 1968) to the upper boundary (the end of 1968) of the group at a height determined by the number of accidents in first half of 1968. Vertical lines then connect this line to the horizontal axis forming a rectangle. The procedure is repeated for each measurement group so that the resulting graph consists of a series of rectangles, similar in appearance to the bar chart in Figure 28.1, but differing from it in that there is no space between the rectangles.

Frequency Polygon. The same information that was used for the histogram could also have been used for making one form of *line graph* known as the frequency polygon (Figure 28.3). The scales on the horizontal and vertical axes would be set up in the same way as for the histogram.

Instead of drawing a line between the upper and lower boundaries of a measurement group, a point is plotted at the height determined by the frequency

FIGURE 28.3
Washtenaw County, Michigan, Late-Night, Single-Vehicle Accidents with Male Drivers 18 to 20 Years Old, 1968 – 1973, in Six-Month Intervals

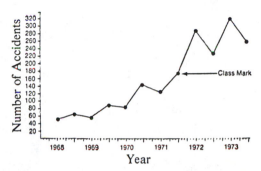

SOURCE: Highway Safety Research Institute, University of Michigan.

of the group, at the midpoint *class mark* of the measurement group. The class mark is the average frequency for the group, as defined by units of the horizontal axis. When the frequencies for each measurement group have been plotted, the points are joined by straight lines. The frequency polygon has an advantage over the histogram in that more than one frequency distribution can be shown on the same graph. A special purpose frequency polygon is a time series.

Time Series. If a graph is to illustrate a time series, points are plotted at a height, according to the scale on the vertical axis, corresponding to the amount that is represented. If the quantity to be plotted is an average, the point is plotted midway between two points on the scale on the horizontal (time) axis. If the frequency being plotted represents totals, such as the accidents in the area with monthly totals for the time period 1968-1973, the series is graphed as in Figure 28.4.

With respect to changes taking place

FIGURE 28.4
Total Washtenaw County, Michigan, Accidents, 1968 – 1973 (August)

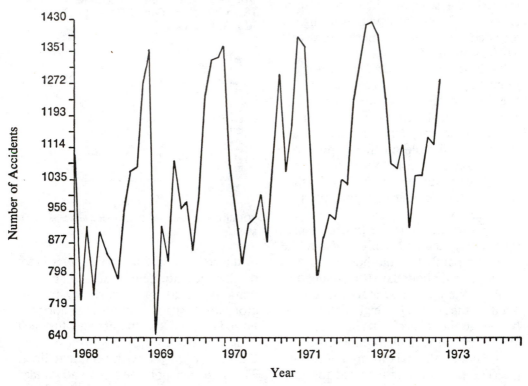

SOURCE: Highway Safety Research Institute, University of Michigan.

over time, there are two techniques to be considered related to the *amount* of change that has taken place and the *rate* at which change has taken place. For example, we might wish to draw a graph to show the changes in the new-home purchase rate from 1960 to 1970. If we were interested in the amount of change, the graph would be drawn with the scale on the vertical axis being an arithmetic scale; if we were concerned with the rate of change, then the scale on the vertical axis would be a logarithmic one (as shown below).

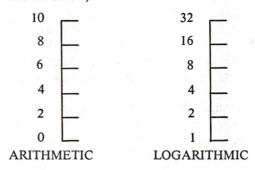

Note that in the scale on the left, equal distances on the scale represent the same *amount* of increase, in this instance, an increase of 2. On the scale on the right, equal distances do not represent the same amount of increase but they do indicate the same *rate* of increase, with each increment representing an increase of 100 percent or doubling of the value.

Most graphs used to show the rate of change will be made on a *semilogarithmic grid;* that is, one on which one scale (the scale on the horizontal axis) will be divided arithmetically, equal lengths of the scale representing the same number of years, while the vertical scale, against which the frequencies are to be plotted, will be scaled logarithmically.

SUMMING UP

I have attempted to suggest ways of thinking about community data, finding such numerical information and ways of presenting such data in tabular or graphical display.

It appears that community services, like other systems in our society, will become increasingly interested in quantitative data in the foreseeable future. I suggest that this trend represents a challenge and an opportunity. If we accept the challenge and become more quantitatively oriented, it is likely that better planning, management, and evaluation of human services will be a visible consequence. Then we will have an opportunity to rationally change, to innovate and improve our community services.

NOTES

1. It should be noted that data collected for a specific purpose may subsequently be used for other purposes, taking on the character of "secondary data." The principal examples are survey data collected by universities and private polling organizations which are stored in libraries and made available to investigators for purposes other than those for which they were originally collected.
2. U.S. Bureau of the Census, *Bureau of the Census Manual of Tabular Presentation,* by Bruce L. Jenkinson (Washington, D.C.: U.S. Government Printing Office, 1949), p. iii.

29. TROUBLESHOOTING GUIDE FOR RESEARCH AND EVALUATION

John Gottman and Robert Clasen

WHY A TROUBLESHOOTING GUIDE?

The idea of this guide is to give you an intuitive feel for what kinds of techniques are available for research and evaluation so that you can be an intelligent seeker of these tools.

I. DESCRIPTIVE STATISTICS

Purpose:

To describe a population from a variable by describing the distribution of that variable in the population.

Example:

Distribution of Income per Month in the Pokohaches Swamp School District. It presents a table of incomes and the percent of the population earning that income.

Useful Concepts:

The *"Mean"* is a measure of central tendency of the distribution (the arithmetic average).

The *"Standard Deviation"* is a measure of the amount of variability of a given variable around the average. If most people have values of the variable

---

Reproduced by permission of the publisher and the authors. From *Evaluation in Education: A Practitioner's Guide*, 1972, pp. 293-312, F. E. Peacock Publishers, Inc., Itasca, Illinois.

close to the average, the standard deviation will be small.

"Probability." It is the likelihood of an event's occurrence, or the relative frequency of a value or set of values of the variable. For example if 80% of the people earn between 4 and 6 thousand dollars a year, the probability is 0.80 that an individual chosen at random from the population will earn between 4 and 6 thousand.

II. INFERENTIAL STATISTICS

Purpose:

To make inferences about a population from knowledge about a random sample or random samples from that population.
Example:
Gallup Poll of opinions.

Useful Concepts:

"Random Sampling." This is a procedure for selecting a group to study which insures that each member of the population will have an equal chance of being selected to be in the sample.

"The Central Limit Theorem" establishes the importance of the normal distribution because the distribution of all sample means of a certain size is normally distributed regardless of the original distribution's shape.

"Statistical Significance" gives the

INDEX TO THE TROUBLESHOOTING GUIDE

maximum risk of generalizing from a sample to the population. Risk is the probability of error. "Statistically significant at p 0.05" means that there is less than a 5% risk in generalizing from sample to population.

The *"Null Hypothesis"* is a hypothesis that the population mean equals a fixed constant $= _0$, or that two samples come from the same population $_1 = _2$.

"A Statistically Significant Result at the 0.05 level" means that there is less than a 5% risk in rejecting the null hypothesis that $= _0$ (or that $_1 = _2$).

The *"Variance Accounted for"* is an index of correlation between two variables. If you account for variance in weight by the variable height, it means that height and weight are correlated. (The square root of the variance accounted for is the correlation coefficient, e.g., 49% variance accounted for is equivalent to a correlation coefficient of 0.70.)

"t-Tests" are tests for comparing the means of two samples to test the hypothesis that they really came from the same population and the observed difference is not larger than sampling error.

The *"Chi-Square Test"* is a test for comparing two samples when the measurement operation is counting. This test compares observed to expected frequencies. In the table below, we can see that in the sample in question, the males were predominantly brown-eyed and the females blue-eyed whereas we would have expected the color of eyes not to be sexlinked.

	Males	Females
Brown Eyes	15	6
Blue Eyes	7	16

III. EXPERIMENTAL DESIGN

Purpose:

To eliminate plausible rival hypotheses that account for observed differences.

Example:

We know that the tested reading comprehension of girls is better than that of boys. One hypothesis is that the observed difference is due to the interest of the material read in school. A design is the detailing of the strategy to be employed in eliminating the rival hypotheses. Designs depend upon many factors including sample size, observation intervals, number of variables, and kind of data.

	Fashion Story	Baseball Story	Total
Boys	25	43	68
Girls	55	20	75
Totals	80	63	

Note that the number in the top, left-hand box is the average score of boys on the fashion story (25). Here we can see that overall girls read better (75 as opposed to 68) but that boys do better on the baseball story than girls.

Someone suggests a plausible rival hypothesis: "How do you know boys don't do better on the baseball story just because they have previous knowledge on the subject and the girls don't? It may not be interest at all." We would then have to control for that variable in our design.

Useful Concepts:

Dependent Variable—This is the variable we are studying. For our example, it's reading comprehension.

Independent Variable—This is the variable we're trying to use to explain the observed variation in the dependent variable. For example, we might hope to explain differences in reading comprehension by the variable of the masculinity or femininity of the story.

Partitioning Variance—The central idea of this procedure is to partition the total variance into independent parts, each of which represents a different variable's effect.

Total Variance in Reading Comprehension = Variance due to Sex Differences + Variance due to Interest Differences in Story Material + An Interaction of Sex and Material + Sampling Error.

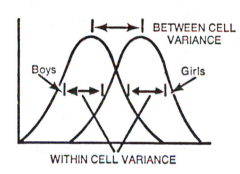 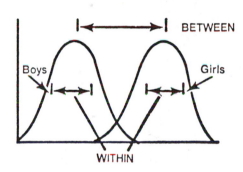

F-Test—This test may be used to compare variances after the total variance is partitioned. For example, does the variance due to sex seem large in relation to sampling error?

The *F*-Test is mainly a ratio of between-cell variance to within-cell variance. In the curves on the left, the within cell variance is large compared to the between cell variance. In the figure on the right, the within-cell variance is small compared to the between-cell variance.

Interaction—In the design given in the example above, we can plot the cell means.

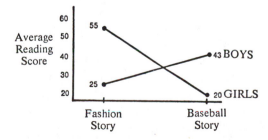

This is an example of interaction. Interaction is zero if the lines are parallel. In this case an interaction of zero would mean that boys (or girls) read better on all stories.

		Fashion Story	Baseball Story
B O Y S	High Socio-Economic Status		
	Low Socio-Economic Status		
G I R L S	High Socio-Economic Status		
	Low Socio-Economic Status		

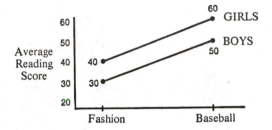

Interactions can cross (be "transverse") or just diverge (be "divergent").

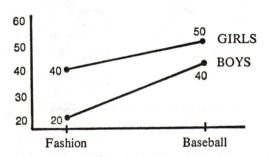

In this case, while girls are still reading better than boys, the difference is reduced in the baseball story.

Analysis of Variance—The analysis of variance is an experimental design for studying differences between cell means or combinations of cell means. The means are compared with respect to a common variance unit.

Blocking—Sometimes we want to split our design by blocking on a variable. For example, we may want to look at that reading data for high and low socioeconomic status children. Then our design would be

We do this hoping to reduce the within-cell variability by introducing a new variable. We also may wish to contend with the plausible rival hypothesis that we have not accounted for socioeconomic status and that perhaps that variable would explain our results.

Analysis of Covariance is a way of trying to control statistically for a variable which we are not able to control experimentally.

For example, two groups may differ in IQ. We could block by IQ, or we could use an analysis of covariance.

Here's how an analysis of covariance works. The dependent variable is related to a *covariate*. (Reading is related to IQ.) We use this relationship to try to predict reading score from IQ. Then we subtract the predicted score from the actual score and analyze the residual. We still hope to reduce the within-cell variability.

[Generally analysis of covariance is inferior to blocking unless the correlation between dependent variable and covariate is greater than 0.60 (Myers, 1966).]

Internal and External Validity—Campbell and Stanley (1963) list sources of plausible rival hypotheses which may jeopardize the conclusions of any experimental design. Please read their excellent article for an elaboration of these and examples of commonly used designs compared on these factors.

Internal Validity—factors representing extraneous variables which will confound the experimental variable if not controlled.

1. *History*—specific events occurring between the first and second measurement in addition to the experimental variable.
2. *Maturation*—processes within the subjects operating as a function of the passage of time, per se (growing older, hungrier, fatigued, or less attentive).
3. *Testing*—the effects of testing upon the scores of a subsequent testing.
4. *Instrumentation*—changes in obtained measurement due to changes in instrument calibration or changes in the observers or judges.
5. Statistical Regression—a phenomenon occurring when groups have been selected on the basis of extreme scores.
6. *Selection*—biases resulting from the differential selection of subjects for the comparison groups.
7. *Experimental Mortality*—the differential loss of subjects from the comparison groups.
8. *Selection-Maturation Interaction, Etc.*—interaction effects between the aforementioned variables which can be mistaken for the effects of the experimental variable.

External Validity—factors which jeopardize the representativeness or one's ability to generalize.

1. *Interaction Effects* of selection biases and the experimental variable.

2. *Reactive or Interaction Effect of Pretesting*—The pretesting modifies the subject in such a way that he responds to the experimental treatment differently than will unpretested persons in the same population.
3. *Reactive Effects of Experimental Procedures*—effects arising from the experimental setting which will not occur in nonexperimental settings.
4. *Multiple-Treatment Interference*—effects due to multiple treatments applied to the same subjects where prior treatments influence subsequent treatments in the series because their effects are not erasable.

Samples of Common Designs

1. One-Shot Case Study
(lousy design)

X	T$_2$
Intervention	Posttest

2. One Group Pretest-Posttest

T$_1$	X	T$_2$
Pretest	Int.	Posttest

3. Randomized Control Group

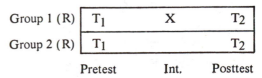

Group 1 (R)	T$_1$	X	T$_2$
Group 2 (R)	T$_1$		T$_2$
	Pretest	Int.	Posttest

(R) = Subjects are randomly assigned to groups. Group 2 gets everything but the intervention, *X*

4. Posttest-Only Design

Group 1 (R)	×	T_2
Group 2 (R)		T_2

Int.　　Posttest

Group 2 gets the posttest only.

5. Solomon Four-Group Design

Group 1 (R)	T_1	×	T_2
Group 2 (R)	T_1		T_2
Group 3 (R)		×	T_2
Group 4 (R)			T_2

Pretest　　Int.　　Posttest

This design is equivalent to a two by two (2 x 2) *factorial design.*

Intervention	Group 1	Group 3
No Intervention	Group 2	Group 4

(Every group gets
a posttest)

This design is recommended as a good experimental design by Campbell and Stanley (1963).

6. Interrupted Time-Series Design

T_1 T_2	T_N × T_{N+1} T_{N+2}	T_{N+M}

7. Time-Lagged Time-Series Design

Group 1	T_1 T_2	T_N × T_{N+1} T_{N+2}	T_{N+M} T_{N+M+1}
Group 2	T_1 T_2	T_N T_{N+1} T_{N+2}	T_{N+M} × T_{N+M+1}

8. Time-Series Flip-Flop Design

Group 1	T_1 T_2	T_N X_Z T_{N+1}	T_{N+M} S_B T_{N+M+1}
Group 2	T_1 T_2	T_N X_B T_{N+1}	T_{N+M} X_A T_{N+M+1}

The time-series designs are recommended by this book as excellent quasi-experimental designs. They can also be used to monitor and assess change in one person (doesn't have to be groups).

IV. MEASUREMENT

Purpose:

We often wish to make the assumption that we are measuring one variable on one continuum. Some techniques in measurement design allow us to test these assumptions.

Example:

Designing an opinionnaire to measure students' attitudes toward school, peers, teachers, studies and teaching methods. A student is asked to register the extent of his agreement with statements such as

	Disagree	Neutral	Agree
School is fun.	1　2　3	4	5　6　7

by circling the number which best represents his opinion. Certain items are clustered as belonging to one scale or another.

Useful Concepts:

Reliability—the extent to which the measurement procedure gives similar results under similar conditions. Methods of assessing:

1. *Stability (test-retest)* correlation between two successive measurements with the same test or inventory must assume times of testing are "similar conditions."
2. *Alternate forms*—two forms are constructed by randomly sampling items

from a domain and a correlation is computed between "equivalent forms."

3. *Split-half*—a procedure used in place of alternate forms by dividing the items in half, hopefully into "equivalent halves."

4. *KR-20 and KR-21* are formulas used to assess an alternate form reliability. Formula 21 is given here (less accurate than formula 20, but easier to compute)

$$r = \frac{K}{K-1}\left(1 - \frac{M(K-M)}{KS^2}\right)$$

where the items are scored 1 if "right," 0 if "wrong," K is number of items, S is standard deviation, and M is the mean of the scale.

Validity is the extent to which a measurement procedure measures what it claims to measure. Methods of assessing:

1. *Content Validity* (snapshot). How well does the individual's performance in this situation correlate with his performance in other similar situations?

2. *Criterion-Related Validity* (motion picture). How well does this individual's performance on this measurement predict his performance in future related situations (how well do achievement test scores predict grades in college?).

3. *Construct Validity.* Does the measurement procedure make sense as measuring what it claims to? Do the items which are supposed to be on one scale "hang together"? This can be assessed empirically by relating the extent to which presumably related constructs explain variation on the instrument in question. Here is an example where this kind of validity is crucial. Suppose you show that 92% of all high school seniors cannot read election

ballots with comprehension. The instrument is *face valid*. It has construct validity and you don't need to show content or criterion validity.

Convergent Operations. Different measurement procedures have different weaknesses. More confidence is obtained in a result when several different measurement procedures point to (or converge to) the same result.

Scales are attempts at quantifying a construct and converting it into a continuum.

1. *Likert Scale.* A scale composed of items each of which the subject rates on a scale. Examples:

a. School is fun. *SA A N D SD (SA* = strongly agree, *A* = agree, *N* = neutral, *D* = disagree, *SD* = strongly disagree)
b. School is (check the blank):
   Fun: — : — : — : — : — : — : Dull

Item *b* is sometimes called a *semantic differential* item. In this kind of item we can put any two words on either side of the line, for example,

strong: — : — : — : — : — : — : weak

2. *Thurstone type* or *equal-appearing interval scales.* These scales scale the items themselves. Items are first sorted by judges into three categories, then each category broken down into three others along a continuum (hostility, favorableness, disruptiveness, assertiveness). Items are eliminated if there is large disagreement between judges. Items are selected to have mean values (across judges) spread across the continuum from 1 to 9, preferably equally spaced. The individual taking the inventory checks those times with which he agrees (or finds hostile or disruptive). He is given the score which is the sum of the

mean judges' ratings for items checked. We might scale situations for the degree of assertiveness required and ask the subject to check the situations which are problems for him. The items not checked could be used to give an assertiveness score for him by adding the average of judged ratings. This places the individual along an assertiveness continuum.

3. *Guttman-Type* scales have items which vary along an attribute. Items can be ordered in difficulty, complexity, or value-loading so that answers to the last item will imply success or approval to all those preceding. Examples:

Difficulty:
I can add two numbers.
I can multiply two numbers.
I can divide two numbers.
I can compute a mean.
I can compute the standard deviation.

Favorableness:
1. Would you object to a retarded person living in your community?
2. Would you object to a retarded person working where you work?
3. Would you object to having lunch with a retarded person at work?
4. Would you object to a retarded person coming to your home for dinner?
5. Would you object to a retarded person marrying a member of your family?

Item Analysis is a procedure for selecting only items which discriminate in the same way the overall instrument is intended to discriminate.

A correlation is computed between each item and the total score on the instrument. For *dichotomous items* (yes, no; pass, fail) a two by two chi-square table is constructed.

For a multiple-choice test we wish there to be a strong relationship between choosing the correct alternative and high total score; also we want there to be a weak relationship between choosing distractors and high total score.

Factor Analysis in Measurement Design is a method for analyzing the extent to which items cluster by studying their intercorrelations. We have confidence in the conclusion that our test has four independent scales if the items within scales correlate highly but items across scales do not correlate very highly (see analysis of data).

	High Total	Low Total
Item 15 Yes		
No		

or

	High Total	Low Total
Item 73 Right		
Wrong		

V. ANALYSIS OF DATA

Purpose:

To study the nature of relationships between variables.

Example:

We wish to determine which variables will predict whether a citizen will vote Republican (or Democrat) in the forthcoming election.

Useful Concepts:

Correlation measures the degree of relationship between two variables. Usually a scatter diagram will provide an index for the eyeball.

The *Correlation Coefficient* gives an index of the degree of association (linear). 0 is no correlation, -1 is strongest negative, 1 is strongest positive correlation.

Partial Correlations involve calculating the correlation coefficient between two variables while statistically holding another variable constant. For example, ice cream sales may correlate with crime rates but not if the average daily temperature were controlled. Since we cannot control average daily temperature experimentally, we do it statistically. The correlation between ice cream sales and crime rate may be high but the partial correlation, controlling average daily temperature, may be quite low. Blaylock uses this technique to argue from correlation to causation.

Regression is a statistical procedure which is like a recipe for converting from one variable to another using the best (least-squares) equation.

Multiple Regression is a statistical procedure like a recipe relating one variable to a set of other variables. For example, if we relate high school dropout rates to school expenditure, teacher experience, and the average number of library books in the classroom, we will have a recipe that says, "our best guess from the multiple regression is that if we spend $3 more per pupil, dropout rates may decline by 2%. We could spend $1 per pupil by buying some books, and the

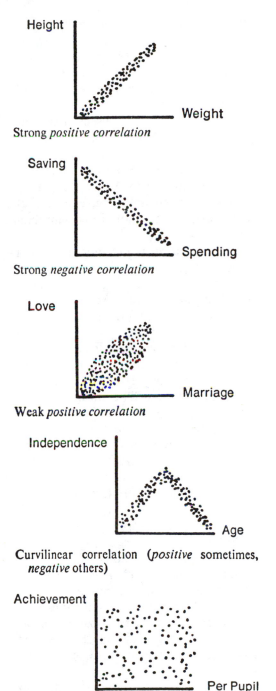

Strong *positive correlation*

Strong *negative correlation*

Weak *positive correlation*

Curvilinear correlation (*positive* sometimes, *negative* others)

No *correlation*

other $2 by hiring more experienced teachers."

The multiple regression gives you a mathematical equation of the relationships between one variable and a set of variables.

It's like a recipe in the sense that how good a cake turns out is related to a host of variables (how much sugar, salt, flour, etc., you add). It differs from a recipe in that you can improve the product by adding more of anything, except that some variables are more important than others.

Factor Analysis is a technique for data reduction. It analyzes the statistical dependencies between a set of variables by looking at the way variables correlate. For example, it may reduce a set of 50 variables into 3 basic variables. Each of the three will be statistically independent (zero correlation if the variables are normally distributed) of the other two. Each of the three will be linear combinations of the original set of fifty. Some of the fifty will "load" more highly on one factor, others will load on other factors. Each factor is a weighted sum of the original fifty.

The three factors should try to account for as much of the variance in the original fifty as possible.

Problem comes in *naming* the factors, i.e., giving them some physical interpretation in the real world. This is where the procedure becomes subjective.

No one has really derived the sampling distributions of factor loading coefficients, so it's not clear how *stable* factors are. (See Principal Components Analysis.)

Principal Components Analysis tries to reduce data by a geometrical transformation of the original variables. An example is a scatterplot in three dimensions which gives a swarm of points in the shape of a football.

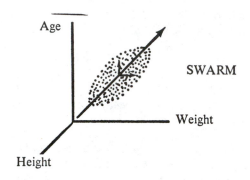

The new axes are those emanating from the swarm. The principal component is the main axis of the football. If most variance in the swarm is along one principal component (which will be a combination of the first three variables), we have reduced our data from three variables (which were correlated) to one variable. In general, we will reduce a large set of variables into a smaller set. Each variable in the smaller set is a linear combination (a weighted sum) of the original variables, and the new smaller set of variables are independent of one another.

The problem comes with interpretations—it's usually worse with principal components than factor analysis although the geometrical meaning is clearer.

Canonical Correlations are a procedure for factor analyzing two batteries of tests simultaneously to extract factors which are uncorrelated within their batteries but which provide high correlation of pairs of factors across batteries. For example, a researcher may have one battery of interest measures and another battery of skill or ability measures and he wants to know the overlap in measurement variance between the two systems of measures.

Multiple Correlation finds the optimal weighting to maximize the correlation between several variables (predictors) and another variable (the criterion).

Multivariate Analysis of Variance is a generalization of the analysis of variance (see section on Research Designs) to the situation where several variables are measured and these variables are statistically related.

The research issue behind the generalized tests is whether two or more sample groups should be thought of as arising from a single multivariate population or from two or more multivariate populations.

Discriminant Function Analysis is a procedure for predicting group membership of an individual on the basis of a set of other variables.

For example, if we can take medical measurements of various kinds, can we find the best way to combine these (weight them) to predict whether or not a person has cancer?

Discriminant function analysis is used extensively in theory construction finding *which* variables in *what* combination predict political party membership or any other group membership.

Time-Series Analysis is a procedure for analyzing observations over time for predicting trends, understanding the basis for fluctuations, and assessing the effects of interventions.

REFERENCES

Blaylock, H. M. *Causal Inferences in Non-experimental Research.* Chapel Hill: University of North Carolina Press, 1961.

Campbell, D. T., and J. Stanley, "Experimental and Quasi-Experimental Designs for Research and Teaching." In Gage, N. L. (ed.), *Handbook of Research on Teaching.* Chicago: Rand McNally, 1963.

Myers, J. L. *Fundamentals of Experimental Design.* Boston: Allyn-Bacon, 1966.

Part Five

Dilemmas of Practice

Introduction

The difficulties of the current situation for community practitioners go far beyond the usual complexities of practice. For organizers and planners, as well as for administrators and managers, the struggle to maintain services and programs with decreasing resources will be difficult at best. High unemployment coupled with reduced benefit levels has negatively affected virtually every major population group—especially those who are poor, of color, old, young, or female. One consequence is a marked trend toward demoralization, cynicism, and pessimism among some groups of practitioners.

At the same time, there is a series of practice dilemmas that confront people in the field which are only exacerbated by these restrictive external conditions. Inattention to these dilemmas—like handling retrenchment and burnout—can spell an early end to almost any change effort. In this section of the book (new in this edition) we try to address certain questions that people in the field feel are critical. Some long-standing and emerging general problems are explored briefly first. The major portion of the section is devoted to a detailed consideration of some of the most pressing and all-encompassing issues.

Personal and Interpersonal Aspects of Practice

Two organizers, who had maintained a stormy personal relationship for years, seemed to be in a constant battle over tactics. At every steering committee meeting of their political organization, each would take opposing positions, leading them to argue through the sessions and into their home hours later. Eventually, their personal relationship ended, but they continued to interact in the same fractious way in meeting after meeting. The process only stopped when the man finally moved to another city. Obviously they had an unhealthy relationship that stormily extended into other, including political, concerns. The only problem with this analysis, however, is the following: as soon as the man had left, the woman at the very next steering committee meeting began to consistently argue with another

409

male member, one with whom she had had cordial relations in the past. No matter how often people spoke to her about her actions, she always found herself intractably locked in constant battle with her former friend. Unable to alter the pattern, her eventual solution was voluntary removal from the committee.[1]

This vignette suggests an important aspect of organizing, planning, and managing that is often overlooked by practitioners and teachers alike. Put simply, it is the personal dimension of community practice. Indeed, many people with long community experience report that it is much more often the personal and interpersonal problems that undermine their effectiveness rather than structural or organizational constraints.

Task and Process Goals

One of the most enduring dilemmas for community practitioners is whether to focus on "task" or "process" goals. As noted earlier in the book, task refers mainly to specific and tangible results—a new program, a policy shift, a conference, a piece of legislation, and so on. Process emphasizes building and strengthening the relationships between and among people involved together in community work. It also directs attention to enhancing the ability of participants to deal with the sociopolitical environment on an ongoing basis. Clearly, in planning and administering, task goals tend to predominate, while in organizing and developing, process goals receive more emphasis. However, there is always a danger of focusing on one kind of goal to the complete exclusion of the other.

In any change effort, our view is that *both* task and process goals must be attended to. Most planning, organizing, managing, and policy making that takes place over time requires the practitioner to do some shifting from one priority set of goals to another in response to client system and to organizational and sociopolitical shifts in the community. Thus, rather than being somehow mutually exclusive, we see task and process as integrally related and most effectively approached as mutually supportive. For example, the practitioner staffing a community-based committee pressing local businesses to more active affirmative action hiring policies must—in some serial fashion—pay attention both to building the interpersonal solidarity, strength, and resolve of the committee while at the same time setting realistic goals for new hires by targeted firms.

Technology, Expertise, and Participation

As Gilbert and Specht have pointed out, there has been an enormous increase in the use of technical expertise in community practice over the last

---

[1]Steve Burghardt, *The Other Side of Organizing* (Cambridge, Mass.: Schenkman, 1982), p. 65.

twenty-five years.[2] One recent illustration is the rapid expansion of instruction in computer technology as an integral part of research at the master's (and sometimes bachelor's) level in social work. Many social agencies, especially those that are larger and better financed, have made extensive use of new data-processing technology.

The rate at which new information is generated by advanced technology suggests that especially those engaged in planning and managing need to be fully aware of its uses (and misuses). The image of the otherwise proud planner, manager, or organizer trembling before the mighty computer needs an early retirement. There is also the very serious question of just how much guidance can be derived from the new technology. The opposite extreme— and the one to which community practitioners have been all too susceptible—is to regard every situation as so unique as to be beyond illumination by application of any set of generalized data. The major dilemma, of course, is to figure out when to leave technocratic problem solving and where to begin using situation-specific information.

A related dilemma, and one which has plagued organizers, planners, and administrators alike since the earliest days of professional social work, is how to balance the requirement for expertise with the humanistic need for participatory decision making. Can all client populations be made into experts on whatever topic may be under consideration? On the other hand, has knowledge become so complex and sophisticated that only well-trained experts can be truly in command of the necessary information for fully informed exploration and selection of alternatives?

While it does not take a genius to conclude that the answer in any given "live" situation is probably somewhere between the two, the practitioner's tendency to lean one way or the other (for ideological or other reasons) may have a direct and lasting bearing on his or her ability to deal both with certain client groups and organization(s) involved in a change process. The health care planning arena, for example, is especially fraught with such questions; consumers often feel undervalued and excluded from decision making and highly trained health care providers expect to exercise their prerogatives as experts.

Practice Theory and Personal Style

Like the advanced medical student who tries to emulate the style of his or her most inspiring professor, many students and beginning planners, organizers, and managers attempt to replicate the theoretical postures and interventive approaches of a favorite practitioner. The appeal of all-encompassing theories and elaborate case materials as guides for action is

---

[2]Neil Gilbert and Harry Specht, "The Integration of Sociopolitical and Technical Knowledge Components in Education for Indirect-Service Practice," paper presented at the Annual Program Meeting of the Council on Social Work Education, Boston, 1979.

undeniable. However, there is no easy or simple fit between available practice theory or "practice wisdom" and the emerging style of each practitioner. As Kramer and Specht note:

> Although the identification of the pace and the complexity of community organization work is important in the development of practice theory, most case histories describe only the writers' personal style of working, and working style is often the unique product of an individual's artistic capacity to integrate his or her personal sensibilities in a given set of sociopolitical circumstances, an important aspect of community work but not a substitute for knowledge. The personal style that a professional uses in practice is something that is developed on an individual basis over several years. We caution aspiring professionals to avoid taking on someone else's way of behaving and take the time needed to develop their own styles.[3]

Balancing what you know (or think you know) and what you do is no easy task. As most veteran practitioners will tell you, this dilemma has no quick or easy solution. In the most literal and important sense, it must be lived through. Anyone who seems to have all the "right" answers has, no doubt, missed some of the important questions.

Other Major Dilemmas

Each of the selections that follow touch on major issues, problems, or questions that community practitioners have found especially significant, challenging or vexing.

The oft-cited but little known National Association of Social Workers (N.A.S.W.) Code of Ethics is a useful guide for a number of basic questions not only of ethics but also of morality. These range from responsibilities to clients to responsibilities to society, from obligations to advocate changes in social policy to prohibitions against sexual involvement with clients. Also included is a commentary prepared by a national office staff member on discussions surrounding preparation of major areas of the code.

Sexism in the profession of social work has been well documented. Chernesky explores the underrepresentation of women in administrative positions and the factors associated with it. Many of the areas she explores are equally important for understanding the disproportionate numbers of women in planning and organizing as well. Specific guidelines for addressing this sex discrimination dilemma are suggested. The need for social work to respond more effectively to Third World people in light of class discrimination and institutional racism are discussed by Morales. He suggests an ecosystems model for practice and explores manpower issues, ethnic agencies, and intervention strategies.

---

[3]Ralph Kramer and Harry Specht (eds.), *Readings in Community Organization Practice,* 3rd ed. (Englewood Cliffs, N.J.: Prentice-Hall, 1983), p. 18.

The last two articles in this final section of the book focus on two pervasive and interrelated problems—retrenchment and burnout. Levine's seminal article on how we address organizational decline highlights many perplexing issues—not the least of which is a misguided approach based upon an expectation of continuing growth. One of the most difficult aspects of this issue is that there are no "right" answers; frequently the question is how to select the least damaging among undesirable options. Finally, there is the question of burnout. Citing their empirical work in this area, Zietz and Erlich explore the meaning, dimensions, and consequences of burnout—along with a surprising amount of job satisfaction—and suggest ways of addressing this most pressing personal and professional dilemma.

John L. Erlich

A. ETHICAL DILEMMAS

30. CODE OF ETHICS OF THE NATIONAL ASSOCIATION OF SOCIAL WORKERS AND COMMENTARY

CONTENTS

PREAMBLE

This code is intended to serve as a guide to the everyday conduct of members of the social work profession and as a basis for the adjudication of issues in ethics when the conduct of social workers is alleged to deviate from the standards expressed or implied in this code. It represents standards of ethical behavior for social workers in professional relationships with those served, with colleagues, with employers, with other individuals and professions, and with the community and society as a whole. It also embodies standards of ethical behavior governing individual conduct to the extent that such conduct is associated with an individual's status and identity as a social worker.

This code is based on the fundamental values of the social work profession that include the worth, dignity, and uniqueness of all persons as well as their rights and opportunities. It is also based on the nature of social work, which fosters conditions that promote these values.

In subscribing to and abiding by this code, the social worker is expected to view ethical responsibility in as inclusive a context as each situation demands and within which ethical judgement is required. The social worker is expected to take into consideration all the principles in this code that have a bearing upon any situation in which ethical judgement is to be exercised and professional intervention or conduct is planned. The course of action that the social worker chooses is expected to be consistent with the spirit as well as the letter of this code.

In itself, this code does not represent a set of rules that will prescribe all the behaviors of social workers in all the complexities of professional life. Rather, it offers general principles to guide conduct, and the judicious appraisal of conduct, in situations that have ethical implications. It provides the basis for making judgements about ethical actions before and after they occur. Frequently, the particular situation determines the ethical principles that apply and the manner of their application. In such cases, not only the particular ethical principles are taken into immediate consideration, but also the entire code and its spirit. Specific applications of ethical principles must be judged within the context in which they are being considered. Ethical behavior in a given situation must satisfy not only the judgement of the individual social worker, but also the judgement of an unbiased jury of professional peers.

This code should not be used as an instrument to deprive any social worker of the opportunity or freedom to practice with complete professional integrity; nor should any disciplinary action be taken on the basis of this code without maximum provision for safeguarding the rights of the social worker affected.

The ethical behavior of social workers results not from edict, but from a personal commitment of the individual. This code is offered to affirm the will and zeal of all social workers to be ethical and to act ethically in all that they do as social workers.

The following codified ethical principles should guide social workers in the various roles and relationships and at the various levels of responsibility in which they function professionally. These principles also serve as a basis for the adjudication by the National Association of Social Workers of issues in ethics.

In subscribing to this code, social workers are required to cooperate in its implementation and abide by any disciplinary rulings based on it. They should also take adequate measures to discourage, prevent, expose, and correct the unethical conduct of colleagues. Finally, social workers should be equally ready to defend and assist colleagues unjustly charged with unethical conduct.

SUMMARY OF MAJOR PRINCIPLES

I. The Social Worker's Conduct and Comportment as a Social Worker

A. Propriety. The social worker should maintain high standards of personal conduct in the capacity or identity as social worker.

B. Competence and Professional Development. The social worker should strive to become and remain proficient in professional practice and the performance of professional functions.

C. Service. The social worker should regard as primary the service obligation of the social work profession.

D. Integrity. The social worker should act in accordance with the highest standards of professional integrity.

E. Scholarship and Research. The social worker engaged in study and research should be guided by the conventions of scholarly inquiry.

II. The Social Worker's Ethical Responsibility to Clients

F. Primacy of Clients' Interests. The social worker's primary responsibility is to clients.

G. Rights and Prerogatives of Clients. The social worker should make every effort to foster maximum self-determination on the part of clients.

H. Confidentiality and Privacy. The social worker should respect the privacy of clients and hold in confidence all information obtained in the course of professional service.

I. Fees. When setting fees, the social worker should ensure that they are fair, reasonable, considerate, and commensurate with the service performed and with due regard for the clients' ability to pay.

III. The Social Worker's Ethical Responsibility to Colleagues

J. Respect, Fairness, and Courtesy. The social worker should treat colleagues with respect, courtesy, fairness, and good faith.

K. Dealing with Colleagues' Clients. The social worker has the responsibility to relate to the clients of colleagues with full professional consideration.

IV. The Social Worker's Ethical Responsibility to Employers and Employing Organizations

L. Commitments to Employing Organizations. The social worker should adhere to commitments made to the employing organizations.

V. The Social Worker's Ethical Responsibility to the Social Work Profession

M. Maintaining the Integrity of the Profession. The social worker should uphold and advance the values, ethics, knowledge, and mission of the profession.

N. Community Service. The social worker should assist the profession in making social services available to the general public.

O. Development of Knowledge. The social worker should take responsibility for identifying, developing, and fully utilizing knowledge for professional practice.

VI. The Social Worker's Ethical Responsibility to Society

P. Promoting the General Welfare. The social worker should promote the general welfare of society.

THE NASW CODE OF ETHICS*

I. The Social Worker's Conduct and Comportment as a Social Worker

A. Propriety—The social worker should maintain high standards of personal conduct in the capacity or identity as social worker.

1. The private conduct of the social worker is a personal matter to the same degree as is any other person's, except when such such conduct compromises the fulfillment of professional responsibilities.

2. The social worker should not participate in, condone, or be associated with dishonesty, fraud, deceit, or misrepresentation.

3. The social worker should distinguish clearly between statements and actions made as a private individual and as a representative of the social work profession or an organization or group.

B. Competence and Professional Development—The social worker should strive to become and remain proficient in professional practice and the performance of professional functions.

1. The social worker should accept responsibility or employment only on the basis of existing competence or the intention to acquire the necessary competence.

2. The social worker should not misrepresent professional qualifications, education, experience, or affiliations.

C. Service—The social worker should regard as primary the service obligation of the social work profession.

1. The social worker should retain ultimate responsibility for the quali-

*Code of Ethics as adopted by the 1979 NASW Delegate Assembly, effective July 1, 1980.

ty and extent of the service that individual assumes, assigns, or performs.

2. The social worker should act to prevent practices that are inhumane or discriminatory against any person or group of persons.

D. Integrity—The social worker should act in accordance with the highest standards of professional integrity and impartiality.

1. The social worker should be alert to and resist the influences and pressures that interfere with the exercise of professional discretion and impartial judgement required for the performance of professional functions.

2. The social worker should not exploit professional relationships for personal gain.

E. Scholarship and Research—The social worker engaged in study and research should be guided by the conventions of scholarly inquiry.

1. The social worker engaged in research should consider carefully its possible consequences for human beings.

2. The social worker engaged in research should ascertain that the consent of participants in the research is voluntary and informed, without any implied deprivation or penalty for refusal to participate, and with due regard for participants' privacy and dignity.

3. The social worker engaged in research should protect participants from unwarranted physical or mental discomfort, distress, harm, danger, or deprivation.

4. The social worker who engages in the evaluation of services or cases

should discuss them only for professional purposes and only with persons directly and professionally concerned with them.

5. Information obtained about participants in research should be treated as confidential.

6. The social worker should take credit only for work actually done in connection with scholarly and research endeavors and credit contributions made by others.

II. The Social Worker's Ethical Responsibility to Clients

F. Primacy of Clients' Interests—The social worker's primary responsibility is to clients.

1. The social worker should serve clients with devotion, loyalty, determination, and the maximum application of professional skill and competence.

2. The social worker should not exploit relationships with clients for personal advantage, or solicit the clients of one's agency for private practice.

3. The social worker should not practice, condone, facilitate or collaborate with any form of discrimination on the basis of race, color, sex, sexual orientation, age, religion, national origin, marital status, political belief, mental or physical handicap, or any other preference or personal characteristic, condition or status.

4. The social worker should avoid relationships or commitments that conflict with the interests of clients.

5. The social worker should under no circumstances engage in sexual activities with clients.

6. The social worker should provide clients with accurate and complete information regarding the extent and nature of the services available to them.

7. The social worker should apprise clients of their risks, rights, opportunities, and obligations associated with social service to them.

8. The social worker should seek advice and counsel of colleagues and supervisors whenever such consultation is in the best interest of clients.

9. The social worker should terminate service to clients, and professional relationships with them, when such service and relationships are no longer required or no longer serve the clients' needs or interests.

10. The social worker should withdraw services precipitously only under unusual circumstances, giving careful consideration to all factors in the situation and taking care to minimize possible adverse effects.

11. The social worker who anticipates the termination or interruption of service to clients should notify clients promptly and seek the transfer, referral, or continuation of service in relation to the clients' needs and preferences.

G. Rights and Prerogatives of Clients— The social worker should make every effort to foster maximum self-determination on the part of clients.

1. When the social worker must act on behalf of a client who has been adjudged legally incompetent, the social worker should safeguard the interests and rights of that client.

2. When another individual has been legally authorized to act in

behalf of a client, the social worker should deal with that person always with the client's best interest in mind.

3. The social worker should not engage in any action that violates or diminishes the civil or legal rights of clients.

H. Confidentiality and Privacy—The social worker should respect the privacy of clients and hold in confidence all information obtained in the course of professional service.

1. The social worker should share with others confidences revealed by clients, without their consent, only for compelling professional reasons.

2. The social worker should inform clients fully about the limits of confidentiality in a given situation, the purposes for which information is obtained, and how it may be used.

3. The social worker should afford clients reasonable access to any official social work records concerning them.

4. When providing clients with access to records, the social worker should take due care to protect the confidences of others contained in those records.

5. The social worker should obtain informed consent of clients before taping, recording, or permitting third party observation of their activities.

I. Fees—When setting fees, the social worker should ensure that they are fair, reasonable, considerate, and commensurate with the service performed and with due regard for the clients' ability to pay.

1. The social worker should not divide a fee or accept or give anything of value for receiving or making a referral.

III. The Social Worker's Ethical Responsibility to Colleagues

J. Respect, Fairness, and Courtesy— The social worker should treat colleagues with respect, courtesy, fairness, and good faith.

1. The social worker should cooperate with colleagues to promote professional interests and concerns.

2. The social worker should respect confidences shared by colleagues in the course of their professional relationships and transactions.

3. The social worker should create and maintain conditions of practice that facilitate ethical and competent professional performance by colleagues.

4. The social worker should treat with respect, and represent accurately and fairly, the qualifications, views, and findings of colleagues and use appropriate channels to express judgements on these matters.

5. The social worker who replaces or is replaced by a colleague in professional practice should act with consideration for the interest, character, and reputation of that colleague.

6. The social worker should not exploit a dispute between a colleague and employers to obtain a position or otherwise advance the social worker's interest.

7. The social worker should seek arbitration or mediation when conflicts with colleagues require resolu-

tion for compelling professional reasons.

8. The social worker should extend to colleagues of other professions the same respect and cooperation that is extended to social work colleagues.

9. The social worker who serves as an employer, supervisor, or mentor to colleagues should make orderly and explicit arrangements regarding the conditions of their continuing professional relationship.

10. The social worker who has the responsibility for employing and evaluating the performance of other staff members, should fulfill such responsibility in a fair, considerate, and equitable manner, on the basis of clearly enunciated criteria.

11. The social worker who has the responsibility for evaluating the performance of employees, supervisees, or students should share evaluations with them.

K. Dealing with Colleagues' Clients— The social worker has the responsibility to relate to the clients of colleagues with full professional consideration.

1. The social worker should not solicit the clients of colleagues.

2. The social worker should not assume professional responsibility for the clients of another agency or a colleague without appropriate communication with that agency or colleague.

3. The social worker who serves the clients of colleagues, during a temporary absence or emergency, should serve those clients with the same consideration as that afforded any client.

IV. The Social Worker's Ethical Responsibility to Employers and Employing Organizations

L. Commitments to Employing Organization—The social worker should adhere to commitments made to the employing organization.

1. The social worker should work to improve the employing agency's policies and procedures, and the efficiency and effectiveness of its services.

2. The social worker should not accept employment or arrange student field placements in an organization which is currently under public sanction by NASW for violating personnel standards, or imposing limitations on or penalties for professional actions on behalf of clients.

3. The social worker should act to prevent and eliminate discrimination in the employing organization's work assignments and in its employment policies and practices.

4. The social worker should use with scrupulous regard, and only for the purpose for which they are intended, the resources of the employing organization.

V. The Social Worker's Ethical Responsibility to the Social Work Profession

M. Maintaining the Integrity of the Profession—The social worker should uphold and advance the values, ethics, knowledge, and mission of the profession.

1. The social worker should protect and enhance the dignity and integri-

ty of the profession and should be responsible and vigorous in discussion and criticism of the profession.

2. The social worker should take action through appropriate channels against unethical conduct by any other member of the profession.

3. The social worker should act to prevent the unauthorized and unqualified practice of social work.

4. The social worker should make no misrepresentation in advertising as to qualifications, competence, service, or results to be achieved.

N. Community Service—The social worker should assist the profession in making social services available to the general public.

1. The social worker should contribute time and professional expertise to activities that promote respect for the utility, the integrity, and the competence of the social work profession.

2. The social worker should support the formulation, development, enactment and implementation of social policies of concern to the profession.

O. Development of Knowledge—The social worker should take responsibility for identifying, developing, and fully utilizing knowledge for professional practice.

1. The social worker should base practice upon recognized knowledge relevant to social work.

2. The social worker should critically examine, and keep current with emerging knowledge relevant to social work.

3. The social worker should contribute to the knowledge base of social work and share research knowledge and practice wisdom with colleagues.

VI. The Social Worker's Ethical Responsibility to Society

P. Promoting the General Welfare— The social worker should promote the general welfare of society.

1. The social worker should act to prevent and eliminate discrimination against any person or group on the basis of race, color, sex, sexual orientation, age, religion, national origin, marital status, political belief, mental or physical handicap, or any other preference or personal characteristic, condition, or status.

2. The social worker should act to ensure that all persons have access to the resources, services, and opportunities which they require.

3. The social worker should act to expand choice and opportunity for all persons, with special regard for disadvantaged or oppressed groups and persons.

4. The social worker should promote conditions that encourage respect for the diversity of cultures which constitute American society.

5. The social worker should provide appropriate professional services in public emergencies.

6. The social worker should advocate changes in policy and legislation to improve social conditions and to promote social justice.

7. The social worker should encourage informed participation by the public in shaping social policies and institutions.

A COMMENTARY

With the adoption of a revised Code of Ethics, NASW's Delegate Assembly took a noteworthy step in the continuing process of developing and extending standards for the social work profession.

Five years after the formation of NASW, the Delegate Assembly in 1960 adopted the association's first Code of Ethics. A principle enjoining discrimination was added in 1967, following which the code remained unaltered for more than a decade. During this period, however, a number of forces militated for revision, including:

- Changes in the profession, including growth in number of independent practitioners; new fields of practice; legal regulation; and expansion of the profession in diversity and size.
- The social and civil rights movements of the '60s and '70s and recognition of "the dissonance which may occur between professional values, agency imperatives and consumer demands."
- Shortcomings in the 1960/67 version, which failed to adequately address the issues such as confidentiality, personal behavior, research, fees, advertising, accountability, collegial obligations, advocacy, and others.
- Difficulties experienced by chapter and national committees on inquiry in adjudicating ethical issues.

Reproduced by permission of the publisher and the author. Commentary by Robert H. Cohen is from the April, May and June 1980 issues of the *NASW News*.

In 1975, a task force was authorized and charged with recommending revisions in the NASW Code of Ethics and presenting them to the 1977 Delegate Assembly.

The task force noted that, although the language of the code needed updating, other areas demanded greater attention. For example, it recommended:

- A comprehensive study of all past complaints of unethical behavior which have come before the Committee on Inquiry.
- Establishment of a clearinghouse to act as an ongoing resource to the association, its units and its members in considering ethical questions.
- Development of a chapter action guide to promote action at the state and local levels.
- Appointment of a task force to initiate, direct, and review the above processes, and allocation of sufficient staff and other resources to support its work.

Although the 1977 Delegate Assembly did not adopt the specific proposals of the task force, it recognized its contribution toward code revision and authorized creation of a successor task force to continue the work and report back to the 1979 Delegate Assembly.

In October 1977, a seven member task force was appointed by President Arthur Katz. Katz wanted to muster "an experienced, scholarly group that would be diverse, representative, and closely enough linked to other parts of the organizational structure to ensure continuity and relevance to association problems and needs."

The task force, led by Charles S. Levy, began by delineating the scope of its efforts and determining to develop a revised code which could serve both as a guide to ethical practice and to the adjudication of ethical issues. The focus was to be on the ethical conduct of social workers in their various roles, responsibilities and professional relationships. Such considerations as implementation, education, and enforcement—as important as these were regarded to be—would not be addressed, but would be left for subsequent consideration and action by others in the NASW leadership structure.

From the outset, attempts were made to involve members and chapter committees in the process of code construction, via the *NASW NEWS* and via direct invitations by task force members and staff. The experience of several other professional organizations, e.g., American Psychological Association, International Federation of Social Workers, American Bar Association, was also taken into consideration.

Approximately three dozen ethical codes of other professions and organizations were identified and subjected to computer-aided scrutiny. Members of the task force identified principles which appeared to have relevance for social workers and grouped these under categories of ethical obligations owed by the social worker (e.g., to clients, colleagues, society, etc.). Data from all of the codes analyzed were fed into a computer and aggregated by category. Eventually, non-relevant items were discarded (or moved to a more appropriate category); duplicative principles were deleted and only one or two of the best formulated ones retained.

A number of criteria guided task force deliberations. Included were the following:

- Ethical principles should be formulated at a level of generality/specificity which would be sufficiently inclusive and precise to provide guidance (to practitioners and adjudicating bodies), yet not attempt to cover every situation and variation thereof.
- The proposed code should not attempt to sort out "inspirational" principles from adjudicatory ones, but should include a mixture of proscribed and preferred behaviors. (This approach was in line with the dual purpose to be served; i.e., as a guide, as well as a basis for adjudication).
- The code should not attempt to formulate principles in a hierarchical arrangement, but should recognize that principles may, and often do, conflict with one another although each may be valid. As stated in the preamble to the proposed code: "Frequently the particular situation determines the ethical principles that apply and the manner of their application. In such cases, not only the particular ethical principles are taken into immediate consideration, but also the entire code and its spirit. . . ."

The code should not be a credo; it should attempt insofar as possible to state principles affirmatively rather than as proscriptions. Sexist language, pejorative terms and jargon should be avoided. Principles should be stated as a series of single declarative sentences and as clearly and concisely as possible.

I. THE SOCIAL WORKER'S CONDUCT AND COMPORTMENT AS A SOCIAL WORKER

Principle A.1:

The private conduct of the social worker is a personal matter to the same degree as is any other person's except when such conduct compromises the fulfillment of professional responsibilities.

Discussion

One viewpoint on private behavior is that, regardless of its nature, it should be considered entirely beyond the reach or coverage of an ethics code—"We shouldn't get into the question of personal conduct or morality."

An opposing view holds that certain behaviors might be so antiethical to social work values (e.g., financial contributions to the Ku Klux Klan), or might reflect such "moral turpitude" that, as professionals, we would be obliged to take action against the member.

In its resolution of these views, the task force agreed that the private or personal behavior of a social worker should be regarded as exactly that (i.e., not subject to the code), except insofar as such conduct might impinge on fulfillment of professional responsibilities. In a situation in which a member would be charged with breach of ethics stemming from private conduct, the critical question would be whether this interfered with carrying out professional responsibility. A jury of peers would have to decide that question, based on the facts of the particular situation.

Principle B.1:

The social worker should accept responsibility or employment only on the basis of existing competence or the intention to acquire the necessary competence.

Discussion

Is it unethical *per se* to assume professional responsibilities or employment for which one is not equipped by training and experience?

For some, this issue goes to the heart of efforts to establish, promulgate, and enforce standards of professional competence and to provide assurance to clients and to the public that the quality of services offered can be relied upon and is commensurate with the task to be performed.

Although none of the task force members disagreed with the vital importance of promoting high standards of professional competence, others contended that the code must provide for those who aspire to more complex and professionally demanding roles; those still in training, in transition, etc. If the principles governing competence and professional development were formulated too stringently, aspirations might be inhibited and professional mobility impaired.

The resulting formulation of the task force attempts to combine the theme of responsibility for one's own undertakings and competency with recognition that latitude must be afforded to those who reach beyond their present capabilities, so long as they intend to acquire the requisite competence.

Principle B.2:

The social worker should not misrepresent professional qualifications, education, experience or affiliations.

Discussion

This provision (along with another later in the code, V. M. 4.) addresses, in part, the issue of "advertising." V. M. 4. emphasizes the product—"The social worker should make no misrepresentations in advertising as to qualifications, competence, service or results to be achieved." I.B.2. deals solely with the person. The way in which the individual holds her/himself out, the accuracy of representation regarding qualifications, background and affiliations, is key here. Advertising, personal or otherwise, thus, is not defined as "good" or "bad," permissible or proscribed. The emphasis is on candor in presenting one's professional credentials properly, and in representing the nature, expectations and limitations of the service to be rendered.

Principle E:

Scholarship and Research. The social worker engaged in study and research should be guided by the conventions of scholarly inquiry.

Discussion

Section I.E., Scholarship and Research, is entirely new and was developed in response to the need of many social workers, especially researchers, academicians and evaluators, who were troubled by the absence of ethical guidelines in an area of practice often affecting the most vulnerable groups.

Although several of the principles set forth in I.E. might have been inferred from provisions in the old code, new concepts were introduced and others that before were implicit at best, have now been spelled out. The whole area of protection of human subjects—brought bluntly to our attention in recent years by revelations of disregard of basic human rights and callous use of unwitting individuals under the banner of scientific research—is addressed. The concept of informed consent and the emphasis on respect for privacy, which extends beyond merely "the people I serve" of the old code, also characterize section E. 1.

II. THE SOCIAL WORKER'S ETHICAL RESPONSIBILITY TO CLIENTS

Principle F.3:

The social worker should not practice, condone, facilitate or collaborate with any form of discrimination on the basis of race, color, sex, sexual orientation, age, religion, national origin, marital status, political belief, mental or physical handicap, or any other preference or personal characteristic, condition or status.

Discussion

This principle, although similar to that contained in the old code, is more extensive in terms both of the nature of the social worker's obligation and the specific bases of proscribed discrimination. Practicing, facilitating or collaborating with *any form of discrimination*, is prohibited. Moreover, in addition to "race, color, religion, age, sex, or national ancestry" (the new code uses the term "national *origin"),* the revised code specifies "sexual orientation," "marital status," "political belief," "mental or physical handicap," or "any other preference or personal characteristic, condition or status."

The singular importance accorded to non-discrimination in the new code is reflected by the reiteration of the principle later, in VI. P. 1., wherein the social worker is called upon, not merely to refrain from "practicing, condoning" discrimination against clients, but also to "act to prevent and eliminate discrimination against any person or group . . ."

Principle F.5:

The social worker should under no circumstances engage in sexual activities with clients.

Discussion

Members of the task force were in agreement that the issue of indulging in sex with clients needed to be addressed. Great damage has been done to clients who have been exploited by trusted physicians, therapists and other "helping" persons, and to the professions (especially in the mental health field) which have seen public confidence in their motives, competence, and integrity steadily eroded.

Thus the task force deliberately used the strongest language of absolute prohibition, "under no circumstances," found any place in the code. However, it was recognized that that which is to be prohibited is not easy to define. Certain-

ly sexual intercourse is intended. But is that all? If the Principle referred to "sexual intercourse," rather than "sexual activities," it might be inferred that other sexual acts might be permissible. An attempt to list proscribed sexual behavior between social workers and clients would be unwieldy, as well as ludicrous.

In using the general term "sexual activities," the task force was aware of its imprecision. Might not a reassuring hug, a pat on the arm, holding a youngster on one's lap, kissing a child, etc., be viewed by some as a "sexual activity"? The task force concluded that the principle as stated would provide guidance where, in essence, there had been none, and that if a situation were brought to adjudication, a jury of peers would be able to determine whether the alleged "sexual activities" were of the sort covered by the prohibition.

Principle H.1:

The social worker should share with others confidences revealed by clients, without their consent, only for compelling professional reasons.

Discussion

If a client refuses to grant permission to the social worker to share confidential communications with others, should this constitute an absolute bar to disclosure by that worker? Some say that confidentiality within the professional helping relationship is of such transcendent importance that it should never be breached without the client's express consent. Others argue that a host of factors—ranging from the need for "case consultation" to the fear of being held legally liable for failure to disclose certain information (e.g., client's suicidal/homicidal tendencies)—militate against the "purist" approach. They contend that allowance for professional discretion should be made.

The formulation hammered out by task force members and delegates at the 1979 Delegate Assembly stresses the general principle—no disclosure without client consent—but allows for some latitude, i.e., "*compelling* (emphasis supplied) professional reasons."

The burden is placed on the worker to justify any breach of confidentiality. The mere assertion that a violation was warranted based on professional judgment would not suffice. The reason must indeed be compelling.

Section III. The Social Worker's Ethical Responsibility to Colleagues

Members of the task force struggled to capture the essence of the ethical obligation owed one's colleagues. "Respect," "courtesy," "fairness," and "good faith" imply a good number of behaviors ranging from regard for social amenities and conventions to more formal notions of fair play, procedural clarity and orderliness. Notions of candor, consideration, and tolerance are also at the heart of the social worker's ethical responsibility to colleagues.

Several of the specific principles adopted extend well beyond the single tenet in the old code, i.e., "I treat with respect the findings, views and actions of colleagues and use appropriate channels to express judgment on these matters." For example, the concept of confidentiality is viewed in a broader context.

The revised code requires that the worker "respect confidences shared by colleagues in the course of their professional relationships and transactions." Clearly this goes beyond merely, "treating with respect the findings, views and actions of colleagues." It carries into the sphere of collegial relationships the regard for privacy/confidentiality contained in the old code: "I respect the privacy of the people I serve." The new code also makes explicit the obligation to extend "to colleagues of other professions the same respect and cooperation" that one is expected to extend to social work colleagues.

Another concept not included in the old code is one which proscribes exploitation of a dispute between a colleague and employer for personal advantage. In part, this principle speaks to troublesome issues which sometime emerge as by-products of labor-management controversies, e.g., "scabbing." The use of the term "exploit" was carefully selected by the task force to provide guidance in the case of a colleague-employer dispute in which employment, promotion or other opportunity may arise. The mere fact that one may directly or indirectly derive some gain as a result of a colleague's misfortune, is not unethical per se. The element of *exploitation* must be present.

Finally, a basic component of sound practice/supervision/administration is reflected in the principle which calls for the worker to share evaluations with those evaluated or supervised. The notion of mutuality and openness with colleagues parallels that incorporated in the "client" section of the code: "The social worker should afford clients reasonable access to any official social work records concerning them."

SECTION IV. THE SOCIAL WORKER'S ETHICAL RESPONSIBILITY TO EMPLOYERS AND EMPLOYING ORGANIZATIONS

The issue of "loyalty" to one's employing organization was particularly vexing. The frequency with which advocacy responsibilities, obligations to clients, and duties owed to colleagues conflict with agency practice or policy was noted.

One view presented was that social workers should avoid bureaucratic adherence to organizational rules and policies whenever these conflict with other professional obligations and values. "Loyalty" to one's employer too often provides a convenient excuse for failure to act, i.e., to "blow the whistle," to "go public," to confront. Social workers are obliged to be agents of change.

One could also argue that the concept of "loyalty" is not a mere abstraction but a basic value upon which trust, mutuality and joint efforts must rest. If one differs so strongly with an agency's policy, practices, and expectations, one should not work there in the first place. Accepting employment and the conditions thereof while harboring serious mental reservations about abiding by them could be viewed as disingenuous if not downright dishonest.

The task force sought to make a distinction between pre-employment knowledge and understandings ("commitments") and subsequent situations. In the first instance, the social worker should be bound by promises, agreements, and prior understandings. This is a matter of basic integrity and presents a different issue from situations which subsequently arise when agency policy, practices and conditions change.

SECTION V. THE SOCIAL WORKER'S ETHICAL RESPONSIBILITY TO THE SOCIAL WORK PROFESSION

The social worker's ethical responsibility to the profession is made more explicit in the revised code. While the old code, for example, imposed an obligation "to *help* (our emphasis) protect the community against unethical practice by any individuals or organizations engaged in social welfare activities," the new code calls upon the social worker to "take *action* through appropriate channels against unethical conduct . . ." The worker is also expected to "*act* to prevent the unauthorized and unqualified practice of social work."

SECTION VI. THE SOCIAL WORKER'S ETHICAL RESPONSIBILITY TO SOCIETY

The principles contained in this section, taken as a whole, are the broadest and the least susceptible to adjudication of any in the code. But despite their almost purely "inspirational" quality, they are vitally important to the total integrity of the code and to our professional posture.

Indeed, the principles included in Section VI are unique reflections of our values, our heritage and our obligations as a profession. The duties to "act to prevent and eliminate discrimination"; "to ensure that all persons have access to the resources, services, and opportunities which they require"; "to expand choice and opportunity for all persons [especially] disadvantaged or oppressed groups and persons"; "to promote conditions that encourage respect for ... diversity of cultures"; "to advocate changes in policy and legislation to improve social conditions and to promote social justice"; and to "encourage informed participation by the public," are lofty principles toward which we set our sights as a profession. They are the essence of our social conscience and the most direct expression of the underlying values upon which our ethical code is grounded.

B. Role Dilemmas

31. WOMEN ADMINISTRATORS IN SOCIAL WORK

Roslyn H. Chernesky

The underrepresentation of women in administrative positions in proportion to their number in the profession is a phenomenon that is not unique to social work and to the social welfare field. Although considered a women's profession, social work shows the same sex role stereotyping found in other professions and fields and pervading society in general. The absence of women administrators in social work may be attributed to complex factors similar to those which lead to deliberate, invidious discrimination in corporations, universities, and other institutions. Some of these factors are related to women and their personal life experiences, training, and decisions;

others stem from institutional constraints or societal barriers placed on women. However, while corporations and universities, faced with sex discrimination lawsuits and affirmative action demands, are finally (albeit, slowly) encouraging women to seek leadership and management positions, the social work profession and social welfare agencies are failing to address the very same issues of discrimination and unequal employment opportunities.

THE PROBLEM

Scope and Magnitude

In recent years attention has been drawn to sexism in the social work profession and the social welfare field.[1] Data have consistently confirmed that male social workers dominate the administrative positions, despite the fact that two thirds of the members of the social work profession are women. Furthermore, studies indicate that the situation appears to be growing worse rather than better. The ratio of female to male administrators is actually declining. One survey of over 800 agencies showed that the percentage of female

The author wishes to express appreciation to her colleagues for their ideas and help with their reactions to the first paper. In particular, Randi Goldstein's work was an important contribution. Evelyn Frankford and Susan Vandiver, as co-chair of the New York City NASW Chapter, Women's Issues Committee, provided the initial forum for much of this material, which was included in a proposal for committee action.

Reproduced by permission of the publisher and the authors. From "Women Administrators in Social Work," by Roslyn H. Chernesky in *Women's Issues and Social Work Practice* by Elaine Norman and Arlene Mancuso, 1980, pp. 241-262. F. E. Peacock Publishers, Inc., Itasca, Illinois.

executives had decreased from 60 percent in 1957 to 16 percent in 1976.[2]

The 1968 study of the membership of the National Association of Social Workers (NASW) showed that 58 percent of the men functioned in some administrative capacity, as did 43 percent of the female social workers. Women were more likely to be located in lower level administrative positions, and, while more than 43 percent of the women listed direct services as their primary job function, only 25 percent of the male workers were in direct services.[3] Employment patterns of social workers derived from NASW membership data in later years showed an even more pronounced disparity. In the 1971-72 survey, 37 percent of the men and 18 percent of the women NASW members identified administration as their primary method, that is, their current job. Of the 1973-75 membership, who are younger and more recent graduates of schools of social work, 11 percent of the men and 5 percent of the women were in administration.[4]

Recent studies of selected agencies and settings provide further evidence for concern. A survey of 20 family agencies in Michigan found a significant relationship between sex and position level, with females more often located in lower level jobs. Women remained longer than men in direct-service positions before being promoted to the first administrative level.[5] An in-house personnel study in 1974 of one state's division of family service found that although well over 50 percent of its women employees were qualified to move into management positions, only 21 percent of all management jobs were held by women.[6]

An investigation on the status of women in the Jewish Communal Services found the vast majority of women were in the lower professional levels of employment and had very limited access to top executive and administrative positions. The survey examined 2,200 social workers across the country. More than half were women, yet less than 1 percent of the women were executives, and only 4 percent were assistant directors. Of the 303 executive positions surveyed, only 3 percent were held by women, and those were chiefly in the smaller agencies.[7]

A study of top administrators in four major national organizations (Family Service Association of America, Child Welfare League of America, federally funded community mental health centers, and the National Jewish Welfare Board) showed that over the last two decades men have replaced women in administrative positions at the rate of 2 percent a year. As noted in the *NASW News* summary of the research, "If the present trend continues, there will be no women in social work leadership positions by the year 1984."[8]

The Social Work Profession

Social work has long been sex-typed as a woman's profession. Not only is the field numerically dominated by women, but there is a general expectation that this is as it should be because the work is considered most appropriate for, or congenial to, "women's nature."[9] Alfred Kadushin makes this same point: "The professional role of social work is, in large measure, an extension of the traditional female functions of nurturing and support, of the traditional female concern with children."[10] The qualities needed for excellence in social work practice are generally considered by society to be feminine qualities. The professional tasks of helping, protecting, and fostering the growth of others continue to be labeled women's functions, requiring feminine or expressive attributes such as warmth, patience, understanding, and sensitivity.

Administration, however, is neither female dominated nor considered to be natural to women. The job requires ability and skill in problem analysis, negotiation and bargaining, fund raising, and decision making. These are all instrumental tasks viewed by society as masculine, and thus the managerial model in social work, as elsewhere, is conceptualized as a male model. The stereotypic sex role categorization leads to a preference for men in management positions because of their "sex-related characteristics," and women are excluded because they are believed to be ill-suited for administration, resulting in direct and indirect discrimination against women in administrative hiring and promotion. There is no reason to believe that the attitudes of male social workers, executives, or board members who make decisions about advancing women are any different or less prejudicial than those of the rest of society. There are generally held beliefs, expressed or not, that women should not have authority over men of equivalent age and social class; the presence of women in the job setting makes social interaction difficult; women are less able to cope with crises than men; women periodically are unable to function dependably and rationally; and men are more effective working with other men. And there is some indication that women share this same bias against women's suitability for and competence in management.[11]

The social welfare field by and large exhibits the characteristic known as sex-linked job pools. Some jobs are socially defined as appropriately held by women, others by men. This division takes on a castelike appearance and quality. Not only are women excluded from high-level positions, but there are separate hierarchical ladders for the male and female job pools. The ranks between the pools are not equivalent—the female pool is of inferior rank—and there is very little mobility between pools; some women make it to the male pool, but hardly any male ever moves to the female job pool.[12] In social welfare, direct-service positions constitute the female pool; men generally move out of their jobs more easily and rapidly than women. Administrative positions are male positions and, although some women break into this pool, they are likely to remain at the lowest positions. Moreover, male social workers tend not to move from administration to direct service; to do so would be negatively viewed, unless, of course, they go into private practice.

Although this sex-based division is not exclusive to social work, the profession has encouraged the channeling by special efforts to recruit men into what has for so long been considered a "woman's field." With the stated purposes of overcoming the profession's female image and raising its status, men have been enticed by offers of high salaries and positions. It is perhaps not coincidental that this goal paralleled the development of community organization/social planning/administration as a concentration in social work education. This new specialization, emphasizing the supposedly more masculine social welfare functions, brought in more men, who were then able to move directly into management positions because of their training, thus bypassing experienced women social workers ready for promotion.

Several possible reasons for the profession's failure to deal with sex discrimination within its ranks have been offered.[13] Bernard Scotch suggests that recognition of the problem and any interest in confronting it may have been overshadowed by issues more significant to the profession in the 1960s, such as racism and poverty. The job market itself, with an undersupply of social workers until very recently, may have made it possible for those who were discriminated against in one agency to move on to another. And, women themselves may have been reluctant to call attention to discriminatory personnel practices or to organize in protest.[14] None of the reasons offered, however, adequately explains how sexism has been allowed to prevail in the social work profession, dominated from the onset by women who were the pioneers in social work theory and practice, dedicated to social change, and committed to improving the lot of women and to overcoming inequality.[15]

An Analysis of the Problem

Why are there so few women administrators? What accounts for the disproportionate numbers of men in executive positions? Is there a lack of interest in administrative responsibilities on the part of women? Are there barriers which prevent women from seeking or attaining administrative jobs? Answers to these questions are currently being sought within and outside of the social work profession. Although there are unique

aspects to the phenomenon, it must be recognized that for all occupations in modern societies, as one approaches the top, the proportion of men increases and the proportion of women decreases.

In an attempt to account for the lack of women administrators, explanations have been sought from a number of theoretical perspectives. Answers have been drawn primarily from the field of psychology. To a lesser extent, sociological analyses have been applied. Both internal and external barriers which women encounter and must therefore overcome have been identified. Mary Flanagan refers to them as internal conflicts, lack of interpersonal support systems, and structural obstacles.[16] The emphasis, in general, has been on internal barriers to explain inequities in employment patterns. The thrust of these theories is summarized in the first part of this section. Although they may contribute to our understanding of why there are so few women administrators, it is posited here that external structural barriers constitute a more significant deterrent force. Despite the apparent impact of external obstacles, they have received much less attention in the literature and research.

Individual Internal Barriers

Internal factors stem primarily from women's socialization into traditional roles, which is said to create attitudes, aspirations, and behaviors that may inhibit women workers from advancing or attaining high levels. These explanations, which draw upon psychological and personal variables, attribute women's apparent failure to aspire to or to hold executive positions to such characteristics as low self-esteem, lack of self-confidence, low achievement motivation, role conflict, and fear of failure or fear of success. The empirical findings on these psychological factors identified as potential barriers to women's mobility do not necessarily support the hypotheses and are generally inconclusive.[17]

The concept of "fear of success" has gained widespread popularity in recent years, adding weight to the emphasis given to internal psychological factors as barriers to women's performance and achievement. Proposed by Matina Horner in 1968 as the "need to avoid success," the concept explained why women college students did not exhibit their wish to achieve in the same way that men did. It is hypothesized that the desire to achieve and the fear of the possible negative consequences of success—such as social rejection or a diminished sense of femininity—combined to create conflicting emotions causing women to feel uneasy and less competent when competing with males.[18] Despite extensive research that both supports and refutes this hypothesis and raises many questions about the initial methodology,[19] the implications of the concept for women's careers and advancement remain ambiguous. Yet the fear syndrome concept continues to be widely accepted, and it has been used to explain women's anxiety about doing well, discouragement with taking risks, avoidance of competitive situations, retreat from ambitious or challenging endeavors, and tendency to downgrade abilities. It thus provides a rationale for why women of excellent ability and potential do not function at their full capacity and fail to achieve top positions.

Considerable emphasis has also been given to the ways in which girls are socialized differently than boys, and how childhood experiences affect the adult woman's assumptions, perceptions, and behavior, as well as her desire to enter and succeed in a man's world and the likelihood of this outcome.[20] This perspective is found in the more popular publications written for the career woman who wants to move ahead. The authors of these seem to agree that women have two major deficiencies stemming from their early socialization: women are not career oriented, and they do not know how to advance to the top.[21] Unlike men, it is said, women do not think in terms of careers and therefore are not attuned to the need for career planning or the techniques of charting a career path. As a result, women tend to make late career decisions and have less time to achieve their goal. Most working women do not look upon their jobs as parts of their careers, nor do they concentrate on achieving long-range goals. Decisions and strategies are made not in terms of their future implications, but rather in relation to the present. Without that future orientation—a vision of where they expect to be in five or ten years—and without a detailed plan for what they will have to do in order to achieve their objectives, women neither see themselves as moving on, nor do they work at it. According to this theory, then, men, by virtue of their early socialization, have an immediate advantage as they move into careers.

Another theory suggests that women suffer an additional disadvantage because they are ignorant of the techniques of career advancement. Recognizing that organizations grow out of a distinctly male culture in which women have not been raised to participate or succeed, it is said that women lack the skills necessary for playing the games of organizational politics and upward mobility. Unsure of the actual game being played, unfamiliar with the rules, and often uncertain if they in fact want to play, women presumably do not have the experience, the preparation, or the skill essential for survival and success in organizations. Men, on the other hand, have been trained to win, to do so as members of teams, and to operate in a male world, with its network of relationships which depend upon persuasion, favors, and compromises.

Other potentially critical factors have been identified in an attempt to locate these childhood and familial experiences that are associated with high achievement among women. The likelihood of women advancing to the top appears to be related to variables such as sibling structure, parental role models, and father-daughter relationships. These factors are thought to influence women's sex role identity and self-concept, and consequently their career aspirations and achievement orientation. Margaret Hennig and Anne Jardim discovered a clear pattern of similarities in these variables among successful women managers.[22]

Women's adult family life is generally viewed as a source of constraint on career advancement. It is commonly held that women interrupt their careers in order to meet family expectations and obligations. The hypothesis wins further support from the fact that many women executives either have remained single or have delayed marriage and family until after significant progress has been gained in their careers. Advancement, it would

appear, is less likely for a woman with the dual roles and responsibilities of marriage/motherhood and career. The extent to which family and parental demands contribute to the disproportionate numbers of women administrators is inconclusive, despite recent research. Studies seem to suggest that although family commitments are an important factor, marital status and family responsibilities do not completely account for the absence of women administrators.[23]

Thus we find an extensive and growing body of literature attributing the absence and underrepresentation of women in administration to the women themselves. Factors within women, that is, internal barriers, are cited to explain the inequities in employment. Women are not in high-level positions either because they do not aspire to those positions or because they lack the inclination and the know-how necessary to compete for and win the positions.

External Barriers

There is considerably less literature that explains women's absence from the professional hierarchy in terms of external factors, barriers that emanate from organizational structures and the professional world itself. Yet, straightforward as well as more subtle forms of discrimination stem from both.

Informal Support System. A major barrier to advancement is the lack of an interpersonal, informal support system, which is deemed essential for moving ahead.[24] At the very least, linkage to others provides access to crucial information, but it also provides contacts, emotional support, visibility, and advice. Learning "the ropes" takes place through informal organizations. In fact, it is the informal system that establishes the rules, the shared values and attitudes, and the patterns of homogeneity and inclusion and exclusion that contribute to the eventual success or failure of an individual. By participation and acceptance in the informal network, a worker establishes legitimacy, a necessary first step in beginning professional advancement. Within this inner circle, ability is identified and individuals are coached and helped to develop and demonstrate competence.

Most importantly, it is through the informal network that individuals identify and locate those persons who can directly affect their mobility. Sandy Albrecht refers to such persons as "structural significant others" which include both "situational definers" and "resource allocators."[25] Situational definers function as role models and provide relevant information about situations, expectations, and appropriate behavior. The greater one's access to situational definers, the better equipped one will be to perform well. Resource allocators are those individuals whose position and influence give them control over various resources that impact upon one's mobility. Their power to recruit, recommend, and promote makes them critical contacts, and access to them is likely to influence one's chances of advancement.

Similarly, the informal network allows for the identification of older, more experienced, and better established colleagues who, as patrons, sponsors, or mentors, provide psychological and tactical assistance and support in moving upward. A number of studies point to the practical importance of linking up with someone who will give valuable advice on how to maximize one's position, act as a sounding board, run interference when necessary, serve as a role model, and encourage and guide the professional development of the newcomer. The existence of a mentor is often cited as a key variable shared by both men and women who have advanced to top positions.[26] Given the number of other barriers confronting women, sponsor figures may be even more important to women's advancement than to men's. However, women usually have a difficult time acquiring sponsors, due at least in part to the dearth of older women who have achieved mentor status, the apparent reluctance of men to take on protegees of the opposite sex, and the reluctance of women to turn to men because of possible sexual implications.

There are two informal organizations that women must enter in order to survive and succeed: the professional community and the organization of employment. Both operate to exclude women, in some cases unintentionally, in others, deliberately. Apparently no insider prefers to communicate with or invite into an inner circle those individuals who not only have lower status, but are unlikely to be helpful and may make others feel anxious or threatened. Yet these are the very reactions women elicit as minority outsiders. Furthermore, there appears to be a natural affinity among similar individuals and a tendency for dominant groups to maintain social distance from minority individuals. These factors may help to explain the differences in accessibility to the informal networks experienced by men and women. Clearly, the informal system favors men to the extent that they are given almost exclusive access to communication networks and information, as well as visibility through presentation of papers at professional conferences, publications in professional journals, and committee chairs in professional associations.[27]

We find that the colleague system in professions and organizations functions as a structural impediment to the career development and advancement of women. Since one's support, assistance, and resources depend on informal associations, without access to the networks there is very little possibility of recognition and acceptance. It is not surprising, therefore, that women fare so poorly.

Organizational Location. Another external barrier to the promotion and advancement of women is the formal structure of organizations. The impact of organizational structure on what one does and how well one does it has only recently been examined, and the results have begun to shed light on why there are so few women administrators. The hypotheses and findings suggest that attitudes, aspirations, and behavior are not necessarily inherent to individuals but are a function of location in a setting. What appear to be sex differences in work behavior emerge as responses to structural conditions, to one's place in the organization. Therefore, the characteristics attributed to women can be explained in terms of women's unique position in the workplace.

The most comprehensive contribution to the theory of structural determinants of behavior in organizations appears in Rosabeth Moss Kanter's book, *Men and Women of the Corporation.*[28] Drawing upon field observations and laboratory experiments, Kanter identifies three distinct but nonetheless interacting dimensions of organizational structure to explain differences in how men and women act in organizations: the structure of opportunity; the structure of power; and the proportional distribution of people of different kinds.

Opportunity refers to the future prospects for mobility and growth of particular positions. Jobs differ in promotion rates, ladder steps, the range and length of career paths, the height of ceilings, and the like. People in positions of low opportunity exhibit characteristics unlike those with jobs of high opportunity. As shown in Table 31.1, individuals with low or blocked mobility tend to scale down their aspirations, seek satisfaction outside of work, dream of escape, and seek rewards and fulfillment from interpersonal relationships rather than accomplishments and performance on the job. Such behavior is viewed as evidence of low commitment and motivation, overinvolvement with persons and peers, and insufficient task and career orientation. These are the same characteristics attributed to women as reasons for their failure to advance in organizations. It would be more accurate, however, to see them as associated with *all* workers who are at the bottom rung of an opportunity structure. But, because women are more often placed in positions with fewer chances for mobility and shorter chains of opportunity, it is not surprising that such behavior is repeatedly thought of as typical of women.

Similarly, characteristics become associated with individuals in accordance with their positions of power. Jobs that

TABLE 31.1
Organizational Behavior and Its Structural Determinants

OPPORTUNITY

People *low in opportunity* would tend to:

Limit their aspirations, not hoping for mobility in general, not valuing more responsibility, more participation.

Have lower self-esteem, value their competence less than adequately.

Seek satisfaction in activities outside of work, dream of escape, and "interrupt" their careers (sometimes as a function of insecurity in the job itself).

Have a "horizontal" orientation, compare themselves with peers.

Be critical of high-power people, of management, or at least fail to identify with them.

Be less likely to protest or seek change; rather to channel grievances into griping or output restriction rather than direct action.

Orient peer groups toward protection and reassurance, with strong loyalty demands, and hence, discourage members of the group from seeking mobility.

Find ways to create a sense of efficacy and worth through personal relationships (as in the case of secretaries) or doing well socially, rather than in terms of task accomplishment.

Be more attached to the local unit than to the larger organization, and, hence, be more parochial.

Resign themselves to staying put.

Be concerned with basic survival and extrinsic rewards: the economic or social payoff of the job.

People *high in opportunity* would tend to:

Have high aspirations.

Have high self-esteem, value or overrate their competence.

Consider work a more central life interest.

Be more committed to the organization, willing to sacrifice for it and believe in its goals.

Be competitive, oriented toward rivalry.

Have a "vertical" orientation, compare themselves upward.

Be more attracted to high power people, seek validation from them, identify with them.

Create power and action-oriented informal groups.

When dissatisfied, engage in active change-oriented forms of protest: collective action, formal meetings, suggestions for change.

Consider themselves members of the larger organization rather than the local unit.

Become impatient or disaffected if they don't keep moving.

Be concerned with the job as an instrument for mobility and growth, and hence with intrinsic aspects such as its potential for learning.

POWER

People *low in organizational power* would tend to:

Foster lower group morale.

Behave in more directive, authoritarian ways.

Try to retain control, restrict opportunities for subordinates' growth or autonomy, supervise too closely.

Use subordinates as their frame of reference for status assessment and enhancement.

Try to hold back talented subordinates, thereby reducing the threat of replacement.

Use more coercive than persuasive power.

Be more insecure and thus more controlling, critical.

Be very concerned about controlling a territory and hang on to that territory, even when inappropriate.

Be less well liked, less talkative in meetings with high-power people.

People *high in organizational* power would tend to:

Foster higher group morale.

Have subordinates who inhibit their negativity and aggressiveness, behaving in more cooperative and less critical ways, thereby reducing the need to exercise strong controls.

Behave in less rigid, directive, authoritarian ways, to delegate more control and allow subordinates more latitude and discretion.

Provide opportunities for subordinates to move along with them, find talented subordinates and groom them for better things.

Have their actions seen more often as helping than hindering.

Be better liked, talk more often, and receive more communications in meetings.

TABLE 31.1 (continued)

PROPORTIONS

People whose type is represented in *very small proportion* would tend to:	People whose type is represented in *very high proportion* would tend to:
Be more visible, be "on display."	Be easily seen as one of the group, a fitting in
Feel more pressure to conform, to make fewer mistakes.	Be preferred for high-communication managerial jobs.
Try to become "socially invisible," not to stand out so much.	Find it easier to earn "credibility" for high uncertainty positions, such as some management jobs.
Find it harder to earn "credibility," particularly in high uncertainty positions such as certain management jobs.	Be more likely to join the informal network, form peer alliances, learn the ropes from peers.
Be more isolated and peripheral.	Be more likely to be sponsored by higher status organization members.
Be more likely to be excluded from informal peer networks, and hence limited in this source of power through alliances.	Be accurately perceived, have a congruent identity and ease in self-presentations.
Have fewer opportunities to be "sponsored" because of the rarity of people like them upward.	Face less personal stress.
Face misperceptions of their identity and role in the organization and hence develop a preference for already established relationships.	
Be stereotyped, be placed in role traps that limit effectiveness.	
Face more personal stress.	

SOURCE: R.M. Kanter, *Men and Women of the Corporation* (New York: Basic Books, 1977), pp. 246-249.

do not enhance an individual's power—that is, the ability to get things done or mobilize resources, accomplish tasks, and achieve goals—produce attitudes and behaviors indicative of a lack of potential for organizational leadership. Women are most often placed in positions where their activities and performance do not allow them to exercise or to increase their power within the organization.

Clearly, some organizational positions are more advantageous than others because of the likelihood that they will lead to advancement. Not surprisingly, the "better" positions are defined more often as appropriate for males and, indeed, are filled by men. The less valuable positions, especially those which are deadend in terms of career, providing no real avenue for advancement, are women's jobs. Typical of the positions that function as organizational barriers to mobility and that are more likely to be filled by women are first-line supervisors, assistant directors, project directors, and coordination and technical assistants. These jobs all have in common one crucial characteristic: They are not perceived by organizations as training areas for higher ranking positions or positions in the male job pool.

Regardless of how well the incumbents of these positions perform, it would still be possible for the organization to maintain that they are not ready for higher (i.e., different) administrative positions. These barrier positions tend to have any one of three major deficiencies: The jobs are not on a managerial ladder; the responsibilities do not allow for the demonstration of skills indicative of the capacity for assuming greater administrative responsibility; and, excellence in these jobs can actually be construed as inability to succeed in higher positions.[29]

In order to be promoted, a higher position must exist to which one can advance. This is not always the case, as many lower level administrative positions do not lead automatically to other positions. Viewed on an organizational chart, it may become apparent that no other positions appear directly above, and, indeed, these positions are more than likely to be set off to the side in the hierarchical structure, a sure sign that they are not even in the mainstream of the organization. Directors of special projects and departments that are not fundamental to the organization's functioning frequently fall into this category. In other situations, organizations may create what appears to be a managerial ladder with positions such as Supervisor I, II, and III, but upon closer inspection it is apparent that advancement to the top does not lead directly to higher executive positions.

In order for an individual to be considered ready for promotion and for higher level work, his or her previous positions would have to provide opportunities to demonstrate a capacity to assume greater responsibility and power. This can only happen if the organizations first perceive the person's previous and current positions as challenging and difficult, requiring aggressiveness, initiative, and leadership. The positions referred to here are generally more routine and less demanding; they are seen as the necessary maintenance tasks. They require the ability to implement the decisions of others rather than making decisions. Assertiveness and creativity are unlikely to be required and would therefore be negatively sanctioned. In fact, the abilities needed to do well in these jobs are usually the qualities that are deemed less desirable in top executives. Excellence in these jobs would therefore suggest, if not confirm, unsuitability for leadership positions. Moreover, these positions place severe limitations upon their incumbents. They restrict visibility, promote specialization at the expense of diversity, do not require or reward interdependent activity, and channel workers away from key organizational concerns.

Placement in positions of blocked mobility, powerlessness, or irrelevancy generates worker attitudes and behaviors which are easily evaluated as ineffective and inappropriate for high management levels. Position is not the only structural barrier imposed by an organization. As noted previously, access to an organization's informal structure is also critical. Organizations can foster or impede the likelihood of interaction and, as a result, the opportunities for becoming known in order to be judged by the inner circle. Physical space—simply where and how offices and lounges are arranged and situated—can direct the flow of traffic and influence the frequency of individuals meeting, influencing, and assisting each other. Common dining facilities, regular staff meetings, and working committees across ranks and positions are examples of how organizations can offer further opportunities. On the other hand, the absence of such viable structural arrangements can isolate and insulate some, especially those who are least likely to interact easily without some structural supports.

Finally, a relationship exists between what may be viewed as "poor management potential" qualities and the distinct behaviors associated with individuals who are in a minority, either in actual numbers or because of characteristics differentiating them from the rest of the organization's members. Being in the limelight, or a token representative, apparently creates a situation of strain and conflict for those in the minority status. The ways minority individuals perceive and experience the situation and respond to their dilemma affect interaction and constrain their behavior. The extent to which organizations contribute to the strain or provide support to the minority workers may be crucial to their ability to do well and consequently to be viewed favorably for promotion.[30]

In reviewing the arguments that attempt to explain why there are so few women administrators, and particularly why there is an underrepresentation of women social work administrators, illustrations of both internal and external barriers have been presented, along with the individual or psychological perspective and the system or structural perspective. Together, the various approaches provide a way of looking at the phenomenon and contribute to our understanding of it. Yet, together or separately, they do not offer a totally convincing explanation. Given the complexity and pervasiveness of the problem, unfortunately, at the present time, there are no fuller or better explanations.

APPROACHES AND SOLUTIONS TO THE PROBLEM

Sexism and the underrepresentation of women administrators in the social work field have been acknowledged as areas of concern by the profession. This recognition is undoubtedly a first step toward solving the problem. A second step would be a commitment to action, and there are some initial signs of this occurring within the profession. The National Association of Social Workers (NASW) has established a National Committee on Women's Issues which has expanded its activities substantially during the past year. Its newsletter, *Woman Power,* provides a forum on issues of concern to women and an exchange of information on local activities, research projects, and relevant publications. The issue of women in administration has been identified as one of the committee's major interests. A research study was commissioned in 1977 to explore possible reasons for the scarcity of women administrators and to examine women's perceptions of barriers to advancement in social work administration. The study's findings are just now becoming available, and it is anticipated they will provide direction for NASW and the local chapters' Women's Issues Committees.[31]

The Council on Social Work Education (CSWE) established a Commission on the Role and Status of Women in Social Work Education. A joint subcommittee of the NASW and CSWE women's committees is presently working on a training program to prepare women for leadership positions in social work practice and social work education. The proposal is designed to cover the internal, external, and structural barriers affecting women who seek to advance to administrative positions. The focus of the training will be on knowledge, skills, and values that will enable women participants to gain: new understanding about role choice and consequences, both personal and professional; knowledge about management functions and organizations; and the skills to carry out management/administrative tasks, including those related to budgeting and finance, communication and relationships, and stress and conflict resolution.[32]

Individual-Oriented Strategies

Not surprisingly, we find the main thrust of the profession's approach to the problem to be individually oriented, emphasizing education as a solution. This approach is consistent with the perception of the cause of the problem as internal. Consequently, programs are directed primarily toward the women themselves, rather than toward the organizations and the external barriers women confront. Social work is not alone in locating the source of the problem within women, and, therefore, neither is it unique in selecting the individual as the point of intervention and solution. Three kinds of programs result from this philosophical orientation.

One educational approach, increasingly found in university-sponsored continuing education programs, focuses on the development of management skills. The workshops and classes are designed primarily for those with no academic background in administration and for women whose training and experience have not adequately prepared them in either the principles of management or the essential administrative skills and functions. These programs, which do not necessarily lead to a degree or certificate of advanced study, are based on two assumptions: managerial competence is essential to advance to administrative positions; and, this competence can be gained in a classroom setting. Both assumptions may be unfounded. Nevertheless, a convincing argument is being made and heard by women that they are not being promoted into administrative positions because they lack necessary management expertise and skills.

If management training is based on the assumption that managerial competence is essential to get ahead, other programs are derived from another premise—competence alone may not be enough. A second approach attempts to impart to women those techniques necessary for advancement. The tactics that are commonly used by men and are especially suited or necessary to women are presented in seminars or offered in counseling and consultation sessions. This approach recognizes that women cannot undo their childhoods, change past events, or make up for lost advantages but asserts that they can, nevertheless, learn how to function effectively in the male world. The popular literature is replete with the "do's and don'ts" for the managerial woman which serve as a basis for these programs.[33] In addition, the workshops draw heavily upon experiential exercises, sensitivity training techniques, and assertiveness training to alter women's behaviors and self-perception.[34]

The third approach is directed toward helping women make career decisions and determine whether they wish to become administrators. These seminars are designed first to enhance women's understanding of what being an administrator entails, and second to enable women to look at themselves as potential administrators by assessing their interest, potential, and readiness. Once the decision to move into management positions is reached, the women are helped to achieve their goals through counseling on how to chart their careers, prepare resumés, locate the right job, handle an interview, and select the most promising positions.

Two recent educational programs for social workers illustrate individual-oriented strategies. One two-day workshop conducted by Louise Bakke and Jean Edson was based on the belief that self-limiting attitudes and behaviors often impede individual upward movement. The workshop was therefore designed to challenge women to explore the pros and cons of moving up, to examine their attitudes about work in relation to their life priorities, and to begin to plan realistically how to acquire the skills and experience needed to meet their personal goals. The workshop leaders found that a problem-solving approach that focuses on skills and strategies useful to women moving up—attitudes about work and career, alternatives in career planning, procedures for obtaining information about job opportunities, writing resumés, preparing for oral examinations—resulted in a change in the participants' perceptions of the barriers within the system. Once they knew more about the system, social workers saw fewer barriers and were then able to make important job changes.[35]

The other program, a nine-week workshop, was designed to help prepare women to assume administrative positions by providing an informal and supportive setting with extensive group process. The format included the sharing of personal experiences and problems participants faced in the performance of administrative tasks, discussion of selected literature, assessment of the individual participants as administrators through problem-solving and role-playing exercises, and presentations by women social work executives. The participants evaluated the workshop highly and commented that they emerged more confident of their own administrative abilities, more aware of the skills they needed to develop, less fearful of taking career risks, and better equipped to reach some decisions about their careers.[36]

System-Oriented Strategies

While a number of programmatic attempts have been initiated to overcome the *internal* barriers that are said to keep women from attaining administrative positions in the social work profession, there have been, to date, no similar efforts to eradicate the *external* organizational or system barriers. Affirmative action efforts have not yet penetrated the social welfare area, and there are no model plans or successful attempts to achieve equal employment opportunity for women. The thrust to increase receptivity and sensitivity to women administrators has occurred in the business world, yet little, if anything, has been done within human service organizations. However, a number of models from outside the field are now available which could be used to open up social welfare agencies to women.[37] Hence, it is possible that agencies could be helped to increase the number of women administrators.

Many agencies are unaware of the extent to which they treat male and female applicants differently, make women feel unwanted, and, in fact, discourage women from taking the administrative positions for which they were recruited. Executives and boards of directors require sensitizing to the biases they hold, which function to discriminate against women. There is some indication that if women were promoted from within agencies, they would probably be in a better bargaining position.[38] Agencies must be helped to examine their own personnel as well as their efforts to groom employees for advancement, instead of looking outside for administrators. Agencies need to restructure their organizations or jobs in such a way as to open up opportunities for advancement, to develop administrative ladders, and to incorporate administrative responsibilities into more positions held by women. Kanter urges that access to more favored positions in organizations be created where necessary. She stresses that attention must be given to the structures of opportunity, power, and numbers in order to achieve equality.[39] Should agencies' commitment to affirmative action planning not be forthcoming, it will be necessary for women's representatives to challenge and confront the organizations. This process is apt to begin with the establishment of ongoing procedures to monitor agencies' employment patterns, to bring to public attention the offenders, and, where appropriate, to initiate sex discrimination action lawsuits.

There is rather strong sentiment that women will have to develop their own informal support system, if not spontaneously then through planned activities.[40] Such a network could provide those essential supports currently available to men and so vital to women who are trying to advance. The Women's Issues Committees of the local chapters of NASW and many of the women's work-shops could be a good source of peer alliance and could represent beginning efforts to lay the groundwork for a national support system.

Another solution may exist in the establishment of mechanisms to link qualified and interested social workers with potential administrative jobs and employers. There have been a number of effective employment exchanges developed for the purpose of putting prospective employees and employers in touch.[41] The intent is to avoid or overcome the familiar situation in which women workers claim they do not know of available positions, and agencies claim they do not know of qualified women to fill their vacancies.

Although many individual women will undoubtedly benefit from efforts to help them overcome internal barriers, and by participating in support networks and employment exchanges, in the long run eradication of sex discrimination in administration will depend on a systemic approach. Only by changing the structure of organizations and the opportunity paths will it be possible to alter the present situation. External as well as internal barriers must be overcome if we expect to increase the numbers of women social workers in administrative positions.

NOTES

1. See, especially, Janet S. Chafetz, "Women in Social Work," *Social Work,* Vol. 17 (September 1972), pp. 12-18; David Fanshel, "Status Differentials: Men and Women in Social Work," *Social Work,* Vol. 21 (November 1976), pp. 448-54; Diane Kravetz, "Sexism in a Women's Profession," *Social Work,* Vol. 21 (November 1976), pp. 421-26; Bernard C. Scotch, "Sex Status in Social Work: Grist for Women's Liberation,"

Social Work, Vol. 16 (July 1971), pp. 5-11; and Martha Williams, Liz Ho, and Lucy Felder, "Career Patterns: More Grist for Women's Liberation," *Social Work,* Vol. 19 (July 1974), pp. 463-66.

2. Juliana Szakacs, "Survey Indicates Social Work Women Losing Ground in Leadership," *NASW News,* Vol. 22 (April 1977), p. 12. Also in *Woman-Power,* February 1977, p. 1.

3. Alfred M. Stamm, "NASW Membership: Characteristics, Deployment, and Salaries," *Personnel Information,* Vol. 12 (May 1969), pp. 34-35.

4. Fanshel, "Status Differentials."

5. Shirley Kuehle Knapman, "Sex Discrimination in Family Agencies," *Social Work,* Vol. 22 (November 1977), pp. 461-65.

6. Louise S. Bakke and Jean B. Edson, "Women in Management: Moving Up?" *Social Work,* Vol. 22 (November 1977), pp. 512-14.

7. Toby Weiner and Sophie Engel, *The Status of Women in Jewish Communal Services,* National Conference of Jewish Communal Services, June 1977.

8. Szakacs, "Survey Indicates Women Losing Ground."

9. For fuller discussion, see Margaret Adams, "The Compassion Trap," in *Woman in Sexist society,* ed. Vivian Gornick and Barbara K. Moran (New York: Basic Books, 1971), pp. 555-75.

10. Alfred Kadushin, "The Prestige of Social Work—Facts and Factors," *Social Work,* Vol. 3 (April 1958), p. 40.

11. Virginia O'Leary, "Some Attitudinal Barriers to Occupational Aspirations for Women," *Psychological Bulletin,* Vol. 81 (1974), pp. 809-26.

12. Harris T. Schrank and John W. Riley, Jr., "Women in Work Organizations," in *Women and the American Economy,* ed. Juanita M. Kreps (New York: The American Assembly, Columbia University, 1976), pp. 82-101.

13. See, for example, Scotch, "Sex Status in Social Work"; Szakacs, "Survey Indicates Women Losing Ground"; and Dorothy Zietz and John L. Erlich, "Sexism in Social Agencies: Practitioner's Perspectives," *Social Work,* Vol. 21 (November 1976), pp. 434-39.

14. Scotch, "Sex Status in Social Work."

15. Brenda McGowan, in a comment to the author, suggests that the answer may rest with the low status of the profession and the desire of these leading women to overcome the image, even if it meant turning the administration of the field over to men.

16. Mary Flanagan, "Women in Social Work: Perceptions of Barriers to Administrative Advancement," *Woman Power,* December 1977, pp. 2-4.

17. O'Leary, "Some Attitudinal Barriers."

18. Matina S. Horner, "Fail! Bright Woman," *Psychology Today,* Vol. 3 (November 1969), pp. 36-41; "Femininity and Successful Achievement: A Basic Inconsistency," in *Feminine Personality and Conflict,* ed. J. M. Bardwick, E. Douvan, M. S. Horner, and D. Guttman (Belmont, Calif.: Brooks/Cole Publishing Co., 1970), pp. 45-74; "Toward an Understanding of Achievement Related Conflicts in Women," *Journal of Social Issues,* Vol. 28, No. 2 (1972), pp. 157-76.

19. For a review of the research and the issues, see Linda Davis, "Fear of Success: Myth and Reality," in *Women in Management,* ed. Meg Gerrard, June S. Oliver, and Martha Williams (Austin: University of Texas, Center for Social Work Research, 1976), pp. 39-45; Lois W. Hoffman, "Fear of Success in Males and Females: 1965-1971," *Journal of Consulting and Clinical Psychology,* Vol. 42, No. 2 (1974), pp. 353-58; and D. Tresemar, "Fear of Success: Popular But Unproven," *Psychology Today,* Vol. 7 (March 1974), pp. 82-85.

20. See, for example, Lois W. Hoffman, "Early Childhood Experiences and Women's Achievement Motives," *Journal of Social Issues,* Vol. 28, No. 2 (1972), pp. 129-55; Eleanor E. Maccoby and Carol Nagy Jacklin, *The Psychology of Sex Differences* (Stanford, Calif.: Stanford University Press, 1974); and Kenneth Dunn and Rita Dunn, *How to Raise Independent and Professionally Successful Daughters* (Englewood Cliffs, N.J.: Prentice-Hall, 1977).

21. See, for example, Betty L. Harragan, *Games Mother Never Taught You* (New

York: Warner Books, 1977); Margaret Hennig and Anne Jardim, *The Managerial Woman* (New York: Doubleday & Co., 1976); and Jane Trahey, *Jane Trahey on Women and Power* (New York: Rawson Associates Publishers, 1977).

22. Hennig and Jardim, *Managerial Woman.*
23. Fanshel, "Status Differentials"; Dorothy Chave Herberg, "A Study of Work Participation by Graduate Female Social Workers: Some Implications for Professional Social Work Training," *Journal of Education for Social Work,* Vol. 9 (Fall 1973), pp. 16-23; Mary Nixon and L. R. Gue, "Women Administrators and Women Teachers: A Comparative Study," *Alberta Journal of Educational Research,* Vol. 21 (September 1975), pp. 196-206; John E. Tropman, "The Married Professional Social Worker," *Journal of Marriage and the Family,* Vol. 30 (November 1968), pp. 661-65; and Williams et al., "Career Patterns."
24. Sandy Albrecht, "Informal Interaction Patterns of Professional Women," in *Women in Management,* ed. Meg Gerrard, June S. Oliver, and Martha Williams (Austin: University of Texas at Austin, 1976), pp. 67-71; Cynthia F. Epstein, "Encountering the Male Establishment: Sex-Status Limits on Women's Careers in the Professions," *American Journal of Sociology,* Vol. 75 (May 1970), pp. 965-82; Patricia A. Yokopenic, Linda B. Bourque, and D. Brogan, "Professional Communication Network: A Case Study of Women in the American Public Health Association," *Social Problems,* Vol. 22 (April 1975), pp. 493-508; Donald W. Zacharias, "Women and the Informal Organization," in *Women in Management,* ed. Gerrard et al., pp. 63-66.
25. Albrecht, "Informal Interaction Patterns of Professional Women."
26. Epstein, "Encountering the Male Establishment"; Hennig and Jardim, *Managerial Woman;* Rosabeth Moss Kanter, *Men and Women of the Corporation* (New York: Basic Books, 1977), pp. 181-84.

27. Aaron Rosenblatt, Eileen M. Turner, Adalene R. Patterson, and Clare K. Rolloson, "Predominance of Male Authors in Social Work Publications," *Social Casework,* Vol. 51 (July 1970), pp. 421-30; Yokopenic et al., "Professional Communication Network."
28. Rosabeth Moss Kanter, "The Impact of Hierarchical Structures on the Work Behavior of Women and Men," *Social Problems,* Vol. 23 (April 1976), pp. 415-27; Rosabeth Moss Kanter, *Men and Women of the Corporation* (New York: Basic Books, 1977).
29. In addition to R. M. Kanter's discussion, these points are also developed by B. L. Harragan, *Games Mother Never Taught You,* and H. T. Schrank and J. W. Riley, "Women in Work Organizations."
30. See also A. W. Herbert, "The Minority Administrator: Problems, Prospects and Challenges," *Public Administration Review,* Vol. 34 (November-December 1974), pp. 556-63; and Alfred Kadushin, "Men in a Women's Profession," *Social Work,* Vol. 21 (November 1976), pp. 440-47.
31. Flanagan, "Women in Social Work."
32. Reported in *Womanpower,* May 1978, p. 14.
33. See, for example, Harragan, *Games Mother Never Taught You;* Hennig and Jardim, *Managerial Woman;* Trahey, *Jane Trahey on Women and Power.* Recent books include Margaret Higginson and Thomas Quick, *The Ambitious Woman's Guide to a Successful Career* (New York: American Management Association, 1975); Nathanial Stewart, *The Effective Woman Manager: Seven Vital Skills for Upward Mobility* (New York: John Wiley & Sons, 1978); Marcille Gray Williams, *The New Executive Woman: A Guide to Business Success* (Radnor, Pa.: Chilton Book Co., 1977); Michael Korda, *Success* (New York: Random House, 1977); and John Molloy, *The Women's Drive for Success Book* (Chicago: Follett Publishing Co., 1977).
34. Barbara S. Brockway, "Assertive Training for Professional Women," *Social Work,* Vol. 21 (November 1976), pp. 498-505.

35. Bakke and Edson, "Women in Management."
36. Roslyn H. Chernesky, "Management Development for Women in Social Work," *Womanpower,* May 1978, p. 3.
37. A number of management consulting and counseling firms are specializing in assisting companies and corporations in the hiring of women executives. A listing of such firms around the country can be found in Cecilia H. Foxley, *Locating, Recruiting and Employing Women: An Equal Opportunity Approach* (Garrett Park, Md.: Garrett Park Press, 1976), pp. 149-53. The book also includes a good summary discussion of how employers can become more effective in working with women and thereby attract and retain more women employees.
38. Williams et al., "Career Patterns."
39. Kanter, *Men and Women of the Corporation,* pp. 265-87.
40. Jane Wilson, "The New Girl Network: A Power System for the Future," *New York,* April 4, 1977, pp. 47-49. One of the projects of the National Women's Education Fund, established in 1972 to increase the numbers and the influence of women in public life, is to expand the resource network which women have begun to develop among themselves.
41. One such exchange is sponsored by Catalyst, a national nonprofit organization which helps to expand career opportunities for college-educated women. Other talent banks, registries, and rosters are listed in Foxley, *Locating, Recruiting and Employing Women.*

32. SOCIAL WORK WITH THIRD-WORLD PEOPLE

Armando Morales

The most recent issue of the *Encyclopedia of Social Work* lists the following groups under the term "minorities": American Indians, Asian Americans, Blacks, Chicanos, Puerto Ricans, and white ethnics.[1] The term "white ethnics" is frequently used to refer to the descendants of eastern and southern European immigrants such as Jewish, Greek, Hungarian, Lithuanian, Italian, Irish, and Scandinavian Americans who came to the United States between 1880 and 1920. They number approximately fifty million persons and are sometimes called "middle Americans."[2] They generally do not share the same socioeconomic characteristics often found in other minority groups. For example, white ethnics have been successfully acculturated into American life, they earn more money than Anglo-American Protestants, and their educational mobility is greater than that of other Americans.[3]

Because white ethnics are less likely than other minorities to be welfare recipients and, therefore, social work clients, this article focuses on the remaining minority groups—Blacks, Hispanics,

Reproduced by permission of the author. From Copyright 1981, National Association of Social Workers, Inc. Reprinted with permission, from *Social Work,* Vol. 26, No. 1 (January 1981), pp. 45-49; 50-51 (excerpts).

Asian Americans, and American Indians, who are frequently referred to as Third-World people.[4]

In 1975, the Third-World population of the United States consisted of 24,000,000 Blacks, approximately 11,200,000 Hispanics, 2,000,000 Asian Americans, and 1,000,000 American Indians.[5] These groups constitute 17 percent of the total U.S. population. The internal segmentation of these groups reflects their diversity. For example, the black population comprises at least three subgroups: those who are born in the United States, those who are born in and emigrate from the West Indies, and those who are born in and emigrate from Africa. The Hispanic population consists of 6,690,000 persons of Mexican descent, 1,600,000 Puerto Ricans, 743,000 Cubans, 671,000 Central Americans, and 1,428,000 persons termed by the census as "other Spanish." All these Hispanic subgroups include persons who are born in or immigrate to the United States. With the exception of the Brazilians who speak Portuguese, these subgroups share a common language—Spanish. However, they are not homogeneous and they have different needs. Asian Americans consist of the following subgroups: Chinese, Japanese, Filipinos, Koreans, Samoans, Guamanians, and Indo-Chinese. In addition to language differences, each of these subgroups has a distinct culture. The American Indian and Alaska Native population is most diverse, consisting of 481 identified tribal groups. Half of all Indians belong to nine tribes; the largest tribal group is the Navajo, with a population of 140,000.

Street has maintained that the increasing racial, ethnic, and political consciousness of these groups binds them together under the term "Third World" and enhances their appreciation of themselves and their relationship with each other.[6] This emerging consciousness has led Third-World groups to coin such catchwords as "black power," "brown power," "yellow power," and "red power," all of which reflect their ideologies, programs, and strategies to achieve power. Their ideologies and strategies, however, differ from and threaten those of white society.

Prager has described an ideology of whiteness that enables whites to protect white privilege.[7] He has found several components that constitute the white ideology, one of which is the rejection of ethnic or racial consciousness expressed through such terms as "Third World," "Chicano," and "Native American." Such ethnic consciousness is viewed as a challenge to what whites perceive as an ideal nonracial, integrated society. Within this ideological context, separatism, language differences, and cultural enhancement are thought to be improper responses for building a society for all. Thus, the ideology of whiteness provides a framework for evading and denying Third-World realities. According to Street, this ideology partly reflects the social science theories on race relations, which affect the planning and implementation of human service programs. Often, these theories constitute barriers to the delivery of services to Third-World people.[8]

INDICATORS OF WELL-BEING

Discrimination and prejudice result in the economic, social, and psychological deprivation of Third-World groups. The economic position of these groups is far inferior to whites.[9] For example, in 1972, the median family income for blacks had declined to 59 percent of that for whites. Over the last twenty years, unemployment rates for blacks were more than twice as high as those for whites. The economic situation for American Indians is even worse. Their current income averages between one-fourth and one-third of the national per capita average. And over the last twenty years, the unemployment rates for Indians were even higher than those for blacks. In some years during this period, Navajo unemployment reached 60 percent. It is a myth that Asian Americans are comparatively better off than other Third-World groups. In 1969, the median income for Chinese men living in urban areas was among the lowest recorded for all groups. The median income for Filipino men was lower than that of the white, black, or Spanish-speaking male for all urban areas except New York and Chicago.

Furthermore, the economic and emotional stability of Third-World families is threatened by arrests, and Third-World people are more likely to be arrested than are whites. In California, for example, the imprisonment of blacks increased 28 percent between 1950 and 1970, although the general black population increased only 2 percent during this period. Among persons institutionalized in California during 1970, blacks had a three-to-one chance of going to prison, and whites had a three-to-one chance of going to a mental institution.[10] Street asserted that

arrest rates are higher in those towns where the police take a defensive or offensive stance toward Third-World people, where they try to protect "whitetown" from "blacktown."[11]

The author compared the number of arrests made for drunkenness and drunken driving in a white community and a Mexican American community in Los Angeles. The two communities had comparable general populations, identical ratios of alcoholism, and identical major crime rates. The author found that Mexican Americans had a nine-to-one greater chance (9,676 to 1,552) of being arrested for their drinking behavior than had whites because of the large number of police assigned to the Mexican American community. Altogether, 375 officers, averaging 13.5 officers per square mile, were assigned to the Mexican American community, as compared to 151 officers assigned to the white community, averaging 3.5 officers per square mile.[12]

Health statistics also reveal that the conditions of life for Third-World people are worse than they are for whites. For example, the rate of infant mortality for all American Indians is 32 per 1,000, compared to 15 for whites, and the rate on the Navajo Reservation is more than twice the national average.[13] Moreover, conditions of life for American Indians are literally the poorest in the nation.

In analyzing national data on the institutionalized population, Gruber found inequality in the social services. He demonstrated how race and class are used by organizations to assign diagnostic categories and award services. The outcome is the propelling of minority and poor persons into institutions in which failure becomes a way of life.[14]

In the areas of health, education, work, and housing in relation to Third-World people, the structure of inequality is glaring. Third-World groups recognize the inequality they face and commit themselves to equalize attainment in these areas. The goal of many of these groups is to improve their life situations by gaining control of self and community. Given the needs of Third-World people and given class discrimination and institutional racism as the causes of inequality, how should the social work profession respond? In addressing this question, the author focuses on an ecosystems model for practice with Third-World people.

ECOSYSTEMS MODEL

Social work practice focuses on the interaction between the person and the environment. The term "person" may refer to an individual or may represent people in the context of a family, large or small group, organization, community, or even larger structures of society. Social work intervention might be directed at the person, the environment, or both. In each case, the social worker seeks to enhance and restore the social functioning of people or to change social conditions that impede the mutually beneficial interaction between people and their environment.

The interaction between Third-World people and their environment involves multiple factors—social, economic, racial, political, and the like—all of which have adverse effects on the life situations of this population. In providing services, the social worker should seek to understand the attitudes of Third-World people about such factors and the impact of these factors on them. This orientation would aid the practitioner in identifying the unique needs of Third-World people and in achieving social work goals—"to enhance and restore social functioning and to improve social conditions."

A major problem in achieving these goals, however, is related to the conceptual constraints imposed by social work methods. In other words, social workers, as Nelson points out, perceive phenomena exclusively and narrowly through the lenses of the methods in which they have been trained.[15] Meyer believes that

the use of any methodological model as an anchoring or conceptual point of reference is like viewing something through the wrong end of the telescope—the view is too restricted and narrow to account for the breadth of the phenomena to be captured.[16]

Meyer adds that for years social work has been offering its well-honored methods to those who could use them instead of first finding out what was needed and then selecting the method from its interventive repertoire or inventing new methods. She believes that the methods framework has been functional in maintaining social work's denial of what had to be done with regard to broader social problems. Meyer proposes the use of an ecosystems orientation to practice. This orientation involves the application of ecology and general systems theory to professional tasks. In explaining the ecosystems perspective, Meyer points out that it

allows social workers to look at psychological phenomena, account for complex variables, assess the dynamic interplay of these variables, draw conceptual boundaries around the unit of attention or the case, and then generate ideas for interventions. At this point methodology enters in; for in any particular case—meaning a particular individual, family, group, institutional unit, or geographical area—any number of practice interventions might be needed.[17]

This model of practice would promote social workers' understanding of the (1) psychosocial problems experienced by

Third-World people, (2) crippling effects of institutional racism, and (3) oppressive neocolonial environments in which Third-World people struggle to survive.

Assuming that social work abandons its constricted methods framework and adopts the ecosystems perspective, this question must be asked: What new objectives should social work seek to fulfill to help Third-World people meet their psychosocial needs more effectively? Social workers should pursue at least three basic objectives. These objectives focus on manpower issues in the profession, the use of Third-World human services agencies, and the development of proactive intervention strategies.

MANPOWER ISSUES

In analyzing the manpower needs of social work, it becomes apparent that bilingual, bicultural practitioners are badly needed. The use of translators interferes with the accuracy of the diagnosis and represents second-class treatment. Furthermore, although one can perceive depression as a universal feeling, its manifestations and course may vary from culture to culture and be further complicated by a person's level of acculturation. In short, the clinical needs of Third-World people require bilingual, bicultural social workers who are familiar with the language and culture of the persons whom they attempt to help. English-speaking social workers can assist the more acculturated English-speaking Third-World persons. A major goal of schools of social work, therefore, must be the active recruitment of students who have a bilingual and bicultural capability.

A related manpower issue concerns education and training. Meyer asserts that graduate schools of social work educate students in accordance with the idiosyncratic interests of their faculties and that students learn one model of practice, especially the clinical model, and not others.[18] Given the emphasis that schools of social work place on the clinical orientation, one must ask whether the theory and practice of clinical social work with Third-World people is being taught by bilingual, bicultural faculty members who have had experience in treating Third-World clients. Furthermore, practitioners with experience in poor communities—labeled "underground social workers" or "weekend activists" by Dean—should become an important part of social work faculties.[19] They should train students to provide services effectively in Third-World communities and teach new and existing theory and practice techniques for handling social problems in those communities. Without this preparation, Dean concludes that the social work profession as a whole will have little to contribute to helping its most troubled clients.

Sanction, the authority and permission for social workers to practice, is another manpower issue that is directly related to the benefits—or lack of benefits—received by Third-World populations. Because a disproportionate number of Third-World people are among those in poverty and in the criminal justice system, it is more likely that they will be involuntary clients than will whites. They will probably encounter social workers who are carrying out a function of social control for the state. Research findings suggest that when social workers practice within a framework of social control with involuntary clients, their interventive efforts may not be as effective as when they work with voluntary clients who are actively seeking their help with a specific problem.[20] In one instance, the state and its sanctioned representatives (the social workers) define the problem and the goals for involuntary clients, and in the other the sanctioning voluntary clients define the problems and goals. Imposing treatment on involuntary clients, which has been known to cause deterioration, raises ethical questions for the profession and its relationship to Third-World people who are involuntary clients. In this respect Third-World people have a right to refuse treatment.

Social workers may find themselves in a dilemma in treating involuntary, Third-World clients because they are given legal sanction to carry out a function of social control that is inconsistent with the value social workers place on self-determination. Preferably, imposed treatment intervention as an act of social control should be used only in serious cases, such as those involving child abuse. Social workers have a role in advocating a person's right to refuse treatment, but this poses still another dilemma for those social workers who have historically asserted their professionalism through the status and authority of their agencies, especially those agencies chiefly concerned with a function of social control. On one hand, such advocacy may threaten the employment status of social workers, and on the other, it may also offer them a new challenge and an opportunity to shift the basis of their relationship with involuntary Third-World clients from that of a social control agent for the state to one of independent employment by clients. An increasing number of people are having their human services paid for by third

parties—Medicare, Medicaid, and private insurance.[21] Third-party insurance coverage for licensed social workers became effective in California in January 1977 under vendorship legislation introduced by Assemblyman Art Torres.

The California law, however, limits licensed social work activities to "psychotherapy of a nonmedical nature."[22] This limitation reintroduces the old issue of clinical treatment versus social action. The Third-World community needs both levels of intervention. The New York law, which has preferable legal sanctions, defines the purpose of licensed social work practice as "helping individuals, groups, and communities to prevent or resolve problems caused by social or emotional stress."[23] This licensing language might be the ideal, since it permits licensed social workers to use a wide range of interventive strategies. The profession, therefore, should seek to make sure that vendorship laws sanction not only clinical intervention but also intervention in larger community systems. Social workers could then use third-party reimbursement in Third-World communities to provide help, upon request, in alleviating and preventing social problems. They would thus derive sanction from Third-World clients. If social workers continue to be licensed and reimbursed for clinical activities only, the profession might be compromising its humanistic values and neglecting some of the social needs of Third-World people.

THIRD-WORLD AGENCY

To help Third-World people meet their psychosocial needs more effectively, bilingual, bicultural social workers should be employed and deployed in traditional human services agencies whenever their skills are indicated. Too often, these agencies lack empathy with Third-World people whose cultural patterns and clinical and social needs differ from established norms. They view ethnicity as a descriptive variable, often with "problem" implications, rather than as a critical ingredient in determining the content of service delivery. According to Jenkins, innovative ethnic agencies, in which ethnic clients and ethnic personnel predominate, incorporate such ethnic factors as culture and consciousness "as positive components of service delivery," not as "problems."[24] Social work should therefore endorse the concept of the Third-World human services agency. However, the profession views the growth of such agencies primarily as a political response to movements for minority rights.

Jenkins, in a systematic study of fifty-four Third-World human services agencies in several states, concluded that these agencies remedied serious deficits in traditional methods of service delivery. She also noted the following:

As we examine "what worked" in the ethnic agencies, it is apparent that many of the examples related to primary-group functions. The ethnic agency stressed family supports, encouraging parents to accept responsibility for their own children, maintenance of own languages, career advancement for own clients, accommodations of traditional myths to meet service needs, and recruitment of minority adoptive and foster parents.[25]

Social workers who oppose the use of Third-World human services agencies might argue that an endorsement of this concept might further polarize Third-World people and whites as well as create a duplication of services, resulting in increased administrative costs. Proponents might argue that Third-World staff members should have decision-making power, that they understand the needs of Third-World people, and that the Third-World agency promotes group survival. The first argument is weak because Third-World people are frequently denied services, directly and indirectly, at traditional human services agencies directed by whites to meet the needs of a white population. Because of their various levels of acculturation and life-style, perhaps Third-World people need access to both traditional human services and ethnic agencies.

INTERVENTION STRATEGIES

Proactive intervention strategies are initiated in anticipation of social problems. Three examples of such strategies are cited in this section to demonstrate their impact on the individual, group, Third-World community, and the larger society. The examples include the concepts of advocacy, empowerment, and "class action social work."

According to Briar, the social worker as advocate is

his client's supporter, his advisor, his champion, and, if need be, his representative in his dealings with the court, the police, the social agency and other organizations that [affect] his well-being.[26]

Briar's definition describes the advocate as one who pleads the cause of an individual. Brager, however, takes another view. His definition describes the advocate as one who represents the interests of an aggrieved class of people:

The worker as advocate identifies with the plight of the disadvantaged. He sees as his primary responsibility the tough-minded and partisan representation of their interests, and this supersedes his fealty to others. This role inevitably requires that the practitioner function as a political tactician.[27]

Third-World communities need both types of advocacy—in behalf of client and class. Although expressing a commitment to advocacy, the NASW Ad Hoc Committee on Advocacy perceived a dilemma concerning the choice between direct intercession by the social worker and mobilization of clients in their own behalf.[28] Some members of the profession might argue that it is a disservice to clients when social workers advocate in their behalf—that advocacy emasculates clients and makes them more dependent. It is difficult to determine whether this argument would be based on solid quantitative data or whether it would represent an intellectual rationalization for remaining uninvolved. Advocacy in behalf of some powerless special populations, such as dependent children or mentally ill jail inmates, might, however, be appropriate. When advocacy is deemed inappropriate, social workers could help clients help themselves through the application of empowerment.

A recent trend evolving in social work relates to the concept of client empowerment, which is defined by Solomon as

a process whereby persons who belong to a stigmatized social category throughout their lives can be assisted to develop and increase skills in the exercise of interpersonal influence and the performance of valued social roles. Power is an interpersonal phenomenon: if it is not interpersonal it probably should be defined as "strength." However, the two concepts—power and strength—are so tightly interrelated that they are often used interchangeably.[29]

According to Solomon, empowerment enables the client to perceive his or her intrinsic and extrinsic worth. It motivates the client to use every personal resource and skill, as well as those of any other person that can be commanded, in the effort to achieve self-determined goals. The social worker attempts to develop in the client a conviction that there are many pathways to goal attainment. Solomon suggests three roles for the practitioner that hold promise for reducing a client's sense of powerlessness and lead to empowerment: the resource consultant role, the sensitizer role, and the teacher-trainer role.

Empowerment as a concept also holds promise in clinical social work. At a recent invitational forum on clinical social work held in Denver in 1979, the author presented a paper in which he demonstrated how the concept of power could be used effectively in clinical social work with persons who find themselves in a powerless or subordinate role to the practitioner in authority.[30] Often these persons are involuntary clients. The act of providing clients with the power to determine whether they wish to participate in treatment is seen as improving the treatment outcome if *they* choose to participate.

The purpose of social work is "to enhance the quality of life for all persons." Social work's impact on social problems, such as poverty and racism, is often limited by the clinical model or inappropriate interventive strategies. A referred client with a "problem" may not really have a problem. The problem may be *in* the referring system. For example, a school may refer a problem student to the social worker to help the student adjust to the requirements of the school system. The school system, however, may have major defects, which are the primary cause of the student's problems. The goal of the social worker should then be to help the school system meet the educational needs of the student. Rather than attempting to work individually with each student to document the deficiencies in the school system, the social worker could deal with one student who represents other students with similar problems. A class action in behalf of the student could then be undertaken to improve conditions in the school. Class action is a legal concept that has promising implications for social work. Closer working relationships will have to be cultivated with the legal profession to enable lawyers to conceptualize broad social work concerns and to translate these concerns into legal class action suits. Such an approach could be called "class action social work." Victories in the courts could provide relief for thousands of poor people.

Collaborative, interdisciplinary efforts involving social workers and lawyers usually have a clinical focus; these professionals serve clients in such areas as premarital or cohabitation counseling, divorce and custody proceedings, and estate planning for the elderly.[31] In some states, social workers have made pioneering efforts to enter the legal arena in behalf of the poor on a broader social scale, which could also be called class action social work. In California, for example, the Greater California Chapter of the National Association of Social Workers presented an award to John Serrano, a social worker, for his actions in the widely publicized *Serrano v. Priest*

case, which argued that the quality of a child's education should not be dependent on the wealth of a school district.[32] In this class action suit filed by the Western Center on Law and Poverty, which had a social worker as president of the corporation, the California Supreme Court ruled that the California public educational financing scheme, which relied heavily on local property taxes, violated the equal protection clause of the Fourteenth Amendment to the U.S. Constitution. In other words, wealthier school districts were favored to the detriment of poorer districts. The significance of *Serrano* transcends California's boundaries because all states, except Hawaii, use similar discriminatory educational financing systems.

Considering the *Serrano* precedent, might not the areas of welfare, health, and mental health services also represent a set of circumstances as unique and compelling as education? A right to public education may not be maximally enjoyed if the child is poorly housed, impoverished, malnourished, and in need of physical and mental health care. *Serrano* may ultimately lead the way for further challenges in a wide range of governmental services, including those in which social workers already have knowledge and experience. The opportunity for class action collaboration between law and social work in behalf of the Third-World community and the oppressed poor is on social work's doorstep and can become a significant tool of social work intervention.

NOTES AND REFERENCES

1. Lloyd Street, "Minorities," in John B. Turner, ed., *Encyclopedia of Social Work,* Vol. 2 (17th issue; Washington,

D.C.: National Association of Social Workers, 1977), pp. 931-984.

2. Special Populations Subpanel on Mental Health of Americans of European Ethnic Origin, *The President's Commission on Mental Health,* Vol. 3 (Washington, D.C.: U.S. Government Printing Office, 1978), p. 879.

3. Andrew M. Greeley, "Minorities: White Ethnics," in Turner, *Encyclopedia of Social Work,* Vol. 1, op. cit., pp. 983-984.

4. The author has used the following sources as background for this article: Joel Fischer, "Is Casework Effective? A Review," *Social Work,* 18 (January 1973), pp. 6-20; Louis L. Knowles and Kenneth Prewitt, eds., *Institutional Racism in America* (Englewood Cliffs, N.J.: Prentice-Hall, 1969); Carol H. Meyer, "What Directions for Direct Practice?" *Social Work,* 24 (July 1979), pp. 267-272; Armando Morales, "The Collective Preconscious and Racism," *Social Casework,* 52 (May 1971), pp. 285-293; Morales, "Beyond Traditional Conceptual Frameworks," *Social Work,* 22 (September 1977), pp. 387-393; Morales and Bradford W. Sheafor, *Social Work: A Profession of Many Faces* (2d ed.; Boston: Allyn & Bacon, 1980); Lloyd Street, "Minorities," op. cit., pp. 931-946; and Bo Thiemann and Mark Battle, *Specialization in Social Work Profession* (Washington, D.C.: National Association of Social Workers, 1974).

5. U.S. Bureau of the Census, *Current Population Reports,* Series P-20, No. 292 (Washington, D.C.: U.S. Department of Commerce, March 1976).

6. Street, op. cit., p. 932.

7. Jeffrey Prager, "The Minds of White Folk: An Analysis of Racism in America," pp. 42-48. Unpublished manuscript, University of California, Berkeley, 1970.

8. *See New York Times,* November 29, 1975, p. 30; and *A Study of Selected Socio-Economic Characteristics of Ethnic Minorities Based on the 1970 Census,* Vol. 2, *Asian Americans* (Washington, D.C.: U.S. Government Printing Office, 1974).

9. *See* Street, op. cit., p. 941.

10. Betty Ogleton, Stephanie Crittendon, and Cozetta Seda, "An Examination of Institutional Racism: Black People in California's Criminal Justice and Mental Health Systems," Monograph No. 2, Faculty Development—Minority Content in Mental Health (Boulder, Colo.: Western Interstate Commission for Higher Education, 1974), pp. 6-7.

11. Street, op. cit., p. 943.

12. Armando Morales, "Institutional Racism in Mental Health and Criminal Justice," *Social Casework,* 59 (July 1978), p. 391.

13. *See* Edgar S. Cahn, *Our Brother's Keeper: The Indian in White America* (New York: World Publishing Co., 1969); and Federal Commission on Civil Rights, "The Navajo Nation: An American Colony" (Washington, D.C.: U.S. Department of Health, Education & Welfare, 1975).

14. Murray L. Gruber, "Inequality in the Social Services," *Social Service Review,* 54 (March 1980), pp. 59-75.

15. Judith C. Nelson, "Social Work's Fields of Practice, Methods, and Models: The Choice to Act," *Social Service Review,* 49 (June 1975), pp. 264-270.

16. Meyer, op. cit., p. 269.

17. Ibid., p. 271.

18. Ibid., p. 268.

19. Walter R. Dean, Jr., "Back to Activism," *Social Work,* 22 (September 1977), p. 373.

20. Fischer, op. cit.

21. George Mace Summers, "Public Sanction and the Professionalization of Social Work," *Clinical Social Work Journal,* 4 (Spring 1976), p. 53.

22. Morales and Sheafor, op. cit., p. 337.

23. Ibid.

24. Shirley Jenkins, "The Ethnic Agency Defined," *Social Service Review,* 54 (June 1980), p. 250. Jenkins's definition of the term "ethnics" included blacks, Puerto Ricans, American Indians, Japanese, Chinese, and Mexican Americans.

25. Ibid., p. 260.

26. Scott Briar, "The Current Crisis in Social Casework," *Social Work Practice, 1967*

(New York: Columbia University Press, 1967), p. 28. *See also* Briar, "The Casework Predicament," *Social Work,* 13 (January 1968), pp. 5-11.

27. George A. Brager, "Advocacy and Political Behavior," *Social Work,* 13 (April 1968), p. 6.
28. The Ad Hoc Committee on Advocacy, "The Social Worker as Advocate: Champion of Social Victims," *Social Work,* 14 (April 1969), pp. 6-22.
29. Barbara Bryant Solomon, *Black Empowerment: Social Work in Oppressed Communities* (New York: Columbia University Press, 1976), p. 6.
30. Armando Morales, "Clinical Social Work with Special Populations," in Patricia L. Ewalt, ed., *Toward a Definition of Clinical Social Work* (Washington, D.C.: National Association of Social Workers, 1980), pp. 66-74.
31. Barton E. Bernstein, "Lawyer and Social Worker as an Interdisciplinary Team," *Social Casework,* 61 (September 1980), pp. 416-422.
32. Morales and Sheafor, op. cit.

C. ORGANIZATIONAL DILEMMAS

33. ORGANIZATIONAL DECLINE AND CUTBACK MANAGEMENT

Charles H. Levine

Government organizations are neither immortal nor unshrinkable.[1] Like growth, organizational decline and death, by erosion or plan, is a form of organizational change; but all the problems of managing organizational change are compounded by a scarcity of slack resources.[2] This feature of declining organizations—the diminution of the cushion of spare resources necessary for coping with uncertainty, risking innovation, and rewarding loyalty and cooperation—presents for government a problem that simultaneously challenges the underlying premises and feasibility of both contemporary management systems and the institutions of pluralist liberal democracy.[3]

Growth and decline are issues of a grand scale usually tackled by only the most brave or foolhardy of macro social theorists. The division of scholarly labor between social theorists and students of management is now so complete that the link between the great questions of

political economy and the more earthly problems of managing public organizations is rarely forged. This bifurcation is more understandable when one acknowledges that managers and organization analysts have for decades (at least since the Roosevelt Administration and the wide acceptance of Keynesian economics) been able to subsume their concern for societal level instability under broad assumptions of abundance and continuous and unlimited economic growth.[4] Indeed, almost all of our public management strategies are predicated on assumptions of the continuing enlargement of public revenues and expenditures. These expansionist assumptions are particularly prevalent in public financial management systems that anticipate budgeting by incremental additions to a secure base.[5] Recent events and gloomy forecasts, however, have called into question the validity and generality of these assumptions, and have created a need to reopen inquiry into the effects of resource scarcity on public organizations and their management systems. These events and forecasts, ranging from taxpayer revolts like California's successful Proposition 13 campaign and financial crises like the near collapse into bankruptcy of New York City's government and the agonizing retrenchment of its bureaucracy, to the foreboding predictions of the "limits of growth" modelers, also relink issues of political economy of the most monumental significance to practices of public management.[6]

We know very little about the decline of public organizations and the management of cutbacks. This may be because even though some federal agencies like the Works Progress Administration, Economic Recovery Administration, Department of Defense, National Aeronautics and Space Administration, the Office of Economic Opportunity, and many state and local agencies have expanded and then contracted,[7] or even died, the public sector as a whole has expanded enormously over the last four decades. In this period of expansion and optimism among proponents of an active government, isolated incidents of zero growth and decline have been considered anomalous; and the difficulties faced by the management of declining agencies coping with retrenchment have been regarded as outside the mainstream of public management concerns. It is a sign of our times—labeled by Kenneth Boulding as the "Era of Slowdown"—that we are now reappraising cases of public organization decline and death as exemplars and forerunners in order to provide strategies for the design and management of *mainstream* public administration in a future dominated by resource scarcity.[8]

The decline and death of government organizations is a symptom, a problem, and a contingency. It is a symptom of resource scarcity at a societal, even global, level that is creating the necessity for governments to terminate some programs, lower the activity level of others, and confront tradeoffs between new demands and old programs rather than to expand whenever a new public problem arises. It is a problem for managers who must maintain organizational capacity by devising new managerial arrangements within prevailing structures that were designed under assumptions of growth. It is a contingency for public employees and clients; employees who must sustain their morale and productivity in the face of increasing control from above and shrinking opportunities for creativity and promotion while clients must find alternative sources for the services governments may no longer be able to provide.

ORGANIZATIONAL DECLINE AND ADMINISTRATIVE THEORY

Growth is a common denominator that links contemporary management theory to its historical antecedents and management practices with public policy choices. William Scott has observed that ". . . organization growth creates organizational abundance, or surplus, which is used by management to buy off internal consensus from the potentially conflicting interest group segments that compete for resources in organizations."[9] As a common denominator, growth has provided a criterion to gauge the acceptability of government policies and has defined many of the problems to be solved by management action and organizational research. So great is our enthusiasm for growth that even when an organizational decline seems inevitable and irreversible, it is nearly impossible to get elected officials, public managers, citizens, or management theorists to confront cutback and decremental planning situations as anything more than temporary slowdowns. Nevertheless, the reality of zero growth and absolute decline, at least in some sectors, regions, communities, and organizations, means that management and public policy theory must be expanded to incorporate non-growth as an initial condition that applies in some cases. If Scott's assertions about the pervasiveness of a growth ideology in management are correct, our management and policy paradigms will have to be replaced or augmented by new frameworks to help to identify critical questions and strategies for action. Put squarely, without growth, how do we manage public organizations?

We have no ready or comprehensive answers to this question, only hunches and shards of evidence to serve as points of departure. Under conditions and assumptions of decline, the ponderables, puzzles, and paradoxes of organizational management take on new complexities. For example, organizations cannot be cut back by merely reversing the sequence of activity and resource allocation by which their parts were originally assembled. Organizations are organic social wholes with emergent qualities which allow their parts to recombine into intricately interwoven semi-lattices when they are brought together. In his study of NASA's growth and drawdown, Paul Schulman has observed that viable public programs must attain "capture points" of public goal and resource commitments, and these organizational thresholds or "critical masses" are characterized by their indivisibility.[10] Therefore, to attempt to disaggregate and cutback on one element of such an intricate and delicate political and organ-

ization arrangement may jeopardize the functioning and equilibrium of an entire organization.

Moreover, retrenchment compounds the choice of management strategies with paradoxes. When slack resources abound, money for the development of management planning, control, information systems, and the conduct of policy analysis is plentiful even though these systems are relatively irrelevant to decision making.[11] Under conditions of abundance, habit, intuition, snap judgments and other forms of informal analysis will suffice for most decisions because the costs of making mistakes can be easily absorbed without threatening the organization's survival.[12] However, in times of austerity, when these control and analytic tools are needed to help to minimize the risk of making mistakes, the money for the development and implementation is unavailable.

Similarly, without slack resources to produce "win-win" consensus-building solutions and to provide side payments to overcome resistance to change, organizations will have difficulty innovating and maintaining flexibility. Yet, these are precisely the activities needed to maintain capacity while contracting, especially when the overriding imperative is to minimize the perturbations of adjusting to new organizational equilibriums at successively lower levels of funding and activity.[13]

Lack of growth also creates a number of serious personnel problems. For example, the need to reward managers for directing organizational contraction and termination is a problem because without growth there are few promotions and rewards available to motivate and retain successful and loyal managers—particularly when compared to job opportunities for talented managers outside the declining organization.[14] Also, without expansion, public organizations that are constrained by merit and career tenure systems are unable to attract and accommodate new young talent. Without an inflow of younger employees, the average age of employees is forced up, and the organization's skill pool becomes frozen at the very time younger, more flexible, more mobile, less expensive and (some would argue) more creative employees are needed.[15]

Decline forces us to set some of our logic for rationally structuring organizations on end and upside down. For instance, under conditions of growth and abundance, one problem for managers and organizational designers is how to set up *exclusionary* mechanisms to prevent *"free riders"* (employees and clients who share in the consumption of the organization's collective benefits without sharing the burden that produced the benefit) from taking advantage of the enriched common pool of resources. In contrast, under conditions of decline and austerity, the problem for managers and organizational designers is how to set up *inclusionary* mechanisms to prevent organizational participants from avoiding the sharing of the *"public bads"* (increased burdens) that result from the depletion of the common pool of resources.[16] In other words, to maintain order and capacity when undergoing decline, organizations need mechanisms like long-term contracts with clauses that make pensions non-portable if broken at the employee's discretion. These mechanisms need to be carefully designed to penalize and constrain *"free exiters"* and cheap exits at the conven-

ience of the employees while still allowing managers to cut and induce into retirement marginally performing and unneeded employees.

As a final example, inflation erodes steady states so that staying even actually requires extracting more resources from the organization's environment and effectuating greater internal economies. The irony of managing decline in the public sector is particularly compelling under conditions of recession or so called "stagflation." During these periods of economic hardship and uncertainty, pressure is put on the federal government to follow Keynesian dictates and spend more through deficit financing; at the same time, critical public opinion and legal mandates require some individual agencies (and many state and local governments) to balance their budgets, and in some instances to spend less.

These characteristics of declining public organizations are like pieces of a subtle jigsaw puzzle whose parameters can only be guessed at and whose abstruseness deepens with each new attempt to fit its edges together. To overcome our tendency to regard decline in public organization as anomalous, we need to develop a catalogue of what we already know about declining public organizations. A typology of *causes* of public organizational decline and corresponding sets of *tactics* and *decision rules* available for managing cutbacks will serve as a beginning.

THE CAUSES OF PUBLIC ORGANIZATION DECLINE

Cutting back any kind of organization is difficult, but a good deal of the problem of cutting back public organizations is compounded by their special status as authoritative, non-market extensions of the state.[17] Public organizations are used to deliver services that usually have no direct or easily measurable monetary value or when market arrangements fail to provide the necessary level of revenues to support the desired level or distribution of services. Since budgets depend on appropriations and not sales, the diminution or termination of public organizations and programs, or conversely their maintenance and survival, are political matters usually calling for the application of the most sophisticated attack or survival tactics in the arsenal of the skilled bureaucrat-politician.[18] These strategies are not universally propitious; they are conditioned by the causes for decline and the hoped-for results.

The causes of public organization decline can be categorized into a four-cell typology as shown in Figure 33.1. The causes are divided along two dimensions: (a) whether they are primarily the result of conditions located either internal or external to the organization, or (b) whether they are principally a product of political or economic/technical conditions.[19] This is admittedly a crude scheme for lumping instances of decline, but it does cover most cases and allows for some abstraction.

FIGURE 33.1
Causes of Public Organization Decline

	INTERNAL	EXTERNAL
Political	Political Vulnerability	Problem Depletion
Economic/ Technical	Organizational Atrophy	Environmental Entropy

Of the four types, *problem depletion* is the most familiar. It covers government involvement in short-term crises like natural disasters such as floods and earthquakes, medium length governmental interventions like war mobilization and countercyclical employment programs, and longer-term public programs like polio research and treatment and space exploration—all of which involve development cycles. These cycles are characterized by a political definition of a problem followed by the extensive commitment of resources to attain critical masses and then contractions after the problem has been solved, alleviated, or has evolved into a less troublesome stage or politically popular issue.[20]

Problem depletion is largely a product of forces beyond the control of the affected organization. Three special forms of problem depletion involve demographic shifts, problem redefinition, and policy termination. The impact of demographic shifts has been vividly demonstrated in the closing of schools in neighborhoods where the school age population has shrunk. While the cause for most school closings is usually neighborhood aging—a factor outside the control of the school system—the decision to close a school is largely political. The effect of problem redefinition on public organizations is most easily illustrated by movements to *de*institutionalize the mentally ill. In these cases, the core bureaucracies responsible for treating these populations in institutions has shrunk as the rising per patient cost of hospitalization has combined with pharmaceutical advances in anti-depressants and tranquilizers to cause public attitudes and professional doctrine to shift.[21]

Policy termination has both theoretical import and policy significance. Theoretically, it is the final phase of a public policy intervention cycle and can be defined as "... the deliberate conclusion or cessation of specific government functions, programs, policies, or organizations."[22] Its policy relevance is underscored by recent experiments and proposals for sunset legislation which would require some programs to undergo extensive evaluations after a period of usually five years and be reauthorized or be terminated rather than be continued indefinitely.[23]

Environmental entropy occurs when the capacity of the environment to support the public organization at prevailing levels of activity erodes.[24] This type of decline covers the now familiar phenomena of financially troubled cities and regions with declining economic bases. Included in this category are: market and technological shifts like the decline in demand for domestic textiles and steel and its effect on the economies and quality of life in places like New England textile towns and steel cities like Gary, Indiana, Bethlehem, Pennsylvania, and Youngstown, Ohio;[25] transportation changes that have turned major railroad hubs and riverports of earlier decades into stagnating and declining economies; mineral depletion which has crippled mining communities; and intrametropolitan shifts of economic activity from central cities to their suburbs.[26] In these cases, population declines often have paralleled general economic declines which erode tax bases and force cities to cut services. One of the tragic side effects of environmental entropy is that it most severely affects those who cannot move.[27] Caught in the declining city and region are the immobile and dependent: the old, the poor, and the unemployable. For these communities, the forced choice of cutting services to an ever more dependent and needy population is the cruel outcome of decline.[28]

Environmental entropy also has a political dimension. As Proposition 13 makes clear, the capacity of a government is as much a function of the willingness of taxpayers to be taxed as it is of the economic base of the taxing region. Since the demand for services and the supply of funds to support them are usually relatively independent in the public sector, taxpayer resistance can produce diminished revenues which force service reductions even though the demand and *need* for services remains high.

The *political vulnerability* of public organizations is an internal property indicating a high level of fragility and precariousness which limits their capacity to resist budget decrements and demands to contract from their environment. Of the factors which contribute to vulnerability, some seem to be more responsible for decline and death than others. Small size, internal conflict, and changes in leadership, for example, seem less telling than the lack of a base of expertise or the absence of a positive self-image and history of excellence. However, an organization's age may be the most accurate predictor of bureaucratic vulnerability. Contrary to biological reasoning, aged organizations are more flexible than young organizations and therefore rarely die or even shrink very much. Herbert Kaufman argues that one of the advantages of organizations over solitary individuals is that they do provide longer institutional memories than a human lifetime, and this means the older organizations ought to have a broader range of adaptive skills, more capacity for learning, more friends and allies, and be more innovative because they have less to fear from making a wrong decision than a younger organization.[29]

Organizational atrophy is a common phenomenon in all organizations but government organizations are particularly vulnerable because they usually lack market generated revenues to signal a malfunction and to pinpoint responsibility. Internal atrophy and declining performance which can lead to resource cutbacks or to a weakening of organizational capacity come from a host of system and management failures almost too numerous to identify. A partial list would include: inconsistent and perverse incentives, differentiation without integration, role confusion, decentralized authority with vague responsibility, too many inappropriate rules, weak oversight, stifled dissent and upward communication, rationalization of performance failure by "blaming the victim," lack of self-evaluating and self-correcting capacity, high turnover, continuous politicking for promotions and not for program resources, continuous reorganization, suspicion of outsiders, and obsolescence caused by routine adherence to past methods and technologies in the face of changing problems. No organization is immune from these problems and no organization is likely to be afflicted by them all at once, but a heavy dose of some of these breakdowns in combination can contribute to an organization's decline and even death.

Identifying and differentiating among these four types of decline situations provides a start toward cataloging and estimating the appropriateness of strategies for managing decline and cutbacks. This activity is useful because when undergoing decline, organizations face three decision tasks: first, management must decide whether it will adopt a strategy to resist decline or smooth it (i.e., reduce the impact of fluctuations in the environment that cause interruptions in the flow of work and poor performance); second, given this choice of maneuvering strategies it will have to decide what tactics are most appropriate;[30] and third, if necessary, it will have to make decisions about how and where cuts will occur. Of course, the cause of a decline will greatly affect these choices.

STRATEGIC CHOICES

Public organizations behave in response to a mix of motives—some aimed at serving national (or state or local) purposes, some aimed at goals for the *organization as a whole,* and others directed toward the particularistic goals of organizational subunits. Under conditions of growth, requests for more resources by subunits usually can be easily concerted with the goals of the organization as a whole and its larger social purposes. Under decline, however, subunits usually respond to requests to make cuts in terms of their particular long-term survival needs (usually defended in terms of the injury which cutbacks would inflict on a program with lofty purposes or on a dependent clientele) irrespective of impacts on the performance of government or the organization as a whole.

The presence of powerful survival instincts in organizational subunits helps to explain why the political leadership of public organizations can be trying to respond to legislative or executive directives to cut back while at the same time the career and program leadership of subunits will be taking action to resist cuts.[31] It also helps to explain why growth can have the appearance of a rational administrative process complete with a hierarchy of objectives and broad consensus, while decline takes on the *appearance* of what James G. March has called a "garbage can problem"—arational, polycentric, fragmented, and dynamic.[32] Finally, it allows us to understand why the official rhetoric about cutbacks—whether it be to "cut the fat," "tighten our belts," "preserve future options," or "engage in a process of orderly and programmed termination"—is often at wide variance with the unofficial conduct of bureau chiefs who talk of "minimizing cutbacks to mitigate catastrophe," or "making token sacrifices until the heat's off."

Retrenchment politics dictate that organizations will respond to decrements with a mix of espoused and operative strategies that are not necessarily consistent.[33] When there is a wide divergence between the official pronouncements about the necessity for cuts and the actual occurrence of cuts, skepticism, cynicism, distrust, and noncompliance will dominate the retrenchment process and cutback management will be an adversarial process pitting top and middle management against one another. In most cases, however, conflict will not be rancorous, and strategies for dealing with decline will be a mixed bag of tactics intended either to *resist* or to *smooth* decline. The logic here is that no organization accedes to cuts with enthusiasm and will try to find a way to resist cuts; but resistance is risky. In addition to the possibility of being charged with nonfeasance, no responsible manager wants to be faced with the prospect of being unable to control where cuts will take place or confront quantum cuts with unpredictable consequences. Instead, managers will choose a less risky course and attempt to protect organizational capacity and procedures by smoothing decline and its effects on the organization.

An inventory of some of these cutback management tactics is presented in Figure 33.2. They are arrayed according to the type of decline problem which they can be employed to solve. This collection of tactics by no means exhausts the possible organizational responses to decline situations, nor are all the tactics exclusively directed toward meeting a single contingency. They are categorized in order to show that many familiar coping tactics correspond, even if only roughly, to an underlying logic. In this way a great deal of information about organizational responses to decline can be aggregated without explicating each tactic in great detail.[34]

The tactics intended to remove or alleviate the external political and economic causes of decline are reasonably straightforward means to revitalize eroded economic bases, reduce environmental uncertainty, protect niches, retain flexibility, or lessen dependence. The tactics for handling the internal causes of decline, however, tend to be more subtle means for strengthening organizations and managerial control. For instance, the management of decline *in the face of resistance* can be smoothed by changes in leadership. When hard unpopular decisions have to be made, new managers can be brought in to make the cuts, take the flak, and move on to another organ-

FIGURE 33.2
Some Cutback Management Tactics

	TACTICS TO RESIST DECLINE	TACTICS TO SMOOTH DECLINE
External Political	(Problem Depletion) 1. Diversify programs, clients and constituents 2. Improve legislation liaison 3. Educate the public about the agency's mission 4. Mobilize dependent clients 5. Become "captured" by a powerful interest group or legislator 6. Threaten to cut vital or popular programs 7. Cut a visible and widespread service a little to demonstrate client dependence	1. Make peace with competing agencies 2. Cut low prestige programs 3. Cut programs to politically weak clients 4. Sell and lend expertise to other agencies 5. Share problems with other agencies
Economic/ Technical	(Environmental Entropy) 1. Find a wider and richer revenue base (e.g., metropolitan reorganization) 2. Develop incentives to prevent disinvestment 3. Seek foundation support 4. Lure new public and private sector investment 5. Adopt user charges for services where possible	1. Improve targeting on problems 2. Plan with preservative objectives 3. Cut losses by distinguishing between capital investments and sunk costs 4. Yield concessions to taxpayers and employers to retain them
Internal Political	(Political Vulnerability) 1. Issue symbolic responses like forming study commissions and task forces 2. "Circle the wagons," i.e., develop a siege mentality to retain esprit de corps 3. Strengthen expertise	1. Change leadership at each stage in the decline process 2. Reorganize at each stage 3. Cut programs run by weak subunits 4. Shift programs to another agency 5. Get temporary exemption from personnel and budgetary regulations which limit discretion
Economic/ Technical	(Organizational Atrophy) 1. Increase hierarchical control 2. Improve productivity 3. Experiment with less costly service delivery systems 4. Automate 5. Stockpile and ration resources	1. Renegotiate long term contracts to regain flexibility 2. Install rational choice techniques like zero-base budgeting and evaluation research 3. Mortgage the future by deferring maintenance and downscaling personnel quality 4. Ask employees to make voluntary sacrifices like taking early retirements and deferring raises 5. Improve forecasting capacity to anticipate further cuts 6. Reassign surplus facilities to other users 7. Sell surplus property, lease back when needed 8. Exploit the exploitable

ization. By rotating managers into and out of the declining organization, interpersonal loyalties built up over the years will not interfere with the cutback process. This is especially useful in implementing a higher level decision to terminate an organization where managers will make the necessary cuts knowing that their next assignments will not depend on their support in the organization to be terminated.

The "exploit the exploitable" tactic also calls for further explanation. Anyone familiar with the personal practices of universities during the 1970's will recognize this tactic. It has been brought about by the glutted market for academic positions which has made many unlucky recent Ph.D's vulnerable and exploitable. This buyers' market has coincided neatly with the need of universities facing steady states and declining enrollments to avoid long-term tenure commitments to expensive faculties. The result is a marked increase in part-time and non-tenure track positions which are renewed on a semester-to-semester basis. So while retrenchment is smoothed and organization flexibility increased, it is attained at considerable cost to the careers and job security of the exploited teachers.

Cutback management is a two-crucible problem: besides selecting tactics for either resisting or smoothing decline, if necessary, management must also select who will be let go and what programs will be curtailed or terminated. Deciding where to make cuts is a test of managerial intelligence and courage because each choice involves tradeoffs and opportunity costs that cannot be erased through the generation of new resources accrued through growth.

As with most issues of public management involving the distribution of

costs, the choice of decision rules to allocate cuts usually involves the tradeoff between equity and efficiency.[35] In this case, "equity" is meant to mean the distribution of cuts across the organization with an equal probability of hurting all units and employees irrespective of impacts on the long term capacity of the organization. "Efficiency" is meant to mean the sorting, sifting, and assignment of cuts to those people and units in the organization so that for a given budget decrement, cuts are allocated to minimize the long-term loss in total benefits to the organization as a whole, irrespective of their distribution.

Making cuts on the basis of equity is easier for managers because it is socially acceptable, easier to justify, and involves few decision making costs. "Sharing the pain" is politically expedient because it appeals to common sense ideals of justice. Further, simple equity decision making avoids costs from sorting, selecting, and negotiating cuts.[36] In contrast, efficiency cuts involve costly triage analysis because the distribution of pain and inconvenience requires that the value of people and subunits to the organization have to be weighed in terms of their expected *future* contributions. In the public sector, of course, things are never quite this clear cut because a host of constraints like career status, veteran's preference, bumping rights, entitlements, and mandated programs limit managers from selecting optimal rules for making cuts. Nevertheless, the values of equity and efficiency are central to allocative decision making and provide useful criteria for judging the appropriateness of cutback rules. By applying these criteria to five of the most commonly used or proposed cutback methods— seniority, hiring freezes, even-percentage-cuts-across-the-board, productivity criteria, and zero base budgeting— we are able to make assessments of their efficacy as managerial tools.

Seniority is the most prevalent and most maligned of the five decision rules. Seniority guarantees have little to do with either equity or efficiency, *per se.* Instead, they are directed at another value of public administration; that is, the need to provide secure career-long employment to neutrally competent civil servants.[37] Because seniority is likely to be spread about the organization unevenly, using seniority criteria for making cuts forces managers to implicitly surrender control over the impact of cuts on services and the capacity of subunits. Furthermore, since seniority usually dictates a "last-in-first-out" retention system, personnel cuts using this decision rule tend to inflict the greatest harm to minorities and women who are recent entrants in most public agencies.

A *hiring freeze* is a convenient short-run strategy to buy time and preserve options. In the short run it hurts no one already employed by the organization because hiring freezes rely on "natural attrition" through resignations, retirements, and death to diminish the size of an organization's work force. In the long run, however, hiring freezes are hardly the most equitable or efficient way to scale down organizational size. First, even though natural and self selection relieves the stress on managers, it also takes control over the decision of whom and where to cut away from management and thereby reduces the possibility of intelligent long range cutback planning. Second, hiring freezes are more likely to harm minorities and women who are more likely to be the next hired rather than the next retired. Third, attrition will

likely occur at different rates among an organization's professional and technical specialties. Since resignations will most likely come from those employees with the most opportunities for employment elsewhere, during a long hiring freeze an organization may find itself short on some critically needed skills yet unable to hire people with these skills even though they may be available.

Even-percentage-cuts-across-the-board are expedient because they transfer decision-making costs lower in the organization, but they tend to be insensitive to the needs, production functions, and contributions of different units. The same percentage cut may call for hardly more than some mild belt tightening in some large unspecialized units but when translated into the elimination of one or two positions in a highly specialized, tightly integrated small unit, it may immobilize that unit.

Criticizing *productivity criteria* is more difficult but nevertheless appropriate, especially when the concept is applied to the practice of cutting low producing units and people based on their *marginal product* per increment of revenue. This method is insensitive to differences in clients served, unit capacity, effort, and need. A more appropriate criterion is one that cuts programs, organization units, and employees so that the *marginal utility* for a decrement of resources is equal across units, individuals, and programs thereby providing for *equal sacrifices* based on the *need* for resources. However, this criterion assumes organizations are fully rational actors, an assumption easily dismissed. More likely, cuts will be distributed by a mix of analysis and political bargaining.

Aggregating incompatible needs and preferences is a political problem and this is why *zero base budgeting* gets such high marks as a method for making decisions about resource allocation under conditions of decline. First, ZBB is future directed; instead of relying on an "inviolate-base-plus-increment" calculus, it allows for the analysis of both existing and proposed new activities. Second, ZBB allows for tradeoffs between programs or units below their present funding levels. Third, ZBB allows a ranking of decision packages by political bargaining and negotiation so that attention is concentrated on those packages or activities most likely to be affected by cuts.[38] As a result, ZBB allows both analysis and politics to enter into cutback decision making and therefore can incorporate an expression of the *intensity of need* for resources by participating managers and clients while also accommodating estimates of how cuts will affect the *activity levels* of their units. Nevertheless, ZBB is not without problems. Its analytic component is likely to be expensive—especially so under conditions of austerity—and to be subject to all the limitations and pitfalls of cost-benefit analysis, while its political component is likely to be costly in political terms as units fight with each other and with central management over rankings, tradeoffs, and the assignment of decrements.[39]

These five decision rules illustrate how strategic choices about cutback management can be made with or without expediency, analysis, courage, consideration of the organization's long term health, or the effect of cuts on the lives of employees and clients. Unfortunately, for some employees and clients, and the public interest, the choice will usually be made by managers to "go along" quietly with across-the-board cuts and exit as soon as possible. The alternative for those who would prefer more responsible and toughminded decision making *to facilitate long run organizational survival* is to develop in managers and employees strong feelings of organizational loyalty and loyalty to clients, to provide disincentives to easy exit, and to encourage participation so that dissenting views on the location of cuts could emerge from the ranks of middle management, lower level employees, and clients.[40]

PONDERABLES

The world of the future is uncertain, but scarcity and tradeoffs seem inevitable. Boulding has argued, "in a stationary society roughly half the society will be experiencing decline while the other half will be experiencing growth."[41] If we are entering an era of general slowdown, this means that the balance in the distribution between expanding and contracting sectors, regions, and organizations will be tipped toward decline. It means that we will need a governmental capacity for developing tradeoffs between growing and declining organizations and for intervening in regional and sectorial economies to avoid the potentially harmful effects of radical perturbations from unmanaged decline.

So far we have managed to get along without having to make conscious tradeoffs between sectors and regions. We have met declines on a "crisis-to-crisis" basis through emergency legislation and financial aid. This is a strategy that assumes declines are special cases of temporary disequilibrium, bounded in time and space, that are usually confined to a single organization, community, or region. A broad scale long-run *societal level* decline, however, is a problem of a different magnitude and to resolve it, patchwork solutions will not suffice.

There seem to be two possible directions in which to seek a way out of immobility. First is the authoritarian possibility; what Robert L. Heilbroner has called the rise of "iron governments" with civil liberties diminished and resources allocated throughout society from the central government without appeal.[42] This is a possibility abhorrent to the democratic tradition, but it comprises a possible future—if not for the United States in the near future, at least for some other less affluent nations. So far we have had little experience with cutting back on rights, entitlements, and privileges; but scarcity may dictate "decoupling" dependent and less powerful clients and overcoming resistance through violent autocratic implementation methods.

The other possible future direction involves new images and assumptions about the nature of man, the state and the ecosystem. It involves changes in values away from material consumption, a gradual withdrawal from our fascination with economic growth, and more efficient use of resources—especially raw materials. For this possibility to occur, we will have to have a confrontation with our propensity for wishful thinking that denies that some declines are permanent. Also required is a widespread acceptance of egalitarian norms and of anti-growth and no growth ideologies which are now only nascent, and the development of a political movement to promote their incorporation into policy making.[43] By backing away from our obsession with growth, we will also be able to diminish the "load" placed on central governments and allow for greater decentralization and the development of functions.[44]

In this way, we may be able to preserve democratic rights and processes while meeting a future of diminished resources.

However, the preferable future might not be the most probable future. This prospect should trouble us deeply.

NOTES

1. The intellectual foundations of this essay are too numerous to list. Three essays in particular sparked my thinking: Herbert Kaufman's *The Limits of Organizational Change* (University, Alabama: The University of Alabama Press, 1971) and *Are Government Organizations Immortal?* (Washington, D.C.: The Brookings Institution, 1976) and Herbert J. Gans, "Planning for Declining and Poor Cities," *Journal of the American Institute of Planners* (September, 1975), pp. 305-307. The concept of "cutback planning" is introduced in the Gans article. My initial interest in this subject stemmed from my work with a panel of the National Academy of Public Administration on a NASA-sponsored project that produced *Report of the Ad Hoc Panel on Attracting New Staff and Retaining Capability During a Period of Declining Manpower Ceilings.*

2. For an explication of the concept of "organizational slack" see Richard M. Cyert and James G. March, *A Behavioral Theory of the Firm* (Englewood Cliffs, N.J.: Prentice-Hall, 1963), pp. 36-38. They argue that because of market imperfections between payments and demands "there is ordinarily a disparity between the resources available to the organization and the payments required to maintain the coalition. This difference between total resources and total necessary payments is what we have called *organizational slack*. Slack consists in payments to members of the coalition in excess of what is required to maintain the organization.... Many forms of slack typically exist: stockholders are paid dividends in excess of those required to keep stockholders (or banks) within the organization; prices are set lower than

necessary to maintain adequate income from buyers; wages in excess of those required to maintain labor are paid; executives are provided with services and personal luxuries in excess of those required to keep them; subunits are permitted to grow without real concern for the relation between additional payments and additional revenue; public services are provided in excess of those required. . . . Slack operates to stabilize the system in two ways: (1) by absorbing excess resources, it retards upward adjustment of aspirations during relatively good times; (2) by providing a pool of emergency resources, it permits aspirations to be maintained (and achieved) during relatively bad times."

3. See William G. Scott, "The Management of Decline," *The Conference Board RECORD* (June, 1976), pp. 56-59 and "Organization Theory: A Reassessment," *Academy of Management Journal* (June, 1974) pp. 242-253; also Rufus E. Miles, Jr., *Awakening from the American Dream: The Social and Political Limits to Growth* (New York: Universal Books, 1976).

4. See Daniel M. Fox, *The Discovery of Abundance: Simon N. Patten and the Transformation of Social Theory* (Ithaca, N.Y.: Cornell University Press, 1967).

5. See Andrew Glassberg, "Organizational Responses to Municipal Budget Decreases," *Public Administration Review* (July/August 1978), pp. 325-331, and Edward H. Potthoff, Jr., "Pre-planning for Budget Reductions," *Public Management* (March, 1975), pp. 13-14.

6. See Donella H. Meadows, Dennis L. Meadows, Jorgen Randers, and William W. Behrens III, *The Limits to Growth* (New York: Universe Books, 1972); also Robert L. Heilbroner, *An Inquiry into the Human Prospect* (New York: W.W. Norton, 1975) and *Business Civilization in Decline* (New York: W.W. Norton, 1976).

7. See Advisory Commission on Intergovernmental Relations, *City Financial Emergencies: The Intergovernmental Dimension* (Washington, D.C.: U.S. Government Printing Office, 1973).

8. Kenneth E. Boulding, "The Management

of Decline," *Change* (June 1975), pp. 8-9 and 64. For extensive analyses of cutback management in the same field that Boulding addresses, university administration, see: Frank M. Bowen and Lyman A. Glenny, *State Budgeting for Higher Education: State Fiscal Stringency and Public Higher Education* (Berkeley, Calif.: Center for Research and Development in Higher Education, 1976); Adam Yarmolinsky, "Institutional Paralysis," *Special Report on American Higher Education: Toward an Uncertain Future* 2 Vol., *Daedalus* 104 (Winter, 1975), pp. 61-67; Frederick E. Balderston, *Varieties of Financial Crisis* (Berkeley, Calif.: Ford Foundation, 1972); The Carnegie Foundation for the Advancement of Teaching, *More Than Survival* (San Francisco: Jossey-Bass, 1975); Earl F. Cheit, *The New Depression in Higher Education* (New York: McGraw-Hill, 1975) and *The New Depression in Higher Education—Two Years Later* (Berkeley, Calif.: The Carnegie Commission on Higher Education, 1973); Lyman A. Glenny, "The Illusions of Steady States," *Change* 6 (December/January 1974-75), pp. 24-28; and John D. Millett, "What Is Economic Health?" *Change* 8 (September 1976), p. 27.

9. Scott, "Organizational Theory: A Reassessment," pp. 245.

10. Paul R. Schulman, "Nonincremental Policy Making: Notes Toward an Alternative Paradigm," *American Political Sciences Review* (December, 1975), pp. 1354-1370.

11. See Naomi Caiden and Aaron Wildavsky, *Planning Budgeting in Poor Countries* (New York: John Wiley & Sons, 1974).

12. See James W. Vaupel, "Muddling Through Analytically," in Willis D. Hawley and David Rogers (eds.), *Improving Urban Management* (Beverly Hills, Calif.: Sage Publications, 1976), pp. 124-146.

13. See Richard M. Cyert, "The Management of Universities of Constant or Decreasing Size," *Public Administration Review* (July/August 1978), pp. 344-349.

14. See National Academy of Public Admin-

istration *Report* and Glassberg, "Organizational Response to Municipal Budget Decreases."

15. See NAPA *Report* and *Cancelled Careers: The Impact of Reduction-In-Force Policies on Middle-Aged Federal Employees,* A Report to the Special Committee on Aging, United States Senate (Washington, D.C.: U.S. Government Printing Office, 1972).

16. See Albert O. Hirschman, *Exit, Voice and Loyalty: Responses to Decline in Firms, Organizations and States* (Cambridge, Mass.: Harvard University Press, 1970); also Mancur Olson, *The Logic of Collective Action* (Cambridge, Mass.: Harvard University Press, 1965).

17. The distinctive features of public organizations are discussed at greater length in Hal G. Rainey, Robert W. Backoff, and Charles H. Levine, "Comparing Public and Private Organization," *Public Administration Review* (March/April, 1976), pp. 223-244.

18. See Robert Behn, "Closing a Government Facility," and Barry Mitnick, "Deregulation as a Process of Organizational Reduction," *Public Administration Review* (July/August 1978), pp. 332-338 & pp. 350-357, and Herbert A. Simon, Donald W. Smithburg, and Victor A. Thompson, *Public Administration* (New York: Knopf, 1950) for discussions of the survival tactics of threatened bureaucrats.

19. This scheme is similar to those presented in Daniel Katz and Robert L. Kahn, *The Social Psychology of Organizations* (John Wiley & Sons, 1966), p. 166, and Gary L. Wamsley and Mayer N. Zald, *The Political Economy of Public Organizations: A Critique and Approach to the Study of Public Administration* (Lexington, Mass.: D. C. Heath, 1973), p. 20.

20. See Schulman, "Nonincremental Policy Making," and Charles O. Jones, "Speculative Augmentation in Federal Air Pollution Policy-Making," *Journal of Politics* (May, 1974), pp. 438-464.

21. See Robert Behn, "Closing the Massachusetts Public Training Schools," *Policy Sciences* (June, 1976), pp. 151-172;

Valarie J. Bradley, "Policy Termination in Mental Health: The Hidden Agenda," *Policy Sciences* (June, 1976), pp. 215-224; and David J. Rothman, "Prisons, Asylums and Other Decaying Institutions," *The Public Interest* (Winter, 1972), pp. 3-17. A similar phenomenon is occurring in some of the fields of regulation policy where deregulation is being made more politically feasible by a combination of technical and economic changes. See Mitnick, "Deregulation as a Process of Organizational Reduction."

22. Peter deLeon, "Public Policy Termination: An End and a Beginning," an essay prepared at the request of the Congressional Research Service as background for the Sunset Act of 1977.

23. There are many variations on the theme of Sunset. Gary Brewer "Termination: Hard Choices-Harder Questions," *Public Administration Review* (July/August 1978), pp. 338-344, identifies a number of problems central to most sunset proposals.

24. For two treatments of this phenomenon in the literature of organization theory see Barry M. Staw and Eugene Szwajkowski, "The Scarcity-Munificence Component of Organizational Environments and the Commission of Illegal Acts," *Administrative Science Quarterly* (September, 1975), pp. 345-354, and Barry Bozeman and E. Allen Slusher, "The Future of Public Organizations Under Assumptions of Environmental Stress," paper presented at the Annual Meeting of the American Society for Public Administration, Phoenix, Arizona, April 9-12, 1978.

25. See Thomas Muller, *Growing and Declining Urban Areas: A Fiscal Comparison* (Washington, D.C.: Urban Institute, 1975).

26. See Richard P. Nathan and Charles Adams, "Understanding Central City Hardship," *Political Science Quarterly* (Spring, 1976), pp. 47-62; Terry Nichols Clark, Irene Sharp Rubin, Lynne C. Pettler, and Erwin Zimmerman, "How Many New Yorks? The New York Fiscal Crisis in Comparative Perspective" (Report No. 72 of Comparative Study of

Community Decision-Making, University of Chicago, April, 1976); and David T. Stanley, "The Most Troubled Cities," a discussion draft prepared for a meeting of the National Urban Policy Roundtable, Academy for Contemporary Problems, Summer, 1976.

27. See Richard Child Hill, "Fiscal Collapse and Political Struggle in Decaying Central Cities in the United States," in William K. Tabb and Larry Sawers (eds.), *Marxism and The Metropolis* (New York: Oxford University Press, 1978); and H. Paul Friesema, "Black Control of Central Cities: The Hollow Prize," *Journal of the American Institute of Planners* (March, 1969), pp. 75-79.

28. See David T. Stanley, "The Most Troubled Cities" and "The Survival of Troubled Cities," a paper prepared for delivery at the 1977 Annual Meeting of the American Political Science Association, The Washington Hilton Hotel, Washington D.C., September 1-4, 1977; and Martin Shefter, "New York City's Fiscal Crisis: The Politics of Inflation and Retrenchment," *The Public Interest* (Summer, 1977), pp. 98-127.

29. See Kaufman, *Are Government Organizations Immortal?* and "The Natural History of Human Organizations," *Administration and Society* (August, 1975), pp. 131-148; I have been working on this question for some time in collaboration with Ross Clayton. Our partially completed manuscript is entitled, "Organizational Aging: Progression or Degeneration." See also Edith Tilton Penrose, "Biological Analogies in the Theory of the Firm," *American Economic Review* (December, 1952), pp. 804-819, and Mason Haire, "Biological Models and Empirical Histories of the Growth of Organizations" in Mason Haire (ed.), *Modern Organization Theory* (New York: John Wiley & Sons, 1959), pp. 272-306.

30. For a fuller explanation of "smoothing" or "leveling," see James D. Thompson, *Organizations in Action* (New York: McGraw-Hill, 1967), pp. 19-24.

31. For recent analyses of related phenomena see Joel D. Aberbach and Bert A. Rockman, "Clashing Beliefs Within the Executive Branch: The Nixon Administration Bureaucracy," *American Political Science Review* (June, 1976), pp. 456-468, and Hugh Heclo, *A Government of Strangers: Executive Politics in Washington* (Washington, D.C.: The Brookings Institution, 1977).

32. See James G. March and Johan P. Olsen, *Ambiguity and Choice in Organizations* (Bergen, Norway: Universitetsforlaget, 1976); and Michael D. Cohen, James G. March, and Johan P. Olsen, "A Garbage Can Model of Organizational Choice," *Administrative Science Quarterly* (March, 1972), pp. 1-25.

33. See Charles Perrow, *Organizational Analysis: A Sociological View* (Belmont, Calif.: Wadsworth Publishing Company, 1970) and Chris Argyris and Donald A. Schon, *Theory in Practice: Increasing Professional Effectiveness* (San Francisco, Calif.: Jossey-Bass, 1974) for discussions of the distinction between espoused and operative (i.e., "theory-in-use") strategies.

34. For extensive treatments of the tactics of bureaucrats, some of which are listed here, see Frances E. Rourke, *Bureaucracy, Politics, and Public Policy* (second edition, Boston: Little, Brown and Company, 1976); Aaron Wildavsky, *The Politics of the Budgetary Process* (second edition, Boston: Little, Brown and Company, 1974); Eugene Lewis, *American Politics in a Bureaucratic Age* (Cambridge, Mass.: Winthrop Publishers, 1977); and Simon, Smithburg and Thompson, *Public Administration*.

35. See Arthur M. Oken, *Equity and Efficiency: The Big Tradeoff* (Washington, D.C.: The Brookings Institution, 1975).

36. For a discussion of the costs of interactive decision making see Charles R. Adrian and Charles Press, "Decision Costs in Coalition Formation," *American Political Science Review* (June, 1968), pp. 556-563.

37. See Herbert Kaufman, "Emerging Conflicts in the Doctrine of Public Administration," *American Political Science Review* (December, 1956), pp. 1057-1073 and Frederick C. Mosher, *Democracy and the Public Service* (New York: Oxford University Press, 1968). Seniority

criteria also have roots in the widespread belief that the organizations ought to recognize people who invest heavily in them by protecting long time employees when layoffs become necessary.

38. See Peter A. Pyhrr, "The Zero-Base Approach to Government Budgeting," *Public Administrative Review* (January/February, 1977), pp. 1-8; Graeme M. Taylor, "Introduction to Zero-base Budgeting," *The Bureaucrat* (Spring, 1977), pp. 33-55.

39. See Brewer, "Termination: Hard Choices—Harder Questions"; Allen Schick, "Zero-base Budgeting and Sunset: Redundancy or Symbiosis?" *The Bureaucrat* (Spring, 1977), pp. 12-32 and "The Road From ZBB," *Public Administration Review* (March/April, 1978), pp. 177-180; and Aaron Wildavsky, "The Political Economy of Efficiency," *Public Administration Review* (December, 1966), pp. 292-310.

40. See Hirschman, *Exit, Voice and Loyalty,* especially Ch. 7, "A Theory of Loyalty," pp. 76-105. Despite the attractiveness of "responsible and toughminded decision making" the constraints on managerial discretion in contraction decisions should not be underestimated. At the local level, for example, managers often have little influence on what federally funded programs will be cut back or terminated. They are often informed after funding cuts have been made in Washington and they are expected to make appropriate adjustments in their local work forces. These downward adjustments often are also outside of a manager's control because in many cities with merit systems, veteran's preference, and strong unions, elaborate rules dictate who will be dismissed and the timing of dismissals.

41. Boulding, "The Management of Decline," p. 8.

42. See Heilbroner, *An Inquiry into the Human Prospect;* also Michael Harrington, *The Twilight of Capitalism* (New York: Simon & Schuster, 1976).

43. For a discussion of anti-growth policies see Harvey Molotch, "The City as a Growth Machine," *American Journal of Sociology* (September, 1976), pp. 309-332.

44. Richard Rose has made a penetrating argument about the potential of governments to become "overloaded" in "Comment: What Can Ungovernability Mean?" *Futures* (April 1977), pp. 92-94. For a more detailed presentation, see his "On the Priorities of Government: A Developmental Analysis of Public Policies," *European Journal of Political Research* (September 1976), pp. 247-290. This theme is also developed by Rose in collaboration with B. Guy Peters in *Can Governments Go Bankrupt?* (New York: Basic Books, 1978).

34. CONFRONTING BURNOUT AND JOB SATISFACTION

Dorothy Zietz and John L. Erlich

We are living in fear of the future. This malaise of uncertainty, confusion, and self-doubt cuts across all divisions of geography, class, culture, race, and political preference in the nation. The pervasiveness of our loss of confidence is all too evident. Its seriousness is reflected in the attention it has received in the media. Indeed, in a radical format departure, *Time* magazine recently devoted twenty-five pages to the subject of "American Renewal,"[1] and Time, Inc., added 135 pages of concurrent coverage in its six other publications.[2] "American Renewal" examines what can be done to restore confidence in ourselves and our future.[3]

Social work is scarcely immune to this distress. In the wholesale (and sometimes headlong) retreat of social programs since the early 1970s, there has emerged a concomitant lack of conviction about the efficacy and value of many of these programs. Certainly our inability to protect from the budget cutters' axe those services directed to the poor and minority oppressed has contributed to our frustration, apathy, and reluctance to act. Unfortunately these external pressures toward stagnation have been met by a sometimes even more destructive tendency toward burnout within social agencies and schools of social work. Edelwich and Brodsky offer a useful definition of burnout:

a progressive loss of idealism, energy and purpose experienced by people in the helping professions as a result of the conditions of their work.[4]

For Pines and Maslach, burnout is

a syndrome of physical and emotional exhaustion, involving the development of negative self-concept, negative job attitudes and loss of concern and feeling for clients.[5]

Recent studies have suggested that burnout is particularly apparent in the human service professions where intense concern for people and their problems is required for sensitive and effective action.[6]

Burnout in job performance has been described in various ways depending upon the setting and psychological environment in which the person works.[7] Often it relates to alienation from initial job expectations as those had been, or continued to be, perceived by individuals in their service-oriented function and institutional goals. Burnout, or performance saturation, may result in physical and multifaceted stress symptoms culminating in the diminution of self-esteem and work pride, fatigue, and disillusionment.[8] The length of time a person can tolerate an unrewarding task experience in which there seems little satisfaction depends upon the individual and, as importantly, upon various factors external to the job itself.[9] No matter what the projected burnout tolerance levels, even if they can be specified, there is little clarity and less

―――――――
Reproduced by permission of the authors. This is an unpublished article presented as a paper at the 1981 Annual Meeting of the Council on Social Work Education.

agreement on what to do about burnout.

Our study is an attempt to bring greater specificity and illumination to the dimensions of job satisfaction and burnout experienced by social workers in the criminal justice system in order to provide direction for ameliorative action. The survey sample consisted of one hundred members of the National Association of Social Workers, selected at random from NASW's 1978 Directory, and employed in the criminal justice field. Each person received a sixty-eight-item questionnaire; seventy-seven of the questionnaires were returned. The respondents consisted of forty men and thirty-seven women, ranging in age from twenty-two to sixty-three.

Line workers represented 40 percent of the total. Supervisors were 22 percent, and administrators made up 38 percent. Only one respondent earned less than $10,000 a year. Earning $10–15,000 were 16 percent; 26 percent earned $15–20,000; 32 percent $20–25,000; 12 percent $25–30,000; and 13 percent were earning over $30,000.

Certain general considerations emerged from a careful review of the quantitative and qualitative information provided by the respondents. It would appear that for social workers in corrections "burnout" is not only self-defined but also is professionally defined as well. Job dissatisfaction arises from two ideological bases: (1) the persistent historical "given" that social work practice is antithetic to the criminal justice model, and (2) that it is difficult for social workers to relate their professional ethos to the legal-political establishment. An example is offered by one respondent:

The agency is responsible to the judge and court administration. Their training and interests render them unreceptive to creative ideas in agency management, evaluation of effectiveness and innovative approaches to service delivery. The agency administrator is appointed by them and therefore carefully screens out approaches he thinks they will disapprove in essence.

The politics of burnout and powerlessness seemed to be more apparent at the top levels of management than line staff. Another person, working in a high level managerial position, wrote, "There are uncontrollable political forces that have a strong impact upon the work climate in which my job is performed."

If top management working within the legal structure does not regard the judicial community as a support system, how are those feelings transmitted, interpreted and communicated to line staff? Does this create a problem that could become a burnout "agitator"? Our study does not indicate that staff relates directly to management concerns but to the insensitivity, status, and salary inequities of the system as it affects them as professional workers. For example, 43 percent felt that they were not receiving adequate pay for the work that they were doing. Concern was also expressed about the undervaluing of the MSW degree. Indicating that they had higher expectations for the work they are doing when they were hired were 45 percent. One person summarized her experience:

When I came to this agency, social workers and parole agents received equal pay. I felt it was unfair as social workers were required to have an MSW. It went from bad to worse. Now, a parole agent I earns better pay than a Supervising Social Worker, which is why I am a Parole Agent II instead of a Supervising Social Worker I. I had to sacrifice my identity for the money.... I am not renewing my membership in NASW this year, it is not worth it to me in this field.

There were other concerns regarding management and administrative staff related to apathy and inability or unwillingness to work with line staff. Another respondent stated:

There is not enough concern from administrators of what staff members' problems are in trying to get cases completed in time. Administration is not a constructive system. It is never interested in general meetings with staff to learn complaints. All communication to staff is passed by memo . . . or through a third person, Judge to Administrator, to Chief to Deputy Chief to supervise the probation office. . . . Do administrators and judges realize that employees are human beings?

Indeed, 66 percent agreed that they encountered a "great deal of bureaucratic hassle on [the] job."

One viewed the relationship between practice, administration and politics this way:

The fickleness of the leadership . . . is seduced by "fly by night" methods of treatment, contrary to what professional education has taught us. There is a constant change of administration with each political election.

A few offered contrary experiences. "[We have] a young, very progressive Chief Probation officer. Excellent, fair and available Chief Justice and competent people make this an outstanding local court."

One social worker seemed to find her position in a police department compatible with her professional training or at least not at odds with it. Describing her job performance: "When I have the opportunity to help someone in a crisis situation or when I catch a criminal, I have feelings of great satisfaction." On the other hand, another noted, "Being an ACSW in the correctional field is a lonesome business at best."

There was a wide variety of problem situations which respondents felt were indigenous to the system. These are listed in order of concern and could be considered the precursors of burnout, if indeed the erosion had not already started. On the list were (1) bureaucratic entanglements, (2) not enough time to work with clients because of heavy paperwork; (3) the paucity of opportunities for advancement for both men and women because promotions were not made from within the agency. Heavy case loads, not enough time for interagency contact that could best serve the client, and prejudice against the MSW worker were also pointed out as serious problems. Respondent reactions to feelings that might be expected to be related to such problems—feeling overworked, tired, angry, depressed, powerless, cynical, worried, bored, and exhausted—followed an interesting and apparently parallel pattern (Table 34.1).

TABLE 34.1
Frequency of Problem Feelings among
Criminal Justice System Social Workers

Feeling	Feel that way sometimes %	Feel that way often %
Overworked	58	17
Tired	53	22
Angry	69	12
Depressed	39	4
Powerless	45	27
Cynical	49	18
Worried	51	13
Bored	30	12
Exhausted	48	10

Despite these serious and substantial problems, there was an unexpected high level of personal satisfaction and the opportunity for innovation and program creativity. Reporting "considerable variety" in their work were 64 percent; 74 percent were in agreement with the statement "I feel I am doing the right kind of work for me," and 66 percent reported that they were "glad to be associated with the Criminal Justice System as it operates in my agency." A typical positive comment was offered by this respondent:

I have been able to develop my supervisory skills via both theory, training and trial and error. The support I received from staff has improved, and I have implemented organizational development concepts to allow maximum involvement of staff.

Receiving support and recognition seems centrally related to the degree of satisfaction and burnout people experience.[10] It was agreed by 73 percent that they received support and recognition for their work from co-workers. All respondents agreed that they got satisfaction from activities outside of work.

Clearly a majority of those surveyed felt that they had opportunity for creative practice and changing some of the procedures they found difficult to deal with. Respondents wrote that they felt their staff worked together closely as a team, and

... there was a sense of accomplishment when clients begin handling things in more constructive ways ... that satisfaction is feeling I can find ways to meet goals without administration's interference.... I receive recognition and support by my peers and supervisors.... weight is given my decisions.... I receive recognition for the quality of my work.... I see client improvement and client and agency appreciation for my work.... I am encouraged to be innovative, as far as that is legally within bounds.... I wish I were more creative, since creativity is encouraged in our system.

A retired worker took the long view:

There were certainly periods of burnout when I was struggling with the limitations of the job, not imposed by the system or the agency, but by the clients themselves. It took me a long time to learn that I was not responsible for them or managing their lives. They were!

In these lean and suspicious times, the authors were somewhat surprised to find the tendency toward burnout not as great as had been anticipated. At the same time, in matters pertaining to pay, work load, and stressful feelings, there was scant cause for optimism. Overall, the picture emerges of both high degrees of job satisfaction and sharp tendencies toward burnout.

The uniqueness of the survey population also needs to be taken into account. Of the population 52 percent was male—in marked contrast with most social agencies. And given the documented sexism of most social agencies (including those related to the justice system), it might be expected that men were more likely to be in more powerful and better paid positions. The nature of our data does not, however, allow us to shed much light on this question. Judging by the number of years the respondents had been in the field, we extrapolated a lower rate of attrition than is true of most of the agencies with which the authors have had experience. Perhaps this is related—as both cause and effect—to salary levels that seemed substantially higher than average (for 1979–80). Despite the dissatisfactions, the fact that almost three-quarters of the respondents felt they were doing the right kind of work (for themselves) was reminiscent of professors reporting that they loved teaching and hated academia.

This study, then, follows the pattern of most work that has been done in the area of burnout—the investigation of particular professional and subprofessional groups and organizations. And the current investigation does present some interesting possibilities for intervention. Perhaps we can begin by looking at the options for intervention in terms of a matrix of job satisfaction and burnout. That is, from a logical standpoint, each may be either high or low in a given situation. The matrix would look like Figure 34.1.

FIGURE 34.1
Matrix of Job Satisfaction and Burnout

Job Satisfaction

		High	Low
	Low	1	2
Burnout			
	High	3	4

The typical way of looking at burnout tends to presume that high burnout leads to low job satisfaction (or perhaps, it's the other way around, but in any case they are regarded as closely related to each other). The focus for intervention is mostly cell 2. While both cell 4 (low job satisfaction and low burnout) and cell 3 (high job satisfaction and low burnout) present interesting possibilities, our focus is cell 1, and to a lesser degree cell 2. The central question seems to be how to sustain the positive aspects of job satisfaction (better yet, build on them), while at the same time mitigating the effects of burnout. The approach that follows is based to a degree on our work with a San Francisco Bay Area Probation Department (with a similar satisfaction burnout profile), and individual experiences of each of the authors in a range of social work settings.

The interventive possibilities explored here consist of three arenas: (I) general preventive maintenance; (II) system intervention by job level; and (III) potential roles for social work faculty.

I. GENERAL PREVENTIVE MAINTENANCE

The authors' experiences suggest that attention needs to be directed to at least four major areas:

1. The Shrinking Social Worker Syndrome

The often noted tendency toward genteel belittling and character assassination must be exposed and discussed. The back-biting and denigration of each other's motivation, intelligence, and willingness to work needs the kind of investigation that makes clear the likely negative consequences in organizational morale and productivity. In the justice setting this often takes the form of snide comments and cynical anecdotes told by probation and parole officers, judges, social workers, paraprofessionals, and law enforcement personnel about each other. The more rampant this sort of behavior is, the more likely it will be to exacerbate such burnout "inducers" as salary inequities, status differentials, and promotional limitations. Special staff meetings, program retreats, and in-service training sessions are places where this demeaning behavior may be effectively addressed.

2. Looking Bad News in the Face

In most areas of the human services, the late 1970s marked a reduction in services and innovative delivery systems. With the 1980s era of "trim, cut, and slash" upon us, the prospects for the immediate future are grim. The justice system is no exception to the unfortunate inclination to wait for disaster until it is upon us. Taking a hard and open look at projected budget cuts and staffing reductions can help to reduce an internecine warfare that almost guarantees future interpersonal grudges and hard feelings (another likely contributor to increased burnout). Staff meetings, retreats, and in-service sessions all have served as vehicles for addressing "bad news."

3. Balancing Expectations and Realities

In our studies, between 45 percent and 66 percent of the respondents indicated that they had higher expectations for their work when hired than they do now. Considered with experiences in a variety of other settings, these data strongly imply that people—at all staff levels—need an opportunity to set out their expectations and participate in the process of evaluating them in light of current (and changing) realities. Even if there are strong disagreements on what the current realities are, we favor this process. Otherwise, the discrepancy between expectation and real possibilities tends to contribute to stressful feelings and burnout. We suggest handling this issue in dyadic or small-group discussions between supervisors and supervisees (including administrators as high up the administrative ladder as is feasible). General patterns of imbalance

can be addressed at unit and general staff meetings.

4. Burnout and Job Satisfaction: The Periodic Check-up

Perhaps above all, and even in the most successful and productive settings, there needs to be a regular internal assessment of both job satisfaction and burnout. Relatively simple assessment instruments—jointly prepared by line staff, supervisors, and administrators—may be used. One important concomitant of this process is an open and clear recognition that certain things are going well, in fact even very well. This, in turn, helps to buttress the system of mutual support (both supervisor and co-worker support and recognition are clearly important positives in our NASW study). Also, administrators, supervisors, and line workers are provided with specific ideas about areas of discontent. Instead of the free-wheeling (and often unproductive) gripe session, there can be problem-area-specific discussion. Small assessment task forces and general staff meetings seem the appropriate locus for the periodic check-up.

II. System Intervention by Job Level

In the human services few efforts to address burnout have taken a systems approach.[11] It is the approach we favor, especially in situations where there are substantial job satisfactions as well. Systems in this case refers to all three of the basic job levels found in most medium to medium-large human services organizations—line workers, supervisors, and administrators. (In smaller organizations—like most schools of social work—administrators and supervisors might be brought together in a single group; and in very large organizations, additional subgroups may be specified.) What it involves is a simultaneous effort to assess the extent of job satisfaction and burnout at each organizational level. We suggest that the assessment effort be planned by democratically selected representatives from each job level, joining together in a committee sufficiently small to allow for active exchange among all members. It probably should not be chaired by an administrator. An outside consultant might make the best "neutral" chairperson, but most often there are no funds for such consultants. The assessment report should illuminate satisfactions and elements of burnout at each job level, and propose at least beginning steps for addressing them. A variant of the survey instrument used in our studies or the Maslach Burnout Inventory[12]—modified to take account of special local conditions—might serve as the major assessment tool. In each case, the emphasis should be on clarifying both the strengths of job satisfaction and weaknesses of burnout.

For example, if the NASW study data can be used for the moment as an agency profile of support and recognition received from supervisors (73 percent) and co-workers (91 percent), clearly something is going "very right." In follow-up meetings to review the survey data, an effort should be made to specify what sort of behaviors contribute to a positive feeling of support and recognition, and clear recommendations made about how to sustain and build on it (that is, encouraging supervisors to give public recognition in staff meetings to effective work being done by their supervisees, or establishing more active written pooling of information about community resources among line staff, and so on). At the same time, attention might be directed to delimiting what makes people at each level feel so powerless (fully 81 percent of our sample felt that way "sometimes" or "often"). Herrick cites the observations of a corrections worker in this regard:

The ability to be creative and have input into new and functional programming is non-existent. The message conveyed is maintain the status quo and cover yourself.[13]

In court-dominated settings, for example, realistic strategies may be developed for dealing with a group of judges who habitually disregard probation reports. Even very modest improvements of this kind, we have noted, sometimes go a long way toward ameliorating feelings of fatigue, cynicism, and powerlessness.

Administrators, in our experience, have been both surprised and pleased to have their contributions and frustrations acknowledged. An open discussion of administrators' views of the adequacy of pay, the extent of "bureaucratic hassle," and the limitations imposed by the wider justice system can really help to defuse hostilities in these arenas. We could go on to describe additional areas of satisfaction and burnout in detail, but the above seems sufficient to make clear the thrust of the approach.

III. INOCULATION AGAINST BURNOUT: ROLES FOR SOCIAL WORK FACULTY

As yet no one has developed a foolproof system for "inoculating" students and practitioners against burnout. Indeed, there is concern about preparing people for more difficult times than they actually experience, thereby creating a self-fulfilling prophecy. On the other hand, looking the other way in matters involving job satisfaction and burnout is not likely to improve either relatively good or deteriorating situations. What might be done? Here again the tendency is to address very bad situations, like those field work settings that get removed from school rosters because they are so poor for student learning. The focus is on catastrophe protection. The high satisfaction, high burnout environment is likely to be treated as some sort of aberration. But, in many different settings, it seems far more prevalent than we might have imagined.

Again, it is our inclination to look at specifics—perhaps by involving students in satisfaction/burnout assessments of their placement agencies. If this is not possible, a second choice would be to use guest lecturers who would share their experiences with an assessment process in their own agencies. Third choice would be a "canned" assessment, like our study. As fate would have it, this is the one with which we've had the most experience. Students are intrigued initially, inclined to be very skeptical, and finally—on a issue-by-issue basis—willing to accept that high satisfaction, high burnout situations may be one of the more desirable alternatives for social agency work in the early and mid-1980s. As Edelwich and Brodsky point out:

The inevitable experience of burnout can be, professionally speaking, a terminal experience or a growth experience. Thinking of frustration or depression as an educational experience may not make it more pleasant, but understanding its place in the rhythm of our development can help us be at peace with it.[14]

Faculty members might also try, as we have, offering themselves as free or low-fee consultants to agencies willing to undertake self-studies of job satisfaction and burnout. The fear of opening "Pandora's box" is still very much with us, as is the tendency to hope that leaving a problem alone is just as likely as anything else to make it go away.

A FINAL WORD

The conventional wisdom has it that "work life" and "personal life" are two separate and distinct worlds (and for the good of both practitioners and clients ought to be kept that way). Cherniss, among others, has pointed out that the two are inextricably intertwined.[15] In studying new public professionals, he noted a clear and reciprocal relationship between work and personal life. Problems and stresses in one "spilled over" into the other. Positive experiences in one, on the other hand, had a positive effect on the other.

In our view, this tendency toward dichotomizing the personal and the professional is especially destructive for those engaged in community practice. Insofar as possible, each needs to reinforce and support the other. To aid in ameliorating the effects of burnout, both are best viewed as vital parts of a single, integrated whole life of the practitioner. The current community climate is just too fraught with strains, stresses, hostilities, and complexities for any other approach to work successfully over time.

Confronting burnout is a place to begin. For the moment, the struggle for real openness in looking at burnout is very much uphill. Perhaps it is well to remember that a balancing of some job satisfactions and tendencies toward burnout is probably inherent in social work as we know it. As one of our respondents summed up her experiences:

Can we love and hate at the same time what we're doing as professionals? I do and that's why I think I'm good at my job.

NOTES

1. John Meyers, "A Letter from the Publisher," *Time,* February 23, 1981, p. 3.
2. Ibid., p. 3.
3. Ibid.
4. Jerry Edelwich with Archie Brodsky, *Burn-out* (New York: Human Sciences Press, 1980), p. 14.
5. Ayala Pines and Christine Maslach, "Characteristics of Staff Burnout in Mental Health Settings," *Hospital and Community Psychiatry* 29, no. 4 (1978), p. 233.
6. Mary Kosenas and M. Richard Wigen, "Factors Associated with Burnout Among Social Workers in Bay Area Veterans' Hospitals," master's thesis, California State University, Sacramento, 1979.
7. For example, see Herbert Freudenberger, "Staff Burnout," *Journal of Social Issues* 30, no. 1 (1974), pp. 159–165; Christina Maslach, "Burned-out," *Human Behavior* 5, no. 9 (1976), 16–20; and Pines and Maslach, "Characteristics of Staff Burn-out in Mental Health Settings," pp. 233–237.
8. For example, see Michael Daley, " 'Burnout': Smoldering Problem in Protective Services," *Social Work* 24, no. 5 (Sept. 1979), 375–379.
9. Ayala Pines and Ditsa Kafry, "Occupational Tedium in the Social Services," *Social Work* 23, no. 6 (Nov. 1978), pp. 499–507.
10. Ibid. Also, see R. Kahn, "Job Burnout: Prevention and Remedies," *Public Welfare,* Vol. 36 (Spring 1978), pp. 61-63.
11. Edelwich with Brodsky, *Burn-out,* pp. 191–194.
12. Christina Maslach and S. E. Jackson, "A Scale Measure to Assess Experienced Burn-out," Paper presented at the meeting of Western Psychological Association, San Francisco, April 1978.
13. Neal Herrick, "How Dissatisfied Is the American Worker?" *Society* 18, no. 2 (Jan/Feb. 1981), p. 26.
14. Edelwich with Brodsky, *Burn-out,* p. 246.
15. Cary Cherniss, *Professional Burnout in Human Service Organizations* (New York: Praeger, 1980), pp. 181–188.

Name Index

Subject Index

BOOK MANUFACTURE

Tactics and Techniques of Community Practice, Second Edition was typeset at Compositors, Cedar Rapids, Iowa. Printing and binding was by Kingsport Press, Kingsport, Tennessee. F. E. Peacock Publishers art department designed the text. The typeface is Times Roman.